AI and Data Engineering Solutions for Effective Marketing

Lhoussaine Alla
Sidi Mohamed Ben Abdellah University, Morocco

Aziz Hmioui
Sidi Mohamed Ben Abdellah University, Morocco

Badr Bentalha
Sidi Mohamed Ben Abdellah University, Morocco

IGI Global
PUBLISHER of TIMELY KNOWLEDGE

A volume in the Advances in Marketing, Customer Relationship Management, and E-Services (AMCRMES) Book Series

Published in the United States of America by
IGI Global
Business Science Reference (an imprint of IGI Global)
701 E. Chocolate Avenue
Hershey PA, USA 17033
Tel: 717-533-8845
Fax: 717-533-8661
E-mail: cust@igi-global.com
Web site: http://www.igi-global.com

Library of Congress Cataloging-in-Publication Data

AI and Data Engineering Solutions for Effective Marketing
Lhoussaine Alla, Aziz Hmioui, Badr Bentalha
2024 Business Science Reference

ISBN: 979-8-3693-3172-9
eISBN: 979-8-3693-3173-6

British Cataloguing in Publication Data
A Cataloguing in Publication record for this book is available from the British Library.

The views expressed in this book are those of the authors, but not necessarily of the publisher.

For electronic access to this publication, please contact: eresources@igi-global.com.

Advances in Marketing, Customer Relationship Management, and E-Services (AMCRMES) Book Series

Eldon Y. Li

National Chengchi University, Taiwan & California Polytechnic State University, USA

ISSN:2327-5502
EISSN:2327-5529

Mission

Business processes, services, and communications are important factors in the management of good customer relationship, which is the foundation of any well organized business. Technology continues to play a vital role in the organization and automation of business processes for marketing, sales, and customer service. These features aid in the attraction of new clients and maintaining existing relationships.

The Advances in Marketing, Customer Relationship Management, and E-Services (AMCRMES) Book Series addresses success factors for customer relationship management, marketing, and electronic services and its performance outcomes. This collection of reference source covers aspects of consumer behavior and marketing business strategies aiming towards researchers, scholars, and practitioners in the fields of marketing management.

Coverage

- CRM in financial services
- CRM strategies
- Database marketing
- E-Service Innovation
- Relationship Marketing
- Online Community Management and Behavior
- Ethical Considerations in E-Marketing
- Cases on Electronic Services
- Mobile CRM
- Telemarketing

IGI Global is currently accepting manuscripts for publication within this series. To submit a proposal for a volume in this series, please contact our Acquisition Editors at Acquisitions@igi-global.com or visit: http://www.igi-global.com/publish/.

Titles in this Series

For a list of additional titles in this series, please visit: www.igi-global.com/book-series

Driving Green Marketing in Fashion and Retail
Theodore K. Tarnanidis (International Hellenic University, Greece) Evridiki Papachristou (International Hellenic University, Greece) Michail Karypidis (International Hellenic University, Greece) and Vasileios Ismyrlis (Hellenic Statistical Authority, Greece)
Business Science Reference • copyright 2024 • 312pp • H/C (ISBN: 9798369330494) • US $295.00 (our price)

Global Perspectives on Social Media Influencers and Strategic Business Communication
Nicky Chang Bi (University of Nebraska at Omaha, USA) and Ruonan Zhang (Rollins College, USA)
Business Science Reference • copyright 2024 • 430pp • H/C (ISBN: 9798369309124) • US $300.00 (our price)

Future of Customer Engagement Through Marketing Intelligence
Mudita Sinha (Christ University, India) Arabinda Bhandari (Presidency University, India) Samant Shant Priya (Lal Bahadur Shastri Institute of Management, India) and Sajal Kabiraj (Häme University of Applied Sciences, Finland)
Business Science Reference • copyright 2024 • 286pp • H/C (ISBN: 9798369323670) • US $355.00 (our price)

New Trends in Marketing and Consumer Science
Theodore K. Tarnanidis (University of Macedonia, Greece) and Nikolaos Sklavounos (International Hellenic University, Greece)
Business Science Reference • copyright 2024 • 516pp • H/C (ISBN: 9798369327548) • US $365.00 (our price)

AI Innovation in Services Marketing
Ricardo Correia (Instituto Politécnico de Bragança, Portugal & CiTUR, Portugal) and Dominyka Venciute (ISM University of Management and Economics, Lithuania)
Business Science Reference • copyright 2024 • 299pp • H/C (ISBN: 9798369321539) • US $285.00 (our price)

Ethical Marketing Through Data Governance Standards and Effective Technology
Shefali Saluja (Chitkara Business School, Chitkara University, India) Varun Nayyar (Center for Distance and Online Education, Chitkara University, India) Kuldeep Rojhe (Center for Distance and Online Education, Chitkara University, India) and Sandhir Sharma (Chitkara Business School, Chitkara University, India)
Business Science Reference • copyright 2024 • 328pp • H/C (ISBN: 9798369322154) • US $285.00 (our price)

IGI Global
PUBLISHER of TIMELY KNOWLEDGE

701 East Chocolate Avenue, Hershey, PA 17033, USA
Tel: 717-533-8845 x100 • Fax: 717-533-8661
E-Mail: cust@igi-global.com • www.igi-global.com

Table of Contents

Dwijendra Nath Dwivedi, Krakow University of Economics, Poland
Ghanashyama Mahanty, Utkal University, India
Varunendra Nath Dwivedi, SRM University, India

Detailed Table of Contents

Chapter 1

    Mustapha Elhissoufi, Sidi Mohamed Ben Abdellah University, Morocco
    Lhoussaine Alla, Sidi Mohamed Ben Abdellah University, Morocco

The objective of this chapter is to explore publications that have addressed the applicability of AI to boost customer acquisition, via bibliometric analysis via VOSViewer. These results reveal an acceleration of research since 2018, a predominance of American institutions, a concentration of publications in marketing and computer science journals, a trend towards the decentralization of research on the uses of AI in customer acquisition and an absence of the emergence of predominant author groups.

Chapter 2

    Mourad Aarabe, National School of Business and Management of Fez, Morocco
    Nouhaila Ben Khizzou, National School of Business and Management of Fez, Morocco
    Lhoussaine Alla, National School of Applied Sciences of Fez, Morocco
    Ahmed Benjelloun, National School of Business and Management of Fez, Morocco

In today's global environment, integrating emerging technologies has become a necessity. This book explores the intersection of technology and marketing, providing an overview of technological advancements and their impact on marketing practices. This chapter proposes a systematic literature review following the PRISMA protocol to explore the breadth and scope of applicability of emerging technology solutions in marketing. The aim is to highlight the key opportunities and challenges for marketing applications of such technologies. This analysis, conducted using Nvivo V12 software, indicates that emerging technologies such as artificial intelligence, augmented reality, the internet of things, blockchain, and data analytics are increasingly important in marketing practices and strategies. These technologies are primarily used to understand and satisfy individual customer needs and improve the customer experience.

Chapter 3

    Ichrak Fahim, Ibn Zohr University, Morocco
    Loubna Haramouni, Ibn Zohr University, Morocco
    Mohamed Khalil Majdi, Ibn Zohr University, Morocco
    Fatima Elkandoussi, Ibn Zohr University, Morocco

Neuromarketing is an interdisciplinary field that combines neuroscience, psychology, and marketing for a better understanding of consumer behaviour. Artificial intelligence (AI) is a discipline that can shape consumers' preferences, leading to better insights for marketing strategies. This chapter aims to identify, evaluate, and summarise the findings of all relevant individual studies on the usage of artificial intelligence in Neuromarketing practices, as well as the different controversial ethical perspectives regarding this discipline. A systematic literature review of research studies published in indexed databases over the past ten years, 58 recent references were studied using a qualitative content analysis approach. The results indicate the application of AI in neuromarketing allows for more accurate and precise analysis of consumer behaviour and decision-making processes. However, the ethical debate of applying AI in neuromarketing is still ongoing, making it a topic of controversy and further research.

Chapter 4

Ibtissam Zejjari, National School of Business and Management of Meknes, Morocco
Issam Benhayoun, National School of Business and Management of Meknes, Morocco

This study aims to provide a review of current research on artificial intelligence use in marketing by examining 661 papers related to AI and marketing from the Web of Science database published in the last twenty years. Using bibliometric analysis, the study sheds light on the present research status, identifies trends, and explores future directions in AI and marketing research. Keyword co-occurrence analysis is utilized to uncover patterns and themes within the literature, offering insights into the field's evolution and emerging research areas. The analysis reveals several significant findings. Notably, it emphasizes the growing importance of AI in marketing, with China and the USA emerging as key contributors. Additionally, a considerable number of papers are funded by agencies and universities, underlining the topic's significance. Based on keyword co-occurrence analysis, four primary research themes are identified: Application of AI in marketing, AI in Marketing Analysis and Forecasting, AI in decision making and optimization, and AI and data analysis.

Chapter 5

Aya Irgui, Ibn Tofail University, Morocco
Mohammed Qmichchou, Ibn Tofail University, Morocco
Ilham El Haraoui, Ibn Tofail University, Morocco

This study outlines the current understanding of augmented reality experiential marketing (AREM), providing a comprehensive overview of the field's state and identifying areas for further investigation. Through a systematic literature review, the authors analyzed 35 articles to develop an integrative framework highlighting both theoretical advancements and practical applications. The review addresses significant research gaps, offering insights and pinpointing challenges in existing knowledge. Key findings demonstrate AREM's influence on consumer behavior and its implications for immersive marketing strategies. Notably, the study calls for a nuanced understanding of AR beyond novelty, advocating for engaging, immersive, and personalized interactions. It emphasizes inclusive demographic approaches and ethical considerations like privacy. Original in its scope, this review lays a foundation for expanding AREM's theoretical landscape, promoting a culturally inclusive and ethically aware marketing approach to enhance consumer experiences in a digital marketplace.

Chapter 6

Tarik Rhardas, National School of Business and Management, Hassan II University of
Casablanca, Morocco

Hanane Rochdane, National School of Business and Management, Hassan II University of Casablanca, Morocco

In many developing countries, smart city initiatives are in their infancy. Like many other developing countries, smart projects in Morocco have been facing several challenges since their launch in 2016. The adoption of smart services requires the commitment and involvement of Moroccan citizens. This chapter focuses on a systematic literature review of the main studies dealing with factors that appear to improve end-user acceptance of services provided by Moroccan smart cities. A specific method known as PRISMA is being adopted to select and synthesize relevant studies in this field. The results obtained from the systematic review indicate that the unified theory of acceptance and use of technology (UTAUT) is the most utilized theory in the literature. Additionally, the examination of existing studies has revealed that successful implementation of smart projects requires decision-makers to consider the following factors: performance expectancy, ease of use, social influence, perceived cost, awareness, trust in technology, and trust in the government.

Agile marketing represents a paradigm shift in strategic marketing, emphasizing the principles of flexibility, speed, and customer-centricity. Originating from software development methodologies that value adaptability and iterative progress, agile practices have been effectively translated into the marketing domain to address the dynamic and fast-paced nature of contemporary markets. This approach focuses on continuous improvement, cross-functional collaboration, and responsiveness to consumer needs and market trends. By integrating diverse methodologies such as Scrum and Kanban, marketing teams enhance their ability to rapidly adapt strategies, execute innovative campaigns, and leverage real-time feedback, thereby ensuring a competitive edge in a constantly evolving business landscape. This chapter aims to explore the transformative potential of Agile Marketing and offers insights into how Agile practices can reshape marketing strategies to be more adaptive, efficient, and aligned with customer expectations, empowering marketers to succeed in today's digital era.

The business environment is constantly changing and evolving, and companies must adapt to remain competitive. Today, companies have no choice but to compete on a global scale by developing products and services that meet the aspirations and needs of consumers. To meet these challenges, companies need to acquire and develop resources that improve their ability to effectively exploit opportunities and avoid threats. Business intelligence and CRM systems help companies do this. Business intelligence and customer relationship management are closely related. Recent studies have explored the benefits of integrating business intelligence and CRM. Today, the integration of business intelligence and CRM has become a key strategy for companies seeking to improve their operational efficiency and customer-centric practices. The purpose of this chapter is to provide a perspective on how the integration of business intelligence and CRM can lead companies to sustainable growth and improved competitiveness. It explores the principles, challenges, and potential benefits of this integration.

In the rapidly evolving technological landscape, the strategic integration of AI becomes imperative, fundamentally altering the dynamics of business-customer interactions. This chapter commences by exploring AI's pivotal role in deciphering complex consumer behavior patterns, providing businesses with invaluable insights to adapt to market dynamics. From there, the focus shifts to AI-powered personalization, highlighting its profound impact on enriching customer experiences and forging deeper connections. Subsequently, the discussion delves into the realm of AI-driven automation, which not only revolutionizes the efficiency but also enhances the quality of customer engagement processes. Lastly, attention is drawn to the ethical considerations and privacy concerns inherent in AI-driven customer engagement, underscoring the importance of responsible AI implementation. In essence, this chapter underscores AI's multifaceted influence on customer engagement strategies, establishing it as a cornerstone for businesses aspiring to achieve sustainable success in the ever-changing marketplace.

Technology is crucial in our daily lives, enabling us to communicate, access information, and engage in various activities through devices like smartphones, tablets, and laptops. Social media platforms facilitate global connectivity and information sharing. The internet has revolutionized access to limitless information, online shopping, education, and job opportunities. Artificial intelligence (AI) advancements have brought innovative solutions to sectors like healthcare, automotive, and finance. This study aims to emphasize the significance of technology and AI in analyzing mobile user behavior and optimizing marketing campaigns. It provides insights into comprehending mobile user behavior, factors influencing it, and the role of AI in marketing research. Moreover, it explores AI's utilization in consumer behavior analysis. The study examines the impact of AI algorithms on mobile user data and discusses personalization through AI. Lastly, it delves into AI-supported campaign optimization and real-time marketing.

In the dynamic transformation of Moroccan e-commerce, AI and marketing convergence reshapes business-consumer engagement. This chapter explores AI's strategic use to enhance marketing in Moroccan e-commerce, spotlighting Jumia Market. Started in 2012 as a Pan-African tech firm, Jumia evolved into a multifaceted entity with marketplace, logistics, and payment services. Competing regionally and globally, Jumia faced challenges but went public on NYSE in 2019, adapting to market shifts. Amidst COVID-19 in 2020, it responded to changing consumer habits, emphasizing adaptability and profitability. This study examines Jumia Market's trajectory, resilience, and performance, showcasing AI's role in refining marketing strategies for optimal customer experiences and sustained growth in Moroccan e-commerce.

Chapter 12

    Ali Tazi Cherti, Sidi Mohamed Ben Abdellah University, Morocco

This research examines the impact of digital marketing (DM), through the integration of artificial intelligence (AI), on business performance (BP) in the Moroccan context. Utilizing a structured questionnaire and the advanced PLS-SEM method for analysis, it uncovers a strong positive correlation between the use of AI in DM and improved BP. This relationship signifies a paradigm shift towards more personalized marketing strategies, data-driven decision-making, and dynamic adaptation to market trends. The research highlights how AI not only enhances operational efficiency but also fosters innovation and value creation, urging Moroccan companies to rethink their digital strategies. It emphasizes AI's pivotal role in transforming the digital marketing landscape, suggesting that its strategic integration is essential for companies aiming to thrive in the digital era. The study's uniqueness stems from its focus on Morocco, offering insights into the adaptation of AI in DM within an African context, thereby contributing to the understanding of digitalization in emerging economies.

Chapter 13

    Youssra Lazrak, Sidi Mohamed Ben Abdellah University, Morocco
    Ouijdane Amrani, High School of Technology of Fez, Sidi Mohamed Ben Abdellah
        University, Morocco
    Amina El Idrissi Tissafi, High School of Technology of Fez, Sidi Mohamed Ben Abdellah
        University, Morocco

This study investigates the impact of big data on online consumer satisfaction and purchasing behavior within the Moroccan context, addressing the gap in understanding its effects on consumer satisfaction in specific markets. Through a quantitative analysis, the authors explore how big data's application in personalized marketing strategies influences consumer behaviors and satisfaction. The research reveals the critical role of product quality and personalized recommendations in enhancing online consumer satisfaction, despite the general assumption of price as a primary factor. These findings suggest that big data, while potent in tailoring marketing efforts, shows varied significance in directly influencing consumer satisfaction levels in Morocco. The study contributes to the digital marketing literature by providing insights into the strategic application of big data in enhancing consumer engagement and satisfaction, offering managerial implications for leveraging technology in marketing strategies.

Chapter 14

Adil Garohe, Mohammed V University in Rabat, Morocco
Rachid Zammar, Mohammed V University in Rabat, Morocco

In the face of escalating customer turnover, Moroccan telecom operators seek robust strategies to retain their customer base. This chapter investigates the dynamics of customer churn and proposes a big data analytic approach to predict and minimize this phenomenon. Through the integration of logistic regression, machine learning techniques, and psychological profiling, the authors provide a comprehensive model for understanding customer behaviors and developing targeted retention strategies. The findings from this study offer a valuable blueprint for telecom companies to not only address the churn but to also pave the way for sustained market success in a competitive digital economy.

Chapter 15

Mohammed Mesbahi, Mohammed V University in Rabat, Morocco
Kaoutar El Menzhi, Mohammed V University in Rabat, Morocco
Mustapha Ait Kassi, Hassan II University of Casablanca, Morocco

For the auditing industry, the advent of digital is not perceived as a simple change, but rather as a genuine revolution redefining the way professionals perform their diligence and maintain their relationships with customers, whose expectations tend to develop. Hence, mastering the digital dimension is necessary for any firm wishing to remain competitive in a fiercely rivalrous sector. This study uses a Delphi approach to provide a prospective overview of audit digitalization and its impact on customer experience optimization, considering the regulatory dimension. Results show that auditing firms, especially the four big ones, are making significant progress in integrating advanced technologies into their processes. Auditors display a certain optimism regarding this transition, as it contributes to optimizing verification procedures while enabling clients to benefit from more efficient and reliable services. However, regulatory reform is crucial to fostering an environment of trust and guiding the ethical use of digital tools.

Chapter 16

Nabil Seghyar, Research Laboratory in Organizational Management Sciences, Ibn Tofail
University, Kenitra, Morocco
Meryem Amane, Artificial Intelligence, Data Science, and Emergent Systems Laboratory,
Sidi Mohamed Ben Abdellah University, Fez, Morocco
Mounir Gouiouez, Psychology, Sociology, and Culture Studies Laboratory, Sidi Mohamed
Ben Abdellah University, Fez, Morocco
Said Hraoui, Artificial Intelligence, Data Science, and Emergent Systems Laboratory, Sidi
Mohamed Ben Abdellah University, Fez, Morocco
Abdelfettah Bouhtati, LRJPE laboratory, Multidisciplinary Faculty of Taza, Sidi Mohamed
Ben Abdellah University, Morocco

This study delves into Moroccan banking's evolving landscape, focusing on client satisfaction through digital tools. Emphasizing digital's pivotal role in service quality, it aims to uncover how emerging tech shapes satisfaction. Employing quantitative methods via tailored questionnaires, it seeks to gauge customer perceptions of digital banking. Examining tech integration, AI-Chatbots, and personalized services, it explores how these enhance satisfaction. Additionally, it probes AI-driven marketing's transformative potential in deepening bank-client connections. By spotlighting digital tool efficacy in client satisfaction, this research offers nuanced insights into Morocco's tech-driven banking paradigm. Its data-driven findings can guide strategic decisions for institutions and policymakers, elevating overall service quality in the digital age.

Chapter 17

Rachid Boudri, Euromed Business School, Euromed University of Fez, Morocco
Badr Bentalha, National School of Business and Management, Sidi Mohammed Ben Abdellah University, Morocco
Omar Benjelloun, Euromed Business School, Euromed University of Fez, Morocco

The physical store provides a shopping experience that can't be replaced by digital means. However, the combination of the two has infinite potential and it's called the phygital shopping experience. In a retail context, phygital marketing is about finding the right amount of digital technology to incorporate into the store, to offer the shopper a unique shopping experience. Moreover, phygital marketing is a recent discipline that lacks practical and theoretical information. This study aims to contribute to the conceptualization of the latter through a netnography, and by linking the practice of phygital marketing to the behavioral science concept which is "the pain of paying." This expression refers to the negative emotions felt during the process of paying for a product. Thus, a thematic content analysis opens the way to define a competitive advantage through phygital marketing.

Chapter 18

Mohamed Amine Gueznai, National School of Commerce and Management, Hassan II University of Casablanca, Morocco
Abdellah Elboussadi, National School of Commerce and Management, Hassan II University of Casablanca, Morocco

Over the past few years, the world of commerce has undergone lightning changes, both in terms of content and form, driven by the democratization of NICT usage. This transformation has led to the emergence of new behaviors, new players, new distribution concepts, and a new shopping experience. The presentation of the commercial offer has given rise to a new in-store experience for customers. The latter can be a source of satisfaction, and consequently of purchase intent. Considering the consumer as a being in search of a sensitive experience, phygital tools combined with experiential marketing have become an essential weapon used by companies to make consumers feel they are living a pleasant and unique experience, provoking in them a sense of belonging and loyalty.

Chapter 19

Mohamed Badouch, Faculty of Sciences, Ibn Zohr University, Agadir, Morocco
Mehdi Boutaounte, National School of Commerce and Management, Ibn Zohr University, Dakhla, Morocco

Accurate hotel recommendations play a crucial role in enhancing the overall travel experience. In recent years, recommendation systems have gained significant popularity in the tourism industry. These systems use various techniques and algorithms to analyze user preferences and provide personalized hotel recommendations. One of the emerging methods in recommendation systems is deep learning, a branch of machine learning that focuses on training neural networks with multiple layers to make accurate predictions or classifications. Deep learning algorithms have shown great success in various domains such as image processing and natural language processing. This chapter aims to propose a hotel recommendation system that utilizes deep learning techniques for analyzing user preferences and providing personalized recommendations. The proposed hotel recommendation system will leverage user reviews and hotel descriptions to extract meaningful features and train a deep learning model.

In the rapidly evolving financial sector, banks face the dual challenge of enhancing customer experience and optimizing marketing strategies. This chapter explores the integration of artificial intelligence (AI) and data engineering in revolutionizing marketing approaches within the banking industry. The core of this study delves into the deployment of AI technologies - including machine learning algorithms, predictive analytics, and natural language processing - to harness vast amounts of banking data for strategic marketing purposes. This research outlines how AI-driven data analysis enables personalized customer experiences, predicting customer needs and behavior with high accuracy. This personalization extends to tailored product recommendations, dynamic pricing models, and targeted marketing campaigns, thereby increasing customer engagement and satisfaction.

Preface

1. OVERVIEW OF THE TOPIC

The increasing use of information technologies and artificial intelligence (AI) in the field of management represents a major evolution for companies, administrations and territories, particularly in logistics, human resources, finance, marketing, etc. Regarding this last dimension, many research questions challenge us in terms of issues, opportunities, mechanisms and impact of recent technological and digital innovations, such as robotics, AI, Internet of Things, Big Data Analytics, IT, ICT, Social Media, Gamification and Mobile Technologies, on the reinvention of emerging marketing research methods and methodologies, the dynamics of reflexivity on the strategic and operational marketing of companies and territories, and the revision of the approaches to evaluate and manage the commercial performance and tourism marketing of these entities.

In particular, the rise of artificial intelligence (AI) and data engineering opens exciting new perspectives for marketing. These disruptive technologies make it possible to deeply rethink marketing practices, from strategy design to campaign optimization and customer relationship management.

Very recently, we are seeing an influx of research into exploring opportunities and opportunities for integrating AI and data engineering solutions throughout the marketing process - from diagnostics to performance measurement (Lies, 2019; Rekha et al., 2016; Yau et al., 2021; Sterne, 2017; Theodoridis & Gkikas, 2019; Verma et al., 2021; Jarek & Mazurek, 2019; Ponomarenko et al., 2024; Kim & Hwang, 2024; George et al., 2024; Eshiett & Eshiett, 2024; …). First, articles by Kim & Hwang (2024), Eshiett & Eshiett (2024), George et al. (2024) and Yau et al. (2021) highlight the growing adoption of AI and data engineering in marketing, both to automate marketing tasks, improve personalization and customer engagement, and optimize marketing campaigns, that to collect, clean and analyze customer data to obtain actionable insights.

Then, articles by George et al. (2024), Eshiett & Eshiett (2024) and Yau et al. (2021) show that AI and data engineering can improve customer satisfaction and marketing performance, This includes understanding customer needs and delivering personalized experiences, targeting marketing campaigns and optimizing marketing spend.

For its part Lies (2019) warns against the risks of manipulation and exploitation of customer data by AI, while Eshiett & Eshiett (2024) raise the issue of job security in the face of automation of marketing tasks, and the responsible and ethical dimensions of AI use and data engineering.

Finally, Sterne (2017), Theodoridis & Gkikas (2019) and Verma et al. (2021) continue to emphasize the potential of AI and data engineering to revolutionize marketing, continuing to play an increasingly important role in personalization, automation and optimization of marketing campaigns. This forces companies, administrations and territories to stay at the forefront of the latest advances in AI and data engineering to make the most of these technologies.

After a series of work on applications and implications of digital, AI and data engineering in the field of logistics (Bentalha, 2020; Bentalha et al., 2019; Badr, 2022; Bentalha et al., 2020; Bentalha & Hmioui, 2021; Bouhtati et al. 2024; Bentalha et al., 2023; Shamim & Bentalha, 2023), our research team very recently contributed to this marketing research, especially in terms of the added value of using Big Data Analytics technologies on the commercial efficiency of tourism companies (Lhoussaine et al., 2022; Alla et al., 2022; Bouhtati et al., 2023a) and on CRM (Bouhtati et al., 2023b). Through these contributions, through literature reviews, we have concluded that big data can help tourism companies improve their customer relationships, develop customer intelligence, optimize their marketing campaigns and improve their ROI. Similarly, and through the fuzzy approach, we have identified promising Big Data opportunities that can help tourism businesses analyze customer data and identify personalization and loyalty opportunities.

These publications offer valuable insights into the potential of big data to improve marketing efficiency in the tourism industry. They highlight the importance of data analytics to understand customer needs and preferences, and to develop targeted marketing campaigns. The authors also discuss the challenges of implementing big data solutions and the need for a strategic approach to ensure success.

Finally, AI and data engineering offer many opportunities to improve the effectiveness of marketing strategies. Companies that exploit these technologies in innovative ways will be better positioned to meet the ever-higher expectations of consumers.

2. CURRENT ISSUES

From the research above, we can summarize the main trends in research on the use of AI and data engineering in marketing as follows:

- Rethink the end-to-end marketing process:

  - → Use AI and data engineering to improve every step of the marketing process, from diagnostics to performance measurement.
  - → Rethinking traditional marketing approaches with these new technologies.

- Improve marketing intelligence:

  - → A better understanding of consumer behaviours through data analysis.
  - → Optimize advertising campaigns more precisely and precisely.
  - → Further customize the customer experience.
  - → Improve customer relationship management throughout its life cycle.

- Addressing organizational, financial and regulatory challenges:

  - → Set up the conditions for successful implementation (leadership, corporate culture, data governance, etc.).

→ Manage the strategic, organizational and ethical implications of adopting these technologies.
→ Develop new business models adapted to these innovations.

• Provide frameworks for analysis and feedback:

→ Provide a theoretical and practical approach to help businesses, administrations and territories take full advantage of AI and data engineering in marketing.
→ Share concrete feedback on the implementation of these innovative solutions.

In summary, the research focuses on how AI and data engineering can profoundly transform marketing practices while addressing the organizational, strategic and ethical challenges associated with this digital transformation.

By exploring the synergies between AI, data engineering and marketing practices, this book offers a unique perspective on how companies and organizations can position themselves to succeed in an ever-changing environment. Its reading is therefore strongly recommended to anyone interested in the transformative impact of digital technologies on the field of marketing.

This book is timely to examine the implications of these innovations and the opportunities they offer to marketing professionals.

The authors highlight theoretical reflections and practical applications that allow rethinking traditional marketing approaches. They highlight both the potential of these technologies to improve marketing intelligence and the organizational, financial and regulatory challenges associated with their implementation.

This book provides valuable insight into the latest advances in this evolving field. It is aimed at both researchers and practitioners, to guide them in adopting these innovative solutions and managing their operational effectiveness. Students will also find a useful reference on emerging trends that will shape the future of marketing.

This book looks in depth at the issues, challenges and best practices related to the adoption and concrete anchoring of these innovative solutions in the field of marketing. It is positioned as an essential scientific and practical reference on the subject.

The book begins with a detailed overview of the impact of AI and data engineering on the different dimensions of marketing. In particular, it explores how these technologies can better understand consumer behaviour, optimize advertising campaigns, personalize the customer experience or improve customer relationship management throughout its life cycle.

Beyond the purely technical aspects, the book also addresses the strategic, organizational and ethical implications of adopting these innovative solutions. It highlights the key conditions for a successful implementation, whether in terms of leadership, corporate culture, data governance or setting up new business models.

Through a theoretical and practical approach, the book provides a comprehensive overview of the issues related to the use of AI and data engineering in marketing. It offers analytical frameworks and concrete feedback to help companies and territories take full advantage of these disruptive technologies.

3. TARGET AUDIENCE AND POTENTIAL USES

The book's central issue aims to identify reflections and applications on the adoption and anchoring of innovative solutions offered by AI and data engineering to improve the efficiency of marketing processes within companies and territories. It is about bridging the gap between theory and practice on the application potential of these technologies to improve marketing and overall performance of organizations.

The book is intended for researchers, practitioners, and students interested in the applications of artificial interest and data engineering in the field of marketing both companies and territories. It is intended as a guide for the implementation of these new marketing management solutions and the management of their operational efficiency. The target audience for this publication is mainly researchers and practitioners in this field, but the book can also be useful to students.

4. OVERALL DESCRIPTION OF CONTRIBUTIONS

The book features a highly selective collection of relevant and advanced scientific research by world-renowned researchers and experts in the field. It aims to provide concise and relevant answers to a wide range of questions at the crossroads of reflexivity on the adoption of innovative solutions in marketing through the mobilization of opportunities offered by data engineering and artificial intelligence, on the approaches to their operational anchoring and the accompanying conditions to be verified, and on the effectiveness of such a strategy and its impact on the commercial and global performance of companies and territories.

The **1st chapter**, "*Artificial Intelligence in Costumer Acquisition: A Bibliometric Study*", seeks to explore, through bibliometric analysis using VOSViewer, publications dealing with the applicability of AI to boost customer acquisition. The results reveal an acceleration of research since 2018, a predominance of American institutions, a concentration of publications in marketing and computer journals, a trend towards decentralization of research on the uses of AI in customer acquisition, and the absence of emergence of predominant author groups. These elements make it possible to draw up an inventory of research in this field.

The **second chapter**, "*Marketing Applications of Emerging Technologies: A Systematic Literature Review*", aims to examine the use and impact of emerging technologies (AI, augmented reality, IoT, blockchain, etc.) on marketing practices and strategies. Based on a systematic review of the literature according to the PRISMA protocol, with qualitative analysis of the results using the NVivo software, The study finds that emerging technologies are increasingly important for understanding and satisfying individual customer needs and improving the customer experience. This presents both opportunities and challenges for marketing applications.

The **third chapter**, "*The Application of AI in Neuromarketing: A Systematic Literature Review*", aims to identify, evaluate and synthesize studies on the use of AI in neuromarketing practices, as well as controversial ethical perspectives. Based on a systematic review of the literature, with qualitative content analysis, the study found that AI allows a more accurate analysis of consumer behaviours and decision-making processes in neuromarketing. However, ethical debates about its use are still ongoing.

The **4th chapter**, "*Artificial Intelligence Applications in Marketing: The State of the Art and Hotspots over 20 years*", focuses on analyzing the current state of AI research in marketing, identifying trends and research areas, and exploring future directions. Through bibliometric analysis, the research identified four main research themes: application of AI in marketing, AI for analysis and forecasting, AI in decision-making and optimization, AI and data analysis. Future perspectives on AI applied to Industry 4.0 and ethical considerations.

The **5th chapter**, "*A Systematic Review of Augmented Reality Experiential Marketing: Conceptual Framework and Research Agenda*", examines the current state of knowledge on experiential marketing in augmented reality (AREM) and identifies areas for further study. Through a methodological approach focused on the systematic review of the literature and the development of an integrative conceptual framework, the study showed that AREM influences consumer behaviour and has important implications for immersive marketing strategies, while noting the need to go beyond mere novelty, towards engaging interactions, personalized and ethically responsible.

For the **6th chapter**, "*Factors Affecting Citizen's Intention to Use Smart City Services in Morocco: A Systematic Literature Review and Conceptual Framework*", the (objective is to identify the main factors influencing the intention of using smart city services by citizens in Morocco, by borrowing a systematic literature review according to the PRISMA method, with an emphasis on the use of the UTAUT theory. Key factors are performance expectations, ease of use, social influence, perceived cost, awareness, trust in technology and trust in government.

The **Chapter 7**, "*Towards Agile Marketing: Transforming Strategies for the Digital Era*", seeks instead to explore the transformative potential of agile marketing and its implications for marketing strategies in the digital age. Based on a literature review and theoretical synthesis on the principles and practices of agile marketing, the study revealed that agile marketing allows greater flexibility, speed and focus on the customer, through the integration of methodologies like Scrum and Kanban.

Regarding the **8th chapter**, "*The Potential Benefits of Integrating Business Intelligence and CRM*", the objective is to examine the principles, challenges and potential benefits of integrating business intelligence and customer relationship management (CRM). With a theoretical and conceptual analysis of the literature on the integration of these two systems., research has found that integrating BI and CRM can improve operational efficiency and customer-centric practices, leading to sustainable growth and improved competitiveness.

For the **9th chapter**, "*Revolutionizing Customer Interactions: Enhancing Customer Engagement Strategies with Artificial Intelligence (AI) Technologies*", the authors seek to better understand the transformative role of AI in customer engagement strategies, from understanding consumer behavior to responsible automation, through a literature review and conceptual analysis of the use of AI to improve customer engagement. They found that AI enables better understanding of consumer behaviours, increased personalization and effective automation, while requiring ethical and privacy-friendly implementation.

Regarding the **10th chapter**, "*Optimizing Marketing Campaigns with AI-Driven Insights on Mobile User Behavior*", the study focuses on using AI to analyze mobile user behavior to optimize marketing campaigns. It explores the factors influencing mobile user behavior and the role of AI in analyzing consumer behavior. The study then analyzes the impact of AI algorithms on mobile user data and examines personalization through AI. Finally, it explores campaign optimization and AI-enabled real-time marketing.

The **11th chapter**, "*Applying Artificial Intelligence to Enhance E-Commerce Marketing Strategies: A Case Study of Jumia Market in Morocco*", studies the strategic use of AI to improve marketing in Moroccan e-commerce, focusing on the Jumia Market case. It traces the trajectory, resilience and performance of Jumia Market, highlighting the role of AI in refining marketing strategies to deliver optimal customer experiences and ensure sustainable growth in Moroccan e-commerce.

The **12th chapter**, *"The Influence of Digital Marketing on Business Performance: A Case Study of Selected Moroccan Companies"*, examines the impact of integrating AI into digital marketing on business performance in Morocco. It reveals a strong positive correlation between the use of AI in digital marketing and performance improvement, highlighting the critical role of AI in transforming the digital marketing landscape. The study focuses on the adaptation of AI in digital marketing in an emerging African context.

In the **13th chapter**, *"Big Data and Consumer Behavior: A Quantitative Study among Moroccan Internet Users"*, the authors seek to examine the impact of Big Data on online consumer satisfaction and purchasing behaviour in Morocco. It reveals the essential role of product quality and personalized recommendations in improving consumer satisfaction online, despite the importance generally given to price. The study sheds light on the strategic application of Big Data to improve consumer engagement and satisfaction, with managerial implications for the use of technology in marketing strategies.

For the **14th chapter**, *"Data-Driven Strategies for Enhancing Customer Retention in Moroccan Telecoms"*, the study examines customer retention dynamics among Moroccan telecoms operators. It proposes an analytical approach of big data to predict and minimize the churn phenomenon, integrating logistic regression, machine learning techniques and psychological profiling. The results provide a valuable framework for telecom companies to not only manage churn, but also ensure their sustainable success in a competitive and digital marketplace.

Regarding the **15th chapter**, *"Digitalization of Auditing Practices and Customer Experience Optimization: A Delphi Analysis of the Moroccan Context"*, the research uses a Delphi approach to provide a forward-looking overview of audit digitization and its impact on customer experience optimization, considering the regulatory dimension. It shows that audit firms, particularly the Big 4, are making significant progress in integrating advanced technologies. While listeners are optimistic about this transition, regulatory reform is crucial to foster an environment of trust and ethical use of digital tools.

The **16th chapter**, *"Client Satisfaction in the Moroccan Banking Sector: The Role of Digitalization"*, explores the role of digital in the satisfaction of banking customers in Morocco. Using quantitative methods, it assesses customer perceptions of technology integration, AI-powered chatbots and personalized services, and examines the transformative potential of AI-driven marketing to deepen bank-customer relationships. The results provide nuanced information on Morocco's digital banking paradigm and can guide the strategic decisions of institutions and policy makers.

For their part, the authors of the **17th chapter**, «*Phygital Marketing and the PAIN of PAYING: An Amazon Go Netnographic Case Study*», aim to contribute to the conceptualization of phygital marketing, by linking it to the concept of "pain of payment" from the science of behavior. Through netnography and thematic content analysis, it paves the way for defining a competitive advantage through phygital marketing, which combines physical store experience and digital technologies to deliver a unique shopping experience.

Regarding the **18th chapter**, *"Exploratory Analysis of the Impact of Phygital on the Customer Experience"*, the study explores the impact of phygital on the customer experience. It shows that the presentation of the commercial offer has given rise to a new in-store experience for customers. Phygital, which combines physical and digital tools, has become an essential weapon for companies to provide consumers with a pleasant and unique experience, creating a sense of belonging and loyalty.

For the **19th chapter**, "*Design and Implementation of a Hotel Recommendation System Using Deep Learning*", the contribution aims to propose a hotel recommendation system using deep learning techniques to analyze user preferences and provide personalized recommendations. The system relies on analysis of user feedback and hotel descriptions to extract relevant features and train a deep learning model.

Finally, for the **final chapter**, "*Innovative Marketing in Banking: The Role of AI and Data Engineering*", the research aims to explore the integration of artificial intelligence (AI) and data engineering to revolutionize marketing approaches in the banking sector. It shows how the analysis of banking data through AI technologies, such as machine learning, predictive analytics and natural language processing, enables personalized customer experiences, accurately predict customer needs and behaviours, and implement targeted marketing campaigns, thereby increasing customer engagement and satisfaction.

5. CONCLUSION

This book is positioned as a scientific reference on reflexivity and applications of data engineering and artificial intelligence techniques and mechanisms in the field of marketing. Through its theoretical modeling and empirical applications, the book aims to make a significant contribution both for managers and decision-makers in business and territorial marketing strategies, as well as for marketing students, trade and territorial management. The originality of this theme lies in the ambition to converge academic and professional research around the issues related to the adoption and anchoring of techniques and mechanisms of data science, Big Data, e-learning, blockchain, augmented and virtual reality and their impact on strategic and operational marketing, customer relationship and life cycle management, business performance management, marketing ethics, etc.

In this sense, this book presents itself as a scientific and practical reference on the integration of AI and data engineering solutions in the field of marketing. It explores the opportunities and challenges associated with this digital transformation, and offers analytical frameworks and concrete feedback to help companies and territories take full advantage of these disruptive technologies.

The focal points for the substantial added value of this book for both the scientific community and the managerial practices of actors and professionals are summarized as follows:

- *News*: The book is timely in examining the implications of AI and data engineering in marketing. It highlights the theoretical reflections and practical applications that make it possible to rethink traditional marketing approaches.
- *Holistic approach:* The book covers the different dimensions of marketing, from understanding consumer behaviours to optimizing advertising campaigns, personalizing the customer experience and managing the customer relationship.
- *Strategic Perspective:* The book highlights the importance of data strategy and governance for successful implementation of AI and data engineering solutions. It also highlights the ethical implications and organizational challenges of adopting them.
- *Frameworks for analysis and feedback:* The book offers frameworks for analysis and concrete feedback to help companies and territories take full advantage of these disruptive technologies.
- *Target audience:* The book is aimed at both researchers and practitioners, as well as marketing students. It is a valuable reference for anyone who wants to understand the marketing implications of AI and data engineering.

In conclusion, the book *AI and Data Engineering For Effective Marketing* is a must-read for anyone who wants to understand the opportunities and challenges of integrating AI and data engineering solutions in the marketing field. It offers a holistic and strategic perspective and offers analytical frameworks and concrete feedback to help companies and territories take full advantage of these disruptive technologies.

Lhoussaine ALLA

National School of Applied Sciences -Fez, Sidi Mohamed Ben Abdellah University, Morocco

Aziz HMIOUI

National School of Business and Management of Fez, Sidi Mohamed Ben Abdellah University, Morocco

Badr BENTALHA

National School of Business and Management of Fez, Sidi Mohamed Ben Abdellah University, Morocco

REFERENCES

Alla, L., Kamal, M., & Bouhtati, N. (2022). Big data and marketing effectiveness of tourism businesses: A literature review. Alternatives Managériales Economiques, *4*. 10.48374/IMIST.PRSM/ame-v1i0.36928

Badr, B. (2022). Smart Technologies for a Sustainable Service Supply Chain: A Prospective Perspective. *Journal of Environmental Issues and Climate Change*, 1(1), 77–89. 10.59110/jeicc.v1i1.81

Bentalha, B. (2020). Big-Data et service supply chain management: Challenges et opportunités. *International Journal of Business and Technology Studies*, 1(3).

Bentalha, B., & Hmioui, A. (2021, November). Smart service supply chain and Just Walk Out technology: a netnographic approach. In *The Proceedings of the International Conference on Smart City Applications* (pp. 223-236). Cham: Springer International Publishing.

Bentalha, B., Hmioui, A., & Alla, L. (2019, October). The digitalization of the supply chain management of service companies: a prospective approach. In *Proceedings of the 4th International Conference on Smart City Applications* (pp. 1-8). ACM. 10.1145/3368756.3369005

Bentalha, B., Hmioui, A., & Alla, L. (2020). Digital service supply chain management: current realities and prospective visions. In *Innovations in Smart Cities Applications Edition 3: The Proceedings of the 4th International Conference on Smart City Applications 4* (pp. 808-822). Springer International Publishing. 10.1007/978-3-030-37629-1_58

Bentalha, B., Hmioui, A., & Alla, L. (Eds.). (2023). *Integrating Intelligence and Sustainability in Supply Chains*. IGI Global. 10.4018/979-8-3693-0225-5

Bouhtati, N., Alla, L., & Bentalhah, B. (2023b). Marketing Big Data Analytics and Customer Relationship Management: A Fuzzy Approach. In *Integrating Intelligence and Sustainability in Supply Chains* (pp. 75-86). IGI Global. . IGI Global.10.4018/979-8-3693-0225-5.ch004

Bouhtati, N., El Yaacoubi, Y., Bentalha, B., & Lhoussaine, A. L. L. A. (2024). Leviers logistiques de promotion du commerce équitable des produits de terroir: Une esquisse de modèle d'analyse. *Alternatives Managériales Economiques*, Vol 6 (Spécial 1), 17-35.

Bouhtati, N., El Yaacoubi, Y., Bentalha, B., & Lhoussaine, A. L. L. A. (2024). Leviers logistiques de promotion du commerce équitable des produits de terroir: Une esquisse de modèle d'analyse. *Alternatives Managériales Economiques, 6*(Spécial 1), 17-35.

Bouhtatit, N., Kamal, M., & Alla, L. (2023a). Big Data and the Effectiveness of Tourism Marketing: A Prospective Review of the Literature. In Farhaoui, Y., Rocha, A., Brahmia, Z., & Bhushab, B. (Eds.), *Artificial Intelligence and Smart Environment. ICAISE 2022. Lecture Notes in Networks and Systems, 635*. Springer. 10.1007/978-3-031-26254-8_40

Eshiett, I. O., & Eshiett, O. E. (2024). Artificial intelligence marketing and customer satisfaction: An employee job security threat review. *World Journal of Advanced Research and Reviews*, 21(1), 446–456. 10.30574/wjarr.2024.21.1.2655

George, S. M., Sasikala, B., Gowthami, T., Sopna, P., Umamaheswari, M., & Dhinakaran, D. P. (2024). Role of Artificial Intelligence in Marketing Strategies and Performance. *Migration Letters : An International Journal of Migration Studies*, 21(S4), 1589–1599.

Jarek, K., & Mazurek, G. (2019). Marketing and artificial intelligence. *Central European Business Review, 8*(2).

Kim, D., & Hwang, G. H. (2024). Machine Learning and Artificial Intelligence Use in Marketing. *International Journal of Intelligent Systems and Applications in Engineering*, 12(5s), 266–272.

Lhoussaine, A. L. L. A., Kamal, M., & Bouhtati, N. (2022). Big data and marketing effectiveness of tourism businesses: A literature review. *Economic Management Alternatives*, 1, 39–58.

Lies, J. (2019). *Marketing intelligence and big data: Digital marketing techniques on their way to becoming social engineering techniques in marketing.*

Ponomarenko, I. V., Pavlenko, V. M., Morhulets, O. B., Ponomarenko, D. V., & Ukhnal, N. M. (2024). Application of artificial intelligence in digital marketing. In *CEUR Workshop Proceedings* (pp. 155-166).

Rekha, A. G., Abdulla, M. S., & Asharaf, S. (2016). Artificial intelligence marketing: An application of a novel lightly trained support vector data description. *Journal of Information and Optimization Sciences*, 37(5), 681–691. 10.1080/02522667.2016.1191186

Shamim, R., & Bentalha, B. (2023). Blockchain-Enabled Machine Learning Framework for Demand Forecasting in Supply Chain Management. In *Integrating Intelligence and Sustainability in Supply Chains* (pp. 28–48). IGI Global. 10.4018/979-8-3693-0225-5.ch002

Sterne, J. (2017). *Artificial intelligence for marketing: practical applications*. John Wiley & Sons. 10.1002/9781119406341

Theodoridis, P. K., & Gkikas, D. C. (2019). How artificial intelligence affects digital marketing. In *Strategic Innovative Marketing and Tourism: 7th ICSIMAT, Athenian Riviera, Greece, 2018* (pp. 1319-1327). Springer International Publishing. 10.1007/978-3-030-12453-3_151

Verma, S., Sharma, R., Deb, S., & Maitra, D. (2021). Artificial intelligence in marketing: Systematic review and future research direction. *International Journal of Information Management Data Insights*, 1(1), 100002. 10.1016/j.jjimei.2020.100002

Yau, K. L. A., Saad, N. M., & Chong, Y. W. (2021). Artificial intelligence marketing (AIM) for enhancing customer relationships. *Applied Sciences (Basel, Switzerland)*, 11(18), 8562. 10.3390/app11188562

Section 1
Bibliometric Studies and Literature Reviews on AI and Marketing

Chapter 1
Artificial Intelligence in Costumer Acquisition:
A Bibliometric Study

Mustapha Elhissoufi

Sidi Mohamed Ben Abdellah University, Morocco

Lhoussaine Alla
http://orcid.org/0000-0002-7238-1792
Sidi Mohamed Ben Abdellah University, Morocco

ABSTRACT

The objective of this chapter is to explore publications that have addressed the applicability of AI to boost customer acquisition, via bibliometric analysis via VOSViewer. These results reveal an acceleration of research since 2018, a predominance of American institutions, a concentration of publications in marketing and computer science journals, a trend towards the decentralization of research on the uses of AI in customer acquisition and an absence of the emergence of predominant author groups.

1. INTRODUCTION

Recent AI advances provide excellent opportunities for marketing practitioners and academic researchers. They have transformed marketing practices (Rangaswamy et al., 2020). These increasingly rely on AI algorithms that mimic human cognitive abilities (Huang & Rust, 2018). These applications bring significant benefits in terms of cost reduction, diversification of service channels, personalization of offers, and innovative, user-friendly solutions (Haenlein & Kaplan, 2019).

In addition, the digitalization of marketing has led to the creation of centralized databases containing structured data (e.g., sales data, customer information) and unstructured data (e.g., videos, images) that require advanced AI models to analyze them (Paschen et al., 2020). Thanks to this ability to obtain and exploit massive and in-depth customer data, AI has become an essential tool in customer relationship management, which has moved from a transactional perspective to a relational one in which customer acquisition plays a fundamental role (Pansari & Kumar, 2017).

DOI: 10.4018/979-8-3693-3172-9.ch001

Customer acquisition is seeking a new customer, i.e., selling a product or service to someone for the first time (Peltokoski, 2022). Acquiring new customers is the backbone of any commercial enterprise (Gopalakrishnan et al., 2022). It has received significant attention in various fields, including marketing, organizational behavior, consumer behavior, and service management (Kumar et al., 2010). The literature often mentions it as a critical element of customer lifetime value (Zheng et al., 2022).

AI is widely used to acquire customers. It provides information to identify their needs, segment them into homogeneous groups, anticipate their concerns, and provide personalized experiences. Overall, AI improves the efficiency and effectiveness of customer acquisition strategies (Castro et al., 2023).

Academically, AI in customer acquisition is an emerging field of research that is developing very rapidly (Feng, 2021). In its early stages, the topics addressed are varied and scattered, such as the use of Big Data as a decision support system for customer acquisition (Alla et al., 2022), applications of various machine learning techniques (Salminen et al.,2019), the use of AI strategically to acquire new customers (Berger et al., 2019), dynamic online pricing (Misra et al., 2019), the automation of acquisition tasks by AI (Thomaz et al., 2020), the impact of AI on retailing (Davenport et al., 2020), the study of psychological and cultural barriers to consumer adoption of autonomous shopping systems (De Bellis & Venkataramani, 2020), the development of explainable automatic product recommendation techniques (Marchand & Marx, 2020), and the impact of AI on customer journeys (Puntoni et al., 2018).

To our knowledge, no bibliometric study of AI in customer acquisition exists. Given its growing importance, we believe this gap provides an opportunity to map, trace, and understand the publications, key terms, authors, institutions, and countries studying AI in this field. As a result, and in order to synthesize research on AI applications in customer acquisition and formulate proposals for future research, in this chapter, we attempt to answer the following research question: ***What are the current trends and future directions in research on AI applications in customer acquisition?*** Therefore, the aim is to conduct a bibliometric analysis of AI and related subjects to identify the main themes studied, the most influential authors, and the networks between authors and subjects. This type of analysis will enable marketers to understand better the forces shaping and advancing AI in customer acquisition as a field of study.

The conceptual framework for our study is set out in the next section, with details of our methodology in section 3. In section 4, we present our bibliometric analysis and discuss limitations and implications for future research in section 5.

2. CONCEPTUAL FRAMEWORK

In recent years, companies have placed increasing importance on artificial intelligence. They are using it to analyze data and make decisions in many areas, including customer acquisition. In this section, we will first define the concepts of artificial intelligence and customer acquisition and then outline the various AI tools applicable to customer acquisition.

2.1 Artificial Intelligence

The driving force behind the fourth industrial revolution, AI, is intelligence manifested by machines. It imitates human intelligence processes by machines, such as decision-making, problem-solving, speech recognition, and imaging (Sagić et al., 2019). Many technologies can perform repetitive tasks, but they cannot think autonomously. They do not think outside their code. In contrast, machine learning, a subset of AI, aims to allow machines to learn a task without pre-existing code (Russel & Norvig,2016). Machines are, therefore, fed problems and examples to learn to perform specific tasks. They learn and adapt to perform activities autonomously as they process these problems and examples. AI experts strive to make the machine capable of using what it has learned by analyzing photographs and different data sets. Data scientists and programmers formulate general-purpose learning algorithms that help machines learn more than one specific task (Verma et al., 2021).

In this research, we adopt Haenlein and Kaplan's (2019, p. 5) definition of AI: "the ability of a system to correctly interpret external data, learn from that data, and use that learning to achieve specific goals and tasks through flexible adaptation." It, therefore, covers a variety of activities and concepts as various types of systems are based on software and algorithms that facilitate or perform tasks that previously required human cognitive abilities (Huang & Rust, 2018; Bouhtati, et al. 2023). As a result, marketing research uses terms such as machine learning, service robots, automation, big data, neural network, natural language processing, and Internet of Things (IoT) to refer to (AI Salminen et al., 2019; Wirtz et al., 2018).

2.2 Customer Acquisition

AI tools have enabled companies to remain competitive in increasingly data-driven marketing landscapes (Lhoussaine et al. 2022), so many companies have invested in them to facilitate various marketing-related tasks of which customer acquisition and one of the most important (Haenlein & Kaplan, 2019; Luo et al., 2019). Customer acquisition is the process of attracting new customers. It involves identifying potential customers, making contact with them, and converting them into buying customers. It is essential for a company's sustainability and growth, enabling it to expand its customer portfolio, increase sales and market share, and improve brand awareness.

According to De Bruyn et al. (2020), customer acquisition consists of targeting potential customers based on their demographic characteristics, interests, and behaviors and contacting them through various marketing channels, such as advertising, social media, and word of mouth. This is the first stage in the customer lifecycle that conditions customer engagement and loyalty (Kumar et al., 2019). Businesses can increase customer loyalty and encourage repeat purchases by building solid customer relationships through personalized communication and exceptional customer service. Companies must invest in effective and efficient customer acquisition strategies to support their growth and competitiveness in the market (Haenlein & Kaplan, 2019). For Huang and Rust (2018), companies can use different methods and strategies only to acquire new customers: online advertising, content marketing, and influencer partnerships. They stress the importance of targeting policies and delivering personalized messages and offers to attract and convert potential customers.

The cost of acquiring customers is much higher than retaining them (Reinartz et al., 2005), and a company's position in the market is more sensitive to acquisition costs than retention costs (Min et al., 2016). To maximize return on investment, companies must understand and control their customer acquisition process to allocate resources effectively and make the best strategic decisions. Indeed, a company's financial value and future sales forecasts largely depend on the size of its customer portfolio (Gupta et al., 2009).

In this research, we adopt a broader definition of customer acquisition. It refers to the consequences of acquiring or converting existing potential customers into new customers. There are two stages in customer acquisition: Prospecting, during which salespeople generate and qualify leads for new customers

(Gopalakrishnan et al., 2022), and conversion (closing sales), during which they attempt to turn these leads into customers. These two activities form the basis of new customer acquisition and are one of the main reasons salespeople are hired (Gopalakrishnan et al., 2022).

According to De Bruyn et al. (2020), customer acquisition consists of targeting potential customers based on their demographic characteristics, interests, and behaviors and contacting them through various marketing channels, such as advertising, social media, and word of mouth. This is the first stage in the customer lifecycle that conditions customer engagement and loyalty (Kumar et al., 2019). Businesses can increase customer loyalty and encourage repeat purchases by building solid customer relationships through personalized communication and exceptional customer service. Companies must invest in effective and efficient customer acquisition strategies to support their growth and competitiveness in the market (Haenlein & Kaplan, 2019). For Huang and Rust (2018), companies can use different methods and strategies only to acquire new customers: online advertising, content marketing, and influencer partnerships. They stress the importance of targeting policies and delivering personalized messages and offers to attract and convert potential customers.

2.3 Customer Acquisition as a Field of Application for AI

In today's business landscape, marked by unprecedented technological upheaval, companies constantly seek innovative ways to acquire customers. One of the most powerful tools available to businesses today is artificial intelligence (AI) (Haleem et al., 2022). AI significantly improves the different phases of the customer journey, with a focus on the customer acquisition phase, by leveraging data analysis, automation, and personalization (Charles et al., 2023). We distinguish several applications of AI to customer acquisition:

- *Generated content:* This functionality can help marketers target potential customers with bespoke and personalized AI-generated messages, promote their brands on social media platforms, and reduce human effort (Miroshnichenko, 2018). AI can generate relevant text, images, and videos for potential customers by analyzing customer activities online, and the system modifies itself based on the feedback it receives from customer actions.
- *Intelligent content curation:* This technique allows marketers to track customers who have purchased products in a specific category (e.g., car accessories) on individual websites. Companies can tap into these potential customers by offering discounts and exclusive deals and approaching them with personalized content (Amatriain & Basilico, 2015). Using AI, companies can provide their potential customers with relevant content at the right time and according to their position in the buying cycle.
- *Programmatic media buying:* This method helps marketers to automatically segment potential customers and target the most exciting groups rather than negotiating directly with customers (Suri et al., 2021).
- *Predictive analytics:* Using this modeling tool, it is possible to predict the likelihood of a potential customer being converted into a value-added customer, assess the price at which a customer is likely to convert, and identify those customers most likely to make repeat purchases (Surendro, 2019)
- *Lead assessment:* AI tools can facilitate the initial gathering of information for lead generation while quickly analyzing unstructured data such as emails, phone conversations, and social messages to identify trends and determine a relevant lead (Marr, 2019). The lead scores generated by these

applications allow salespeople to measure their potential and determine whether they should devote their time to them.

- *Targeted advertising:* AI algorithms can use information from potential customers to analyze the products they seek at different times. In this way, creative content can target potential customer's at the most appropriate time and place while enabling real-time bidding by presenting a specific ad to a specific user based on their previous browsing behavior (Coffin, 2022). This method can also anticipate a customer's future purchase by examining sales data and identifying frequent links between items in previous transactions. As a result, it is possible to target the customer with advertisements and promotions associated with the anticipated purchase.

3. METHODOLOGY

This section will present our methodological approach and data collection and analysis protocol.

3.1. Methodological Approach

Bibliometric analysis objectively and quantitatively examines research on a subject objectively and quantitatively, assessing its scientific quality and influence on the literature. Thanks to this quantitative study, it is possible to grasp the internal structure of knowledge on a subject (Real, 2020) and to carry out a scientific assessment of the literature and its influence on the body of knowledge (Merigoù et al., 2015). According to Samiee and Chabowski (2012), the comprehensive collection of material for bibliometric analysis provides nuanced and accurate information, contributing to the literature's advancement. Researchers have employed bibliometric analysis to analyse the composition of research on digital mediation in business-to-business marketing and key account management (Kumar et al., 2020).

Our methodological approach consists of a bibliometric analysis of 216 articles on AI applications in customer acquisition. Researchers use bibliometric analysis to assess the quality, impact, and influence of authors, journals, and institutions in a specific research area (Lowry et al., 2013). It has also been widely used to understand trends in AI research on specific domains (Zhao, Lou et al., 2020). In this chapter, we conducted this type of analysis to understand research trends on AI applications in customer acquisition using the approach proposed by Aria and Cuccurullo (2017). This methodology comprises three main phases: data collection, analysis, and visualization.

3.2. Methodological Protocol

The data collection phase involves querying, selecting, and exporting data from selected databases. The data sample for this study was obtained by querying the central Scopus databases for publications from 2000 to 2023. This database was chosen over others such as Google Scholar or WoS because Scopus provides better quality bibliometric information due to its poly-disciplinary nature, which fits well with the nature of our theme, and better coverage of high-impact journals (Aghaei Chadegani et al., 2013).

The following search string was used to query the title, keywords, and abstracts of all the documents in the Scopus collection: (("customer acquisition" OR prospecting OR conversion) AND ("artificial intelligence "OR "Deep learning" OR "Expert system" OR "Machine learning " OR "Big data " OR "IoT")).

This search chain led to 1060 documents. For quality reasons, only document types labeled as articles published in newspapers or journals since 2000 and written in English were selected for this study as they are most likely to have undergone a rigorous peer review process before publication (Milian et al., 2019). Thus, editorial material, letters, news items, meeting abstracts, and retracted publications were removed from the dataset, leaving 216 documents constituting the final bibliometric analysis dataset. Figure 1 summarises the data collection phase.

Query database

(title, keywords, abstract) using pre-defined search string

Select relevant documents: Articles, Journals, and reviews

Figure 1. Summary of the data collection phase

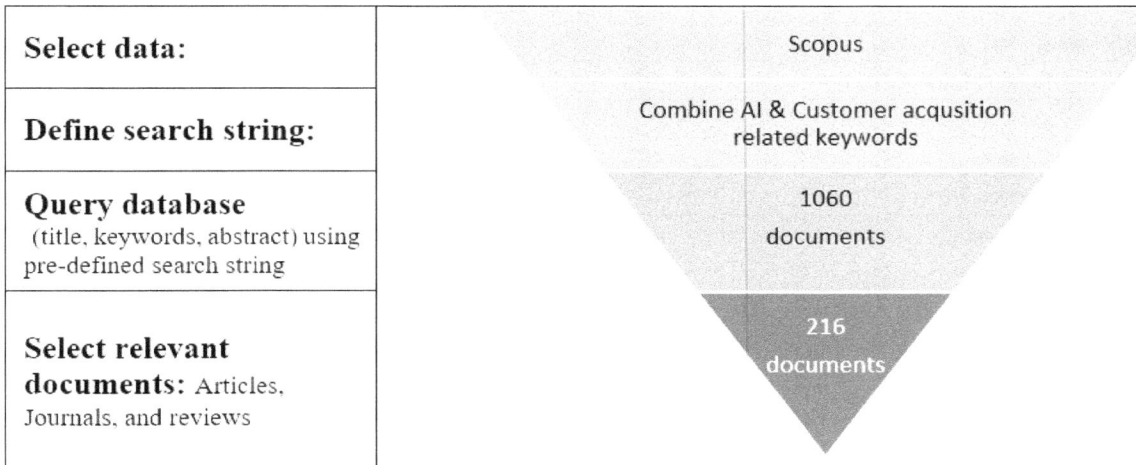

Table 1 summarizes the primary information on the dataset concerning duration, document sources, document types, document content, authors, and author collaborations. The dataset consists of documents from 155 sources, published by 426 authors and 4409 references.

Bibliographic analysis and visualization of the data generated by Scopus are carried out using VOSViewer software. VOSViewer is free software that can generate graphically representative maps with different priorities, such as co-authors, citations, keywords; bibliographic linkage, etc. (van Eck & Waltman, 2010). VOSViewer maps use lines to connect objects (such as articles, authors, organizations, and countries) that share strong connections, while the physical distance represents the relatedness between nodes. Different colors are used for each cluster to differentiate each network. These visualization features are designed to make it relatively easy for researchers to interpret the results of the bibliometric analysis (Wong, 2018).

Table 1. Key information about the dataset

Description	Results
Timespan	2000 - 2023
Sources (journals, books, etc.)	155
Number of organisations	474
Number of documents	216
Average years from publication	4.53
Average citations per doc	7.54
Average citations per year per doc	1.01
References	18040
Author's keywords	78
Authors	210
Author appearances	646
Authors of single-authored documents	88
Authors of multi-authored documents	128
Documents per author	1,03
Co-authors per documents	1,97

Source: Compiled by us

4. BIBLIOMETRIC ANALYSIS

In this section, we present the results generated by VOSViewer concerning co-author analysis, co-occurrence analysis, citation analysis, and co-citation analysis.

In the early 2000s, researchers and marketing practitioners should have paid more attention to using AI in customer acquisition. However, the situation has changed rapidly in recent times, as illustrated by the graph in Figure 2, which shows that the number of articles on the subject was negligible until 2013, when interest in the topic began to change. The trend accelerated rapidly from 2019, with 25 articles published, to reach the peak of publications in 2020, with 36 articles published and, by mid-2020, 41 articles had already appeared. After declining in 2021 and 2022, publications increased in 2023 to 29 articles.

Figure 2. Number of articles on AI in customer acquisition (2000-2023)

The results of the four types of analysis mentioned above (co-authors, co-occurrence, citations, and co-citation) are presented in this section, together with the visualizations created in VOSViewer and our interpretations of these maps.

4.1 Analysis of Co.Authors

The aim is to examine the links between authors, institutions, and countries by identifying and exploring the extent of their collaboration as authors;

• Analysis By Author

Two hundred ten authors have published articles on AI in customer acquisition in the Scopus database. In order to draw up a more meaningful map of co-authors, we only consider authors who have published more than two articles. Only 13 authors meet this threshold: Stadlman, Zehetner, Kannan, Ma, Neslin, Rust, Huang, Hanssens, Dekimpe, Zhang, He, Li, and Chen. Figure 3 shows a map of co-authors generated by VOSViewer for the 13 authors. The network is very dispersed, and all the researchers produced two articles each. Zhang, He, Li, and Chen are the most cited, with six citations. These results indicate that the landscape of authors researching AI in customer acquisition is still decentralized. As a result, newcomers to the field can join many existing nodes of researchers or conduct their research without having to join an existing network of authors.

Figure 3. Co-authorship by author

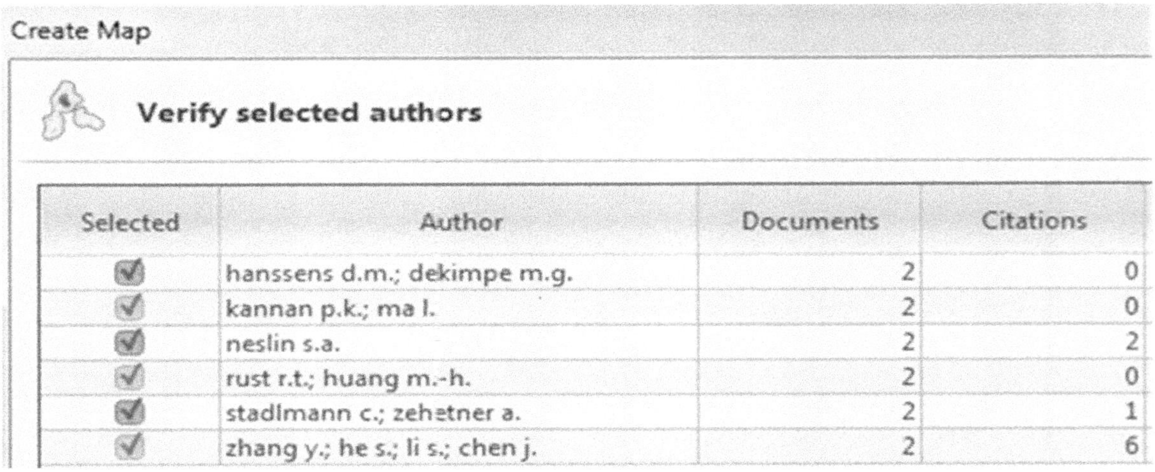

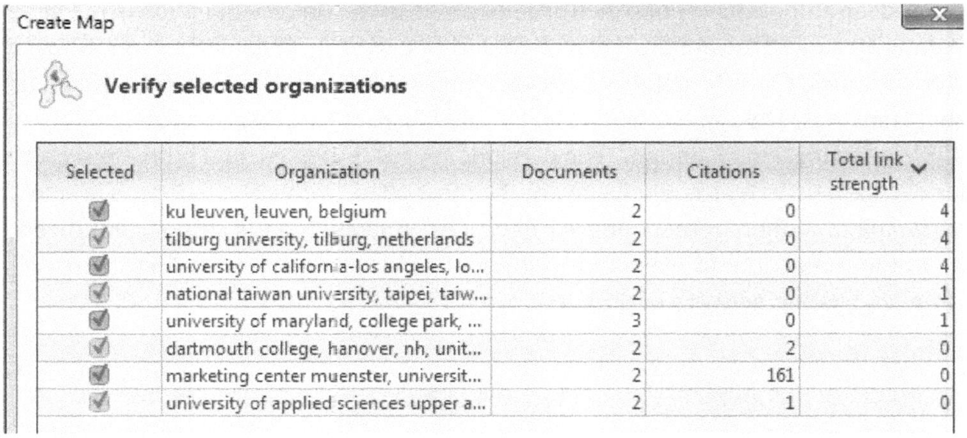

Create Map			
Verify selected authors			
Selected	Author	Documents	Citations
☑	hanssens d.m.; dekimpe m.g.	2	0
☑	kannan p.k.; ma l.	2	0
☑	neslin s.a.	2	2
☑	rust r.t.; huang m.-h.	2	0
☑	stadlmann c.; zehetner a.	2	1
☑	zhang y.; he s.; li s.; chen j.	2	6

• *Analysis By Organization*

Similarly, to obtain a more meaningful map of organizations, we limit ourselves to those who have published more than two articles. In total, 474 organizations are involved in publishing work on topics related to AI in customer acquisition. Eight organizations met the two-paper requirement, as shown in Figure 4. The most productive university is the University of Maryland (3 papers), and all other universities published two papers.

Figure 4. Co-authors by organization

Create Map				X
Verify selected organizations				
Selected	Organization	Documents	Citations	Total link strength
☑	ku leuven, leuven, belgium	2	0	4
☑	tilburg university, tilburg, netherlands	2	0	4
☑	university of california-los angeles, lo...	2	0	4
☑	national taiwan university, taipei, taiw...	2	0	1
☑	university of maryland, college park, ...	3	0	1
☑	dartmouth college, hanover, nh, unit...	2	2	0
☑	marketing center muenster, universit...	2	161	0
☑	university of applied sciences upper a...	2	1	0

• *Country Analysis*

When it comes to international collaboration, we look at which countries are cooperating to publish topics related to AI in customer acquisition. Researchers from 59 countries have published activities in this area. For a more illustrative map, we set a minimum of 5 publications per country. Sixteen countries meet this minimum threshold. As Figure 5 shows, there are strong links between countries working together on AI issues in customer acquisition, as the 16 countries form a considerable group centered on the US. US researchers have collaborated with academics from every other country on this map and have published the most papers (65 publications). Clearly, the US dominates this field, producing half of the publications in our sample, followed by China (29 publications), the UK (18 publications), and India (12 publications).

Figure 5. Co-authors by country

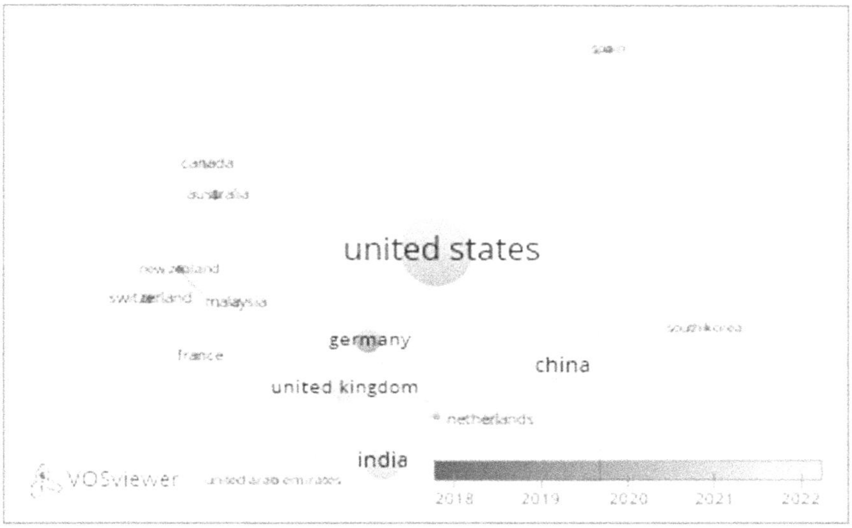

4.2 Co-Occurrence Analysis

Co-occurrence analysis aims to examine the links between keywords and the terms most frequently used in searches in order to deepen our understanding of researchers' common areas of interest. VOSViewer can identify the most commonly used keywords in articles, allowing us to identify the terms associated with the main themes.

Figure 6 shows the 20 keywords, each of which has at least seven occurrences, are closely related to each other. The ten most frequent keywords are: "sales" (38 occurrences), "artificial intelligence" (31 occurrences), "machine learning" (29 occurrences), "marketing" (23 occurrences), "commerce" (19 occurrences), "data mining" (14 occurrences), "deep learning" (11 occurrences), "CRM" (9 occurrences), "public relations", "customer acquistion" (7).

Figure 6. Co-occurrence of all keywords

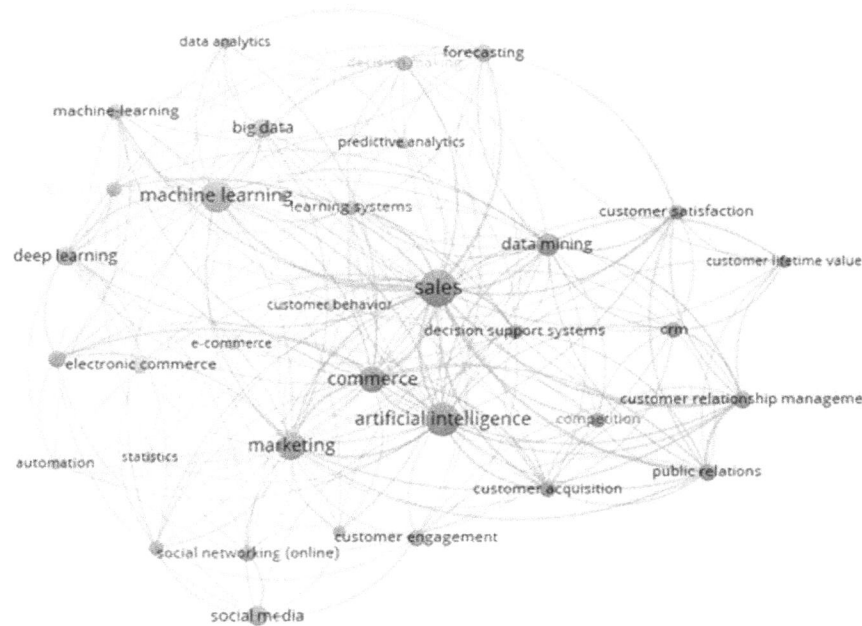

Examining the groups of different colors allows us to understand which keywords share the most vital links. The map reveals three main groups: a red group that directly concerns our studies and brings together the ten most frequent keywords. "sales," "artificial intelligence," and "customer acquisition," indicating that these terms are used closely together. The blue group includes the keywords "marketing", "cutomer engagement", "social media," and "electronic commerce". The green group contains mainly IT-related keywords.

4.3 The Analysis of Quotations

In this section, we assess the strength of the links between articles, authors, journals, institutions, and countries by calculating the number of times they cite each other. Indeed, VOSViewer performs citation analysis by measuring the number of times that two elements (articles, authors, journals, institutions, and countries) cite each other to identify the strength of the links between them.

In this part, we examine the power of the links between articles, authors, journals, institutions, and countries by studying the number of times they cite each other. For this purpose, VOSViewer's citation analysis function measures the number of times two elements (articles, authors, journals, institutions, and countries) mention each other to assess the strength of the links between them. In order to exclude low-impact articles, we have set the minimum number of citations at 20, and 42 articles meet this requirement. As shown in Figure 7, the largest group contains ten items rotated by the article by Wang and Goldfarb (2017).

Figure 7. Top ten AI-related articles in customer acquisition

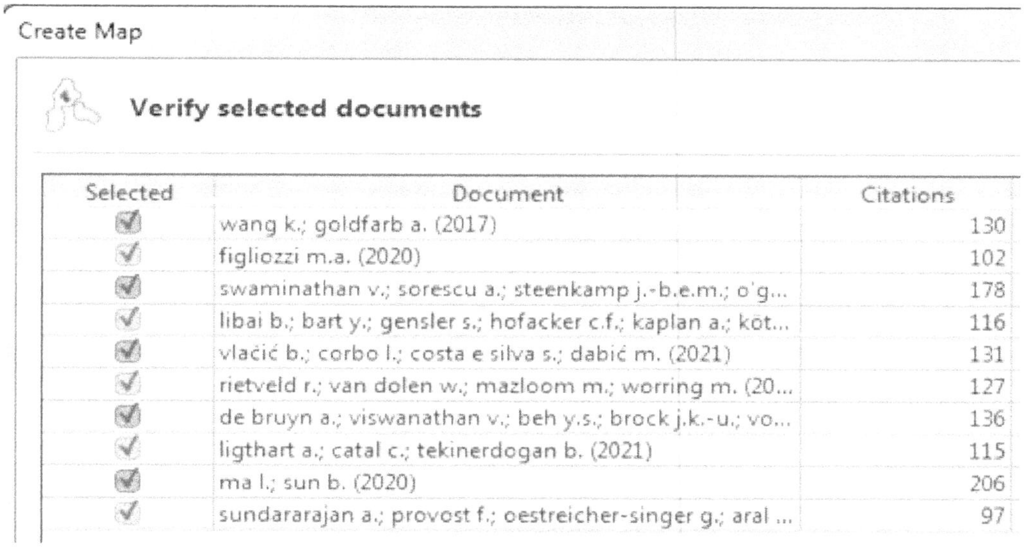

Create Map		
Verify selected documents		
Selected	Document	Citations
☑	wang k.; goldfarb a. (2017)	130
☑	figliozzi m.a. (2020)	102
☑	swaminathan v.; sorescu a.; steenkamp j.-b.e.m.; o'g...	178
☑	libai b.; bart y.; gensler s.; hofacker c.f.; kaplan a.; kot...	116
☑	vlačić b.; corbo l.; costa e silva s.; dabić m. (2021)	131
☑	rietveld r.; van dolen w.; mazloom m.; worring m. (20...	127
☑	de bruyn a.; viswanathan v.; beh y.s.; brock j.k.-u.; vo...	136
☑	ligthart a.; catal c.; tekinerdogan b. (2021)	115
☑	ma l.; sun b. (2020)	206
☑	sundararajan a.; provost f.; oestreicher-singer g.; aral ...	97

To analyze the relationship between the different journals, we required that one Journal have at least three articles on the central themes to be included, and 14 met this threshold. As shown in Figure 8, the Journal of Interactive Marketing Research has the highest number of citations (514) with six publications, followed by the Journal of Marketing with 264 citations and four publications.

Figure 8. Citation analysis by source

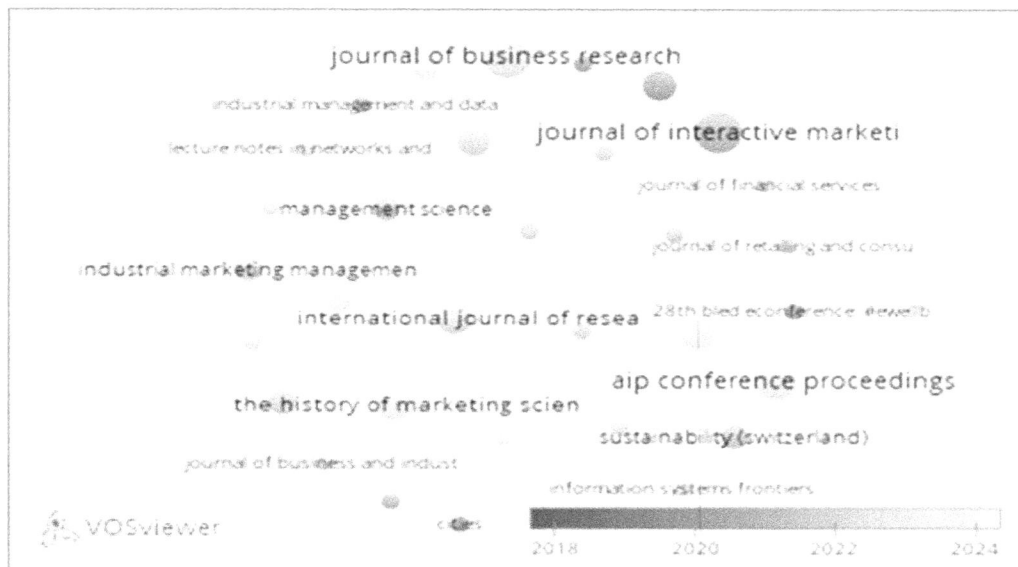

We also analyzed the links between the different organizations. We required each university to have at least two publications to be included, which resulted in the eight institutions shown on the map in Figure 9.

Figure 9. Citation analysis by organization

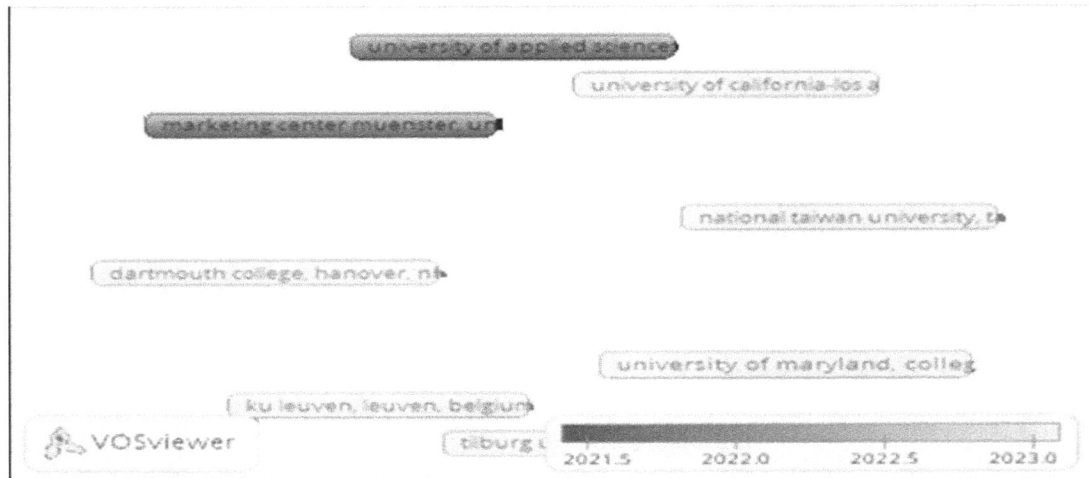

In conclusion, of this citation analysis, although articles, authors, journals, and institutions are all based on primary groups of developing authors, each other's networks are generally disseminated through many other networks outside primary groups. This indicates that research on AI applications in customer acquisition is still booming that there are many new or complementary research opportunities, and that potential authors should not rely on existing author networks or journals to publish their work

4.4 The Analysis of Co-Citation

The objective of this analysis is to highlight the links between articles, authors, institutions, and countries by studying the number of times they are simultaneously used by another work. It is an analysis that assesses the strength of the links between articles, authors, and journals by examining how often they are cited together. To do this, VOSViewer explores the list of citations for each article in the sample and analyzes articles that do not necessarily appear in the selected database. This allows us to examine the links between AI-related customer acquisition topics and other areas.

18,040 references were returned by VOSViewer, of which 25 remained after we set the criterion that an item must be cited at least six times to be included. As shown in Figure 10, the articles in our sample are grouped into three clusters. The first is red and consists of 9 articles federated by the work of Schwartz and Bradlaw (2017), cited 12 times, and which focuses on customer acquisition through display advertising through multi-armed bandit experiences. The second is green in color and consists of eight articles revolving around the work of Becker et al. (2019), quoted eight times and relating to authenticity in television advertising. The blue third consists of seven articles that cluster on the work of Meire et al. (2107), cited 12 times, and he worked on the benefit of social media data in B2B customer acquisition systems.

Figure 10. Co-citation analysis by reference

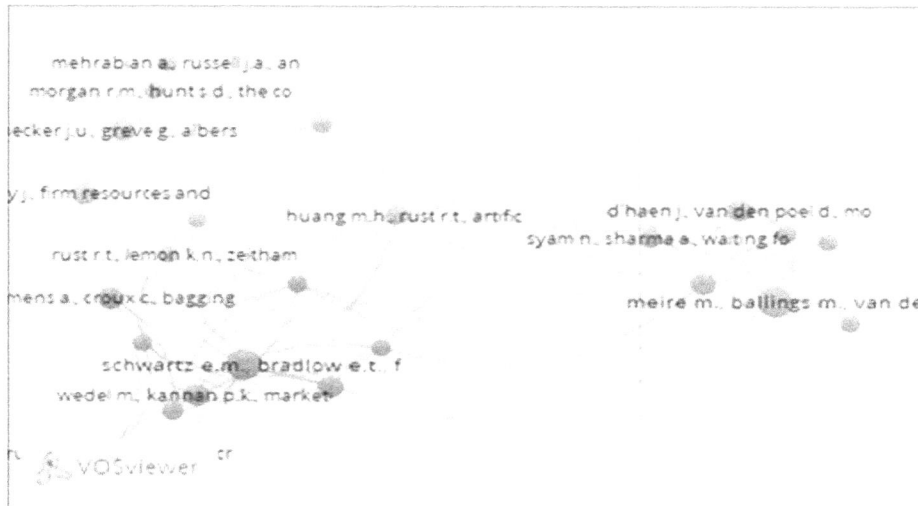

We also studied the co-citation relations of the 24971 authors cited in the selected works in our database. An author had to be cited at least 30 times to be included, and 79 authors reached this threshold. The five most cited authors in our database are Rust (178 times), Kumar (188 times), Verhoef (116 times), Gupta (99 times) and Neslin (89 times). They are the most essential authors in AI studies related to customer acquisition, and they influence other researchers in this field. As shown in Figure 11, authors such as Rust, Kumar, Verhoef, and Gupta are at the center of the map and have the most numerous and most vital links with other works, while Smith is relatively poorly connected to this network.

According to this co-citation analysis, it is clear that author groups are playing an increasingly crucial role in AI research in the field of customer acquisition. Kumar, Verhoef, and Gupta are frequently mentioned in collaboration. Although two of these three authors are not mentioned in collaboration, one of them is often mentioned in collaboration with another author. Despite the uncertainty about the consequences of this trend at present, it is conceivable that the writings of these authors will become "traditional" or mandatory citations as this area continues to progress.

Figure 11. Analysis of co-citations by author

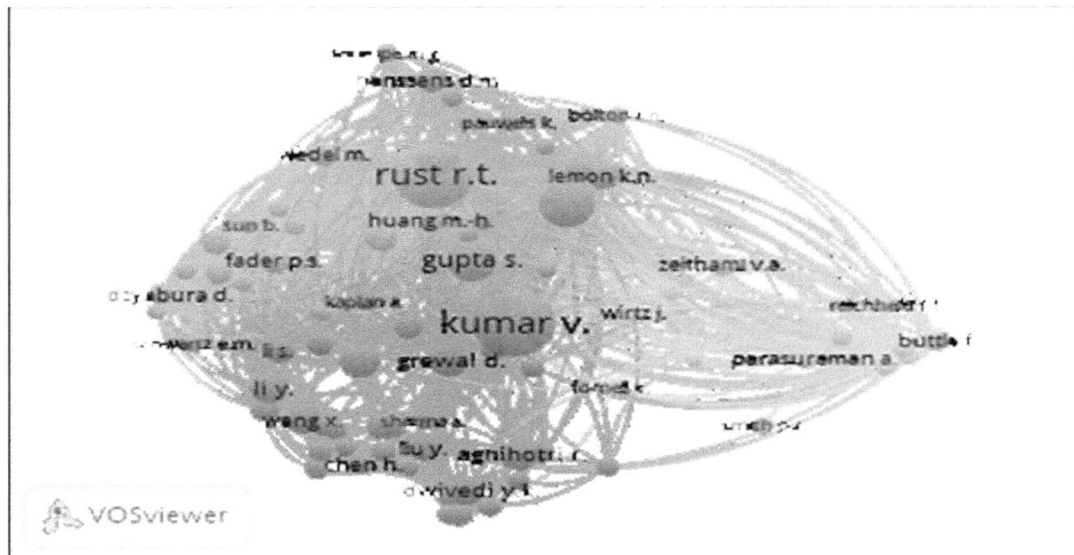

5. DISCUSSION AND MANAGERIAL CONTRIBUTIONS

This chapter examines the state of research on AI applications in client research using a bibliometric approach. Using VOSViewer software, we analyzed authors, citations, publication volumes, institutional origins and other parameters related to articles on this topic from the Scopus database. VOSViewer provided information without the need for manual analysis and coding required by other content analysis tools.

Our first observation is that, over time, we observe a significant increase in the number of articles on AI in customer acquisition, with a particular acceleration after 2018. While the journals in the sample have a reasonable distribution of the most cited articles, the Journal of Interactive Marketing Research has the highest number of citations (514) with six publications and is currently the most influential in the work on the subject. Similarly, researchers from the United States, China and England currently dominate the literature on this topic, both in terms of research results and influence.

Our second observation is that, overall, research on the uses of AI in the field of customer acquisition is rather decentralized. Despite the emergence of co-authors, there has yet to be a clearly identified group of authors that predominates in the corpus of literature. Similarly, many opportunities remain to be explored in this area, as citation sources are scattered, and there still seems to be no close link between articles, authors or institutions.

On the other hand, we see an increase in the concentration of themes and keywords in the field of AI in customer acquisition, in line with the technical keywords used in the traditional field of computing. This observation is also confirmed by the study carried out by Ledro et al. (2022) by identifying three main sub-domains of the literature on AI in the field of the RCMP (Big et al. as a database, AI and machine learning techniques applied to CRM activities and strategic management of AI-CRM integrations). This suggests a probable relationship with the technical concepts that have been studied in the field of computer science. In addition, so far, work in this area has tended to focus on four key areas, namely "sales," "artificial intelligence," "machine learning," and "marketing." Among the different disciplines outside of marketing, most research has been conducted by academics in computer science and management information systems.

VOSViewer's capabilities in manipulating very large databases with a large number of items, it would be quite simple to incorporate them into the subsequent study on the uses of AI in customer acquisition. It would also be relevant to review our work at a later date by adding more publications. These avenues of research are destined for the future. We contribute to all the literature on this subject by listing the paths taken by marketing experts in their research on this subject. We believe this bibliometric study will allow marketers to determine which areas are important to AI applications in customer acquisition.

The integration of AI in customer acquisition has the potential to revolutionize customer engagement for businesses, but it also raises significant ethical concerns (Brynjolfsson & McAfee, 2014). AI algorithms can collect vast amounts of customer data, leading to personalized marketing strategies that may enhance sales but also raise privacy issues (Mittelstadt, et al., 2016).. The opacity of AI algorithms can create distrust among customers and pose challenges for businesses in maintaining ethical standards (Mittelstadt, et al., 2016). Additionally, there is a risk of discriminatory practices against certain demographic groups, which can lead to unfair treatment and decreased trust in businesses (Crawford, 2016).

This study also develops the different applications of AI in customer acquisition, which can help, on the one hand, researchers to further deepen knowledge in this field and managers to plan an appropriate and coherent strategy. For researchers, such a study can provide insights into the effectiveness of AI technologies in customer acquisition, offering opportunities to deepen their understanding of consumer behavior, market trends, and the impact of AI on business outcomes. By examining real-world applications and case studies, researchers can identify best practices, challenges, and areas for further investigation, contributing to the advancement of knowledge in this field. For managers, the study can serve as a valuable resource for planning strategic initiatives related to customer acquisition. By understanding the capabilities and limitations of AI tools, managers can make informed decisions on implementing AI-driven solutions to optimize customer targeting, engagement, and conversion. The study can help managers identify key performance indicators, develop tailored strategies, and align resources effectively to enhance customer acquisition efforts.

6. CONCLUSION, LIMITS, AND PERSPECTIVES

The use of artificial intelligence in customer acquisition is an emerging, multidisciplinary and very promising field of research. The number of publications is constantly increasing; the work tends to focus on specific themes and a reasonable distribution of articles by journals, organization and country. Artificial intelligence will continue to transform the customer acquisition landscape by revolutionizing data analytics, automating tasks by improving their ability to understand and target their customers, and delivering personalized experiences. Therefore, many research opportunities still need to be explored in this area, as citation sources are scattered, and there still seems to be no close link between articles, authors or institutions.

Our study presents a main limitation based on Scopus as the main data source. Despite its extensive coverage and rigorous structure, this database only lists some publications. Any article published on this topic in journals and newspapers outside Scopus would not be included in our sample. It is, therefore, possible that the conclusions of this study only partially reflect all the work done so far on the uses of AI in customer acquisition. A second methodological limitation concerns the number of articles analyzed which remains limited by contribution to the analytical capabilities of VOSViewer.

This study paves the way for future research to advance knowledge, foster innovation and promote responsible use of AI technologies in customer engagement strategies. Researchers can identify emerging trends in AI-enabled customer acquisition, explore industry-specific applications and assess the impact and effectiveness of AI strategies through empirical studies. This research provides valuable insights to businesses by assessing the return on investment of AI technologies, customer satisfaction levels, conversion rates and other key performance indicators to guide decision-making and strategy development.

REFERENCES

Aghaei Chadegani, A., Salehi, H., Md Yunus, M. M., Farhadi, H., Fooladi, M., Farhadi, M., & Ale Ebrahim, N. (2013). A comparison between two main academic literature collections: Web of science and scopus databases. *Asian Social Science*, 9(5), 18–26. 10.5539/ass.v9n5p18

Alalwan, A. A., Algharabat, R. S., Baabdullah, A. M., Rana, N. P., Qasem, Z., & Dwivedi, Y. K. (2020). Examining the impact of mobile interactivity on customer engagement in the context of mobile shopping. *Journal of Enterprise Information Management*, 33(3), 627–653. 10.1108/JEIM-07-2019-0194

Alla, L., Kamal, M., & Bouhtati, N. (2022). Big data et efficacité marketing des entreprises touristiques : Une revue de littérature. *Alternatives Managériales Economiques, 4*.10.48374/IMIST.PRSM/ame-v1i0 .36928

Amatriain, X., & Basilico, J. (2015). Recommender systems in industry: A netflix case study. In *Recommender systems handbook* (pp. 385–419). Springer US. 10.1007/978-1-4899-7637-6_11

Aria, M., & Cuccurullo, C. (2017). bibliometrix: An R-tool for comprehensive science mapping analysis. *Journal of Informetrics*, 11(4), 959–975. 10.1016/j.joi.2017.08.007

Barari, M., Ross, M., Thaichon, S., & Surachartkumtonkun, J. (2021). A meta-analysis of customer engagement behaviour. *International Journal of Consumer Studies*, 45(4), 457–477. 10.1111/ijcs.12609

Becker, M., Wiegand, N., & Reinartz, W. J. (2019). Does it pay to be real? Understanding authenticity in TV advertising. *Journal of Marketing*, 83(1), 24–50. 10.1177/0022242918815880

Berger, J., Humphreys, A., Ludwig, S., Moe, W. W., Netzer, O., & Schweidel, D. A. (2019). Uniting the tribes: Using text for marketing insight. *Journal of Marketing*, 84(1), 1–25. 10.1177/0022242919873106

Bouhtati, N. alla, L., & bentalha, B. (2023). Marketing Big Data Analytics and Customer Relationship Management: A Fuzzy Approach. In *Integrating Intelligence and Sustainability in Supply Chains* (pp. 75-86). DOI: . IGI Global.10.4018/979-8-3693-0225-5.ch004

Brynjolfsson, E., & McAfee, A. (2014). *The second machine age: Work, progress, and prosperity in a time of brilliant technologies*. WW Norton & Company.

Castro, S. L. C., Del Pozo Durango Rodrigo Humberto, V., Paúl, A. C., & Estefanía, A. T. P. (2023). Impact of Artificial Intelligence on Market Behavior Analysis: A Comprehensive Approach to Marketing. *Remittances Review, 8*(4).

Charles, V., Rana, N. P., Pappas, I. O., Kamphaug, M., Siau, K., & Engø-Monsen, K. (2023). The Next 'Deep' Thing in X to Z Marketing: An Artificial Intelligence-Driven Approach. *Information Systems Frontiers*, 1–6.

Coffin, J. (2022). Asking questions of AI advertising: A maieutic approach. *Journal of Advertising*, 51(5), 608–623. 10.1080/00913367.2022.2111728

Colicev, A., Kumar, A., & O'Connor, P. (2019). Modeling the relationship between firm and user generated content and the stages of the marketing funnel. *International Journal of Research in Marketing*, 36(1), 100–116. 10.1016/j.ijresmar.2018.09.005

Crawford, K., Whittaker, M., Elish, M. C., Barocas, S., Plasek, A., & Ferryman, K. (2016). The AI now report. *The Social and Economic Implications of Artificial Intelligence Technologies in the Near-Term, 2*.

Davenport, T., Guha, A., Grewal, D., & Bressgott, T. (2020). How artificial intelligence will change the future of marketing. *Journal of the Academy of Marketing Science*, 48(2), 24–42. 10.1007/s11747-019-00696-0

De Bellis, E., & Johar, G. V. (2020). Autonomous shopping systems: Identifying and overcoming barriers to consumer adoption. *Journal of Retailing*, 96(1), 74–87. 10.1016/j.jretai.2019.12.004

De Bruyn, A., Viswanathan, V., Beh, Y. S., Brock, J. K. U., & von Wangenheim, F. (2020). Artificial intelligence and marketing: Pitfalls and opportunities. *Journal of Interactive Marketing*, 51, 91–105. 10.1016/j.intmar.2020.04.007

Dolega, L., Rowe, F., & Branagan, E. (2021). Going digital? The impact of social media marketing on retail website traffic, orders and sales. *Journal of Retailing and Consumer Services*, 60, 60. 10.1016/j.jretconser.2021.102501

Feng, C. M., Park, A., Pitt, L., Kietzmann, J., & Northey, G. (2021). Artificial intelligence in marketing: A bibliographic perspective. *Australasian Marketing Journal*, 29(3), 252–263. 10.1016/j.ausmj.2020.07.006

Fernandes T., Remelhe P. (2016). How to engage customers in co-creation: customers' motivations for collaborative innovation. *J. Strat. Market., 24*.

Gopalakrishna, S., Crecelius, A. T., & Patil, A. (2022). Hunting for new customers: Assessing the drivers of effective salesperson prospecting and conversion. *Journal of Business Research*, 149, 916–926. 10.1016/j.jbusres.2022.05.008

Gopalakrishna, S., Crecelius, A. T., & Patil, A. (2022). Hunting for new customers: Assessing the drivers of effective salesperson prospecting and conversion. *Journal of Business Research*, 149, 916–926. 10.1016/j.jbusres.2022.05.008

Gupta, S. (2009). Customer-based valuation. *Journal of Interactive Marketing*, 23(2), 169–178. 10.1016/j.intmar.2009.02.006

Haenlein, M., & Kaplan, A. (2019). A brief history of artificial intelligence: On the past, present, and future of artificial intelligence. *California Management Review*, 61(4), 5–14. 10.1177/0008125619864925

Haleem, A., Javaid, M., Qadri, M. A., Singh, R. P., & Suman, R. (2022). Artificial intelligence (AI) applications for marketing: A literature-based study. *International Journal of Intelligent Networks*.

Huang, M.-H., & Rust, R. T. (2018). Artificial Intelligence in Service. *Journal of Service Research*, 21(2), 155–172. 10.1177/1094670517752459

Huang, Y., Zhang, X., & Zhu, H. (2022). How do customers engage in social media-based brand communities: The moderator role of the brand's country of origin? *Journal of Retailing and Consumer Services*, 68.

Islam, J. U., Rahman, Z., & Hollebeek, L. D. (2017). Personality factors as predictors of online consumer engagement: An empirical investigation. *Marketing Intelligence & Planning*, 35(4), 510–528. 10.1108/MIP-10-2016-0193

Juric, B., Smith, S. D., & Wilks, G. (2015). Negative customer brand engagement: an overview of conceptual and blog-based findings. *Customer Engagement: Contemporary Issues and Challenges,* pp. 278-294.

Kumar, V., Aksoy, L., Donkers, B., Venkatesan, R., Wiesel, T., & Tillmanns, S. (2010). Undervalued or overvalued customers: Capturing total customer engagement value. J. Serv. *Journal of Service Research,* 13(3), 297–310. 10.1177/1094670510375602

Kumar, V., Aksoy, L., Donkers, B., Venkatesan, R., Wiesel, T., & Tillmanns, S. (2019). Customer engagement: The construct, antecedents, and consequences. *Journal of the Academy of Marketing Science,* 47(2), 252–277.

Kumar, V., Rajan, B., Venkatesan, R., & Lecinski, J. (2019). Understanding the role of artificial intelligence in personalized engagement marketing. *California Management Review,* 61(4), 135–155. 10.1177/0008125619859317

Ledro, C., Nosella, A., & Vinelli, A. (2022). Artificial intelligence in customer relationship management: Literature review and future research directions. *Journal of Business and Industrial Marketing,* 37(13), 48–63. 10.1108/JBIM-07-2021-0332

Lhoussaine, A. (2022). Big data et efficacité marketing des entreprises touristiques: Une revue de littérature. *Alternatives Managériales Economiques,* 1, 39–58.

Lowry, P. B., Moody, G. D., Gaskin, J., Galletta, D., Humphreys, S., Barlow, J. B., & Wilson, D. (2013). Evaluating Journal Quality and the Association for Information Systems Senior Scholars' Journal Basket via Bibliometric Measures: Do Expert Journal Assessments Add Value? (SSRN Scholarly Paper ID 2186798). 10.25300/MISQ/2013/37.4.01

Luo, X., Tong, S., Fang, Z., & Qu, Z. (2019). Frontiers: machines vs. humans: The impact of artificial intelligence chatbot disclosure on customer purchases. *Marketing Science,* 38(6), 937–947. 10.1287/mksc.2019.1192

Marchand, A., & Marx, P. (2020). Automated product recommendations with preference-based explanations. *Journal of Retailing,* 96(3), 328–343. 10.1016/j.jretai.2020.01.001

Marr, B. (2019). *Artificial intelligence in practice: how 50 successful companies used AI and machine learning to solve problems.* John Wiley & Sons.

Meire, M., Ballings, M., & van den Poel, D. (2017). The Added Value of Social Media Data in B2B Customer Acquisition Systems: A Real-Life Experiment. *Decision Support Systems,* 104, 26–37. 10.1016/j.dss.2017.09.010

Mikalef, P., Pappas, I. O., Krogstie, J., & Pavlou, P. A. (2020). Big data and business analytics: A research agenda for realizing business value. *Information & Management,* 57(1), 1. 10.1016/j.im.2019.103237

Miroshnichenko, I. V., Sheremet, M. A., Oztop, H. F., & Abu-Hamdeh, N. (2018). Natural convection of Al2O3/H2O nanofluid in an open inclined cavity with a heat-generating element. *International Journal of Heat and Mass Transfer,* 126, 184–191. 10.1016/j.ijheatmasstransfer.2018.05.146

Misra, K., Schwartz, E. M., & Abernethy, J. (2019). Dynamic online pricing with incomplete information using multiarmed bandit experiments. *Marketing Science,* 38(2), 226–252. 10.1287/mksc.2018.1129

Mittelstadt, B. D., Allo, P., Taddeo, M., Wachter, S., & Floridi, L. (2016). The ethics of algorithms: Mapping the debate. *Big Data & Society*. 3(2), 2053951716679679. 10.1177/2053951716679679

Muhammad, S. S., Dey, B. L., & Weerakkody, V. (2018). Analysis of factors that influence customers' willingness to leave big data digital footprints on social media: A systematic review of literature. *Information Systems Frontiers*, 20(3), 559–575. 10.1007/s10796-017-9802-y

Pansari, A., & Kumar, V. (2017). Customer engagement: The construct, antecedents, and consequences. *Journal of the Academy of Marketing Science*, 45(3), 294–311. 10.1007/s11747-016-0485-6

Paschen, J., Wilson, M., & Ferreira, J. J. (2020). Collaborative intelligence: How human and artificial intelligence create value along the B2B sales funnel. *Business Horizons*, 63(3), 403–414. 10.1016/j.bushor.2020.01.003

Raisch, S., & Krakowski, S. (2021). Artificial intelligence and management: The automation augmentation paradox. *Academy of Management Review*, 46(1), 192–210. 10.5465/amr.2018.0072

Rangaswamy, A., Moch, N., Felten, C., van Bruggen, G., Wieringa, J. E., & Wirtz, J. (2020). The role of marketing in digital business platforms. *Journal of Interactive Marketing*, 51(August), 72–90. 10.1016/j.intmar.2020.04.006

Reinartz, W., Thomas, J. S., & Kumar, V. (2005). Balancing acquisition and retention resources to maximize customer profitability. *Journal of Marketing*, 69(1), 63–79. 10.1509/jmkg.69.1.63.55511

Rowley, J., & Slack, F. (2004). Conducting a literature review. *Management Research News*, 27(6), 31–39. 10.1108/01409170410784185

Salminen, J., Yoganathan, V., Corporan, J., Jansen, B. J., & Jung, S.-G. (2019). Machine-learning approach to auto-tagging online content for content marketing efficiency: A comparative analysis between methods and content type. *Journal of Business Research*, 101, 203–217. 10.1016/j.jbusres.2019.04.018

Sanchez-Hernandez, G., Chiclana, F., Agell, N., & Carlos, J. (2013). Ranking and selection of unsupervised learning marketing segmentation. *Knowledge-Based Systems*, 44, 20–33. 10.1016/j.knosys.2013.01.012

Schwartz Eric, M., Bradlow Eric, T., & Fader Peter, S. (2017). Customer acquisition via display advertising using multiarmed bandit experiments. *Marketing Science*, 36(4), 500–522. 10.1287/mksc.2016.1023

Surendro, K. (2019, March). Predictive analytics for predicting customer behavior. In *2019 International Conference of Artificial Intelligence and Information Technology (ICAIIT)* (pp. 230-233). IEEE.

Suri, A., Jones, B. C., Ng, G., Anabaraonye, N., Beyrer, P., Domi, A., Choi, G., Tang, S., Terry, A., Leichner, T., Fathali, I., Bastin, N., Chesnais, H., & Rajapakse, C. S. (2021). A deep learning system for automated, multi-modality 2D segmentation of vertebral bodies and intervertebral discs. *Bone*, 149, 115972. 10.1016/j.bone.2021.11597233892175

Thomaz, F., Salge, C., Karahanna, E., & Hulland, J. (2020). Learning from the dark web: Leveraging conversational agents in the era of hyper-privacy to enhance marketing. *Journal of the Academy of Marketing Science*, 48(2), 43–63. 10.1007/s11747-019-00704-3

Van Eck, N. J., & Waltman, L. (2010). Software survey: VOSviewer, a computer program for bibliometric mapping. *Scientometrics*, 84(2), 523–538. 10.1007/s11192-009-0146-320585380

Wang, R. J., Krishnamurthi, L., & Mathouse, E. C. (2018). When reward convenience meets mobile app: Increasing customer participation in a coalition loyalty program [V.M. Landers.]. *Journal of the Association for Consumer Research*, 3(3), 314–329. 10.1086/698331

Wirtz, J., & Zeithaml, V. (2018). Cost-effective service excellence. *Journal of the Academy of Marketing Science*, 46(1), 59–80. 10.1007/s11747-017-0560-7

Zhao, L., Tang, Z., & Zou, X. (2019). Mapping the knowledge domain of smart-city research: A bibliometric and scientometric analysis. *Sustainability*, 11(23), 1–28. 10.3390/su12010001

Zheng, R., Li, Z., & Na, S. (2022). How customer engagement in the live-streaming affects purchase intention and customer acquisition, E-tailer's perspective. *Journal of Retailing and Consumer Services*, 68, 103015. 10.1016/j.jretconser.2022.103015

Chapter 2
Marketing Applications of Emerging Technologies:
A Systematic Literature Review

Mourad Aarabe
http://orcid.org/0009-0003-9772-6683
National School of Business and Management of Fez, Morocco

Nouhaila Ben Khizzou
National School of Business and Management of Fez, Morocco

Lhoussaine Alla
http://orcid.org/0000-0002-7238-1792
National School of Applied Sciences of Fez, Morocco

Ahmed Benjelloun
National School of Business and Management of Fez, Morocco

ABSTRACT

In today's global environment, integrating emerging technologies has become a necessity. This book explores the intersection of technology and marketing, providing an overview of technological advancements and their impact on marketing practices. This chapter proposes a systematic literature review following the PRISMA protocol to explore the breadth and scope of applicability of emerging technology solutions in marketing. The aim is to highlight the key opportunities and challenges for marketing applications of such technologies. This analysis, conducted using Nvivo V12 software, indicates that emerging technologies such as artificial intelligence, augmented reality, the internet of things, blockchain, and data analytics are increasingly important in marketing practices and strategies. These technologies are primarily used to understand and satisfy individual customer needs and improve the customer experience.

DOI: 10.4018/979-8-3693-3172-9.ch002

1. INTRODUCTION

In today's hyperconnected world, marketing has been greatly impacted by the rapid development of emerging technologies (Grewal et al., 2020; Kumar et al., 2021; Shah & Murthi, 2021). The adoption of these technologies, including augmented reality, artificial intelligence, the internet of things, blockchain, and big data analytics, presents unique opportunities and challenges for both practitioners and theorists.

Research into the marketing applications of emerging technologies is an area that has not been explored sufficiently despite its importance. The stakes, opportunities, risks, and marketing performance expected and actually acquired through the adoption and embedding of the solutions offered by these technologies have not been highlighted enough (Hoffman et al., 2022; Sharma et al., 2023).

Our contribution thus seeks to review the most relevant empirical and theoretical studies published in this field, with the main objective of conducting a systematic literature review to explore the impact of emerging technologies on marketing. Our mission is to identify the main trends, benefits, challenges and practical and theoretical implications of the marketing adoption of these technological advances.

To achieve our objective, our research is guided by the following central question: What are the main marketing applications of emerging technologies, and what are the implications of these transformations for managers and researchers in this field?

To answer these questions, we conducted a systematic literature review, taking a holistic perspective of marketing applications. Our goal is to cover a broad range of topics, such as augmented reality and customer experience, personalization using AI-based technologies, customer relationship management through the Internet of Things, marketing decision-making through big data analytics, and the use of various other technologies in different marketing aspects. Our literature search will follow the PRISMA protocol to select relevant studies from reputable academic databases. We will analyze the collected data using Nvivo version 12 software.

This chapter presents a theoretical framework highlighting the evolution of the marketing concept, emerging marketing technologies, and their applications. We then present the methodology and results of our systematic literature review. Following the results, we discuss the implications, limitations, and prospects for future research.

2. LITERATURE REVIEW

2.1. Marketing: A Field Constantly Seeking Intelligence

In response to technological, strategic, economic, and environmental changes and developments, the concept of marketing has evolved over time. Kotler, one of the founders of modern marketing, and others in their series of books on marketing have classified marketing perspectives into five phases, from Marketing 1.0 to Marketing 5.0 (Kotler et al., 2021).

Marketing 1.0 focused solely on the product. In this era of mass production, companies aimed to efficiently distribute standardized products to meet strong market demand. The role of marketing was to inform consumers about product features and benefits to stimulate sales (Kotler et al., 2010). However, with the advent of the internet and social media, the marketing paradigm shifted to focus on the customer, marking the beginning of marketing 2.0. The purpose of marketing is to utilize digital platforms to encourage engagement and interaction with customers (Kotler et al., 2010). In the third phase of marketing (Marketing 3.0), values and emotions have become the defining characteristics, with companies striving to establish emotional connections with consumers as part of a corporate social responsibility strategy (Kotler et al., 2010).

The use of digital technologies, including AI, data analytics, the Internet of Things, and automation, has contributed to the emergence of Marketing 4.0 (Khargharia et al., 2023; Kotler et al., 2016). This approach to marketing emphasizes the importance of data and algorithms in providing personalized and targeted experiences to customers (Kotler et al., 2016).

From this revolutionary perspective, human-centered marketing 5.0 is no longer solely about a transaction between the customer and the brand. Instead, it focuses on creating memorable experiences that meet people's emotional and spiritual needs (Kotler et al., 2021).

This evolution demonstrates a gradual shift from a focus on products and transactions to a focus on relationships and experiences. There is a clear trend towards more intelligent marketing, incorporating solutions from various emerging technologies. The table below summarizes the progression from Marketing 1.0 to Marketing 5.0.

Table 1. Summary of the evolution of marketing

	Optics	Business conditions	Marketing's role	Objective
Marketing 1.0	Product	Mass production Increased demand	Product promotion	Boosting sales
Marketing 2.0	Customer	Internet and social media	Commitment to customers	Creating personalized relationships
Marketing 3.0	Values	Corporate social responsibility	Making emotional connections with consumers	Promoting human fulfillment
Marketing 4.0	Digital	Proliferation of digital technologies	Advanced customization	Offer consumers more targeted and individualized marketing experiences
Marketing 5.0	Human	Emerging technologies Post-Covid 19	Deep connection with the consumer	Create meaningful experiences that meet people's emotional and spiritual needs

Source: Inspired by (Kotler et al., 2010, 2016, 2021)

The role and objectives of marketing have undergone significant changes over time, from various perspectives (Kotler et al., 2010, 2016, 2021). This transformation is part of an unprecedented evolution of the marketing landscape, aimed at adapting to the changing needs of consumers and society (Dash et al., 2021; Grewal et al., 2020; Rust, 2020). In this context, studying emerging technologies in marketing can help us strategically integrate these tools to strengthen customer relationships, create value, and foster a more human and authentic experience.

2.2. Emerging Technologies on Marketing

The impact of emerging technologies on modern marketing is significant and presents both new opportunities and challenges for professionals (Kotler et al., 2021). However, previous research has been insufficient in fully understanding this impact. Emerging technologies, as defined by (Godé, 2021), are innovative solutions that rapidly emerge and evolve. These technologies are still developing and have the potential to disrupt traditional marketing practices (Kocaman et al., 2023; Lo & Campos, 2018; Rauschnabel et al., 2022; Verma et al., 2021). Anastassova, (2006) characterizes these technologies as innovative, rapidly scalable, and capable of introducing significant transformations in business models and consumer behavior (Bobillier Chaumon, 2021).

The marketing industry has seen the introduction of a number of innovations. Artificial intelligence is notable for its ability to utilize big data collected from multiple connected devices through Internet of Things (IoT) technology. Blockchain technology provides security and transparency for transactions and data. Huang & Rust, (2021) propose a comprehensive perspective on the role of Artificial Intelligence in marketing. AI has transformed marketing by enabling experts to gather and analyze data to comprehend market trends and consumer behavior (Campbell et al., 2020; Castro et al., 2023). Huang & Rust, (2021) and Stone et al., (2020) propose that AI can enhance strategic marketing by enabling effective and relevant marketing actions through segmentation, targeting, and positioning. This facilitates the personalization of messages and offers (Haleem et al., 2022), which has a significant effect on consumers' perceived value and purchase intent (Yin & Qiu, 2021). Artificial intelligence systems can encourage customer interaction and foster future engagement (Perez-Vega et al., 2021).

Several works have demonstrated the growing importance of artificial intelligence and machine learning applications in marketing. Ma & Sun, (2020) emphasize the potential benefits of these methods for enhancing marketing research. ML employs algorithms and statistical models to enable computers to learn and improve from data without explicit programming (Campbell et al., 2020). This approach aims to identify trends to better understand behavior and generate insights for informed decision-making (Ma & Sun, 2020). De Mauro et al., (2022) proposed taxonomy of eleven[1] recurring uses of machine learning in marketing, grouped into four improvement families. "Purchasing principles and consumer experiences" refer to the experiences of consumers, while "decision-making and financial applications" refer to the experiences of businesses. These technologies enable companies to improve customer experience and competitiveness (Keegan et al., 2022; Volkmar et al., 2022).

Chatbots and virtual assistants are becoming increasingly popular in marketing and customer service practices (Ngai et al., 2021). These devices utilize artificial intelligence to enhance customer experiences (Kushwaha et al., 2021) by providing round-the-clock support for customer requests, resulting in faster response times and reduced human effort (Ngai et al., 2021). Selamat & Windasari, (2021) found that anthropomorphism, perceived pleasure, and perceived usefulness positively impact customers' purchase intention when using chatbots.

However, some authors have noted the difficulties marketers face with AI errors, as well as the human biases that can compromise their systems (Volkmar et al., 2022). The environmental and ethical impacts of AI use require particular attention (Huang & Rust, 2021).

Augmented reality (AR) (Rauschnabel et al., 2022), virtual reality (VR) (Adeola et al., 2022; Berberović et al., 2022), extended reality (XR) (Wagner & Cozmiuc, 2022), and mixed reality (MR) (Bec et al., 2021) offer great potential for marketing. Integrating virtual elements into the physical world enables companies to offer interactive and immersive experiences to their customers, which can positively influence their behavior and perception (Flavián et al., 2019; Wedel et al., 2020). For instance, the utilization of augmented reality eases product preview and adjustment, thereby decreasing customer uncertainty (Gallardo et al., 2018) and perceived risk (Lim et al., 2024). As a result, this impacts customer satisfaction, commitment (Wagner & Cozmiuc, 2022), and purchase intention (Kazmi et al., 2021).

In the field of marketing, the Internet of Things (IoT) represents a significant advancement. It enables real-time data collection via connected sensors and smart objects, providing marketers with useful information on consumer behavior (Grewal et al., 2020; Khargharia et al., 2023). Lo & Campos, (2018) suggest that IoT solutions can be used to explore new market segments while driving value creation and customer engagement (Wagner & Cozmiuc, 2022). It is also a vector for relationship marketing, which is achieved through the creation and development of lasting relationships and positive experiences for customers (Lo & Campos, 2018).

Blockchain has revolutionized modern marketing by providing a transparent and secure way to conduct transactions (Gleim & Stevens, 2021). This technology is characterized by trust, immutability, and confidence in the recording of data, which reduces the risk of fraud and counterfeiting without the need for intermediaries (Stallone et al., 2021).

2.3. Marketing Applications of Emerging Technologies

Several authors have noted the significant potential of emerging technologies in marketing (Plangger et al., 2022; Rust, 2020) and customer relations (Kumar et al., 2021). In addition, some authors have highlighted their impact on consumer decision-making (Sharma et al., 2023). These technologies offer marketers unprecedented opportunities to engage with consumers and create more personalized, immersive, and engaging experiences (Perez-Vega et al., 2021). The table below summarizes the various marketing applications of the main emerging technologies.

Table 2. Main marketing applications for emerging technologies

Authors	Emerging technology	Marketing applications	Marketing objectives
(Blasco-Arcas et al., 2022; Buhalis & Moldavska, 2022; Campbell et al., 2020; Castro et al., 2023; Huang & Rust, 2021; Kushwaha et al., 2021; Ngai et al., 2021; Perez-Vega et al., 2021; Selamat & Windasari, 2021; Vlačić et al., 2021)	Artificial intelligence	• AI-based CRM • Customer data analysis • Marketing automation • Chatbots • Voice assistants • Virtual assistants • Automated interaction	• Value creation • Customer relationship management • Personalization • Segmentation • Loyalty • Analysis of market behavior • Reduced response time • Improving the customer experience
(Gallardo et al., 2018; Jessen et al., 2020; Lim et al., 2024; Nikhashemi et al., 2021; Rauschnabel et al., 2022; Wedel et al., 2020; Yu et al., 2023)	Augmented reality	• AR applications • Interactive experience design	• Commitment • Personalization • Value creation • Inspiration
(Jonny et al., 2021; Lo & Campos, 2018; Wagner & Cozmiuc, 2022)	Internet of Things	• Connected devices • Instant data collection and analysis	• Exploring new segments • Customer relationship management • Optimizing marketing campaigns
(Gleim & Stevens, 2021; Peres et al., 2023; Stallone et al., 2021)	Blockchain	• blockchain applications	• Transparency • Security • Traceability • Trust
(De Mauro et al., 2022; Li et al., 2019; Miklosik et al., 2019; Volkmar et al., 2022)	Automatic learning	• Predictive analysis • Market segmentation • Personalized recommendations	• Personalization • Identifying market trends • Strategy optimization
(Alla et al., 2022; Amado et al., 2018; Bouhtati, Alla, et al., 2023; Bouhtati, Kamal, et al., 2023; Lhoussaine et al., 2022; Liu et al., 2023; Rosário & Dias, 2023; Shah & Murthi, 2021)	Big data	• Data analysis • Predictive modeling • Advanced segmentation	• Detecting market trends • Predicting consumer behavior • Customize marketing strategies

Source: authors

The integration of emerging technologies has become a necessity, transforming marketing strategies and customer interactions (Kumar et al., 2021). These advances also provide competitive advantages to organizations (IBM Institute for Business Value, 2023; Sharma et al., 2023). They enable personalized interactions with consumers, targeted advertising, and tailored experiences (Plangger et al., 2022). Systematic literature review is useful for analyzing previous research, identifying trends, and highlighting knowledge gaps.

3. METHODOLOGY

3.1. Protocol for Setting up the Reference Sample

In order to summarize and synthesize the current trends, challenges, and future prospects of marketing applications of emerging technologies (Donthu et al., 2021) a systematic literature review was conducted using the PRISMA protocol. This protocol is a methodological framework for systematic reviews that facilitates the identification, selection, and analysis of relevant references. The PRISMA protocol establishes clear inclusion and exclusion criteria to ensure the completeness and reproducibility of the analysis (Page et al., 2021). It requires a thorough evaluation of methodological quality to ensure the reliability and validity of the data, reinforcing the strength of the conclusions. By presenting comprehensive results transparently, the PRISMA protocol enhances the credibility of the research and facilitates comparison with other studies. Adhering to this protocol ensures a sound and transparent methodological approach to marketing research(Mateo, 2020).

As a first step, we conducted a comprehensive search of the existing literature in well-known scientific databases, such as SCOPUS, WOS, ScienceDirect, and Springer, using relevant keywords combined in the following equation: ('Marketing applications' OR 'Marketing strategies') AND ('emerging technologies' OR 'new technologies'). This query yielded 10,982 references after removing duplicates and excluding references published before 2018. To refine our results, we applied an inclusion criterion that limited publications to the fields of management and social sciences. This yielded 4,542 references. We then eliminated publications for which the full text was not available, resulting in a corpus of 213 publications. We conducted a meta-analysis based on titles, abstracts, and keywords to obtain a definitive corpus of 90 references.

Figure 1. Information flow in the different phases of the systematic review

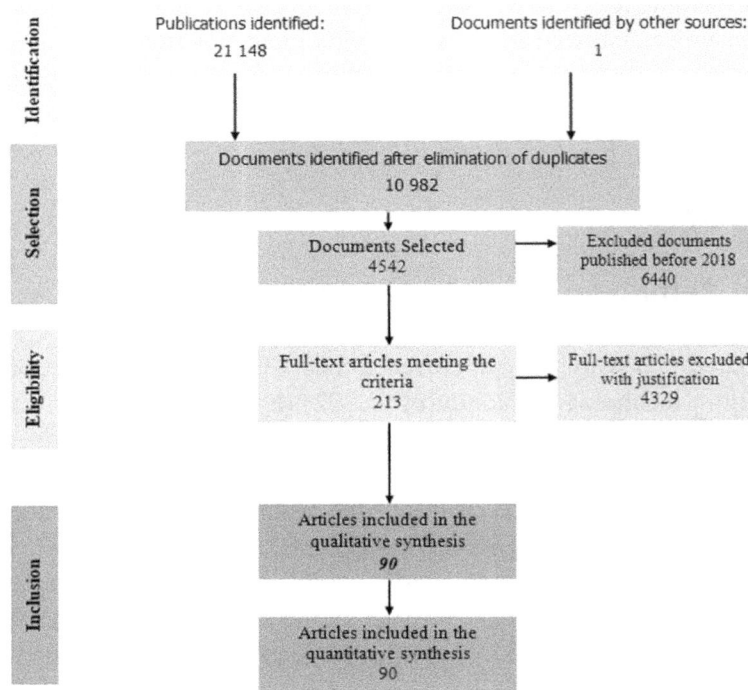

| | Publications identified: 21 148 | Documents identified by other sources: 1 |

Identification

Selection

Eligibility

Inclusion

Documents identified after elimination of duplicates
10 982

Documents Selected
4542

Excluded documents published before 2018
6440

Full-text articles meeting the criteria
213

Full-text articles excluded with justification
4329

Articles included in the qualitative synthesis
90

Articles included in the quantitative synthesis
90

Source: adapted from (Moher et al., 2009)

To organize and analyze our corpus, we utilized the Zotero bibliographic reference management tool to facilitate citation and source document management. We exported the 90 references from Zotero in RIS format and imported them into NVIVO V 12 for qualitative analysis of the data extracted from our corpus. To ensure accuracy, we created several codes for systematic analysis.

The analysis of the sample profile allows for an assessment of the representativeness and relevance of the selected references, an outline of methodological decisions, and information for future research.

3.2. Profile of Reference Sample

The purpose of analyzing the reference sample for our study is to provide an overview of its main characteristics, including the breakdown by year of publication, type of document, database, journal title, and nature of the study conducted. This analysis will help us understand the composition and diversity of the sample and identify significant trends or patterns.

3.2.1 Breakdown of References by Database

Figure 2, created with Nvivo, presents a breakdown of bibliographic references by database. The analysis shows a significant predominance of large, reputable databases such as Sciendirect, which accounts for 51 references or 57% of all references. Elsevier Scopus and Springer complete the list with a total of 29 references.

Figure 2. Distribution of references by database

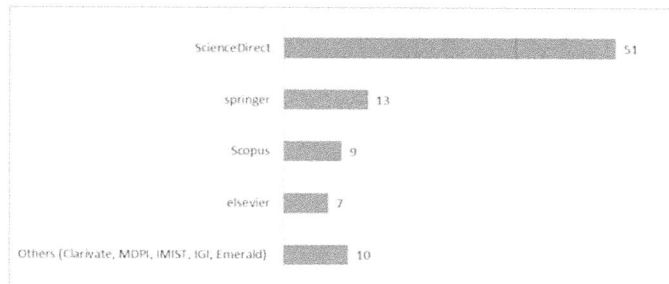

Source: Authors

The study's credibility is reinforced by the rigorous and exhaustive data collection achieved through the use of diverse references. The corpus includes specialized and less conventional resources, with an 'other' category containing 10 references from sources such as Clarivate, MDPI, IMIST, IGI, and Emerald.

3.2.2 References by Year of Publication

The data indicate a significant increase in research on the subject from 2018 onwards, with a peak of 25 sources in 2021 (Figure 3).

Figure 3. Distribution of references by year of publication

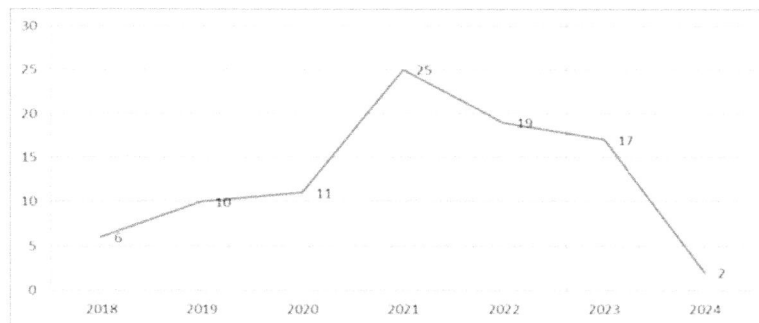

Source: Authors

This may indicate an increase in research efforts or greater availability of data this year. However, there is a slight decrease in the number of sources in 2022 and 2023, although the number remains significant because the full text of some recent sources is not available in open access. The literature review was conducted from January to February, which explains the limited number of sources used in 2024.

3.2.3 References by Publication Type

Analysis of the corpus produced a table displaying the distribution of references by type. The results indicate a significant predominance of journal articles, accounting for 96% of the total references, highlighting their importance in scientific research. Additionally, the presence of other reference types, such as papers, chapters, or books, demonstrates the diversity of resources used and enriches our study.

Table 3. Breakdown of references by publication type

Reference type	Occurrences	Frequencies
Articles	86	96%
Conference papers	1	1%
Book chapters	2	2%
books	1	1%
Total	**90**	**100%**

Source: Authors

3.2.4 Distribution of References by Journal Titles

In order to get an overview of the journals of interest for our field of research, we have extracted the following table showing the distribution of the various references by journal. According to the results, the "Journal of Business Research" leads the list with 18 references, underlining its central importance in our field of research. Several journals, including the "International Journal of Research in Marketing", the "Journal of the Academy of Marketing Science", the "Journal of Retailing and Consumer Services" and "Industrial Marketing Management", also play an important role. Some journals contribute more modestly, with only 2 or 3 references, and there is also a category called "Other" for journals that have published only one article.

Table 4. Distribution of references by journal title

Article titles	Occurrences	Frequencies
Journal of Business Research	18	20%
International Journal of Research in Marketing	7	8%
Journal of the Academy of Marketing Science	6	7%
Journal of Retailing and Consumer Services	5	6%
Industrial Marketing Management	5	6%
Computers in Human Behavior	3	3%

continued on following page

Table 4. Continued

Article titles	Occurrences	Frequencies
Technological Forecasting and Social Change	3	3%
International Journal of Information Management Data Insights	2	2%
Sustainability (Switzerland)	2	2%
Journal of Interactive Marketing	2	2%
Business Horizons	2	2%
International Journal of Information Management	2	2%
Italian Journal of Marketing	2	2%
Journal of Destination Marketing & Management	2	2%
Marketing Letters	2	2%
others	27	30%
Total	90	100%

Source: Authors

After acknowledging the diversity and multidisciplinary nature of the studies, it is important to focus on the type of study conducted. This includes determining whether the study is theoretical, based on literature reviews of previous studies, or empirical, using primary data.

3.2.5 Breakdown of References by Study Type

The type of research is an important aspect to consider in our literature review. The figure below shows a balanced distribution between theoretical studies (46 references) and empirical studies (44 references).

Figure 4. Distribution of references by study type

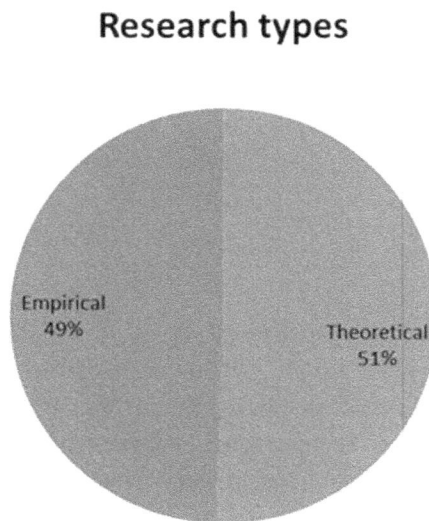

Research types

Empirical 49%

Theoretical 51%

Source: Authors

This balance allows for a holistic methodological approach based on solid theoretical foundations supported by tangible empirical data. It is important to note the abundance of theoretical studies that require empirical validation.

4. FINDINGS

4.1. Descriptive Analysis

This analysis consists in deciphering the co-occurrence of keywords in order to gain insight into the main trends and relevance of our corpus. In addition, this section includes a textual analysis of emerging technologies applied to marketing and the dimensions of marketing affected by emerging technologies.

4.1.1 Decoding the Study Text

Incorporating search criteria such as lexical words and synonyms, and looking for "texts" from "all sources" that were "created or modified by any user," we used the word frequency query on Nvivo to display the 100 most frequent words. The resulting word cloud is shown below.

Figure 5. Word cloud

Source: Nvivo V 12 results

The word cloud and table below distinguish three categories of words. Brown words such as "marketing," "data," "consumer," "positive," "virtual," "behavior," and "advertising" highlight the importance of data, digital platforms, and user experience in marketing, consumer behavior, and preferences. In the second category, in blue, terms such as "experience," "augmented," "use," "intelligence," and "chatbots" demonstrate the growing importance of emerging technologies in marketing. In the third category, in light blue, key words such as "technology," "customer," "future," and "analytics" indicate the importance of emerging technologies in marketing and customer relationship management, as well as future trends and emerging analytical methods. The table below shows the top 20 words.

Table 5. The top 20 keywords in the literature

Rank	Word	Occurrences	Rank	Word	Occurrences
1	Marketing	12051	11	Design	5673
2	Use	11548	12	Technology	5418
3	Study	9390	13	Consumer	5339
4	Data	8125	14	Experience	5222
5	Research	7928	15	Business	5215
6	Customer	7733	16	Learning	4927
7	Making	7625	17	Management	4865
8	Positive	6731	18	Based	4659
9	Results	6010	19	Process	4545
10	Intelligence	5856	20	Product	4533

- Source: Based on Nvivo V12 results

4.1.2 Textual Analysis of Emerging Technology Solutions Applied to Marketing

Textual analysis using Nvivo allowed us to create a matrix that reconciles the emerging technologies most cited in the literature (presented in rows) with marketing (presented in columns). This approach facilitates the identification of trends and relationships between the main emerging themes and concepts. Upon analyzing our matrix, it is evident that artificial intelligence (AI), augmented/virtual/extended/ mixed reality (AR/VR/ER/MR), and machine learning (ML) are crucial in comprehending the emerging technology landscape and its impact on marketing. Additionally, other emerging technologies, such as the Internet of Things (IoT), blockchain, and big data, may also have a significant role in transforming the marketing landscape. This systematic approach allows us to position our work within a wider context, identifying current trends and future research opportunities.

Table 6. Textual analysis matrix of technological solutions applied in marketing

	Occurrences
1: Emerging technologies	13
2: ML	8
3: IoT	2
4: AI	23
5: Blockchain	3
6: Big data	8
7: AR/VR/ER/MR	22
...	...

Source: Based on Nvivo V12 results

4.1.3 Textual Analysis of Marketing Dimensions Affected by Emerging Technologies

Statistical analysis of the marketing dimensions affected by emerging technologies reveals significant trends. The frequency of key terms in the analyzed documents was examined using Vosviewer software (Figure 5), which provides a visual representation of the relationships between marketing dimensions and emerging technologies.

Figure 6. Keyword Co-occurrence

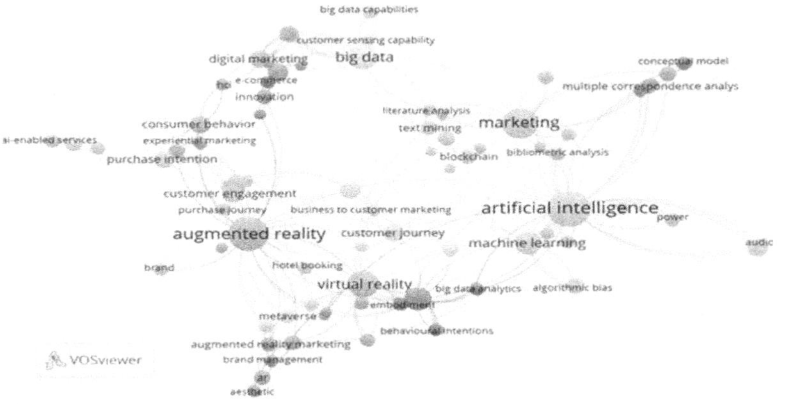

Source: VOSviewer results

The results highlight the facets of marketing that are most affected by these technologies. The adoption of emerging technologies has an impact on several dimensions of marketing, namely behavioral intention, customer relationship management, consumer behavior, engagement, brand management, customer experience, and strategic marketing.

4.1.4 Textual Analysis of the Theories Used

The creation of nodes has allowed us to obtain an analytical grid in the form of a table that brings together all the important elements for the analysis of our corpus, i.e. the problem, the questions and objectives, the theories mobilized, the research proposals and hypotheses, the methodology, the results, the contributions, the limitations, the perspectives and the managerial implications. This provides an overview of the most mature methodologies and theories in the field.

Table 7. Major theories used

Theories used	Occurrences
TRA	5
UTAUT	4
Stimulus-Organism-Response (SOR theory)	3

continued on following page

Table 7. Continued

Theories used	Occurrences
TAM	3
Uses and gratification theory	2
Commitment-trust theory	2
Dynamic capabilities theory	2
Affordance theory	1
Theory of ELM	1
Technology continuance theory (TCT)	1
Broaden-and-build theory	1
Risk-benefit models	1
Flow theory	1
…	…

Source: Based on Nvivo V12 results

With this in mind, we used Nvivo to conduct an in-depth study of the different theories used by the authors in our corpus. The results show that a variety of approaches, theories, and models are widely used. The Theory of Reasoned Action (TRA) is the most cited, with 5 corresponding sources. This is followed by the Unified Theory of Acceptance and Use of Technology (UTAUT), which is also frequently cited, with 4 sources. The Stimulus-Organism-Response theory (SOR theory), the Technology Acceptance Model (TAM), and the Uses and gratification theory are also well represented, each with 3 corresponding sources. Other theories such as the Commitment-Trust Theory, the Dynamic Capabilities Theory, and the Affordance Theory were also mobilized, although less frequently.

4.2. Thematic Analysis of Application Trends Marketing Emerging Technologies

To complete our study, we have summarized the results of the major empirical studies in the table below. These results show the authors' main contributions to the marketing applications of emerging technologies with empirical validation.

Table 8. Summary of Key Findings

Authors	Technology solutions	Marketing application dimensions
(Li et al., 2019)	• Machine learning prediction algorithms	• Consumer behavior • Customer satisfaction
(Huang & Rust, 2021)	• Automating data analysis with artificial intelligence	• Marketing research (data collection, market analysis, customer understanding) • Strategic marketing (segmentation, targeting, positioning) • Operational marketing (standardization, personalization, relationalization)
(Yin & Qiu, 2021)	• Recognition and analysis (voice, images, text) • User-machine interaction	• Consumer behavior and intentions • Customer experience

continued on following page

Table 8. Continued

Authors	Technology solutions	Marketing application dimensions
(Volkmar et al., 2022)	• Artificial intelligence • Automatic learning	• Customer relationship management
(Mishra et al., 2022)	• Chatbots • Recommendation systems • Data processing	• Customer experience • Operational efficiency • Communication
(Lim et al., 2024)	• Augmented reality • Virtual reality	• Customer experience
(Nikhashemi et al., 2021; Vieira et al., 2022)	• Augmented reality	• Consumer behavior
(Rauschnabel et al., 2019)	• Augmented reality mobile applications	• Brand attitude and commitment
(Lo & Campos, 2018)	• Internet of Things	• Relationship marketing
(Selamat & Windasari, 2021)	• Chatbots	• Customer experience
(Tseng, 2023)	• Big data	• Market research
(Sharma et al., 2023)	• Artificial intelligence • RV/RA/RM • Internet and mobile platforms	• Consumer decision-making process
(Kaur et al., 2023)	• Gamification platforms	• Purchase intention and behavior • Customer experience
(Marasco et al., 2018)	• Virtual reality	• Customer experience
(Wagner & Cozmiuc, 2022)	• Extended reality	• Customer relationship management • Customer experience
(Kang et al., 2020)	• 3D virtual reality	• Purchasing decision process
(Castro et al., 2023)	• AI in marketing • Marketing Automation	• Market behavior and personalization • Customer experience
(Buhalis & Moldavska, 2022)	• Voice assistants	• Customer service
(Kumar et al., 2021)	• Internet of Things • Automatic learning • Artificial intelligence • Blockchain	• Strategic marketing • Customer relationship management
(Kautish & Khare, 2022)	• Artificial intelligence	• Customer experience
(Brewis et al., 2023)	• Big data	• Strategic marketing
(Perez-Vega et al., 2021)	• Artificial intelligence system	• Customer engagement behavior
(Kazmi et al., 2021)	• Augmented reality	• consumer behavior and decision-making
(Saura et al., 2021)	• artificial intelligence	• Customer relationship management • B2B digital marketing
(Flavián et al., 2019)	• VR/AR/MR	• Customer experience
(Jessen et al., 2020)	• Augmented reality	• Customer commitment and satisfaction
(Miklosik et al., 2019)	• Automatic learning	• Digital marketing strategies • Market research • Decision-making process
(Scholz & Duffy, 2018)	• Augmented reality	• Consumer-brand relations
(Kushwaha et al., 2021)	• Chatbots • Big data analysis	• Customer experience

Source: Authors

The chart illustrates the emerging technologies that have transformed the modern marketing landscape. These advances have revolutionized the entire marketing process, from the collection and analysis of market data to the implementation of strategies such as segmentation, targeting, positioning, standardization, personalization, and relationalization. Following the analysis, we will discuss the findings, contextualize them, and place them in the broader landscape of modern marketing.

5. DISCUSSION AND SUMMARY

5.1. Discussion of Findings

The in-depth analysis of our literature review has enabled us to highlight the major current trends in the various marketing uses of emerging technologies. The results of our research clearly show that the scale of adoption of these technologies, such as artificial intelligence, augmented reality, and the Internet of Things, is reshaping the way companies do business and offering significant opportunities for managers to rethink their marketing strategies and improve the customer experience.

New technologies have revolutionized marketing practices. Effective integration of these technologies enables companies to optimize the marketing process through increased personalization of offers (Gallardo et al., 2018; Moradi & Dass, 2022; Nikhashemi et al., 2021) and better understanding and prediction of customer needs (Liu et al., 2023). For example, AI-powered chatbots and voice assistants can improve the efficiency of customer service (Buhalis & Moldavska, 2022). Augmented reality provides a more immersive way to interact with products (Cowan & Ketron, 2019) and reduces consumer uncertainty (Sun et al., 2022).

This literature review provides a better understanding of existing concepts, theories, and models related to emerging technologies and marketing. It also highlights the important role of customer data in marketing decisions, in parallel with the adoption of these new technologies and new market dynamics (Rosário & Dias, 2023). Blockchain technology demonstrates its importance in terms of data security, reliability and confidentiality (Stallone et al., 2021).

The reconciliation of the different results shows a convergence on several points, namely personalization, process optimization and improvement of the customer experience. There is also agreement on the challenges associated with the adoption of new technologies, mainly confidentiality, ethics, and potential human and algorithmic biases. However, divergences can be discussed, generally related to specific contexts.

5.2. Design of the Analysis Model

The figure below outlines a conceptual model that explains the relationship between emerging technologies and marketing performance. These technologies have a direct impact on an organization's marketing practices and strategies, and the customer experience is improved by enhancing the quality of interactions through the use of these technologies. Satisfaction, trust, and retention are key dimensions of a successful customer experience. Improved customer experience can also be enhanced through customer knowledge. Marketing performance is the result of deep customer knowledge and improved customer experience.

Figure 7. Sketch of the conceptual model

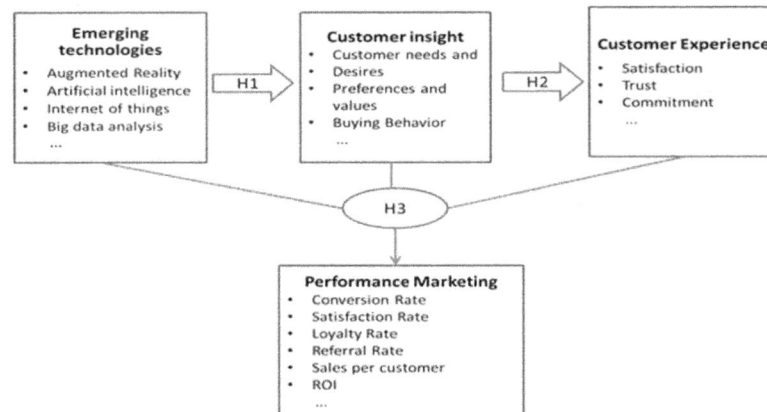

Having sketched out the conceptual model, it's clear that emerging technologies such as augmented reality, artificial intelligence, the Internet of Things, and big data analytics are opening up new perspectives for businesses. They enable them to gain a deeper understanding of their customers' buying behavior, preferences, and needs. This evolution promises a significant improvement in the customer experience, with a notable impact on marketing performance, particularly in terms of conversion rates, return on investment and customer loyalty. Several hypotheses emerge from these considerations:

- **H1**: The adoption of innovative solutions based on emerging technologies fosters a better understanding of the customer.
- **H2**: Improved customer insight, fostered by the integration of innovative emerging technology solutions, contributes to the development of the customer experience.
- **H3**: The relationship between emerging technologies and marketing performance is mediated by customer knowledge and experience.

This attempt to model the impact of emerging technologies on improving the marketing performance of firms highlights the variety of innovative solutions that can be mobilized to develop customer knowledge and enhance their experience, and the opportunities that can be seized to further improve the various dimensions of marketing performance of these firms.

6. CONCLUSION, LIMITATIONS, AND PERSPECTIVES

At the end of our literature review, we can draw several conclusions about the marketing applications of emerging technologies. The main finding is that augmented reality, artificial intelligence, the Internet of Things, and big data are emerging technologies that have had a profound impact on marketing practices and strategies.

Analysis of the findings included in this review demonstrates the important role these technologies play in enhancing the customer experience, personalizing offers, and optimizing marketing campaigns. Studies have linked augmented reality to increased customer satisfaction (Lim et al., 2024), purchase intention (Bilgili & Aydin, 2019), and reduced product uncertainty (Sun et al., 2022), while the performance of customer service systems can be enhanced by chatbots and virtual assistants with artificial intelligence (Buhalis & Moldavska, 2022; Kushwaha et al., 2021).

As with all research, this literature review has theoretical, methodological, and practical limitations. There are theoretical gaps in defining concepts that evolve and vary according to different contexts. In addition, the understanding of the underlying mechanisms of adoption and acceptance of emerging technologies, as well as their integration into existing marketing theories, needs to be further developed. From a methodological point of view, there is a risk of irrelevance of the selected references. In addition, the general conceptual framework does not take into account the unique characteristics of sector marketing, company size, industry, environment, management education and culture.

Today's practitioners understand that the successful adoption of new technologies is everyone's business - a culture that requires a strategic approach. To take full advantage of these innovative tools, it is also essential to invest in training and developing technology skills, as well as raising awareness of ethical and deontological use. To remain competitive, practitioners must be alert to technological changes and market trends.

In this rapidly evolving field, there are several research avenues to explore. Future research could focus on developing a sound theoretical framework for understanding how the combination of emerging technologies can revolutionize marketing strategies and practices. The model can then be empirically tested to understand the mechanisms by which emerging technologies can be adopted in marketing, and the practical and strategic aspects of marketing that are affected by this adoption. In addition, it is important to pay special attention to the ethical and social considerations surrounding the use of these technologies. The goal is to ensure that consumers and brands benefit from these technologies in an ethical and responsible manner.

REFERENCES

Adeola, O., Evans, O., Ndubuisi Edeh, J., & Adisa, I. (2022). The Future of Marketing : Artificial Intelligence, Virtual Reality, and Neuromarketing. In *Marketing Communications and Brand Development in Emerging Economies* (Vol. I, pp. 253–280). Palgrave Macmillan. 10.1007/978-3-030-88678-3_12

Alla, L., Kamal, M., & Bouhtati, N. (2022). Big data et efficacité marketing des entreprises touristiques : Une revue de littérature. *Alternatives Managériales Economiques, 4*(0), Article 0. 10.48374/IMIST .PRSM/ame-v1i0.36928

Amado, A., Cortez, P., Rita, P., & Moro, S. (2018). Research trends on Big Data in Marketing : A text mining and topic modeling based literature analysis. *European Research on Management and Business Economics*, 24(1), 1–7. 10.1016/j.iedeen.2017.06.002

Anastassova, M. (2006). *L'analyse ergonomique des besoins en amont de la conception de technologies émergente : Le cas de la Réalité Augmentée pour la formation à la maintenance automobile* [PhD Thesis, Université René Descartes-Paris V]. https://theses.hal.science/tel-00340103

Bec, A., Moyle, B., Schaffer, V., & Timms, K. (2021). Virtual reality and mixed reality for second chance tourism. *Tourism Management*, 83, 104256. 10.1016/j.tourman.2020.104256

Berberović, D., Alić, A., & Činjarević, M. (2022). Virtual Reality in Marketing : Consumer and Retail Perspectives. *Lecture Notes in Networks and Systems, 472 LNNS*, 1093-1102. *Scopus*, 472, 1093–1102. 10.1007/978-3-031-05230-9_129

Bilgili, S. S., & Aydin, K. (2019). Marketing Communications and Experiential Marketing in the Context of Augmented Reality. In Grima, S., Özen, E., Boz, H., Spiteri, J., & Thalassinos, E. (Eds.), *Contemporary Issues in Behavioral Finance* (Vol. 101, pp. 153–162). Emerald Publishing Limited. 10.1108/ S1569-375920190000101010

Blasco-Arcas, L., Lee, H.-H. M., Kastarakis, M. N., Alcañiz, M., & Reyes-Menendez, A. (2022). The role of consumer data in marketing : A research agenda. *Journal of Business Research*, 146, 436–452. 10.1016/j.jbusres.2022.03.054

Bobillier Chaumon, M.-É. (2021). Technologies émergentes et transformations digitales de l'activité : Enjeux pour l'activité et la santé au travail. *Psychologie du Travail et des Organisations*, 27(1), 17–32. 10.1016/j.pto.2021.01.002

Bouhtati, N., Alla, L., & Bentalha, B. (2023). Marketing Big Data Analytics and Customer Relationship Management : A Fuzzy Approach. In *Integrating Intelligence and Sustainability in Supply Chains* (p. 75-86). IGI Global. https://www.igi-global.com/chapter/marketing-big-data-analytics-and-customer -relationship-management/331980

Bouhtati, N., Kamal, M., & Alla, L. (2023). Big Data and the Effectiveness of Tourism Marketing : A Prospective Review of the Literature. *Artificial Intelligence and Smart Environment*, 287-292. 10.1007/978-3-031-26254-8_40

Brewis, C., Dibb, S., & Meadows, M. (2023). Leveraging big data for strategic marketing : A dynamic capabilities model for incumbent firms. *Technological Forecasting and Social Change*, 190, 122402. 10.1016/j.techfore.2023.122402

Buhalis, D., & Moldavska, I. (2022). Voice assistants in hospitality : Using artificial intelligence for customer service. *Journal of Hospitality and Tourism Technology, 13*(3), 386-403. *Scopus*. Advance online publication. 10.1108/JHTT-03-2021-0104

Campbell, C., Sands, S., Ferraro, C., Tsao, H.-Y. (Jody), & Mavrommatis, A. (2020). From data to action : How marketers can leverage AI. *ARTIFICIAL INTELLIGENCE AND MACHINE LEARNING, 63*(2), 227-243. 10.1016/j.bushor.2019.12.002

Castro, S. L. C., Humberto, D. P. D. R., Paúl, V. A. C., & Estefanía, A. T. P. (2023). Impact of Artificial Intelligence on Market Behavior Analysis : A Comprehensive Approach to Marketing. *Remittances Review, 8*(4). https://remittancesreview.com/menu-script/index.php/remittances/article/view/742

Cowan, K., & Ketron, S. (2019). Prioritizing marketing research in virtual reality : Development of an immersion/fantasy typology. *European Journal of Marketing, 53*(8), 1585-1611. *Scopus*. 10.1108/EJM-10-2017-0733

Dash, G., Kiefer, K., & Paul, J. (2021). Marketing-to-Millennials : Marketing 4.0, customer satisfaction and purchase intention. *Journal of Business Research*, 122, 608–620. 10.1016/j.jbusres.2020.10.016

De Mauro, A., Sestino, A., & Bacconi, A. (2022). Machine learning and artificial intelligence use in marketing : A general taxonomy. *Italian Journal of Marketing*, 2022(4), 439–457. 10.1007/s43039-022-00057-w

Donthu, N., Kumar, S., Mukherjee, D., Pandey, N., & Lim, W. M. (2021). How to conduct a bibliometric analysis : An overview and guidelines. *Journal of Business Research*, 133, 285–296. 10.1016/j.jbusres.2021.04.070

Flavián, C., Ibáñez-Sánchez, S., & Orús, C. (2019). The impact of virtual, augmented and mixed reality technologies on the customer experience. *Journal of Business Research*, 100, 547–560. 10.1016/j.jbusres.2018.10.050

Gallardo, C., Rodríguez, S. P., Chango, I. E., Quevedo, W. X., Santana, J., Acosta, A. G., Tapia, J. C., & Andaluz, V. H. (2018). Augmented reality as a new marketing strategy. *Lecture Notes in Computer Science (Including Subseries Lecture Notes in Artificial Intelligence and Lecture Notes in Bioinformatics), 10850 LNCS*, 351-362. *Lecture Notes in Computer Science*, 10850, 351–362. 10.1007/978-3-319-95270-3_29

Gleim, M., & Stevens, J. (2021). Blockchain : A game changer for marketers? *Marketing Letters*, 32(1), 1–6. 10.1007/s11002-021-09557-9

Godé, C. (2021). Propos introductif : Technologies émergentes et digitalisation des organisations. *Recherche et Cas en Sciences de Gestion*, (22). 10.3917/rcsg.022.0007

Grewal, D., Hulland, J., Kopalle, P. K., & Karahanna, E. (2020). The future of technology and marketing : A multidisciplinary perspective. *Journal of the Academy of Marketing Science*, 48(1), 1–8. 10.1007/s11747-019-00711-4

Haleem, A., Javaid, M., Asim Qadri, M., Pratap Singh, R., & Suman, R. (2022). Artificial intelligence (AI) applications for marketing : A literature-based study. *International Journal of Intelligent Networks*, 3, 119–132. 10.1016/j.ijin.2022.08.005

Hoffman, D. L., Moreau, C. P., Stremersch, S., & Wedel, M. (2022). The Rise of New Technologies in Marketing : A Framework and Outlook. *Journal of Marketing*, 86(1), 1–6. 10.1177/00222429211061636

Huang, M.-H., & Rust, R. T. (2021). A strategic framework for artificial intelligence in marketing. *Journal of the Academy of Marketing Science*, 49(1), 30–50. 10.1007/s11747-020-00749-9

IBM Institute for Business Value. (2023). *2023 Chief Executive Officer Study : Decision-making in the age of AI*. IBM. https://www.ibm.com/thought-leadership/institute-business-value/en-us/report/2023-ceo

Jessen, A., Hilken, T., Chylinski, M., Mahr, D., Heller, J., Keeling, D. I., & de Ruyter, K. (2020). The playground effect : How augmented reality drives creative customer engagement. *Journal of Business Research*, 116, 85–98. 10.1016/j.jbusres.2020.05.002

Jonny, Kriswanto, & Toshio, M. (2021). Building an Implementation Model of IoT and Big Data and Its Improvement. *INTERNATIONAL JOURNAL OF TECHNOLOGY, 12*(5), 1000-1008. 10.14716/ijtech.v12i5.5178

Kang, H. J., Shin, J., & Ponto, K. (2020). How 3D Virtual Reality Stores Can Shape Consumer Purchase Decisions : The Roles of Informativeness and Playfulness. *Journal of Interactive Marketing*, 49(1), 70–85. 10.1016/j.intmar.2019.07.002

Kaur, J., Lavuri, R., Parida, R., & Singh, S. V. (2023). Exploring the Impact of Gamification Elements in Brand Apps on the Purchase Intention of Consumers. *Journal of Global Information Management, 31*(1). *Journal of Global Information Management*, 31(1), 1–30. 10.4018/JGIM.317216

Kautish, P., & Khare, A. (2022). Investigating the moderating role of AI-enabled services on flow and awe experience. *International Journal of Information Management*, 66, 102519. 10.1016/j.ijinfomgt.2022.102519

Kazmi, S. H. A., Ahmed, R. R., Soomro, K. A., Hashem, E. A. R., Akhtar, H., & Parmar, V. (2021). Role of augmented reality in changing consumer behavior and decision making : Case of Pakistan. *Sustainability (Switzerland), 13*(24). *Sustainability (Basel)*, 13(24), 14064. 10.3390/su132414064

Keegan, B. J., Canhoto, A. I., & Yen, D. A. (2022). Power negotiation on the tango dancefloor : The adoption of AI in B2B marketing. *Industrial Marketing Management*, 100, 36–48. 10.1016/j.indmarman.2021.11.001

Khargharia, H. S., Rehman, M. H., Banerjee, A., Montori, F., Forkan, A. R. M., & Jayaraman, P. P. (2023). Towards Marketing 4.0 : Vision and Survey on the Role of IoT and Data Science. *Societies (Basel, Switzerland)*, 13(4), 4. 10.3390/soc13040100

Kocaman, B., Gelper, S., & Langerak, F. (2023). Till the cloud do us part : Technological disruption and brand retention in the enterprise software industry. *International Journal of Research in Marketing*, 40(2), 316–341. 10.1016/j.ijresmar.2022.11.001

Kotler, P., Kartajaya, H., & Setiawan, I. (2010). *Marketing 3.0 : Produits, clients, facteur humain*. Wiley. 10.1002/9781118257883

Kotler, P., Kartajaya, H., & Setiawan, I. (2016). *Marketing 4.0 : Moving from Traditional to Digital*. John Wiley & Sons.

Kotler, P., Kartajaya, H., & Setiawan, I. (2021). *Marketing 5.0 : Technology for Humanity*. John Wiley & Sons.

Kumar, V., Ramachandran, D., & Kumar, B. (2021). Influence of new-age technologies on marketing : A research agenda. *Journal of Business Research*, 125, 864–877. 10.1016/j.jbusres.2020.01.007

Kushwaha, A. K., Kumar, P., & Kar, A. K. (2021). What impacts customer experience for B2B enterprises on using AI-enabled chatbots? Insights from Big data analytics. *Industrial Marketing Management*, 98, 207–221. 10.1016/j.indmarman.2021.08.011

Lhoussaine, A., Kamal, M., & Bouhtati, N. (2022). Big data et efficacité marketing des entreprises touristiques : Une revue de littérature. *Alternatives Managériales Economiques*, 1, 39–58.

Li, J., Pan, S., Huang, L., & Zhu, X. (2019). A machine learning based method for customer behavior prediction. *Tehnicki Vjesnik, 26*(6), 1670-1676. *Scopus*. 10.17559/TV-20190603165825

Lim, W. M., Mohamed Jasim, K., & Das, M. (2024). Augmented and virtual reality in hotels : Impact on tourist satisfaction and intention to stay and return. *International Journal of Hospitality Management*, 116, 103631. 10.1016/j.ijhm.2023.103631

Liu, C.-H., Horng, J.-S., Chou, S.-F., Yu, T.-Y., Huang, Y.-C., & Lin, J.-Y. (2023). Integrating big data and marketing concepts into tourism, hospitality operations and strategy development. *Quality & Quantity*, 57(2), 1905–1922. 10.1007/s11135-022-01426-535729961

Lo, F.-Y., & Campos, N. (2018). Blending Internet-of-Things (IoT) solutions into relationship marketing strategies. *Technological Forecasting and Social Change, 137*, 10-18. *Scopus*. 10.1016/j.techfore.2018.09.029

Ma, L., & Sun, B. (2020). Machine learning and AI in marketing–Connecting computing power to human insights. *International Journal of Research in Marketing*, 37(3), 481–504. 10.1016/j.ijresmar.2020.04.005

Marasco, A., Buonincontri, P., van Niekerk, M., Orlowski, M., & Okumus, F. (2018). Exploring the role of next-generation virtual technologies in destination marketing. *Journal of Destination Marketing & Management*, 9, 138–148. 10.1016/j.jdmm.2017.12.002

Mateo, S. (2020). Procédure pour conduire avec succès une revue de littérature selon la méthode PRISMA. *Kinésithérapie, la Revue*, 20(226), 29–37. 10.1016/j.kine.2020.05.019

Miklosik, A., Kuchta, M., Evans, N., & Zak, S. (2019). Towards the Adoption of Machine Learning-Based Analytical Tools in Digital Marketing. *IEEE Access, 7*, 85705-85718. *Scopus*. 10.1109/ACCESS.2019.2924425

Mishra, S., Ewing, M. T., & Cooper, H. B. (2022). Artificial intelligence focus and firm performance. *Journal of the Academy of Marketing Science*, 50(6), 1176–1197. 10.1007/s11747-022-00876-5

Moher, D., Liberati, A., Tetzlaff, J., & Altman, D. G.The PRISMA Group. (2009). Preferred Reporting Items for Systematic Reviews and Meta-Analyses : The PRISMA Statement. *PLoS Medicine*, 6(7), e1000097. 10.1371/journal.pmed.100009719621072

Moradi, M., & Dass, M. (2022). Applications of artificial intelligence in B2B marketing : Challenges and future directions. *Industrial Marketing Management*, 107, 300–314. 10.1016/j.indmarman.2022.10.016

Ngai, E. W. T., Lee, M. C. M., Luo, M., Chan, P. S. L., & Liang, T. (2021). An intelligent knowledge-based chatbot for customer service. *Electronic Commerce Research and Applications*, 50, 101098. 10.1016/j.elerap.2021.101098

Nikhashemi, S. R., Knight, H. H., Nusair, K., & Liat, C. B. (2021). Augmented reality in smart retailing : A (n) (A) Symmetric Approach to continuous intention to use retail brands' mobile AR apps. *Journal of Retailing and Consumer Services*, 60, 102464. 10.1016/j.jretconser.2021.102464

Page, M. J., McKenzie, J. E., Bossuyt, P. M., Boutron, I., Hoffmann, T. C., Mulrow, C. D., Shamseer, L., Tetzlaff, J. M., Akl, E. A., & Brennan, S. E. (2021). The PRISMA 2020 statement : An updated guideline for reporting systematic reviews. *BMJ (Clinical Research Ed.)*, 372. https://www.bmj.com/content/372/bmj.n71.short33782057

Peres, R., Schreier, M., Schweidel, D. A., & Sorescu, A. (2023). Blockchain meets marketing : Opportunities, threats, and avenues for future research. *International Journal of Research in Marketing*, 40(1), 1–11. 10.1016/j.ijresmar.2022.08.001

Perez-Vega, R., Kaartemo, V., Lages, C. R., Borghei Razavi, N., & Männistö, J. (2021). Reshaping the contexts of online customer engagement behavior via artificial intelligence : A conceptual framework. *Journal of Business Research*, 129, 902–910. 10.1016/j.jbusres.2020.11.002

Plangger, K., Grewal, D., de Ruyter, K., & Tucker, C. (2022). The future of digital technologies in marketing : A conceptual framework and an overview. *Journal of the Academy of Marketing Science*, 50(6), 1125–1134. 10.1007/s11747-022-00906-2

Rauschnabel, P. A., Babin, B. J., tom Dieck, M. C., Krey, N., & Jung, T. (2022). What is augmented reality marketing? Its definition, complexity, and future. *Journal of Business Research, 142*, 1140-1150. *Scopus*. 10.1016/j.jbusres.2021.12.084

Rauschnabel, P. A., Felix, R., & Hinsch, C. (2019). Augmented reality marketing : How mobile AR-apps can improve brands through inspiration. *Journal of Retailing and Consumer Services*, 49, 43–53. 10.1016/j.jretconser.2019.03.004

Rosário, A. T., & Dias, J. C. (2023). How has data-driven marketing evolved : Challenges and opportunities with emerging technologies. *International Journal of Information Management Data Insights*, 3(2), 100203. 10.1016/j.jjimei.2023.100203

Rust, R. T. (2020). The future of marketing. *International Journal of Research in Marketing*, 37(1), 15–26. 10.1016/j.ijresmar.2019.08.002

Saura, J. R., Ribeiro-Soriano, D., & Palacios-Marqués, D. (2021). Setting B2B digital marketing in artificial intelligence-based CRMs : A review and directions for future research. *Industrial Marketing Management*, 98, 161–178. 10.1016/j.indmarman.2021.08.006

Scholz, J., & Duffy, K. (2018). We ARe at home : How augmented reality reshapes mobile marketing and consumer-brand relationships. *Journal of Retailing and Consumer Services*, 44, 11–23. 10.1016/j.jretconser.2018.05.004

Selamat, M. A., & Windasari, N. A. (2021). Chatbot for SMEs : Integrating customer and business owner perspectives. *Technology in Society*, 66, 101685. 10.1016/j.techsoc.2021.101685

Shah, D., & Murthi, B. P. S. (2021). Marketing in a data-driven digital world : Implications for the role and scope of marketing. *Journal of Business Research*, 125, 772–779. 10.1016/j.jbusres.2020.06.062

Sharma, P., Ueno, A., Dennis, C., & Turan, C. P. (2023). Emerging digital technologies and consumer decision-making in retail sector : Towards an integrative conceptual framework. *Computers in Human Behavior*, 148, 107913. 10.1016/j.chb.2023.107913

Stallone, V., Wetzels, M., & Klaas, M. (2021). Applications of Blockchain Technology in marketing—A systematic review of marketing technology companies. *Blockchain: Research and Applications*, 2(3), 100023. 10.1016/j.bcra.2021.100023

Stone, M., Aravopoulou, E., Ekinci, Y., Evans, G., Hobbs, M., Labib, A., Laughlin, P., Machtynger, J., & Machtynger, L. (2020). Artificial intelligence (AI) in strategic marketing decision-making : A research agenda. *The Bottom Line (New York, N.Y.)*, 33(2), 183–200. 10.1108/BL-03-2020-0022

Sun, C., Fang, Y., Kong, M., Chen, X., & Liu, Y. (2022). Influence of augmented reality product display on consumers' product attitudes : A product uncertainty reduction perspective. *Journal of Retailing and Consumer Services, 64.Journal of Retailing and Consumer Services*, 64, 102828. 10.1016/j.jretconser.2021.102828

Tseng, H.-T. (2023). Customer-centered data power : Sensing and responding capability in big data analytics. *Journal of Business Research*, 158, 113689. 10.1016/j.jbusres.2023.113689

Verma, S., Sharma, R., Deb, S., & Maitra, D. (2021). Artificial intelligence in marketing : Systematic review and future research direction. *International Journal of Information Management Data Insights*, 1(1), 100002. 10.1016/j.jjimei.2020.100002

Vieira, V. A., Rafael, D. N., & Agnihotri, R. (2022). Augmented reality generalizations : A meta-analytical review on consumer-related outcomes and the mediating role of hedonic and utilitarian values. *Journal of Business Research*, 151, 170–184. 10.1016/j.jbusres.2022.06.030

Vlačić, B., Corbo, L., Costa e Silva, S., & Dabić, M. (2021). The evolving role of artificial intelligence in marketing : A review and research agenda. *Journal of Business Research*, 128, 187–203. 10.1016/j.jbusres.2021.01.055

Volkmar, G., Fischer, P. M., & Reinecke, S. (2022). Artificial Intelligence and Machine Learning : Exploring drivers, barriers, and future developments in marketing management. *Journal of Business Research*, 149, 599–614. 10.1016/j.jbusres.2022.04.007

Wagner, R., & Cozmiuc, D. (2022). Extended Reality in Marketing—A Multiple Case Study on Internet of Things Platforms. *Information (Switzerland), 13*(6). *Information (Basel)*, 13(6), 278. 10.3390/info13060278

Wedel, M., Bigné, E., & Zhang, J. (2020). Virtual and augmented reality : Advancing research in consumer marketing. *International Journal of Research in Marketing*, 37(3), 443–465. 10.1016/j.ijresmar.2020.04.004

Yin, J., & Qiu, X. (2021). Ai technology and online purchase intention : Structural equation model based on perceived value. *Sustainability (Switzerland), 13*(10). *Sustainability (Basel)*, 13(10), 567110.3390/su13105671

Yu, Y., Kwong, S. C. M., & Bannasilp, A. (2023). Virtual idol marketing : Benefits, risks, and an integrated framework of the emerging marketing field. *Heliyon*, 9(11), e22164. 10.1016/j.heliyon.2023.e2216438053914

Chapter 3
The Application of AI in Neuromarketing:
A Systematic Literature Review

Ichrak Fahim
Ibn Zohr University, Morocco

Loubna Haramouni
http://orcid.org/0000-0003-4510-3305
Ibn Zohr University, Morocco

Mohamed Khalil Majdi
Ibn Zohr University, Morocco

Fatima Elkandoussi
Ibn Zohr University, Morocco

ABSTRACT

Neuromarketing is an interdisciplinary field that combines neuroscience, psychology, and marketing for a better understanding of consumer behaviour. Artificial intelligence (AI) is a discipline that can shape consumers' preferences, leading to better insights for marketing strategies. This chapter aims to identify, evaluate, and summarise the findings of all relevant individual studies on the usage of artificial intelligence in Neuromarketing practices, as well as the different controversial ethical perspectives regarding this discipline. A systematic literature review of research studies published in indexed databases over the past ten years, 58 recent references were studied using a qualitative content analysis approach. The results indicate the application of AI in neuromarketing allows for more accurate and precise analysis of consumer behaviour and decision-making processes. However, the ethical debate of applying AI in neuromarketing is still ongoing, making it a topic of controversy and further research.

DOI: 10.4018/979-8-3693-3172-9.ch003

1. INTRODUCTION

The field of neuromarketing is an evolving field that integrates marketing, psychology, and neuroscience to comprehend customer behavior and decision-making processes. Artificial intelligence (AI) has become an increasingly important tool in the field of neuromarketing, allowing researchers to analyse large amounts of data quickly and efficiently. These two disciplines enable businesses to make more informed marketing decisions based on the generated consumer behaviour data.

According to Forbes, neuromarketing insights can increase sales by up to 20 By understanding the unconscious factors that drive consumer behavior, businesses can create more effective marketing campaigns. These campaigns will resonate better with their target audience. Additionally, research revealed that companies that use AI in their marketing strategies are more likely to outperform their competitors. According to a study by McKinsey, AI-powered companies saw a 5-10% increase in sales and a 20-30% decrease in marketing costs. However, there is a lack of references that merge both of these disciplines. With this paper, we dive to explore the usage of AI in neuromarketing practices.

The term "neuromarketing" was coined by Smidts in 2002. However, it wasn't until 2004, with McClure et al.'s pioneering fMRI investigation, that neuromarketing transitioned from theoretical study to practical research. Drawing from diverse fields such as neuroscience, marketing, and psychology (Javor et al., 2013; Sebastian, 2014), neuromarketing holds promise as a multidisciplinary area. Its goal is to uncover valuable insights into unconscious consumer behavior, enhancing the effectiveness of marketing strategies like promotion, advertising, and pricing. Research within neuromarketing has increasingly delved into the underlying neural responses of consumers towards the marketing mix, encompassing areas such as advertising research (Alsharif et al., 2023). The tools employed in neuromarketing aim to unveil decision-making processes that elude direct observation. Through the application of scientific methods, not only can we comprehend the decision-making process, but we can also gain insights into the entire shopping experience. With advancements in neuroscience, the field has embraced the use of 2D and 3D models, providing effective tools for analyzing these processes (Duque-Hurtado et al., 2020).

From an IT perspective, Artificial Intelligence (AI) is characterized as a technology that empowers machines to mimic human intelligenc Its core objective is to endow computers with the capacity to solve real-world problems using the same formal reasoning and decision-making capabilities as humans. This transformative technology has permeated diverse facets of human life. It spans industries, businesses, education, healthcare, and consumer gcod of human life, spanning industries, businesses, education, healthcare, and consumer goods. Virtually every domain has witnessed the integration of AI, offered intelligent solutions and left no aspect of human life untouched by its influence. Consequently, AI holds the potential to revolutionize marketing strategies and reshape how businesses interact with their customers (Bansal & Gupta, 2023). The infusion of AI into marketing presents a significant opportunity to enhance analytical methods for addressing a wide array of marketing challenges. As emphasized by De Bruyn et al. (2020), AI facilitates improved analysis of massive datasets, a deeper understanding of consumer behavior throughout the entire purchasing process, and elevated user experiences. AI empowers marketers to more accurately predict consumer expectations, enabling them to make pricing decisions with increased confidence and efficiency.

The primary aim of this study is to conduct an in-depth exploration of the contemporary literature pertaining to the utilization of Artificial Intelligence (AI) in the field of neuromarketing, while concurrently investigating the diverse ethical perspectives entwined with the deployment of AI in analyzing consumer behavior. To achieve this objective, a rigorous examination of scholarly articles published over the past decade across various databases has been undertaken. The methodology employed in this research involves a comprehensive analysis of a broad spectrum of literature sourced from reputable academic databases. Articles selected for inclusion underwent meticulous scrutiny to ensure relevance and rigor in addressing the nexus of AI and neuromarketing. Utilizing a qualitative content analysis approach, these selected articles were scrutinized to discern prevailing trends and patterns concerning the integration of AI within neuromarketing practices. Furthermore, to provide a comprehensive under-standing of the subject matter, particular attention was devoted to delineating the ethical considerations inherent in employing AI to scrutinize consumer behavior within the context of neuromarketing. These ethical dimensions were critically examined and synthesized alongside the empirical findings to offer nuanced insights into the ethical implications of AI utilization in this domain. By synthesizing and analyzing the extant literature, this study endeavors to contribute to the elucidation of the burgeoning field of neuromarketing and its intersection with AI, while also shedding light on the ethical dimensions inherent in this symbiotic relationship. Through a systematic examination of the literature, this research aims to provide valuable insights for both academia and industry practitioners, thereby fostering informed discourse and guiding future research endeavors in this dynamic domain.

2. RESEARCH METHODOLOGY

We performed a systematic literature review (SLR) for this study. SLR follows a transparent, scientific, and replicable process. The benefits of SLR include: repeatable actions used throughout the review process, and higher quality review processes and outcomes that minimize bias and errors and increase the validity of the process. SLR offers a framework that integrates current knowledge for academics and practitioners, as well as data synthesis and literature mapping of a particular research field. The two research steps in our methodology are as follows: an exploratory research phase for identifying, reading, and comprehending significant publications, and an extended research phase of the selected references for an in-depth content analysis addressing our research question.

Gathering references is the first step in creating a literature review. One effective method for achieving this is to search academic databases with relevant keywords such as "Neuromarketing" and "Artificial Intelligence." We used Boolean operators to form queries like "Artificial Intelligence AND Neuro-marketing" to access references addressing both keywords, we also used abbreviations such as "AI" to further enhance our findings. Additionally, we limited our search to only include studies published within the last thirteen years (2010–2023). The main databases leveraged are: Scopus, Web of Science, ScienceDirect, and Google Scholar as they are mostly used in social science disciplines. Other articles sources were also consulted like Springer and ResearchGate. The precise selection criteria for articles used in this procedure are listed in Table 1 below.

Table 1. Criteria for Selecting and Refining References

Keywords	Publication year	Academic Database	Document Indexing	Language
Neuromarketing, Artificial Intelligence (AI), Consumer Behavior	[2010-2023]	Web of Science, Scopus, ScienceDirect, Google Scholar, Springer, ResearchGate	SJR: Scientific Journal Ranking Q1, Q2, Q3	English

Source: Author's processing

The search query "The Usage of Artificial Intelligence in Neuromarketing" was launched in ScienceDirect and it extracted 37 results. 31 results were found in Scopus by using the query: "Artificial Intelligence AND Neuromarketing", and 24 results in web of science for the same query. Google scholar on the other hand displayed 4860 results with the query "The Usage of Artificial Intelligence in Neuromarketing" by filtering dates to range from 2010 to 2023. According to the selection Criteria we reached 58 references of different document types.

2.1 Exploratory Literature Review

We can examine all the relevant references within the study topic by doing an exploratory systematic literature review, from which we can select and read only the most pertinent ones. In order to proceed with this, we must put in place a reference management system that will let us cite them throughout the writing process and maintain our database in a systematic way. We chose to implement Zotero since it is useful, free to use, and open source. In short, we completed the construction of our reference database using Excel MS by inputting the following: country, source, abstract, author(s), journal/publisher, document type, publication date, and reference number. The references listed below are the most pertinent ones:

Table 2. Types of relevant references

Document Type	Number of References
Journal article	46
Conference article	6
Book chapter	5
Book	1
Total	58

Source: Author's processing

The references compiled encompass a diverse array of secondary data documents, as detailed in Table 2, contributing to a comprehensive and insightful review. Journal papers play a pivotal role as the primary building blocks and the foundational elements of this study. Conference articles are incorporated to provide the latest updates on the research topic, while book chapters and books contribute to a deeper understanding of the fundamentals, historical context of neuromarketing, and the ethical considerations associated with the usage of AI in this field. To facilitate organization and analysis, all gathered documents from the online Zotero library were downloaded and transferred to NVivo, a qualitative data analysis program. NVivo is instrumental in aiding researchers in the organization and analysis of qualitative data, which can range from text and audio files to images and videos. In this particular study, a full-text analysis was conducted using NVivo to extract valuable insights and patterns from the collected data.

2.1.1 Word Could

The most frequent words in the texts of the publications selected from databases are highlighted in Figure 1: Word Cloud. Only the word's frequency in the chosen articles determines the size of the words in the image. The study's keywords, Neuromarketing, and AI, are in the figure's central location. In the references, the term "neuromarketing" appears 6774 times, followed by the word "AI" standing for artificial intelligence which appears 4388 times. The word "Research" is also revealed to be frequently used since the correlation nature between neuromarketing and AI is to research and understand consumer behaviour.

Figure 1. Word Cloud

Source: Processed with Nvivo

This word cloud figure makes it easier to find references where the searched terms are used most frequently. By condensing complex textual information into a visually accessible format, the word cloud enables us to recognize prominent trends, prioritize key topics for further investigation, and uncover connections and patterns that might not be immediately apparent through traditional textual analysis alone. In this case, the keywords neuromarketing, AI and research are strongly intertwined, meaning that neuromarketing practices are dependent on scientific research outcomes by leveraging artificial intelligence tools to analyze the consumer's brain.

2.1.2 Exploratory Review Data Analysis

Table 3. Most Frequent Words in the References' Full-Text

Word	Length	Count
Research	8	6774
Neuromarketing	14	6364
AI	2	4388
Marketing	9	4148
Consumer	8	2959
Brain	5	2557
Data	4	2174

Source: Processed with Nvivo

As per the word frequency query outcomes obtained from NVivo, the initial quartet of words, namely "research," "neuromarketing," and "AI," emerged as the most frequently occurring terms within the entirety of the referenced texts. This observation underscores their elevated significance as pivotal criteria for document filtration in the ensuing phase. It's worth reiterating that the compilation of references encompassed a broad spectrum of origins and scholarly databases. The emphasis was placed on research papers due to their efficient encapsulation of the existing research landscape, ultimately saving substantial research time and effort in comprehending our designated subject of study.

Table 4. References' Database Sources

Sources of references	Rate in %
Google scholar	15 (25,86%)
ScienceDirect	12 (20,68%)
Scopus	10 (17,24%)
Springer	10 (17,24%)
Web of science	2 (3,44%)
Other	9 (15,51%)

Source: Author's processing

The majority of the sources listed here are accessible through subscription services. Nevertheless, freely available databases such as Google Scholar, offer valuable resources, representing 25% of the references' origins, a substantial portion of which comprises well-regarded journal articles. Following closely are ScienceDirect, Scopus and Springer, each contributing between 20% to 17%. Materials obtained from Scopus and ScienceDirect encompass book chapters, as well as conference and journal articles. The remaining sources comprise offline materials or platforms facilitating access to paywalled papers.

Given the refining options in most databases, our search efforts centered on documents released between 2010 and 2023. The field of neuromarketing, and neuroscience has garnered significant interest worldwide among researchers, even more with the technology developments of artificial intelligence.

Figure 2. Number of References Collected by Year of Publication

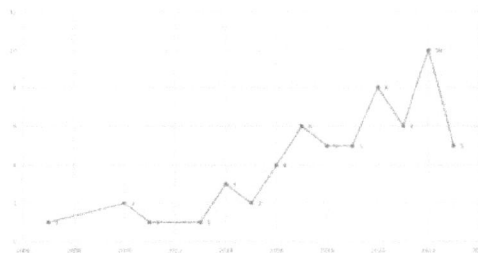

Source: Author's processing

Our approach to selection employs qualitative techniques, primarily involving the examination of abstracts to carefully select our literature review basis by excluding irrelevant publications. It's not uncommon for the keywords we search for to appear in the abstracts of many documents. However, the core focus of these documents may diverge from our research objectives. Additionally, throughout our research and refinement process, we placed emphasis on the most frequently cited papers and reputable journals within the field.

Given that journal articles constitute the predominant reference type, understanding the journals in which these articles are published becomes crucial. This encompasses considerations such as their H-Index, impact factor, and scientific ranking (SJR), which offers a means to assess journals' significance within the scholarly landscape. It's worth noting that some high-quality journals might lack an impact factor or SJR, especially if they are relatively new, which does not necessarily reflect their limited contribution to the realm of scientific inquiry.

2.2 Extended Literature Review

Table 5.

Year	Author	Journal	Reference Type	Subtopic	Aims and findings	Methodology
2023	Sheikh, H., Prins, C., Schrijvers, E	Mission AI	Book Chapter	Artificial Intelligence, history	This book chapter explain the emergence of AI, so it discusses the different definitions of AI, the myths, the theories and the history of this field	Qualitative study
2023	Shikha Bhardwaj, Gunjan A Rana, Abhishek Behl, Santiago Juan Gallego de Caceres	Journal of Business Research	Article	SLM, consumer neuroscience	This study presents a systematic review using the PRISMA method to investigate the boundaries of Neuromarketing and highlight the neuromarketing effect as the centre of consumer decision making.	Qualitative study: Systematic literature review
2023	(Alsh Ahmed H.Alsharif, Nor Zafir Md Salleh, Mazilah Abdullah, Ahmad Khraiwish, and Azmirul Ashaari	Sage Open	Article	SLR, PRISMA, Neuromarketing	This paper constitutes a systematic literature review aimed at categorizing contemporary neuromarketing tools employed in the Marketing Mix. The results of the review indicate that Electroencephalography (EEG) emerges as the predominant tool utilized in the Marketing Mix.	Qualitative study: Systematic literature Review
2023	Shashank Vaid, Stefano Puntoni, AbdulRahman Khodr	Journal of Business Research	Article	AI, Consumer Research, Marketing	This paper examines the adoption of AI techniques in consumer research in order to stimulate boundary breaking research and explain the potential of collaboration between AI experts and consumer researchers.	Qualitative study
2023	WCuicui Wang, Yiyang Li, Weizhong Fu, Jia Jin	Journal of Retailing and Consumer service	Article	AI,Chatbots, Consumers	The study explores consumer perceptions of AI chatbot services in e-commerce, focusing on trust implications and emotional interactions, suggesting e-retailers enhance chatbots' emotional service for objective customer service tasks.	Quantitative Study
2023	Shubhi Bansal, Monika Gupta	International Journal of Business and Globalization	Article	Artificial Intelligence, Neuromarketing	The study explores the integration of artificial intelligence in neuromarketing, highlighting its potential to enhance customer understanding, bias-free judgments, and enhance brand recognition.	Qualitative study
2023	Gaia Rancati, Isabella Maggioni	Journal of Services Marketing	Article	Neuroscience, Immersion,	The study explores customer immersion in human-robot interactions and their impact on store visit duration, finding that robot interaction enhances immersion during welcome and surprise moments.	Quantitative study
2022	Zeren Zhu, Yuanqing Jin1Yushun Su, Kan Jia, Chien-Liang Lin and Xiaoxin Liu	Frontiers in Psychology	Article	Neuromarketing trends 2020	The research, based on a bibliometric review from 2010-2021, reveals that the Journal of Consumer Psychology and the Journal of Marketing Research are key publishers, with Pieters et al. (2010) being the most cited.	Qualitative study:
2022	Lucília Cardoso, Meng-Mei Chen 2, Arthur Araújo, Giovana Goretti Feijó de Almeida, Francisco Dias and Luiz Moutinho	Behavioral Science	Article	SciValtopic prominence, neuromarketing, gaps	This paper aims to determine and evaluate the overall performance and efficacy of neuromarketing research. This study provides insights in terms of gaps for researchers for future studies.	Qualitative study: a bibliometric analysis through a mixed method approach
2022	Nikolina Ljepava	TEM JOURNAL -	Article	SLR, Marketing, AI, decision making	This paper reviews 2020-2022 articles on AI's marketing application, revealing its primary use in understanding consumer behavior needs and developing marketing mix strategies.	Qualitative study: SLR

continued on following page

Table 5. Continued

Year	Author	Journal	Reference Type	Subtopic	Aims and findings	Methodology
2022	Abid Haleem, Mohd Javaid,, Mohd Asim Qadri, Ravi Pratap Singh, Rajiv Suman	International Journal of Intelligent Networks	Article	Artificial Intelligence, Decision making, Data analytics	This paper explores the application of AI in marketing, focusing on deep learning and machine learning techniques. AI aids in data analysis, consumer insights, and efficient decision-making, ensuring better organization and efficiency.	Qualitative study: Review of journal articles and books
2022	Rupali Gill, Jaiteg Singh	Materials Today: Proceedings	Article	Neuromarketing, Emotions	The paper suggests that neuromarketing techniques are crucial for sustainable future and business growth, as there is limited research on integrated frameworks, allowing for innovation.	Qualitative study
2022	Peter Varghese	UJ Journal of Management	Article	Artificial intelligence, eye tracking, neuromarketing	This paper aims to explain the potential of combining AI with Neuromarketing.	Qualitative study
2022	Marcelo Royo-Vela and Ákos Varga	Encyclopedia of Social Sciences	Article	Neuromarketing, uses and attitudes; academic research	This paper examines neuromarketing's current state, applications, and definitions, distinguishing between traditional and neuromarketing methods, and predicts a gradual increase in its use alongside other research techniques.	Qualitative study
2022	Ogechi Adeola, Olaniyi Evans, Jude Ndubuisi Edeh & Isaiah Adisa	Marketing Communications and Brand Development in Emerging Economies Volume	Book Chapter	Artificial Intelligence, Neuromarketing, Virtual Reality	This chapter evaluates literature on AI, Virtual Reality, and neuromarketing to guide future marketing decisions. AI enhances consumer analysis and targeting, Virtual Reality enhances customer experience, and neuromarketing allows informed forecasting of purchasing behaviour by recording subconscious cognitive and emotional reactions.	Qualitative study
2021	Ahmed H. Alsharif, Nor Zafir Md Salleh, Rohaizat Baharun, Yahia H. Alsharif, Hassan Abuhassna	International Journal of Academic Research in	Article	Consumer neuroscience, Neuromarketing, Prisma	This paper provides a bibliometric analysis of neuromarketing to understand global trends, productive journals, cited authors, and countries producing research in this field.	Qualitative study:
2021	Ahmad F. Klaib *, Nawaf O. Alsrehin, Wasen Y. Melhem, Haneen O. Bashtawi, Aws A. Magableh	Experts systems with applications	Article	Eye tracking, technology, artificial intelligence	This paper explores eye tracking concepts, methods, and effectiveness using artificial intelligence like Machine Learning, IoT, and Cloud computing, revealing their importance in evolving eye tracking applications and achieving more efficient results.	Systematic Qualitative approach
2021	Andrea Owe· Seth D. Baum	AI and Ethics	Article	Artificial Intelligence, Non humans, Ethics	This paper explains that Ethics in AI should value non-human across all stages of the AI cycle from collecting data to using it, Non humans also deserve consideration for how much they benefit humans.	Qualitative study
2021	C. Luna-Nevarez	Journal of Consumer Policy	Article	Ethics, Social media, neuromarketing	The study explores consumer opinions on neuromarketing and ethics concerns, finding positive sentiments but highlighting concerns about the regulation of this field to protect consumers.	Content Analysis
2021	Vlačić, B., Corbo, L., e Silva, S. C., & Dabić, M.	Journal of Business Research	Article	Artificial Intelligence, Intelligent System, Marketing,	This paper is a systematic literature review to outline the combination of AI and Marketing, the acceptance, adoption and use of AI in marketing research.	Qualitative study
2021	Christopher Collins a, Denis Dennehy, Kieran Conboy, Patrick Mikalef	International Journal of Information Management	Article	Artificial Intelligence, Systematic Literature Review	This systematic literature review explores AI research in information systems, identifying its business value, contribution, use, and impactful opportunities in research.	Qualitative study

continued on following page

Table 5. Continued

Year	Author	Journal	Reference Type	Subtopic	Aims and findings	Methodology
2020	Rupali Gill, Jaiteg Singh	Materials Today Proceedings	Article	Neuroimaging	This paper aims to propose a cost-efficient framework for neuromarketing.	Qualitative study
2020	Bogdan Glova Ivan Mudryk	Third International Conference on Data Stream Mining & Processing (DSMP)	Conference paper	Machine learning, neuromarketing	The paper explores the use of machine learning in neurosciences and its potential in neuromarketing. It highlights the real-time recording of subconscious reactions and external factors influencing research, allowing for quantifiable perception and unbiased evaluation.	Quantitative study
2020	Chowdhury Rabith Amin; Mirza Farhan Hasin; Tasin Shafi Leon; Abrar Bareque Aurko; Tasmi Tamanna	IEEE Symposium Series on Computational Intelligence (SSCI)	Conference Paper	EEG, Consumer Decision	The paper presents a model analysing EEG signals to understand consumer behaviour, outperforming existing techniques in accuracy, sensitivity, and specificity, potentially aiding practitioners in improving marketing strategies.	Quantitative study
2020	Assunta Di Vaio, Rosa Palladino, Rohail Hassan, Octavio Escoba	Journal of Business Research	Article	Artificial intelligence, Sustainable Business Model	This paper explores the connection between AI and sustainable business models, highlighting the significance of AI and the role of knowledge management systems in facilitating this adaptation.	Qualitative study
2020	Thomas Davenport1 & Abhijit Guha2 & Dhruv Grewal3 & Timna Bressgott	Journal of the Academy of Marketing Science	Article	Ethics, Artificial Intelligence, Marketing	This paper explores the future impact of AI on marketing, highlighting its potential to enhance customer insights, predict pricing, offer price promotions, and predict consumer behaviour.	Qualitative study
2020	Pedro Duque-Hurtado	Estudios Gerenciales	Article	neuromarketing; consumer neuroscience; bibliometrics;	This paper reviews neuromarketing trends through science mapping tools, revealing it as an immature and incipient area with limited theoretical census.	Qualitative study
2020	Ferdousi Sabera Rawnaque*, Khandoker Mahmudur Rahman, Syed Ferhat Anwar, Ravi Vaidyanathan, Tom Chau, Farhana Sarker and Khondaker Abdullah Al Mamu	Brain Informatics	Article	Systematic literature review, machine learning, neuromarketing	This paper reviews technological advancements in Neuromarketing, focusing on consumer goods stimuli and social advertisement. Researchers focus on frontal and prefrontal cortex for cognitive and emotional inquiries, with EEG becoming more popular in Neuromarketing experiments.	Qualitative study
2020	Bahman PEYRAVI, Julija NEKROŠIENĖ, Liudmila LOBANOVA	Business: Theory and Practice	Article	artificial intelligence, marketing, marketing automation,	This systematic review explores the impact of AI in marketing, highlighting its theoretical background, current trends, and tools used, emphasizing their potential to enhance marketing managers' performance and strategy.	Systematic literature review
2020	Arabinda Bhandari	Analyzing the Strategic Role of Neuromarketing and Consumer Neuroscience	Book Chapter	Neuromarketing	This chapter explores the origins, applications, and opportunities of neuromarketing in understanding consumer behaviour using various technologies within organizations.	Qualitative study
2019	Filip Filipovic,	Artificial Intelligence: Applications and Innovations (IC-AIAI)	Conference paper	AI, neuromarketing, neural network	The paper explores the use of AI in neuromarketing for emotion detection using a webcam application, demonstrating precise identification of user emotions during advertisement viewing.	Quantitative study
2019	Kristina Kaličanin*, Milica Čolović, Angelina Njeguš, Vladimir Mitić	International Scientific Conference on Information Technology and Data Related Research	Conference Paper	machine learning, marketing intelligence, smart application	This paper explores the use of AI in marketing, highlighting its applications in Machine Learning and Deep Learning, enabling marketers to deliver personalized experiences to customers.	Qualitative study

continued on following page

Table 5. Continued

Year	Author	Journal	Reference Type	Subtopic	Aims and findings	Methodology
2019	Milica Slijepčević1, Nevenka Popović Šević2, Ivana Radojević	Journal of Innovative Business and Management	Article	Consumer behaviour, neuroscience, academicians, Neuromarketing research	This paper explores the limitations of neuromarketing research, including high costs, difficulty in finding respondents, and potential manipulation of attitudes, confirming that neuromarketing is a modern method with ethical principles.	Quantitative Study
2019	Yahia Mouammine, Hassan Azdimousa	International Journal of Business & Economic Strategy (IJBES)	Article	AI, Neuromarketing	This paper is a literature review about AI and Neuromarketing, the current emergence of AI in marketing studies. The findings explain that thanks to the combination of AI and Neuromarketing, many limitations may disappear and the neuromarketing tools will be more accessible and less costly	Qualitative study
2019	Md.Hafez,	Pacific Business Review International	Article	Neuromarketing, Branding, Advertisement, fMRI, EEG, MEG	This paper explores neuromarketing's application in brand building and advertisement, suggesting a new model based on empirical findings to explore people's emotions and feelings towards a brand or advertisement.	Exploratory Study
2018	Weng Marc Lim	Journal of Business Research	Article	Neuromarketing Neuroscience Marketing science	This article is a systematic review to explain the concept, the methods, the ethical consideration regarding neuromarketing.	Qualitative study: Content Analysis
2018	Olga Burukina,, Svetlana Karpova, and Nikolas Koro	International Conference on Human Systems Engineering and Design: Future Trends and Applications	Conference Paper	Ethical Issues, Artificial Intelligence	The paper explores the current trends in human users' attitudes towards AI, focusing on their satisfaction with AI applications, concerns about AI's impact on jobs and society, preferences for AI-human collaboration, and attitudes towards data privacy and security through surveys, interviews, and studies.	Mixed Method Approach
2018	Norbert Wirth	International Journal of Market Research	Article	Artificial Intelligence	This paper defines artificial intelligence (AI) in three forms: narrow, hybrid, and strong, and highlights its potential in marketing, emphasizing the need for its adoption.	Exploratory study
2018	Bogart Yail Márquez, José Sergio Magdaleno Palencia, Arnulfo Alanís Garza, Karina Romero Alvarado	Proceedings of the 2018 International Conference on Algorithms, Computing and Artificial Intelligence	Conference Paper	EEG	This project aims to create a classification algorithm to measure what we like and what we don't like as consumers using the EEG tool. This classification will help neuromarketing to understand consumer behaviour.	Quantitative study
2018	Lee, Nick, Chamberlain, Laura and Brandes, Le	European Journal of Marketing	Article	Neuromarketing, Consumer neuroscience	This paper aims to explain whether the existing body of Neuromarketing literature can support such growth within the parameters of the field.	Experimental study
2017	Lisa-Charlotte Wolter, David Hensel, and Judith Znanewitz	Ethics and Neuromarketing	Book Chapter	Ethics, Neuromarketing	This chapter aims to develop a framework guideline to use neuromarketing for researchers and practitioners	Qualitative study: Review of journal articles and books
2017	caro Luiz dos Santos Jordão,	Int. J. Business Forecasting and Marketing Intelligence	Article	Consumer neuroscience, literature review	This paper presents an integrative literature review of neuromarketing applied to consumer behaviour studies from 2010 to 2015.	Integrative literature review
2017	Bakardjieva	Ethics & Behavior	Article	neuromarketing research, research ethics, ethical ideology	Two studies reveal that neuromarketing research attitudes, ethicality, and willingness to participate are influenced by factors such as knowledge, attitudes towards science, technology, and ethical ideology, and can be influenced by demographics and third-party sources.	Quantitative Study

continued on following page

Table 5. Continued

Year	Author	Journal	Reference Type	Subtopic	Aims and findings	Methodology
(Sebastian, 2014)2017	Steven J. Stanton, Walter Sinnott-Armstrong, Scott A. Huettel	Journal of Business Ethics	Article	Ethics, Neuroscience	The paper addresses ethical concerns in neuromarketing, emphasizing transparency, quality certification, and privacy to reduce consumer concerns, while highlighting its potential positive impacts on consumers and society.	Qualitative study
2016	Prof. (Dr.) Manish Madan1, Ankita Popli	Journal of Business and Management	Article	Neuromarketing, Acceptance, Interpretive Structural Modelling	This paper aims to identify the variables that influence the acceptance of emerging Neuromarketing in the Indian market,	Qualitative study
2016	Erick Valencia Editors: Dos Santos	Applying Neuroscience to Business Practice	Book Chapter	Neuroscience, Neuroeconomics, tools, brain	This chapter explores neuromarketing, brain structure, tools for measuring techniques, neuroeconomics, and 10 steps companies should adopt for effective neuromarketing.	Qualitative study
2016	Cassiana Maris Lima Cruz, Janine Fleith De Medeiros, Lisiane Caroline Rodrigues Hermes, Arthur Marcon and Érico Marcon	Int. J. Business and Globalization,	Article	neuromarketing, consumer neuroscience, SLM	This study reviews literature on neuromarketing, focusing on consumer behaviour research in neuroscience and psychology, highlighting significant insights from scholarly studies.	Qualitative study: Literature Review
2016	Dijana Ćosić	Interdisciplinary Description of Complex Systems	Article	Eye tracking, Neuromarketing	The paper explores the ethical implications of neuromarketing, analysing a market research study using eye trackers, which revealed a particular scene in the commercial drew more attention.	Quantitative study
2015	Monica Diana Bercea Olteanu	Neuroethics	Article	Ethics, regulations	This paper reviews the ethics issues regarding neuromarketing and suggests the regulations that must be applied to improve the development of this field.	Review Study
2015	Cüneyt Dirican	Procedia - Social and Behavioral Sciences	Article	Robotics, Artificial Intelligence	This study explores the future of robots, mechatronics, and artificial intelligence, analysing various sources and suggesting further academic research for business and economic impacts.	Qualitative study
2014	Vitor Costa Rozan Fortunato, Janaina de Moura Engracia Giraldi, Jorge Henrique Caldeira de Oliveira	Journal of Management Research	Article	Neuromarketing, techniques, ethics	This paper explores the definitions, significance, advantages, ethics, applications, and limitations of neuromarketing, highlighting its role in marketing studies and its potential over traditional techniques.	Qualitative study
2014	Jason Flores, Arne Baruca, Robert Saldiviar	Journal of Legal, Ethical and Regulatory Issues	Article	Consumers, Ethics, Neuromarketing	The study investigates consumer's ethical perception of neuromarketing, finding that while profit-driven neuromarketing is considered unethical, non-profit neuromarketing is considered ethical.	Quantitative Study
2014	Vlăsceanu Sebastian	Procedia - Social and Behavioral Sciences	Article	Neuromarketing neuroethics neuroimaging	The paper explores neuroethics in neuromarketing, highlighting its benefits in reducing unnecessary spending, promoting self-discovery, and reducing impulsive shopping, while also highlighting its compatibility with consumer interests.	Qualitative study
2013	Khalid Ait Hammou, Md Hasan Galib, Jihane Melloul	Journal of Management Research	Article	Neuroimaging, consumer behaviour	This paper explores the potential of neuromarketing in understanding consumer behaviour, reviews its history, limitations, and areas for further exploration.	Review Study
2011	Christophe Morin	Symposium: Consumer Culture in Global Perspective	Article	Neuromarketing. Advertising.. Consumer behaviour	This paper introduces Neuromarketing, a science of consumer behaviour, and its potential to enhance the effectiveness of commercial and cause-related advertising worldwide.	Qualitative study

continued on following page

Table 5. Continued

Year	Author	Journal	Reference Type	Subtopic	Aims and findings	Methodology
2010	Carl Erik Fisher, MD, Lisa Chin, EdD, JD, MA, MPH, and Robert Klitzman, MD	Harv Rev Psychiatry	Article	Neuroeconomics, neuroethics, practitioners	This article aims to review the history of neuromarketing and to review websites of neuromarketing companies to uncover the policy and the ethics of professionals in this field.	Exploratory research
2010	Dan Ariely, Gregory S. Berns	Nature Reviews Neuroscience	Article	Neuroimaging, consumer behaviour	The paper explores the potential of Neuromarketing, a strategy that may offer hidden insights into consumer experiences, though its effectiveness remains uncertain.	Qualitative study
2007	Nick Lee, Amanda J. Broderick, Laura Chamberlain	International Journal of Psychophysiology	Article	Neuroscience; Neuromarketing; Neuroeconomics;	This article provides a perspective on neuromarketing which concerned developing to understand consumer behaviour and have an impact on the human society	Exploratory study

3. FINDINGS AND DISCUSSION

AI is increasingly playing a pivotal role in neuromarketing, aiding in the comprehension and prediction of customer behavior, refining marketing mix strategies, and even detecting emotions through the utilization of webcams (Filipovic et al., 2019). Machine Learning (ML) and Deep Learning (DL) stand out as the predominant AI tools in the field of neuromarketing, enabling marketers to discern patterns within vast datasets and deliver personalized experiences (Glova & Mudryk, 2020). Eye tracking emerges as a significant technique in neuromarketing studies, and when coupled with AI technologies such as machine learning, the internet of things, and cloud computing, its efficacy is substantially enhanced (Klaib et al., 2021). AI is also instrumental in deciphering customer desires, predicting pricing strategies, and offering targeted price promotions. For instance, AI aids businesses in making more accurate predictions about customer needs, potentially driving a shift towards a model where shipping precedes the shopping experience (Davenport et al., 2020; Peyravi et al., 2020). While Deep Learning (DL) has not yet been extensively applied to understand consumer influences on purchasing decisions, its unique capability to autonomously extract features in real-time holds promise for identifying factors influencing purchases among a vast array of auto-generated variables (Vaid et al., 2023). Neuromarketing proponents advocate for company-specific market research utilizing neurophysiological technologies such as EEG, fMRI, eye-tracking, and skin conductance. These tools facilitate the measurement of consumer emotions, generate unbiased assessments, and leverage artificial intelligence to efficiently gather pertinent data on how brain signals respond to specific stimuli (Mouammine & Azdimousa, 2019; Varghese, 2022).

Ethical perspectives of consumers towards neuromarketing and AI have been centred on the business implications, with concerns about transparency, customer manipulation, and the lack of regulations. Marketers should inform consumers about the type of study being conducted, distinguish between scientific and marketing research, and warn them of any hazards (Cosic, 2016). The most commonly cited consumer concerns are autonomy, privacy, and control; therefore, the actions neuromarketers should take to alleviate these issues are transparency, quality certification, and privacy. Considering these factors, neuromarketing undoubtedly holds promise for beneficial impacts on both consumers and the broader community (Stanton et al., 2017). Despite these concerns, neuromarketing holds promise for beneficial impacts on both consumers and the broader community. It is essential for neuromarketing businesses to self-regulate or sign on to a code of ethics, ensuring that nonhumans are given more wide and consistent moral consideration in AI ethics (Sebastian, 2014).

To summarize, the integration of AI within neuromarketing constitutes a pivotal advancement, offering profound insights into consumer behavior and preferences. This synthesis, as elucidated by the referenced literature, encompasses several salient dimensions: Firstly, the utilization of machine learning (ML) and deep learning (DL) algorithms enables marketers to meticulously parse through extensive datasets, discerning intricate patterns that inform highly personalized marketing strategies tailored to individual consumer proclivities. Secondly, the integration of AI technologies, such as emotion detection via webcams, furnishes marketers with real-time insights into consumer emotional responses during marketing interactions, thereby facilitating adaptive strategies that resonate more profoundly with target audiences. Moreover, the fusion of eye tracking methodologies with AI further amplifies the efficacy of neuromarketing endeavors. By harnessing machine learning in conjunction with the Internet of Things (IoT) and cloud computing, marketers glean deeper insights into consumer attentional dynamics and engagement patterns. Additionally, AI augments the predictive capabilities of marketers, enabling more precise forecasts of customer needs and preferences. Consequently, this predictive prowess holds the potential to engender a paradigm shift towards preemptive product dissemination, where goods are dispatched prior to consumers initiating the shopping experience. Ethically, consumer apprehensions regarding neuromarketing and AI center on issues of transparency, privacy, and autonomy. It is imperative for marketers to assuage these concerns through transparent practices, quality certification mechanisms, and robust privacy safeguards, thereby fostering trust and credibility among consumers. Furthermore, the imperative of self-regulation and ethical conduct within neuromarketing enterprises cannot be overstated. Adherence to ethical codes and regulatory frameworks ensures the protection of consumer interests and promotes a more conscientious approach towards the ethical implications of AI in marketing endeavors. In summation, the integration of AI into neuromarketing holds immense promise for unraveling consumer behaviors and preferences. However, its ethical deployment is paramount, necessitating a steadfast commitment to transparency, privacy protection, and adherence to ethical principles to foster trust and safeguard consumer welfare.

4. CONCLUSION

AI and Neuromarketing is a relatively nascent field of research. Neuromarketing and artificial intelligence are related topics that can complement one another. To comprehend customer behaviour, emotions, and decision-making processes, neuromarketing makes use of psychological and neuroscience findings. By offering cutting-edge tools and methods for gathering, analysing, and interpreting data relevant to customer responses and preferences, AI technologies improve neuromarketing procedures.

This paper undertakes a systematic literature review to explore the applications of AI in Neuromarketing practices, employing a two-part research approach. The initial phase involves an exploratory systematic literature review, followed by refinement of titles, abstracts, and keywords. In this step, documents are filtered based on predefined inclusion and exclusion criteria to eliminate irrelevant topics. Subsequently, the second method, known as the extended systematic literature review, entails a comprehensive examination of the entire texts. This phase involves reading, understanding, and retaining the complete content while conducting a detailed analysis of the references' substance.

The results indicate that AI will assist Neuromarketing technologies such as EEG, fMRI, eye-tracking, and skin conductance with analysing a massive amount of data.

Analysis of the articles shows also that to interpret subtle hints from customers, AI can be used with eye-tracking technology. AI, for example, can examine eye movement patterns and facial expressions to identify the elements of an advertisement or product that are grabbing consumers' attention and evoking strong feelings. To develop individualised marketing plans, AI algorithms can study the behaviour and preferences of certain customers. Marketers can customise commercials and product offerings to fit specific needs by learning what neurologically connects with each customer. On the other hand, the ethical debate about AI and neuromarketing is still ongoing making it an important topic that needs further study.

Our results will serve as a roadmap for upcoming researchers to navigate and delve into opportunities within this domain more effectively.

REFERENCES

Adeola, O. (2022). The Future of Marketing: Artificial Intelligence, Virtual Reality, and Neuromarketing. O. Adeola, R.E. Hinson, and A.M. Sakkthivel (eds) *Marketing Communications and Brand Development in Emerging Economies Volume I: Contemporary and Future Perspectives*. Cham: Springer International Publishing (Palgrave Studies of Marketing in Emerging Economies), pp. 253–280. 10.1007/978-3-030-88678-3_12

Ait Hammou, K., Galib, M. H., & Melloul, J. (2013). The Contributions of Neuromarketing in Marketing Research. *Journal of Management Research*, 5(4), 20. 10.5296/jmr.v5i4.4023

Alsharif, A. H. (2021). 'A Bibliometric Analysis of Neuromarketing: Current Status, Development and Future Directions', International Journal of Academic Research in Accounting. *Finance and Management Business Sciences*, 11(3), 828–847.

Alsharif, A. H., Salleh, N. Z. M., Abdullah, M., Khraiwish, A., & Ashaari, A. (2023). Neuromarketing Tools Used in the Marketing Mix: A Systematic Literature and Future Research Agenda. *SAGE Open*, 13(1), 215824402311565. 10.1177/21582440231156563

Amin, C. R. (2020). Consumer Behavior Analysis using EEG Signals for Neuromarketing Application. *2020 IEEE Symposium Series on Computational Intelligence (SSCI)*. IEEE. 10.1109/SSCI47803.2020.9308358

Ariely, D., & Berns, G. S. (2010). Neuromarketing: The hope and hype of neuroimaging in business. *Nature Reviews. Neuroscience*, 11(4), 284–292. 10.1038/nrn279520197790

Bakardjieva, E., & Kimmel, A. J. (2017). Neuromarketing Research Practices: Attitudes, Ethics, and Behavioral Intentions. *Ethics & Behavior*, 27(3), 179–200. 10.1080/10508422.2016.1162719

Bansal, S., & Gupta, M. (2023). Towards Using Artificial Intelligence in Neuromarketing. In *Promoting Consumer Engagement Through Emotional Branding and Sensory Marketing* (pp. 16–23). IGI Global., 10.4018/978-1-6684-5897-6.ch002

Bercea Olteanu, M. D. (2015). Neuroethics and responsibility in conducting neuromarketing research. *Neuroethics*, 8(2), 191–202. 10.1007/s12152-014-9227-y

Bhandari, A. (2020). Neuromarketing Trends and Opportunities for Companies. In *Artificial intelligence in information systems research: A systematic literature review and research agenda* (pp. 82–103). IGI Global.

Bhardwaj, S., Rana, G. A., Behl, A., & Gallego de Caceres, S. J. (2023). Exploring the boundaries of Neuromarketing through systematic investigation. *Journal of Business Research*, 154, 113371. 10.1016/j.jbusres.2022.113371

Burukina, O., Karpova, S., & Koro, N. (2019). Ethical Problems of Introducing Artificial Intelligence into the Contemporary Society. T. Ahram, W. Karwowski, and R. Taiar (eds) *Human Systems Engineering and Design*. Cham: Springer International Publishing (Advances in Intelligent Systems and Computing). 10.1007/978-3-030-02053-8_98

Cardoso, L., Chen, M.-M., Araújo, A., de Almeida, G. G. F., Dias, F., & Moutinho, L. (2022). Accessing Neuromarketing Scientific Performance: Research Gaps and Emerging Topics. *Behavioral Sciences (Basel, Switzerland)*, 12(2), 55. 10.3390/bs1202005535200306

Collins, C., Dennehy, D., Conboy, K., & Mikalef, P. (2021). Artificial intelligence in information systems research: A systematic literature review and research agenda. *International Journal of Information Management*, 60, 102383. 10.1016/j.ijinfomgt.2021.102383

Cosic, D. (2016). Neuromarketing in Market Research. *Interdisciplinary Description of Complex Systems*, 14(2), 139–147. 10.7906/indecs.14.2.3

Cruz, C. M. L., Medeiros, J. F. D., Hermes, L. C. R., Marcon, A., & Marcon, É. (2016). Neuromarketing and the advances in the consumer behaviour studies: A systematic review of the literature. *International Journal of Business and Globalisation*, 17(3), 330. 10.1504/IJBG.2016.078842

Daugherty, T., & Hoffman, E. (2017). Neuromarketing: Understanding the Application of Neuroscientific Methods Within Marketing Research. In Thomas, A. R., (Eds.), *Ethics and Neuromarketing* (pp. 5–30). Springer International Publishing. 10.1007/978-3-319-45609-6_2

Davenport, T., Guha, A., Grewal, D., & Bressgott, T. (2020). How artificial intelligence will change the future of marketing. *Journal of the Academy of Marketing Science*, 48(1), 24–42. 10.1007/s11747-019-00696-0

De Bruyn, A., Viswanathan, V., Beh, Y. S., Brock, J. K.-U., & von Wangenheim, F. (2020). Artificial Intelligence and Marketing: Pitfalls and Opportunities. *Journal of Interactive Marketing*, 51, 91–105. 10.1016/j.intmar.2020.04.007

Di Vaio, A., Palladino, R., Hassan, R., & Escobar, O. (2020). Artificial intelligence and business models in the sustainable development goals perspective: A systematic literature review. *Journal of Business Research*, 121, 283–314. 10.1016/j.jbusres.2020.08.019

Dirican, C. (2015). The Impacts of Robotics, Artificial Intelligence On Business and Economics. *Procedia: Social and Behavioral Sciences*, 195, 564–573. 10.1016/j.sbspro.2015.06.134

Dos Santos, M. A. (Ed.). (2017). *Advances in Business Strategy and Competitive Advantage*. Applying Neuroscience to Business Practice. IGI Global. 10.4018/978-1-5225-1028-4

Duque-Hurtado, P. (2020a). *Neuromarketing: Its current status and research perspectives*. Estudios Gerenciales. 10.18046/j.estger.2020.157.3890

Duque-Hurtado, P. (2020b). Neuromarketing: Its current status and research perspectives. Estudios Gerenciales. 10.18046/j.estger.2020.157.3890

Filipovic, F. (2019). An Application of Artificial Intelligence for Detecting Emotions in Neuromarketing. *2019 International Conference on Artificial Intelligence: Applications and Innovations (IC-AIAI)*. IEEE. 10.1109/IC-AIAI48757.2019.00016

Fisher, C. E., Chin, L., & Klitzman, R. (2010). Defining Neuromarketing: Practices and Professional Challenges. *Harvard Review of Psychiatry*, 18(4), 230–237. 10.3109/10673229.2010.49662320597593

Fortunato, V. C. R., Giraldi, J. D. M. E., & De Oliveira, J. H. C. (2014). A Review of Studies on Neuromarketing: Practical Results, Techniques, Contributions and Limitations. *Journal of Management Research*, 6(2), 201. 10.5296/jmr.v6i2.5446

Gill, R., & Singh, J. (2022). A study of neuromarketing techniques for proposing cost effective information driven framework for decision making. *Materials Today: Proceedings*, 49, 2969–2981. 10.1016/j.matpr.2020.08.730

Glova, B., & Mudryk, I. (2020). Application of Deep Learning in Neuromarketing Studies of the Effects of Unconscious Reactions on Consumer Behavior. *2020 IEEE Third International Conference on Data Stream Mining & Processing (DSMP)*. IEEE. 10.1109/DSMP47368.2020.9204192

Hafez, M. (2019). Neuromarketing: A new avatar in branding and advertisement. *Pac. Bus. Rev. Int*, 12(4), 58–64.

Haleem, A., Javaid, M., Asim Qadri, M., Pratap Singh, R., & Suman, R. (2022). Artificial intelligence (AI) applications for marketing: A literature-based study. *International Journal of Intelligent Networks*, 3, 119–132. 10.1016/j.ijin.2022.08.005

Hensel, D., Wolter, L.-C., & Znanewitz, J. (2017). *A guideline for ethical aspects in conducting neuromarketing studies. Ethics and neuromarketing: Implications for market research and business practice.* Research Gate.

Javor, A., Koller, M., Lee, N., Chamberlain, L., & Ransmayr, G. (2013). Neuromarketing and consumer neuroscience: Contributions to neurology. *BMC Neurology*, 13(1), 13. 10.1186/1471-2377-13-1323383650

Kaličanin, K. (2019). Benefits of Artificial Intelligence and Machine Learning in Marketing. *Proceedings of the International Scientific Conference - Sinteza 2019*. Novi Sad, Serbia: Singidunum University. 10.15308/Sinteza-2019-472-477

Klaib, A. F., Alsrehin, N. O., Melhem, W. Y., Bashtawi, H. O., & Magableh, A. A. (2021). Eye tracking algorithms, techniques, tools, and applications with an emphasis on machine learning and Internet of Things technologies. *Expert Systems with Applications*, 166, 114037. 10.1016/j.eswa.2020.114037

Lee, N., Broderick, A. J., & Chamberlain, L. (2007). What is "neuromarketing"? A discussion and agenda for future research. *International Journal of Psychophysiology*, 63(2), 199–204. 10.1016/j.ijpsycho.2006.03.00716769143

Lee, N., Chamberlain, L., & Brandes, L. (2018). Welcome to the jungle! The neuromarketing literature through the eyes of a newcomer. *European Journal of Marketing*, 52(1/2), 4–38. 10.1108/EJM-02-2017-0122

Lim, W. M. (2018). Demystifying neuromarketing. *Journal of Business Research*, 91, 205–220. 10.1016/j.jbusres.2018.05.036

Ljepava, N. (2022). AI-enabled marketing solutions in Marketing Decision making: AI application in different stages of marketing process. *TEM Journal*, 11(3), 1308–1315. 10.18421/TEM113-40

Luna-Nevarez, C. (2021). Neuromarketing, Ethics, and Regulation: An Exploratory Analysis of Consumer Opinions and Sentiment on Blogs and Social Media. *Journal of Consumer Policy*, 44(4), 559–583. 10.1007/s10603-021-09496-y

Márquez, B. Y. (2018). Neural Network Algorithm to Measure the Human Emotion. *Proceedings of the 2018 International Conference on Algorithms, Computing and Artificial Intelligence*. ACM. 10.1145/3302425.3302441

McClure, S. M., Li, J., Tomlin, D., Cypert, K. S., Montague, L. M., & Montague, P. R. (2004a). Neural correlates of behavioral preference for culturally familiar drinks. *Neuron*, 44(2), 379–387. 10.1016/j.neuron.2004.09.01915473974

McClure, S. M., Li, J., Tomlin, D., Cypert, K. S., Montague, L. M., & Montague, P. R. (2004b). Neural correlates of behavioral preference for culturally familiar drinks. *Neuron*, 44(2), 379–387. 10.1016/j.neuron.2004.09.01915473974

Morin, C. (2011). Neuromarketing: The New Science of Consumer Behavior. *Society*, 48(2), 131–135. 10.1007/s12115-010-9408-1

Mouammine, Y. & Azdimousa, H. (2019a). *Using Neuromarketing and AI to collect and analyse consumer's emotion: Literature review and perspectives.*

Owe, A., & Baum, S. D. (2021). Moral consideration of nonhumans in the ethics of artificial intelligence. *AI and Ethics*, 1(4), 517–528. 10.1007/s43681-021-00065-0

Peyravi, B., Nekrošienė, J., & Lobanova, L. (2020). 'Revolutionised technologies for marketing: Theoretical review with focus on artificial intelligence', Business. *Business: Theory and Practice*, 21(2), 827–834. 10.3846/btp.2020.12313

Rancati, G., & Maggioni, I. (2023). Neurophysiological responses to robot–human interactions in retail stores. *Journal of Services Marketing*, 37(3), 261–275. 10.1108/JSM-04-2021-0126

Rawnaque, F. S., Rahman, K. M., Anwar, S. F., Vaidyanathan, R., Chau, T., Sarker, F., & Mamun, K. A. A. (2020). Technological advancements and opportunities in Neuromarketing: A systematic review. *Brain Informatics*, 7(1), 10. 10.1186/s40708-020-00109-x32955675

Royo-Vela, M., & Varga, Á. (2022). Unveiling Neuromarketing and Its Research Methodology. *Encyclopedia*, 2(2), 729–751. 10.3390/encyclopedia2020051

Sebastian, V. (2014a). Neuromarketing and Evaluation of Cognitive and Emotional Responses of Consumers to Marketing Stimuli. *Procedia: Social and Behavioral Sciences*, 127, 753–757. 10.1016/j.sbspro.2014.03.349

Sebastian, V. (2014b). Neuromarketing and Neuroethics. *Procedia: Social and Behavioral Sciences*, 127, 763–768. 10.1016/j.sbspro.2014.03.351

Sheikh, H., Prins, C., & Schrijvers, E. (2023). 'Artificial Intelligence: Definition and Background', in Sheikh, H., Prins, C., and Schrijvers, E., Mission AI. Cham: Springer International Publishing. *Research Policy*, 15–41. 10.1007/978-3-031-21448-6_2

Slijepčević, M., Šević, N.P. and Radojević, I. (2019) 'Limiting Aspects of Neuromarketing Research', Mednarodno inovativno poslovanje= Journal of Innovative Business and Management, 11(1), pp. 72–83.

Stanton, S. J., Sinnott-Armstrong, W., & Huettel, S. A. (2017). Neuromarketing: Ethical implications of its use and potential misuse. *Journal of Business Ethics*, 144(4), 799–811. 10.1007/s10551-016-3059-0

Thomas, A. R. (2017a). *'Ethics and neuromarketing', Implications for Market Research and Business Practice*. Springer. 10.1007/978-3-319-45609-6

Thomas, A. R. (Eds.). (2017b). *Ethics and Neuromarketing: Implications for Market Research and Business Practice*. Springer International Publishing. 10.1007/978-3-319-45609-6

Vaid, S., Puntoni, S., & Khodr, A. (2023). Artificial intelligence and empirical consumer research: A topic modeling analysis. *Journal of Business Research*, 166, 114110. 10.1016/j.jbusres.2023.114110

Varghese, P. (2022). *Neuromarketing and Artificial Intelligence for Effective Future Business*.

Vlačić, B., Corbo, L., Costa e Silva, S., & Dabić, M. (2021). The evolving role of artificial intelligence in marketing: A review and research agenda. *Journal of Business Research*, 128, 187–203. 10.1016/j.jbusres.2021.01.055

Wang, C., Li, Y., Fu, W., & Jin, J. (2023). Whether to trust chatbots: Applying the event-related approach to understand consumers' emotional experiences in interactions with chatbots in e-commerce. *Journal of Retailing and Consumer Services*, 73, 103325. 10.1016/j.jretconser.2023.103325

Wirth, N. (2018). Hello marketing, what can artificial intelligence help you with? *International Journal of Market Research*, 60(5), 435–438. 10.1177/1470785318776841

Zhu, Z., Jin, Y., Su, Y., Jia, K., Lin, C.-L., & Liu, X. (2022). Bibliometric-Based Evaluation of the Neuromarketing Research Trend: 2010–2021. *Frontiers in Psychology*, 13, 872468. 10.3389/fpsyg.2022.87246835983212

KEY TERMS AND DEFINITIONS

AI, or Artificial Intelligence: The development of computer systems capable of performing tasks that typically require human intelligence. These tasks include learning, reasoning, problem-solving, perception, and language understanding. AI technologies can range from rule-based systems to advanced machine learning and deep learning algorithms, enabling computers to analyze data, recognize patterns, and make decisions.

Consumer Behavior: The study of how individuals make decisions regarding the acquisition, use, and disposal of goods and services, influenced by psychological, social, cultural, and economic factors. Essential for businesses to tailor products and marketing strategies to meet consumer needs.

Consumer Data Analysis: The examination of information about consumer behavior, preferences, and interactions. Using statistical methods and technologies like data mining, machinelearning, businesses extract insights from large datasets to make informed decisions, refine marketing strategies, and enhance overall customer experiences.

Consumer Neuroscience: A specialized field within neuromarketing that employs neuroscience techniques to study and understand the neural processes underlying consumer behavior. It involves using technologies such as brain imaging (e.g., fMRI, EEG), eye tracking, and biometrics to gain insights into how individuals' brains respond to marketing stimuli.

Neuromarketing Ethics: The set of principles and standards that guide responsible and morally sound practices in the application of neuroscience techniques within the field of marketing. The focus is on conducting research and applying insights in a manner that respects individuals and upholds ethical values in marketing practices.

Neuromarketing: Neuromarketing is a field that uses neuroscience and psychological insights to analyze and influence consumer behavior It employs techniques like brain imaging to understand how individuals' brains respond to marketing stimuli, aiming to optimize marketing strategies and enhance the effectiveness of campaigns by tapping into subconscious decision-making processes.

Systematic Literature Review: A comprehensive and structured approach to gather: evaluate, and synthesize existing research on a specific topic. It involves systematically searching for, selecting, and appraising relevant studies from various sources, followed by a rigorous analysis and synthesis of their findings. The goal is to provide a comprehensive and unbiased summary of the current state of knowledge on a particular subject, helping researchers, practitioners, and policymakers make informed decisions and identify gaps in existing research.

APPENDIX

Selected journals and corresponding papers

Journals	Number of Corresponding Papers
Journal of Business Research	5
Journal of Management Research	2
Procedia - Social and Behavioral Sciences	2
Int. J. Business and Globalization,	1
Int. J. Business Forecasting and Marketing Intelligence,	1
Journal of Consumer Policy	1
Estudios Gerenciales	1
European Journal of Marketing	1
International Journal of Psychophysiology	1
Harvard Review Psychiatry	1
International Journal of Business & Economic Strategy	1
Interdisciplinary Description of Complex Systems	1
IUJ Journal of Management	1
International Journal of Academic Research in Accounting, Finance and Management Sciences	1
Pacific Business Review International	1
Encyclopedia of Social Sciences	1
Computer Law & Security Review	1
Journal of Retailing and Consumer service	1
Journal of Business Ethics	1
Nature Reviews Neuroscience	1
Journal of Business and Management	1
International Journal of Marketing Research	1
Expert Systems with Applications	1
Behavioral Science	1
Journal of Innovative Business Research	1
Journal of Legal, Ethical and Regulatory Issues	1
Journal of the Academy of Marketing Science	1
International Journal of Information Management	1
TEM Journal - Technology, Education, Management, Informatics	1
International Journal of Intelligent Networks	1
Journal of Services Marketing	1
Total	37

Chapter 4
Artificial Intelligence Applications in Marketing:
The State of the Art and Hotspots Over 20 Years

Ibtissam Zejjari

National School of Business and Management of Meknes, Morocco

Issam Benhayoun
http://orcid.org/0000-0001-5118-1524

National School of Business and Management of Meknes, Morocco

ABSTRACT

This study aims to provide a review of current research on artificial intelligence use in marketing by examining 661 papers related to AI and marketing from the Web of Science database published in the last twenty years. Using bibliometric analysis, the study sheds light on the present research status, identifies trends, and explores future directions in AI and marketing research. Keyword co-occurrence analysis is utilized to uncover patterns and themes within the literature, offering insights into the field's evolution and emerging research areas. The analysis reveals several significant findings. Notably, it emphasizes the growing importance of AI in marketing, with China and the USA emerging as key contributors. Additionally, a considerable number of papers are funded by agencies and universities, underlining the topic's significance. Based on keyword co-occurrence analysis, four primary research themes are identified: Application of AI in marketing, AI in Marketing Analysis and Forecasting, AI in decision making and optimization, and AI and data analysis.

1. INTRODUCTION

The explosive growth of artificial intelligence (AI) is transforming industries across the globe, and marketing is with no exception (Huang and Rust, 2018). From automating repetitive tasks to personalizing customer experiences, AI promises to revolutionize the way brands engage with audiences (Davenport et al., 2020). However, with the rapid influx of research and applications, understanding the key directions

DOI: 10.4018/979-8-3693-3172-9.ch004

and emerging trends within AI-powered marketing can be challenging yet crucial for guiding future publications (Haenlein and Kaplan, 2019).

Artificial intelligence (AI) is the ability of machines to perform tasks that normally require human intelligence, such as learning, reasoning, and decision making (Russell and Norvig, 2016). Marketing is the process of creating, delivering, and exchanging value for customers, partners, and society at large (Kotler and Keller, 2016). AI and marketing are two fields that have been increasingly intertwined in recent years, as AI offers new opportunities and challenges for marketing research and practice (Stone et *al.,* 2020; Alla, Kamal and Bouhtati, 2022). According to a report by McKinsey, AI has the potential to create up to $2.6 trillion of value in marketing and sales by 2025, through enhancing customer experience, personalization, segmentation, targeting, and analytics (Chui et *al.,* 2018).

In recent times, there has been a noticeable uptick in the utilization of bibliometric analysis as a scientific research tool (Moral-Muñoz et *al.,* 2020). This approach, distinct from traditional literature review methods, demonstrates the capacity to handle substantial volumes of literature, examining it from diverse angles while concurrently generating dependable data analysis and visualized outcomes (Zupic and Čater, 2015). The increasing influence of bibliometric analysis is underscored, positioning it as an effective means to assess scientific achievements (Donthu et *al.,* 2021).

In an era characterized by rapid technological advancements and dynamic market landscapes, understanding the trajectory of AI in marketing becomes imperative for both scholars and practitioners. This paper aims to provide a bibliometric analysis of 661 papers related to AI and marketing, published until January of 2024, using VOSviewer, a software tool for constructing and visualizing bibliometric networks. The paper identifies the publication trends, main themes, research subjects and the most productive countries, authors and journals. Furthermore, a co-citation keywords analysis was performed to assess the main research areas and future agenda. This bibliometric analysis not only provides a retrospective lens on the existing literature but also serves as a foundational resource for shaping the trajectory of future research in this burgeoning field.

The paper is structured as follows: The first section offers a concise theoretical framework concerning AI and Marketing. This is followed by a detailed description of the setup in the Methodology section. Subsequently, the Results section delves into the findings of the study. Finally, the Discussion and Conclusions sections provide an in-depth discussion of the results and offers concluding remarks.

2. THEORETICAL FRAMEWORK

Marketing, among various business domains, has become a focal point for the integration of Artificial Intelligence (AI), attracting considerable attention from both researchers and practitioners (Loureiro et *al.,* 2020). As companies strive to maintain a competitive edge, the adoption of AI tools has become imperative in navigating the complexities of the evolving business landscape (Bouhtati, Kamal and Alla, 2023; Nunan and Di Domenico, 2013).

The historical trajectory of AI in marketing dates back to the 1980s when early studies primarily focused on systems and robots (Chablo, 1994; Davenport, 2018). However, a significant paradigm shift occurred in subsequent decades with the advent of big data and the widespread application of advanced AI tools by marketers and practitioners. This transformative shift necessitates an urgent adaptation of existing literature to reflect the current marketing landscape shaped by the integration of AI technologies.

Rust (2020) identifies three major forces influencing the future of marketing: technological trends, socioeconomic trends, and geopolitical trends. Central to these forces is the development of AI algorithms, revealing their transformative potential across marketing research, education, and practice. In this context, AI emerges as a dynamic force that not only adapts to these trends but actively shapes the future landscape of marketing practices.

Defining AI in the marketing context is fundamental to understanding its implications. AI is described by Poole and Mackworth (2010) as "computational agents that act intelligently." More specifically, Overgoor et al. (2019) provide a nuanced definition for Marketing AI as "the development of artificial agents that, given information about consumers, competitors, and the focal company, suggest and/or take marketing actions to achieve the best marketing outcome." These definitions lay the groundwork for comprehending the multifaceted role AI plays within marketing frameworks (Kim et *al.,* 2023; Alla, Kamal and Bouhtati, 2022).

The integration of AI into marketing practices holds profound implications. Loureiro et *al.,* (2020) underscore the increasing attention devoted to understanding AI's impact on consumer behavior, market segmentation, and personalized marketing strategies. AI's capacity to process extensive data sets and generate actionable insights empowers marketers to make informed decisions, enhancing campaign effectiveness and customer engagement (Gao and Liu, 2023; Amoako et *al.,* 2021).

As we can notice, literature on AI in marketing has evolved dynamically (Bouhtati, Alla and Bentalha, 2023), mirroring the advancements in technology and the shifting business landscape. From its origins in the 1980s to the present day. AI has emerged as a pivotal element shaping the future of marketing.

3. METHODOLOGY

In conducting this bibliometric analysis, we curated a dataset by retrieving articles from the Web of Science database, chosen for its extensive coverage and reliability in academic research (Donthu et *al.,* 2021; Verma and Gustafsson, 2020; Benhayoun et al., 2019). We focused on papers where either "AI" or "Artificial Intelligence" and "Marketing" were mentioned in titles, abstracts, or keywords, ensuring direct relevance to the subject matter. This targeted search yielded a substantial dataset of over 1700 documents. Two filters were then applied: the first, related to language, limited the selection to English papers; the second filter ensured the inclusion of only open-access articles. Selecting an open-access dataset aligns with principles of transparency and reproducibility, allowing unrestricted access to the research corpus and fostering inclusivity in scientific inquiry. This approach ensures the accessibility of our findings to a broader audience.

This process resulted in a dataset of 661 publications at the nexus of Artificial Intelligence (AI) and Marketing as of January 25, 2024. The collected data, encompassing titles, abstracts, keywords, authors, journals, and publication years, was exported as CSV document. Subsequently, this document was uploaded to VOSviewer software for bibliometric analysis (Donthu et *al.,* 2021; Emich et *al.,* 2020; Zhao et *al.,* 2019).

Figure 1 recapitulate the tools used to perform our bibliometric analysis. We will first examine the temporal analysis to reveal growth patterns in AI and Marketing research over time. We will then categorize research subjects and topics to capture the diverse themes within the dataset. Co-authorship networks will be examined to uncover collaborative patterns among authors, highlighting key contributors and the collaborative nature of the field. Visualization of authors affiliations will help identify global research distribution and regional hotspots. Identifying funding agencies is also crucial for understanding research support, ensuring ethical acknowledgment. Keyword co-citation analysis will be performed to provide intuitive insights into thematic clusters and interconnections among keywords.

Figure 1. The bibliometric analysis toolbox

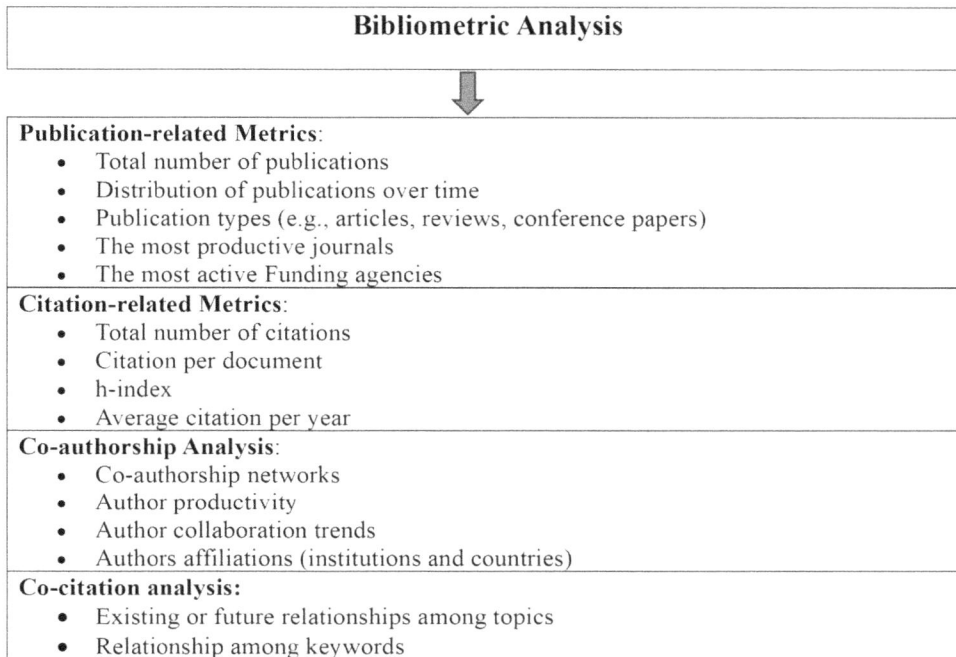

Bibliometric Analysis

Publication-related Metrics:
- Total number of publications
- Distribution of publications over time
- Publication types (e.g., articles, reviews, conference papers)
- The most productive journals
- The most active Funding agencies

Citation-related Metrics:
- Total number of citations
- Citation per document
- h-index
- Average citation per year

Co-authorship Analysis:
- Co-authorship networks
- Author productivity
- Author collaboration trends
- Authors affiliations (institutions and countries)

Co-citation analysis:
- Existing or future relationships among topics
- Relationship among keywords

4. RESULTS

4.1. Publication and Citation Related Metrics

4.1.1. Document Type and Subject Categories Overview

In accordance with our investigative endeavors, a total of 661 papers were extracted from the Web of Science Database (Table I). A predominant fraction of 493 papers constitutes articles, representing 75% of the selected corpus. Concurrently, 130 papers are identified as Proceeding Papers, accounting for 20%, while 38 and 18 papers are discerned as review articles and editorial papers, respectively, contributing to 3% of the aggregate.

In terms of subject categorization, our analysis reveals the exploration of the topic across 20 distinct study areas. The primary focus is observed within the realm of Computer Science constituting 41% (n=274) of the collected papers. Subsequently, Business and Engineering emerge as significant contributors, comprising respectively 25% (n=165) and 17% (n=117) of the corpus.

Additional subject categories hosting a significant presence include Telecommunications (n=48), Science Technology (n=43) and Social Sciences (n=17). Conversely, subject domains such as Educational Research and Psychology exhibit a comparatively lower representation in the dataset with less than 7 papers.

Table 1. Top five research areas

Research Areas	Record Count	%
Computer Science	274	41,45
Business	165	24,96
Engineering	117	17,7
Telecommunications	48	7,26
Science Technology	43	6,50

4.1.2. Trends of Publications and Citations

Figure 2. Times cited and publications over time

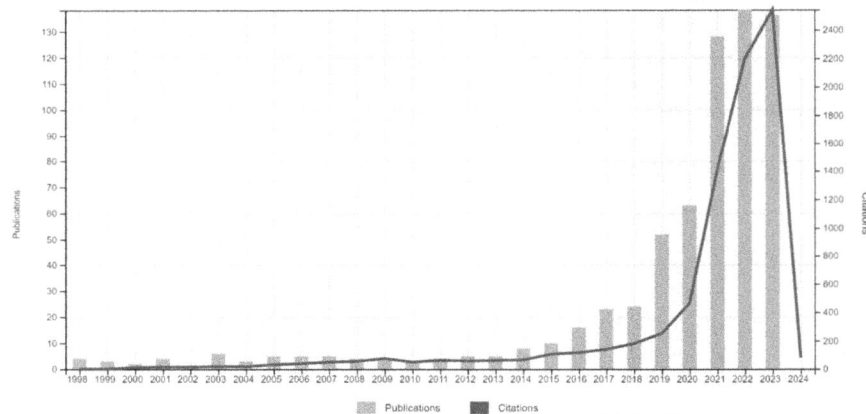

The annual publication count serves as a barometer for gauging the developmental trajectory of specific research domains within the context of this study. The graphical representation in Figure 2 illustrates an upward trajectory in both publication and citation trends within the realm of Marketing and Artificial Intelligence. Notably, prior to 2014, the annual output was modest, with fewer than ten documents disseminated each year.

A discernible surge in publications unfolded from 2014 to 2020, with a pronounced escalation in 2019, wherein the publication count (n=52) more than doubled compared to the preceding year (n=24). During this period, the mean annual publication rate stood at 32. A remarkable upswing in literature output was particularly evident post-2020, reaching its zenith in 2022, with 210 published papers.

The trend in citation patterns mirrors the trajectory observed in publications. A substantial increase in citations manifested post-2020, with the cumulative citations tallying 8120, and 7856 when excluding self-citations. This culminates in an average citation rate of 312.77 per year and 12.28 per document. The H-Index, standing at 40, indicates that 40 papers out of the 661 garnered a minimum of 40 citations, underscoring the impact and scholarly resonance of the research contributions in this corpus.

4.1.3. Most Active Journals and Funding Agencies

The number of relevant papers published and the number of citations can reflect the importance of a journal in a particular research field. In particular, the number of publications and citations is directly proportional to the contribution. Table II shows the top ten publishers in terms of publication volume in the field of Marketing and AI. Their publication volume accounts for 20% of all relevant literature. The largest number of related papers were published in Sustainability (N=27, 3.79%).

Table 2. The most productive journals in the field

Journal Title	Number of Publications	Percentage (%)
Sustainability	27	3.792%
Wireless Communications Mobile Computing	17	2.388%
IEEE Access	16	2.247%
Mobile Information Systems	13	1.826%
Applied Sciences Basel	11	1.545%
Computational Intelligence and Neuroscience	11	1.545%
Energies	11	1.545%
Journal of Business Research	9	1.264%
Frontiers in Artificial Intelligence	8	1.124%
Industrial Marketing Management	8	1.124%

A noteworthy facet of the corpus under consideration is the financial underpinning of the research endeavors, with 40% of the published papers being supported by various funding agencies. Table III represents the most active funding agencies in this field.

At the apex of this hierarchy is the National Natural Science Foundation of China (NSFC), featuring prominently with a sponsorship of 37 papers. Following is the Fundação para a Ciência e a Tecnologia (FCT), contributing to the research landscape with 16 funded papers. Subsequently, a confluence of support is observed from entities such as the European Union and the Spanish government, each for 13 documents. Furthermore, other agencies emanating from Korea, Taiwan, and the United Kingdom exhibit substantial involvement, funding more than 5 papers each. This empirical representation underscores the pivotal role played by diverse funding entities in sustaining the scholarly output within the domain of inquiry.

Table 3. The most active funding agencies related to AI and marketing

Funding agency	Number of Publications	Percentage (%)
The National Natural Science Foundation of China	37	5.60
The Fundação Para A Ciência E A Tecnologia	16	2.49
European Union Eu	13	1.97
Spanish Government	13	1.97
National Science Foundation Nsf	10	1.51
Ministry of Science and Technology Taiwan	7	1.06
National Research Foundation of Korea	7	1.06

4.2. Co-Authorship Analysis

4.2.1. Countries Co-Autorship Analysis

This analysis endeavors to delineate the most prolific countries in the respective field. The outcomes of the co-authorship analysis, conducted using VOSviewer, are portrayed in Figure 3. Node size, proportionate to the volume of publications, signifies that larger nodes correspond to a higher number of publications. The thickness of interconnecting lines in the figure serves as an indicator of the closely interlinked nature of research collaboration between countries.

Figure 3. Visualization of country co-occurrence

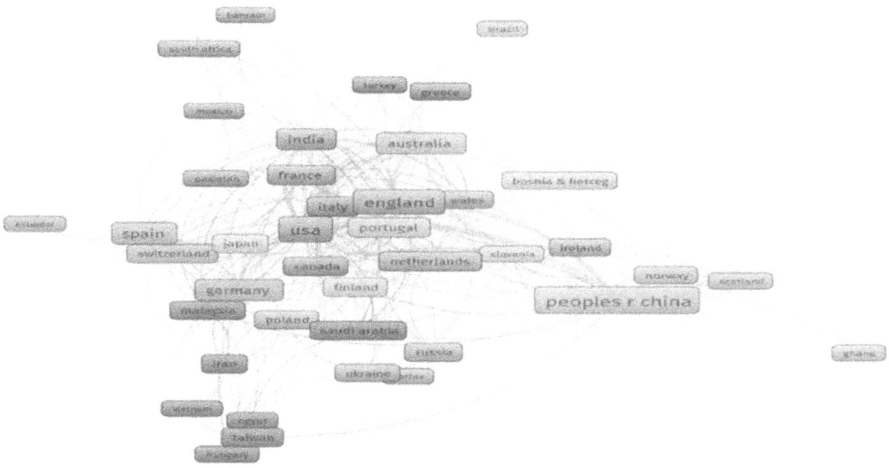

A total of 661 papers emanated from the collaborative efforts of 78 countries, with 62 of them contributing a minimum of 2 papers. Topping the list is China, having contributed by 117 papers, succeeded by the United States with 99 papers, England with 83 papers, Spain with 52, and India with 48 publications.

In terms of citations (Table IV), the United States takes the lead with a count of 2980 citations, coupled with the highest level of collaboration denoted by a total link strength of 113.

Additionally, Figure 3 underscores the concentration of these studies in economically developed countries and regions. A discernible pattern reveals fewer studies emanating from emerging economies in Latin America, Africa, and the Middle East, signaling a potential area for future exploration and collaborative research initiatives.

Table 4. The most productive countries in the field of AI and marketing

Country	Documents	Citations	Total Link Strength
China	117	1143	76
USA	99	2980	113
UK	83	1362	108
Spain	52	749	36
India	48	1000	62
Australia	41	1247	62
Germany	39	995	53
France	28	874	57
Italy	28	372	39
Portugal	28	371	21

4.2.2. Authors Productivity

The research papers under consideration emanate from the collective efforts of 2071 authors, a noteworthy subset of which includes 129 authors contributing to at least 2 publications, while 27 of them produced a minimum of 3 papers. In Table V we listed authors who have delved into the intersection of Artificial Intelligence (AI) and Marketing and published a substantial 4 or more papers in this domain.

The most productive authors with the highest citation counts have diverse geographical origins—namely, Portugal, Bosnia and Herzegovina, and the United Kingdom. Despite Portugal occupying the lowest rung in terms of the sheer quantity of published papers (28 documents), it distinguishes itself by boasting the most cited authors. As a example the author Vale Vita, who has published 11 documents at the intersection of Marketing and AI. Notably, Vita boasts an impressive H-index of 42, coupled with over 7000 citations, underscoring the profound impact of her scholarly output.

Furthermore, the landscape of collaboration in this topic unveils alliances, with particularly noteworthy synergies observed among authors Vale Vita, Pinto Tiago, and Praca Isabelle. Significantly, these authors share not only the same national affiliation, hailing from Portugal, but are also affiliated with the same institution.

Table 5. The most productive authors in AI and marketing

Authors	Documents	Citations	Total Link Strength
Vale, Zita	11	158	27
Pinto Tiago	10	139	26
Badnjevic, Almir	8	2	14
Pokvic, Lejla Gurbeta	8	2	14
Deumic, Amar	6	2	12
Praca, Isabelle	5	98	12
Santos, Gabriel	5	107	17
Faia, Ricardo	5	50	9
Dwivedi, Yogesh K.	5	555	1

4.2.3. Authors Universities of Affiliation

The presented data enumerates the affiliations of authors contributing to the corpus under scrutiny, revealing a spectrum of institutional representation (Table VI). The University of London emerges with the highest record count, encompassing 16 papers, constituting 2.42% of the total affiliations. Following closely, the Instituto Politécnico do Porto, with 14 papers at 2.11%, establishes itself as a substantial contributor to the scholarly output. Notably, the Ministry of Education Science of Ukraine is represented by 12 records, corresponding to 1.81%, attesting the international participation in the research endeavor.

Chinese Academy of Sciences, Southwestern University of Finance and Economics (China), and the University of Oxford each exhibit 9 papers, constituting 1.36% of the affiliations. This confluence of international affiliations reflects a diverse array of scholarly contributions.

Among other affiliations, King's College London, Swansea University, and the University of Michigan each demonstrate 8 papers, representing 1.21% of the affiliations. These affiliations underscore a distributed and varied landscape of scholarly engagement.

The delineation of affiliations in this manner provides a quantitative glimpse into the institutional fabric of the scholarly community, revealing both concentrated and dispersed centers of academic contribution.

Table 6. the most productive universities in the topic

Affiliations	Record Count	%
University of London	16	2.42
Instituto Politecnico Do Porto	14	2.11
Ministry of Education Science of Ukrane	12	1.81
Chinese Academy of Sciences	9	1.36
Southwestern University of Finance Economics China	9	1.36
University of Oxford	9	1.36
King s College London	8	1.21
Swansea University	8	1.21
University of Michigan	8	1.21

4.3. Keywords Co-Citation Analysis

Figure 4. Network visualization of keyword co-occurrence

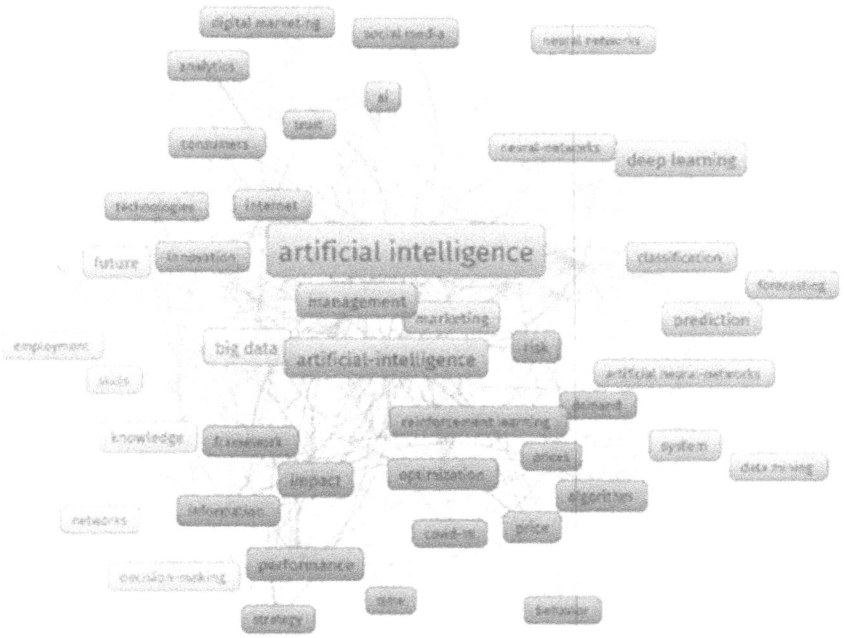

A comprehensive analysis of 2810 keywords was conducted, revealing noteworthy patterns in their citation frequencies. Among these, 158 keywords garnered citations at least five times, with 58 of them achieving a minimum of ten citations. Notably, the preeminent keyword, "Artificial Intelligence," stands out with 190 occurrences, establishing over 300 connections with other keywords.

Figure 4 performed by VOSviewer visually portrays the interplay of concepts, particularly highlighting the centrality and intricate interconnections among "Artificial Intelligence," "Marketing," and "Management." This substantiates the direct relevance of the selected papers to the domains of AI and marketing management. The graphical representation delineates four distinct clusters, each denoted by a unique color. The observed clustering signifies thematic cohesion (Al Husaeni and Nandiyanto, 2022), indicating that keywords within each cluster share inherent relationships and collectively contribute to a specialized facet of the overarching research domain. Each cluster reveil a specific research area related to AI and Marketing.

Blue Cluster: Within the domain of AI and marketing, this cluster presents a compelling array of eleven interconnected themes namely: digital marketing, AI, social media, analytics, trust, consumers, innovation, management, Internet and technology. At the core is the profound impact of technology and innovation on digital marketing strategies and also application of AI in marketing. Researchers are delving into the utilization of vast datasets to gain comprehensive insights into consumer behaviors, market trends, and campaign effectiveness (Hermann, 2022;Zintso et *al.,* 2023;Guercini, 2023).

Green cluster: this cluster reveals eleven interconnected keywords—big data, marketing, deep learning, AI, neural networks, data mining, prediction, and forecasting—So the dominant topic is: AI in marketing analysis and Forecasting. In fact, prediction and forecasting are one of the most valuable advantages offered by AI to Marketing, as it is needed to enhance the effectiveness of marketing strategies (Kowalkowski et *al.,* 2023; Ma et *al.,* 2023)

Yellow cluster: this cluster intricately weaves together seven keywords related to themes of decision-making, big data, networks, skills, and employment, forming a nexus where technological advancements intersect with the decision making and optimization (Ashrafi et *al.,* 2023 ; Badnjevic et *al.,* 2023).

Red cluster: In the realm of AI and marketing, this cluster reveals a synergistic convergence of fifteen key themes like price, demand, behavior, control, optimization and performance, which suggest that this cluster is focused on demand and pricing strategies, control mechanisms, optimization techniques and performance metrics in AI-driven marketing all related to AI and Data analytics (Vicente et *al.,* 2023 ; Wang, 2023).

Other conclusions can be drawn from the network visualization co-citation analysis:

- The most cited keyword in the documents related to AI and marketing is "artificial intelligence", which is also the largest node in the graph.
- The second most cited keyword is "digital marketing", which is also the largest node in the blue cluster. This suggests that digital marketing is the most prominent subdomain of AI and marketing, and that it has a lot of research potential and interest.
- The yellow cluster has the most connections with the other clusters, especially the green and red ones. This implies that technology and innovation are the key drivers and enablers of AI and marketing, and that they have a strong influence on the development and application of AI technologies and optimization techniques in marketing.
- The red cluster has the least connections with the other clusters, especially the blue one. This means that pricing and optimization are relatively independent and specialized areas of AI and marketing, and that they have less relevance and interaction with the online and digital aspects of marketing.

5. DISCUSSION

5.1. Evolution of Research on AI and Marketing

The substantiation of interest in a specific topic finds validation through the discernment of both the quantity of publications and citations it accrues. A higher count in these metrics correlates with heightened interest in the subject matter ((Donthu et *al.,* 2021). Our bibliometric analysis unveils a discernible surge in interest pertaining to Artificial Intelligence (AI) in Marketing. This escalating trend, which predates the year 2000, has experienced exponential growth in recent years. The undertaking of this bibliometric analysis is thus justified, serving as a crucial tool to remain abreast of evolving publication trends and areas of heightened interest. Furthermore, the burgeoning interest is evidenced not only by the high number of publications but also by the increasing number of citations received. This dynamic evolution underscores the significance of comprehending the landscape of AI in Marketing, as it continues to shape and influence scholarly discourse.

Additionally, the proliferation of conferences dedicated to this thematic domain further validates the burgeoning interest among both academics and practitioners. The presence of a significant number of proceeding papers within these conferences accentuates the emphasis on emerging and novel research themes. This convergence of scholarly and practical attention substantiates the contemporary relevance of AI in Marketing, highlighting its position as a focal point for collaborative exploration and knowledge dissemination within the academic and professional communities. Furthermore, the results of our citation analysis highlighted four main research areas presented in Table VII.

Table 7. Key topics explored in the literature on AI and marketing

Topics	References
Application of AI in marketing	(Cui, 2023), (Hermann, 2022), (Keegan et *al.,* 2022), (Ballestar, 2022) (Guercini, 2023), (Ameen et *al.,* 2022), (Barnes and Ruyter, 2022), (Zintso et *al.,* 2023), (Moon and Iacobucci, 2022), Gerlich, Elsayed and Sokolovskiy, 2023)
AI in market analysis and forecasting	(Badnjevic et *al.,* 2023), (Cui, 2023), (Fakharchian, 2023), (Ghosh et al., 2023), (Haftor et al., 2023), (Kowalkowski et al., 2023), (Leal et al., 2023), (Ma et al., 2023), (Mohammed et al., 2023), (Petrescu and Krishen, 2023), (Ruggeri et al., 2023), (Shaban et al., 2023), (Steinberg and Hohenberger, 2023), (Vicente et al., 2023), (Wang, 2023)
AI in decision making and optimization	(Ashrafi et al., 2023), (Badnjevic et al., 2023), (Cui, 2023), (El Helou et al., 2023), (Ghosh et al., 2023), (Leal et al., 2023), (Shaban et al., 2023)
AI and data analytics	(Badnjevic et al., 2023), (Cui, 2023), (Fakharchian, 2023), (Ghosh et al., 2023), (Haftor et al., 2023), (Leal et al., 2023), (Ma et al., 2023), (Mohammed et al., 2023), (Petrescu and Krishen, 2023), (Ruggeri et al., 2023), (Shaban et al., 2023), (Steinberg and Hohenberger, 2023), (Vicente et al., 2023), (Wang, 2023)

Application of AI in Marketing: this category covers the use of AI to understand consumer behavior, preferences, needs and emotions. Some of the applications include customer segmentation, churn prediction, sentiment analysis and personalization.

AI in Market Analysis and Forecasting: This category covers the use of AI to enhance the customer journey, satisfaction, loyalty and engagement. Some of the applications include recommender systems, chatbots, voice assistants and augmented reality.

AI in Decision Making and Optimization: This category covers the use of AI to support marketing decisions, strategies and actions. Some of the applications include forecasting, pricing, promotion, advertising and optimization. Researchers can delve into the ways in which organizations utilize big data to inform decision-making, understanding how data-driven insights contribute to strategic choices, resource allocation, and overall organizational performance.

AI and Data Analytics: this category covers the use of AI to measure and improve the financial performance and outcomes of marketing activities. Some of the applications include attribution, return on investment, customer lifetime value and profitability.

5.2. Future of Research Trends on AI and Marketing

The research trends in a given field can be analyzed by analyzing keywords in recent publications (Hjørland, 2013; Chang et *al.,* 2015; Pingxiu and Hassan, 2023). However, considering the rapid evolution of AI and marketing, we focused on publications from the last three years to capture the most current trends and potential future research directions. We conducted a keyword co-occurrence analysis based on titles and abstracts. By identifying the most frequently occurring and highly cited keywords related to AI and marketing, we were able to discern two promising research directions, summarized in Table VIII.

Table 8. future research agenda on AI and marketing

Topics	References
Ethical and social implications of AI in marketing	(Niet et *al.,* 2023), (behera et *al.*, 2022), Nikam, R. J. (2023), Predel and steger, 2021),
AI in industry 4.0 and emerging technologies	(Badnjevic et *al.*, 2023), (Cui, 2023), (El Helou et *al.*, 2023), (Ghosh et *al.*, 2023), (Leal et *al.*, 2023)

The first direction is concentrated on the Ethical and Social Implications of AI in Marketing. This area of research explores the ethical considerations surrounding the integration of AI technologies in marketing practices. It investigates issues such as data privacy, algorithmic bias, transparency, and accountability in AI-driven marketing strategies. Consumer Well-being must also be taken into account. This aspect focuses on the impact of AI-driven marketing on consumer well-being, including concerns related to psychological manipulation, digital addiction, and the exacerbation of societal inequalities. Researchers assess the unintended consequences of AI-based marketing interventions on vulnerable populations.

In addition, there is another research direction worthy of attention: AI in Industry 4.0 and Emerging Technologies. This research direction explores how AI technologies are transforming marketing practices in the context of Industry 4.0. It examines the application of machine learning, natural language processing, and predictive analytics in areas such as customer segmentation, personalized content creation, and marketing automation. Scholars should investigate the synergies between AI and other emerging technologies, such as the Internet of Things (IoT), augmented reality (AR), and virtual reality (VR), in enhancing marketing effectiveness and customer engagement. They explore innovative applications and interdisciplinary collaborations to drive digital transformation in marketing.

CONCLUSION

This study conducted an extensive bibliometric analysis on a dataset comprising 661 documents related to the intersection of AI and Marketing. The findings reveal a discernible surge in scholarly attention to this domain starting from 2014, with a pronounced elevation in significance after 2020, marking it as a research hotspot.

The geographical concentration of these studies primarily resides in economically developed countries and regions, with China leading in the number of published documents and the USA taking the forefront in total citations. The prevalence of these documents in conferences underscores the enduring importance of this topic and its evolving trajectory. Noteworthy is the fact that over 40% of the published documents receive funding from various agencies and governmental institutions, underscoring the broader societal and institutional recognition of the topic's significance.

Within this field, four prominent research topics have emerged: application of AI in marketing, AI in Marketing Analysis and Forecasting, AI in Decision Making and Optimization and AI and Data Analytics. Furthermore, the study identifies two potential future research directions that merit exploration: Ethical and Social Implications of AI in Marketing and AI in Industry 4.0 and Emerging Technologies.

However, this study is not without limitations. Firstly, the data collection is confined to literature available in the Web of Science database and is limited to English publications, potentially introducing biases. Additionally, focusing exclusively on open-access articles, while ensuring accessibility, may limit insights that non-open access articles could provide. Finally, the retrieved literature is predominantly concentrated in developed countries, with limited representation from emerging markets. To address these limitations, future researchers are encouraged to diversify data sources, explore non-English literature, such as Chinese literature, and employ more inclusive search strategies for a more comprehensive understanding of the subject matter.

REFERENCES

Abbasi, G. A., Rahim, N. F. A., Wu, H. Y., Iranmanesh, M., & Keong, B. N. C. (2022). Determinants of SME's Social Media Marketing Adoption: Competitive Industry as a Moderator. *SAGE Open*, 12(1). 10.1177/21582440211067220

Al Husaeni, D. F., & Nandiyanto, A. B. D. (2022). Bibliometric using Vosviewer with Publish or Perish (using google scholar data): From step-by-step processing for users to the practical examples in the analysis of digital learning articles in pre and post Covid-19 pandemic. *ASEAN Journal of Science and Engineering*, 2(1), 19–46. 10.17509/ajse.v2i1.37368

Albayati, M. G., De Oliveira, J., Patil, P., Gorthala, R., & Thompson, A. E. (2022, November). A market study of early adopters of fault detection and diagnosis tools for rooftop HVAC systems. *Energy Reports*, 8, 14915–14933. 10.1016/j.egyr.2022.11.017

Alla, L., Kamal, M., & Bouhtati, N. (2022). Big data and marketing effectiveness of tourism businesses: A literature review. Alternatives Managériales Economiques, 4(0). 10.48374/IMIST.PRSM/ame-v1i0.36928

Ameen, N., Sharma, G. D., Tarba, S., Rao, A., & Chopra, R. (2022). Toward advancing theory on creativity in marketing and artificial intelligence. *Psychology and Marketing*, 39(9), 1802–1825. 10.1002/mar.21699

Ballestar, M. T., Martín-Llaguno, M., & Sainz, J. (2022). An artificial intelligence analysis of climate-change influencers' marketing on Twitter. *Psychology and Marketing*, 39(12), 2273–2283. 10.1002/mar.21735

Barnes, S., & de Ruyter, K. (2022). Guest editorial: Artificial intelligence as a market-facing technology: getting closer to the consumer through innovation and insight. *European Journal of Marketing*, 56(6), 1585–1589. Advance online publication. 10.1108/EJM-05-2022-979

Bouhtati, N., Alla, L., & Bentalhah, B. (2023). Marketing Big Data Analytics and Customer Relationship Management: A Fuzzy Approach. In *Integrating Intelligence and Sustainability in Supply Chains* (pp. 75-86). DOI: . IGI Global.10.4018/979-8-3693-0225-5.ch004

Bouhtatit, N., Kamal, M., & Alla, L. (2023). Big Data and the Effectiveness of Tourism Marketing: A Prospective Review of the Literature. In Farhaoui, Y., Rocha, A., Brahmia, Z., & Bhushab, B. (Eds.), *Artificial Intelligence and Smart Environment. ICAISE 2022. Lecture Notes in Networks and Systems, 635*. Springer. 10.1007/978-3-031-26254-8_40

Chablo, A. (1994). Potential Applications of Artificial Intelligence in Telecommunications. *Technovation*, 14(7), 431–435. 10.1016/0166-4972(94)90001-9

Chang, Y. W., Huang, M. H., & Lin, C. W. (2015). Evolution of research subjects in library and information science based on keyword, bibliographical coupling, and co-citation analyses. *Scientometrics*, 105(3), 2071–2087. 10.1007/s11192-015-1762-8

Chui, M., Henke, N., & Miremadi, M. (2018). Most of AI's business uses will be in two areas. *Harvard Business Review*, 3–7. https://hbr.org/2018/07/most-of-ais-business-uses-will-be-in-two-areas

Cui, H. (2023). RETRACTION: Construction and Development of Modern Brand Marketing Management Mode Based on Artificial Intelligence. *Journal of Sensors*, 2023, 1. 10.1155/2023/9758414

Davenport, T. (2018). *The AI Advantage: How to put the artificial intelligence revolution to work*. MIT Press. 10.7551/mitpress/11781.001.0001

Davenport, T., Guha, A., Grewal, D., & Bressgott, T. (2020). How artificial intelligence will change the future of marketing. *Journal of the Academy of Marketing Science*, 48(1), 24–42. 10.1007/s11747-019-00696-0

Davenport, T. H., & Ronanki, R. (2018). Artificial intelligence for the real world. *Harvard Business Review*, 96(1), 108–116.

Donthu, N., Kumar, S., Mukherjee, D., Pandey, N., & Lim, W. M. (2021). How to conduct a bibliometric analysis: An overview and guidelines. *Journal of Business Research*, 133, 285–296. 10.1016/j.jbusres.2021.04.070

El Helou, R., Lee, K. Y., Wu, D. Q., Xie, L., Shakkottai, S., & Subramanian, V. (2023). OpenGridGym: An Open-Source AI-Friendly Toolkit for Distribution Market Simulation. *IEEE Transactions on Smart Grid*, 14(2), 1555–1565. 10.1109/TSG.2022.3213240

Fakharchian, S. (2023). Designing a forecasting assistant of the Bitcoin price based on deep learning using market sentiment analysis and multiple feature extraction. *Soft Computing*, 27(24), 18803–18827. 10.1007/s00500-023-09028-5

Gao, Y. J., & Liu, H. F. (2023). Artificial intelligence-enabled personalization in interactive marketing: A customer journey perspective. *Journal of Research in Interactive Marketing*, 17(5), 663–680. 10.1108/JRIM-01-2022-0023

Gerlich, M., Elsayed, W., & Sokolovskiy, K. (2023). Artificial intelligence as toolset for analysis of public opinion and social interaction in marketing: Identification of micro and nano influencers. *Frontiers in Communication*, 8, 1075654. 10.3389/fcomm.2023.1075654

Ghosh, I., Alfaro-Cortés, E., Gámez, M., & García-Rubio, N. (2023). COVID-19 Media Chatter and Macroeconomic Reflectors on Black Swan: A Spanish and Indian Stock Markets Comparison. *Risks*, 11(5), 94. 10.3390/risks11050094

Guercini, S. (2023). Marketing automation and the scope of marketers' heuristics. *Management Decision*, 61(13), 295–320. 10.1108/MD-07-2022-0909

Haftor, D. M., Costa-Climent, R., & Navarrete, S. R. (2023). A pathway to bypassing market entry barriers from data network effects: A case study of a start-up's use of machine learning. *Journal of Business Research*, 168, 114244. 10.1016/j.jbusres.2023.114244

Hermann, E. (2022). Leveraging Artificial Intelligence in Marketing for Social Good-An Ethical Perspective. *Journal of Business Ethics*, 179(1), 43–61. 10.1007/s10551-021-04843-y34054170

Hjørland, B. (2013). Facet analysis: The logical approach to knowledge organization. *Information Processing & Management*, 49(2), 545–557. 10.1016/j.ipm.2012.10.001

Kaplan, A., & Haenlein, M. (2019). Siri, Siri, in my hand: Who's the fairest in the land? On the interpretations, illustrations, and implications of artificial intelligence. *Business Horizons*, 62(1), 15–25. 10.1016/j.bushor.2018.08.004

Keegan, B. J., Dennehy, D., & Naudé, P. (2022). Implementing Artificial Intelligence in Traditional B2B Marketing Practices: An Activity Theory Perspective. *Information Systems Frontiers*, 15. Advance online publication. 10.1007/s10796-022-10294-135637917

Kim, T., Usman, U., Garvey, A., & Duhachek, A. (2023). Artificial Intelligence in Marketing and Consumer Behavior Research. *Foundations and Trends in Marketing*, 18(1), 1–93. Advance online publication. 10.1561/1700000078

Lhoussaine, A. L. L. A., Kamal, M., & Bouhtati, N. (2022). Big data and marketing effectiveness of tourism businesses: A literature review. *Economic Management Alternatives*, 1, 39–58.

Li, P., & Hassan, S. H. (2023). Mapping the literature on Gen Z purchasing behavior: A bibliometric analysis using VOSviewer. *Innovative Marketing*, 19(3), 62–73. 10.21511/im.19(3).2023.06

Loureiro, S. M. C., Bilro, R. G., & Japutra, A. (2019). The effect of consumer-generated media stimuli on emotions and consumer brand engagement. *Journal of Product and Brand Management*, 29(3), 387–408. 10.1108/JPBM-11-2018-2120

Mohammed, T., Naas, S. A., Sigg, S., & Di Francesco, M. (2023). Knowledge Sharing in AI Services: A Market-Based Approach. *IEEE Internet of Things Journal*, 10(2), 1320–1331. 10.1109/JIOT.2022.3206585

Moon, S., & Iacobucci, D. (2022). Social Media Analytics and Its Applications in Marketing. *Foundations and Trends in Marketing*, 15(4), 213–292. 10.1561/1700000073

Nikam, R. J. (2023). Legality of usage of Artificial Intelligence and Machine Learnings by Share Market Intermediary. *Passagens-International Review of Political History and Legal Culture*, 15(2), 319–339. 10.15175/1984-2503-202315207

Nunan, D., & Di Domenico, M. (2013). Market Research and the Ethics of Big Data. *International Journal of Market Research*, 55(4), 505–520. 10.2501/IJMR-2013-015

Overgoor, G., Chica, M., Rand, W., & Weishampel, A. (2019). Letting the Computers Take Over: Using AI to Solve Marketing Problems. *California Management Review*, 61(4), 156–185. 10.1177/0008125619859318

Petrescu, M., & Krishen, A. S. (2023). Hybrid intelligence: human-AI collaboration in marketing analytics. *Journal of Marketing Analytics*, 2023(3), 263–274. 10.1057/s41270-023-00245-3

Poole, D. L., & Mackworth, A. K. (2010). *Artificial Intelligence: Foundations of Computational Agents*. Cambridge University Press. 10.1017/CBO9780511794797

Rust, R. T. (2020). The Future of Marketing. *International Journal of Research in Marketing*, 37(1), 15–26. 10.1016/j.ijresmar.2019.08.002

Verma, S., & Gustafsson, A. (2020). Investigating the Emerging COVID-19 Research Trends in the Field of Business and Management: A Bibliometric Analysis Approach. *Journal of Business Research*, 118, 253–261. 10.1016/j.jbusres.2020.06.05732834211

Vicente, O. F., Fernández, F., & García, J. (2023). Automated market maker inventory management with deep reinforcement learning. *Applied Intelligence*, 53(19), 22249–22266. 10.1007/s10489-023-04647-9

Wang, F. R., & Zhao, L. (2022). A Hybrid Model for Commercial Brand Marketing Prediction Based on Multiple Features with Image Processing. *Security and Communication Networks*, 2022, 1–10. 10.1155/2022/5455745

Wang, M. M., & Pan, X. M. (2022). Drivers of Artificial Intelligence and Their Effects on Supply Chain Resilience and Performance: An Empirical Analysis on an Emerging Market. *Sustainability (Basel)*, 14(24), 16836. 10.3390/su142416836

Zintso, Y., Fedorishina, I., Zaiachkovska, H., Kovalchuk, O., & Tyagunova, Z. (2023). Analysis of current trends in the use of digital marketing for the successful promotion of goods and services in Ukraine. *Financial and Credit Activity-Problems of Theory and Practice*, 3(50). 10.55643/fcaptp.3.50.2023.4080

Zupic, I., & Čater, T. (2015). Bibliometric Methods in Management and Organization. *Organizational Research Methods*, 18(3), 429–472. 10.1177/1094428114562629

Chapter 5
A Systematic Review of Augmented Reality Experiential Marketing:
Conceptual Framework and Research Agenda

Aya Irgui
http://orcid.org/0000-0003-3254-2843
Ibn Tofail University, Morocco

Mohammed Qmichchou
Ibn Tofail University, Morocco

Ilham El Haraoui
http://orcid.org/0000-0002-5962-6409
Ibn Tofail University, Morocco

ABSTRACT

This study outlines the current understanding of augmented reality experiential marketing (AREM), providing a comprehensive overview of the field's state and identifying areas for further investigation. Through a systematic literature review, the authors analyzed 35 articles to develop an integrative framework highlighting both theoretical advancements and practical applications. The review addresses significant research gaps, offering insights and pinpointing challenges in existing knowledge. Key findings demonstrate AREM's influence on consumer behavior and its implications for immersive marketing strategies. Notably, the study calls for a nuanced understanding of AR beyond novelty, advocating for engaging, immersive, and personalized interactions. It emphasizes inclusive demographic approaches and ethical considerations like privacy. Original in its scope, this review lays a foundation for expanding AREM's theoretical landscape, promoting a culturally inclusive and ethically aware marketing approach to enhance consumer experiences in a digital marketplace.

DOI: 10.4018/979-8-3693-3172-9.ch005

INTRODUCTION

In recent years, the importance of technological innovation within organizations has captured the focus of a growing body of academic research. This increased focus is driven by companies' rapid adoption of technology to boost both their innovativeness and overall performance (Kim et al., 2024), Concurrently, there's a noticeable shift in consumer behavior, with preferences increasingly tilting towards digital consumption, underscoring the evolving landscape of consumer habits in the digital age (Shah & Murthi, 2021).

Amidst this evolution, immersive technologies such as Augmented Reality (AR), Virtual Reality (VR), and Mixed Reality (MR) are emerging as frontiers for consumer engagement. This surge in interest is further catalyzed by significant investments from tech giants like Facebook, and Apple, suggesting a high interest in the potential these technologies hold in shaping the future consumer market (Dieck et al., 2022). In the retail sector, the application of AR for experiential marketing is on the rise. A notable array of companies, including but not limited to IKEA, Amazon, Apple, and L'Oréal, are adopting AR solutions to craft unique and engaging customer experiences. This underscores a broader industry recognition of the imperative to generate customer value through immersive and experiential interactions (Haumer et al., 2020). Hence, it is crucial to explore how the marketing landscape is evolving due to the adoption and integration of these digital advancements (Hilken et al., 2018).

Several studies have made contributions to understanding the role of AR in retail and marketing, highlighting the evolving nature of consumer interaction with digital innovations. Javornik (2016) was among the pioneers, examining how AR enhances the characteristics of interactive media within the retail sector, though his approach was not methodically systematic. Following this, Perannagari and Chakrabarti (2019) systematically reviewed AR's adoption in retail, noting its ability to enrich customer experiences and stimulate positive behavioral intentions through its unique characteristics and media quality.

Further expanding the scope, Du et al. (2022) observed the burgeoning application of AR across diverse fields such as retail, tourism, and advertising, crediting its capacity to significantly affect consumer behavior and responses. Similarly, Lavoye et al. (2021) offered a comprehensive overview of consumer behavior in the context of AR retail, proposing a conceptual framework that encapsulates critical consumer behaviors, their consequences, and avenues for future research. This study particularly emphasizes AR's dual potential to augment utilitarian and hedonic experiences, thereby refining decision-making processes and personalizing consumer experiences. In a more recent systematic review, Walenteka and Ziora (2023) conducted a systematic review focusing on AR's implications for performance and data management, as well as its influence on small business and business development strategies. Similarly, Kumar (2022) assessed the utilization of AR in online retailing from a consumer perspective, highlighting the technology's role in reshaping retail experiences.

Despite these contributions, a comprehensive understanding of consumer behavior towards AR as an experiential marketing tool remains elusive. The existing literature, while expansive, points to a significant gap in integrating AR's experiential aspects with its impact on consumer behavior, underscoring the need for a holistic exploration of this dynamic field. Furthermore; existing research reveals a significant gap in the field of Augmented Reality Experiential Marketing (AREM), particularly concerning its formal definition and conceptualization. While Rauschnabel et al. (2019) and Yaoyuneyong et al. (2016) both highlight the ongoing efforts to develop a working definition of AR marketing, indicating that the academic community has not yet reached a consensus. This is further evidenced by the tendency of existing research to focus more on the underlying concepts of AREM rather than on providing a clear, comprehensive definition. Thus, this review will address the following research questions:

RQ1. How is AR experiential marketing defined in the literature?
RQ2. What are the dimensions/influential factors and key outcomes of AR experiential marketing?
RQ3. What are the methodologies/theories adopted in studies of AR Experiential Marketing?
RQ4. What are the key research gaps and new future research directions in AR experiential marketing?

Therefore, this study aims to critically analyze and synthesize the existing literature on AREM. This entails a systematic exploration and synthesis of existing knowledge in the domains of AR marketing and experiential marketing. It focuses on outlining the current understanding in these areas, while also identifying potential areas in need of further investigation, establishing a comprehensive overview of the current state of AREM research, offering valuable insights, and identifying significant challenges and gaps in existing knowledge.

BACKGROUND

Augmented Reality (AR) is defined as a sophisticated technology that amalgamates computer-generated virtual images with our physical world, establishing an integrated interface between the virtual and the real, making it more meaningful through the ability to interact with it (Yoon & Oh, 2022; Oyman et al., 2022; Sun & Yuan, 2024). This innovation is transforming a variety of sectors; it has particularly revolutionized medical education, enabling immersive training experiences, and is equally influential in architecture and interior design, where it aids professionals in visualizing end products within real-world contexts (Kim et al., 2024).

In commerce, AR is increasingly harnessed as a strategic component of intelligent retailing initiatives, offering a distinctive immersive environment that augments the customer experience, with several brands across varied industries integrating AR to engage consumers dynamically (Wang & Ameen, 2023; Hsu et al., 2021). This synergy within smart retailing strategies signifies a transformative approach in the industry, underscoring its potential to reshape traditional consumer interactions and environments. Beyond retail, AR's applicability extends to tourism, where it enhances visitor experiences by providing interactive and contextual information about destinations, and to education, where it transforms learning by enabling interactive, real-world applications of theoretical concepts. In fitness, AR exercise apps engage users by allowing them to visually align their movements and postures with virtual scenes in real-time, thus facilitating more natural and effective exercise training (Sun & Yuan, 2024). These applications, ranging from furniture arrangement with IKEA Place to virtual try-ons with beauty brands like L'oreal and Sephora, demonstrate AR's ability to facilitate interactive experiences with virtual objects in real-time.

Building on this technological foundation, experiential marketing with AR brings a novel dimension to consumer experience and engagement. Holbrook and Hirschman (1982) initially introduced the concept of 'experiential' in marketing, by highlighting its focus on the continuous flow of consumer fantasies, feelings, and fun. They emphasized how experiential marketing involves engaging consumers through playful activities, sensory pleasures, aesthetic enjoyment, and emotional responses. Over the years, experiential marketing has evolved from being a peripheral concept to becoming a core component of brand strategy. It transcends traditional marketing by not only addressing consumer needs and desires but also offering personalized attention, stimulation, and emotional engagement, which fosters deeper brand-consumer relationships (Carmo et al., 2022).

With the rising trend towards more immersive marketing experiences and the growing popularity of AR, the integration of this technology is redefining retail strategies. AR enhances experiential marketing by allowing customers to interact with virtual products, seamlessly blending the physical and digital realms and enriching the shopping experience to make it fun, memorable, and exciting (Kim et al., 2024). This not only enhances functional utility but also elevates the overall consumer experience, potentially increasing satisfaction and loyalty (Haumer et al., 2020).

Diverging from the all-encompassing immersion of Virtual Reality (VR) which creates an entirely new digital environment, AR introduces interactive digital elements to the user's physical environment, thereby not replacing, but augmenting the real world, by allowing consumers to engage with products in a novel manner, providing a layered experience that enriches the conventional shopping experience (Hilken et al., 2018; Alimamy & Nadeem, 2022). The growing proliferation of mobile AR applications by retailers, including Gucci and Burberry, reflects an ongoing trend towards leveraging AR to elevate the customer experience, marking its growing significance in the consumer market.

Thus, the examination of AR in marketing, as indicated by the compilation of publications from Scopus and the Web of Science (**Figure 1**), highlights an escalating academic curiosity and publication frequency over the past two decades. It traces the trajectory from the year 2000 to April 2024, offering a lens into the research community's interest in this domain.

Figure 1. Number of publications in the WoS and Scopus databases on AR marketing over the years

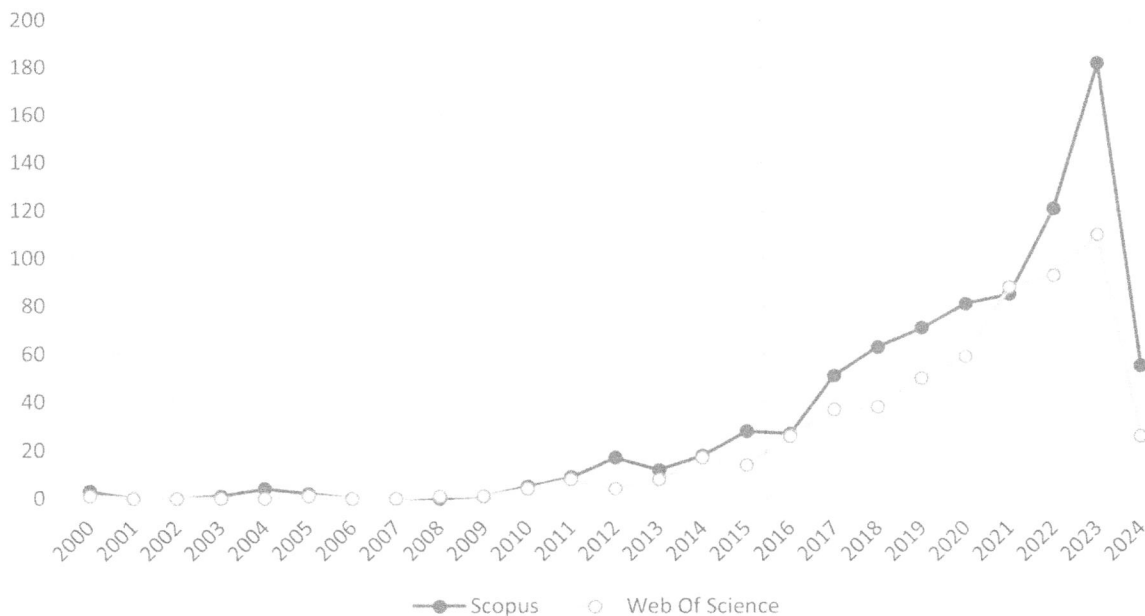

In the initial years (2000-2006), the nascent state of AR technology is reflected by minimal research output, with only a few publications noted in Scopus and Web of Science, and annual publications remaining in single digits across both databases. Research activity began to gradually increase after 2010, highlighting a rising awareness of AR's potential in marketing. The year 2012 marks a notable jump, with Scopus recording 17 publications and the Web of Science 4, with continued growth in research activity in subsequent years. By 2017, there is a significant leap, with Scopus and the Web of Science documenting 51 and 37 publications, respectively. This upward momentum continues, with both databases recording steady annual increases in publications. The peak of scholarly interest in AR marketing is shown by 2023 data, with Scopus reporting 182 publications and Web of Science 110, marking the highest research output in the field. This increase highlights the growth of AR technologies and their integration into mainstream marketing and the research community's efforts to explore and leverage these developments. For 2024, preliminary data as of April shows 55 publications in Scopus and 26 in Web of Science. The publication patterns suggest that research output is not evenly distributed throughout the year but rather accumulates progressively.

Therefore, the current numbers for 2024 are expected to rise as the year progresses, following the collection and indexing of new research within the databases. In light of the evidenced growth, the surge in the popularity of AR marketing practices over the last few years underlines its potential as a disruptive technology that not only enriches consumer experiences and perceptions of value but also transforms marketing strategies in different sectors (tourism, m-commerce, gaming....), inciting businesses to explore innovative strategies based on a customer-centric approach to engage and retain their customers. In this context, the focus of this SLR on AR experiential marketing is timely. Thus, this review aims to identify the characteristics/dimensions of experiential AR marketing, identify the research gaps and the used theories, and highlight and understand the key factors of AREM influencing consumer behavior in marketing and brand experiences, using a defined protocol. In doing so, the study not only addresses research gaps but also offers valuable insights for practitioners and potential avenues for further exploration.

METHODOLOGY OF THE SYSTEMATIC REVIEW

A Systematic Literature Review (SLR) meticulously compiles relevant studies to answer defined research questions, detailing search methods and inclusion criteria transparently. It aims to impartially consolidate knowledge and draw comprehensive conclusions from the literature (Williams Jr. et al., 2021). Thus, this study adopts an SLR methodology, drawing on established guidelines by Paul and Criado (2020), Denyer and Tranfield (2009), and Williams Jr. et al. (2021), to comprehensively examine and synthesize research on AR Experiential Marketing. This approach enables us to methodically aggregate and evaluate the existing literature, identifying research gaps and opportunities for future investigation in the realm of AREM. The SLR process consists of several key stages, including identification, screening, eligibility, and synthesis, as illustrated in **Figure 2**. The analysis process was facilitated by the use of NVivo software, which enabled a systematic coding procedure throughout the study. After exporting the selected studies from Zotero to NVivo, we capitalized on the software's analytical tools, including Text Search Queries, Query Results, and Node Coding. These features allowed for the consolidation of all relevant studies into a unified dataset, thereby enhancing the thoroughness of the examination and reducing the likelihood of omitting critical data.

Figure 2. Systematic literature review process

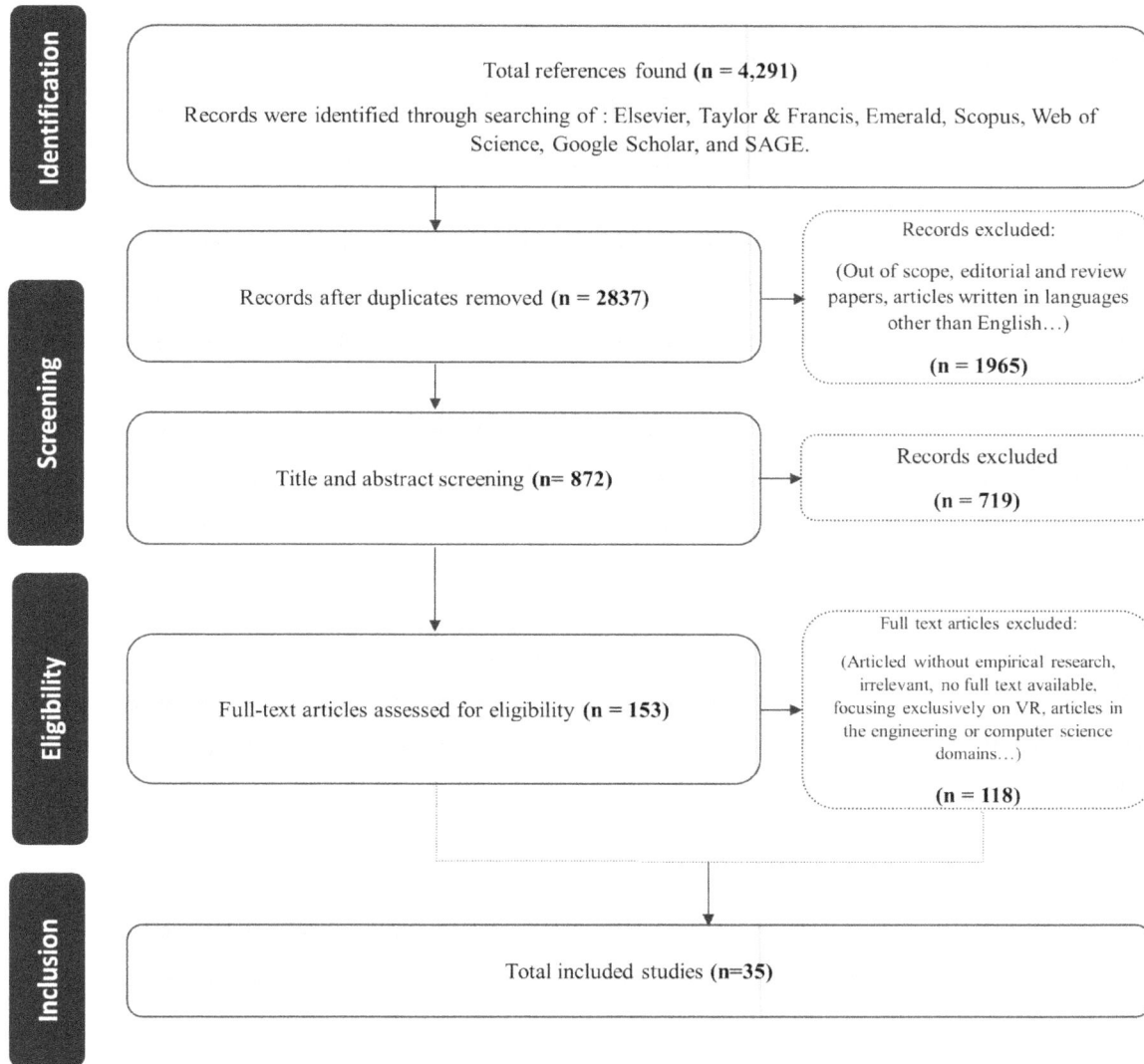

Identification

Total references found **(n = 4,291)**

Records were identified through searching of : Elsevier, Taylor & Francis, Emerald, Scopus, Web of Science, Google Scholar, and SAGE.

Screening

Records after duplicates removed **(n = 2837)**

Records excluded:
(Out of scope, editorial and review papers, articles written in languages other than English...)
(n = 1965)

Title and abstract screening **(n= 872)**

Records excluded
(n = 719)

Eligibility

Full-text articles assessed for eligibility **(n = 153)**

Full text articles excluded:
(Articled without empirical research, irrelevant, no full text available, focusing exclusively on VR, articles in the engineering or computer science domains...)
(n = 118)

Inclusion

Total included studies **(n=35)**

To identify relevant literature, we used a multi-technique approach, conducting an extensive keyword search in prominent academic databases, including Elsevier, Taylor & Francis, Emerald, Scopus, Web of Science, Google Scholar, and SAGE. We also applied backward and forward snowballing methods. Our search was not restricted by publication time frame, allowing for a comprehensive collection of literature across all relevant periods (Rebouças & Soares, 2020). Our keyword strategy involved using a combination of Boolean operators ("AND", "OR") to capture literature pertinent to AREM, with terms including "Augmented reality," "AR," "experiential marketing/value," "Consumer/customer behavior," "Customer/consumer experience," "experiential augmented reality," and related variations. The search yielded 4,292 publications relevant to AREM. Backward snowballing involved examining references within selected studies, while forward snowballing aimed to find newer studies citing the initially reviewed articles. Our inclusion criteria focused on empirical, peer-reviewed articles published in English, without time restrictions. Articles were required to present empirical research with clearly articulated constructs and methodologies (Paul & Benito, 2018), aligning with the PRISMA method standards for SLRs across various disciplines.

Exclusion criteria were set to omit theoretical models, qualitative literature reviews, conceptual contributions, case studies, and articles primarily in the engineering or computer science domains. Additionally, theses, short reports, workshop and work-in-progress papers, editorials, practice guidelines, and conference-related publications, such as proceedings, posters, and abstracts, were excluded from our review. Furthermore, as our focus is exclusively on AR in the context of experiential marketing, articles that primarily or exclusively focus on VR were also excluded. After eliminating duplicate entries to ensure dataset integrity, the screening phase was conducted; articles were evaluated based on the screening of titles and abstracts using our predefined inclusion and exclusion criteria. 153 papers were selected for full-text screening. Articles that did not meet the predefined criteria or were not relevant to the research objectives were eliminated from consideration. Following this, a total of 35 articles were included in the systematic literature review.

RESULTS AND DISCUSSION

General Overview

Table 1 of our SLR provides a summary of general information from 35 selected studies on AR experiential marketing published between 2015 and 2024; it highlights the authors, year of publication, country of study, AR applications studied, research methods employed, and the sample sizes involved. These studies reflect an international research effort adopting a quantitative approach, primarily through the use of surveys often paired with experimental designs, using statistical methods such as SEM (Structural Equation Modeling), ANOVA (Analysis of Variance), and Multiple regression analysis. Sample sizes vary significantly, with a range from 96 to 801 participants, indicating diverse research scales from more focused group analyses to broader population insights. The scope of research extends across various product sectors, from fashion and cosmetics to furniture and tourism, involving specific AR applications by renowned brands that are commercially available—including IKEA, Ray-Ban, and a variety of beauty brands—as well as AR apps developed specifically for research purposes. Additionally, some studies have compared the effects of AR and non-AR apps (e.g., Kim et al., 2024; Arghashi, 2022), aiming to understand the unique influence of AR in shaping consumer behavior and its potential in creating immersive brand experiences. Kim et al. (2023) also compared the functional mechanisms of AR and VR, examining their impacts on perceptions and behaviors from the users' perspectives.

Table 1. Overview of studies included in the SLR

Author, Year	Country of Study	Product Category/Brands	Research Method	Sample Size
Alimamy & Nadeem (2022)	Randomly recruited (Amazon Mechanical Turk)	Ikea Place	Survey (SEM)	266
Arghashi (2022)	Turkey	Wanna Kicks AR app & Nike Non-AR app	Survey +Experiment (SEM)	297
Arghashi et al. (2022)	Turkey	Wanna Kicks AR app	Survey (SEM)	350
Barhorst, et al., (2021)	United Kingdom	Commercially available AR App	Survey +Experiment (SEM)	500
Chen & Chou (2022)	Taiwan	Wanna Kicks & FitGlasses	Survey +Experiment (SEM)	193
Daassi & Debbabi (2021)	France	YouCam Makeup	Survey (SEM)	224
Dieck et al. (2023)	United Kingdom	Ikea Place & Wanna Kicks & Specsavers	Survey +Experiment (SEM)	173 (High-Immersion), 222 (Low-Immersion)
Erdmann et al., (2023)	Spain	Commercially available AR App	Survey +Experiment (SEM)	253
Eru et al. (2022)	Turkey	Commercially available AR App	Survey (SEM)	319
Han et al. (2021)	Randomly recruited (Amazon Mechanical Turk)	Commercially available AR App	Survey (SEM)	355
Haumer et al. (2020)	Munich	Ikea Place	Survey +Experiment (Factorial analysis of variance & Multiple regression analysis)	100
Hsu et al. (2021)	Taiwan	YouCam Makeup app	Survey (SEM)	437
Hu et al.(2021)	China	Fantawild AR app	Survey(SEM)	917
Huang & Liao (2015)	Taiwan	Commercially available AR App	Survey(SEM)	220
Kazmi et al. (2021)	Karachi	Ray-Ban virtual mirror	Survey +Experiment (SEM)	100
Kim et al. (2023)	Randomly recruited (Amazon Mechanical Turk)	IKEA Place (AR vs VR)	Survey +Experiment (SEM)	116 AR & 146 VR
Kim et al. (2024)	South Korea	AR & Non-AR APP	Survey (SEM)	302
Kowalczuk et al. (2021)	Germany	IKEA Place	Survey +Experiment (SEM)	400
Lee et al. (2022)	United States	Commercially available AR App	Survey(SEM)	352
McLean & Wilson (2019)	United Kingdom	Amazon, ASOS, IKEA	Survey(SEM)	441
Poushneh &Vasquez-Parraga (2017)	United States	Ray-Ban virtual mirror	Survey +Experiment (SEM)	99
Qin et al. (2021)	United States	IKEA Place and Ray-ban	Survey(SEM)	316

continued on following page

Table 1. Continued

Author, Year	Country of Study	Product Category/Brands	Research Method	Sample Size
Singh et al. (2024)	India	Commercially available AR App	Mixed-method – Qual (semi-structured interviews+in-depth interviews)	25 (Qual) & 350 (Quant)
Sun & Yuan (2024)	China	Tiantian Rope Skipping AREA	Survey(SEM)	398
Sung (2021)	United States	Developed an AR app	Survey(SEM)	62
Trivedi et al. (2022)	India	Commercially available AR App	quasi-experimental method + Survey (SEM)	343
Tsang et al. (2023)	Taiwan	Commercially available AR App	Survey (SEM)	557
Vo et al. (2022)	Vietnam	YouCam Makeup & FormexTryOn	Survey (SEM)	322
VONGURAI (2021)	Thailand	Commercially available AR App	Survey (SEM)	550
Wang et al. (2023)	United Kingdom	Commercially available AR App	Survey (SEM)	253
Watson et al. (2018)	Swiss	AR makeup app (AR vs Non-AR)	Survey +Experiment (SEM)	162
Whang et al. (2021)	South Korea	MakeupPlus	Survey +Experiment (SEM)	106
Yang (2021)	China	Commercially available AR App	Survey (SEM)	248
Yim et al. (2017)	United States	AR vs Web	Survey +Experiment (SEM)	801
Zanger et al. (2022)	Germany & United Kingdom	Amazon and Essie (AR vs Non AR)	Survey +Experiment (SEM)	238 students (Study 1), 251 female panelists (Study 2)

Source: Authors' own elaboration

AR Applications Studied

The findings from our review highlight that the AR application IKEA Place has been the subject of considerable academic scrutiny, being the focus of 7 studies. This focus reflects its innovative use of AR technology in the furniture retailing sector, which aligns with the current trend towards enhancing customer experience through immersive technologies (Vaidyanathan & Henningsson, 2023). Similarly, Wanna Kicks, which offers a virtual shoe try-on experience, has a notable presence in the research as well, constituting 10% of the selected studies, indicating a significant interest in AR apps that enhance online shopping for footwear, offering insights into how such technology can innovate the try-before-you-buy experience and suggests a broader applicability of AR in fashion and retail.

AR apps like YouCam Makeup and Ray-Ban Virtual Try-On, with 7% each, allow consumers to virtually test makeup and glasses, providing a personalized and real-time shopping experience without needing physical samples. Moreover, the largest segment of the research, involving 16 studies, focuses on commercially available AR apps that have not been specified by name, indicating that a significant portion of the research is dedicated to exploring the broad implications of AR in marketing rather than focusing on specific apps or brands. Additionally, Amazon's AR app, with a 5% share, reflects its role in the broader context of e-commerce, where AR can add value to the online shopping experience by enabling a virtual preview of products. The remainder of the selected studies is distributed among various other AR apps, including Essie, FitGlasses, AREA... pointing to the technology's potential across various sectors, including tourism and fitness, and sports sectors, as illustrated in **Figure 3.**

Figure 3. AR applications studied

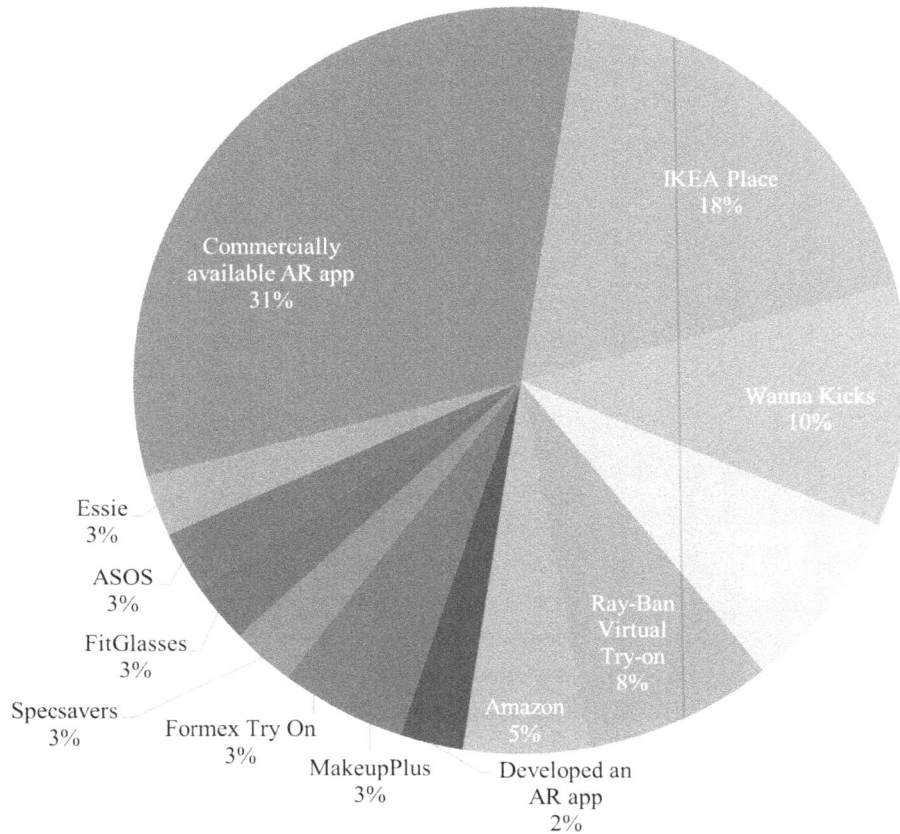

Publications by Country

The geographical distribution of research articles on AR experiential marketing, as gathered from our review (**Figure 4**), reveals a predominant focus on a select few countries, primarily centered on the US and the UK, with these countries being the subject of 5 studies each, followed by Taiwan accounting for 4 studies, this reflects the significant advancements and uptake of AR technologies within these markets. Additionally, 3 studies used Amazon Mechanical Turk, to randomly recruit participants with AR experience, reflecting a broader international though non-specific geographical sampling, that extends beyond a single country. Turkey, China, and Germany each account for three studies. Significantly less represented are South Korea, and India with two articles each, while Spain, Southern Pakistan, France,

Vietnam, Thailand, and Switzerland are each the focus of single studies. The limited geographic spread, with a heavy skew towards Western nations, identifies a research gap and suggests an opportunity for future research to understand the implications and applications of AREM within emerging markets and countries with different cultures, which would potentially provide a richer, more nuanced understanding of consumers' response to AR experiential technologies.

Figure 4. Studied populations

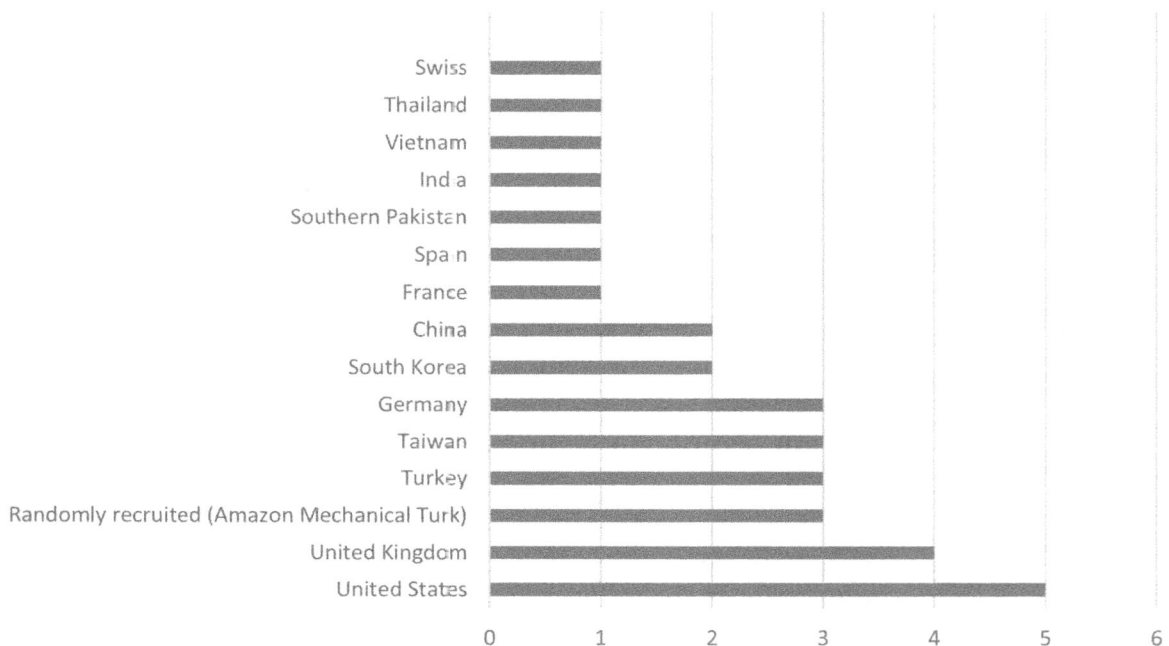

Theoretical Lenses

Drawing from our review, it is evident that a diverse array of theoretical lenses has been utilized to understand and explore AR experiential marketing (**Table 2**). Notably, the Stimulus-Organism-Response (SOR) framework is a prevalent theory, guiding research into how sensory stimuli provided by AR affect consumer internal states and lead to certain behavioral responses (e.g., Arghashi, 2022; Sun & Yuan, 2024). Its relevance is heightened by AR's capacity to alter perceptions of reality, invoking both cognitive and emotional reactions that can lead to enhanced consumer engagement or behavioral intentions. Similarly, the Technology Acceptance Model (TAM) is another dominant theory in examining the acceptance and use of AR technologies in marketing, highlighting its ability to predict users' attitudes and intentions towards new technologies (e.g., McLean & Wilson, 2019; Chen & Chou, 2022; Vo et al., 2022). With AR being a relatively recent innovation, TAM's focus on perceived usefulness and ease of use offers a lens through which researchers analyze consumer readiness to adopt AR and integrate it into their shopping and consumption behaviors.

Furthermore, building upon the theoretical framework of experiential marketing, studies utilizing AR technologies in commerce have adopted experiential value constructs rooted in seminal works by Mathwick et al. (2001) and Holbrook and Hirschman (1982). Researchers emphasize the importance of engaging consumers on an emotional level, proposing that AR technologies can potentially enhance the experiential value of shopping by offering immersive and interactive experiences that go beyond traditional consumption (Eru et al., 2022), often emphasizing values such as visual appeal, entertainment, enjoyment, and escapism to evaluate consumer responses (Han et al., 2021; Hsu et al., 2021). Consequently, the lens of experiential marketing provides valuable insights into how AR can create memorable experiences that contribute to brand differentiation and customer loyalty.

Additionally, the Telepresence theory has garnered attention, underscoring how AR technologies can create a vivid sense of presence and immersion that significantly affects consumer attitudes and behaviors (e.g., Wang et al., 2023; Daassi & Debabi, 2021). Equally, Flow theory has been essential in understanding consumer psychology, showing how AR can create immersive experiences, that resonate with consumers' abilities and challenges, leading to positive affective states that can elevate consumer trust and engagement (e.g., Arghashi et al., 2022; Barhorst et al., 2021). Other theoretical lenses, such as Media Richness Theory, Experience Economy Theory, Uses and Gratification Theory, Schmitt's Customer Experience Model, the Cognition-Affect-Conation (C-A-C) Framework, the Unified Theory of Acceptance and Use of Technology, and Social Cognitive Theory (SCT) surface infrequently in our SLR. These perspectives, while less prevalent, offer rich insights into the multifaceted nature of consumer interaction with AR technologies—from the media communication richness to the psychological underpinnings of technology adoption and user experience. Thus, given their capacity to unpack the complexities of AREM, these theories merit deeper exploration in future research

Therefore, despite the richness of theoretical applications, it reveals a promising but still maturing scholarly domain. For a more comprehensive understanding of experiential AR's impact, there is a need for further theoretical integration and cross-disciplinary research. This should draw from areas such as social sciences, information technology, psychology, and sociology, among others. Specifically, cognitive psychology could provide insights into AR's effects on consumer perception and decision-making. Moreover, considering cultural dimensions, such as those proposed by Hofstede (2001), could offer valuable insights into how AR experiential marketing is perceived across different national cultures, which might inform future research directions. Additionally, environmental and ethical considerations are becoming increasingly important, highlighting the need for research on the sustainability and ethical aspects of AR in marketing, in response to growing consumer awareness and concern.

Table 2. Theories used

Theories	References
Stimulus-organism-response framework	Arghashi (2022), Daassi & Debbabi (2021), Hsu et al., (2021), Kim et al. (2023), Lee et al. (2022), Trivedi et al. (2022), Watson et al. (2018), Yang (2021), Sun & Yuan (2024)
Flow Theory	Arghashi et al. (2022), Barhorst, et al. (2021), Dieck et al. (2023)
Technology acceptance model	Chen & Chou (2022), McLean & Wilson (2019), Qin et al. (2021), Vo et al. (2022), Daassi & Debbabi (2021), Eru et al. (2022); Huang & Liao (2015)
Schmitt's Customer Experience Model/ User Experience Model	Chen & Chou (2022), Kazmi et al. (2021)
Value-based adoption model	Erdmann et al. (2023)
Regulatory engagement theory	Arghashi et al. (2022)
Self-determination theory	Arghashi et al. (2022)
Consumer-based brand equity	Haumer et al. (2020)
Experiential marketing/Experiential value/Experiential quality	Eru et al. (2022), Haumer et al. (2020), Barhorst, et al. (2021), Yang (2021), Han et al. (2021), VONGURAI (2021), Hsu et al. (2021), Huang & Liao (2015), Kim et al. (2024), Kazmi et al. (2021), Hu et al. (2021), Tsang et al. (2023), Wang et al. (2023);
Cocreation of value theory	Alimamy & Nadeem (2022)
Uses and Gratification Theory	Kazmi et al. (2021), Kowalczuk et al. (2021)
Experiential hierarchy model	Kowalczuk et al. (2021)
Unified Theory of Acceptance and Use of Technology	McLean & Wilson (2019)
Cognition-affect-conation framework	Qin et al. (2021)
The motivation theory	Trivedi et al. (2022);
The theory of planned behavior	Vo et al. (2022), Daassi & Debbabi (2021), Tsang et al. (2023)
Affect-as-Information Theory	Zanger et al., (2022)
Telepresence theory	Whang et al. (2021), Daassi & Debbabi (2021) ; Kim et al. (2023), Dieck et al. (2023), Yang (2021)
Media richness theory	VONGURAI (2021)
Feelings-as-information theory	Kowalczuk et al. (2021)
Experience economy theory	Sung (2021), Singh et al. (2024)
Habituation–tedium theory	Yim et al. (2017)
Transcendent Experience Perspective:	Hu et al. (2021)
Social cognitive theory	Singh et al (2024)
Human value orientation theory	Wang et al (2023)
Consumption value theory	Wang et al. (2023)

Source: Authors' own elaboration

AR Experiential Marketing Definition

AR Experiential Marketing represents a paradigm shift in the marketing domain, pushing the boundaries of traditional approaches to forge deeper, more immersive connections between brands and consumers. The definitions across the literature paint AREM as a multifaceted strategy, leveraging AR technology to create experiences that are not only immersive and interactive but also highly personalized and sensory-stimulating. This review draws upon diverse definitions and insights from the literature to offer a comprehensive understanding of AREM.

Haumer et al. (2020), define AR as an experiential marketing form that focuses on crafting an all-encompassing experience centered around the user, offering innovative, brand-interactive, and immersive experiences. This perspective highlights AREM's ability to elevate product and brand knowledge, its viral potential, and the level of immersion it can create in a real-world context, through vivid depiction and personalization. The emphasis on the accessibility of AR through devices like smartphones significantly broadens the reach of this marketing strategy, making AREM's engaging experiences a widely accessible, cost-effective strategy for immersive marketing (Haumer et al. 2020).

Central to the definition of AREM is the concept of experiential value, which is derived from the user's interaction with AR technology and the dynamic elements of the created experience (Han et al., 2021). The capacity of AR to simulate direct product experiences enables consumers to gain more information and develop a deeper interest, such realism offers experiential value that simulates close-to-real in-store shopping experiences, thereby engaging consumers more positively compared to traditional strategies (Li et al. 2008; Daassi & Debbabi, 2021; Kim et al. 2024). Moreover, researchers emphasize the importance of experiential authenticity in shaping the overall value perceived by users through personal interpretations of their interactions with AR technologies, encouraging active participation and integration of user inputs with the brand's offerings, and directly influencing decision-making (Han et al. 2021). This authenticity, when integrated with the sensory richness of AREM, not only deepens the user's emotional connection with the brand but also elevates the product's perceived value by offering a more engaging, sensory-stimulating experience than conventional marketing and advertising methods (Alimamy & Nadeem, 2022; Chen & Chou, 2022). Additionally, AREM is distinguished by its potential for personalization and interactivity, which enriches the consumer's experiential value, through personalized AR experiences tailored to meet individual consumer needs and preferences, thus enhancing engagement and satisfaction, and fostering a deeper connection with the marketing content (Javornik, 2016; Sung, 2021). Tsang et al. (2023) expand on the concept of experiential value in the context of tourism, describing it as sensory experiences derived from the use of AR technologies and applications, emphasizing the role of interactivity and flow experience in enhancing customer experiential value.

Moreover, the literature identifies specific elements that enrich the experiential value offered by AREM, such as informative, personalization, and interactivity features (Hsu et al. 2021; Javornik, 2016). Researchers argue that AR can alleviate online shopping unease through immersive experiences that connect pre- and post-consumption expectations with emotional embodiment like playfulness and excitement (Poushneh & Vasquez-Parraga, 2017; Sung, 2021; Hsu et al. 2021). Kim et al. (2024) expanded on this, highlighting AR's role in creating immersive experiences, making shopping fun, memorable, and exciting. It transcends its functional utility to become a source of hedonic pleasure and enjoyment, involving consumers in playful activities and eliciting emotional responses, thereby deepening the emotional engagement and trust in making purchases. Similarly, Kazmi et al. (2021) describe AR's role in experiential marketing as creating holistic consumer experiences that transcend mere service provision, reflecting on the entire user journey. Furthermore, Huang & Liao (2015) advocate for viewing AR as a persuasive technology that delivers experiential value, improving online shopping by increasing consumer trust and mitigating perceived risks. Thus, experiential value is crucial in enhancing online shopping experience and facilitating the decision-making process through the provision of vivid, aesthetically appealing product information (Poushneh & Vasquez-Parraga, 2017; Qin et al. 2021)

Eru et al. (2022) further enrich this discourse by defining AREM as a strategic marketing approach that blends digital and physical elements to align with business goals and enhance consumer experiences, marking it as a pivotal innovation in the marketing field. They highlight AR as a dimension of experiential marketing that enhances customer experiences through a comprehensive, holistic marketing approach, aimed at augmenting customer satisfaction, loyalty, and purchase intent, resulting in enhanced value perceptions and potential behavioral responses (Eru et al. 2022; Yang 2021). Furthermore, AREM provides businesses with a competitive edge, boosting their ability to capture consumer attention, influence buying decisions, and foster innovative engagement.

The consensus among researchers underscores AREM as a multidimensional approach that simulates realistic product interactions and environments, leveraging AR technology to create immersive, interactive, and highly personalized customer-centric experiences, thereby fostering authentic connections between brands and consumers, and sensory-rich experiences that transcend the limitations of conventional marketing strategies. The recurring theme across the literature highlights the transformational impact of AR technology in marketing, enabling brands to offer experiential value that resonates deeply with consumers on a personal and emotional level. The strategic integration of AR within experiential marketing initiatives not only elevates the consumer experience but also provides businesses with a competitive edge, leveraging the power of digital innovation to forge meaningful, lasting connections with their target audience. As such, the discourse surrounding AREM encapsulates a broad spectrum of applications and benefits, heralding a new era of experiential marketing that is poised to redefine the boundaries of consumer-brand interactions in the digital age.

AREM Framework

The integrative framework illustrated in **Figure 5** synthesizes findings from our SLR on AR Experiential Marketing and aims to clarify the complex phenomenon that AR brings to experiential marketing strategies. Our thematic analysis has underscored the multidimensional aspects of AREM, informed by a range of studies, including Chen & Chou (2022), Haumer et al. (2020), and Han et al. (2021), leading to a structured depiction of the various elements involved.

We adopt an antecedents-consequences logic. Antecedents contributing to effective AREM are organized into key categories: Experiential AR features, such as interactivity and immersion; Experiential AR value, capturing elements like entertainment and escapism. These are complemented by considerations of media richness and quality, as well as potential negative factors like information overload. The consequences of AREM are bifurcated into behavioral intentions—encompassing purchase intention (e.g., Kazmi et al., 2021; Arghashi, 2022) and word-of-mouth (WOM) intention (e.g., Zanger et al., 2022) and brand outcomes, which include brand equity and sustainable brand relationship behavior (e.g., Arghashi & Yuksel, 2022; Haumer et al., 2020). Furthermore, consumer behavior outcomes such as loyalty (e.g., Kim et al., 2024; Eru et al., 2022) and satisfaction (e.g., Dieck et al., 2023; Sun & Yuan, 2024) are acknowledged as critical indicators of AR's impact.

To articulate the connections between these antecedents and consequences, we examine underlying mechanisms. These mechanisms include mediators such as trust (Arghashi & Yuksel, 2022), engagement, ethical perceptions (Alimamy & Nadeem, 2022), and experiential value encompassing both the functional, utilitarian value and the enjoyment-related, hedonic value (e.g., Hsu et al., 2021; Yang, 2021), which bridge the initial impact of AR features with their eventual outcomes on consumer behavior. Moderators, including technological familiarity and cultural dimensions, and control variables like AR familiarity, privacy concerns, and demographic details, further refine our understanding of when and how AREM exerts its influence.

The framework serves as a comprehensive model for mapping the effects of AR on consumer responses, considering the full array of influencing factors and outcomes. It is intended as a dynamic tool, evolving as new research emerges, to guide future research on AREM. Moreover, the framework presents practitioners with a nuanced perspective of AR as an experiential marketing tool, urging marketers to consider a broader array of factors when crafting their AR marketing strategies to align with the complex interplay of technology, consumer psychology, and market dynamics depicted in our review.

Figure 5: Integrative framework of AREM

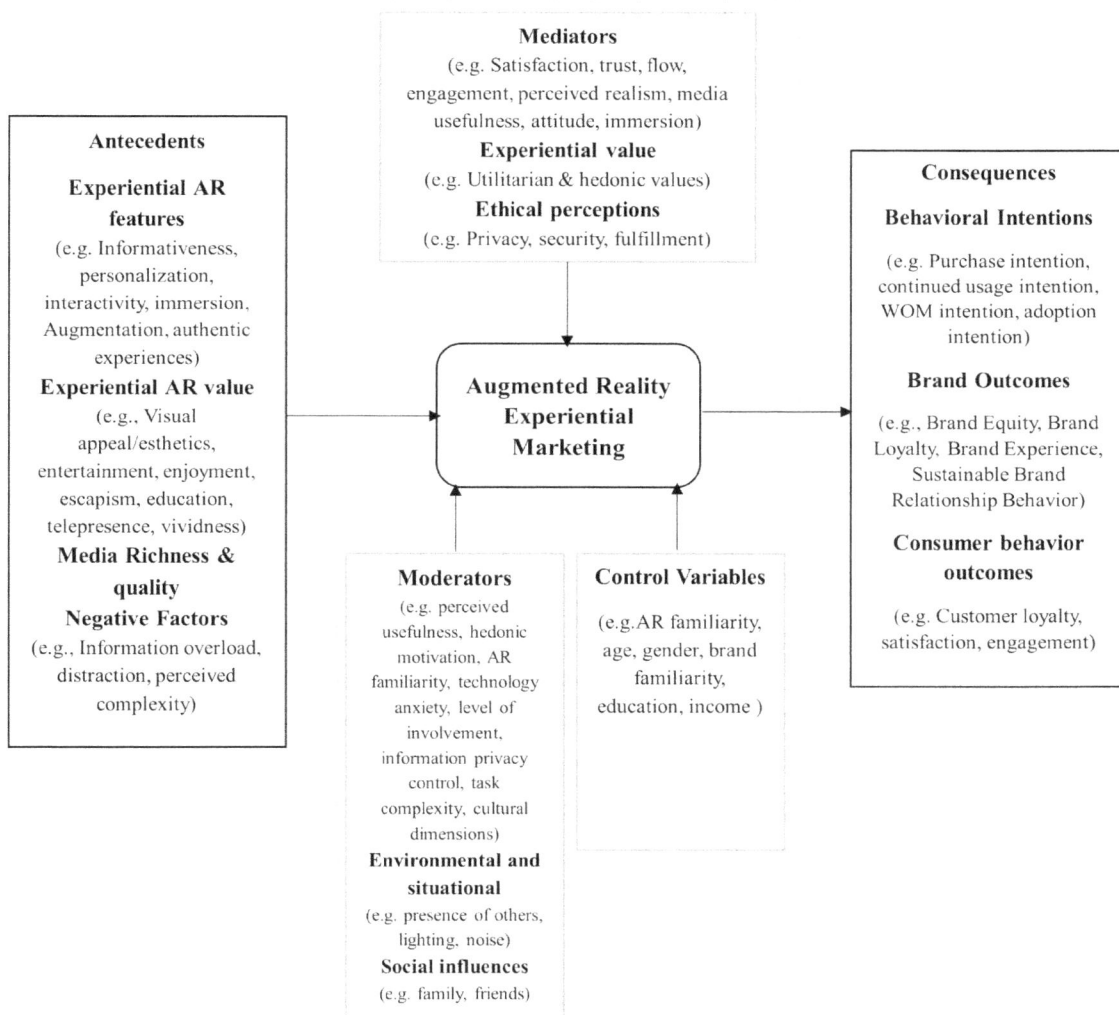

Limitations and Research Agenda

The current landscape of AR experiential marketing research, as illuminated by recent studies, showcases numerous gaps and future research directions. Our SLR has revealed a range of unexplored aspects and opportunities within AREM. These gaps underscore the need for comprehensive exploration to deepen our understanding of AR's multifaceted effects on consumers, brands, and the broader market. A recurrent theme from the studies, including those by Chen & Chou (2022) and Haumer et al. (2020), is the call for longitudinal research to comprehend the temporal effects of AR. The longitudinal approach is particularly pivotal to grasping the evolution of consumer-brand relationships facilitated by AR experiences over time. Furthermore, such research could illuminate the role of AR in the customer journey, from initial contact through post-purchase stages. Additionally, they pinpoint a significant gap in the demographic range of respondents, predominantly limited to young adults familiar with mobile technology. This demography exhibits particular behaviors and receptiveness to AR, potentially skewing the applicability of findings across a broader population. Extending the age range of respondents and incorporating diverse segments including Generation X and Baby Boomers, would contribute to a more inclusive understanding of AR's appeal and utility.

Han et al. (2021) underscored the potential of a multidimensional approach to experiential value, suggesting the integration of intrinsic-extrinsic and active-reactive values to capture the full spectrum of consumer experiences. This notion is echoed in the call for investigating the relationship between experiential value and customer satisfaction, to enhance customer purchase decisions (Han et al., 2021). Moreover, Hsu et al. (2021) propose the exploration of additional experiential AR app attributes, such as augmentation quality and novelty, and their effects on consumer outcomes, alongside the examination of varying user interfaces and their impact on usage behavior across different AR experiences. Kim et al. (2023) advocate for deploying AR research across diverse environments to deepen our understanding of its experiential value, while Kowalczuk et al. (2021) emphasized the significance of experiential factors like enjoyment and immersion, suggesting the need for qualitative research to explore cognitive and behavioral states related to AR in retail. Watson et al. (2018) suggest exploring the differential effects of AR features in various retail settings to understand how they create distinct experiential values and influence consumer responses. Lastly, Hu et al. (2021) highlight the importance of examining the relationship between AR experiential quality and behavioral constructs, such as word of mouth and revisit intentions.

Furthermore, several scholars have highlighted the need for a detailed examination of AR features, suggesting that the exploration should extend beyond the mere presence or absence of AR to encompass a wide range of features and tools. By determining which AR aspects—such as interactivity levels, realism, and multi-sensory integration—most effectively captivate consumers, researchers could uncover a variety of experiential nuances, thereby deepening our understanding of consumer behavior, as suggested by Haumer et al. (2020) and Barhorst et al. (2021). Moreover, the existing literature often overlooks the influence of cultural and country-of-origin effects, as well as contextual and environmental dimensions on technology adoption and AREM effectiveness. Thus researchers, have underscored the necessity for cross-cultural studies to elucidate how different cultural dimensions shape the global acceptance and impact of AR in marketing (Haumer et al., 2020; Arghashi, 2022; Hsu et al., 2021; Whang et al., 2021). Furthermore, studies also emphasize the importance of AR's impact on cognitive and affective consumer processes. Daassi & Debbabi (2021) and Hu et al. (2021) underscore the need for developing robust measures for perceived realism and integrating affective reactions, thereby crafting a more comprehensive understanding of the AR experience from a psychological standpoint. Despite the extensive focus on retail and tourism, other sectors like healthcare and education emerge as less-charted territories, as indicated by Kazmi et al. (2021). These domains present unique challenges and opportunities for AR's application, prompting questions about its educational efficacy, ethical considerations, and broader social implications.

Another significant observation is the scarce exploration of AR's dark side and ethical concerns related to privacy, self-disclosure (Chen & Chou, 2022), and the overall influence of AR on consumer-brand relationships. Notably, Alimamy & Nadeem (2022) investigated the mediating influence of perceived ethics within the co-creation process, specifically investigating how perceived ethics mediates customers' intention to co-create value through authentic experiences with AR. This underscores the importance of ethical considerations in shaping consumer engagement and trust in AR-enabled environments. Similarly, Vo et al., (2022) highlighted privacy concerns as a significant factor, treated as a control variable in their study. Their findings indicate a positive effect of privacy concerns on the adoption intention towards mobile augmented reality (MAR) applications, suggesting that effectively managing these concerns can enhance user acceptance and willingness to adopt AR technologies. Furthermore, Alimamy & Nadeem (2022) and Whang et al., (2021) emphasized the need to understand how AR can foster authentic experiences and sustainable relationships between brands and consumers, considering ethical implications. This underscores the broader imperative for future research to delve deeper into the ethical dimensions of AR, ensuring that its integration in experiential marketing respects consumer privacy and fosters trust.

Arghashi (2022) further elaborates on the role of AR features in driving consumer behavior, advocating for a nuanced evaluation of the 'wow-effect' and its varying degrees. This psychological and emotional impact, coupled with the influence of social aspects like family and friends in AR adoption, can significantly affect shopping motivations and decisions. Additionally, while studies have confirmed AR's influence on purchase intentions through mechanisms like telepresence and augmentation, systematic research evaluating these media characteristics on a wider array of consumer responses is lacking (Watson et al., 2018). The differential impact of AR across various brands and industries, as well as its role in co-creation processes and consumer engagement, remains an underdeveloped field ripe for scholarly exploration (Alimamy & Nadeem, 2022; Whang et al., 2021).

Therefore, these studies point towards a comprehensive and nuanced exploration of AREM, emphasizing the need for multidimensional, qualitative, and context-specific research approaches to unlock the full potential of AREM in engaging consumers and influencing their behavior. **Table 3** presents a structured research agenda, synthesizing these research directions and presenting them alongside illustrative questions that could guide future empirical research. The table not only serves as a roadmap for upcoming studies but also as a reflection of the multifarious nature of AR's intersection with experiential marketing—a domain rich with academic and practical promise. The critical analysis presented here underscores the nascent stage of AR research in this field and the pressing need for comprehensive, nuanced, and ethically-informed scholarly attention.

Table 3. Future research agenda and directions

Area	Future Research Direction	Example Research Questions
Methodology	• Explore the global acceptance of AREM features. • Analyze changes over time with AR interactions, and examine the impact of frequency and duration of AR exposure. • Experimental designs for causal effects, and test AR interactions. • The lack of standardized measures for perceived realism in AR environments • Development and validation of measures for AR-related constructs. • Conduct qualitative and mixed-methods studies to understand consumer cognitive and emotional processes and identify context-specific constructs. • Conduct systematic research evaluating AR media characteristics on purchase intentions	• What are the long-term impacts of AR on consumer purchase behavior and brand engagement? • How do repeated AR experiences influence consumer brand perception and loyalty? • How does the novelty effect of AR influence consumer behavior in the short-term vs long-term? • What qualitative insights can be gained about the emotional impact of AR in experiential tourism?
Consumer Segmentation	• Analysis of AREM's impact across different consumer segments, including psychographics, and behavioral traits. • The moderating role of factors like age, gender, and education level	• To what extent do psychographic and demographic traits moderate the relationship between AR experiences and consumer responsiveness? • How do personal characteristics such as technological self-efficacy and interest in cultural heritage sites influence the effectiveness of AREM strategies across different age groups? • What impact does AREM have on brand identity perception and customer participation among various generational cohorts, and how might this inform targeted marketing campaigns?
Cultural, Contextual, Social Influences	• The role of culture in AR technology adoption • Assess AR adoption in multicultural environments. • The moderating effect of cultural dimensions on consumer behavior • Cross-Cultural acceptance and impact of AR in Marketing • Shifting the focus from a pure B2C to a B2B context • The role of social aspects like family and friends in AR adoption and their impact on consumer decision-making • Impact of environmental and contextual factors on AR content perception and UX through the lens of the Affect-as-Information Theory	• How do cultural values, such as interdependence and conformity, moderate the perception of technology value in AR marketing across different cultures? • How do cultural dimensions influence the acceptance and effectiveness of experiential AR applications in marketing, and what are the differences in usage behaviors between Eastern and Western countries? • How do environmental and situational factors, such as the presence of others, lighting, and noise, alongside the visualization and processing of AR content, influence users' mood and stress levels? • How does AR adoption vary across cultures with different levels of technological advancement? And how do social influences, such as feedback from family and friends, affect the adoption and impact of AR in shopping?

continued on following page

Table 3. Continued

Area	Future Research Direction	Example Research Questions
AR and Consumer Behavior & Characteristics	• Consumer characteristics influencing AREM effectiveness. • Identify features that make AR apps enjoyable. • Varying levels of 'wow-effect' in AR and its influence on consumer behavior. • The role of consumer innovation, enjoyment, and familiarity with technology in AR experiences • AREM and consumer behavior outcomes, including shopping motivation and product involvement • Influence of AREM on loyalty, consumer journey stages, and actual purchase behavior, beyond behavioral intentions	• How do different intensities of the 'wow-effect' in AR influence impulse buying behavior? • What makes AR apps enjoyable? • Does familiarity with AR technology enhance or detract from the consumer flow experience, and how does it influence their affective responses? • Does AR influence the consumer decision-making process for high-involvement products differently than for low-involvement products?
AR and Brand Relationships	• AREM's effect on brand-focused affective variables like brand love or brand admiration and brand images • Influence of AR experience in the pre-purchase stage on brand switching behavior and loyalty. • Influence of AREM on building and sustaining consumer-brand relationships. • Identify AR attributes influencing brand engagement • Examine whether the influence of AR applies to all brands and industries and explore potential moderators that could enhance or weaken AR's contribution • Other traits like product/brand familiarity could also influence consumer adoption of AR	• How can brands specifically use AR to build sustainable long-term relationships, such as brand love with consumers? (Zanger et al., 2022) • How does AREM influence consumers' willingness to switch to or from a brand? • What specific attributes of AR contribute most significantly to enhancing brand engagement, and do these attributes vary in effectiveness across different brands and industries? • To what extent do product or brand familiarity moderate the effectiveness of AREM in influencing consumer adoption and engagement, and are there other critical traits that either amplify or diminish this impact?

continued on following page

Table 3. Continued

Area	Future Research Direction	Example Research Questions
AR Features, and Experiential Value	• Investigate the role of AREM factors such as enjoyment, immersion, experiential value, and a broad range of AR features and tools. • AR's capability to create authentic experiences. • AR's influence on consumer hedonic and utilitarian values. • Examine how AR features generate different types of experiential value, their relationship with customer satisfaction, and their impact on affective and behavioral responses. • Investigate the relationships between AR experiential quality and behavioral constructs like e-WOM, revisit intention, and willingness to pay a premium • Consider a multidimensional structure of experiential values integrating both intrinsic-extrinsic and active-reactive values • Additional attributes such as augmentation quality, spatial presence, and novelty could be explored to understand their impact on consumer outcomes. • Bifurcating user satisfaction into pre-purchase, purchase, and post-purchase sub-variables to assess the effect of AREM. • Examine how inspiration can trigger tourists to engage in ex-situ AR tours, expanding the understanding of AR technology adoption in tourism.	• How do specific AR features contribute to creating different dimensions of experiential value in retail settings, and how do these experiential values, influence consumer affective responses, behavioral intentions (such as word of mouth, revisit intention), and willingness to pay a premium? • Which specific AREM features are most effective in enhancing consumer shopping experiences? • Do AR experiences in public spaces lead to different consumer behaviors compared to private settings? • What experiential factors are most influential in driving consumer engagement with AR technologies in retailing?
Ethical Considerations and AR Dark Side	• In-depth exploration of the ethical concerns related to AR, including consumer privacy concerns, data security, and the overall impact on consumer well-being. • Identification and exploration of negative factors related to AR use, moving beyond privacy and security concerns to other potential adverse impacts on consumers, such as data sharing and dizziness, self-disclosure… • Identify barriers and challenges that could impede AR's adoption, such as technological disparities and the need for significant content innovation (from both consumer and business perspectives)	• What are consumer perceptions of privacy concerning AR marketing practices? • How do ethical concerns impact the trust and acceptance of AR among consumers? • How can marketers ethically leverage AR without compromising user data security and privacy? • What are consumer reactions to AR data collection practices, and how does transparency in AR applications affect consumer trust and intentions? • How does AR contribute to consumer decision fatigue or skepticism, and what mitigation strategies can be developed? • What are the unexplored negative consequences of AR use, such as psychological discomfort or dependency, and how do they impact consumer welfare?

Source: Authors' own elaboration

CONCLUSION AND LIMITATIONS

This review has revealed a promising ground for future research, characterized by both theoretical advancements and practical applications. Drawing from key studies including Chen & Chou (2022), Haumer et al. (2020), and Kim et al. (2023), among others, we conduct a comprehensive examination of AR experiential marketing across various sectors such as retail, advertising, and tourism. This exploration has served to capture and define the vibrant academic discourse surrounding AR's application in experiential marketing practices. Moreover, we have developed an integrative framework consolidating the diverse aspects of AREM, providing a cohesive reference for both academic and practical applications. Additionally, this investigation has yielded numerous scholarly and theoretical contributions at the nexus of AR and experiential marketing. The integration of theories such as experiential value constructs and telepresence theory enriches our comprehension of AR's immersive experiences. Future research should aim to further integrate and cross-validate these theories across diverse contexts and cultures, thereby broadening the theoretical landscape of AR in marketing. Additionally, this review highlights the need for businesses to adopt a more nuanced understanding of AR features that go beyond novelty, focusing on creating genuinely engaging, immersive, and personalized experiences for consumers. The identification of demographic gaps, such as the predominance of young adult respondents in existing studies, suggests the necessity for marketers to broaden their approach to include older demographics and diverse cultural contexts. Furthermore, exploring the dark side of AR, including privacy and ethical concerns, offers critical insights for developing responsible AR applications that respect consumer boundaries and foster trust.

Moreover, by establishing a comprehensive research agenda, this study highlights novel AREM research directions and questions, requiring in-depth future exploration. From examining the long-term impacts of AR on consumer behavior to understanding the role of AR in the consumer journey and its integration with brand strategies, there's a wealth of avenues for future scholarly investigation. Ethical considerations, particularly around privacy and the psychological impacts of AR, also present critical areas for future study. This confluence shapes a comprehensive, critical, and forward-looking synthesis of the existing body of work, establishing a foundation for both theoretical enhancements and practical advancements in AREM. Addressing the outlined research directions will significantly improve the integration of AR in marketing, leading to enhanced consumer experiences in an increasingly digital marketplace.

Despite its extensive contributions, this SLR has limitations due to the applied inclusion and exclusion criteria. Notably, the exclusion of conference proceedings, books, dissertations, and non-empirical studies, as well as publications in languages other than English. Addressing these limitations in future reviews, by incorporating a wider array of sources and languages, could enrich the understanding and application of AR experiential marketing. Moreover, not conducting a meta-analysis in this study is a limitation. As a statistical method that aggregates findings from multiple studies, it could offer a more comprehensive understanding of AREM's effects by statistically summarizing diverse research.

REFERENCES

Alimamy, S., & Nadeem, W. (2022). Is this real? Cocreation of value through authentic experiential augmented reality: The mediating effect of perceived ethics and customer engagement. *Information Technology & People*, 35(2), 577–599. 10.1108/ITP-07-2020-0455

Arghashi, V. (2022). Shopping with augmented reality: How wow-effect changes the equations! *Electronic Commerce Research and Applications*, 54, 101166. 10.1016/j.elerap.2022.101166

Arghashi, V., & Yuksel, C. A. (2022). Interactivity, Inspiration, and Perceived Usefulness! How retailers' AR-apps improve consumer engagement through flow. *Journal of Retailing and Consumer Services*, 64, 102756. 10.1016/j.jretconser.2021.102756

Barhorst, J. B., McLean, G., Shah, E., & Mack, R. (2021). Blending the real world and the virtual world: Exploring the role of flow in augmented reality experiences. *Journal of Business Research*, 122, 423–436. 10.1016/j.jbusres.2020.08.041

Bouhtati, N., Alla, L., & Bentalha, B. (2023). Marketing Big Data Analytics and Customer Relationship Management: A Fuzzy Approach. In *Integrating Intelligence and Sustainability in Supply Chains* (pp. 75-86). IGI Global. 10.4018/979-8-3693-0225-5.ch004

Bouhtati, N., Kamal, M., & Alla, L. (2022). Big Data and the Effectiveness of Tourism Marketing: A Prospective Review of the Literature. In *The International Conference on Artificial Intelligence and Smart Environment* (pp. 287-292). Cham: Springer International Publishing.

Carmo, I. S. D., Marques, S., & Dias, Á. (2022). The influence of experiential marketing on customer satisfaction and loyalty. *Journal of Promotion Management*, 28(7), 994–1018. 10.1080/10496491.2022.2054903

Chen, S. C., Chou, T. H., Hongsuchon, T., Ruangkanjanases, A., Kittikowit, S., & Lee, T. C. (2022). The mediation effect of marketing activities toward augmented reality: The perspective of extended customer experience. *Journal of Hospitality and Tourism Technology*, 13(3), 461–480. 10.1108/JHTT-03-2021-0093

Daassi, M., & Debbabi, S. (2021). Intention to reuse AR-based apps: The combined role of the sense of immersion, product presence and perceived realism. *Information & Management*, 58(4), 103453. 10.1016/j.im.2021.103453

Erdmann, A., Mas, J. M., & Arilla, R. (2023). Value-based adoption of augmented reality: A study on the influence on online purchase intention in retail. *Journal of Consumer Behaviour*, 22(4), 912–932. 10.1002/cb.1993

Eru, O., Topuz, Y. V., & Ruziye, C. O. P. (2022). The Effect of Augmented Reality Experience on Loyalty and Purchasing Intent: An Application on the Retail Sector. *Sosyoekonomi*, 30(52), 129–155. 10.17233/sosyoekonomi.2022.02.08

Han, S., Yoon, J. H., & Kwon, J. (2021). Impact of experiential value of augmented reality: The context of heritage tourism. *Sustainability (Basel)*, 13(8), 4147. 10.3390/su13084147

Haumer, F., Kolo, C., & Reiners, S. (2020). The impact of augmented reality experiential marketing on brand equity and buying intention. *Journal of Brand Strategy*, 8(4), 368–387.

Hilken, T., Heller, J., Chylinski, M., Keeling, D. I., Mahr, D., & de Ruyter, K. (2018). Making omni-channel an augmented reality: The current and future state of the art. *Journal of Research in Interactive Marketing*, 12(4), 509–523. 10.1108/JRIM-01-2018-0023

Holbrook, M. B., & Hirschman, E. C. (1982). The experiential aspects of consumption: Consumer fantasies, feelings, and fun. *The Journal of Consumer Research*, 9(2), 132–140. 10.1086/208906

Hsu, S. H. Y., Tsou, H. T., & Chen, J. S. (2021). "Yes, we do. Why not use augmented reality?" customer responses to experiential presentations of AR-based applications. *Journal of Retailing and Consumer Services*, 62, 102649. 10.1016/j.jretconser.2021.102649

Hu, R., Wang, C., Zhang, T., Nguyen, T., Shapoval, V., & Zhai, L. (2021). Applying augmented reality (AR) technologies in theatrical performances in theme parks: A transcendent experience perspective. *Tourism Management Perspectives*, 40, 100889. 10.1016/j.tmp.2021.100889

Huang, T. L., & Liao, S. (2015). A model of acceptance of augmented-reality interactive technology: The moderating role of cognitive innovativeness. *Electronic Commerce Research*, 15(2), 269–295. 10.1007/s10660-014-9163-2

Irgui, , AQmichchou, , M. (2023). Contextual marketing and information privacy concerns in m-commerce and their impact on consumer loyalty. *Arab Gulf Journal of Scientific Research*. 10.1108/AGJSR-09-2022-0198

Irgui, , AQmichchou, , M., & ElHaraoui, , I. (2024). Phygital learning in Moroccan higher education and its impact on student satisfaction. *Revue Management & Innovation, (3)*, 110-129. 10.3917/rmi.209.0110

Javornik, A. (2016). Augmented reality: Research agenda for studying the impact of its media characteristics on consumer behaviour. *Journal of Retailing and Consumer Services*, 30, 252–261. 10.1016/j.jretconser.2016.02.004

Kazmi, S. H. A., Ahmed, R. R., Soomro, K. A., Hashem, E. A. R., Akhtar, H., & Parmar, V. (2021). Role of augmented reality in changing consumer behavior and decision making: Case of Pakistan. *Sustainability (Basel)*, 13(24), 14064. 10.3390/su132414064

Kim, J. H., Kim, M., Park, M., & Yoo, J. (2023). Immersive interactive technologies and virtual shopping experiences: Differences in consumer perceptions between augmented reality (AR) and virtual reality (VR). *Telematics and Informatics*, 77, 101936. 10.1016/j.tele.2022.101936

Kim, J. H., Kim, M., Yoo, J., & Park, M. (2024). Augmented reality in delivering experiential values: Moderating role of task complexity. *Virtual Reality (Waltham Cross)*, 28(1), 19. 10.1007/s10055-023-00896-8

Kowalczuk, P., Siepmann, C., & Adler, J. (2021). Cognitive, affective, and behavioral consumer responses to augmented reality in e-commerce: A comparative study. *Journal of Business Research*, 124, 357–373. 10.1016/j.jbusres.2020.10.050

Kumar, H. (2022). Augmented reality in online retailing: A systematic review and research agenda. *International Journal of Retail & Distribution Management*, 50(4), 537–559. 10.1108/IJRDM-06-2021-0287

Lavoye, V., Mero, J., & Tarkiainen, A. (2021). Consumer behavior with augmented reality in retail: A review and research agenda. *International Review of Retail, Distribution and Consumer Research*, 31(3), 299–329. 10.1080/09593969.2021.1901765

Lee, H., Xu, Y., & Porterfield, A. (2022). Antecedents and moderators of consumer adoption toward AR-enhanced virtual try-on technology: A stimulus-organism-response approach. *International Journal of Consumer Studies*, 46(4), 1319–1338. 10.1111/ijcs.12760

Lhoussaine, A., Kamal, M., & Bouhtati, N. (2022). Big data and marketing effectiveness of tourism businesses: A literature review. *Economic Management Alternatives*, 1, 39–58.

Mathwick, C., Malhotra, N., & Rigdon, E. (2001). Experiential value: Conceptualization, measurement and application in the catalog and Internet shopping environment☆. *Journal of Retailing*, 77(1), 39–56. 10.1016/S0022-4359(00)00045-2

McLean, G., & Wilson, A. (2019). Shopping in the digital world: Examining customer engagement through augmented reality mobile applications. *Computers in Human Behavior*, 101, 210–224. 10.1016/j.chb.2019.07.002

Oyman, M., Bal, D., & Ozer, S. (2022). Extending the technology acceptance model to explain how perceived augmented reality affects consumers' perceptions. *Computers in Human Behavior*, 128, 107127. 10.1016/j.chb.2021.107127

Paul, J., & Criado, A. R. (2020). The art of writing literature review: What do we know and what do we need to know? *International Business Review*, 29(4), 101717. 10.1016/j.ibusrev.2020.101717

Perannagari, K. T., & Chakrabarti, S. (2019). Factors influencing acceptance of augmented reality in retail: Insights from thematic analysis. *International Journal of Retail & Distribution Management*, 48(1), 18–34. 10.1108/IJRDM-02-2019-0063

Poushneh, A., & Vasquez-Parraga, A. Z. (2017). Discernible impact of augmented reality on retail customer's experience, satisfaction and willingness to buy. *Journal of Retailing and Consumer Services*, 34, 229–234. 10.1016/j.jretconser.2016.10.005

Qin, H., Osatuyi, B., & Xu, L. (2021). How mobile augmented reality applications affect continuous use and purchase intentions: A cognition-affect-conation perspective. *Journal of Retailing and Consumer Services*, 63, 102680. 10.1016/j.jretconser.2021.102680

Shah, D., & Murthi, B. P. S. (2021). Marketing in a data-driven digital world: Implications for the role and scope of marketing. *Journal of Business Research*, 125, 772–779. 10.1016/j.jbusres.2020.06.062

Singh, P., Sharma, M., & Daim, T. (2024). Envisaging AR travel revolution for visiting heritage sites: A mixed-method approach. *Technology in Society*, 76, 102439. 10.1016/j.techsoc.2023.102439

Sun, Y., & Yuan, Z. (2024). A virtual gym in your pocket: The influence of augmented reality exercise app characteristics on user's continuance intention. *Virtual Reality (Waltham Cross)*, 28(1), 1–20. 10.1007/s10055-024-00959-4

Sung, E. C. (2021). The effects of augmented reality mobile app advertising: Viral marketing via shared social experience. *Journal of Business Research*, 122, 75–87. 10.1016/j.jbusres.2020.08.034

Tom Dieck, M. C., Cranmer, E., Prim, A. L., & Bamford, D. (2023). The effects of augmented reality shopping experiences: immersion, presence and satisfaction. *Journal of Research in Interactive Marketing*, (ahead-of-print).

Tom Dieck, M. C., & Han, D. I. D. (2022). The role of immersive technology in Customer Experience Management. *Journal of Marketing Theory and Practice*, 30(1), 108–119. 10.1080/10696679.2021.1891939

Trivedi, J., Kasilingam, D., Arora, P., & Soni, S. (2022). The effect of augmented reality in mobile applications on consumers' online impulse purchase intention: The mediating role of perceived value. *Journal of Consumer Behaviour*, 21(4), 896–908. 10.1002/cb.2047

Tsang, S. S., Kuo, C., Hu, T. K., & Wang, W. C. (2023). Exploring impacts of AR on group package tours: Destination image, perceived certainty, and experiential value. *Journal of Vacation Marketing*, 29(1), 84–102. 10.1177/13567667221078244

Vaidyanathan, N., & Henningsson, S. (2023). Designing augmented reality services for enhanced customer experiences in retail. *Journal of Service Management*, 34(1), 78–99. 10.1108/JOSM-01-2022-0004

Vo, K. N., Le, A. N. H., Thanh Tam, L., & Ho Xuan, H. (2022). Immersive experience and customer responses towards mobile augmented reality applications: The moderating role of technology anxiety. *Cogent Business & Management*, 9(1), 2063778. 10.1080/23311975.2022.2063778

Vongurai, R. (2021). Factors influencing experiential value toward using cosmetic AR try-on feature in Thailand. *Journal of Distribution Science*, 19(1), 75–87.

Walentek, D., & Ziora, L. (2023). A systematic review on the use of augmented reality in management and business. *Procedia Computer Science*, 225, 861–871. 10.1016/j.procs.2023.10.073

Wang, W., Cao, D., & Ameen, N. (2023). Understanding customer satisfaction of augmented reality in retail: A human value orientation and consumption value perspective. *Information Technology & People*, 36(6), 2211–2233. 10.1108/ITP-04-2021-0293

Watson, A., Alexander, B., & Salavati, L. (2018). The impact of experiential augmented reality applications on fashion purchase intention. *International Journal of Retail & Distribution Management*, 48(5), 433–451. 10.1108/IJRDM-06-2017-0117

Whang, J. B., Song, J. H., Choi, B., & Lee, J. H. (2021). The effect of Augmented Reality on purchase intention of beauty products: The roles of consumers' control. *Journal of Business Research*, 133, 275–284. 10.1016/j.jbusres.2021.04.057

Williams, R. I.Jr, Clark, L. A., Clark, W. R., & Raffo, D. M. (2021). Re-examining systematic literature review in management research: Additional benefits and execution protocols. *European Management Journal*, 39(4), 521–533. 10.1016/j.emj.2020.09.007

Yang, X. (2021). Augmented reality in experiential marketing: The effects on consumer utilitarian and hedonic perceptions and behavioural responses. *Information technology in organisations and societies: Multidisciplinary perspectives from AI to Technostress*, 147-174.

Yaoyuneyong, G., Foster, J., Johnson, E., & Johnson, D. (2016). Augmented reality marketing: Consumer preferences and attitudes toward hypermedia print ads. *Journal of Interactive Advertising*, 16(1), 16–30. 10.1080/15252019.2015.1125316

Yim, M. Y. C., Chu, S. C., & Sauer, P. L. (2017). Is augmented reality technology an effective tool for e-commerce? An interactivity and vividness perspective. *Journal of Interactive Marketing*, 39(1), 89–103. 10.1016/j.intmar.2017.04.001

Yoon, S., & Oh, J. (2022). A theory-based approach to the usability of augmented reality technology: A cost-benefit perspective. *Technology in Society*, 68, 101860. 10.1016/j.techsoc.2022.101860

Zanger, V., Meißner, M., & Rauschnabel, P. A. (2022). Beyond the gimmick: How affective responses drive brand attitudes and intentions in augmented reality marketing. *Psychology and Marketing*, 39(7), 1285–1301. 10.1002/mar.21641

Chapter 6
Factors Affecting Citizen Intention to Use Smart City Services in Morocco:
A Systematic Literature Review and Conceptual Framework

Tarik Rhardas
http://orcid.org/0009-0004-3271-3213

National School of Business and Management, Hassan II University of Casablanca, Morocco

Hanane Rochdane

National School of Business and Management, Hassan II University of Casablanca, Morocco

ABSTRACT

In many developing countries, smart city initiatives are in their infancy. Like many other developing countries, smart projects in Morocco have been facing several challenges since their launch in 2016. The adoption of smart services requires the commitment and involvement of Moroccan citizens. This chapter focuses on a systematic literature review of the main studies dealing with factors that appear to improve end-user acceptance of services provided by Moroccan smart cities. A specific method known as PRISMA is being adopted to select and synthesize relevant studies in this field. The results obtained from the systematic review indicate that the unified theory of acceptance and use of technology (UTAUT) is the most utilized theory in the literature. Additionally, the examination of existing studies has revealed that successful implementation of smart projects requires decision-makers to consider the following factors: performance expectancy, ease of use, social influence, perceived cost, awareness, trust in technology, and trust in the government.

1. INTRODUCTION

In recent years, smart cities have been more popular than ever because they provide new solutions in the areas of mobility, environment, economy, governance, quality of life, and education, thanks to the innovative use of Information and Communication Technologies (ICT)(Nassereddine & Khang, 2024).

DOI: 10.4018/979-8-3693-3172-9.ch006

Generally, the interest in smart cities is closely linked to the rise of new information technologies such as mobile devices, semantic web, cloud computing, and the Internet of Things(Syed et al., 2021). The term "smart city" was adopted in 2005 by a number of technology companies offering complex information systems to their clients, aimed at integrating the operations of urban infrastructur(Savastano et al., 2023). Several other non-technological factors have led to the broader adoption of a smart city strategy: the increase in city size, the need to protect the environment from pollution and energy consumption, or the increased demands of citizens for public services(Jebaraj et al., 2023).

Although the technological aspects of smart cities have been well covered in the literature, the crucial role of citizens in these cities has often been overlooked(Jebaraj et al., 2023). Too often, smart cities have not achieved their goals because citizens have not been adequately involved in their definition or because the impact on their daily lives has not been taken into account(Del-Real et al., 2023).

In the field of research on smart cities, many authors have emphasized the importance of discussing citizen participation in a smart city. However, until now, very little has been written about the various facilitators of citizen participation in the context of a smart city.

A smart city is an innovative urban area that leverages Information and Communication Technologies (ICT) to promote robust economic activity, enhance the overall quality of life, and foster sustainable development. We are currently observing a highly interconnected and complex world, necessitating the development of improved methods for exchanging and transmitting information across many participants in common spaces, such as urban areas.

ICT infrastructure has a crucial role in enhancing and facilitating social and urban development, fostering public engagement, and boosting government efficiency in smart city contexts. From the viewpoint of the citizens, the integration of Information and Communication Technology (ICT) is crucial for the functioning of intelligent cities and enterprises. Smart city services enhance the living environment and enhance the quality of life for citizens. Smart city services encompass a wide range of applications that address common challenges including mobility, public services, and security. The pandemic problem has recently emphasized the crucial importance of these smart city services.

Cities are compelled to adopt new methods of urban management in order to fulfill the demands of territorial competitiveness. Currently, there is a global inclination to adopt smart city standards by investing in the digitalization of diverse public services in urban areas. Recently, numerous endeavors have been undertaken in various Moroccan cities to enhance their appeal by engaging in a process of promoting and enhancing their territories through the execution of substantial infrastructure projects and the digitalization of municipal administration(Haj, 2020).

Morocco is betting on transforming six cities into smart cities by 2026 (Ministry of Industry, 2013). The project has already begun in Casablanca in 2016, with Marrakech, Rabat, Tangier, Ifrane, Berkane, and Fez to follow. Morocco aims to create a new model of urban management at a lower cost, improve the efficiency of urban planning, and achieve sustainable social development that meets citizens' needs in terms of transportation, energy, green economy, security, and housing.

However, for these smart administration initiatives to be successful, citizens must understand and accept online administration services(Del-Real et al., 2023; Junaidi et al., 2024). The effectiveness of adopting intelligent public services relies on the perception of the online administration effort by end-users. The end-users may not have a positive reception of the currently available technology. The existence of a smart city is rendered pointless if end-users do not successfully utilize online administration services.

Researchers point out that few studies have focused on citizen participation in smart cities, such as smart practices or activities (Suryawan & Lee, 2023). The authors argue that there is a gap between recent policy approaches that emphasize citizen engagement in smart cities and relevant research on this issue. In fact, smart cities differ from digital cities in that smart cities focus on the relationships between actors and related entities and their contribution to the success of all(Jiang et al., 2023).

Empirical literature on citizen engagement in smart cities in developing countries is still scarce(Bernardin & Jeannot, 2019; Braga et al., 2022). Thus, this article contributes to expanding research on this topic. Building on this reflection, this study provides some understanding and explores factors explaining citizens' intention in smart initiatives and projects.

The main objective of this article is to review and synthesize previous studies on factors explaining citizen engagement in smart activities during the period 2013-2023. Additionally, the paper aims to analyze some characteristics of key publications such as spatial distribution of studies, evolution of publications, etc. To achieve these objectives, we will undertake a systematic review using the PRISMA (Preferred Reporting Items for Systematic Reviews and Meta-Analyses) method and a quantitative analysis of the main characteristics of these studies.

Moreover, systematic quantitative literature review is a trend in research work(Perez-Vega et al., 2022). It provides a comprehensive, structured, and analytical way to accurately organize reviews. Additionally, it effectively identifies research gaps in the literature(Paul & Criado, 2020). Widely adopted in the broader social sciences and particularly in management and marketing research. Similarly, it offers several advantages, including the ability to develop flexible article databases that can be easily updated and queried(Kumar, 2022).

The purpose of this document is to identify the factors that determine the successful adoption of smart services and to develop a conceptual framework for the implementation of smart cities in Morocco. Our study will be based on research conducted in countries with similar characteristics to the Moroccan case.

This systematic review will be organized into three sections. We will begin with a literature review on the key concepts of our issue. Then, we will focus on the methodology and approach adopted in the review in question. Finally, a third section will be dedicated to the analysis and discussion of the main findings.

2. LITERATURE REVIEW

2.1. In Search of a Definition of the Smart City

The phrase "Smart City" emerged in the late 1990s with the development of urbanisation, particularly in relation to Information and Communication Technology(Anthopoulos et al., 2022). The notion of Smart City, popularised by private IT companies such as IBM and Cisco, has attracted the attention of numerous researchers and practitioners (Anthopoulos, 2017).

Despite the many definitions in the literature, researchers agree that the use of ICT remains the most crucial feature of the Smart City(Bibri, 2018). Indeed, according to (Kandt & Batty, 2021), the concept of the Smart City primarily refers to how technologies could enhance the functioning of cities, their efficiency, their competitiveness, and provide new ways to address various economic problems. If this dimension appears unavoidable, we dispute the recurring use of the technological dimension by authors to define the Smart City.

Indeed, although Information and Communication Technologies (ICT) are a fundamental and inseparable part of the Smart City idea(Bibri et al., 2023), it is important to note that a Smart City is not limited to being a digital or numerical city. For example, (Cocchia, 2014a)emphasises the need to broaden the scope of smart cities in order to make them more balanced and inclusive, highlighting the need of considering the various environmental, social, and economic components of the city. Indeed, according to (Albino et al., 2015), the notion of the Smart City is closely linked to that of sustainability, since it is now crucial to address the significant challenges posed by widespread urbanisation, which brings about heavy environmental and economic constraints.

Multiple definitions of the Smart City exist in the literature, without any of them reaching a consensus so far (Cocchia, 2014b). However, we adhere to (Anthopoulos, 2017)definition, which we consider to be the most comprehensive and up-to-date, as it encompasses the various elements of the Smart City and highlights its main objectives.

The concept of the Smart City involves the utilisation of ICT and innovation by cities (both new and existing) as a means to achieve economic, social, and environmental sustainability and address various concerns across six dimensions: people, economy, governance, mobility, environment, and quality of life(Giffinger, 2015; Koz\lowski & Suwar, 2021).

The existing literature on the development of smart cities highlights two main objectives for them: the improvement of citizens' quality of life through the provision of new services (Bakici et al., 2013) and the preservation of the environment (Bibri et al., 2023). Indeed, (Dameri, 2013) define the Smart City as "an urban environment that, supported by ubiquitous ICT systems, is capable of providing new services to citizens, thereby improving the overall quality of their lives." For example, the urban mobility service effectively demonstrates how ICT has enhanced citizens' mobility experience and facilitated their movements in the city by providing accurate real-time information through various media outlets within the city. (Bibri et al., 2023)report that the adoption of new technologies will enable cities to redefine and reorganise urban areas at various spatial scales in order to achieve the required level of sustainability and supportability. This implies the implementation of a set of measures aimed at addressing the many economic, as well as environmental, social, and cultural objectives of cities. Here, intelligence should primarily be focused on sustainable development goals rather than on technology and the efficiency of smart solutions.

The Smart City must therefore prioritise a sustainable and pleasant environment for its citizens by placing them at the forefront of its concerns.

The term "smart city" is defined to enhance our understanding of the various facets of this phenomenon. In order to offer a more tangible demonstration of this particular element, the subsequent portion of this study will present a comprehensive examination of the smart city in Morocco, which is widely acknowledged as a noteworthy exemplar in this domain. This serves as a prototype for numerous other African cities.

2.2. Moroccan Cities in the Era of the Smart City

The Moroccan city possesses significant factors that can be invested to succeed in its smart transformation process: a sufficiently connected population, efforts towards digitizing administrations and public institutions, the existence of a national digitization strategy. All these elements are potential factors for such success, provided that local authorities successfully mobilize other stakeholders involved in this project, secure financing for large restructuring projects, ensure the presence of a quality and diversified transportation network, establish innovation and research and development hubs, institutions for youth and creativity, and define a strategy for the city that projects into its future territorial intelligence.

The transformation of the Moroccan city into a "smart city" requires more than the mentioned elements; it necessitates total mobilization of actors and stakeholders in the city. In this regard, it is important to consider the establishment of a code of good practices that outlines country-specific standards for smart cities. This will enable territorial competition between cities and thus ensure continuous attractiveness to investors and tourists(Alla et al., 2023), consequently guaranteeing the success of the regionalization project and the participation of territories in the country's development.

It is worth mentioning that the government, in its role as the lawmaker, has the ability to intervene by enacting laws that define the methods and procedures for territorial transformation. These laws would establish the requirements and actions necessary to earn the designation of a Moroccan smart city.

In Morocco, a reflection on the metropolitan development of Casablanca(El Assal & Rochdane, 2023), emphasizing the reinforcement of its national and international competitiveness to make it a true technological hub, has begun. A very ambitious project called "Casablanca Smart City" has been launched. This project aims to transform the metropolis of Casablanca into a smart city through digital projects that enable optimal analysis of the informational wealth of collected and analyzed data, with the aim of bringing administration and users closer by offering them tailored public services.

The smart city approach is based on the use of mobile and ubiquitous ICT infrastructures, such as information and communication systems, smartphones, and other mobile devices, to develop interconnected applications, services, and pilot projects.

The objective is to progressively establish an innovation ecosystem that is social, sustainable, and collaborative. This will be achieved through networked applications, services, and pilot projects, which will build an environment of an interconnected smart city. Consequently, implementing the Smart City initiative in Casablanca would necessitate a person who possesses a high level of intelligence(El Assal & Rochdane, 2023). Put simply, individuals must showcase their agility and cognitive abilities in order to use digital technology, since they will be responsible for creating and consuming digital data(Bouhtati, Kamal, et al., 2023).

Nevertheless, concerning statistics indicate that there are substantial barriers impeding the acceptance and utilization of technologies, particularly the internet and technological assistance. The metropolis exhibits notable inequalities, especially between affluent neighborhoods and outlying areas where there is a significant digital divide. In addition, a significant percentage of the population is unable to afford the cost of accessing technology. According to a 2020 estimate by the World Bank, a typical household from the poorest 54% of the Moroccan population would need to spend 36% of its income in order to access mobile broadband. The household in question would need to allocate 32% of its disposable income in order to afford fixed broadband.

In addition to these obstacles, illiteracy prevents a large portion of citizens from manipulating technology.

2.3. The Role of Citizens in Smart Cities

While the concept of citizen participation is not limited to smart cities, these cities have brought a fresh perspective to this concept and offer innovative methods to facilitate such participation. Smart cities are currently receiving substantial financial assistance from both governmental and commercial groups, leading to a notable increase in their popularity. Cities must strategically plan and implement smart city initiatives by harnessing the wide range of technological opportunities available to them. This involves making informed decisions on how to utilize and enhance their information and communication technology (ICT) infrastructure, while also maximizing the use of their resources. A key difficulty is to effectively execute these measures in collaboration with inhabitants, with the ultimate objective of constructing a smart city that may significantly improve their quality of life. (Hollands, 2020) highlights the significance of individuals and critiques the technology-focused approach of smart cities. In addition, he argues that smart cities must have a foundation that goes beyond the mere utilization of information and communication technology (ICT) in order to facilitate progress in social, environmental, economic, and cultural aspects. Hollands argues that an authentic smart city should prioritize the residents and their skills, and utilize information technology to encourage democratic discussions about the kind of city that the people want. This critical analysis has sparked a new trend in scientific publications. A new definition of the smart city has integrated the various dimensions of a smart city and the critique (Rudolf Giffinger & Gudrun Haindlmaier, 2018): A city can be defined as "smart" when investments in human and social capital and information and communication technologies (ICT) are sufficient and fuel sustainable economic development and high quality of life, with wise management of natural resources through participatory governance. This definition is widely accepted and used in scientific literature and in practice (for example, smart cities like Amsterdam have used this definition as the basis for their sustainable development strategy). Building on previous literature and the analysis of some of the most well-known and successful smart cities (such as Ghent or Santander), we formalize citizen participation into three main categories(Berntzen & Johannessen, 2016; Simonofski et al., 2021). First, citizens can be democratic participants in the city's decision-making process(EL JAOUHARI & Lhoussaine, 2021). By being involved in the decision-making process, citizens can become familiar with difficult technical issues and become subject matter experts(Irvin & Stansbury, 2004). Second, citizens can be co-creators to propose better solutions and ideas and reduce the risk of failure early in the process (Nguyen et al., 2018). Finally, During the post-implementation phase, citizens have the opportunity to actively engage with information and communication technology (ICT) as users. They can proactively utilize the smart city infrastructure, creating a sense of being immersed in technology.

Empirical research by (Alipour et al., 2020; Oukarfi & Bercheq, 2020a) consistently highlight the importance of individuals' socioeconomic and regional circumstances in determining their decisions regarding technology adoption. The econometric study undertaken by (Diallo et al., 2010)in Africa analysed data from a household survey conducted in 17 sub-Saharan countries. The study examined how individual traits and household factors influence the adoption of ICT (Information and Communication Technology). The study posits that there is a greater probability of adopting when there is a better level of education, a larger number of children, and a higher household income.

Moreover, the utilisation of the Internet may be directly linked to the lifestyle or technological characteristics of the participants. Possessing computer equipment such as tablets, desktop and laptop computers, and gaming consoles would incentivize the choice to acquire a home internet connection. Research suggests the presence of individuals known as "technophiles" who often engage with information and communication technology (ICT) and have a stronger and more consistent inclination to connect to the Internet (Oukarfi & Bercheq, 2020b; Sebei et al., 2018).

2.4. Models Used to Measure Adoption of New Technologies

To explore the factors impacting end users' behaviors towards technology, an analysis of various models and contributions by researchers has been undertaken. This includes Davis's Technology Acceptance Model (TAM)(Davis, 1989), Rogers's Diffusion of Innovations (DOI) model(Rogers Everett, 1995), as well as Venkatesh et al.'s Unified Theory of Acceptance and Use of Technology (UTAUT) (Venkatesh et al., 2003). Other examined models include Trust model(Belanger et al., 2002), Citizen Adoption model(AlNuaimi et al., 2011), and Rehman and Esichaikul's model(Rehman & Esichaikul, 2011), which proposed a third Citizen Adoption model based on integrated models adapted from TAM, DOI, and UTAUT. Studying these models has helped identify potential factors that could influence Moroccan citizens in their adoption of electronic services.

3. METHODOLOGY

To conduct this systematic research, we adhered to a well-defined approach consisting of a set of steps. The following point will be dedicated to explaining this process.

The course of this study was carried out by adopting a method that takes into account four essential steps, inspired by the PRISMA method. The choice of this method is justified by its ability to select and identify relevant references to include in qualitative or quantitative analysis. In the first step, we identified all references related to our main subject. To do this, we chose databases such as Scopus, Cairn, Google Scholar, and ScienceDirect, as they contain the majority of indexed references(Zhao & Strotmann, 2015). Accordingly, we selected a research period ranging from 2013 to 2023.

The choice of the research period is justified by several essential factors. Firstly, this period is temporally relevant, covering a significant decade in the field of marketing research. Additionally, it allows for consideration of major technological advancements, particularly in social media development. By choosing this period, we also ensure access to available data and updated information, thereby facilitating analysis and synthesis of research findings.

Furthermore, we restricted the scope of the study to countries with economic, technological, and sociocultural traits similar to those of Morocco.

Moreover, we used a combination of all the aforementioned keywords by adopting the boolean operator "AND" in fields related to "articles," "abstracts," and "keywords" derived from our main theme, namely "citizen participation," "smart city," and "adoption factors." The objective remains to collect a maximum of references addressing the aforementioned keywords. Subsequently, the selected references underwent an initial filtering process involving comparison of articles found in the chosen databases (Scopus, Cairn, Google Scholar, and ScienceDirect). This comparison aimed to identify and eliminate repetitive references within the consulted databases. Then, we proceeded to select articles based on well-defined criteria, as summarized in the table below.

Table 1. Exclusion and inclusion criteria for articles

Levels	Inclusion criteria	exclusion criteria
Type of references	Journal articles	Conference papers, collective works
Years selected	3013-2023	Articles published outside the selected period
Type of stadies	Qualitative, Quantitative, Mixed	Review articles
Kyewords	Smart cities, smart citizen, adoption facors,	Other keywords
Study area	Developing countries	Developed countries

Source: Authors

Next, an in-depth analysis of the full articles will allow us to select the relevant articles closely related to our research question. Finally, we will proceed with a quantitative analysis of the list of selected references to address the posed questions. The following figure summarizes the various steps chosen to conduct our systematic review.

Figure 1. PRISMA flowchart

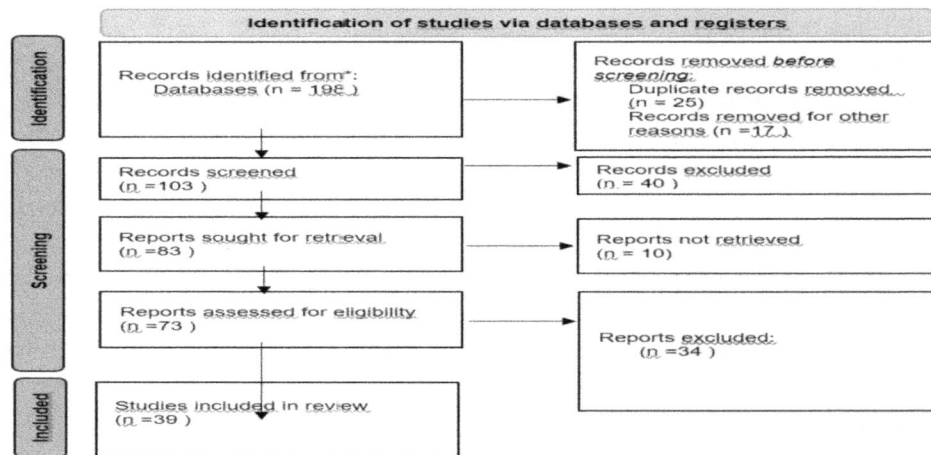

This approach initially allowed us to identify a sample of 198 references collected from the various aforementioned databases. Secondly, we reduced the number of articles to 103 after eliminating observed duplicates. Subsequently, the review of abstracts and titles identified a sample of 83 references. Then, we proceeded with the reading of the full text to ensure relevance to our main topic. This final step led us to limit the number of references to a definitive set of 39 articles (Table 2). The final stage will focus on the inclusion of articles in the analysis and discussions. This inclusion phase in the quantitative analysis aims to study trends in previous studies to address the aforementioned questions.

Table 2. The factors influencing the adoption of smart city services

Authors	Cuntrie	THEORIE	FINDING
Raihan, 2023	Saudi Arabia	TAM	The factors influencing students' intentions towards using ICT in education sustainability are computer self-efficacy, subjective norms, perceived enjoyment, perceived ease of use, perceived usefulness, and attitudes towards computer use
Lakmal et al, 2023	Sri Linka	UTAUT	The research adopted quantitative method to explore factors and the results showed that Performance Expectancy, Effort Expectancy and Social Influence were positively influencing the citizens' Intention and Use Behaviour of e-Government services
Ullah et al, 2023	Pakistan	TAM	In this paper, the authors investigated the various roles that ICTs can play in enhancing SME efficiency, by adopting and extending the Technology Acceptance Model, and then identifying several factors to achieve their adoption.
Zirabaet al, 2023	Zimbabwe	TAM	factors that slow the acceptance, adoption and use of e-government services in Zimbabwe are numerous, our results show that various cultural dimensions influenced people's intent to use egovernment services. The key contribution of our study is that the adoption and acceptance of e-government services is greatly influenced by cultural values of the end users and recipients of that technology
Chandavarkar, 2023	India	TAM	The paper identifies complexity as the main factor influencing the adoption of information and communication technology (ICT) by Indian SMEs. Other significant factors include technological, organizational, and environmental factors.
Srimulyani, 2023	Indonesia	UTAUT,TAM	The factors influencing ICT adoption in Indonesian SMEs are internal factors such as management characteristics and organizational factors, as well as external factors such as technology and environment.
Hoque et al, 2016	Bangladesh	UTAUT	The factors that influence the adoption of information and communication technology (ICT) in small and medium enterprises (SMEs) in rural areas of Bangladesh are awareness of benefits, government support, top management support, and financial support
Yusuf et al, 2016	Malaysia	UTAUT	The paper investigates factors that influence ICT usage among Malaysian agro-based SMEs, including performance expectancy, effort expectancy, and facilitating conditions.
Al-Haddad et al, 2023	Jordanie	TRA,TAM	In this article, the authors studied the factors that affect individuals' intentions and actual e-government usage, including attitudes toward behavior, credibility, and subjective norms that are derived from perceived usefulness, ease of use, awareness, trust in the government, incentives, trustin service delivery, transactional security, and social influence.
Nofal et al, 2021	Jordanie	TAM	In this article, the mediating roles of perceived usefulness (PU), perceived ease of use (PEOU), and trust, as well as the moderating role of transparency, in citizens' adoption of e-government services in the Jordanian public sector institutes.
Al-dmour, 2021	Jordanie	TAM,UTAUT	In this article, the main factors associated with consumers' intentions to adopt electronic payment systems (EPS) in Jordan were identified, including perceived usefulness, ease of use, security, self-efficacy, and trust.
Oumlil, 2020	Morocco	UTAUT	Expected performance, expected effort, Perceived cost, and social influence
Hassan, 2020	Jordanie	UTAT 2	Behavioral intention is influenced by performance expectancy, hedonic motivation, price value, and perceived risk. - Social influences do not have a significant influence on behavioral intention
Alryalat et al, 2020	Jordanie	TAM	- Factors such as relative advantage, perceived trust, computer self-efficacy, and perceived awareness positively influence behavioral intentions to adopt e-government services. - Resistance to change negatively influences citizens' behavioral intentions to adopt e-government services.
Almaiah et al, 2019	Jordanie	UTAUT	Factors such as website quality, trust of internet, trust of government, performance expectancy, effort expectancy, and facilitating conditions have a positive effect on the adoption of e-government services among Jordanian citizens. - Social influence does not significantly influence the intention to use e-government services.
Amin et al, 2022	Saudi Arabia	UTAUT	, the authors examined the adoption of E-Government systems using the Unified Theory of Acceptance and Use of Technology (UTAUT) in Saudi Arabia, and the results of the hypothesis testing reveal several meaningful relationships, including relative benefits, compatibility, security, management support, performance expectations, perceived Usefulness of EGovernment, ease of use by reducing uncertainty to e-Government, and IT infrastructure by reducing language on EGovernment adoption
Alnemer, 2018	Saudi Arabia	TAM	Perceived ease of use and perceived usefulness have a positive effect on digital banking adoption. - Trust has a negative effect on digital banking adoption
Elatrachi et al, 2020	Morocco	UTAUT	The paper discusses the determinants of ICT integration by teachers in higher education in Morocco, but it does not specifically mention the factors of ICT adoption in Morocco
Hassan et al, 2017	Morocco	TRA,TAM,UTAUT	Effort expectancy had no influence on adoption of the IS. - Performance expectancy had a positive effect on adoption of the IS.
Ezzahid, 2021	Morocco	TAM	These online government services are influenced by various factors such as technology, government policies, user behavior, and socioeconomic barriers that can impact their quality and use.
Xiao et al, 2015	China	UTAUT,TAM	Perceived usefulness and perceived credibility influence adoption of e-banking - Resistance to e-banking due to difficulty, unnecessary, and security concerns

continued on following page

Table 2. Continued

Authors	Cuntrie	THEORIE	FINDING
Alzaidi et al, 2021	Saudi Arabia	UTAUT,TAM	- Relative advantage, trialability, observability positively influence citizens' adoption of smart government services. - Complexity and privacy concerns negatively impact citizens' adoption of smart government services
Huang et al, 2019	China	UTAUT	The paper discusses the factors affecting the adoption intention of smart community services (SCS) by residents, including perceived usefulness, perceived enjoyment, and affective community commitment.
Kusdibyo et al, 2023	Indoesia	TAM,TPA	The paper does not specifically mention the adoption factor for smart activities. The paper focuses on the adoption of smart tourism technology in influencing visiting tourism destinations.
Nusir et al, 2023	Jordanie	UTAUT, TAM	The paper investigates factors that influence citizens' intention to adopt smart city technologies in Jordan, including perceived ease of use and ICT infrastructure and Internet connectivity.
Fernando et al, 2021	Indonesia	UTAUT2	The variables used are based on existing theories, so this study uses the variables Facilitating Conditions, Hedonic Motivations, Performance Expectancy, Effort Expectancy, Social Influence, Price Value, Habit, Trust, and risk.
Fernando et al, 2021	Jordanie	UTAUT	The paper discusses factors affecting the intention to adopt and use smart government services, including relative advantage, trialability, and observability.
Al-shafi, 2013	Qatar	UTAUT	The findings reveal that effort expectancy and social influences determine citizens' behavioural intention towards e-government. Additionally, facilitating conditions and behavioural intention were found to determine citizens' use of e-government services in Qatar.
Anwar, 2021	Iraq	TAM	Increases in perceptions of ease of use an electronic government should lead to increased perceptions of usefulness in an electronic government. It was found that increases in the perceived ease of use of an electronic government will lead to increases behavioural intention to use electronic government. Positive attitude toward an electronic government will lead to increases behavioural intention to use electronic government.
Radwan, 2023	Uae	UTAUT,TAM	The findings revealed that participants greatly appreciate and trust the electronic services provided via smart applications; they particularly appreciate the ease of use and the quality of the information posted. Respondents highlighted some of the factors that motivated their use, such as information disclosure strategy, and interactivity
Almuraqab, 2016	Uae	TAM, UTAUT	This study found that the following factors, namely perceived usefulness, perceived ease of use, social influence, awareness, trust in technology, trust in government, influence social, perceived risk, facilitating conditions are significant for the adoption of smart government by citizens and their determination to accept these services placed on mobile applications.
Abu-shanab, 2015	Jordanie	TAM	This study used the TAM model to investigate factors, i.e. perceived usefulness, social influence, perceived ease of use, perceived responsiveness, perceived compatibility and perceived the cost of services. These five factors are important whereas the perceived cost of services was deemed to be insignificant.
Abdelghaffar, 2014	Egypt	UTAUT, TAM	This research found five factors are significant determinants of m-government adoption, namely compatibility, perceived usefulness, social influence awareness, and face-to-face interactions. They all significantly contribute to predicting the intention of m-government use. Internet experience, perceived ease of use, trust and personal connections insignificantly contribute to predicting the intention to use m-government
Jasimuddin, 2017	Uae	TAM	This study used the TAM model (Perceived Usefulness, Perceived Ease of Use) and extendedintegration with Social influence, facilitating conditions, Perceived cost, Awareness, Trust in government, and Trust in Technology. It found that factors may influence end-user's adoption of smart government in the UAE.
Almarashdeh, 2018	Saudi Arabia	TAM,UTAUT,TRA	This study reported the results of all factors, i.e. perceived usefulness, social influence, cost of service, perceived ease of use and perceived trust. They all wield an important and direct impact on intention to use m-government and indirect impact on actual use behavior.
Archer et al, 2013	India	TAM,DOI,TRA	This study developed a model for integrating TAM, DOI, and TRA theories and concluded that perceived ease of use, perceived security, perceived reliability, perceived empathy, and relative advantage are important factors that influence users' adoption of m-government in India.
Babullah et al, 2015	Saudi Arabia	UTAUT	This study employed a descriptive analysis of 600 participants and showed that performance expectancy, effort expectancy, social influence, facilitating condition, hedonic motivation, and price value influenced the adoption of m-government by Saudi citizens.
Mutambik et al, 2023	Saudi Arabia	UTAUT,TAM	The results showed that information availability has a direct and positive effect on an individual's engagement behaviour, while perceived benefits, responsibility and social norms have an indirect effect on engagement, by positively impacting the attitude of residents. Practical implications, based on these findings, are discussed.
Alderete, 2021	Argentina	UTAUT	A higher levels of ICT use are associated with higher levels of smart-city commitment and that higher awareness of the smart-city concept is related to higher levels of smart-city commitment. Sociodemographic factors such as age and labor condition also explain ICT use.
Alotaibi, 2016	Saudi Arabia	TAM	This research was based on the TAM model with four constructs (Perceived usefulness, Perceived Ease of Use, Attitude towards to use, Perceived mobility, Perceived trustworthiness, Perceived service quality, and User's satisfaction. It found there is a significant relationship between the use of m-government services and all factors.

Source: Authors

This final step has resulted in reducing the total number of references to 39 articles. The next step will be to incorporate these articles into the analysis and discussions. This phase of inclusion, focused on quantitative analysis, aims to explore the main trends from previous studies in order to understand the key factors influencing the adoption of smart city services.

Haut du formulaire

4. RESULTS AND DISCUSSIONS

In this section, we will conduct a quantitative analysis of the general characteristics of the articles selected for the study focusing on articles by author frequency, year of publication, the publication zone, and an analysis by the main factors cited in the selected references and offer an appropriate conceptual model at the end.

4.1. Distribution by Authors

The first feature to analyze in this review concerns publications by author. The goal is to highlight the most active authors in the relevant field. The following figure illustrates the distribution of publications by author.

Figure 2. Distribution of articles by author

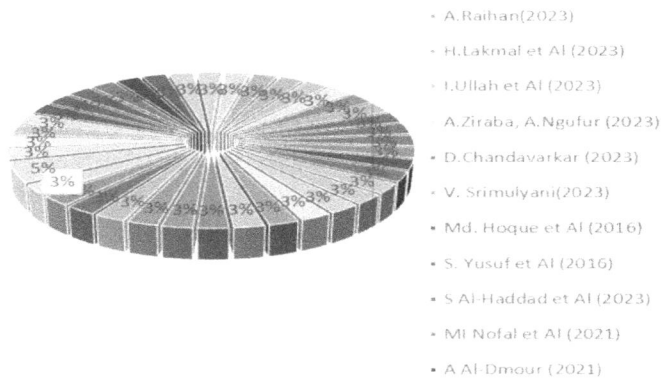

Figure 2: Distribution of articles by author

- A.Raihan(2023)
- H.Lakmal et Al (2023)
- I.Ullah et Al (2023)
- A.Ziraba, A.Ngufur (2023)
- D.Chandavarkar (2023)
- V. Srimulyani(2023)
- Md. Hoque et Al (2016)
- S. Yusuf et Al (2016)
- S Al-Haddad et Al (2023)
- MI Nofal et Al (2021)
- A Al-Dmour (2021)

Source: Authors

Author-based statistics reveal an equitable distribution of authors for the period under study. Indeed, out of a total of 39 authors, each author represents 3% of the references. However, this analysis only considers one author per published article. If we consider the total number of publications over the period, it appears that some authors have contributed to multiple articles, whether as lead author or co-author. This indicates that Erick Fernando has a more pronounced presence in the studied field. To gain a better understanding of authors who have more influence in this field, it would be preferable to refer to statistics on the number of citations per reference.

4.2. Distribution by Year of Publication

To analyze the evolution of publications on the topic of citizen participation in the smart city, it is essential to focus on the trend of references published by year. The results of this analysis are summarized in the figure below.

Figure 3. Distribution by publication year

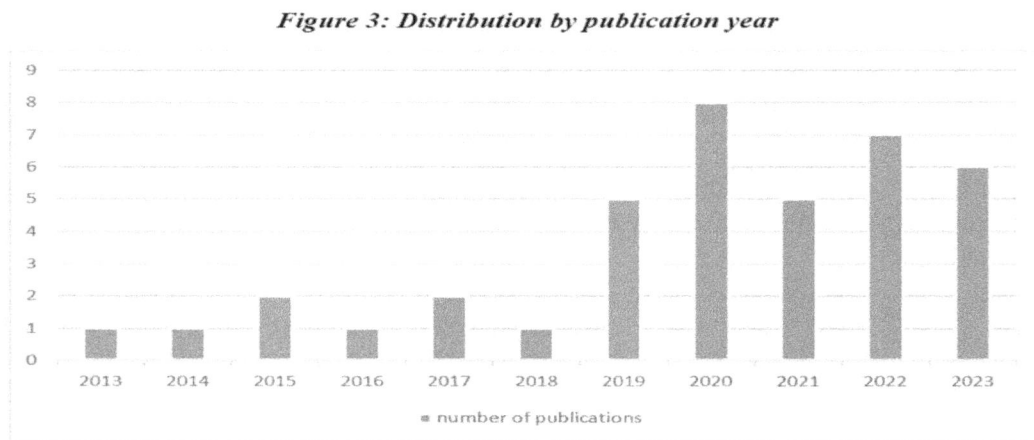

Figure 3: Distribution by publication year

Source: Authors

Publications by year highlight an acceleration of studies over the last few years, compared to the early years of the period studied. Particularly, studies conducted in the last five years (2019, 2020, 2021, 2022, and 2023) together account for nearly two-thirds of the work done during the considered period (67% of publications). Therefore, we can conclude that the trend of publications has increased, underscoring the importance of the subject, especially in developing countries. Moreover, these results highlight the extent of interest in citizen participation in smart cities within the academic community.

4.3. The Distribution of Articles by Geographical Publications

The results regarding the distribution of references by country will be summarized in the figure below.

Figure 4. Distribution by country of study

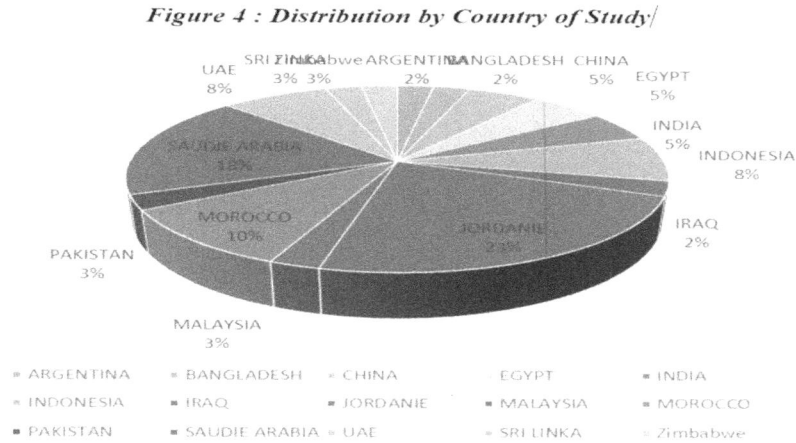

Figure 4 : Distribution by Country of Study

Source: Authors

Regarding the geographical distribution of publications, it was found that Asian countries dominate the sample of publications, with 25 studies out of a total of 39 articles published. For the African continent, only 8 studies were conducted in this context. Finally, we note that in Morocco, only 3 studies were conducted within this framework. This observation leads us to conclude that studies conducted in the African context, particularly in Morocco, are scarce, which constitutes a research gap to be explored to investigate the subject in the Moroccan context.

4.4. The Distribution of Articles by Theories

The results regarding the main theories mobilized in the context of our review will be summarized in the figure below.

Figure 5. Distribution by country of study

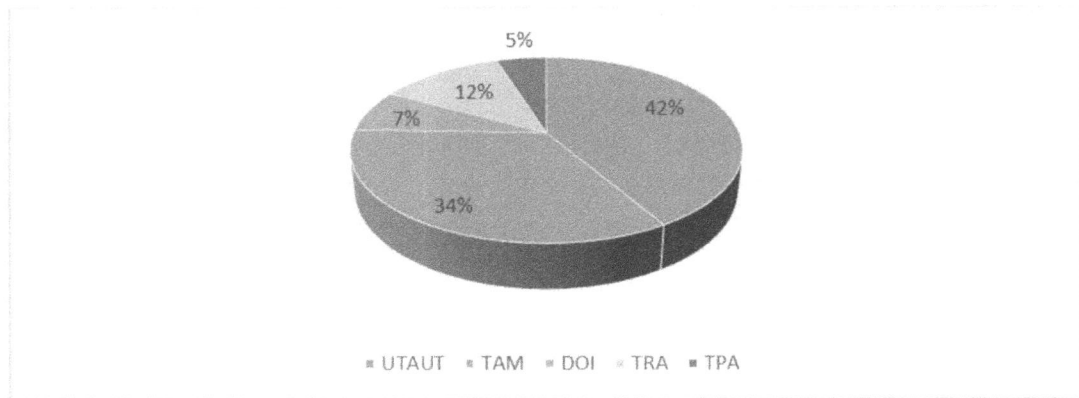

Figure 5 : Distribution by theories

Source: Authors

The UTAUT model, standing for Unified Theory of Acceptance and Use of Technology, has become an essential reference for deciphering the factors that influence technology adoption. Since its inception in the early 2000s by Venkatesh and his colleagues(Venkatesh et al., 2003), this model has garnered significant empirical support, with over 60,000 citations on Google Scholar as of January 2024. Venkatesh and his team designed the UTAUT with the aim of synthesizing the numerous existing models on technological acceptance, including the famous TAM. They extracted and analyzed the key components of 8 major models in this field to develop the UTAUT, which identifies four main factors influencing intention and usage of technologies, as well as four moderators of these influences. This integrated approach and its applicability to various information contexts make UTAUT a valuable tool for our study, allowing us to explore in depth the dynamics between elements such as perceived usefulness, ease of use, and intention to use. Venkatesh and his colleagues also identified four moderating factors - gender, age, experience with technology, and the voluntary or mandatory nature of use that can influence the relationship between the determinants and the intention or usage of technologies. They propose hypotheses on how these moderators might affect the relationships between variables, based on a thorough analysis of the existing literature.

4.5. Research Hypothesis and Conceptual Model

The review of the selected references in our study allowed us to identify the main factors addressed in empirical studies.

The results of this analysis are summarized in the following figure.

Figure 6. Distribution by influencing factor

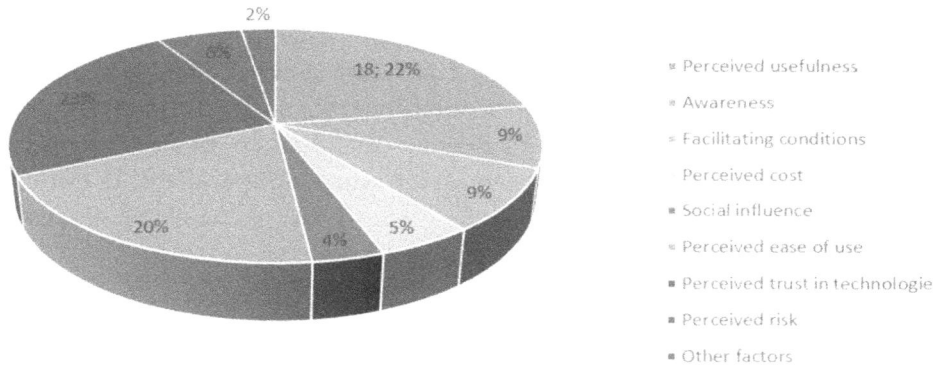

Figure 6 : Distribution by Influencing Factor

Source: Authors

Eight key factors identified play a predominant role in the decision to adopt a technology:

Expected Performance: This factor assesses an individual's belief that using a specific technology will enhance their performance(Chen & Aklikokou, 2020). The stronger this belief, the more likely the individual is to adopt the technology(Fernando et al., 2021). This echoes the notion of perceived usefulness in the TAM and TAM2 models. Taken the above together, this work posits the following hypothesis:

H1: Expected Performance will have a positive influence on behavioral intention to use smart services.

Expected Effort: This refers to the perception of ease or difficulty of using the technology. A technology perceived as complex and difficult to use is less likely to be adopted. This concept is similar to that of ease of use in the TAM and TAM2 models. According to Davis (1989), perceived ease of use is the degree to which a person believes that a particular system is user-friendly. It is the second main concept of TAM, which has been used in previous studies on technology adoption and the adoption of online administration. Researchers (Almuraqab & Jasimuddin, 2017; Alonazi et al., 2020) have found that end-users may prefer to use a service because it is convenient, simple, easy to access, less complicated, and easy to use. Other studies have indicated that perceived ease of use has a significant impact on the adoption of m-government services(Choi & Song, 2020). Therefore, the following hypothesis was developed.

H2: Expected Effort will have a positive influence on behavioral intention to use smart services.

Social Influence: This factor reflects the pressure exerted by an individual's social circle on their choice to use or not use technology. If a person perceives that the use of technology is valued by their social circle, they will be more inclined to adopt it(Ranaweera, 2016). This corresponds to the notion of subjective norm in the TAM2 model. According to (Venkatesh et al., 2003), it is the extent to which an individual believes it is important that others (for example, their family and friends) think they should use the new system. Social influence emerges as a factor in the intention to use government services.

These three factors directly influence a person's intention to use a technology, which in turn determines their actual use. So, based on these findings, the following hypothesis was developed:

H3: Social influence will have a positive influence on the behavioral intention to use smart services.

The fourth factor, **Facilitating Conditions**, though it does not directly affect the intention to use, plays a crucial role in the actual use of technology, such as the availability of documentation or technical support. According to Venkatesh et al. (2003), facilitating conditions are related to the extent to which an individual believes that there is an organizational and technical infrastructure to support the use of the system(Bouhtati, Alla, et al., 2023). Facilitating conditions are also defined as a person's belief in the extent to which a governmental and technical infrastructure is available to facilitate the system(Almuraqab & Jasimuddin, 2017; Babullah et al., 2015). Based on the above discussion, the following hypothesis can be formulated:

H4: Facilitating conditions will affect individual behavior of using smart services.

Perceived risk is defined as a citizen's subjective expectation of suffering a loss in pursuit of a favored outcome(Carter & Bélanger, 2005). Citizens' behavior is strongly influenced by risk perception. End-users are often uncertain about the consequences of a decision or action. Moreover, it has been revealed that end-users tend to minimize risk rather than maximize utility. The end-user's subjective perception of risk can largely explain their behavio(Eid et al., 2021; Zhou et al., 2023). Therefore, we hypothesise:

H5: The perceived risk will have a negative impact on users' intentions to use smart services.

Awareness is the understanding people have of technology and the availability of e-services(Venkatesh et al., 2003). (Abdelghaffar & Magdy, 2012) feel that fostering awareness is the initial stage for users to become cognisant of the government's provision of services over the internet. Several studies have indicated that individuals' knowledge of smart government services and the accessibility of electronic resources is a significant issue. Undoubtedly, a deficiency in understanding has a detrimental effect on citizens' willingness to embrace e-government and m-government services(Almuraqab & Jasimuddin, 2017; Alryalat et al., 2023).

H6: Perceived awareness has a positive and significant influence on citizens' intention to use smart services.

Perceived cost is a crucial consideration. Access devices must be affordable, and the cost of accessing online public services must be low. The cost of mobile services is one of the main factors influencing end-users' intentions to use m-government services(Almuraqab & Jasimuddin, 2017; Eid et al., 2021). Perceived cost has a negative effect on users' intentions to adopt m-government services. In the context of citizen behavior, price is considered a very important factor (Oumlil & Aderkaoui, 2020). This work posits the following hypothesis:

H7: The perceived cost will have a negative impact on users' intentions to use smart services.

Perceived trust in technology is consistently recognized as a key factor in the adoption of m-services. This type of trust is often referred to as institutional trust. According to(McKnight et al., 2002), it refers to an individual's perceptions of the institutional environment, which contains the structures and principles that make the environment safe. In this regard, (Carter & Bélanger, 2005) emphasize that citizens must have trust in enabling technologies. Furthermore, (Pavlou & Gefen, 2004)suggest that institution-based trust is a very critical form of trust in objective financial environments where the sense of a community with shared values is important(Chen & Aklikokou, 2020; Tavitiyaman et al., 2021). As a result, rooted in UTAUT, this study hypothesizes:

H8: Perceived trust in technology will have a positive impact on users' intents to use smart services.
    Based on the above discussion, a modified UTAUT modelis proposed which is depicted in figure 7.

Figure 7. Adapted conceptual model

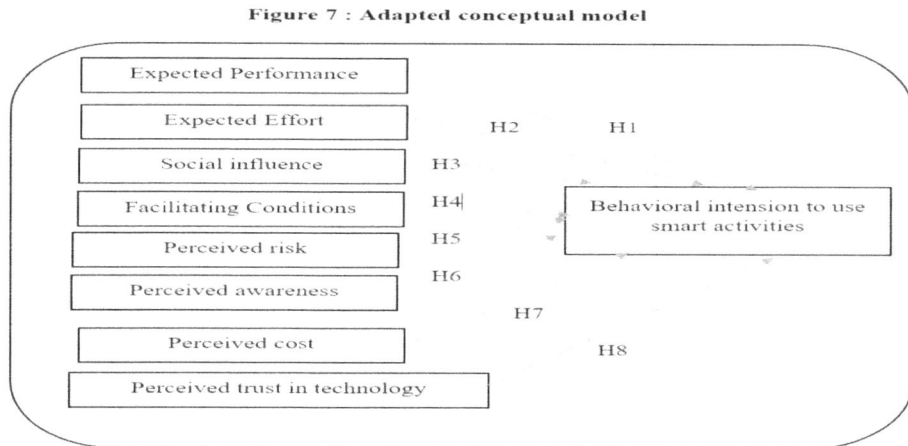

Figure 7 : Adapted conceptual model

Source : Authors

Source: Authors

The present study aims to expand the UTAUT model by integrating expected performance, perceived cost, trust in technology, expected effort, social influence, awareness, facilitating conditions, and perceived risk as independent variables that influence the behavioral intention to use smart services (dependent variable). However, it is necessary to evolve it to take into account primarily the moderating factors and confront it with the reality of the field within the framework of an empirical study in order to get an empirical model from it.

In summary, analyzing the key features of our sample comprised of 39 articles over a 10-year period has allowed us to draw several conclusions, notably about the trends in publications over time, the theories mobilized within the framework of our literature review, the different geographical areas that have been covered, The main factors influencing a citizen's intention to use smart activities are identified and a conceptual model is adapted based on the UTAUT paradigm.

4.6. Discussions

This article brings a new perspective on citizen engagement in the context of smart cities in Morocco. It highlights the importance of examining factors influencing active citizen participation in these initiatives, in an environment where infrastructure and technological conditions differ significantly from those in developed countries. The study also aims to enlighten local decision-makers, providing them with crucial data to develop effective policies and strategies in favor of citizen engagement in the digital era(Alla et al., 2022).

In terms of practical implicaons, local governments should prioritise the promotion of the proactive utilisation of Information and Communication Technology (ICT) and increasing public knowledge of the smart city idea. Advancing towards smart cities requires closing the gap in ICT use known as the digital divide. Mere implementation of local policies to ensure Wi-Fi and internet access for everybody is inadequate to enhance the utilisation of ICT. Moreover, implementing a plan to enhance the utilisation of Information and Communication Technology (ICT) would be advantageous in promoting smart city endeavours or undertakings.

Technological trends in smart cities, such as high-speed mobile connectivity, open data, urban interfaces, and cloud computing, among others, are advancing rapidly. ICT plays a key role in smart cities by connecting infrastructure, government, and citizens. (Alderete, 2021) emphasized that a smart city relies on "utilizing" the benefits offered by information and communication technologies.

ICT enables the provision of online public services, facilitates easy access to public information, and allows individuals to collaborate in order to exchange their interests and concerns. Moreover, the utilisation of ICT can enhance and encourage decision-making and citizen engagement in public affairs.

Trust in technology and trust in government are crucial elements in technology adoption. However, the latest technologies and devices are exposed to cybercrime, viruses, and malware, which prompts people to think twice before accessing smart applications for transactions. Additionally, people are concerned about the privacy of their data, which has been observed and supported by previous research and needs to be tested in the context of smart services in Morocco.

This conceptual essay aims to identify the factors that influence moroccan citizens in their decision-making process regarding the use or intention to use services offered by smart cities. This allows us to deduce a set of hypotheses to be tested in a future project.

5. CONCLUSION AND PERSPECTIVES

This systematic exploration of research has enlightened us on the fundamental empirical studies conducted between 2013 and 2023, which have scrutinized the relevant questions surrounding the adoption of smart governance by citizens and their relationship with people's intentions to accept smart city services. Relying on the PRISMA method, we selected 39 key references. Our quantitative analysis of these articles revealed salient aspects such as the authors, the years of publication, the theories mobilized, the countries where these studies were conducted, and the factors influencing a citizen's decision towards adopting smart services. This analysis not only allowed us to answer our initial questions but also highlighted avenues for further research.

Furthermore, our research study provides several significant contributions. First, the present systematic review helps fill the scarcity of studies in this genre, particularly in identifying determinants of smart services adoption to avoid failures in smart projects implementation. Similarly, our systematic review offers several advantages, including the ability to provide a flexible reference base that can be easily updated and queried. Additionally, quantitative analysis serves as a tool to accurately capture publication trends in the smart city domain while focusing on certain characteristics of previous empirical studies such as geographical distribution and publication years. The in-depth study of the literature highlighted the widespread adoption of the UTAUT model in the contexts of developing countries. Our analysis led to the formulation of eight essential propositions, which reveal the determining factors encouraging the adoption of smart city services by users in Morocco.

However, this present systematic review has some limitations. Firstly, despite the use of precise inclusion and exclusion criteria, it is possible that relevant studies may not have been identified or included, which could introduce bias if some relevant studies are missed. Secondly, the study duration was limited to the last decade, which may potentially lead to the exclusion of certain studies. Finally, we did not conduct a qualitative analysis of the selected references. Consequently, this may limit the overall understanding of the phenomenon under study and the ability to explore the subjective experiences of individuals involved in smart activities. In future studies, it would be important to consider a sufficiently long period to cover all studies addressing the topic of smart cities and citizen engagement. By choosing an adequately long search period, future studies can benefit from a more comprehensive and updated overview of the field.

Our research brings several key contributions. Firstly, this systematic review addresses the lack of studies, especially concerning the analysis of factors explaining citizens' engagement in electronic services in countries with similar economic, socio-cultural, and technological characteristics to Morocco. It also proposes a modifiable reference base, a major asset, allowing for easy updates and inquiries. From a theoretical perspective, this study aims to enhance models and theories on technology acceptance and use, especially the UTAUT model and related frameworks. Managerially, it highlights the need to understand and consider factors influencing citizens' usage and behavioral intentions across various sectors.

Firstly, digital service providers should focus on performance enhancement to meet user expectations and deliver optimal e-services, emphasizing user-friendly, intuitive, and accessible applications. Social influence can be leveraged through positive word-of-mouth and user testimonials.

Additionally, smart service providers might adopt pricing strategies aligned with their target audience's financial concerns and expectations. Establishing trust in technology, particularly through secure e-transactions, is also deemed crucial.

Nevertheless, our review has some limitations. Despite our rigorous inclusion and exclusion criteria, relevant studies may have been omitted, potentially introducing bias. The temporal coverage of our study, limited to the last decade, may also exclude significant research. Furthermore, the absence of qualitative analysis of the selected references may restrict our overall understanding of the subject under study and does not allow for exploration of the subjective experiences of individuals who have used smart activities.

This research, which is still in its early stages, presents a theoretical model for analysing the determinants of acceptance and usage of intelligent services in Morocco. The proposed model is based on existing approaches. The objective is to develop a more integrative approach that would relate to the Moroccan setting. We intend to conduct an exploratory-explanatory investigation based on the proposed model. Data will be collected by relying on observations, interviews, and questionnaires. The future research model must also incorporate the four moderators (gender, age, experience, and voluntariness) included in the original UTAUT model. The collected data will be analysed and presented in the form of numbers, graphs, and descriptive statements illustrating the relationships between the different variables of the proposed model.

REFERENCES

Abdelghaffar, H., & Magdy, Y. (2012). The adoption of mobile government services in developing countries : The case of Egypt. *International Journal of Information and* Communication *Technology Research, 2*(4). https://www.researchgate.net/profile/Hany-Abdelghaffar/publication/268393482_The_Adoption_of_Mobile_Government_Services_in_Developing_Countries_The_Case_of_Egypt/links/5da6e6b84585159bc3d0d031/The-Adoption-of-Mobile-Government-Services-in-Developing-Countries-The-Case-of-Egypt.pdf

Albino, V., Berardi, U., & Dangelico, R. M. (2015). Smart Cities : Definitions, Dimensions, Performance, and Initiatives. *Journal of Urban Technology*, 22(1), 3–21. 10.1080/10630732.2014.942092

Alderete, M. V. (2021). Determinants of smart city commitment among citizens from a middle city in Argentina. *Smart Cities*, 4(3), 1113–1129. 10.3390/smartcities4030059

Alipour, M., Salim, H., Stewart, R. A., & Sahin, O. (2020). Predictors, taxonomy of predictors, and correlations of predictors with the decision behaviour of residential solar photovoltaics adoption : A review. *Renewable & Sustainable Energy Reviews*, 123, 109749. 10.1016/j.rser.2020.109749

Alla, L., Bentalha, B., & Elyoussfi, A. (2023). Intelligence territoriale et positionnement stratégique des régions au Maroc : Le cas de la région de Fès Meknes en perspective. *Le concept de l'intéligence en sciences juridiques, économiques et sociales*, 215-237.

Alla, L., Kamal, M., & Bouhtati, N. (2022). Big data et efficacité marketing des entreprises touristiques : Une revue de littérature. *Alternatives Managériales Economiques, 4*, 39-58. 10.48374/IMIST.PRSM/ame-v1i0.36928

Almuraqab, N. A. S., & Jasimuddin, S. M. (2017). Factors that Influence End-Users' Adoption of Smart Government Services in the UAE : A Conceptual Framework. *Electronic Journal of Information Systems Evaluation*, 20(1), 11–23.

AlNuaimi, M., Shaalan, K., Alnuaimi, M., & Alnuaimi, K. (2011). Barriers to electronic government citizens' adoption : A case of municipal sector in the emirate of abu dhabi. *2011 Developments in E-systems Engineering*, 398-403. https://ieeexplore.ieee.org/abstract/document/6150013/

Alonazi, M., Beloff, N., & White, M. (2020). Perceptions Towards the Adoption and Utilization of M-Government Services : A Study from the Citizens' Perspective in Saudi Arabia. In Ziemba, E. (Ed.), *Information Technology for Management : Current Research and Future Directions* (Vol. 380, pp. 3–26). Springer International Publishing. 10.1007/978-3-030-43353-6_1

Alryalat, M., Alryalat, H., Alhamzi, K., & Hewahi, N. (2023). E-Government Services Adoption Assessment From the Citizen Perspective in Jordan. [IJEGR]. *International Journal of Electronic Government Research*, 19(1), 1–17. 10.4018/IJEGR.322440

Anthopoulos, L. G. (2017). *Understanding Smart Cities : A Tool for Smart Government or an Industrial Trick?* (Vol. 22). Springer International Publishing. 10.1007/978-3-319-57015-0

Anthopoulos, L. G., Pourzolfaghar, Z., Lemmer, K., Siebenlist, T., Niehaves, B., & Nikolaou, I. (2022). Smart cities as hubs : Connect, collect and control city flows. *Cities (London, England)*, 125, 103660. 10.1016/j.cities.2022.103660

Babullah, A., Dwivedi, Y., & Williams, M. (2015). *Saudi citizens' perceptions on mobile government (mGov) adoption factors.* AISEL. https://aisel.aisnet.org/ukais2015/8/

Bakici, T., Almirall, E., & Wareham, J. (2013). A smart city initiative : The case of Barcelona. *Journal of the Knowledge Economy*, 4(2), 135–148. 10.1007/s13132-012-0084-9

Belanger, F., Hiller, J. S., & Smith, W. J. (2002). Trustworthiness in electronic commerce : The role of privacy, security, and site attributes. *The Journal of Strategic Information Systems*, 11(3-4), 245–270. 10.1016/S0963-8687(02)00018-5

Bernardin, S., & Jeannot, G. (2019). La ville intelligente sans les villes? Interopérabilité, ouvertures et maîtrise des données publiques au sein des administrations municipales. *Reseaux (London)*, 6, 9–37.

Berntzen, L., & Johannessen, M. R. (2016). The Role of Citizen Participation in Municipal Smart City Projects : Lessons Learned from Norway. In Gil-Garcia, J. R., Pardo, T. A., & Nam, T. (Eds.), *Smarter as the New Urban Agenda* (Vol. 11, pp. 299–314). Springer International Publishing. 10.1007/978-3-319-17620-8_16

Bibri, S. E. (2018). The IoT for smart sustainable cities of the future : An analytical framework for sensor-based big data applications for environmental sustainability. *Sustainable Cities and Society*, 38, 230–253. 10.1016/j.scs.2017.12.034

Bibri, S. E., Alexandre, A., Sharifi, A., & Krogstie, J. (2023). Environmentally sustainable smart cities and their converging AI, IoT, and big data technologies and solutions : An integrated approach to an extensive literature review. *Energy Informatics*, 6(1), 9. 10.1186/s42162-023-00259-237032812

Bouhtati, N., Alla, L., & Bentalha, B. (2023). Marketing Big Data Analytics and Customer Relationship Management : A Fuzzy Approach. In *Integrating Intelligence and Sustainability in Supply Chains* (p. 75-86). IGI Global. https://www.igi-global.com/chapter/marketing-big-data-analytics-and-customer -relationship-management/331980

Bouhtati, N., Kamal, M., & Alla, L. (2023). Big Data and the Effectiveness of Tourism Marketing : A Prospective Review of the Literature. In Farhaoui, Y., Rocha, A., Brahmia, Z., & Bhushab, B. (Eds.), *Artificial Intelligence and Smart Environment* (pp. 287–292). Springer International Publishing., 10.1007/978-3-031-26254-8_40

Braga, S., Zacarias, S. L., & Champoski, L. H. (2022). *APLICACIONES MÓVILES Y GOBERNANZA DIGITAL EN BRASIL: ESTUDIO DE CASO DEL "PROYECTO PIÁ", DEL ESTADO DE PARANÁ. 38.*

Carter, L., & Bélanger, F. (2005). The utilization of e-government services : Citizen trust, innovation and acceptance factors*. *Information Systems Journal*, 15(1), 5–25. 10.1111/j.1365-2575.2005.00183.x

Chen, L., & Aklikokou, A. K. (2020). Determinants of E-government Adoption : Testing the Mediating Effects of Perceived Usefulness and Perceived Ease of Use. *International Journal of Public Administration*, 43(10), 850–865. 10.1080/01900692.2019.1660989

Choi, J.-C., & Song, C. (2020). Factors explaining why some citizens engage in E-participation, while others do not. *Government Information Quarterly*, 37(4), 101524. 10.1016/j.giq.2020.101524

Cocchia, A. (2014a). Smart and Digital City : A Systematic Literature Review. In Dameri, R. P., & Rosenthal-Sabroux, C. (Eds.), *Smart City* (pp. 13–43). Springer International Publishing. 10.1007/978-3-319-06160-3_2

Dameri, R. P. (2013). Searching for smart city definition : A comprehensive proposal. *International Journal of Computers and Technology*, 11(5), 2544–2551. 10.24297/ijct.v11i5.1142

Davis, F. D. (1989). Perceived Usefulness, Perceived Ease of Use, and User Acceptance of Information Technology. *Management Information Systems Quarterly*, 13(3), 319. 10.2307/249008

Del-Real, C., Ward, C., & Sartipi, M. (2023). What do people want in a smart city? Exploring the stakeholders' opinions, priorities and perceived barriers in a medium-sized city in the United States. *International Journal of Urban Sciences, 27*(sup1), 50-74. 10.1080/12265934.2021.1968939

Diallo, M., Fall, A. K., Diallo, I., Diédhiou, I., Ba, P. S., Diagne, M., Ndiaye, B., Ndiaye, A. R., Niang, A., & Gning, S. B. (2010). Dermatomyosites et polymyosites : 21 cas au Sénégal. *Médecine Tropicale*, 70(2), 166.20486354

Eid, R., Selim, H., & El-Kassrawy, Y. (2021). Understanding citizen intention to use m-government services : An empirical study in the UAE. *Transforming Government: People. Process and Policy*, 15(4), 463–482.

El Assal, Z., & Rochdane, H. (2023). L'intérêt des citoyens de Casablanca envers l'utilisation des énergies renouvelables dans le contexte de la ville intelligente. *SHS Web of Conferences, 175*, 01036. https://www.shs-conferences.org/articles/shsconf/abs/2023/24/shsconf_mh2s2023_01036/shsconf_mh2s2023_01036.html

El Jaouhari, S. & Lhoussaine, A. (2021). Approche participative en tourisme et gouvernance territoriale, quel apport pour le développement territorial? *Alternatives Managériales Economiques*, 3(2), 257–277.

Fernando, E., Ikhsan, R. B., Condrobimo, A. R., Daniel, H., & Halim, S. K. (2021). Concept model : Analysis of factors on intention and decisions on the use of smart tourism applications. *2021 International Conference on Information Management and Technology (ICIMTech), 1*, 154-158. https://ieeexplore.ieee.org/abstract/document/9534933/

Giffinger, R. (2015). Smart City Concepts : Chances and Risks of Energy Efficient Urban Development. In Helfert, M., Krempels, K.-H., Klein, C., Donellan, B., & Guiskhin, O. (Eds.), *Smart Cities, Green Technologies, and Intelligent Transport Systems* (Vol. 579, pp. 3–16). Springer International Publishing. 10.1007/978-3-319-27753-0_1

Giffinger, R., & Haindlmaier, G. (2018). Benchmarking the Smart City : A Sound Tool for Policy-Making? *Scienze Regionali*, 1, 115–122. 10.14650/88820

Haj, D. A. E. (2020). La ville marocaine et la nécessité d'une transformation à l'ère de la Smart City : Analyse des cas des villes de Tanger, Casablanca et Marrakech. *Geopolitics and Geostrategic Intelligence, 3*(2), Article 2.

Hollands, R. G. (2020). Will the real smart city please stand up?: Intelligent, progressive or entrepreneurial? In *The Routledge companion to smart cities* (pp. 179–199). Routledge. https://www.taylorfrancis.com/chapters/edit/10.4324/9781315178387-13/real-smart-city-please-stand-robert-hollands10.4324/9781315178387-13

Irvin, R. A., & Stansbury, J. (2004). Citizen Participation in Decision Making : Is It Worth the Effort? *Public Administration Review*, 64(1), 55–65. 10.1111/j.1540-6210.2004.00346.x

Jebaraj, L., Khang, A., Chandrasekar, V., Pravin, A. R., & Sriram, K. (2023). Smart City : Concepts, Models, Technologies and Applications. In *Smart Cities* (p. 1-20). CRC Press. https://www.taylorfrancis.com/chapters/edit/10.1201/9781003376064-1/smart-city-concepts-models-technologies-applications-luke-jebaraj-alex-khang-vadivelraju-chandrasekar-antony-richard-pravin-kumar-sriram

Jiang, H., Geertman, S., & Witte, P. (2023). The contextualization of smart city technologies : An international comparison. *Journal of Urban Management*, 12(1), 33–43. 10.1016/j.jum.2022.09.001

Junaidi, A., Basrowi, B., Sabtohadi, J., Wibowo, A., Wibowo, S., Asgar, A., Pramono, E., & Yenti, E. (2024). The role of public administration and social media educational socialization in influencing public satisfaction on population services : The mediating role of population literacy awareness. *International Journal of Data and Network Science*, 8(1), 345–356. 10.5267/j.ijdns.2023.9.019

Kandt, J., & Batty, M. (2021). Smart cities, big data and urban policy : Towards urban analytics for the long run. *Cities (London, England)*, 109, 102992. 10.1016/j.cities.2020.102992

Koz\lowski, W., & Suwar, K. (2021). *Smart city : Definitions, dimensions, and initiatives*. UM. https://www.um.edu.mt/library/oar/handle/123456789/105179

Kumar, A. (2022). Sustainable smart cities. In Kumar, A. (Ed.), *Ecosystem-Based Adaptation* (pp. 325–416). Elsevier. 10.1016/B978-0-12-815025-2.00007-1

Lytras, M. D., & Visvizi, A. (2018). Who uses smart city services and what to make of it : Toward interdisciplinary smart cities research. *Sustainability (Basel)*, 10(6), 1998. 10.3390/su10061998

McKnight, D. H., Choudhury, V., & Kacmar, C. (2002). Developing and Validating Trust Measures for e-Commerce : An Integrative Typology. *Information Systems Research*, 13(3), 334–359. 10.1287/isre.13.3.334.81

Nassereddine, M., & Khang, A. (2024). Applications of Internet of Things (IoT) in smart cities. In *Advanced IoT Technologies and Applications in the Industry 4.0 Digital Economy* (pp. 109–136). CRC Press. https://www.taylorfrancis.com/chapters/edit/10.1201/9781003434269-6/applications-internet-things-iot-smart-cities-mohamed-nassereddine-alex-khang10.1201/9781003434269-6

Nguyen, C. T.-L., Bleus, H., Van Bockhaven, J., Crutzen, N., & Basile, C. (2018). *Smart City-Le Guide Pratique-Tome 2-Comment Rendre le Citoyen Acteur de son Territoire?* Bitstream. https://orbi.uliege.be/bitstream/2268/229265/1/smart-city-le-guide-pratique-tome-2.pdf

Oukarfi, S., & Bercheq, A. (2020a). Les déterminants socioéconomiques et géographiques de l'achat en ligne au Maroc. *Revue d'Economie Industrielle*, 171(3), 139–182. 10.4000/rei.9308

Oukarfi, S., & Bercheq, A. (2020b). Les déterminants socioéconomiques et géographiques de l'achat en ligne au Maroc. *Revue d'Economie Industrielle*, 139–182. 10.4000/rei.9308

Oumlil, R., & Aderkaoui, A. (2020). Technology Acceptance, a relevant step to digitalize Moroccan human development public organizations. *Revue Management & Innovation*, 20(1), 119–136. 10.3917/rmi.201.0119

Paul, J., & Criado, A. R. (2020). The art of writing literature review : What do we know and what do we need to know? *International Business Review*, 29(4), 101717. 10.1016/j.ibusrev.2020.101717

Pavlou, P. A., & Gefen, D. (2004). Building Effective Online Marketplaces with Institution-Based Trust. *Information Systems Research*, 15(1), 37–59. 10.1287/isre.1040.0015

Perez-Vega, R., Hopkinson, P., Singhal, A., & Mariani, M. M. (2022). From CRM to social CRM : A bibliometric review and research agenda for consumer research. *Journal of Business Research*, 151, 1–16. 10.1016/j.jbusres.2022.06.028

Ranaweera, H. M. B. P. (2016). Perspective of trust towards e-government initiatives in Sri Lanka. *SpringerPlus*, 5(1), 22. 10.1186/s40064-015-1650-y26759761

Rehman, M., & Esichaikul, V. (2011). Factors influencing the adoption of e-government in Pakistan. *2011 International Conference on E-Business and E-Government (ICEE)*, (pp. 1-4). IEEE. https://ieeexplore.ieee.org/abstract/document/5887093/

Rogers Everett, M. (1995). *Diffusion of innovations*.

Savastano, M., Suciu, M.-C., Gorelova, I., & Stativă, G.-A. (2023). How smart is mobility in smart cities? An analysis of citizens' value perceptions through ICT applications. *Cities (London, England)*, 132, 104071. 10.1016/j.cities.2022.104071

Sebei, H., Hadj Taieb, M. A., & Ben Aouicha, M. (2018). Review of social media analytics process and Big Data pipeline. *Social Network Analysis and Mining*, 8(1), 30. 10.1007/s13278-018-0507-0

Simonofski, A., Vallé, T., Serral, E., & Wautelet, Y. (2021). Investigating context factors in citizen participation strategies : A comparative analysis of Swedish and Belgian smart cities. *International Journal of Information Management*, 56, 102011. 10.1016/j.ijinfomgt.2019.09.007

Suryawan, I. W. K., & Lee, C.-H. (2023). Citizens' willingness to pay for adaptive municipal solid waste management services in Jakarta, Indonesia. *Sustainable Cities and Society*, 97, 104765. 10.1016/j.scs.2023.104765

Syed, A. S., Sierra-Sosa, D., Kumar, A., & Elmaghraby, A. (2021). IoT in smart cities : A survey of technologies, practices and challenges. *Smart Cities*, 4(2), 429–475. 10.3390/smartcities4020024

Tavitiyaman, P., Qu, H., Tsang, W. L., & Lam, C. R. (2021). The influence of smart tourism applications on perceived destination image and behavioral intention : The moderating role of information search behavior. *Journal of Hospitality and Tourism Management*, 46, 476–487. 10.1016/j.jhtm.2021.02.003

Venkatesh, V., Morris, M. G., Davis, G. B., & Davis, F. D. (2003). User acceptance of information technology : Toward a unified view. *Management Information Systems Quarterly*, 27(3), 425–478. 10.2307/30036540

Zhao, D., & Strotmann, A. (2015). *Analysis and visualization of citation networks*. Morgan & Claypool Publishers. 10.1007/978-3-031-02291-3

Zhou, P., Zhao, S., Ma, Y., Liang, C., & Zhu, J. (2023). What influences user participation in an online health community? The stimulus-organism-response model perspective. *Aslib Journal of Information Management*, 75(2), 364–389. 10.1108/AJIM-12-2021-0383

Section 2
Integrating AI and Digital Into Marketing Strategies

Chapter 7
Towards Agile Marketing:
Transforming Strategies for the Digital Era

Busra Ozdenizci Kose
http://orcid.org/0000-0002-8414-5252
Gebze Technical University, Turkey

ABSTRACT

Agile marketing represents a paradigm shift in strategic marketing, emphasizing the principles of flexibility, speed, and customer-centricity. Originating from software development methodologies that value adaptability and iterative progress, agile practices have been effectively translated into the marketing domain to address the dynamic and fast-paced nature of contemporary markets. This approach focuses on continuous improvement, cross-functional collaboration, and responsiveness to consumer needs and market trends. By integrating diverse methodologies such as Scrum and Kanban, marketing teams enhance their ability to rapidly adapt strategies, execute innovative campaigns, and leverage real-time feedback, thereby ensuring a competitive edge in a constantly evolving business landscape. This chapter aims to explore the transformative potential of Agile Marketing and offers insights into how Agile practices can reshape marketing strategies to be more adaptive, efficient, and aligned with customer expectations, empowering marketers to succeed in today's digital era.

1. INTRODUCTION

Agile is a project management and software development methodology that originated in response to the limitations of traditional, plan-driven approaches, such as the Waterfall model. It was formalized in 2001 with the creation of the Agile Manifesto by a group of software developers who emphasize flexibility, collaboration, and customer satisfaction over rigid planning and execution (Flewelling, 2018; Atawneh, 2019). Unlike the linear, sequential approach of Waterfall, Agile promotes adaptive planning, evolutionary development, early delivery, and continual improvement, ensuring that processes and products remain responsive to changing requirements and environments. By encouraging cross-functional teamwork and organizing work into short, iterative cycles known as sprints, Agile methodologies facilitate rapid delivery of high-quality products and enable teams to quickly adapt to change. This makes Agile

DOI: 10.4018/979-8-3693-3172-9.ch007

especially effective in dynamic environments where project requirements and goals are likely to evolve (Kalenda et al., 2018; Duka, 2013; Ramos & Pavhlichenko, 2022).

The formal advent of Agile methodologies occurred in February 2001 when 17 software developers convened at a ski resort in Snowbird, Utah. This meeting aimed at discussing lightweight development methods and led to the creation of the "Manifesto for Agile Software Development", known as the Agile Manifesto (Winter & Winter, 2015; Patary, 2019; Hohl et al., 2018). This document outlined four core values and twelve principles that suggest being flexible, focusing on people, working closely with customers, and being open to changes is better than sticking strictly to detailed plans, lots of paperwork, formal agreements, and not changing course. This document marked the start of using Agile methods in software development and started to change how projects are managed to be more adaptable and people-friendly.

Following the introduction of the Agile Manifesto, various methodologies inspired by its core values started to emerge and become popular. Scrum, Extreme Programming (XP), Lean Software Development, Kanban, and Feature-Driven Development (FDD) are among the most notable (Merzouk et al. 2018; Matharu et al., 2015). Each method provides a distinct approach to implement the Agile values and principles in practical, real-world settings. These methodologies share a common foundation in iterative development, team collaboration, and a focus on delivering value to customers, but differ in their specific practices, roles, and terminologies.

Agile has evolved beyond its origins as a software development methodology to become a comprehensive philosophy that shapes the way organizations operate and thrive in a dynamic, rapidly changing environment (Highsmith, 2002; Kelly, 2008; Ramos & Pavhlichenko, 2022). It's a philosophy that has seen widespread adoption across various industries that continually refines and expands the set of tools, frameworks, and best practices for implementing Agile principles. At the heart of this evolution is the Agile mindset which is a critical component for effectively leveraging Agile methodologies. This mindset is about following specific practices or guidelines; and also embodies a way of thinking characterized by flexibility, continuous improvement, and a focus on delivering value to customers.

Today, there is a noticeable shift towards the adoption of Agile in marketing, which reflects a transformative approach to planning and executing marketing strategies (Perkin, 2023; Thümler, 2023). This trend signifies how marketing teams are increasingly embracing the principles of rapid iteration, customer-centric planning, and responsiveness to market changes. By integrating Agile mindset, -such as short, focused work cycles and data-driven decision-making- marketing departments can swiftly adjust their strategies, experiment with innovative ideas, and improve their campaigns based on real-time feedback (Barbosa et al., 2022; Ewel, 2020; Gera et al., 2019). Agile adoption enhances the agility and effectiveness of marketing efforts and also cultivates a culture of collaboration and ongoing improvement. Consequently, organizations are better positioned to meet the evolving demands of their customers and maintain a competitive edge in the dynamic business landscape.

This chapter explores the transformative potential of Agile Marketing, a strategic approach that emphasizes flexibility, speed, and customer-centricity in marketing operations. It focuses on the core values and principles of Agile, such as iterative development, continuous improvement, and cross-functional collaboration, which have been instrumental in reshaping marketing strategies to be more adaptive and responsive. By integrating Agile practices, including frameworks like Scrum and Kanban, marketing teams can significantly enhance their flexibility and responsiveness to rapidly changing market conditions and consumer preferences. This chapter offers valuable insights into how Agile methodologies, originally devised for the software industry, can be effectively adapted for the marketing domain. This chapter is designed to empower researchers, practitioners, and marketers by providing them with the insights and methodologies needed to excel within the dynamic field of marketing.

2. TOWARDS AGILE MARKETING

Agile marketing is a strategic approach that applies the principles of Agile development to the marketing domain, emphasizing speed, flexibility, and customer focus (Yusoff et al., 2019; Moi et al., 2018; Ewel, 2020). Instead of relying on long-term plans and big campaigns, it aims to improve the responsiveness of marketing teams to changes in consumer preferences and market dynamics. Agile marketing adopts practices such as iterative planning, frequent adaptation, and collaborative team efforts to execute campaigns that can quickly pivot based on real-time feedback and insights (Vassileva, 2017; Hoogveld & Koster, 2016; Katare 2022). This method allows for more transparent, measurable, and efficient marketing efforts, and enables teams to achieve better results and alignment with customer needs.

The Agile Marketing Manifesto (https://agilemarketingmanifesto.org) was introduced in 2012. This marked a pivotal moment in adapting Agile principles specifically for the marketing industry. It aims to improve how marketing teams respond to change, collaborate, and ultimately serve their customers in a rapidly evolving digital landscape. While it shares the core spirit of the original Agile Manifesto, the Agile Marketing Manifesto focuses on five essential values as shown in Figure 1.

Figure 1. Core values of agile marketing

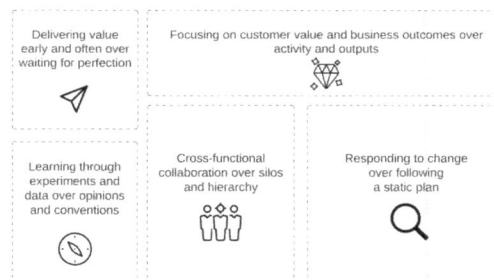

The Agile Marketing Manifesto (2012) tailored to address the unique challenges and opportunities in the marketing field. While it draws inspiration from the original Agile Manifesto for software development, it specifically emphasizes the principles that foster a more adaptive and customer-centric marketing approach. It was created as a response to the need for marketing teams to be more flexible, data-driven, and iterative in their work, which highlights the rapidly changing landscape of digital marketing and consumer engagement.

2.1 Understanding Core Values of Agile Marketing

In accordance with the Agile Marketing Manifesto (2012), the values of Agile marketing represent a shift in focus from traditional marketing practices to more dynamic and responsive approaches. These values guide how marketing teams prioritize tasks, make decisions, and measure success:

(1) *Focusing on customer value and business outcomes over activity and outputs:* This value focuses on delivering significant benefits to customers and achieving meaningful business outcomes, rather than completing tasks or generating a high volume of content and campaigns. Agile marketing teams are dedicated to ensuring their actions translate into real value for customers and measurable results for the business. By prioritizing the needs of customers and the objectives of the business, marketing efforts become more targeted and relevant, and create the 'right things' rather than just 'more things.' This approach helps avoid the common pitfall of engaging in marketing activities for their own sake. With a commitment to this value, teams are guided to concentrate on initiatives that offer the greatest value to customers, which can positively influence the business in the long run.

(2) *Delivering value early and often over waiting for perfection:* This value emphasizes delivering customer value early and often, moving away from the quest for perfection to adopt a rapid and iterative approach in marketing. Agile marketing supports launching campaigns and projects in their simplest form and refining them based on feedback and data. This method accelerates the learning process, identifying what works and quickly adjusting what does not, thereby saving time and resources on strategies that do not yield results. Focusing on early delivery opens up opportunities to learn from customers, continually improving and adding value based on these insights. Waiting for perfection can lead to missed learning opportunities, resulting in long production cycles and a big-bang approach that may not meet customer needs. Instead, prioritizing frequent and incremental value delivery enables a more accurate meeting of customer needs and enhances the effectiveness of marketing efforts over time.

(3) *Learning through experiments and data over opinions and conventions:* This value places a strong emphasis on data-driven decision-making and continuous experimentation over following traditional methods or relying on subjective opinions. In Agile marketing, the focus is on conducting experiments and using the resulting data to make informed decisions. It cultivates a culture of innovation and learning, where decisions are grounded in evidence and actual performance metrics, not just assumptions or the traditional way of doing things. Engaging in this cycle of experimentation, measurement, and learning -rather than adhering to the opinion of the highest paid person in the room (HIPPO) or blindly following established conventions- ensures that marketing efforts are always aligned with what works best. By validating learnings through a continuous implement-measure-learn feedback loop, this value guides teams towards more effective and impactful marketing strategies, and ensures resources are used efficiently to engage audiences meaningfully.

(4) *Cross-functional collaboration over silos and hierarchies:* This core value focuses on the superiority of cross-functional collaboration, centered on customer needs, over working in isolated silos and strictly adhering to hierarchical decision-making. Agile marketing highlights the contributions from team members across various functions and levels, and fosters close cooperation as a cohesive unit. Such collaboration breaks down the barriers that typically separate departments like marketing, sales, product development, and customer service, and promotes a unified, customer-focused strategy. By bringing together diverse skills and viewpoints, teams are empowered to craft more creative solutions and adapt more swiftly to shifts in the marketplace. In contrast, operating in silos can trap

essential knowledge within departmental confines, leading to a disconnect from what customers truly need. Therefore, fostering collaboration that centers on understanding and meeting customer demands results in more effective marketing outcomes than when efforts are compartmentalized and constrained by rigid organizational structures.

(5) *Responding to change over following a static plan*: This value, drawing inspiration from the original Manifesto for Agile Software Development introduced by developers in 2001, emphasizes the critical need for adaptability in the face of market volatility. The addition of 'static' to describe traditional plans enhances its relevance to the marketing sphere, and highlights the dangers of inflexibility. In a landscape where buyer preferences, market conditions, and global dynamics can shift dramatically, the ability to change from a rigid, unchanging plan is essential. Agile marketing teams, by prioritizing responsiveness over strict adherence to a predetermined plan, position themselves to better serve their audiences, capitalize on emerging opportunities, mitigate potential risks, and maintain alignment with customer needs and preferences. This commitment to flexibility ensures that marketing efforts remain effective and relevant.

2.2 Understanding Principles of Agile Marketing

The Agile Marketing Manifesto (2012) presents several key principles that are designed to guide marketers in adopting a more flexible, responsive, and customer-focused approach. The commonly recognized Agile Marketing Principles are described hereunder:

Figure 2. Principles of agile marketing

(1) *Customer Focus and Early Delivery:* Agile marketing prioritizes the customer's needs and preferences, and aims to deliver value as early as possible. This principle emphasizes understanding the customer journey, using insights and feedback to guide marketing strategies, and rapidly iterating offerings to meet customer demands more effectively. By focusing on the customer, marketers can adjust campaigns in real time, and also they can ensure that marketing efforts are always aligned with what the customer values most.

(2) *Embrace Change:* In an ever-evolving market landscape, the ability to adapt to change is crucial. Agile marketing encourages teams to remain flexible, and views changes in customer behavior, market conditions, or business objectives not as obstacles but as opportunities to evolve and improve. This

mindset ensures that marketing strategies stay relevant and can pivot quickly in response to new information, which in turn keeps the organization competitive and responsive.

(3) *Incremental Marketing Efforts:* Agile marketing breaks down large campaigns into smaller, manageable pieces of work that can be completed in short cycles or sprints. This approach allows teams to test hypotheses, measure results, and refine strategies in a continuous loop of feedback and improvement. By focusing on incremental progress, marketers can achieve valuable gains in performance and effectiveness, while also reducing the risk associated with large, complex projects.

(4) *Collaborative Teams:* Collaboration is at the heart of Agile marketing, with cross-functional teams working closely together to plan, execute, and review marketing initiatives. This principle emphasizes open communication, shared objectives, and collective responsibility for outcomes. By breaking down silos and encouraging diverse perspectives, Agile marketing teams can harness the full range of skills, experiences, and ideas available to them.

(5) *Empowering Team Members:* Agile marketing relies on the premise that the people doing the work are best positioned to understand how to accomplish it efficiently and effectively. This principle advocates for empowering team members with the autonomy to make decisions, manage their workflows, and take ownership of their contributions. When team members feel supported and trusted, they are more engaged, motivated, and likely to produce their best work.

(6) *Face-to-Face Communication:* Agile marketing values direct, face-to-face interactions as the most efficient and effective method of conveying information. Whether through in-person meetings or video conferencing, this principle presents the importance of personal connection and clear communication. It helps in building stronger team dynamics and ensures that everyone is aligned on goals and expectations.

(7) *Functional Deliverables:* The focus on producing tangible, functional deliverables is a core aspect of Agile marketing. Instead of heavy processes or documentation, the goal is to create marketing outputs that have a real impact on the market or the customer. This principle emphasizes the importance of actionable results, such as launched campaigns, published content, or executed events.

(8) *Sustainable Pace:* Agile marketing promotes working at a sustainable pace to ensure long-term success. This principle acknowledges that burnout and overwork are counterproductive. It highlights balanced workloads, reasonable expectations, and regular intervals of work and rest. By maintaining a sustainable pace, teams can remain creative, productive, and motivated over time.

(9) *Continuous Improvement:* The principle of continuous improvement is fundamental to Agile marketing, which seeks to constantly refine and enhance marketing practices. Through regular retrospectives and feedback loops, teams assess their performance, identify areas for improvement, and implement changes to processes, strategies, and tactics. This commitment to ongoing optimization ensures that marketing efforts remain effective and efficient; teams can adapt to new challenges and opportunities.

(10) *Self-Organizing Teams:* This principle supports the idea that teams are most effective when they have the freedom to organize their own work. Agile marketing encourages teams to set their own goals, manage their tasks, and determine the best approach to their work. This self-organization leads to higher levels of engagement, creativity, and accountability, as team members take full ownership of their projects and outcomes.

(11) *Regular Reflection and Adaptation:* Agile marketing places a strong emphasis on the importance of regular reflection and adaptation. Teams are encouraged to periodically review their processes, strategies, and results, openly discussing what worked, what did not, and how they can improve.

This principle ensures that lessons learned are integrated into future efforts, presenting a culture of continuous learning.

(12) *Simplicity in Focus:* Lastly, Agile marketing emphasizes simplicity, encouraging teams to focus on what truly matters and eliminate unnecessary tasks or complexities. This principle can be described as streamlining efforts, prioritizing high-impact activities, and minimizing waste. By concentrating on simplicity, marketers can allocate their resources more effectively, and ensures that every effort contributes directly to achieving business objectives.

3. TRANSITIONING FROM TRADITIONAL TO AGILE MARKETING APPROACHES

Traditional marketing is characterized by its systematic approach to planning and executing marketing strategies. It emphasizes comprehensive market research, detailed planning, and the execution of campaigns over longer periods (Bhayani & Vachhani, 2014; Durmaz & Efendioglu, 2016; Alla et al., 2022; Bouhtatit et al., 2023). Traditional marketing methods often focus on mass media advertising, print media, direct mail, and other broad-reaching strategies aimed at building brand awareness and positioning over time. This approach relies heavily on predicting consumer behavior and planning campaigns well in advance, with a significant emphasis on consistency and message control.

Integrating Agile methodologies with traditional marketing practices represents a significant 'shift' towards more dynamic, responsive, and customer-centric marketing operations. Some key strategies with specific examples are presented hereunder to illustrate how embracing these shifts can substantially enhance a marketing team's effectiveness in the rapidly evolving digital landscape (Perkin, 2023; Barbosa et al., 2022; Katare 2022; Ewel, 2020; Gera et al., 2019; Poolton et al., 2006; Lewnes, 2021).

3.1 From Big Campaigns to Small Iterations

Traditional marketing often focuses on large, inflexible campaigns planned far in advance. The shift to Agile marketing encourages smaller, more manageable iterations that can be adjusted and optimized based on real-time data and feedback. This approach allows marketing teams to be more adaptive, testing what works and what does not, and making continuous improvements to their strategies. An example of this shift can be a company which is launching a digital ad campaign on a modest scale to initially test its assumptions. By closely monitoring the campaign's performance through real-time feedback and analytics, the team can make data-driven decisions to iteratively refine the campaign's messaging, targeting, and creative elements. This iterative approach not only reduces the risk associated with larger campaigns but also ensures that marketing resources are allocated more efficiently towards strategies.

3.2 From Output to Outcome Focus

The shift from focusing on the quantity of marketing outputs to prioritizing tangible outcomes marks a significant change in how marketing success is measured. Traditionally, the emphasis was on the volume of activities, like campaigns and ads, without fully assessing their impact on essential business goals such as customer engagement and profitability. This move towards an outcome-focused approach requires a reevaluation of strategies to ensure marketing efforts align with specific, measurable objectives like improving customer engagement and conversion rates. It is a strategic shift that demands a deeper understanding of what success means for the business and a commitment to continuously refine marketing strategies based on actual performance data. For example, instead of just counting how many emails are sent in a campaign, the emphasis shifts to understanding how those emails lead to more website visits or more sales. This approach ensures that marketing is not just busy work but is effectively contributing to the company's success. By prioritizing outcomes over simple output, marketing teams can use their resources more wisely, respond better to what customers want and need, and clearly show how their work benefits the company.

3.3 From Isolated Functions to Cross-Functional Collaboration

The shift from operating in isolated marketing functions to fostering cross-functional collaboration marks a significant change in approach. This approach aims to bridge gaps and create a unified strategy that aligns with the overarching goals of the business. In traditional marketing setups, departments often work independently, focusing solely on their specific objectives without a comprehensive view of the business's collective goals. This siloed approach can lead to disjointed strategies and misaligned objectives.

The Agile mindset introduces a transformative shift towards collaborative efforts, and breaks down the barriers between marketing and other critical departments such as sales, customer service, and product development. An example of this collaborative approach is the formation of cross-functional teams for new product launches. These teams bring together diverse expertise from marketing, sales, product development, and customer support to ensure a cohesive strategy from conception to launch. So that, messaging is streamlined across all customer touchpoints, goals are synchronized across departments, and the collective insights and skills of various teams are harnessed. This holistic approach improves internal alignment and also elevates the customer experience, driving better business outcomes through a unified, strategic effort.

3.4 From Rigid Planning to Flexibility and Adaptability

Agile marketing emphasizes flexibility and adaptability, with plans that are viewed as dynamic guides rather than fixed blueprints in traditional marketing plans. This shift allows teams to respond quickly to new opportunities or challenges, and ensures that their marketing efforts remain relevant and effective. For instance, consider a marketing team that has outlined a content strategy for the year but recognizes the need to pivot their focus or change distribution channels through based on new trends or direct feedback from their audience. Such adaptability ensures that marketing initiatives stay relevant and resonate with the target audience, and also maximizes the impact of marketing efforts by allowing for real-time adjustments to strategy. This shift towards a more flexible and responsive planning process marks a significant departure from the traditional, more static approach to marketing strategy.

3.5 From Top-Down Decisions to Empowered Teams

In traditional settings, decisions are typically made at the top and cascaded down through the organization. Agile marketing empowers teams to make informed decisions quickly based on their close understanding of the projects, market conditions, and customer feedback. This bottom-up approach encourages ownership, innovation, and a more responsive marketing strategy, as decisions are made by those closest to the work and the customer. For example, if a marketing team notices early signs that a campaign is not performing as expected, they have the autonomy under an agile framework to adjust the campaign's direction without the need for approval processes from higher management. This bottom-up approach speeds up the response time to emerging challenges and also encourages a sense of ownership and innovation among team members.

4. KEY AGILE FRAMEWORKS AND PRACTICES FOR MARKETING

The Agile practices in marketing is rich and diverse, and offers valuable methodologies that can significantly enhance the adaptability and efficiency of marketing teams. This section explores the integration of Agile into marketing, highlights popular key frameworks and details the practices that can help marketing teams become more adaptive, innovative, and effective in their campaigns.

4.1 Scrum Based Agile Marketing

The term Scrum, from the perspective of original Agile principles, is a framework that embodies the core Agile philosophy of flexibility, iterative development, and customer-centricity (Schwaber, 2004; Rubin, 2012). It organizes work into small, manageable units called "sprints," typically lasting two to four weeks. Scrum approach allows teams to focus on delivering specific features or components of a project in a time-boxed manner. It encourages regular reflection and adaptation through daily stand-up meetings, sprint reviews, and retrospectives. This ensures continuous improvement and responsiveness to change, aligns closely with the Agile Manifesto's values of individuals and interactions over processes and tools, working solutions over comprehensive documentation, customer collaboration over contract negotiation, and responding to change over following a plan (Fowler & Highsmith, 2001; Batra et al., 2017).

From Agile Marketing perspective, by adapting Scrum principles, marketing teams can break down large projects into manageable sprints, and can develop a collaborative environment that thrives on incremental progress and flexibility. This approach ensures that marketing initiatives are continuously aligned with customer needs and market dynamics, enabling teams to adjust strategies swiftly based on feedback and performance analytics.

Under the Scrum-based Agile marketing framework, several key practices are pivotal for enhancing team dynamics, ensuring alignment with customer expectations, and driving marketing success (Figure 3). These practices are described hereunder:

- Daily Stand-ups: These brief, focused meetings serve as a platform for marketing team members to share their progress, outline plans for the day, and address any challenges. This practice supports team alignment and enables swift resolution of issues, and ensures that campaigns stay on track. For instance, a team might discuss adjustments to a digital ad campaign based on the latest engagement metrics.
- Sprint Planning: In this critical preparatory session, the team collaborates to select high-priority items from the marketing backlog that align with the upcoming sprint's goals. Setting clear objectives and success criteria, such as expected increase in lead generation or website traffic, provides focused efforts and strategic decision-making.

- Backlog Refinement: This ongoing process involves the prioritization and clarification of the backlog. It ensures that each task is well-defined, valuable, and strategically aligned. For example, refining could involve deciding to prioritize the development of a new email marketing campaign over updating existing social media ads based on ROI analysis.

- User Stories: Using stories that focus on the user helps align marketing objectives with what the target audience truly needs and wants. Developing stories such as "As a young professional, I want to find quick healthy meal options" helps in shaping marketing communications and content approaches that deeply connect with the audience.

- Sprint Reviews: At the end of each sprint, the team shares its progress with important participants, highlighting finished tasks and collecting comments. This can include reviewing the performance of a new product launch campaign across various channels and discussing customer reactions and sales data.

- Retrospectives: These sessions offer a chance to assess the sprint's overall process, acknowledging successes and identifying areas for improvement. For example, a retrospective may reveal the need for better coordination between content creators and graphic designers to streamline content production.

- Burndown Charts: By visually tracking completed versus remaining tasks within a sprint, burndown charts provide a clear overview of the team's progress and any discrepancies from the plan. This tool helps in adjusting workloads to meet sprint goals, such as completing all planned blog posts and SEO (Search Engine Optimization) on schedule.

Figure 3. Scrum based agile marketing process

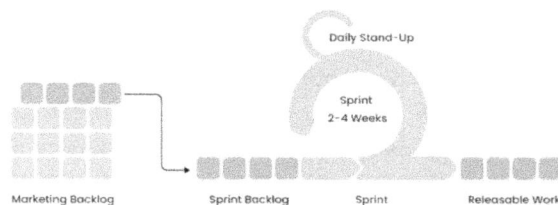

(Source: Intuz, 2022)

4.2 Kanban-Based Agile Marketing

Kanban is a lean management method that enhances efficiency through visual management. Originating from Japanese manufacturing sectors, it's especially useful in managing complex tasks by visualizing the entire workflow on a Kanban board (Ahmad et al., 2013; Senapathi & Drury-Grogan, 2021). It focuses on maximizing efficiency and minimizing waste by visualizing work, limiting Work In Progress (WIP), managing flow, and making process policies explicit. At its core, Kanban uses a board and cards to represent tasks, moving them across columns that represent different stages of the process, from "To Do" to "Doing" to "Done". This visualization helps teams monitor their workflow and identify bottlenecks, enabling continuous improvement and adaptability to changing priorities (Alaidaros et al., 2021; Senapathi & Drury-Grogan, 2021).

In the realm of marketing, adopting a Kanban-based Agile marketing approach translates Kanban principles to manage and improve marketing processes. By visualizing marketing tasks on a Kanban board, teams can easily see what needs to be done, what is in progress, and what has been completed. This clarity allows for better prioritization of tasks, ensuring that marketing efforts are aligned with business goals and customer needs. It also facilitates smoother collaboration among team members, as everyone has a clear understanding of the workflow and can identify areas where they can contribute or where bottlenecks might be forming. By limiting work in progress, marketing teams can concentrate on completing tasks efficiently, thereby increasing productivity and reducing the time to market for campaigns and initiatives. Kanban-based Agile marketing supports a more dynamic and responsive marketing strategy, enabling teams to adapt quickly to feedback and market changes without overcommitting resources.

Under the Kanban-based Agile marketing framework, several key practices are pivotal for streamlining marketing operations and enhancing team productivity:

- Visualizing the Workflow: Using a Kanban board to map out all marketing tasks, from conceptualizing social media campaigns to launching email marketing sequences, provides transparency and also allows for dynamic strategy adjustments. This practice ensures that all stakeholders, from content creators to digital strategists, are aligned and can monitor the progress of tasks, such as the development of a new product launch or seasonal advertising push, from start to finish.
- Limiting Work in Progress: Imposing limits on active tasks in each stage of the workflow encourages teams to concentrate on completing ongoing initiatives, like finalizing a series of blog posts or optimizing a PPC campaign. This approach improves focus and output quality, and facilitates more efficient transitions between tasks, significantly reducing the risk of project bottlenecks and team burnout.
- Managing Flow: Continuously analyzing the movement of tasks, such as the progression of a video marketing project or the execution of a market research plan through the Kanban board, helps identify delays early. By addressing these delays promptly, marketing teams can refine their processes, ensuring that initiatives like new brand partnerships or influencer collaborations are delivered more swiftly and effectively.
- Making Process Policies Explicit: Establishing clear criteria for advancing tasks from ideation to completion ensures that everyone, from graphic designers to SEO specialists, understands their responsibilities. This clarity streamlines the workflow, minimizing misunderstandings and improving the marketing activities, such as content publication schedules or event marketing preparations.
- Feedback Loops: Regularly revisiting the marketing workflow and analyzing campaign outcomes, like the engagement rate of a recent social media ad or the conversion metrics of an email campaign, encourages ongoing learning and iteration. This adaptive approach allows teams to refine their strategies in alignment with customer feedback and market trends.
- Collaborative Prioritization: Engaging the whole marketing team in prioritizing tasks ensures that resources are allocated to the most impactful initiatives, such as a high-stakes product launch or a strategic content marketing pivot. This collective decision-making process enhances team commitment, and also ensures that marketing efforts are strategically aligned with broader business goals, maximizing ROI and driving sustainable growth.

Kanban tools are essential for implementing the Kanban methodology effectively, providing visual management of tasks and workflows that facilitate better planning, tracking, and collaboration. These tools, such as Trello, Asana, and Jira, offer digital platforms designed to enhance project visibility and collaboration for marketing teams (Figure 4). With features like customizable workflows, task assignments, and progress tracking, Kanban tools facilitate efficient workflow management. They enable teams to prioritize work, identify bottlenecks, and adjust strategies swiftly, making them indispensable for managing diverse marketing projects and ensuring seamless communication among remote or in-office teams.

Figure 4. An example of Kanban Board of Trello

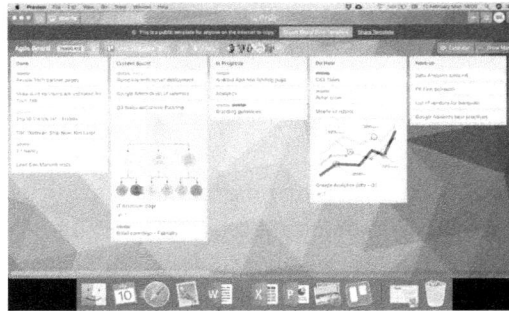

(Atlassian Trello, 2024)

4.3 Scrumban Based Agile Marketing

Scrumban combines two leading Agile methodologies -Scrum and Kanban- into a single process for getting work done (Atlassian, 2024). Scrumban as a hybrid Agile methodology merges the structured sprint approach of Scrum with the continuous flow and flexibility of Kanban. It is designed to provide teams with the framework to prioritize work more effectively, adapt to changing priorities, and improve the delivery process continuously. As presented in Table 1, by integrating Scrum's structured planning sessions and reviews with Kanban's focus on visualizing work and limiting work in progress, Scrumban allows teams to manage their tasks with greater agility and responsiveness. This methodology is particularly beneficial in environments where work priorities frequently shift, or where the scope of projects can change rapidly, offering a balanced approach that maximizes efficiency and adaptability.

For agile marketing teams, Scrumban offers a tailored approach that supports the dynamic nature of marketing projects and campaigns. By adopting Scrumban, marketing teams can leverage Scrum's sprint planning to outline major initiatives and campaign launches, while employing Kanban's visualization to track ongoing tasks like content creation, social media management, and event planning. This blend facilitates a more adaptive workflow that can swiftly accommodate new market opportunities or customer feedback without disrupting the overall marketing strategy. Moreover, Scrumban's emphasis on continuous improvement and team collaboration makes it an ideal choice for marketing departments looking to innovate and stay competitive in a fast-paced industry.

Table 1. *Scrum, Kanban, and Scrumban (Source: Atlassian, 2024)*

Criteria	Scrum	Kanban	Scrumban
Methodology	Fixed length sprints Fixed roles Consistent delivery	Limit work in progress Track tasks visually Continuous flow of work	Fixed length sprints Limit work in progress Track tasks visually Continuous flow of work
Roles	Product Owner Scrum Master Development team	None	None
Artifacts	Product backlog Sprint backlog Increment finished	Kanban board Kanban cards	Scrumban board Scrumban cards
Events	Sprint planning Daily standup Sprint review Sprint retrospective	Kanban meeting	Sprint planning Daily standup Sprint retrospective
Process flow	Product backlog Sprint backlog In progress Review Done	To Do In Progress Done	To Do In Progress Done

As described in Table 1, the key practices of Scrumban for Agile marketing teams effectively combines Scrum's structured approach with Kanban's adaptability, and provides a robust framework tailored for the dynamic needs of marketing. These practices include:

- Structured Sprints for Marketing Projects: Integrating Scrum's sprint concept, Scrumban allows marketing teams to define work periods -generally two weeks- for completing sets of tasks. This structure provides a clear timeframe for campaign development, content production, and other marketing initiatives, promoting focus and timely delivery.
- Daily Standup Meetings for Team Alignment: Borrowing from Scrum, daily standups are crucial in Scrumban, providing a platform for marketing team members to synchronize daily activities. These brief meetings enhance clarity on individual contributions, progress on tasks, and identification of any obstacles.
- Retrospective Meetings for Continuous Improvement: At the end of each sprint, marketing teams conduct retrospectives to evaluate their processes and outcomes. This practice enables teams to reflect on what worked well and what did not, and applies lessons learned to optimize future marketing strategies and operations.
- Kanban Boards for Visual Management: The Kanban board, with columns like "To Do", "In Progress", and "Done", visually tracks the progress of marketing tasks. This transparency allows for real-time adjustments and ensures all team members are aware of the campaign's status and priorities.
- Task Cards for Detailed Tracking: Utilizing cards on the Kanban board to represent individual marketing tasks -from ideation to execution- facilitates detailed tracking of progress and accountability. Each card's journey from "To Do" to "Done" shows the workflow of marketing deliverables, such as email campaigns, blog posts, or social media updates.

- WIP Limits to Prevent Overload: Adopting Kanban's WIP limits ensures marketing teams do not take on more than they can handle, maintaining high-quality output and preventing burnout. By limiting the number of active tasks, teams can focus on completing current projects before initiating new ones.
- Collaborative Task Prioritization: Combining Scrum's collaborative planning with Kanban's flexibility, Scrumban encourages marketing teams to jointly prioritize tasks based on strategic objectives and current market dynamics. This collective decision-making ensures that high-impact projects are addressed promptly, and aligns marketing efforts with overall business goals.

Figure 5. Context of Scrumban process flow

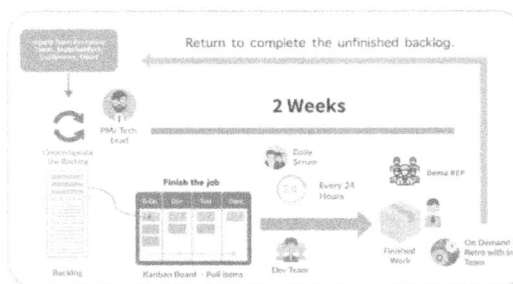

(Source: Aini et al., 2021)

While the Scrumban methodology offers a flexible and efficient framework for managing work, it comes with its own set of limitations. The hybrid nature of Scrumban can introduce complexity and ambiguity for teams new to Agile practices. Also, the novelty of Scrumban means that there is less documented guidance and fewer established best practices available, potentially leading to challenges in implementation. Additionally, the lack of traditional Scrum roles and the emphasis on self-management may result in confusion regarding task responsibilities and decision-making authority. These limitations highlight the importance of clear communication and the need for teams to invest time in understanding and adapting the methodology to their specific context and workflows.

4.4 Lean Agile Marketing

Lean Management is a methodology derived from Lean Manufacturing principles, initially developed in the automotive industry to maximize value for customers while minimizing waste (Anvari et al., 2011; Bhamu et al., 2014). It focuses on streamlining operations, improving process efficiency, and enhancing product quality by systematically removing non-value adding activities and reducing variability in production processes. Key elements of Lean Management include continuous improvement (Kaizen), respect for people, and optimizing the flow of products and services through the value stream (Pinto et al., 2018; Deshmukh et al., 2010). The goal is to create more value with fewer resources, increase customer satisfaction, and develop a collaborative culture and continuous learning within organizations.

When Lean principles are applied to Agile marketing, in other words when deploying Lean Agile Marketing, the focus shifts to maximizing customer value in marketing activities while maintaining the agility to respond to market changes swiftly. This approach combines the waste reduction and efficiency focus of Lean with the flexibility and rapid iteration of Agile methodologies. Benefits of Lean Agile Marketing include improved responsiveness to customer needs, enhanced team productivity through the elimination of unnecessary tasks, and a stronger alignment between marketing activities and overall business objectives. It enables marketing teams to more effectively adapt to the digital landscape, where consumer preferences can change rapidly, and data-driven insights are crucial for success. The key practices of Lean Agile Marketing are described below:

- Emphasizing Customer Value: This practice focuses on prioritizing marketing initiatives that deliver the most significant value to customers. It involves using feedback and data analytics to make informed decisions, and ensures that marketing efforts are always aligned with customer needs and preferences.
- Streamlining Marketing Processes: This practice focuses on identifying and eliminating non-value adding processes in marketing activities. The goal is to streamline operations, reduce waste, and enhance overall efficiency, leading to more focused and effective marketing efforts. For example, by implementing an automation software, a company can streamline its email marketing efforts, automatically segmenting its audience based on their behavior and preferences, and sending personalized emails at scale, thereby enhancing efficiency and engagement while reducing the time to market for new campaigns.
- Utilizing Data-Driven Decision Making: This practice emphasizes making informed marketing decisions based on data analysis and insights. It ensures that marketing strategies are only aligned with actual performance metrics and customer preferences and are also optimized for effectiveness and efficiency. For example, a digital marketing team utilizes A/B testing to experiment with two variations of call-to-action (CTA) phrases on their product page. By analyzing the click-through and conversion data, they identify the CTA that better engages their audience, which in turn results in a significant increase in conversion rates.
- Maintaining Flexibility and Adaptability: This practice focuses on keeping marketing strategies flexible, allows for swift pivots in response to changing market conditions and consumer feedback. The objective is to ensure that marketing efforts remain relevant and impactful, regardless of external changes.

4.5 Alternative Agile Frameworks for Marketing Success

While Scrum, Kanban, Scrumban and Lean Agile are among the most popular frameworks adapted for marketing, there are indeed other methodologies and approaches that can significantly enhance the agility and effectiveness of marketing teams.

Today, Design Thinking approach in marketing offers a powerful framework for tackling complex marketing challenges and enhancing the development of customer-centric marketing strategies. (Knight, 2021). By deeply understanding customer needs, brainstorming innovative solutions, and rapidly prototyping and testing ideas, teams can develop marketing strategies and solutions that not only meet but exceed customer expectations. For example, a company focusing on launch a new product line may begin with Design Thinking workshops to deeply empathize with potential customers, identifying their core needs and pain points. Leveraging these insights, the marketing team can then employ Agile methodologies to rapidly prototype various marketing messages and channels, testing them in real-world scenarios to see which works most. Based on real-time feedback and data analytics, the team iteratively refines their approach, and ensures the final marketing campaign is both innovative and highly tailored to the target audience's preferences. This blend of Design Thinking and Agile allows for a more dynamic, responsive marketing process that can adapt to changing customer expectations and market conditions, ultimately leading to more effective and successful marketing outcomes.

Another valuable Agile framework, Feature-Driven Development (FDD) can be used for marketing practices as well. It emphasizes a structured approach to delivering key features or initiatives (Hunt, 2006; Palmer & Felsing, 2001). FDD principles can lead to more organized and impact-driven marketing campaigns. It focuses on planning, building, and delivering marketing projects in a systematic, efficient manner. Through FDD approach in marketing, each feature contributes significantly to the overall marketing objectives and delivers tangible value to the business and its customers. For example, in case of the launch of a new product line, the marketing team breaks down the launch into key features, such as targeted social media campaigns, influencer partnerships, and email marketing sequences. Each feature is then developed and executed in a structured manner, with specific timelines, responsibilities, and measurable goals. This approach allows for detailed tracking of each initiative's success and provides clear insights into which marketing efforts are most effective at driving engagement and sales. By focusing on discrete, high-value features, the team can allocate resources more efficiently, adapt quickly based on real-time feedback, and enhance the effectiveness of the product launch strategy.

5. STRATEGIES FOR AGILE METHODOLOGIES IN MARKETING

Adopting Agile methodologies in the marketing domain introduces several challenges such as cultural resistance within organizations, a lack of Agile expertise, difficulties in dynamic resource allocation, skill gaps across teams, challenges in scaling Agile practices, integrating Agile within non-Agile departments, and redefining success metrics to fit Agile marketing efforts. Each of these issues requires targeted strategies to overcome, ensuring the successful implementation and optimization of Agile methodologies in marketing environments. Overcoming the challenges of implementing Agile marketing needs a multifaceted approach, focusing on leadership, culture, and processes:

5.1 Agile Leadership and Support for Agile Marketing

Effective Agile transformation is rooted in leadership that adopts Agile principles and also actively demonstrates and supports these practices. Leaders play a pivotal role in navigating their teams through the Agile transition, acting not as traditional authoritative figures but as facilitators who empower their teams. They are responsible for cultivating a culture that values open dialogue, teamwork, and continuous improvement. Essential to this process is obtaining executive support, which ensures the allocation of necessary resources and reinforces the organization's commitment to Agile practices. This support from top management is crucial for handling challenges and making sure the Agile project gets the attention it needs to succeed. Also, it is important to develop Agile leaders within teams. These leaders act as guides and supporters of Agile methods, spreading the Agile way of thinking throughout the marketing team and the wider organization, which helps Agile practices blend seamlessly into the company's operations.

5.2 Fostering an Agile Culture in Marketing

Building an Agile culture requires continuous training and education to deepen the team's understanding of Agile practices. This ensures a deep understanding of Agile methods and how they can be applied in marketing. This foundational knowledge empowers teams to fully embrace Agile values and practices. Emphasizing cross-functional collaboration is particularly vital in the diverse world of marketing, as it brings together varied skills and perspectives, from creative to analytical, enhancing team dynamics and output quality. Promoting a mindset of experimentation and viewing both successes and failures as chances to learn is key to fostering a truly Agile environment. In marketing, this approach promotes a culture of innovation and adaptability, allowing teams to swiftly respond to market changes, consumer trends, and feedback loops. This environment of continuous improvement and flexibility is key to achieving sustained marketing success and driving meaningful engagement with target audiences.

5.3 Streamlining Agile Processes and Metrics for Marketing Excellence

Optimizing Agile tools and methodologies to suit the specific needs of marketing teams and their projects is essential for maximizing efficiency and effectiveness. The adoption of Agile project management tools, such as Trello, Asana, or Jira, is critical in facilitating task organization, workflow visualization, and team collaboration. Moreover, refining performance metrics to prioritize Agile values, such as customer engagement, campaign adaptability, and speed to market, ensures that evaluation criteria are aligned with the objectives of Agile marketing. Adopting iterative planning enables marketing teams to remain flexible, quickly adapting to consumer feedback and changing market trends, ensuring their efforts stay relevant and effective.

Additionally, establishing well-defined processes and clear communication channels is key to enhancing collaboration with departments that may not operate under Agile principles. This cross-departmental synergy is crucial for ensuring that marketing strategies are coherent with the company's overall goals and strategies. By streamlining these Agile processes and metrics with a marketing-centric approach, teams can launch campaigns that are more focused, adaptable, and aligned with customer needs. So that, it leads better marketing ROI and continuous business growth.

5.4 Real-World Agile Marketing Success Stories

Some examples are presented that highlight how Agile Marketing principles have been applied across various industries, showcasing their broad applicability and effectiveness in driving marketing success (Faster Capital, 2024; Marketing Insider Group, 2024; PepsiCo Partners, 2024; Denning, S., 2019; Coca Cola Company, 2019):

- Microsoft has applied Agile Marketing principles through the use of growth hacking teams across its product lines. These teams use data-driven approaches to experiment rapidly with marketing tactics, optimizing in real-time based on performance metrics. This method has allowed for more personalized customer engagement and faster adaptation to market changes.

- Coca-Cola embraced Agile methodologies by establishing smaller, cross-functional teams focused on content creation, allowing for rapid development and deployment of marketing campaigns. This shift enabled them to quickly adapt to changing consumer preferences and social media trends, resulting in more relevant and engaging content.
- Amazon's marketing strategy is a prime example of Agile Marketing in action. By leveraging vast amounts of customer data, Amazon continuously tests and optimizes its marketing messages and channels. This data-driven approach enables them to be incredibly responsive to customer needs and preferences, customizes their offerings and improves the customer experience.
- ING Bank adopted the Agile "Tribe" model to reorganize its workforce, including marketing teams. This structure consists of cross-functional groups that work autonomously on specific customer-centric projects, enabling faster decision-making, quicker adaptation to market changes, and enhanced collaboration.
- Unilever implemented Agile methodologies in its digital marketing efforts to better respond to the fast-changing digital landscape. This approach has enabled Unilever to more effectively test different digital marketing tactics, analyze performance data, and iterate on their strategies, resulting in higher engagement rates and improved ROI on digital campaigns.
- PepsiCo launched a Digital Lab partnership program with startups to test and scale new digital capabilities, including data analytics, AI for personalization, and digital vending experiences. This initiative allows PepsiCo to stay at the forefront of digital marketing innovations, rapidly experimenting with and implementing new technologies to enhance customer engagement.

6. CONCLUSION

Adopting the Agile mindset is a key step towards harnessing the transformative power of Agile methodologies in marketing. This approach emphasizes flexibility, customer focus, and collaboration, promoting the continuous improvement of marketing strategies through feedback and learning. Agile marketing values transparency and adaptability, and enables teams to quickly adjust to market changes and consumer needs. By aligning marketing efforts with strategic goals, organizations foster innovation and responsiveness, and also improves their ability to navigate market challenges effectively.

The integration of Agile methodologies, such as Scrum, Kanban, Scrumban, and Lean into marketing practices marks a shift towards more dynamic and customer-oriented strategies. This shift requires strong leadership, a culture of continuous learning, and a willingness to experiment. Despite potential obstacles like cultural resistance and skill gaps, focusing on Agile leadership and collaborative practices can lead organizations to more effective and agile marketing outcomes. Looking forward, the adoption of Agile in marketing promises a future of innovation, resilience, and a stronger connection with customers, and drives the marketing field towards greater excellence and adaptability.

REFERENCES

Ahmad, M. O., Markkula, J., & Oivo, M. (2013, September). Kanban In Software Development: A Systematic Literature Review. In *2013 39th Euromicro Conference On Software Engineering And Advanced Applications* (Pp. 9-16). IEEE. 10.1109/SEAA.2013.28

Aini, Q., Budiarto, M., Putra, P. O. H., & Santoso, N. P. L. (2021). Gamification-Based The Kampus Merdeka Learning In 4.0 Era. [Indonesian Journal Of Computing And Cybernetics Systems]. *IJCCS*, 15(1), 31–42. 10.22146/ijccs.59023

Alaidaros, H., Omar, M., & Romli, R. (2021). The State Of The Art Of Agile Kanban Method: Challenges And Opportunities. *Independent Journal of Management & Production*, 12(8), 2535–2550. 10.14807/ijmp.v12i8.1482

Alla, L., Kamal, M., & Bouhtati, N. (2022). Big data and marketing effectiveness of tourism businesses: A literature review. *Alternatives Managériales Economiques, 4*(0). 10.48374/IMIST.PRSM/ame-v1i0.36928

Anvari, A., Ismail, Y., & Hojjati, S. M. H. (2011). A Study On Total Quality Management And Lean Manufacturing: Through Lean Thinking Approach. *World Applied Sciences Journal*, 12(9), 1585–1596.

Atawneh, S. (2019). The Analysis Of Current State Of Agile Software Development. *Journal of Theoretical and Applied Information Technology*, 97(22), 3197–3028.

Atlassian. (2024). *Scrumban: Mastering Two Agile Methodologies*. Atlassian. Https://Www.Atlassian.Com/Agile/Project-Management/Scrumban

Barbosa, A. T., Da Silva, C. C., Caetano, R. L., Da Silva, D. P. S., Barbosa, J. V., & Pinto, Z. T. (2022). Agile Methodologies: And Its Applicability In The Marketing AREA. Revista Ibero-Americana De Humanidades. *Ciência & Educação (Bauru)*, 8(3), 1659–1669.

Batra, D., Xia, W., & Zhang, M. (2017). Collaboration In Agile Software Development: Concept And Dimensions. *Communications of the Association for Information Systems*, 41(1), 20. 10.17705/1CAIS.04120

Bhamu, J., & Singh Sangwan, K. (2014). Lean Manufacturing: Literature Review And Research Issues. *International Journal of Operations & Production Management*, 34(7), 876–940. 10.1108/IJOPM-08-2012-0315

Bhayani, S., & Vachhani, N. V. (2014). Internet Marketing Vs Traditional Marketing: A Comparative Analysis. *FIIB Business Review*, 3(3), 53–63. 10.1177/2455265820140309

Bouhtati, N., Alla, L., & Bentalhah, B. (2023). Marketing Big Data Analytics and Customer Relationship Management: A Fuzzy Approach. In *Integrating Intelligence and Sustainability in Supply Chains* (pp. 75-86). IGI Global. .10.4018/979-8-3693-0225-5.ch004

Coca Cola Company. (2019). *Building A Growth Culture At Coke Includes Empowering All Employees To Drive Company's Innovation Agenda*. Coca Cola Company. Https://Www.Coca-Colacompany.Com/Media-Center/Growth-Culture-At-Coke-Empowers-Employees

Denning, S. (2019). How Amazon Became Agile. *Forbes*. Https://Www.Forbes.Com/Sites/Stevedenning/2019/06/02/How-Amazon-Became-Agile/?Sh=495af40031aa

Deshmukh, S. G., Upadhye, N., & Garg, S. (2010). Lean Manufacturing For Sustainable Development. *Glob. Bus. Manag. Res. Int. J*, 2(1), 125.

Duka, D. (2013, May). Adoption Of Agile Methodology In Software Development. In *2013 36th International Convention On Information And Communication Technology, Electronics And Microelectronics (MIPRO)* (Pp. 426-430). IEEE.

Durmaz, Y., & Efendioglu, I. H. (2016). Travel From Traditional Marketing To Digital Marketing. *Global Journal of Management and Business Research*, 16(2), 34–40. 10.34257/GJMBREVOL22IS2PG35

Flewelling, P. (2018). *The The Agile Developer's Handbook: Get More Value From Your Software Development: Get The Best Out Of The Agile Methodology*. Packt Publishing Ltd.

Fowler, M., & Highsmith, J. (2001). The Agile Manifesto. *Software Development*, 9(8), 28–35.

Gera, G., Gera, B., & Mishra, A. (2019). Role Of Agile Marketing In The Present Era. *International Journal Of Technical Research & Science*, 4(5), 40–44. 10.30780/IJTRS.V04.I05.006

Highsmith, J. A. (2002). *Agile Software Development Ecosystems*. Addison-Wesley Professional.

Hoogveld, M., & Koster, J. (2016). Measuring The Agility Of Omnichannel Operations: An Agile Marketing Maturity Model. *SSRG International Journal Of Economics And Management Studies (SSRG-IJEMS)*, 3(10), 5-14.

Hunt, J. (2006). Feature-Driven Development. *Agile Software Construction*, 161-182.

Intuz (2022). *An Ultimate Guide On Adopting Agile Marketing Methodology*. Intuz. Https://Www.Intuz.Com/Guide-On-Agile-Marketing-Methodology

Kalenda, M., Hyna, P., & Rossi, B. (2018). Scaling Agile In Large Organizations: Practices, Challenges, And Success Factors. *Journal of Software (Malden, MA)*, 30(10), E1954. 10.1002/smr.1954

Kelly, A. (2008). *Changing Software Development: Learning To Become Agile*. John Wiley & Sons.

Knight, W. (2021). *How To Use Design Thinking In Marketing*. Warren-Night. Https://Warren-Knight.Com/2021/04/08/How-To-Use-Design-Thinking-In-Marketing/

Lewnes, A. (2021). Commentary: The Future Of Marketing Is Agile. *Journal of Marketing*, 85(1), 64–67. 10.1177/0022242920972022

Marketing Insider Group. (2024). *Case Studies*. Marketing Insider Group. Https://Marketinginsidergroup.Com/Agile-Marketing/Agile-Marketing-Examples-Case-Studies/

Matharu, G. S., Mishra, A., Singh, H., & Upadhyay, P. (2015). Empirical Study Of Agile Software Development Methodologies: A Comparative Analysis. *Software Engineering Notes*, 40(1), 1–6. 10.1145/2693208.2693233

Moi, L., & Cabiddu, F. (2021). An Agile Marketing Capability Maturity Framework. *Tourism Management*, 86, 104347. 10.1016/j.tourman.2021.104347

Palmer, S. R., & Felsing, M. (2001). *A Practical Guide To Feature-Driven Development*. Pearson Education.

Patary, C. L. (2019). *The Scrum Master Guidebook: A Reference For Obtaining Mastery.* Notion Press.

Perkin, N. (2023). *Agile Transformation: Structures, Processes And Mindsets For The Digital Age.* Kogan Page Publishers.

Pinto, J. L. Q., Matias, J. C. O., Pimentel, C., Azevedo, S. G., Govindan, K., Pinto, J. L. Q., & Govindan, K. (2018). Lean Manufacturing And Kaizen. *Just In Time Factory: Implementation Through Lean Manufacturing Tools*, 5-24.

Poolton, J., Ismail, H. S., Reid, I. R., & Arokiam, I. C. (2006). Agile Marketing For The Manufacturing-Based SME. *Marketing Intelligence & Planning*, 24(7), 681–693. 10.1108/02634500610711851

Ramos, C., & Pavhlichenko, I. (2022). *Creating Agile Organizations: A Systemic Approach.* Addison-Wesley Professional.

Rubin, K. S. (2012). *Essential Scrum: A Practical Guide To The Most Popular Agile Process.* Addison-Wesley.

Schwaber, K. (2004). *Agile Project Management With Scrum.* Microsoft Press.

Senapathi, M., & Drury-Grogan, M. L. (2021). Systems Thinking Approach To Implementing Kanban: A Case Study. *Journal of Software (Malden, MA)*, 33(4), E2322. 10.1002/smr.2322

Thümler, N. (2023). Agility In Marketing: A Bibliometric Analysis. *Business: Theory and Practice*, 24(1), 173–182. 10.3846/btp.2023.17090

Vassileva, B. (2017). *Agile Marketing Strategies: How To Transform The Customer-Brand Dynamics In Services.* Bucharest.

Winter, B., & Winter, B. (2015). *The Basics Of Agile. Agile Performance Improvement: The New Synergy Of Agile And Human Performance Technology*, 85-120.

Yusoff, Y., Alias, Z., Abdullah, M., & Mansor, Z. (2019). Agile Marketing Conceptual Framework For Private Higher Education Institutions. *International Journal of Academic Research in Business & Social Sciences*, 9(1). 10.6007/IJARBSS/v9-i1/5896

Chapter 8
The Potential Benefits of Integrating Business Intelligence and CRM

Abdelhak Ait Touil

http://orcid.org/0000-0003-4816-1420

National School of Business and Management, Meknes, Morocco

ABSTRACT

The business environment is constantly changing and evolving, and companies must adapt to remain competitive. Today, companies have no choice but to compete on a global scale by developing products and services that meet the aspirations and needs of consumers. To meet these challenges, companies need to acquire and develop resources that improve their ability to effectively exploit opportunities and avoid threats. Business intelligence and CRM systems help companies do this. Business intelligence and customer relationship management are closely related. Recent studies have explored the benefits of integrating business intelligence and CRM. Today, the integration of business intelligence and CRM has become a key strategy for companies seeking to improve their operational efficiency and customer-centric practices. The purpose of this chapter is to provide a perspective on how the integration of business intelligence and CRM can lead companies to sustainable growth and improved competitiveness. It explores the principles, challenges, and potential benefits of this integration.

1. INTRODUCTION

The business environment is constantly changing and evolving, and companies must adapt to remain competitive. Globalization has intensified international competition in all sectors. Companies now have no choice but to compete on a global scale, developing products and services that meet the aspirations and needs of consumers in different parts of the world. What's more, the increasing use of digital technologies, such as transaction systems, business intelligence, and artificial intelligence, is drastically changing the way companies compete. Companies have a growing interest in adopting this type of technology to stay competitive and deliver a value proposition. Customers are increasingly demanding and have high expectations of products. Companies must be able to respond quickly to these changing preferences to remain competitive. In addition, there is strong pressure on companies to adopt responsible

DOI: 10.4018/979-8-3693-3172-9.ch008

and sustainable practices, such as reducing their carbon footprint and using environmentally friendly materials (Jhamb and Turcanu, 2022).

To meet these challenges, companies need to acquire and develop resources that are likely to improve their ability to effectively exploit opportunities and avoid threats to their performance (Murat et al., 2023). One way to do this is the implementation and use of business systems. BI aims to help companies make informed decisions by providing timely, accurate, and relevant information for their operational and strategic processes. Business Intelligence consists of collecting and analyzing large volumes of data from many sources, such as sales data, customer data, and data from social networks, to identify trends and insights that can help companies improve their performance and competitiveness.

BI can help companies track key performance indicators (KPIs) such as sales growth, customer satisfaction, and profitability in real-time, enabling them to make fast, informed decisions. BI can also identify new opportunities for growth and innovation by analyzing market trends and consumer behavior. BI is increasingly used in conjunction with other technologies such as Artificial Intelligence, machine learning, and big data analytics to provide advanced insights and predictive capabilities.

Business Intelligence is a perfect fit for CRM processes. The goal of CRM is to manage and improve the interactions between the company and its customers. CRM is a strategy that companies use to understand their customers' needs and preferences and to build strong, lasting relationships with them. For doing so, CRM involves collecting data about customers, such as their purchase history, preferences, and feedback, and using this information to personalize marketing, offers, and service to customers to best meet their expectations (Fernandes et al., 2023). The ultimate goal of CRM is to improve customer satisfaction and loyalty, which can sustainably increase sales and revenues. CRM can also help companies respond more quickly to customer complaints and problems to build a relationship of trust with customers. By building a relationship of trust with their customers, companies can create and develop a competitive advantage that is difficult for competitors to imitate.

Business Intelligence and Customer Relationship Management are closely related. Business Intelligence can improve the effectiveness of CRM initiatives. Using BI tools, companies can analyze data collected about consumers and gain in-depth knowledge of consumer behavior, which can increase and improve the effectiveness of CRM initiatives. For example, by analyzing consumer data, companies can determine which products sell best, which consumers are most profitable, and which marketing companies are most effective. This information can help companies make data-driven decisions about how to allocate resources, which products to promote, and which customers to target. What's more, Business Intelligence can help companies identify trends and patterns in customer data that they might not otherwise see. For example, by analyzing customer data. Companies can see which customers are most likely to go to the competition, or which product is more likely to be sold with another product.

A case study presented by Lehman shows how business and real-time data warehousing helped "Continental Airlines" change its position in the industry from "worst to best" and then from "best to favorite". In fact, with a $30 million investment in hardware and software over six years, Continental realized $500 million in reduced costs and increased revenue in areas such as marketing, fraud detection, and demand forecasting. As a result, the company moved from 10th place in the market to the recognized leader that customers prefer (Lehman et al., 2008).

One of the strongest reasons why organizations invest in business intelligence tools is to create new customer relationships and improve existing ones (Olszak, 2016). It can be argued that this is the primary need that organizations are trying to satisfy with the BI systems. This is possible because BI can provide significant support for processing large, structured volumes of data from transactional systems such as ERP and CRM, or unstructured data from the Web and social networks. In his seminal article "Competing on Analytics," Davenport emphasized the importance of customer relationships and showed that BI&A-based companies, which he calls "analytic competitors," have an advantage over their rivals because they know their customers better than others (Davenport and Harris, 2006). In addition, BI tools can be useful for identifying and profiling new customers through network data analysis. As a result, companies can invest in business intelligence to address a range of sales and marketing needs (Olszak, 2016).

As companies continue to digitize their CRM processes, the link between CRM and business intelligence is becoming increasingly important. By integrating CRM with business intelligence, companies can further improve customer relationship management. Business intelligence provides advanced tools for analyzing customer data so that users and decision-makers have the right information, at the right time, in the right place, to improve performance.

Recent studies have examined the benefits of integrating business intelligence and CRM. For example, Rathod et al. found that integrating artificial intelligence and CRM can help companies improve their sales and marketing strategy and increase customer satisfaction (Rathod et al., 2024). Similarly, Ledro et al. provided a review of the literature on the topic, identifying gaps and suggesting interesting avenues for research (Ledro et al., 2022). In a case study, Alikhani and Kazemi have shown that BI has several beneficial effects on CRM, such as improving the decision-making process at strategic and operational levels, reducing the costs of CRM processes, and identifying new opportunities by analyzing customer data (Alikhani et al., 2021).

It seems then that the harmonious and intelligent use of these two systems simultaneously offers enormous opportunities. This raises the following research question: what are the potential benefits of integrating BI and CRM capabilities? And what are the main challenges of this integration?

What we mean by "integration of BI and CRM capabilities" is the possible use of BI resources and capabilities in CRM processes and vice versa. Resources are the productive assets owned by the firm; capabilities are what the firm can do. On their own, individual resources do not confer a competitive advantage; they must work together to create organizational capability (Grant, 2018). It is necessary to clarify here that by integration we do not mean the erasure of the two systems to give rise to a single one, but rather the possible use by each of the two systems of the resources and capabilities of the other.

Today, integrating business intelligence and CRM has become a key strategy for companies seeking to improve their operational efficiency and customer-centric strategy. The primary objective of this chapter is to explore the relationship between business intelligence and CRM processes and the benefits that result when these two essential components of today's competitive environment are seamlessly merged. By understanding how to integrate these two technologies, companies can use data-driven insights to improve customer relationship management and strategic decision-making. We, therefore, propose to carry out a prospective study based on a review of the literature and presenting the state of the art in terms of BI and CRM integration.

To carry out this study, we adopted an unorthodox methodology that is neither a narrative literature review nor a systematic literature review. It is a hybrid literature review augmented by artificial intelligence. Hybrid because it meets some of the requirements of a systematic literature review. In this sense, before any research procedure, we set a clear research question that was subdivided into three major partial research questions (the ones that gave shape to the structure of the chapter elucidated in the plan announcement), which guided the process of selecting the studies to be included and excluded. Next came the data collection phase, which was carried out not in the traditional way by searching the various databases available, but with the help of search engines powered by artificial intelligence. The search engines used were Typset.io, scholar-chat.com, consensus.app and connectedpapers.com[1]. These four search engines offer several different and complementary functions, such as keyword searches, searches by search question, sorting of results by recency and number of citations, and the ability to discuss and analyze a particular paper. The fourth engine (connectedpapers) provides a graphical presentation of all the papers and articles linked (whether they are sources or cite the article) to a specific article. Throughout the search process, we used three hierarchical criteria: the degree of proximity to the research question, the number of citations, and the recency of the article (focusing on post-2020 articles and studies). This search process enabled us to select 109 articles and studies, from which we were able to use 64 articles. The main criterion for elimination was the degree of proximity to the research question.

The purpose of this chapter is to provide a perspective on how the integration of business intelligence and CRM can lead companies to sustainable growth and improved competitiveness. It explores the principles, challenges, and potential benefits of this integration.

This chapter is organized as follows. The first part of the chapter examines the fundamentals of CRM and Business Intelligence and their integration, highlighting the key components and processes of both systems and the need for them to work together harmoniously. It then discusses the benefits of integrating business intelligence and CRM, showing how this integration improves customer relationship management and data-driven decision-making. The chapter will also outline the challenges of integrating Business Intelligence and CRM and propose some solutions to overcome these obstacles and challenges. By discussing these key points, the chapter aims to provide readers with a general understanding of the successful integration of business intelligence and CRM.

2. UNDERSTANDING THE INTEGRATION OF CRM AND BI

2.1 Overview of CRM Processes

2.1.1 Definition and Components of CRM

Customer Relationship Management is the process of managing and improving interactions between a company and its customers. It's a strategy that companies use to understand their customer's preferences and needs and to build a strong, lasting relationship with them. CRM involves collecting data about consumers, their preferences, and their purchase history, and using it to personalize marketing, sales offer, and customer service to better meet their needs. The ultimate goal is to increase customer loyalty and satisfaction and to drive sustainable growth in sales and revenue. By building a strong relationship with customers, CRM also aims to respond better and faster to their complaints, thereby increasing their confidence in the company and its products.

Customer relationship management is a set of processes that combines strategy, technology, and human resources to manage customer interactions. It enables companies to effectively manage customer accounts, resulting in a better customer experience and increased loyalty(Aulia, 2022). The main components of CRM include (Piert Espinoza et al., 2023) customer data management (collecting, storing, and analyzing customer data to better understand their behaviors and preferences), sales automation (this component includes automating sales processes such as lead generation and order processing), marketing automation (automating marketing processes such as customer segmentation and managing more targeted campaigns), customer support (handling complaints, managing returns and refunds, and providing technical support), and reporting and analytics (using data to gain insights into customer behaviors and preferences).

These different CRM components support a set of fundamental processes that enable better relationship management throughout the customer lifecycle. These processes are summarized in Table 1:

Table 1. The main processus of CRM

Process	Description
Lead management	The lead management process consists of capturing and qualifying leads for presentation to sales reps and tracking them through the sales pipeline. For this purpose, Stefanov et al. suggest the use of specialized lead management software (Stefanov et al., 2023).
Sales management	According to Kucera, CRM systems help optimize sales processes(Kučera and Cmuntová, 2023). Sales management encompasses the management of customer interactions throughout the sales cycle (order processing and customer account management).
Marketing management	This process involves creating and executing marketing campaigns that target specific customer segments. Berestetska et al. found that CRM systems can be used to develop and implement digital communication strategies for brands. (Berestetska et al., 2023) .
Customer service management	This process involves managing customer interactions after the sale. It includes handling customer complaints, managing returns and refunds, and providing technical support after the sale. In this sense, Espinoza points out that s-CRM and e-CRM can be used to improve customer service management processes (Piert Espinoza et al., 2023).

In short, CRM is designed to help companies manage their interactions with customers throughout the entire customer lifecycle, from awareness to recommendation (El Mokretar and Adman, 2023).

2.1.2 Importance of CRM in Enhancing Customer Relationships

It is becoming increasingly difficult for companies to acquire new customers (Malik and Ghai, 2023). In an increasingly competitive environment, retaining existing customers and attracting new ones is critical to a company's ability to survive and gain a competitive advantage. CRM plays a crucial role in this context. It can improve customer relationships by making them more personal. By using CRM systems, it is possible to use stored customer data to personalize the customer experience, for example, by offering customized product recommendations and communication content tailored to each customer. For example, Mohammed Mohammed et al. found that e-CRM systems can enhance personalization, leading to greater customer loyalty and satisfaction (Mohamed Mohamed et al., 2022).

Based on a single source of customer data accessible to all users, CRM also facilitates communication between the company and its customers. Based on this single version of the truth, which centralizes all available information about customers regardless of their point of contact with the company, CRM systems improve customer response time and reduce customer frustration. Fernando et al (2023), in their systematic review of the literature on CRM trends and challenges, found that CRM has the effect of improving communication with customers, thereby positively influencing the customer experience (Fernando et al., 2023).

Finally, when problems arise and customers have complaints or are dissatisfied with the company's services in some way, CRM enables companies to respond quickly and effectively to customer complaints. By tracking customer complaints and their resolution, CRM enables companies to identify the sources of problems in customer relationships, make the customer experience more user-friendly and satisfying, and thus prevent future problems. Fowler (2023) has shown that service recovery (the process by which companies respond to customer complaints and resolve problems) in the hospitality industry through CRM significantly improves customer loyalty and satisfaction.

2.2 Introduction to Business Intelligence

2.2.1 Definition and Key Elements of BI

There is no standard or agreed-upon definition of Business Intelligence. There are two main approaches to defining the concept: the business approach and the technical approach. If the latter was historically the first to be adopted, it's because BI is first and foremost a technical system, falling within the domain of technology-dominated information systems proposed by an engineer(Luhn, 1958). To this day, technology-dominated definitions persist even within the discipline of management, not just engineering. An example of a definition that seems useful for this section is that of Wixom and Watson: "Business Intelligence is a broad category of technologies, applications, and processes for collecting, storing, accessing, and analyzing data to help users make better decisions" (Wixom and Watson, 2010).

There are several aspects of this definition worth discussing. While BI is sometimes thought of in terms of applications such as dashboards, reporting, and visualization, this definition emphasizes that BI has a much broader scope. For Wixom and Watson, BI is primarily a broad category of technologies that allow users to (get data in) through technologies such as (data mart) and (data warehouse) and (get data out) through technologies or applications that meet a user's desired objective. BI therefore includes both BI applications and the BI technologies used to develop those applications.

The typical architecture of a BI system can be roughly depicted as shown in Figure 1. Data is first extracted from multiple internal and external sources and then integrated into a data warehouse using ETL (extract, transform, and load) processes. It should be noted that BI systems do not produce the data themselves; they simply work on the data that already exists in transactional systems (ERP, CRM, SCM...) and external sources (Web, sensors, social networks...). This data is then processed and analyzed, either directly in the data warehouse or in specialized data marts, to generate information and knowledge that can be accessed by applications and end users through visualization tools (Getting data out).

Figure 1. Typical BI system architecture

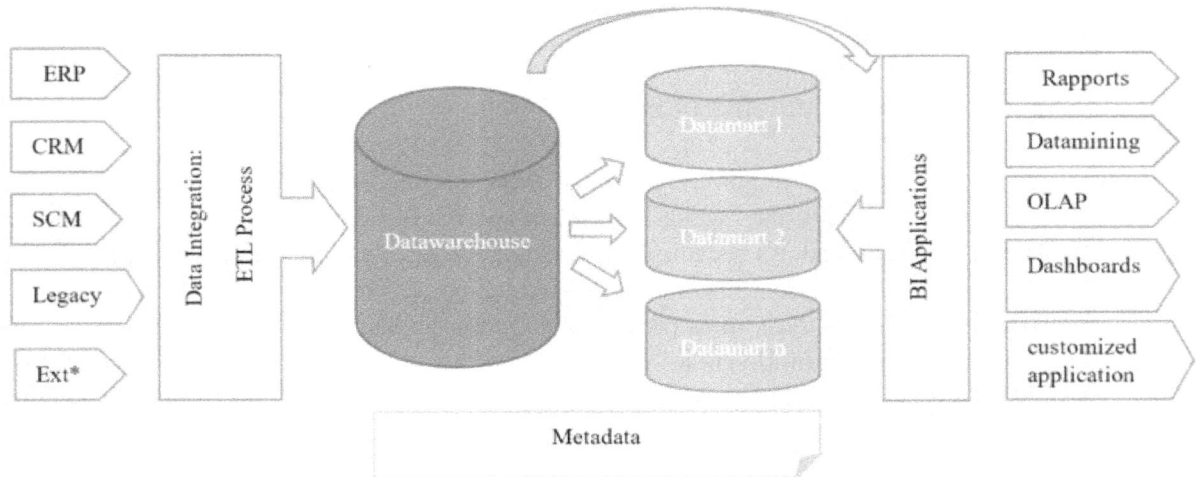

*: External sources

(adapted from Wixom and Watson, 2010)

2.2.3 Benefits of Using Business Intelligence

Through business intelligence, organizations are leveraging their data assets by using and experimenting with increasingly sophisticated data analysis techniques to make decisions. As Chaudhuri et al. point out, it's hard to find a successful company today that hasn't used BI technology to improve its business (Chaudhuri et al., 2011). In fact, with an effectively executed BI system, companies can compete by being better than the competition at using information to improve profits and performance (Williams and Williams, 2008).

BI supports a variety of decisions related to different processes that can lead to benefits for organizations. However, researchers have found that benefits are difficult to define and measure. The difficulty exists because benefits include intangible effects. Studies have suggested that the benefits of BI may be significant, but not necessarily simple or easy to quantify (Watson et al., 2002). As a result, it is difficult to find in the literature a consensus or shared vision of the benefits to be derived from BI, let alone how to achieve them.

According to a systematic literature review (Trieu, 2017) on how to "leverage business intelligence systems," the impact of BI has been the focus of BI research over the past 15 years. Specifically, researchers have shown that BI can be used to: 1) Improve an organization's operational efficiency 2) Transform business processes 3) Enrich organizational knowledge 4) Develop new or improved products and services. The list of BI benefits is long. To remedy this, Watson and Wixom (2010) proposed a taxonomy of benefits that highlights several levels of BI impact. These levels are listed according to their impact on the organization (local to global) and their tangibility and measurability (easy to difficult). This taxonomy is consistent with Watson and Wixom's observations of practitioners (Figure 2).

Figure 2. Benefits of BI

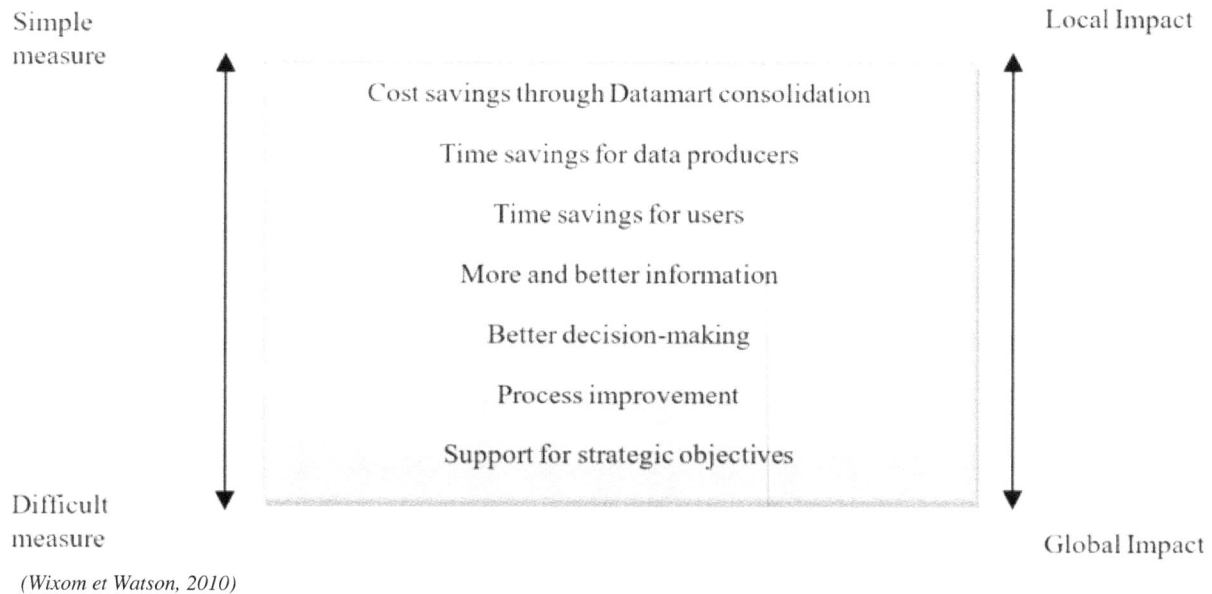

Simple
measure

Local Impact

Cost savings through Datamart consolidation

Time savings for data producers

Time savings for users

More and better information

Better decision-making

Process improvement

Support for strategic objectives

Difficult
measure

Global Impact

(Wixom et Watson, 2010)

The first two benefits, "time savings" and "more and better information," are the most tangible on the list. The "time savings" category assumes that people are performing much the same tasks and arriving at the same conclusions or results, but that they are doing so more quickly with a BI system. In the case of information quantity and quality, we can recognize that more and better information is available, but it is more difficult to specify the decisions affected by it or to quantify its impact on those particular decisions (Wixom and Watson, 2010).

In the third category, it is possible to identify specific decisions or categories of decisions that are better than previous decisions. This is because a BI system helps managers identify problems and opportunities more quickly, deepen their analysis, and make better decisions. Finally, the greatest benefits of BI applications occur when they are used to redefine business processes to make them more efficient and effective and to support the company's strategic goals.

In a study of the BI market by Dresner (2020), companies were asked to rate their perception of the performance and benefits of their BI systems (Dresner, 2020)(Figure 3).

Figure 3. Business intelligence achievements

Business Intelligence Achievement

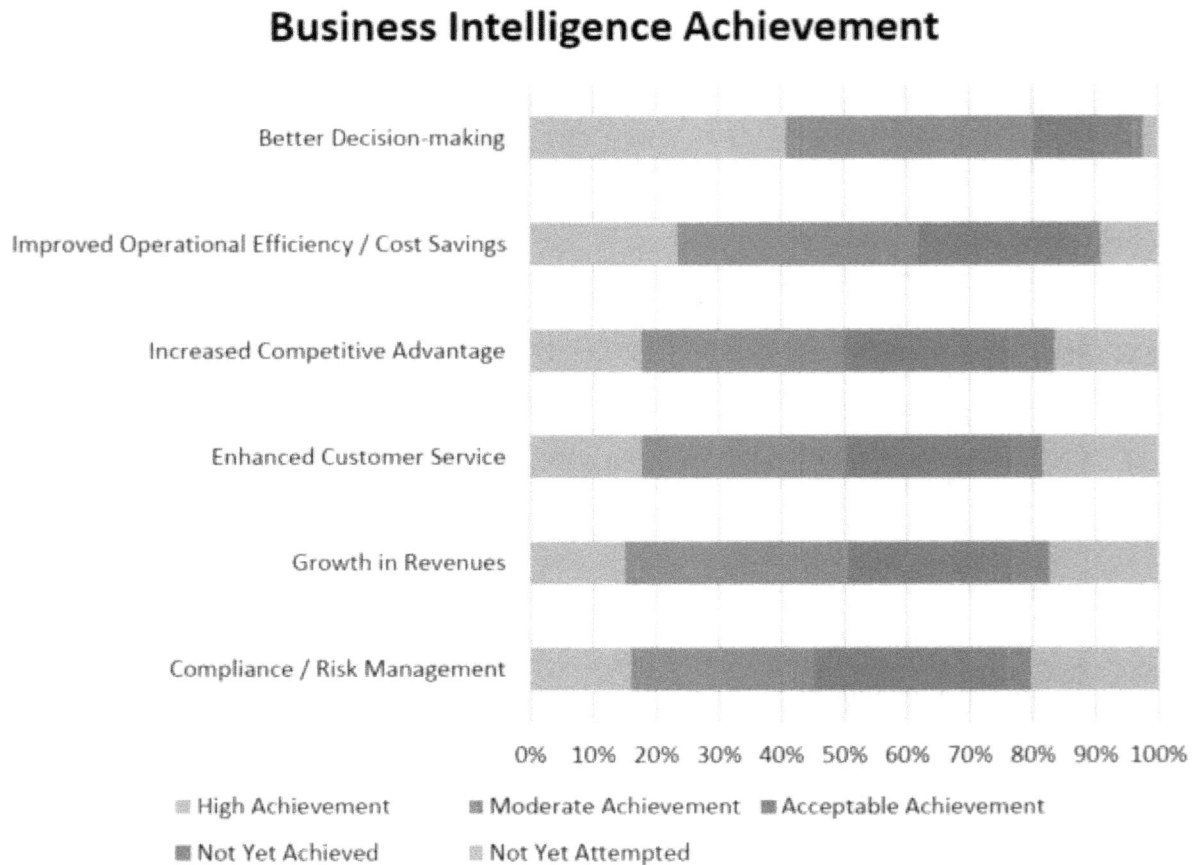

(Dressner, 2020)

The results of the study show that 80% of companies succeed in achieving one of the main goals of BI, which is to improve decision-making. However, it is worth noting that improving customer service ranks 4th among the main benefits of BI, even though it is not one of the top priorities for companies when investing in BI (in fact, it ranks 5th according to the same study). This demonstrates the rational link between BI and CRM.

2.3 Rationale for Integration

Customers are becoming more empowered, thanks to increasingly easy access to information on the Internet in general and social networks in particular. This makes them both more demanding and more volatile. The same can be said of competitors, who are becoming more flexible and better able to respond effectively to changes in the environment, thanks to available and effective technologies. In this context,

CRM systems take on their full strategic importance. They can provide a competitive advantage when used in harmony with BI systems.

By adopting a restrictive and narrow view of CRM systems, which are often seen as simple software solutions to be implemented, organizations struggle to take full advantage of these systems. By siloing them within the organization, they miss the opportunity for potential synergies with other systems that are often available but have their databases and dedicated teams, such as BI. Studies show that even industries that consider themselves customer-centric, such as banking, and have implemented several CRM initiatives, are seeing limited benefits. Peppard's research, for example, found that banks derive limited benefits from their CRM systems in isolation, and proposed a general framework for integrating CRM with other systems, such as ERP and BI, to overcome this limitation(Peppard, 2000). For their part, Zaby and Wilde have pointed out that ERP/BI and CRM systems, when implemented separately without an integrative approach, create problems of consistency, redundancy, and data quality (Zaby and Wilde, 2018). Therefore, it is essential to integrate CRM systems that provide customer data with the analytical capabilities of BI to provide a more consistent and richer view of consumer characteristics, needs, preferences, and desires to improve the effectiveness of customer relationships (Handzic et al., 2014).

Figure 1 shows that BI systems feed transactional (operational) CRM systems to perform analytics through the various BI tools. If the company can create a closed loop between these two systems, with one feeding the other with customer data and the other with customer insights, customer actions, and strategies will be optimized and improved (Zaby and Wilde, 2018). This is possible when BI systems provide timely, informed insights every time decisions need to be made at the operational CRM level. In this way, BI becomes an essential decision support for customer processes.

The integration of BI and CRM can lead to the creation of several synergies that can improve overall business performance and the effectiveness of these marketing efforts. For example, by providing decision-makers with up-to-date, real-time data on inventory, by using big data to better understand customers and predict their behavior, or by using artificial intelligence to automate tasks and facilitate business decisions. By combining CRM data and BI tools, companies can develop a deep understanding of consumer behavior, preferences, and trends. For example, Rygielski et al. found that data mining techniques enable companies to identify profitable customers, predict future behavior, and be proactive by making informed decisions based on facts and historical data (Rygielski et al., 2002). What's more, the integration of BI and CRM systems also enables the personalization of customer interactions. This is made possible by applying business analytics to CRM data. This makes it possible to propose customized offers that ensure better engagement of targeted customers and strengthen their loyalty (Rathod et al., 2024). Moreover, the benefits of this integration can extend to optimizing the effectiveness of marketing strategies by improving the targeting of communication campaigns and the selection of communication messages at the right time and through the best channel (Ponyiam and Arch-int, 2018).

In short, it can be said that the combination of CRM and BI systems has the potential to enable synergies that affect a better understanding of consumers, personalized relationships with them, and more effective marketing strategies. This will be discussed in more detail in the following section.

3. BENEFITS OF INTEGRATING CRM WITH BI

3.1 Improved Customer Relationship Management

3.1.1 How BI Enhances the Understanding of Customer Behavior

Knowing your customers is the cornerstone of any business that wants to respond to their needs and preferences. The better a company knows its customers, the better it can adapt its marketing strategies and actions to influence their behavior in its favor. As we have seen, Business Intelligence collects data through ETL processes from multiple sources, both internal and external, both structured (from company databases, such as sales data, customer feedback, and complaints) and unstructured (from social networks, such as reviews and comments on company products). By analyzing all of this data, we can increase and enrich our knowledge of consumer behavior and gain insights to improve the effectiveness of our business actions.

The use of BI techniques in CRM processes could increase revenue by tracking and analyzing customer transactions to make appropriate, personalized offers at the right time. This could improve the return on investment in both systems by increasing and optimizing the revenue generated from each customer (Gessner and Volonino, 2005). In this way, customer profitability increases and attrition rates decrease through the use of BI, enabling marketing teams to know exactly when to propose sales opportunities and personalized offers (Zaki et al., 2021). The study by ALLA et al. showed that Big Data techniques can increase sales and improve return on investment by optimizing marketing campaigns and promotions, thereby improving ROI(ALLA et al., 2022).

By processing and analyzing this data, BI tools can identify trends and patterns in consumer behavior that would otherwise be undetectable. For example, Zhang et al. used BI techniques to analyze and predict the risk of customer churn in the Chinese automotive sector. Using publicly available data on churn in China and data mining techniques, they were able to show that companies can identify the various factors that increase the risk of churn, such as poor customer service or lack of product variety (Zhang et al., 2023). This would allow companies to be proactive and take targeted actions to retain customers at risk of churn.

Another benefit of BI in customer relationship management is its ability to discover and identify the most profitable customers and best-selling products, enabling companies to tailor their marketing and sales efforts to better meet the needs and preferences of these customers. For example, a telecommunications company that identifies a loyal customer who regularly pays his subscriptions would have a lot to lose by sending him a less-than-cordial message warning him of a late payment. On the contrary, if the customer is identified by BI tools as a loyal and diligent customer, a personalized message highlighting his value to the company and granting an extension will act as positive reinforcement and consolidate the specificity of the customer relationship. It's in this sense that the study by L. Fiiwe et al. shows that CRM initiatives supported by Business Intelligence can increase customer satisfaction and retention while reducing advertising expenditures and efforts to acquire new customers (L et al., 2023).

Finally, one of the key areas for improving customer satisfaction and retention is complaint management. It is becoming increasingly difficult for companies to keep track of their customer's complaints, especially when there are so many of them. To understand the root causes of customer dissatisfaction, it's critical to have an individualized understanding of each consumer's problem to resolve it satisfactorily. This in-depth knowledge of each consumer's dissatisfaction enables the company to respond effectively and individually to each complaint. In addition, an analysis of the history of these complaints allows the company to propose and improve its offers, avoiding the root causes of dissatisfaction. Companies that can do this build a relationship of trust and loyalty with their customers, ensuring sustainable revenue growth. For example, Kunathikornkit et al., who used BI techniques such as text mining for language behavior analysis and sentiment analysis to identify the sources of customer complaints in real-time in the banking sector, found that implementing a BI-enabled CRM promotes organizational behaviors that improve post-purchase customer satisfaction and thus customer retention and loyalty (Kunathikornkit et al., 2023).

In short, the use of BI techniques in CRM processes enables companies to gain in-depth knowledge of consumer behavior and preferences by developing insights and trends in customer data, thus improving customer retention and trust, and monitoring their satisfaction in real-time.

3.1.2 Leveraging BI Insights for Personalized Customer Experiences

Leveraging the knowledge generated by BI through the analysis of CRM transactional data can help companies deliver unique, personalized customer experiences based on each customer's preferences and desires. The understanding of consumer behavior made possible by business intelligence tools and their effective use can create tailored customer experiences. For example, Sharma et al. found that using BI and AI techniques in e-commerce to predict consumer behavior made it possible to personalize the shopping experience (Sharma, 2023). By using AI and BI techniques, the authors concluded that it is possible to improve predictions and increase conversion rates through personalized recommendations that match e-shoppers' desires and preferences.

In addition, customer satisfaction and loyalty can be greatly improved by identifying consumer complaints early and responding to them quickly, as customers become more impatient. A study by Malki et al. of 340 car owners in Algeria with brands that have social media CRM initiatives showed that social CRM increases customer satisfaction and loyalty (Malki et al., 2023). This study shows that CRM initiatives supported by BI techniques can improve customer satisfaction and consequently loyalty through an engaging and personalized user experience. Furthermore, through a review of the literature, Alla et al have shown that the use of Big Data techniques enables companies to improve the effectiveness of their marketing by allowing them to better personalize their offers and positively enhance the customer experience (Bouhtati et al., 2023).

By leveraging business intelligence insights about customers, companies can deliver personalized customer experiences. In a cross-channel and multi-channel marketing environment, collecting and analyzing customer data from the various customer touch points enables hyper-personalization of the customer experience. Valdez and Flores found that this hyper-personalization relies on companies' ability to collect and transform data to personalize customer experiences. This has the effect of both personalizing customer experiences and increasing the number of people who benefit from these personalized experiences (Valdez Mendia and Flores-Cuautle, 2022), creating a close and special relationship between customers and the company. Predictive analytics modeling techniques fueled by machine learning help improve the understanding of consumer behavior and provide them with a unique experience tailored to their desires and preferences (Gupta and Joshi, 2022; Velu, 2021).

3.2 Business Intelligence Tools for Commercial Performance

3.2.1 Overview of BI Tools Suitable for Optimizing Commercial Performance

Companies that use BI tools generally achieve better business performance than those that don't. BI tools help companies improve business processes, define and achieve goals, and are likely to create a competitive advantage (Maaitah, 2023). The implementation and use of BI have a strong impact on the bottom line, which is an important determinant of business performance.

BI tools differ from traditional data analysis tools in several ways. Business intelligence systems process both real-time transactional data and historical data using tools that provide relevant information and knowledge to decision-makers (Zamlynskyi Viktor et al., 2023). The goal is to increase the timeliness and quality of data so that managers can better understand their organizations.

There are several business intelligence solutions on the market that companies can use to enhance and improve their business performance. All of them can collect, analyze, and visualize information in real-time to provide insight into consumer behavior and market trends. One of the most popular solutions is Microsoft Power BI, which allows users to create reports and dashboards to visualize their performance in real-time. According to Lishchynska et al, Microsoft Power BI can support up to 100 local and cloud data sources. It also supports DAX, Power Query, SQL, R, and Python. One of the strengths of Power BI is its compatibility with other Microsoft solutions, such as data lake integration (Azure Data Lake Storage Gen2), support for real-time data flows using the Power BI REST API, and integration with Azure machine learning (Lishchynska et al., 2022).

Another popular business intelligence solution is Tableau. This BI solution is best known for its unmatched visualization capabilities, enabling the creation of dashboards that provide a better understanding of operations and processes. This solution offers the ability to preview individual areas of the dashboard and connect to data sets based on location. What's more, Tableau Online lets you connect to databases in the cloud. It also offers integration with Amazon Redshift and Google BigQuery (Lishchynska et al., 2022). This promising and fashionable BI solution was acquired by the CRM giant Salesforce in 2019.

Other open-source BI solutions, such as Apache Hadoop, Orange, and OpenRefine, simplify working with unstructured data, support multiple file formats, facilitate machine learning, and enable the processing of large data sets to provide valuable insights into consumer behavior, preferences, and desires. For example, Taleb et al. used big data technologies to combine internal CRM data with data from the external environment on consumer behavior and purchasing patterns. They showed that the use of these BI tools increases the efficiency of CRM systems (Taleb et al., 2020).

In short, there are several BI solutions that companies can use to optimize their sales performance. These solutions enable companies to better capture the complexity of consumer behavior, better understand their desires and preferences, and track their performance in real time.

3.2.2 Some Successful Case Studies of Integrating BI and CRM

The literature is replete with success stories showing how analytic competitors have managed to leapfrog the competition by using advanced customer data analysis to gain a sustainable competitive advantage (Davenport and Harris, 2006). In the introduction, we cited the example of Continental Airlines, which went from tenth place in the market with completely dissatisfied customers to not only the market leader but also the "favorite" of its customers by implementing BI systems focused on customer data (Lehman et al., 2008). Other success stories are also worth mentioning. Netflix, for example, is a prime example of a company that can leverage BI technologies to better personalize the customer experience. As early as 2006, it launched a competition open to all machine learning researchers, promising $1 million for any algorithm that could improve its recommendation system by 10% by 2011 (Greene, 2006). By mining customer data and using the right BI tools, Netflix can make personalized recommendations that match each customer's choices and tastes, thereby improving their streaming experience and satisfaction.

Another example of a company that has successfully integrated business intelligence into its CRM strategy is Amazon. This platform can track consumer behavior and identify their preferences using BI tools and artificial intelligence to personalize the recommendation system both on its e-commerce platform and for its Netflix-competing service, Amazon Prime(Larry Hardesty, 2019). By relying on a recommendation system based on customers' purchase history, Amazon can provide relevant product recommendations, making the customer experience more rewarding and increasing customer satisfaction. Finally, let's look at the case of the hospitality company Hilton, which, thanks to the successful integration of business intelligence tools to process customer data, can personalize the customer experience in a way that always puts the guest at the center of its concerns, thus succeeding in proposing innovative solutions, including digital services, that radically change the customer experience (Escobar, 2021).

All of these cases demonstrate how companies can optimize the use of their business intelligence systems as part of their CRM strategies to analyze customer data and identify trends and buying patterns to create unique, personalized customer experiences. These CRM giants are developing a competitive advantage and succeeding in retaining their customers for as long as possible not because of their products or price, but because of the unique customer experience they provide to their customers (Ayyagari, 2019).

3.3 Enhancing Decision-Making Through CRM Data

It's hard to imagine a successful, high-performing company without being customer-centric. Without satisfying customer needs and preferences, it's unlikely that a company will survive in the marketplace (Baboolal-Frank, 2021). That's why companies are doing everything they can to satisfy and retain their customers, including CRM strategies and business intelligence systems. We saw above that BI systems collect data from a variety of sources, including transactional systems such as ERP, SCM, and CRM, as well as external sources. This data is then transferred through ETL processes to a data warehouse, where it is analyzed using various BI techniques such as OLAP and data mining to support decision-making.

Data from CRM systems can help increase the efficiency of BI-supported decision-making processes by providing critical customer data to guide decisions (Ayyagari, 2019). The analysis of customer data by BI systems can lead to increased customer satisfaction and loyalty, thereby improving competitiveness and commercial and financial performance (Rygielski et al., 2002; Trabelsi and Akrout, 2022). CRM data can improve the efficiency of decision-making processes in several ways. For example, through a literature review, Ledro et al. found that integrating artificial intelligence and CRM can help companies increase sales and refine marketing strategies, thereby increasing customer satisfaction(Ledro et al., 2022). By using customer data to feed AI algorithms, companies can determine which products sell best, which customers are most profitable, and which marketing campaigns are most effective. This type of information can enable companies to create more targeted communication campaigns, thereby improving customer acquisition and retention.

What's more, customer data has the potential to enable companies to identify all possible sources of business process improvement. For example, a study by Rathod et al. found that using customer data in AI algorithms embedded in BI can track consumer complaints to identify areas and processes for improvement, such as product quality and customer service (Rathod et al., 2024). By addressing these issues, companies can improve their business performance through increased customer satisfaction. Customer data can therefore be used to identify new opportunities for growth and additional product and service innovation.

From another perspective, CRM data can improve decision-making at both the strategic and tactical levels. By providing insights into customer behavior, preferences, and desires, CRM data helps optimize current operations. For example, Rathod et al. found that the use of CRM data enables the tracking of customer complaints and claims to help companies improve their customer service and thus avoid attrition (Rathod et al., 2024). Similarly, Cristescu et al, in a study of the impact of CRM data on revenue improvement in the European Union, found that the use of CRM data combined with big data techniques helped optimize supply chain management and increase revenues (Cristescu et al., 2023).

CRM data can also inform strategic decision-making by providing insights into long-term market trends and potential opportunities for the company. Ledro et al. found that using CRM data in artificial intelligence algorithms can help companies improve their sales and marketing strategy and increase customer satisfaction in the long run (Ledro et al., 2022). Gräser et al. found that integrating CRM, ERP, and BI data increases the efficiency of data-driven decision-making by providing a complete view of customer interactions, sales data, and operations through social CRM (Gräser et al., 2023).

In short, CRM data positively impacts BI decision support processes in a variety of ways, supporting both strategic and operational decisions.

4. IMPLEMENTATION STRATEGIES

After discussing the benefits and possible synergies of integrating CRM and Business Intelligence in the previous section, it's time to focus on the challenges companies may face when attempting this endeavor. Integrating CRM and BI is not an easy task, as it requires companies to address several issues. Separate databases, redundant data, and incompatible infrastructures, not to mention the problem of data inconsistency.

4.1 Common Challenges in Integrating CRM and BI

Organizations typically have CRM applications with databases that are separate from the rest of their information systems. When companies want to integrate CRM data into BI data warehouses, they face many obstacles.

One of the biggest issues companies face is data quality. Ensuring that the data collected by CRM and BI systems is accurate and complete is a critical challenge. Poor data quality often leads to incorrect insights and inefficient decision-making processes. Data quality refers to cleansed data that is meaningful to the organization (Khan et al., 2012). Generally speaking, quality data is data that meets the needs and intended use of the organization (Ait Touil and Jabraoui, 2023). Data quality is such an important issue for organizations that most BI maturity models consider it a critical dimension (Ait Touil and Jabraoui, 2022). Kegan et al. found that one of the biggest challenges to overcome when integrating AI into CRM systems is comprehensive and fluid access to high-quality data sets (Keegan et al., 2022). Unlike stand-alone AI systems with their own training and test data sets, AI systems based on CRM data require fluid, unfettered access to CRM platforms and their databases(Ledro et al., 2023).

Another problem with integrating CRM and BI is data integration. The variety of sources where data is stored requires considerable effort to integrate them so that they can all be used in processing and analysis processes. Li et al. found that this problem of integrating data from different sources, especially when the data sets are large and complex, is one of the major challenges of integrating CRM and BI systems (Li et al., 2023). What's more, integrating BI and CRM requires significant investment in hardware and software infrastructure, which poses a financial challenge for companies and raises the issue of return on investment, which in turn challenges companies' ability to weigh the expected costs and benefits of such investments (Li et al, 2023), making it difficult to justify this type of project.

However, one of the key challenges in this quest for integration is culture. One of the reasons why individual BI and CRM systems fail is organizational culture. A lack of commitment and involvement from top management, or a low level of cooperation and understanding between the BI and CRM teams on the one hand, and between them and the various business units on the other, can jeopardize all the investment and effort put into integrating BI and CRM systems. Kumar et al. found that organizational culture is a significant challenge when it comes to integrating CRM and BI(Kumar and Reinartz, 2018).

4.2 Best Practices to Overcome These Challenges

To address these challenges, organizations can leverage existing best practices. For example, the issue of data quality can be addressed by implementing data governance systems. Data governance refers to the overall process of managing the availability, security, use, and integrity of data within an organization. Organizations in the 21st century must treat data as a strategic resource. It is a key success factor for any data-driven initiative, especially BI and CRM initiatives. The role that data governance can play in the context of BI and CRM integration is critical because data governance sets standards for data quality and ensures that the extracted data used in either system meets those standards. In this way, organizations can ensure fluidity and continuity in the use and exploitation of reliable data without encountering problems with data redundancy, inconsistency, or accuracy. Li et al. suggested that data quality in the context of CRM and BI integration can be greatly improved through the implementation of data governance (Li et al., 2023). Ahmad et al. discussed the importance of unified data governance when data is distributed across different on-premises and cloud databases, and emphasized the role of data stewardship and data owners in maintaining integrity and accountability across multiple integrated systems such as CRM and BI (Ahmad et al., 2023).

To avoid infrastructure-related problems, companies are well advised to invest in a scalable, flexible, and extensible technology infrastructure that enables the integration of BI and CRM systems. This makes these investments profitable and improves their return on investment. Cloud-based SaaS CRM and BI solutions can also provide a solution to this infrastructure problem, as these systems have the advantage of adapting to changing business needs. For this reason, Li et al (2023) suggest that companies invest in these types of solutions to avoid the problems of technological infrastructure, which remains an important dimension in improving data quality in the context of BI (Ait Touil and Jabraoui, 2023) and, by extension, in that of CRM.

The problem of organizational culture is one of the most difficult to solve. Creating a data-driven culture is one of the biggest challenges, even for those organizations that are aware of it and have initiatives in place to promote it. Davenport and Bean have highlighted the slowness with which organizations attempt to implement a data-driven culture. Their study found that 90% of the organizations surveyed said they were working to instill this culture, but only one-third admitted to being successful (Davenport and Bean, 2018). However, to successfully integrate CRM and BI, organizations have no choice but to persist in this quest. They can do this by implementing policies and procedures that foster a culture of collaboration and sharing across departments and business teams, and by rewarding the use of data and testing in decision-making processes in general and CRM in particular. In addition, a major effort is needed to raise awareness of the benefits of fact-based, data-driven decision-making. According to Kumar and Reinartz (2018), data literacy can help overcome cultural issues in organizations that want to integrate BI and CRM systems.

5. CONCLUSION

Throughout this chapter, we've tried to show why companies should integrate their BI and CRM systems and take advantage of the resulting synergies. The integration of CRM and BI systems promises to have a positive impact on companies in today's highly competitive environment, where customers are increasingly difficult to please. As a result, BI and CRM integration has become a key strategy for companies seeking to improve their operational efficiency and customer-centric practices.

By presenting the key processes and components of both BI and CRM, we were able to identify potential synergies between the two systems. Since CRM is a strategy used by companies to understand their customers' preferences and needs and to build a strong, lasting relationship with them, it gives rise to a set of processes such as lead management, sales management, marketing management, and customer service management. BI, for its part, has been presented as a broad category of technologies, applications, and processes designed to help users make better decisions by collecting data from a variety of internal and external sources, storing it in data warehouses, and applying a range of analytical techniques such as OLAP, data mining, and machine learning.

This work is of particular interest to managers. From the point of view of managerial implications, it presents the logic behind the usefulness of synchronizing CRM and BI systems. The chapter has drawn on existing literature to show that integrating these two systems offers several possible synergies, helping to make managers aware of the importance of such an initiative. Throughout the chapter, we have explained that the combination of CRM data and BI techniques helps companies develop a deep understanding of consumer behavior, preferences, and desires. This helps guide sales and marketing efforts, enabling companies to personalize products and services, respond effectively to customer complaints, increase customer satisfaction and loyalty, and reduce churn. The result is improved business performance through increased revenue and reduced churn and customer acquisition costs. The customer experience is not left out, as the use of artificial intelligence techniques in various sectors such as e-commerce, hospitality, and streaming, for example, makes it possible to individualize these experiences on the one hand, and to increase the effectiveness of recommendation systems to match customer desires and preferences on the other. To this end, we have presented success stories from companies currently considered to be CRM giants, such as Netflix, Amazon, and Hilton.

The chapter also discussed the usefulness of using CRM data in BI processes, and how this is critical for generating insights that are essential for effective decision-making, both strategic and operational. For example, customer data can enable companies to identify all possible sources of improvement in business processes, such as customer service and product quality, and to explore new opportunities for innovation in the company's products and services. CRM data can also inform strategic decisions by providing insight into long-term market trends and opportunities that the company can capitalize on.

Another contribution of this chapter for managers is that it has highlighted the challenges that organizations must overcome to integrate these two systems at both operational and organizational/strategic levels. Indeed, not all of these potential synergies come automatically to the enterprise, as the integration of BI and CRM systems presents companies with challenges and obstacles that can derail these initiatives. Challenges such as data quality, infrastructure compatibility, integrating data from disparate sources, and difficulties related to organizational culture when it is not data-driven. To that end, we have presented a set of best practices that have the potential to overcome these challenges.

While of particular importance to managers, these challenges may provide fertile ground for future research avenues for the research community. Even if the question of data quality or infrastructure compatibility, in addition to the challenges of change management and the Data-driven culture and involvement of top management, are subjects widely adopted in the literature, their analysis in the context of CRM and BI integration may show particular specificities due to the strategic importance of these two processes. It is also essential to note that despite the abundance of literature on CRM and BI separately, the integration of these two systems still suffers from a lack of studies, especially empirical ones, that shed light on how companies could undertake this type of initiative in an enlightened way. For example, the field of information systems could be enriched by studies on what artificial intelligence and machine learning can contribute to improving the integration of these two systems, thereby increasing the benefits derived by companies. Research into best practices in data governance, especially in the context of BI and CRM integration, would also ensure integration with secure, high-quality data. Finally, we recommend research into the impact of integrating these two systems on overall business performance, customer satisfaction and loyalty, and financial results.

From a methodological point of view, this work adopted an innovative approach midway between the narrative literature review and the systematic literature review, relying on search tools powered by artificial intelligence which are gradually making their entry into the field of academic research, and are admittedly in an embryonic phase and require in-depth discussion by academics as to how they can be used with rigor and credibility. However, it has to be acknowledged that the main limitation of this study is the difficulty of its reproducibility by the scientific community.

REFERENCES

Ahmad, S., Arumugam, D., Bozovic, S., Degefa, E., Duvvuri, S., Gott, S., Gupta, N., Hammer, J., Kaluskar, N., Kaushik, R., Khanduja, R., Mujumdar, P., Malhotra, G., Naik, P., Ogg, N., Parthasarthy, K. K., Ramakrishnan, R., Rodriguez, V., Sharma, R., & Wolter, A. (2023). Microsoft Purview: A System for Central Governance of Data. *Proceedings of the VLDB Endowment International Conference on Very Large Data Bases*, 16(12), 3624–3635. 10.14778/3611540.3611552

Ait Touil, A., & Jabraoui, S. (2022). Les modèles de maturité de la business intelligence Analyse comparative. *Revue Marocaine de la Prospective en Sciences de Gestion*, 2022(4), 16.

Ait Touil, A., & Jabraoui, S. (2023). Information Quality of Business Intelligence Systems: A Maturity-based Assessment. *Journal of Information Systems Engineering and Business Intelligence*, 9(2), 276–287. 10.20473/jisebi.9.2.276-287

Alikhani, M., Naderi, N., & Kazemi Eskeri, F. (2021). The Impact Of Business Intelligence On CRM Case of study: Shuttle Companies' Group. *Science and Technology Policy Letters*. https://stpl.ristip.sharif.ir/article_22232.html?lang=en

Alla, L., Kamal, M., & Bouhtati, N. (2022). Big data et efficacité marketing des entreprises touristiques: Une revue de littérature. *Alternatives Managériales Economiques, Numéro spécial 1*, 39–58. 10.48374/IMIST.PRSM/ame-v1i0.36928

Aulia, D. (2022). ENHANCEMENTS IN THE MANAGEMENT OF RELATIONSHIPS WITH CUSTOMERS AS A MEANS OF PRESERVING SALES PERFORMANCE. [JAMB]. *Journal of Applied Management and Business*, 3(1). 10.37802/jamb.v3i1.242

Ayyagari, M. R. (2019). A Framework for Analytical CRM Assessments Challenges and Recommendations. *International Journal of Business and Social Science*, 10(6). Advance online publication. 10.30845/ijbss.v10n6p2

Baboolal-Frank, R. (2021). *ANALYSIS OF AMAZON: CUSTOMER CENTRIC APPROACH, 20*(2).

Berestetska, O., Iankovets, T., Orozonova, A., Voitovych, S., Parmanasova, A., & Medvedieva, K. (2023). Using Crm Systems for the Development and Implementation of Communication Strategies for Digital Brand Management and Internet Marketing: Eu Experience. *International Journal of Professional Business Review*, 8(4), e01613. 10.26668/businessreview/2023.v8i4.1613

Bouhtati, N., Kamal, M., & Alla, L. (2023). Big Data and the Effectiveness of Tourism Marketing: A Prospective Review of the Literature. In Brahmia, Z., & Bhushab, B. (Eds.), *Artificial Intelligence and Smart Environment* (pp. 287–292). Springer International Publishing. 10.1007/978-3-031-26254-8_40

Chaudhuri, S., Dayal, U., & Narasayya, V. (2011). An overview of business intelligence technology. *Communications of the ACM*, 54(8), 88–98. 10.1145/1978542.1978562

Cristescu, M. P., Mara, D. A., Culda, L. C., Neri anu, R. A., Bâra, A., & Oprea, S.-V. (2023). The Impact of Data Science Solutions on the Company Turnover. *Information (Basel)*, 14(10), 573. 10.3390/info14100573

Davenport, T. H., and Bean, R. (2018). *Big Companies Are Embracing Analytics, But Most Still Don't Have a Data-Driven Culture.*

Davenport, T. H., & Harris, J. G. (2006, January 1). Competing on Analytics. *Harvard Business Review.* https://hbr.org/2006/01/competing-on-analytics

Dresner, H. (2020). *Wisdom of crowds business intelligence market study report* (Survey 2020 Edition; p. 183). Dresner Advisory Services. https://www.pyramidanalytics.com/docs/default-source/downloads/wisdom_of_crowds-__business_intelligence_market_study_report__-_licensed_to_pyramid_analytics_-_-_2020_dresner_advisory_services.pdf?sfvrsn=cd68f8c9_0

El Mokretar, L., & Adman, M. (2023). Developing a growth marketing approach to B2B customer retention: Case Algeria. *Marketing Science & Inspirations*, 18(3), 36–46. 10.46286/msi.2023.18.3.4

Escobar, M. C. (2021, October 21). *Hilton Introduces Tech Enhancements to Improve Guest Experience.* Hospitality Technology. https://hospitalitytech.com/hilton-introduces-tech-enhancements-improve-guest-experience

Fernandes, N., & Lim, J., Raymond, Eddison, T., & Hasan, G. (2023). The Impact of Customer Relationship Management (CRM) on Company Performance in Three Segments (Finance, Marketing and Operations). *Jurnal Minfo Polgan*, 12(1), 1. 10.33395/jmp.v12i1.12431

Fernando, E., Sutomo, R., Prabowo, Y. D., Gatc, J., & Winanti, W. (2023). Exploring Customer Relationship Management: Trends, Challenges, and Innovations. *Journal of Information Systems and Informatics*, 5(3), 984–1001. 10.51519/journalisi.v5i3.541

Gessner, G. H., & Volonino, L. (2005). Quick Response Improves Returns on Business Intelligence Investments. *Information Systems Management*, 22(3), 66–74. 10.1201/1078/45317.22.3.20050601/88746.8

Grant, R. M. (2018). *Contemporary strategy analysis* (10th ed.). Wiley & Sons.

Gräser, M., Harris, C., Alt, R., & Reinhold, O. (2023). How Integrated Social CRM Affects Business Success: Learnings from a Literature Analysis. *2023 IEEE/WIC International Conference on Web Intelligence and Intelligent Agent Technology (WI-IAT)*, (pp. 547–554). IEEE. 10.1109/WI-IAT59888.2023.00091

Greene, K. (2006). *The $1 Million Netflix Challenge*. MIT Technology Review. https://www.technologyreview.com/2006/10/06/273459/the-1-million-netflix-challenge/

Gupta, S., & Joshi, S. (2022). Predictive Analytic Techniques for enhancing marketing performance and Personalized Customer Experience. *2022 International Interdisciplinary Humanitarian Conference for Sustainability (IIHC)*, (pp. 16–22). IEEE. 10.1109/IIHC55949.2022.10060286

Handzic, M., Ozlen, K., & Durmic, N. (2014). Improving Customer Relationship Management Through Business Intelligence. *Journal of Information & Knowledge Management*, 13(02), 1450015. 10.1142/S0219649214500154

Hardesty, L. (2019, November 22). *The history of Amazon's recommendation algorithm.* Amazon Science. https://www.amazon.science/the-history-of-amazons-recommendation-algorithm

Jhamb, S., & Turcanu, R. (2022). A Scholarly Review of Global Business Indications and Economic Trends: Understanding International Competitiveness, Economic Globalization, and Digitization Through the Lens of the COVID-19 Pandemic and the New Normal. *Journal of Marketing Development and Competitiveness*, 16(3). 10.33423/jmdc.v16i3.5584

Keegan, B. J., Canhoto, A. I., & Yen, D. A. (2022). Power negotiation on the tango dancefloor: The adoption of AI in B2B marketing. *Industrial Marketing Management*, 100, 36–48. 10.1016/j.indmarman.2021.11.001

Khan, A., Ehsan, N., Mirza, E., & Sarwar, S. Z. (2012). Integration between Customer Relationship Management (CRM) and Data Warehousing. *Procedia Technology*, 1, 239–249. 10.1016/j.protcy.2012.02.050

Kučera, P., & Cmuntová, D. (2023). Design and implementation of a CRM system to optimize business processes of a trading company. *Entrepreneurship and Sustainability Issues*, 11(2), 363–380. 10.9770/jesi.2023.11.2(25)

Kumar, V., & Reinartz, W. (2018). *Customer Relationship Management*. Springer Berlin Heidelberg., 10.1007/978-3-662-55381-7

Kunathikornkit, S., Piriyakul, I., & Piriyakul, R. (2023). One-to-one marketing management via customer complaint. *Social Network Analysis and Mining*, 13(1), 83. 10.1007/s13278-023-01082-z

L, F., J., E., E., A., U., O., J., and O., O., B. (2023). Customer Relationship Management and Customers Repeat Purchase Behavior in Nigeria. *Scholars Journal of Economics, Business and Management, 10*(1), 19–28. 10.36347/sjebm.2023.v10i01.002

Ledro, C., Nosella, A., & Dalla Pozza, I. (2023). Integration of AI in CRM: Challenges and guidelines. *Journal of Open Innovation*, 9(4), 100151. 10.1016/j.joitmc.2023.100151

Ledro, C., Nosella, A., & Vinelli, A. (2022). Artificial intelligence in customer relationship management: Literature review and future research directions. *Journal of Business and Industrial Marketing*, 37(13), 48–63. 10.1108/JBIM-07-2021-0332

Lehman, R. A., Watson, H. J., Wixom, B. H., & Hoffer, J. A. (2008). Continental Airlines Flies High with Real-time Business Intelligence. *MIS Quarterly Executive*, 3(4), 30.

Li, L., Lin, J., & Luo, W. (2023). INVESTIGATING THE EFFECT OF ARTIFICIAL INTELLIGENCE ON CUSTOMER RELATIONSHIP MANAGEMENT PERFORMANCE IN E-COMMERCE ENTERPRISES. *Journal of Electronic Commerce Research*, 24(1).

Lishchynska, L., & Dobrovolska, N. (2022). PROSPECTIVE SOFTWARE TOOLS FOR DATA ANALYSIS IN BUSINESS. *Herald of Khmelnytskyi National University*, 305(1), 78–83. 10.31891/2307-5732-2022-305-1-78-79

Luhn, H. P. (1958). A Business Intelligence System. *IBM Journal of Research and Development*, 2(4), 314–319. 10.1147/rd.24.0314

Maaitah, T. (2023). The Role of Business Intelligence Tools in the Decision Making Process and Performance. *Journal of Intelligence Studies in Business*, 13(1), 43–52. 10.37380/jisib.v13i1.990

Malik, A., & Ghai, S. (2023). Role of CRM in Customer Loyalty and Repeat Purchase Intention: An Analytical Study. *Journal of Informatics Education and Research*, 3(1), 1. 10.52783/jier.v3i1.60

Mohamed Mohamed, S., Yehia, E., & Marie, M. (2022). Relationship between E-CRM, Service Quality, Customer Satisfaction, Trust, and Loyalty in banking Industry. *Future Computing and Informatics Journal*, 7(2), 51–74. 10.54623/fue.fcij.7.2.5

Murat, A., Saida, S., & Timurlan, S. (2023). Global Digital Transformation Trends in Real Sectors of the Economy. *SHS Web of Conferences, 172*, 02014. 10.1051/shsconf/202317202014

Olszak, C. M. (2016). Toward Better Understanding and Use of Business Intelligence in Organizations. *Information Systems Management*, 33(2), 105–123. 10.1080/10580530.2016.1155946

Peppard, J. (2000). Customer Relationship Management (CRM) in financial services. *European Management Journal*, 18(3), 312–327. 10.1016/S0263-2373(00)00013-X

Piert Espinoza, J., Cardenas Yactayo, D., & Chavez Ugaz, R. (2023, October 10). CRM Implementation in SMEs Management Processes: The Role of e-CRM and s-CRM. *Proceedings of the International Conference on Industrial Engineering and Operations Management*. IEEE. 10.46254/EV01.20230213

Ponyiam, P., & Arch-int, S. (2018). Customer Behavior Analysis Using Data Mining Techniques. *2018 International Seminar on Application for Technology of Information and Communication*, (pp. 549–554). IEEE. 10.1109/ISEMANTIC.2018.8549803

Rathod, H. D., Rajawat, D., Ahmed, M., Dagur, Y., & Rajpurohit, K. (2024). A Study to Know Impact of AI on CRM. *Interantional Journal Of Scientific Research In Engineering And Management*, 08(02), 1–13. 10.55041/IJSREM31253

Rygielski, C., Wang, J.-C., & Yen, D. C. (2002). Data mining techniques for customer relationship management. *Technology in Society*, 24(4), 483–502. 10.1016/S0160-791X(02)00038-6

Sharma, A. (2023). Analyzing the Role of Artificial Intelligence in Predicting Customer Behavior and Personalizing the Shopping Experience in Ecommerce. *Interantional Journal Of Scientific Research In Engineering And Management*, 07(02). 10.55041/IJSREM17839

Stefanov, T., Varbanova, S., Stefanova, M., & Ivanov, I. (2023). CRM System as a Necessary Tool for Managing Commercial and Production Processes. *TEM Journal*, 785–797. https://doi.org/10.18421/TEM122-23

Taleb, N., Salahat, M., & Ali, L. (2020). Impacts of Big-Data Technologies in Enhancing CRM Performance. *2020 6th International Conference on Information Management (ICIM)*, (pp. 257–263). IEEE. 10.1109/ICIM49319.2020.244708

Trabelsi, L., & Akrout, F. (2022). *Data Mining for CRM: Extracting Customer Knowledge From Data.* IGI Global. Https://Services.Igi-Global.Com/Resolvedoi/Resolve.Aspx?Doi=10.4018/978-1-7998-9553-4.Ch008

Trieu, V.-H. (2017). Getting value from Business Intelligence systems: A review and research agenda. *Decision Support Systems*, 93, 111–124. 10.1016/j.dss.2016.09.019

Valdez Mendia, J. M., & Flores-Cuautle, J. J. A. (2022). Toward customer hyper-personalization experience—A data-driven approach. *Cogent Business & Management*, 9(1), 2041384. 10.1080/23311975.2022.2041384

Velu, A. (2021). *Machine Learning Techniques for Customer Relationship Management.* 9(6).

Viktor, Z., Alla, S., & Ol'ga, Z. (2023, April 23). Features and characteristics of business intelligence (BI)-systems as a tool for improving the efficiency of company activities. *Ukrainian Journal of Applied Economics and Technology.* http://ujae.org.ua/en/features-and-characteristics-of-business-intelligence-bi-systems-as-a-tool-for-improving-the-efficiency-of-company-activities/

Watson, H. J., Goodhue, D. L., & Wixom, B. H. (2002). The benefits of data warehousing: Why some organizations realize exceptional payoffs. *Information & Management*, 39(6), 491–502. 10.1016/S0378-7206(01)00120-3

Williams, S., & Williams, N. (2008). *The Profit Impact of Business Intelligence* (Updated and rev.[New ed.]). Elsevier/Morgan Kaufmann Publishers.

Wixom, B., & Watson, H. (2010). The BI-Based Organization. *International Journal of Business Intelligence Research*, 1(1), 13–28. 10.4018/jbir.2010071702

Zaby, C., & Wilde, K. D. (2018). Intelligent Business Processes in CRM: Exemplified by Complaint Management. *Business & Information Systems Engineering*, 60(4), 289–304. 10.1007/s12599-017-0480-6

Zaki, S., Ismail, M. M., Rashad, H., & Ibrahim, M. (2021). Optimizing Customer Relationship Management through Business Intelligence for Sustainable Business Practices. *American Journal of Business and Operations Research*, 3(1), 70–79. 10.54216/AJBOR.030105

Zhang, D., Zhang, C., & Zheng, C. (2023). Prediction and Analysis of Customer Churn of Automobile Dealers Based on BI. *2023 IEEE 6th Information Technology, Networking, Electronic and Automation Control Conference (ITNEC).* IEEE. 10.1109/ITNEC56291.2023.10082554

ENDNOTE

[1]   AI Chat for scientific PDFs | SciSpace (typeset.io) ; Scholar-Chat ; Search - Consensus: AI Search Engine for Research ; Connected Papers | Find and explore academic papers

Chapter 9
Unleashing the Potential of Artificial Intelligence (AI) in Customer Engagement

Farid Huseynov
http://orcid.org/0000-0002-9936-0596
Gebze Technical University, Turkey

ABSTRACT

In the rapidly evolving technological landscape, the strategic integration of AI becomes imperative, fundamentally altering the dynamics of business-customer interactions. This chapter commences by exploring AI's pivotal role in deciphering complex consumer behavior patterns, providing businesses with invaluable insights to adapt to market dynamics. From there, the focus shifts to AI-powered personalization, highlighting its profound impact on enriching customer experiences and forging deeper connections. Subsequently, the discussion delves into the realm of AI-driven automation, which not only revolutionizes the efficiency but also enhances the quality of customer engagement processes. Lastly, attention is drawn to the ethical considerations and privacy concerns inherent in AI-driven customer engagement, underscoring the importance of responsible AI implementation. In essence, this chapter underscores AI's multifaceted influence on customer engagement strategies, establishing it as a cornerstone for businesses aspiring to achieve sustainable success in the ever-changing marketplace.

1. INTRODUCTION

Artificial Intelligence (AI) refers to the development of computer systems that possess the ability to perform activities typically requiring human intelligence (Garg, 2021; Sarker, 2022). These abilities include the acquisition of knowledge from experience, the interpretation of spoken communication, the recognition of recurring patterns, and solving of complex problems. AI seeks to build systems that are capable of self-improvement and data-driven decision-making, allowing them to function independently without explicit programming. It includes a variety of technologies, including robotics, machine learn-

DOI: 10.4018/979-8-3693-3172-9.ch009

ing, and natural language processing. Its applications range from recommendation engines and virtual assistants to self-driving cars and sophisticated medical diagnostics.

Customer interaction refers to the communication and engagement between a business or brand and its customers (Nüesch & Puschmann, 2015; Jian & Liu, 2016; Hydle et al. 2021). It includes all points of contact between clients and the business, such as face-to-face meetings, emails, phone conversations, and correspondence via other media. Effective customer interaction involves understanding and responding to customer needs, providing assistance, and creating positive experiences to build and maintain strong relationships with customers. It plays a crucial role in shaping customer satisfaction, loyalty, and overall perception of a brand. Customer engagement, on the other hand, extends beyond individual interactions and emphasizes building a long-term relationship between the customer and the brand. It involves creating meaningful connections, fostering loyalty, and maintaining ongoing communication to ensure a positive and enduring customer experience (Bowden, 2009; Rasool et al., 2021). Engaged customers are more likely to interact with the brand consistently and advocate for its products or services.

In the rapidly evolving landscape of customer interactions and engagements, businesses face the pressing challenge of meeting and surpassing modern consumers' expectations in an increasingly digital marketplace. Traditional methods are proving inadequate for satisfying the demand for personalized, efficient, and seamless experiences, exacerbating the difficulty of staying competitive. The absence of AI integration further compounds this problem, posing a significant obstacle that risks businesses falling behind competitors and jeopardizing their ability to establish meaningful, long-term relationships with customers. In this dynamic environment, where technology-driven, individualized interactions are the new standard, the strategic integration of AI emerges as a critical catalyst for revolutionizing traditional customer interaction paradigms. This represents not just an adaptation but a fundamental change in consumer perception and interaction. This chapter explores the intersection of cutting-edge AI technologies and the evolving field of customer engagement, revealing how companies can address this problem, exceed expectations, and ensure a more seamless and fulfilling experience for all involved.

The methodology employed in this chapter employs a systematic approach to delve into the convergence of AI and customer engagement. This involves conducting a meticulous literature review to scrutinize existing research on AI technologies and their role in customer engagement. The review encompasses a wide array of sources, including academic journals, conference proceedings, and industry reports, to unearth key concepts and empirical findings pertinent to the subject matter. By gathering information from diverse sources, the chapter ensures a robust foundation for discussion and analysis, thereby facilitating a thorough examination of the transformative impact of AI on contemporary customer interaction paradigms.

This chapter approaches the above stated problem from four dimensions depicted in Figure 1, each clarifying a unique aspect of this transformative endeavor.

Figure 1. Dimensions of AI-driven customer engagement

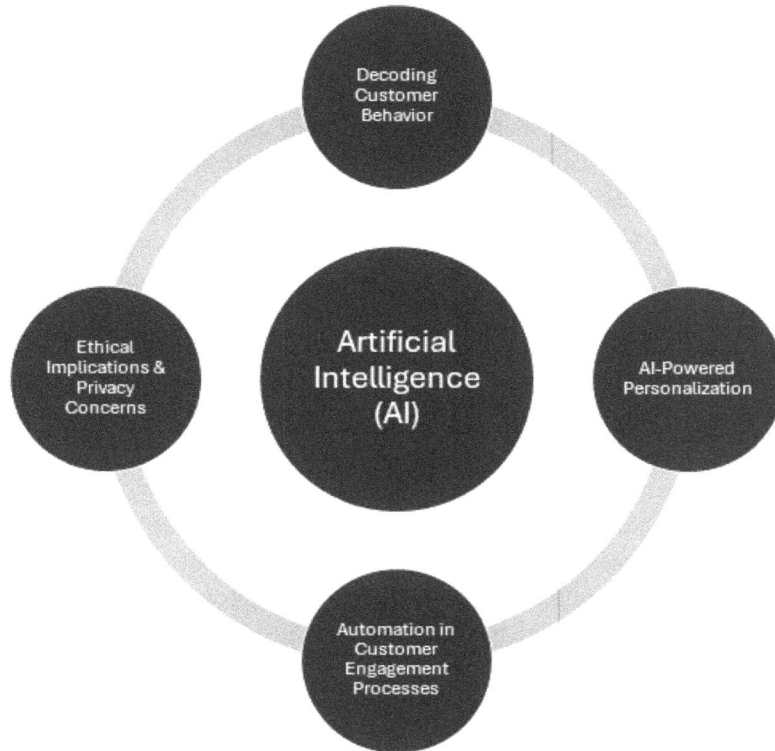

In the first dimension, the exploration commences with decoding consumer behavior through AI-powered insights, delving into the invaluable contribution of AI in unraveling the complex patterns of consumer behavior. By harnessing the capabilities of AI-driven analytics, businesses not only gain unprecedented insights into the intricate nuances of customer preferences but are also equipped to strategically adapt to the ever-changing dynamics of the market. This section serves as a gateway to understanding how AI becomes an indispensable tool, empowering enterprises to make informed decisions and stay agile in response to the evolving landscape of consumer demands and market trends.

The second dimension delves into AI-powered personalization to enhance brand-consumer bonds, exploring the profound connection established between brands and consumers facilitated by AI-powered personalization. In an era where personalized experiences hold significant importance, AI technologies play a pivotal role in enabling brands to customize their interactions with customers in careful detail. This capability not only enhances the overall customer experience but also nurtures a deeper and more meaningful connection between brands and consumers, emphasizing the importance of individual preferences and fostering a more tailored and resonant engagement.

The third dimension elucidates the pivotal role of automation in reshaping the landscape of customer engagement processes. From instant responses provided by chatbots to complex processes streamlined through sophisticated workflows, AI-driven automation not only enhances the efficiency and overall quality of customer engagement but actively elevates it. Beyond mere technological advancement, the strategic implementation of AI-powered automation showcases a fundamental reshaping of how businesses and customers interact in the contemporary digital landscape, where operational processes are seamlessly integrated to ensure a more efficient, responsive, and ultimately satisfying customer experience.

In the final dimension, ethical implications and privacy concerns in AI-driven customer engagement are thoroughly examined. This includes responsible handling of customer data, ensuring transparency, and addressing issues such as algorithmic bias and potential manipulation of consumer behavior. The section delves into the complexities of data privacy when AI algorithms analyze sensitive information, and it emphasizes the importance of implementing robust data protection measures. Moreover, it discusses the ethical challenges posed by algorithmic bias and the potential for AI-powered systems to manipulate consumer behavior for commercial gain.

Together, these dimensions carefully unravel the multifaceted impact of AI technologies on customer engagement processes, providing a comprehensive illustration of how these advancements can be leveraged by businesses not only to meet but also to surpass customer expectations. As this exploration is undertaken, it becomes increasingly evident that the integration of AI into customer engagement strategies is not merely a trend but signifies a profound paradigm shift, holding the key to unlocking new dimensions of success in the contemporary business landscape. The transformative potential of AI extends beyond the conventional boundaries of customer-business relationships, ushering in an era where adaptability, personalized experiences, and streamlined interactions are not just desired but imperative for staying competitive and achieving sustainable growth. This chapter serves as a guide, revealing the transformative power of AI in shaping the future of customer engagement and emphasizing its pivotal role as a strategic cornerstone for businesses seeking to thrive in the evolving dynamics of the modern marketplace.

2. DECODING CONSUMER BEHAVIOR THROUGH AI-POWERED INSIGHTS

Understanding customer behavior has become an essential component of making strategic decisions in the constantly changing business environment. AI has become an invaluable tool for understanding the complex nature of consumer behavior. It provides organizations with unique knowledge about customer preferences, motivations, and trends (Khrais, 2020; Puntoni et al., 2021; Sarabhai et al., 2023). This section explores the foundational role of AI in understanding consumer behavior and how businesses can extract meaningful insights from vast datasets for strategic adaptation. AI plays a crucial role in understanding customer behavior by being able to evaluate large datasets quickly, accurately, and flexibly. Traditional methods of market research often struggled to keep pace with the dynamic nature of consumer preferences and the sheer volume of data generated in today's digital age. AI, however, excels in processing large datasets, identifying patterns, and discerning subtle correlations that may elude human analysis. One foundational aspect of AI's role in understanding consumer behavior lies in its ability to recognize and interpret complex patterns. Machine learning is a field of AI where systems learn from data to make predictions or decisions without being explicitly programmed (Dhall et al.,2020; Cohen, 2021). Machine learning algorithms can sift through massive datasets, discerning correlations and uncovering hidden relationships between variables. This enables businesses to move beyond surface-level insights and gain a deeper understanding of the factors influencing consumer choices (Zhou et al., 2020; Feldman et al., 2022). For instance, AI can identify patterns in online shopping behavior, aiding businesses in understanding the factors driving purchasing decisions and customer loyalty. Take Amazon's Anticipatory Shipping Model as an example; it's a predictive strategy employed by the e-commerce giant to reduce delivery times and enhance customer satisfaction (Borgi et al., 2017; Ogbuke et al., 2022). This model leverages data analytics and machine learning algorithms to anticipate customer orders before they are placed. By analyzing various factors such as past purchasing behavior, browsing history, and demographic information, Amazon predicts which products customers are likely to order in specific regions. These anticipated orders are then pre-packaged and dispatched to fulfillment centers closer to the projected delivery locations. This proactive approach enables Amazon to expedite the shipping process, significantly reducing delivery times and ensuring that products are readily available for prompt dispatch once orders are confirmed. The anticipatory shipping model epitomizes Amazon's commitment to harnessing advanced technologies to optimize logistics and deliver exceptional customer experiences.

Coca-Cola is another company that is very successful in decoding consumer behavior. Coca-Cola utilizes data collected from its fountain machines, which dispense various Coca-Cola beverages in restaurants, convenience stores, and similar locations, to gain insights into consumer preferences and behaviors (Tang et al., 2022). This data encompasses details such as the types of drinks consumed, how often they are consumed, and where they are popular. AI tools are then utilized to analyze this data, employing machine learning algorithms to detect patterns, trends, and correlations within consumption patterns. By leveraging AI to process this fountain machine consumption data, Coca-Cola can extract valuable insights into emerging consumer preferences, market trends, and potential opportunities. For instance, AI algorithms may uncover growing demand for specific flavor combinations or beverage categories in certain geographic regions or demographic segments. With these insights, Coca-Cola can tailor new product development to meet consumer needs and seize market opportunities. Moreover, AI-driven analysis of fountain machine data enables Coca-Cola to adjust its product offerings and marketing strategies in real time. By continuously monitoring consumption patterns and customer feedback, the company can refine its product lineup, adapt pricing strategies, and launch targeted marketing campaigns to drive sales and enhance brand loyalty. Overall, leveraging fountain machine consumption data with AI tools empowers Coca-Cola to make data-driven decisions, innovate more effectively, and stay ahead of evolving consumer preferences in the competitive beverage market.

Moreover, AI facilitates real-time analysis of consumer interactions across various touchpoints. From social media engagement to online browsing behavior, AI can aggregate and analyze data swiftly, providing businesses with up-to-the-minute insights. The real-time aspect is extremely helpful in a dynamic environment where consumer tastes can change quickly. It enables firms to instantly adjust their plans and maintain a competitive edge. Without the assistance of AI, extracting valuable insights from large datasets can be a challenging endeavor. The vast amount and intricate nature of data produced in the digital world require sophisticated analytical capabilities. AI technologies, such as natural language processing and sentiment analysis, allow organizations to analyze unstructured data sources such as customer reviews, social media comments, and online forums. This not only facilitates comprehension of consumer sentiment but also offers detailed insights into the particular facets of products or services that resonate most strongly with customers. One real example of using natural language processing and sentiment analysis to understand consumer sentiment is how companies like Airbnb analyze customer reviews. Airbnb utilizes AI-powered tools to process the vast amount of text-based reviews left by guests on their platform. By analyzing the language used in these reviews, as well as the sentiment expressed (positive, negative, or neutral), Airbnb gains valuable insights into the aspects of their accommodations and services that guests appreciate most and areas where improvements may be needed. This allows Airbnb to enhance the overall guest experience, tailor their offerings to better meet customer preferences, and maintain high levels of satisfaction among their user base.

An important benefit of AI-driven insights is the capability to generate comprehensive consumer profiles. Businesses can create detailed profiles of their target audience by examining many data points such as purchase history, online behavior, and demographic information (Huseynov & Yıldırım, 2017; Huseynov & Özkan Yıldırım, 2019; Liao et al.,2021; Haleem et al., 2022). These profiles go beyond conventional demographic segmentation by including behavioral and psychographic characteristics. By having a comprehensive understanding of customers, firms may customize their marketing strategies, product offers, and customer experiences to match the tastes of certain consumer categories. Strategic adaptation, driven by AI-powered insights, is a fluid procedure that entails ongoing surveillance and modification. AI can be utilized by businesses to execute focused interventions using up-to-date data, thereby optimizing marketing campaigns, improving product features, and upgrading customer experiences. For example, if AI analysis detects a change in customer preferences towards sustainability, a company can quickly adjust its product offerings or marketing communication to correspond with this trend, thereby earning a competitive advantage in the market.

Another example of decoding consumer behavior using AI is seen in how retail stores use computer vision technology to understand shopper behavior. Retailers install sensors and cameras equipped with AI algorithms that analyze customer movements and interactions within the store (Saßnick et al., 2023; Knof et al., 2023). These systems can track factors like foot traffic patterns, dwell times at specific product displays, and even facial expressions to gauge shopper interest and engagement. By collecting and analyzing this data, retailers gain insights into which areas of the store are most popular, which products attract the most attention, and how shoppers navigate through the space. This information helps retailers optimize store layouts, product placements, and marketing strategies to better meet the needs and preferences of their customers, ultimately leading to improved sales and customer satisfaction.

In conclusion, using AI-powered insights to decipher customer behavior is a revolutionary approach that enables companies to remain competitive, responsive, and flexible in the ever-evolving business environment of today. AI's fundamental capacity to decipher intricate patterns, examine enormous datasets, and offer real-time insights is what makes it so valuable for comprehending customer behavior. By extracting valuable information from diverse sources, enterprises can generate comprehensive insights about customer behavior and make strategic adjustments accordingly. It's likely that the future of business will be significantly influenced by the integration of AI and consumer behavior analysis. This integration will enable businesses to adopt more individualized, flexible, and customer-focused strategies as technology continues to evolve.

3. AI-POWERED PERSONALIZATION TO ENHANCE BRAND-CONSUMER BONDS

Conventional marketing strategies often leaned on broad segmentation, simplifying the diverse tapestry of consumer groups into seemingly homogeneous entities. However, it's crucial to recognize that within a broad consumer audience, there exists a rich tapestry of heterogeneity. This diversity manifests in distinct needs, varied requirements, and unique preferences among different segments. In the dynamic landscape of modern marketing, the evolution from broad segmentation to more nuanced and targeted approaches is imperative. Understanding the intricate layers of consumer diversity allows businesses to tailor their strategies, crafting messaging and offerings that resonate on a deeper level with specific segments. This shift towards recognizing heterogeneity unlocks the potential for more personalized and effective marketing campaigns. By acknowledging and catering to the diverse needs within the consumer base, businesses can create tailored experiences that foster stronger connections and brand loyalty. This personalized approach not only enhances customer satisfaction but also positions companies strategically in an era where consumers increasingly seek individualized interactions with brands. In essence, departing from the traditional one-size-fits-all model enables businesses to embrace the complexity inherent in diverse consumer groups. This shift is not just a response to changing market dynamics; it is a proactive strategy to stay relevant and competitive in an environment where consumers value personalized, meaningful engagements. The acknowledgment of heterogeneity within a broad consumer audience is, therefore, a crucial step towards building lasting and authentic relationships between brands and their diverse customer base.

In the era of digital marketing, personalization has become a cornerstone for building meaningful connections between brands and consumers. The advent of AI has revolutionized the landscape, empowering businesses to tailor their marketing efforts to individual preferences with unprecedented precision. At the heart of AI-driven personalization lies the ability to analyze vast datasets and extract actionable insights. AI excels in processing intricate details, understanding nuanced preferences, and predicting individual behavior based on historical data. This transformative power enables businesses to move beyond one-size-fits-all strategies and deliver highly targeted and relevant content to each consumer. The utilization of machine learning algorithms allows brands to create sophisticated customer profiles, capturing not only demographic information but also behavioral patterns, purchase history, and even sentiment analysis from social media interactions. This holistic understanding of the consumer journey empowers brands to craft personalized experiences that resonate on a deeper level. For instance, an e-commerce platform can use AI to analyze a customer's past purchases, browsing history, and preferences to curate a personalized product recommendation, creating a seamless and enjoyable shopping experience.

Today, recommender systems play a crucial role in delivering personalized services to customers in various sectors. These intelligent software solutions harness AI to offer tailored content to users, leveraging information collected about customers, whether implicitly or explicitly. There are different types of recommender systems, including collaborative filtering recommender systems, content-based recommender systems, knowledge-based recommender systems, utility-based recommender systems, demographic-based recommender systems, and hybrid recommender systems (Huseynov, 2020a). Each type offers unique approaches to understanding user preferences and effectively tailoring recommendations to meet individual needs and preferences, thereby enhancing user experience and satisfaction across various domains.

Cutting-edge personalization techniques powered by AI extend across various industries, leaving a profound impact on customer engagement and satisfaction. In the realm of online streaming services, algorithms analyze viewing habits, genre preferences, and even viewer ratings to offer personalized content recommendations. This not only enhances user experience but also keeps subscribers engaged, fostering loyalty and reducing churn rates. Netflix, the world's leading internet entertainment service, employs a sophisticated recommender system to cater to its over 260 million paid subscribers, blending collaborative filtering and content-based approaches. This system generates personalized recommendations based on user interactions, preferences, and content attributes, considering factors such as viewing history, ratings, and similarities with other users. While demographic information is not factored in, Netflix's recommender system also analyzes factors like time of day, viewing devices, and duration to enhance the viewing experience for its subscribers (Huseynov, 2020a). Similarly, YouTube and Spotify utilize AI-driven recommendation algorithms to suggest videos and music tracks tailored to each user's preferences and browsing history, thereby enhancing user satisfaction and engagement.

In the field of education, the integration of cutting-edge personalization techniques driven by AI is revolutionizing the learning experience. Through advanced algorithms, educational platforms analyze students' learning behaviors, academic performance, and individual preferences to provide tailored recommendations and resources (Kaswan et al., 2024). Whether it's suggesting relevant study materials, adaptive learning modules, or personalized feedback, these systems aim to optimize student engagement and learning outcomes. Moreover, AI-powered educational tools can adapt to each student's pace and learning style, fostering a more inclusive and effective learning environment (Rane et al., 2023). By harnessing the power of personalized recommendations, educational institutions can enhance student satisfaction, retention rates, and overall academic success, ultimately shaping a brighter future for learners worldwide. For example, platforms like Khan Academy and Duolingo utilize AI algorithms to analyze user interactions and performance data, providing personalized recommendations for study materials and learning activities. These platforms adapt to each learner's pace, skill level, and learning style, offering customized lessons and practice exercises to optimize learning outcomes. By harnessing the power of AI, educational institutions can create more engaging and effective learning experiences, ultimately improving student satisfaction and academic success.

Similarly, in the healthcare industry, AI-driven personalization is making waves. Personalized treatment plans based on individual health data, genetic information, and lifestyle choices are becoming more prevalent (Sahu et al., 2022; Batra & Dave, 2024; Javanmard, 2024). Patients receive tailored recommendations, medication plans, and preventive measures, creating a more patient-centric approach to healthcare. This not only improves health outcomes but also strengthens the bond between healthcare providers and their patients.

In another innovative approach, online retailers combine AI with gamification elements to revolutionize its customer engagement strategy. Gamification is the integration of game mechanics and elements into non-game contexts to enhance engagement, motivation, and participation, by applying features like challenges, rewards, competition, and achievement systems (Alsawaier, 2018). By leveraging AI-powered algorithms, retailers personalize the gamified experiences to each customer's preferences and behavior, enhancing the overall effectiveness of the strategy. Through sophisticated AI-driven analytics, retailers gain valuable insights into individual customer preferences and shopping habits, allowing for the creation of tailored gamification challenges and rewards. These personalized experiences not only increase customer engagement but also foster stronger connections between the brand and its customers (Huseynov, 2020b). The integration of AI and gamification proved to be a winning combination, driving higher levels of participation, satisfaction, and loyalty among the retailer's customer base.

The hospitality sector has embraced AI to deepen connections with customers. Hotels and travel agencies utilize AI to analyze customer preferences regarding destinations, accommodation styles, and amenities. This data enables them to offer personalized travel packages, room preferences, and exclusive deals, ensuring a memorable and tailored experience for each guest (Doborjeh et al., 2022; Said, 2023). For instance, hotels utilize AI-powered concierges like Hilton's Connie and chatbots like Rose at The Cosmopolitan in Las Vegas to assist guests with various inquiries and recommendations. Additionally, AI enhances in-room experiences, as demonstrated by Marriott International's experiments with AI-powered assistants that allow guests to control room settings through voice commands, providing tailored experiences based on individual preferences. These real-world examples illustrate the potential of AI to enhance guest satisfaction and anticipate future applications in the hospitality industry.

The impact of AI-driven personalization is not limited to consumer-facing industries; B2B enterprises are also leveraging these techniques to enhance client relationships (Latinovic & Chatterjee, 2022; Khvatova et al., 2023). By understanding the unique needs and challenges of each business client, AI helps companies deliver targeted solutions, content, and services. This approach fosters trust, loyalty, and long-term partnerships in the competitive B2B landscape.

In conclusion, AI has ushered in a new era of personalization, revolutionizing the way brands and consumers interact. The transformative power of AI in tailoring marketing efforts to individual preferences is reshaping diverse industries, from entertainment and healthcare to hospitality and B2B enterprises. Cutting-edge personalization techniques powered by AI have the potential to deepen the bond between brands and consumers, creating more meaningful and personalized experiences that drive customer satisfaction, loyalty, and long-term success. As technology continues to advance, the landscape of personalization will evolve, presenting new opportunities and challenges for businesses seeking to navigate the ever-changing terrain of consumer engagement.

4. AUTOMATION'S ROLE IN MODERN CUSTOMER ENGAGEMENTS

Automation plays a crucial part in modern consumer engagement in the continuously changing business and technology environment. Organizations are increasingly adopting AI-powered automation to optimize marketing processes, improve operational efficiency, and enhance consumer experiences. This shift in paradigm not only enables cost reduction but also allows for unprecedented scalability and agility. AI-powered automation is crucial for optimizing and expanding marketing operations. Conventional marketing strategies frequently depend on manual interventions, leading to inefficiencies, inaccuracies, and constraints in scalability. Nevertheless, the incorporation of automation technology brings about a fundamental change by automating repetitive operations, improving workflows, and facilitating customized client interactions on a large scale. An essential factor is the capacity to rapidly evaluate huge quantities of client data. Artificial intelligence algorithms have the ability to analyze data points, recognize trends, and extract useful insights that may be used to develop specific marketing plans. This not only optimizes efficiency but also guarantees that marketing endeavors are based on data and tailored to meet the specific needs of each customer. Utilizing automation in data analysis enables organizations to customize their marketing messaging, ensuring a more individualized and impactful strategy. Moreover, automation is essential in the implementation of marketing initiatives across several platforms. Artificial intelligence solutions can efficiently plan and carry out campaigns, guaranteeing prompt and uniform connection with customers. Automation improves the efficiency and accuracy of activities such as email marketing, social media outreach, and personalized content recommendations. This not only allows for the allocation of human resources to more strategic activities, but also decreases the probability of errors that are linked to manual execution.

Real-world case studies offer compelling evidence of the transformative impact of automation on operational efficiency and customer experience. Companies across industries have witnessed significant improvements by embracing AI-driven solutions. For instance, leading e-commerce platforms implement chatbot automation to handle routine customer queries. Chatbots are computer software designed to simulate human conversation through spoken or written language, serving as virtual assistants for online customers (Luo et al., 2019; Kaczorowska-Spychalska, 2019). The chatbots efficiently address common issues, providing instant responses and freeing up customer support agents to focus on more complex and nuanced inquiries (Huseynov, 2023). This not only reduc response times but also enhanc the overall customer experience. According to Schuetzler et al. (2020), chatbots with human-like features such as perceived humanness and engaging behavior can improve user experience. Similarly, Adam et al. (2020) suggests that chatbots displaying humanization traits like identity, empathy, and the ability to handle simple requests are more likely to succeed in gaining user cooperation. Furthermore, Shumanov and Johnson (2021) discovered that consumers tend to engage with chatbots for extended durations when the chatbot's personality matches their own.

Robotic Process Automation (RPA) is a highly effective technique for automating client interaction and engagement. RPA utilizes software robots or "bots" to automate repetitive and rule-driven process-es across different systems and applications (Devarajan, 2018; Ivančić et al., 2019; Syed et al., 2020). When it comes to interacting with customers, RPA can be used to make backend procedures like order processing, billing, and account management more efficient. For instance, RPA bots can be coded to retrieve pertinent customer data from various databases, modify CRM records, and produce custom-ized communication such as order confirmations or delivery reminders. RPA allows for the automation of repetitive operations, enabling human agents to dedicate their time to more intricate and valuable activities. These activities may involve handling client concerns that need empathy, problem-solving abilities, or critical thinking skills (Syed et al., 2020). In addition, RPA guarantees precision and con-sistency in customer engagements, mitigating the possibility of mistakes or delays and enhancing the overall quality of service. As organizations strive to enhance efficiency and agility in customer service operations, they are increasingly turning to RPA as a means to automate repetitive work and improve the customer experience.

Nevertheless, the integration of automation in customer engagement is not without difficulties. Businesses must find an appropriate balance between automation and human interaction. Although au-tomation is highly effective in managing repetitive tasks, human involvement is still crucial for dealing with complicated issues, establishing authentic relationships, and preserving a brand's emotional appeal. Ultimately, automation has proven to be a transformative force in contemporary customer engagement. Organizations achieve exceptional efficiency and scalability by utilizing AI-driven automation for mar-keting processes. As businesses adapt to the ever-changing environment, incorporating automation is no more optional but a necessary strategic move for long-term success in customer engagement.

5. ETHICAL IMPLICATIONS AND PRIVACY CONCERNS IN AI-DRIVEN CUSTOMER ENGAGEMENT

Ethical implications and privacy concerns in AI-driven customer engagement are critical consider-ations in today's digital landscape. As businesses increasingly leverage AI technologies to interact with customers, issues surrounding ethics and privacy come to the forefront. While AI has the potential to enhance customer experiences and streamline processes, it also raises questions about data privacy, con-sent, bias, and transparency (Du & Xie, 2021). Prominent concerns regarding AI are depicted in Figure 2.

Figure 2. Ethical concerns in AI-driven customer engagement

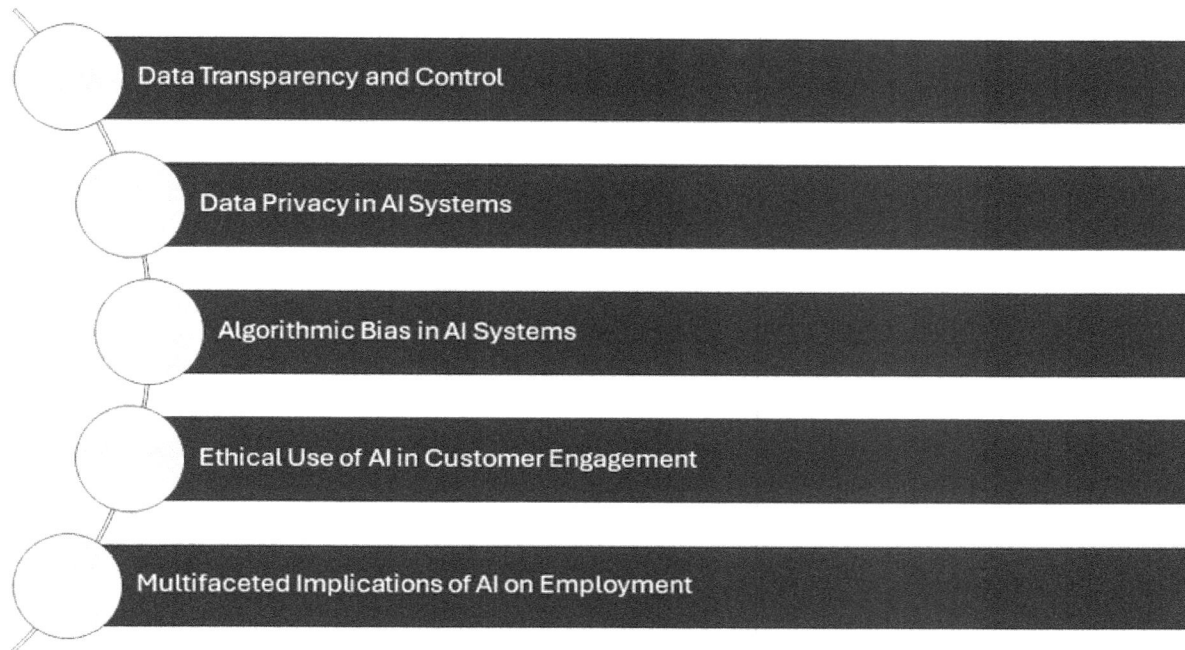

One of the primary ethical concerns in AI-driven customer engagement is the responsible handling of customer data. AI systems rely on vast amounts of data to make predictions and recommendations (Alla et al., 2022; Lhoussaine et al., 2022; Bouhtatit et al., 2023a; Bouhtatit et al., 2023b; Blanco-Gonzalez et al., 2023). However, collecting and processing this data can raise privacy issues if not done transparently or if customers are unaware of how their data is being used. Companies must be transparent about the types of data they collect, how it is used, and provide customers with clear options for controlling their data.

Moreover, ensuring data privacy becomes even more complex when AI algorithms are employed to analyze sensitive information, such as personal preferences, behaviors, or health data. There's a fine line between personalization and intrusion, and companies must tread carefully to respect customer privacy while still delivering personalized experiences. This involves implementing robust data protection measures, including encryption, anonymization, and strict access controls.

Another ethical consideration is the potential for algorithmic bias in AI-driven customer engagement. AI systems are only as unbiased as the data they are trained on. If the training data is skewed or reflects existing biases, AI algorithms can perpetuate and even exacerbate discriminatory outcomes (Ferrara, 2023; Giovanola & Tiribelli, 2023). For example, biased algorithms in customer engagement systems may inadvertently discriminate against certain demographic groups in product recommendations or pricing strategies. To mitigate bias, companies need to regularly audit their AI systems, diversify their training data, and employ techniques like fairness-aware learning.

Additionally, there are ethical implications surrounding the use of AI in customer engagement for manipulative purposes. AI-powered systems can analyze vast amounts of data to influence consumer behavior through targeted advertising, persuasive messaging, or personalized recommendations. While these tactics can increase sales and engagement, they also raise concerns about manipulation and autonomy (Ienca, 2023). Companies must ensure that their use of AI in customer engagement aligns with ethical principles and respects customer autonomy and agency.

In the face of the impending AI revolution and its significant impact on the job landscape, it is imperative to recognize the multifaceted nature of employment beyond mere economic implications. As AI continues to automate tasks across various industries, the potential disruption to employment extends beyond financial concerns to encompass psychological, social, and even political dimensions (Du & Xie, 2021). Given the ethical responsibility of companies to safeguard the interests of their employees, proactive measures are essential to address the challenges posed by AI-driven job displacement. Initiatives focused on reskilling and lifelong learning can empower employees to adapt and thrive in a rapidly evolving job market. Companies could allocate resources towards establishing corporate learning academies or funds dedicated to supporting employees in acquiring digital skills and navigating job transitions (Du & Xie, 2021). Furthermore, governments play a crucial role in addressing societal issues stemming from AI-induced unemployment. Research into regulatory frameworks and policies is vital to ensure equitable distribution of the benefits of AI technologies and mitigate the potential negative consequences of widespread job displacement. By prioritizing ethical considerations and collaborative efforts between corporations and governments, society can navigate the challenges and opportunities presented by the AI revolution in a responsible and sustainable manner.

In conclusion, ethical considerations and privacy concerns are paramount in AI-driven customer engagement. Companies must prioritize transparency, data privacy, fairness, and respect for customer autonomy to build trust and maintain ethical standards in their AI initiatives. By addressing these concerns proactively, businesses can leverage AI to enhance customer experiences while upholding ethical values.

6. CONCLUSION

Throughout this chapter, the pressing challenge or problem outlined in the introduction— the need for businesses to meet and surpass modern consumers' expectations in an increasingly digital marketplace— has been thoroughly addressed. Solutions to this challenge have been presented through the lens of AI, which serves as a catalyst for revolutionizing traditional customer interaction paradigms. From decoding consumer behavior to revolutionizing personalization and streamlining customer engagements through automation, each section of this chapter has offered insights and strategies to exceed expectations and ensure seamless experiences for customers. Embracing AI technologies responsibly and strategically allows businesses to navigate the complexities of the digital era, foster meaningful relationships with customers, and secure their position in an ever-evolving marketplace.

In the exploration of the dynamic intersection between AI technologies and customer engagement, it becomes evident that the strategic integration of AI is not merely a response to technological progress but a profound paradigm shift. This chapter unveil the transformative potential of AI in reshaping the landscape of customer-business relationships. The foundational role of AI in decoding consumer behavior proves indispensable for strategic adaptation. AI's capacity to analyze extensive datasets, recognize complex patterns, and provide real-time insights empowers businesses to understand and respond to ever-changing consumer dynamics swiftly. This not only enhances decision-making processes but also allows for strategic adaptation to market trends and consumer preferences. The ability to extract meaningful insights from vast datasets is a game-changer, providing businesses with a competitive edge in understanding and meeting customer expectations.

The exploration of AI's role in revolutionizing personalization emphasizes the profound connection established between brands and consumers. Cutting-edge personalization techniques, powered by AI, enable businesses to create detailed customer profiles, delivering highly targeted and relevant content. This not only enhances the overall customer experience but also fosters a more profound and meaningful connection between brands and consumers.

Automation plays a pivotal role in modern customer interaction, revolutionizing marketing processes, operational efficiency, and overall customer experiences. Through AI-driven automation, organizations achieve cost savings, scalability, and agility, streamlining marketing efforts and enhancing customer engagement. By automating repetitive tasks and analyzing vast customer data, AI algorithms inform targeted marketing strategies, ensuring personalized and relevant interactions. Transformative impact of automation, such as the implementation of chatbot technology in e-commerce platforms, significantly reduces response times and enriches the overall customer journey. Additionally, RPA streamlines back-end processes, freeing up human agents to focus on complex inquiries and enhancing service quality. However, businesses must balance automation with human touchpoints to address intricate issues and maintain authentic connections. Ultimately, embracing automation becomes imperative for sustained success in modern customer interaction, driving efficiency and delivering exceptional experiences.

Amidst the transformative potential of AI in customer engagement, it is crucial to acknowledge potential drawbacks and challenges. Privacy concerns, data security, and ethical considerations surrounding customer information necessitate careful handling. That is, it is essential to address challenges related to privacy concerns and data security, ensuring a delicate balance between personalized experiences and individual privacy. Businesses must prioritize transparency and responsible AI use to maintain customer trust. Moreover, the risk of over-reliance on AI without human intervention poses challenges in addressing complex and nuanced customer inquiries.

Looking forward, the future presents exciting opportunities for businesses that harness the potential of AI in customer engagement. As technology continues to advance, AI algorithms can evolve to provide even more sophisticated insights and personalized experiences. The integration of AI in customer engagement strategies is poised to become not just a trend but a fundamental aspect of maintaining competitiveness and achieving sustainable growth. Moreover, ongoing research and development in AI technologies may unveil innovative solutions to address current challenges, fostering a more seamless and harmonious integration between AI and human interactions. The exploration of AI's impact on customer interaction reveals a transformative journey that goes beyond adaptation to signify a seismic shift in how businesses understand, connect with, and serve their customers. The strategic imperative of AI in customer engagement is not just a response to the demands of the digital era but a proactive approach to stay relevant, competitive, and successful in a landscape where personalized, efficient, and technology-driven interactions are imperative. The future holds immense potential for businesses that embrace AI, striking a balance between automation and human touch while navigating challenges to build lasting and authentic relationships with their diverse customer base.

In conclusion, while this chapter provides a comprehensive exploration of the intersection between AI technologies and customer engagement, it's important to acknowledge some limitations. Firstly, the scope of this chapter may not cover every aspect of AI-driven customer interaction, as the field is vast and constantly evolving. Certain emerging technologies or niche applications of AI in customer engagement may not have been fully addressed. Additionally, the examples provided are illustrative but not exhaustive, and there may be other noteworthy examples that could further enrich the discussion. Also, the ethical considerations and privacy concerns discussed are complex and multifaceted, and a more in-depth examination of these issues could provide additional insights. Overall, while this chapter offers valuable insights into the transformative potential of AI in customer engagement, it is important to recognize its limitations and continue exploring this dynamic field.

REFERENCES

Adam, M., Wessel, M., & Benlian, A. (2021). AI-based chatbots in customer service and their effects on user compliance. *Electronic Markets*, 31(2), 427–445. 10.1007/s12525-020-00414-7

Alla, L., Kamal, M., & Bouhtati, N. (2022). Big data and marketing effectiveness of tourism businesses: A literature review. Alternatives Managériales Economiques, 4(0), Article 0. 10.48374/IMIST.PRSM/ame-v1i0.36928

Alsawaier, R. S. (2018). The effect of gamification on motivation and engagement. *The International Journal of Information and Learning Technology*, 35(1), 56–79. 10.1108/IJILT-02-2017-0009

Batra, P., & Dave, D. M. (2024). Revolutionizing Healthcare Platforms: The Impact of AI on Patient Engagement and Treatment Efficacy. *International Journal of Science and Research (IJSR)*, 13(10.21275), 613-624.

Blanco-Gonzalez, A., Cabezon, A., Seco-Gonzalez, A., Conde-Torres, D., Antelo-Riveiro, P., Pineiro, A., & Garcia-Fandino, R. (2023). The role of ai in drug discovery: Challenges, opportunities, and strategies. *Pharmaceuticals (Basel, Switzerland)*, 16(6), 891. 10.3390/ph1606089137375838

Borgi, T., Zoghlami, N., & Abed, M. (2017, January). Big data for transport and logistics: A review. In *2017 International Conference on Advanced Systems and Electric Technologies (IC_ASET)* (pp. 44-49). IEEE. 10.1109/ASET.2017.7983742

Bouhtati, N., Alla, L., & Bentalhah, B. (2023a). Marketing Big Data Analytics and Customer Relationship Management: A Fuzzy Approach. In *Integrating Intelligence and Sustainability in Supply Chains* (pp. 75-86). IGI Global.10.4018/979-8-3693-0225-5.ch004

Bouhtatit, N., Kamal, M., & Alla, L. (2023b). Big Data and the Effectiveness of Tourism Marketing: A Prospective Review of the Literature. In Farhaoui, Y., Rocha, A., Brahmia, Z., & Bhushab, B. (Eds.), *Artificial Intelligence and Smart Environment. ICAISE 2022. Lecture Notes in Networks and Systems, 635*. Springer. 10.1007/978-3-031-26254-8_40

Bowden, J. L. H. (2009). The process of customer engagement: A conceptual framework. *Journal of Marketing Theory and Practice*, 17(1), 63–74. 10.2753/MTP1069-6679170105

Cohen, S. (2021). The basics of machine learning: strategies and techniques. In *Artificial intelligence and deep learning in pathology* (pp. 13–40). Elsevier. 10.1016/B978-0-323-67538-3.00002-6

Devarajan, Y. (2018). A study of robotic process automation use cases today for tomorrow's business. *International Journal of Computers and Technology*, 5(6), 12–18.

Dhall, D., Kaur, R., & Juneja, M. (2020). Machine learning: a review of the algorithms and its applications. *Proceedings of ICRIC 2019: Recent innovations in computing*, (pp. 47-63). Springer. 10.1007/978-3-030-29407-6_5

Doborjeh, Z., Hemmington, N., Doborjeh, M., & Kasabov, N. (2022). Artificial intelligence: A systematic review of methods and applications in hospitality and tourism. *International Journal of Contemporary Hospitality Management*, 34(3), 1154–1176. 10.1108/IJCHM-06-2021-0767

Du, S., & Xie, C. (2021). Paradoxes of artificial intelligence in consumer markets: Ethical challenges and opportunities. *Journal of Business Research*, 129, 961–974. 10.1016/j.jbusres.2020.08.024

Feldman, J., Zhang, D. J., Liu, X., & Zhang, N. (2022). Customer choice models vs. machine learning: Finding optimal product displays on Alibaba. *Operations Research*, 70(1), 309–328. 10.1287/opre.2021.2158

Ferrara, E. (2023). Fairness and bias in artificial intelligence: A brief survey of sources, impacts, and mitigation strategies. *Sci*, 6(1), 3. 10.3390/sci6010003

Garg, P. K. (2021). Overview of artificial intelligence. In *Artificial intelligence* (pp. 3–18). Chapman and Hall/CRC. 10.1201/9781003140351-2

Giovanola, B., & Tiribelli, S. (2023). Beyond bias and discrimination: Redefining the AI ethics principle of fairness in healthcare machine-learning algorithms. *AI & Society*, 38(2), 549–563. 10.1007/s00146-022-01455-635615443

Haleem, A., Javaid, M., Qadri, M. A., Singh, R. P., & Suman, R. (2022). Artificial intelligence (AI) applications for marketing: A literature-based study. *International Journal of Intelligent Networks*, 3, 119–132. 10.1016/j.ijin.2022.08.005

Huseynov, F. (2020a). Intelligent Recommender Systems in E-Commerce: Opportunities and Challenges for Online Customers. *Handbook of Research on IT Applications for Strategic Competitive Advantage and Decision Making,* 36-51. Springer.

Huseynov, F. (2020b). Gamification in e-commerce: Enhancing digital customer engagement through game elements. In *Digital innovations for customer engagement, management, and organizational improvement* (pp. 144–161). IGI Global. 10.4018/978-1-7998-5171-4.ch008

Huseynov, F. (2023). Chatbots in digital marketing: Enhanced customer experience and reduced customer service costs. In *Contemporary Approaches of Digital Marketing and the Role of Machine Intelligence* (pp. 46–72). IGI Global. 10.4018/978-1-6684-7735-9.ch003

Huseynov, F., & Özkan Yıldırım, S. (2019). Online consumer typologies and their shopping behaviors in B2C e-commerce platforms. *SAGE Open*, 9(2), 2158244019854639. 10.1177/2158244019854639

Huseynov, F., & Yıldırım, S. Ö. (2017). Behavioural segmentation analysis of online consumer audience in Turkey by using real e-commerce transaction data. *International Journal of Economics and Business Research*, 14(1), 12–28. 10.1504/IJEBR.2017.085549

Hydle, K. M., Hellström, M., Aas, T. H., & Breunig, K. J. (2021). *Digital servitization: strategies for handling customization and customer interaction. The Palgrave Handbook of Servitization,* (pp. 355-372). Palgrave.

Ienca, M. (2023). On Artificial Intelligence and Manipulation. *Topoi*, 42(3), 833–842. 10.1007/s11245-023-09940-3

Ivančić, L., Suša Vugec, D., & Bosilj Vukšić, V. (2019). Robotic process automation: systematic literature review. In *Business Process Management: Blockchain and Central and Eastern Europe Forum*. Springer.

Javanmard, S. (2024). Revolutionizing Medical Practice: The Impact of Artificial Intelligence (AI) on Healthcare. *OA J Applied Sci Technol, 2*(1), 01-16.

Jian, Z., & Liu, Y. (2016). The Impacts of Customer Interaction and Social Capital on New Service Development Performance. *American Journal of Industrial and Business Management, 6*(12), 1133–1145. 10.4236/ajibm.2016.612106

Kaczorowska-Spychalska, D. (2019). Chatbots in marketing. *Management, 23*(1), 251–270. 10.2478/manment-2019-0015

Kaswan, K. S., Dhatterwal, J. S., & Ojha, R. P. (2024). AI in personalized learning. In *Advances in Technological Innovations in Higher Education* (pp. 103–117). CRC Press. 10.1201/9781003376699-9

Khrais, L. T. (2020). Role of artificial intelligence in shaping consumer demand in E-commerce. *Future Internet, 12*(12), 226. 10.3390/fi12120226

Khvatova, T., Appio, F. P., Ray, S., & Schiavone, F. (2023). Exploring the Role of AI in B2B Customer Journey Management: Towards an IPO Model. *IEEE Transactions on Engineering Management*. IEEE.

Knof, M., Stock-Homburg, R., & Schurer, J. (2023). How in-store sensor technologies can help retailers to understand their customers: Overview on two decades of research. *International Review of Retail, Distribution and Consumer Research*, 1–18.

Latinovic, Z., & Chatterjee, S. C. (2022). Achieving the promise of AI and ML in delivering economic and relational customer value in B2B. *Journal of Business Research*, 144, 966–974. 10.1016/j.jbusres.2022.01.052

Lhoussaine, A. L. L. A., Kamal, M., & Bouhtati, N. (2022). Big data and marketing effectiveness of tourism businesses: A literature review. *Economic Management Alternatives*, 1, 39–58.

Liao, S. H., Widowati, R., & Hsieh, Y. C. (2021). Investigating online social media users' behaviors for social commerce recommendations. *Technology in Society*, 66, 101655. 10.1016/j.techsoc.2021.101655

Luo, X., Tong, S., Fang, Z., & Qu, Z. (2019). Frontiers: Machines vs humans: The impact of artificial intelligence chatbot disclosure on customer purchases. *Marketing Science, 38*(6), 937–947. 10.1287/mksc.2019.1192

Nüesch, R., Alt, R., & Puschmann, T. (2015). Hybrid customer interaction. *Business & Information Systems Engineering, 57*(1), 73–78. 10.1007/s12599-014-0366-9

Ogbuke, N. J., Yusuf, Y. Y., Dharma, K., & Mercangoz, B. A. (2022). Big data supply chain analytics: Ethical, privacy and security challenges posed to business, industries and society. *Production Planning and Control, 33*(2-3), 123–137. 10.1080/09537287.2020.1810764

Puntoni, S., Reczek, R. W., Giesler, M., & Botti, S. (2021). Consumers and artificial intelligence: An experiential perspective. *Journal of Marketing, 85*(1), 131–151. 10.1177/0022242920953847

Rane, N., Choudhary, S., & Rane, J. (2023). Education 4.0 and 5.0: Integrating Artificial Intelligence (AI) for personalized and adaptive learning. Available at *SSRN* 4638365. 10.2139/ssrn.4638365

Rasool, A., Shah, F. A., & Tanveer, M. (2021). Relational dynamics between customer engagement, brand experience, and customer loyalty: An empirical investigation. *Journal of Internet Commerce*, 20(3), 273–292. 10.1080/15332861.2021.1889818

Sahu, M., Gupta, R., Ambasta, R. K., & Kumar, P. (2022). Artificial intelligence and machine learning in precision medicine: A paradigm shift in big data analysis. *Progress in Molecular Biology and Translational Science*, 190(1), 57–100. 10.1016/bs.pmbts.2022.03.00236008002

Said, S. (2023). The Role of Artificial Intelligence (AI) and Data Analytics in Enhancing Guest Personalization in Hospitality. *Journal of Modern Hospitality*, 2(1), 1–13. 10.47941/jmh.1556

Sarabhai, S., Chakraborty, M., Batra, M., Kler, R., Banerjee, S., & Mishra, S. (2023, November). Using AI and Machine Learning to Predict Consumer Buying Behavior: Insights from Behavioral Economics in Case of Alcoholic Beverages. In *2023 3rd International Conference on Technological Advancements in Computational Sciences (ICTACS)* (pp. 980-986). IEEE.

Sarker, I. H. (2022). AI-based modeling: Techniques, applications and research issues towards automation, intelligent and smart systems. *SN Computer Science*, 3(2), 158. 10.1007/s42979-022-01043-x35194580

Saßnick, O., Zniva, R., Schlager, C., Horn, M., Kozlica, R., Neureiter, T., & Nöbauer, J. (2023, April). Analyzing customer behavior in-store: A review of available technologies. In *Digital Marketing & eCommerce Conference* (pp. 243–252). Springer Nature Switzerland. 10.1007/978-3-031-31836-8_25

Schuetzler, R. M., Grimes, G. M., & Scott Giboney, J. (2020). The impact of chatbot conversational skill on engagement and perceived humanness. *Journal of Management Information Systems*, 37(3), 875–900. 10.1080/07421222.2020.1790204

Shumanov, M., & Johnson, L. (2021). Making conversations with chatbots more personalized. *Computers in Human Behavior*, *117*, 106627. doi:. chb.2020.10662710.1016/j

Syed, R., Suriadi, S., Adams, M., Bandara, W., Leemans, S. J., Ouyang, C., ter Hofstede, A. H. M., van de Weerd, I., Wynn, M. T., & Reijers, H. A. (2020). Robotic process automation: Contemporary themes and challenges. *Computers in Industry*, 115, 103162. 10.1016/j.compind.2019.103162

Tang, Z., Xu, X., Song, Y., & Yang, H. (2022, March). Data Analytics Applications in the Soda Industry. In *International Conference on Business and Policy Studies* (pp. 677-688). Singapore: Springer Nature Singapore. 10.1007/978-981-19-5727-7_69

Zhou, F., Ayoub, J., Xu, Q., & Jessie Yang, X. (2020). A machine learning approach to customer needs analysis for product ecosystems. *Journal of Mechanical Design*, 142(1), 011101. 10.1115/1.4044435

ADDITIONAL READING

Perez-Vega, R., Kaartemo, V., Lages, C. R., Razavi, N. B., & Männistö, J. (2021). Reshaping the contexts of online customer engagement behavior via artificial intelligence: A conceptual framework. *Journal of Business Research*, 129, 902–910. 10.1016/j.jbusres.2020.11.002

Yin, D., Li, M., & Qiu, H. (2023). Do customers exhibit engagement behaviors in AI environments? The role of psychological benefits and technology readiness. *Tourism Management*, 97, 104745. 10.1016/j.tourman.2023.104745

Zhang, J., Chen, Q., Lu, J., Wang, X., Liu, L., & Feng, Y. (2024). Emotional expression by artificial intelligence chatbots to improve customer satisfaction: Underlying mechanism and boundary conditions. *Tourism Management, 100*, 104835.

KEY TERMS AND DEFINITIONS

Artificial Intelligence (AI): AI involves the replication of human-like intelligence in machines, usually achieved through computer systems. This enables machines to carry out tasks that traditionally necessitate human intelligence, including learning, solving problems, and making decisions.

Gamification: Gamification involves integrating game-like elements and mechanics into non-game environments to increase engagement, motivation, and participation. This is accomplished by incorporating features such as challenges, rewards, competition, and achievement systems.

Robotic Process Automation (RPA): RPA utilizes software robots or "bots" to automate repetitive and rule-based tasks across multiple systems and applications.

Chapter 10
Optimizing Marketing Campaigns With AI–Driven Insights on Mobile User Behavior

Nurullah Tas
http://orcid.org/0000-0001-6221-0204
Gebze Technical University, Turkey

Farid Huseynov
http://orcid.org/0000-0002-9936-0596
Gebze Technical University, Turkey

Büşra Özdenizci Köse
http://orcid.org/0000-0002-8414-5252
Gebze Technical University, Turkey

ABSTRACT

Technology is crucial in our daily lives, enabling us to communicate, access information, and engage in various activities through devices like smartphones, tablets, and laptops. Social media platforms facilitate global connectivity and information sharing. The internet has revolutionized access to limitless information, online shopping, education, and job opportunities. Artificial intelligence (AI) advancements have brought innovative solutions to sectors like healthcare, automotive, and finance. This study aims to emphasize the significance of technology and AI in analyzing mobile user behavior and optimizing marketing campaigns. It provides insights into comprehending mobile user behavior, factors influencing it, and the role of AI in marketing research. Moreover, it explores AI's utilization in consumer behavior analysis. The study examines the impact of AI algorithms on mobile user data and discusses personalization through AI. Lastly, it delves into AI-supported campaign optimization and real-time marketing.

DOI: 10.4018/979-8-3693-3172-9.ch010

1. INTRODUCTION

Today, technology has assumed a role that affects the behavior of its users. This situation may cause customers who are dissatisfied with their shopping experience to prefer other platforms regardless of any loyalty (Özmen, 2003). This is due to the convenience of shopping regardless of time and place. Mobile devices such as smartphones, tablets and computers offer this convenience (Barutçu, 2008). Artificial intelligence (AI) tools, which are very useful for businesses, are extremely useful in identifying customer expectations and making a plan for the future. Studies show that AI-based systems can analyze customer behavior and predict their preferences (Wisetsri et al., 2021).

Artificial intelligence traces its origins back to philosophers such as Descartes and Leibniz. Although it goes back this far, the focus on artificial intelligence has been focused on in later years. The Dartmouth Conference held in 1956 was an important development point for artificial intelligence as its goals and methods began to take shape (McCarthy, 2007). With the developments, artificial intelligence enables data to be processed and interpreted more systematically. They also have the ability to adapt optimally to capture to achieve the set goals. Businesses benefit from artificial intelligence innovations by using these capabilities. In this way, they can analyze customer data and develop personalized marketing strategies for them (Kaplan and Haenlein, 2019).

Artificial intelligence can be defined as the ability of machines to imitate human intelligence and perform various tasks (Garg, 2021). The goals of AI include learning, reasoning and performing tasks. Basic concepts such as machine learning, deep learning and neural networks form the basis of artificial intelligence. These concepts contribute greatly to the advancement of fields such as data mining, natural language processing and software development (Wisetsri et al., 2021). It is argued that artificial intelligence will create a significant transformation in the field of marketing (Davenport et al., 2020).

Understanding mobile user behavior is critical for businesses. With the rapid advancement of mobile technologies, users' interactions and preferences on mobile devices have become more important. Understanding mobile user behavior enables businesses to optimize marketing strategies, improve user experience and gain competitive advantage. Technologies such as artificial intelligence and data analytics play an important role in understanding and predicting user behavior by processing large amounts of data. By better understanding users' needs, businesses can offer personalized services and increase customer satisfaction. Understanding mobile user behavior is an indispensable factor for businesses to succeed in the competitive market. In this section, information about the increase in mobile device usage and its impact on our lives will be presented and the importance of mobile user behavior and the factors affecting these factors will be discussed. Then, the role of artificial intelligence in mobile user behavior analysis and the use of artificial intelligence techniques in optimizing marketing campaigns for mobile users will be discussed.

2. UNDERSTANDING MOBILE USER BEHAVIOR

Mobile marketing aims to increase the promotion and sales of products through the delivery of personal information to consumers regardless of time and place (Haghirian et al., 2005). Mobile marketing offers businesses the opportunity for customer segmentation and customized marketing strategies can be created for target audiences based on factors such as gender, age, geographic location and interests (Constantiou and Mahnke, 2010). With the rapid advancement of technology, there have been great changes in the field of mobile marketing. Mobile devices and applications offer advantages such as offering interactive content, providing visual and audio experiences, and interacting with the user. This increases the effectiveness of mobile marketing. For example, mobile ads can be made visually appealing with rich media content and offer users interactive experiences. At the same time, marketing messages such as personalized notifications, promotions and discounts can be easily delivered to consumers through mobile devices. However, mobile marketing is not without its challenges. Technical constraints on mobile devices, such as limited screen size and connection speed, can affect content delivery and user experience. In addition, factors such as consumers developing insensitivity or discomfort towards mobile advertisements can reduce the effectiveness of mobile marketing (Park et al., 2008).

The mobile marketing literature has many important studies on the understanding and analysis of mobile user behavior. Mobile marketing enables real-time communication with consumers regardless of time and place (Waldt et al., 2009). Hence, factors such as entertainment, personalization and inconvenience are seen as the most important factors that determine advertising effectiveness and consumer attitudes through mobile marketing and affect mobile marketing (Haghirian and Madlberger, 2005). Trust and personalization are also critical factors affecting mobile marketing (Al-alak and Alnawas, 2010).

Much of the research on mobile marketing has focused on understanding mobile phone users' attitudes towards mobile advertising and examining their behavior in this regard. According to the results of these studies, it has been observed that there is a positive attitude towards personalized, reliable, informative and entertaining mobile marketing applications. However, consumers react negatively to annoying, repetitive and mechanical messages. While showing interest in entertaining messages, experiencing a negative reaction to annoying messages may cause consumers to form negative opinions about the brand (Tsang et al., 2004).

In this context, it can be stated that there are many factors that affect mobile user behavior. User experience and usability factors, application interface, performance and user-friendly content, personalization and customization options, content presentation according to users' preferences, social interactions, security and privacy, economic factors and demographic factors are among the factors that affect mobile user behavior. The following section will elaborate on these factors.

3. FACTORS AFFECTING MOBILE USER BEHAVIOR

Personal variables are important factors affecting the behavior of mobile users. These variables consist of the consumer's personal characteristics, income, age, gender, marital status and occupation (Köseoğlu, 2002; Orhan, 2002; Penpece, 2006): These can affect people's purchasing behavior. For example, consumers' interest may shift to different products according to age groups. While young people are mostly interested in clothing, more middle-aged individuals may be interested in household goods or electronics. On the other hand, gender is also important for mobile consumer behavior. Depending on gender, preferences for product categories may change. On the other hand, the occupation of the person is another important variable.

Socio-cultural factors are also of great importance among the factors affecting mobile user behavior. An individual's needs, desires, beliefs, cultural values and abilities are among the factors that shape mobile usage. In addition, the family has an important role in the consumption process in terms of both earning and spending. The social class to which people belong is also a factor affecting the behavior of the individual and can have a decisive impact on consumption preferences, product choices and spending habits (Odabaşı and Barış, 2003).

Another important factor shaping the purchasing behavior of mobile consumers is economic factors. Factors such as income level, prices and economic conditions are factors that influence consumers' purchasing decisions. In addition, the economic factor, which is directly related to factors such as social status, environment and culture, can play a guiding role in purchasing decisions for users (Penpece, 2006).

An important factor affecting mobile user behavior is the acceptance of mobile technology. Nowadays, mobile technology is a very important part of a lifestyle where consumers interact with mobile marketing technologies and their acceptance of these technologies is increasing (Al-Meshai and Almotairi, 2013). Consumers' acceptance of mobile technology is vital for mobile marketing strategies to achieve their goals (Bauer et al., 2005). Apart from these; there are many variables that affect the acceptance of mobile marketing such as perceived benefit, individual commitment, innovativeness, perception of risk, attitude towards mobile marketing, perception of value, access to content, ability to share content, perception of ease of information acquisition and use (Gao et al., 2010; Jayawardhena et al., 2009).

In the field of mobile marketing, risk perception has a great importance among the factors affecting mobile user behavior. Risk perception refers to the likelihood of users obtaining personal information for online situations. The likelihood of individuals sharing personal information to participate in online marketing campaigns is related to risk perception. Research shows that security concerns can be reduced by ensuring trust and control over the protection of personal information. This suggests that privacy is critical for the successful implementation of mobile marketing strategies (Gao et al., 2010).

Another important factor influencing mobile user behavior is personal commitment. This is associated with consumers' desire to personalize their mobile phones and express themselves in a unique way. It is emphasized that mobile phones are used with individualized features to represent individuals themselves (Du, 2012). In addition, the acceptance of these devices as an inextricably critical part of a person's life is also considered as an indicator of personal attachment (Rohm et al., 2012).

Perceived value, a factor that has an impact on mobile users' attitudes, shows the belief in the usefulness of a system in fulfilling its mission. Perceived value elements of smartphones, such as communication and access to information, can also be directly related to attitudes towards mobile marketing. Innovativeness, on the other hand, is another factor. Innovativeness can be measured by consumers' acceptance of and interest in new mobile applications. Likewise, attitudes towards mobile marketing include emotional and belief elements such as taking advantage of mobile marketing incentives and obtaining information from brands (Gao et al., 2012).

Based on all these, it can be said that artificial intelligence has a wide range of applications in marketing. Today, thanks to advanced algorithms and data analytics techniques, businesses can use AI models to understand customer behavior, make them feel more special with personalized products, and strengthen customer relationships through targeting. Ultimately, AI applications enable businesses to create more effective marketing strategies and offer more customized experiences to their customers. Below, more detailed information on the use of AI in marketing research will be provided.

4. ARTIFICIAL INTELLIGENCE IN MARKETING RESEARCH

In marketing mix management, AI is of great importance and plays an influential role in various areas. From a product management perspective, AI-based marketing analytics tools can determine the level of customer satisfaction by assessing how well the product design matches customer needs (Dekimpe, 2020). In addition, AI can also make great contributions to service innovations and offer innovative solutions by using subject modeling and design capabilities (Antons and Breidbach, 2018). On the other hand, AI can identify customer preferences during the product search process, enabling them to actively use product recommendation systems to improve their marketing strategies (Dzyabura and Hauser, 2019).

Dynamic pricing algorithms have the ability to optimize pricing by taking into account customer preferences, competitor strategies, and the supply network (Dekimpe, 2020). Artificial intelligence methods offer the possibility to realize dynamic price adjustments (Misra et al., 2019). Moreover, with machine learning algorithms, it is possible to quickly align pricing scenarios with competitor prices (Bauer and Jannach, 2018).

Artificial intelligence also provides significant benefits in distribution. In terms of access to products, AI methods optimize processes such as packaging, delivery, order tracking and portfolio management. It also offers new opportunities in customer interaction. In addition, the use of service robots increases customer satisfaction (Verma et al., 2021). At the same time, AI-powered tools such as cobots and drones enhance service quality by improving location management (Huang and Rust, 2022).

In the field of promotion, AI provides the ability to deliver personalized customer-based messages (Huang and Rust, 2022). Content informatics and emotional AI algorithms can monitor customer behavior in real time. At the same time, analysis of social media content offers the opportunity to create strategies in line with customer preferences (Verma et al., 2021). Artificial intelligence contributes greatly to the creation of customer-centered and effective communication strategies in the field of marketing communication.

AI is playing a major role in several critical areas of marketing, such as analyzing the performance of campaigns and setting customer expectations (Haleem et al., 2022) and analyzing customer habits, buying behaviors and preferences (Chatterjee et al., 2019). AI is being used to support strategic decisions such as segmentation, targeting and positioning. Through the use of computational algorithms such as sentiment analysis and deep learning, social media data can be analyzed in a meaningful way. These can provide consumer insights and contribute to marketing decisions (Verma et al., 2021).

The analysis of consumer behavior is undergoing a significant transformation with AI-enabled methods. AI enables us to understand consumer preferences, trends and needs more effectively by using big data analysis and machine learning techniques. This gives businesses a huge advantage in creating more effective marketing strategies and delivering personalized experiences. With AI, businesses can gain deeper insights into consumer behavior and deliver this information in a customized way to their target audiences. Below, more detailed information on the use of AI in analyzing consumer behavior will be provided.

5. ARTIFICIAL INTELLIGENCE IN ANALYZING CONSUMER BEHAVIOR

Artificial intelligence plays a vital role in analyzing consumer behavior. The use of AI is radically changing the way businesses and customers interact and enabling marketers to pay more attention to their customers (Hoyer et al., 2020). By quickly analyzing the data they collect and generate, AI algorithms have the ability to determine which strategies to use to target content to customers. This ensures that customer needs can be met in real time and experiences can be personalized (Haleem et al., 2022). On the other hand, artificial intelligence offers marketers the opportunity to better understand their customers' behavior and develop more effective marketing strategies accordingly.

Consumers are interacting with AI as they adapt to rapidly changing technology and innovations (Verma et al., 2021). Artificial intelligence optimizes business processes, generates data-driven insights and produces algorithms for consumer and market analysis (Davenport et al., 2020). AI technologies such as machine learning, deep learning and natural language processing are significantly impacting digital marketing strategies by analyzing big data (Haleem et al., 2022). In this way, and using further developments, businesses can better understand consumer behavior, optimize their marketing strategies, and deliver personalized experiences to customers.

In the field of marketing, the demand for marketing research has increased in order to predict transformations in the AI-driven consumer market. Marketing research has radically changed marketing research processes by adapting to technological changes. Companies attach great importance to market research to better understand their target audiences, develop their products, improve user experience and create an effective marketing strategy (Emeritus, 2023). In this way, businesses can better meet customer demands and strengthen their leading position in the market.

Artificial intelligence is indispensable in the analysis of consumer behavior. This technology offers businesses the opportunity to meet customers' needs in real time. Moreover, when personalized experiences are offered, the use of AI is observed to increase consumers' propensity to purchase. Consumers who interact with various AI tools show remarkable behavioral changes. AI has the ability to automate business processes, extract meaningful insights from data and generate market insights. It also includes various fields such as machine learning, deep learning and natural language processing. Among these, machine learning has a significant impact on digital marketing scenarios thanks to its capacity to analyze big data and provide analytical tools in marketing (Haleem et al., 2022). Accordingly, businesses are using artificial intelligence to gain competitive advantage and create successful marketing strategies.

Market research offers companies significant advantages. First, it provides guidance on how to focus on customer needs and increase customer satisfaction. The data enables brands to understand consumers' needs and make customer-oriented decisions. It also provides an opportunity to improve brand image and strengthen market positioning. By identifying the preferences of target audiences, market research enables companies to offer products and services tailored to the customer. It also plays an important role in mitigating risks. It prepares companies to adapt to market changes by providing information on market trends, competitor strategies and customer requirements. On the other hand, market research enables leaders to make data-driven decisions and identify the right products, marketing strategies and target markets. The market research process is carried out through primary and secondary market research, which includes two different methods. Primary market research is research conducted internally within companies and aims to identify needs and wants through direct communication with customers. These methods include focus groups, interviews, observation-based research, buyer personality surveys and market segmentation research. Secondary market research is research conducted by third parties and is based on previously collected, analyzed and published data. This method includes information from sources such as company websites, industry statistics, white papers and government agency data (Emeritus, 2023).

However, marketing research has undergone a radical transformation with the adoption of artificial intelligence. In order to survive in a competitive market, the analysis of consumer behavior is of paramount importance. Market research involves the process of collecting, analyzing and interpreting data and provides companies with an overview of evolving market trends, consumer behavior and market conditions. The purposes of conducting market research include assessing the feasibility of a new business or product, identifying potential new markets, tracking marketing trends, and testing demand for new products (Emeritus, 2023).

Artificial intelligence greatly benefits from the power of algorithms used in marketing and many other fields. Advanced algorithms can identify complex patterns, analyze data and make predictions using big data analysis and machine learning techniques. These algorithms can quickly process large datasets to understand user behavior, preferences and trends. It can also be used to deliver personalized content, product recommendations or targeted ads to users using the results of data analysis. AI algorithms give businesses a significant advantage in making more effective decisions, optimizing marketing strategies and improving the customer experience. Below, we will provide more detailed insights into the impact of AI algorithms on mobile user data.

6. IMPACT OF ARTIFICIAL INTELLIGENCE ALGORITHMS ON MOBILE USER DATA

Artificial intelligence, defined as machines that can successfully perform human-like cognitive tasks, has become an important part of digital marketing and social media (Galloway and Swiatek, 2018). The algorithms that AI uses to work need a large amount and variety of data to evolve. Users' activities on various digital platforms such as social media, email, websites and search engines play an important role in the creation of this data (Pavlik et al., 2022). This data plays an important role in the creation of personalized flows and experiences. These large pools of data are known as the information available online and stored in the cloud (Mosco, 2014, citing Fuchs, 2014). Artificial intelligence algorithms have a huge impact on mobile user data and these algorithms are used by popular platforms such as Facebook, Google, Amazon (Koenig, 2020). These companies use algorithms by focusing on users' digital activities and create personalized environments based on data collected, archived, analyzed and interpreted through different activities (Willson, 2016).

In relation to digital marketing activities, there are debates on the unethical aspects of data collection processes (Palmer, 2005). Understanding the functioning and implications of algorithms in personalized digital platforms is becoming increasingly important (Swart, 2021, citing Head et al., 2020). Algorithms are defined as a set of instructions that produce output based on a given input (Gillespie, 2014). Nowadays, there is a great reliance on algorithms for decisions and analysis (Doneda and Almeida, 2016).

Personalization is an important feature of AI, providing the ability to better understand users' preferences and behaviors to deliver tailored experiences. By analyzing data such as users' past interactions, buying habits and demographics, AI algorithms can deliver tailored content, product recommendations or targeted marketing messages. In this way, users can more easily access their interests and needs and feel more valued. Personalization increases customer satisfaction and offers the potential for businesses to generate higher conversion rates and loyalty. Artificial intelligence has become an important tool to support personalization using big data analysis and learning algorithms, helping to shape marketing strategies more effectively. More detailed information on personalization will be provided below.

7. PERSONALIZATION WITH ARTIFICIAL INTELLIGENCE

Personalization is offered as a feature developed to provide convenience, speed and practicality for users. This feature allows users to access the content they want quickly and easily by preventing them from getting lost among thousands of content. Personalization is useful in creating a content stream that better reflects the wants, expectations and needs of internet users. Therefore, personalization is thought to have positive effects on issues such as brand loyalty and sales orientation (Kuş, 2021).

With the advancement of artificial intelligence technologies, personalization is evolving to a structure based on user data. However, the frequent exposure of popular platforms to privacy violations related to user data raises concerns among users about this structure. However, with personalization's functional features and customer satisfaction, users are becoming more willing to share data. Users start to find personalization and data processes more acceptable when they realize that personalization increases their benefits, facilitates decision-making in various areas, puts them in control, and makes them happy with their experience (Kotler et al., 2022).

Personalization can be defined in a user-centric way and has the potential to offer great advantages by saving users time and making their experience more targeted and enjoyable. However, it is a topic that should be approached hesitantly due to certain situations and therefore problems. The personalization paradigms of social media platforms may cause users to be limited to content produced by users similar to themselves. This may eliminate the possibility of encountering different perspectives that will help overcome personal and social prejudices and may lead to the deepening of prejudices (Narin, 2018).

In the field of marketing, artificial intelligence is of great importance for campaign optimization and real-time marketing. Artificial intelligence algorithms, big data analysis and continuous learning capabilities allow marketing campaigns to be optimized more effectively and respond quickly to users' instant interactions. This gives businesses a strategic and competitive advantage. Below, more detailed information on AI-powered campaign optimization and real-time marketing will be provided.

8. AI-POWERED CAMPAIGN OPTIMIZATION AND REAL-TIME MARKETING

AI-powered customer experience is an area where marketers are using AI to better understand customers and deliver the best experience (Haleem et al., 2022). AI has the potential to increase ROI without spending on ineffective initiatives through analyzing consumer data, and also offers the possibility to avoid annoying advertising (Peyravi et al., 2020). AI technology is also gaining attention for its ability to process customer data to provide personalized services and product recommendations (Ameen et al., 2021). AI-powered customer experience offers efficiency benefits in terms of reduced labor resources and automation of routine tasks (Murgai, 2018).

Customers begin to trust brands and the technology used, especially when AI-powered services are personalized, convenient and high-quality (Ameen et al., 2021). AI customer experience improves every touchpoint in the customer journey through the seamless integration of advanced technologies and human insight (Villegas, 2024). AI-powered experiences can increase customers' determination to maintain an ongoing relationship with brands and help customers develop positive experiences with brands (Ameen et al., 2021).

AI technologies such as machine learning and natural language processing can help retailers analyze customer sentiment and feedback at a scale that humans cannot achieve (Gartner, 2020). This makes AI an important tool for retailers to stay competitive and continuously improve the customer experience (Newman, 2019). AI technology, when combined with other technologies such as augmented reality, image recognition and inventory management, has the potential to significantly improve retailers' customer experience (Saponaro et al., 2018). In this way, personalized services are provided by better responding to customers' needs. This makes the shopping experience more immersive. In addition, AI-powered analytics help retailers to better understand consumer behavior and make effective strategic decisions.

AI-powered customer experience uses customer data and profiles to help businesses learn the best ways to interact with customers. In this way, businesses can better understand customer preferences, save time by automating routine tasks, and provide personalized experiences by offering tailored recommendations (Villegas, 2024). However, these technologies should always be under control to avoid ethical problems. This is because issues such as data privacy, security and transparency are important issues in AI-supported customer experience applications. Therefore, businesses should protect customer data appropriately and comply with ethical rules.

In the future, artificial intelligence will spread rapidly and will be used in wider areas. With the advancement of emerging technologies and AI algorithms, businesses will prefer more efficient and intelligent systems. In healthcare, automotive, retail, manufacturing and many other sectors, AI-based solutions will be more widely adopted, offering great opportunities to optimize business processes, improve decision-making and deliver personalized experiences.

Research is a valuable source of information on how AI can complement and enhance marketing strategies (Haleem et al., 2022). The diversity and increasing interest of research in the field of marketing shows that AI can be used in different approaches to marketing strategies. The development of new methods in AI-based marketing research, such as microtext analysis and anaphora analysis, offers more capabilities to future researchers (Poria et al., 2015). Future work can improve emotional predictability by enhancing emotional analysis through the use of deep learning and linguistic patterns (Verma et al., 2021). In this way, AI algorithms can better understand emotional expressions and effectively use customer emotions in marketing strategies.

Future AI research offers important insights into how AI can be used in the development and completion of marketing strategies (Haleem et al., 2022). This research aims to increase the capabilities of future researchers by focusing on topics such as the development of emotional analytics, microtext analysis and collaborative market intelligence. Furthermore, integrating AI technologies with other fields, such as big data analysis and emotional dictionaries, could lead to significant advances in the field of marketing.

9. OPTIMIZATION DIMENSIONS THAT CAN BE GENERATED BY ARTIFICIAL INTELLIGENCE

Artificial intelligence can offer optimization in many aspects of ad optimization. For example, AI can contribute to the development of important dimensions such as cost reduction, targeting quality, content relevance and media effectiveness. First of all, cost reduction is an important aspect of AI-supported ad optimization. AI algorithms can provide decision support on pricing strategies and budget allocation to make the most optimal use of the advertising budget. In this way, lower cost, higher recycling and more effective advertising campaigns can be carried out (Ever & Demircioğlu, 2022).

Targeting quality can be seen as another advantage of artificial intelligence in ad optimization. Thanks to big data analysis and learning capabilities, advertising options with more accurate and precise targeting can be offered. By analyzing information such as consumer preferences, behaviors and demographic data, AI can ensure that advertising messages reach the right target audience. This offers advertisers higher conversion rates and more effective marketing strategies (Bateni et al., 2017).

Another optimization dimension developed by AI solutions is content relevance and media effectiveness. By utilizing artificial intelligence, content analysis and recommendation systems can be developed to ensure that advertising content is relevant to the target audience. In this way, more engaging and personalized content can be created and the consumer experience can be enhanced. In addition, AI-supported media optimization can increase ad effectiveness by ensuring that ads are shown on the right channels and at the right times (Dalenberg, 2018). Some more explanatory information on this topic is shared in the following sections.

10. SEGMENTATION AND POSITIONING OF ADVERTISING ACTIONS SUPPORTED BY ARTIFICIAL INTELLIGENCE

Customer knowledge is an increasingly important strategic element (Bouhtati et al., 2023a). AI-supported advertising actions are also important for marketing segmentation and positioning processes for customers. Today, AI can provide more precise and accurate segmentation thanks to its big data analysis and learning capabilities. Thus, by analyzing a lot of information together, the target audience can be divided into different groups and advertising messages can be customized for these groups (Choi and Lim, 2020).

Utilizing artificial intelligence in segmentation provides significant advantages for advertisers in terms of marketing positioning. Artificial intelligence can help determine the position of products or services in the market by evaluating factors such as consumer preferences, market trends and competitive analysis. Thus, advertisers can identify unique selling points and differentiating positioning strategies and create effective messages and campaigns for the target audience (Theodoridis and Gkikas, 2019).

In addition, artificial intelligence can continuously improve itself by analyzing real-time data. This allows segmentation and positioning strategies to be improved over time. AI-driven dynamic segmentation and positioning enables rapid response to potential changes (Ziafat and Shakeri, 2014).

11. APPLICATION OF ARTIFICIAL INTELLIGENCE IN AD OPTIMIZATION AND TARGETING

Artificial intelligence helps advertisers with technologies such as real-time bidding. Thus, the most optimal bids can be determined by analyzing user behavior and ad performance. In this way, the advertising budget is used more efficiently and the target audience can be reached more effectively (Nikolajeva & Teilans, 2021).

On the other hand, artificial intelligence can determine which ads are effective by analyzing big data. By optimizing ad content and strategies, advertisers can create more effective campaigns (Gupta et al., 2020). It can also optimize ad content, frequency, placement and timing by monitoring ad performance. This enables effective budget management (Mühlhoff and Willem, 2023).

On the other hand, AI also plays an important role in ad targeting. By analyzing consumer data, different customer groups can be identified and ads can be shown only to those relevant user segments. In addition, by using artificial intelligence, advertising campaigns can be expanded by finding new potential customers with similar characteristics. Thus, it can reach a wider audience and optimize marketing strategies (Bhatt, 2020). Thanks to big data, personalized advertising experiences are also offered (Lhoussaine et al., 2022).

With advancing technology, artificial intelligence can also provide more effective targeting by analyzing the content and placement of ads. It can also optimize ad placements by evaluating user scenarios (Haleem et al., 2022). Furthermore, AI can also increase the effectiveness of advertising campaigns. With AI, ad performance can be continuously monitored by analyzing real-time data (Ziafat and Shakeri, 2014).

12. ETHICAL CONSIDERATIONS IN ARTIFICIAL INTELLIGENCE SUPPORTED MOBILE MARKETING APPLICATIONS

In addition to its many benefits, artificial intelligence brings some challenges. One of these is ethical considerations. The marketing discipline needs big data to improve customer experience, personalize and tailor offers (Bouhtatit et al., 2023b). Artificial intelligence used for this purpose can lead to biases and unintended dissemination of information. This can have negative impacts on people's lives. The need for large amounts of data for artificial intelligence raises privacy concerns. At this point, consumer data should be used ethically, privacy rights should be respected, and users should be given the right to choose how their data is shared (Munjal, 2016).

The transparency and interpretability of AI algorithms has focused on a number of privacy concerns, including societal values, ethical and legal issues. While there are many ethical guidelines on AI issues, keeping and presenting information transparently is a common problem. AI entails such security shortcomings and a number of regulatory and restrictive legal challenges (Larsson and Heintz, 2020).

For these reasons, consultation and collaboration between advertisers, researchers, policymakers and other relevant stakeholders is essential for the ethical and responsible use of AI. These collaborations aim to maximize the benefits and minimize the risks, as well as to ensure the ethical use of AI.

13. CONCLUSION

The proliferation of mobile devices has created new opportunities in marketing, and the collection and analysis of mobile usage data has gained importance. Artificial intelligence applications play a critical role in analyzing and understanding mobile user behavior. By processing large datasets, AI algorithms can understandably reveal and predict user behavior. AI techniques such as machine learning and deep learning model user behavior and help create the most appropriate marketing strategies.

Optimizing the mobile app user experience is of great importance for marketing. By analyzing users' app experiences, AI can help design more user-friendly interfaces and manage feedback effectively. In addition, sentiment analysis techniques can be used to understand customers' emotional reactions and develop marketing strategies based on this information.

Measuring the effectiveness of mobile marketing campaigns is an important issue and AI can be used in this area. Using AI techniques, marketers can evaluate the results of marketing campaigns, perform real-time analyses and optimize future strategies. By using predictive models, customer behavior can be predicted in advance and based on this, the most appropriate marketing strategies can be developed.

As a result, artificial intelligence is of great importance in the mobile marketing industry. More effective and competitive marketing strategies can be developed by using artificial intelligence techniques in areas such as analyzing mobile usage data, understanding user behavior, optimizing application experiences and measuring the effectiveness of marketing campaigns.

REFERENCES

Al-alak, B. A., & Alnawas, I. A. (2010). Examining the Impact of Trust, Privacy Concern and Consumers' Attitudes on Intention to Purchase. *International Journal of Business and Management*, 5(3), 28–41. 10.5539/ijbm.v5n3p28

Al-Meshal, S., & Almotairi, M. (2013). Consumer Acceptance of Mobile Marketing: An Empirical Study on the Saudi Female. *International Journal of Marketing Studies.*, 5(5). Advance online publication. 10.5539/ijms.v5n5p94

Ameen, N., Tarhini, A., Reppel, A., & Anand, A. (2021). Customer experiences in the age of artificial intelligence. *Computers in Human Behavior*, 114, 106548. 10.1016/j.chb.2020.10654832905175

Antons, D., & Breidbach, C. F. (2018). Big data, big insights? Advancing service innovation and design with machine learning. *Journal of Service Research*, 21(1), 17–39. 10.1177/1094670517738373

Barutçu, S. (2008). *Mobil Pazarlama Güncel Pazarlama Yaklaşımlarından Seçmeler.*

Bateni, M., Esfandiary, H., Mirrokni, V., & Seddighin, S. (2017, February). *A study of compact reserve pricing languages [Conference session].* Proceedings of the AAAI Conference on Artificial Intelligence, San Francisco, CA, USA.

Bauer, H., Reichardt, T., Barnes, S., & Neumann, M. (2005). Driving consumer acceptance of mobile marketing: A theoretical framework and empirical study. *Journal of Electronic Commerce Research*, 6.

Bauer, J., & Jannach, D. (2018). Optimal pricing in e-commerce based on sparse and noisy data. *Decision Support Systems*, 106, 53–63. 10.1016/j.dss.2017.12.002

Bhatt, V. K. (2021). Assessing the significance and impact of artificial intelligence and machine learning in placement of advertisements [Conference session]. *2021 IEEE International Conference on Technology Management, Operations and Decisions (ICTMOD),* (pp. 1–6). IEEE.

Bouhtati, N., Alla, L., & Bentalhah, B. (2023a). Marketing Big Data Analytics and Customer Relationship Management: A Fuzzy Approach. In *Integrating Intelligence and Sustainability in Supply Chains* (pp. 75-86). DOI: . IGI Global.10.4018/979-8-3693-0225-5.ch004

Bouhtatit, N., Kamal, M., & Alla, L. (2023b). Big Data and the Effectiveness of Tourism Marketing: A Prospective Review of the Literature. In Farhaoui, Y., Rocha, A., Brahmia, Z., & Bhushab, B. (Eds.), *Artificial Intelligence and Smart Environment. ICAISE 2022. Lecture Notes in Networks and Systems, 635*. Springer. 10.1007/978-3-031-26254-8_40

Chatterjee, S., Ghosh, S. K., Chaudhuri, R., & Nguyen, B. (2019). Are CRM systems ready for AI integration? A conceptual framework of organizational readiness for effective AI-CRM integration. *The Bottom Line (New York, N.Y.)*, 32(2), 144–157. 10.1108/BL-02-2019-0069

Choi, J. A., & Lim, K. (2020). Identifying machine learning techniques for classification of target advertising. *ICT Express*, 6(3), 175–180. 10.1016/j.icte.2020.04.012

Constantiou, I. D., & Mahnke, V. (2010). Consumer Behaviour and Mobile TV Services: Do Men Differ from Women in Their Adoption Intentions? *Journal of Electronic Commerce Research*, 11(2).

Dalenberg, D. J. (2018). Preventing discrimination in the automated targeting of job advertisements. *Computer Law & Security Report*, 34(3), 615–627. 10.1016/j.clsr.2017.11.009

Davenport, T., Guha, A., Grewal, D., & Bressgott, T. (2020). How artificial intelligence will change the future of marketing. *Journal of the Academy of Marketing Science*, 48(1), 24–42. 10.1007/s11747-019-00696-0

Dekimpe, M. G. (2020). Retailing and retailing research in the age of big data analytics. *International Journal of Research in Marketing*, 37(1), 3–14. 10.1016/j.ijresmar.2019.09.001

Doneda, D., & Almeida, V. A. F. (2016, July-August). What Is Algorithm Governance? *IEEE Internet Computing*, 20(4), 60–63. 10.1109/MIC.2016.79

Dzyabura, D., & Hauser, J. R. (2019). Recommending products when consumers learn their preference weights. *Marketing Science*, 38(3), 417–441. 10.1287/mksc.2018.1144

Emeritus. (2023). *What is Market Research? Definition and Types*. Emeritus. https://emeritus.org/in/learn/what-is-market-research-and-why-is-it-important/)

Ever, D., & Demircioğlu, E. N. (2022). *Yapay Zekâ Teknolojilerinin Kalite Maliyetleri Üzerine Etkisi, Çukurova Üniversitesi Sosyal Bilimler Enstitüsü Dergisi*, 31(1), 59–72.

Fuchs, C. (2014). *Sosyal Medya Eleştirel Bir Giriş*. Notabene Yayınları.

Galloway, C., & Swıatek, L. (2018). Public Relations and Artificial Intelligence: It's Not (Just) About Robots. *Public Relations Review*, 44(5), 734–740. 10.1016/j.pubrev.2018.10.008

Gao, T., Rohm, A. J., Sultan, F., & Huang, S. (2012). Antecedents of consumer attitudes toward mobile marketing: A comparative study of youth markets in the United States and China. *Thunderbird International Business Review*, 54(2), 211–224. 10.1002/tie.21452

Gao, T., Sultan, F., & Rohm, A. J. (2010). Factors influencing Chinese youth consumers' acceptance of mobile marketing. *Journal of Consumer Marketing*, 27(7), 574–583. 10.1108/07363761011086326

Garg, P. K. (2021). Overview of artificial intelligence. In *Artificial intelligence* (pp. 3–18). Chapman and Hall/CRC. 10.1201/9781003140351-2

Gillespie, T. (2014). Relevance of Algorithms. In Gillespie, T., Boczkowski, P. J., & Foot, K. A. (Eds.), *Inside Technology. Media Technologies: Essays on Communication, Materiality, and Society* (pp. 167–194). The MIT Press. 10.7551/mitpress/9042.003.0013

Gupta, S., Gupta, A., Savjani, P., & Kumar, R. (2020). Optimizing creative allocations in digital marketing [Conferece session]. *International conference on advances in computing and data sciences, Singapore* (pp. 419–429). Springer Singapore.

Haghirian, P., & Madlberger, M. (2005). Consumer Attitude toward Advertising via Mobile Devices. *European Conference on Information Systems*, (pp. 447–458). IEEE.

Haghirian, P., Madlberger, M., & Tanuskova, A. (2005). Increasing Advertising Value of Mobile Marketing - An Empirical Study of Antecedents. *Proceedings of the 38th Annual Hawaii International Conference on System Sciences* (pp. 32c-32c). IEEE. 10.1109/HICSS.2005.311

Haleem, A., Javaid, M., Qadri, M. A., Singh, R. P., & Suman, R. (2022). Artificial intelligence (AI) applications for marketing: A literature-based study. *International Journal of Intelligent Networks*.

Head, A. J., Fister, B., & Macmillan, M. (2020, January 15). *Information Literacy in the Age of Algorithms: Student Experiences With News and Information, and The Need for Change.* Project Information Literacy. https://files.eric.ed.gov/fulltext/ ED605109.pdf

Hoyer, W. D., Kroschke, M., Schmitt, B., Kraume, K., & Shankar, V. (2020). Transforming the customer experience through new technologies. *Journal of Interactive Marketing*, 51(1), 57–71. 10.1016/j.intmar.2020.04.001

Huang, M. H., & Rust, R. T. (2022). A framework for collaborative artificial intelligence in marketing. *Journal of Retailing*, 98(2), 209–223. 10.1016/j.jretai.2021.03.001

Jayawardhena, C., Kuckertz, A., Karjaluoto, H., & Kautonen, T. (2007). Antecedents to Permission Based Mobile Marketing: An Initial Examination. *European Journal of Marketing*, 43(3/4), 473–499. 10.1108/03090560910935541

Kaplan, A., & Haenlein, M. (2019). ve Haenlein, M., "Siri, Siri, in my hand: Who's the fairest in the land? On the interpretations, illustrations, and implications of artificial intelligence". *Business Horizons*, 62(1), 15–25. 10.1016/j.bushor.2018.08.004

Köseoğlu, Ö. (2002). *Değişim Fenomeni Karşısında Markalaşma Süreci ve Bu Süreçte Halkla İlişkilerin Rolü.* Yüksek Lisans Tezi. Ege Üniversitesi Sosyal Bilimler Enstitüsü Halkla İlişkiler Anabilim Dalı, İzmir.

Kotler, P., Kartajaya, H., & Setiawan, I. (2022). *Pazarlama 5.0.* Nişantaşı Üniversitesi Yayınları.

Kuş, O. (2021). *Algoritmaları Dehümanizasyon Çerçevesinde Tartışmak (Der. Oğuz Kuş). Algoritmaların Gölgesinde Toplum Ve İletişim.* Alternatif Bilişim Derneği.

Larsson, S., & Heintz, F. (2020). Transparency in artificial intelligence. *Internet Policy Review*, 9(2), 1–16. 10.14763/2020.2.1469

Lhoussaine, A. L. L. A., Kamal, M., & Bouhtati, N. (2022). Big data and marketing effectiveness of tourism businesses: A literature review. *Economic Management Alternatives*, 1, 39–58.

McCarthy, J. (2007). From here to human-level AI. *Artificial Intelligence*, 171(18), 1174–1182. 10.1016/j.artint.2007.10.009

Misra, K., Schwartz, E. M., & Abernethy, J. (2019). Dynamic online pricing with incomplete information using multiarmed bandit experiments. *Marketing Science*, 38(2), 226–252. 10.1287/mksc.2018.1129

Mühlhoff, R., & Willem, T. (2023). Social media advertising for clinical studies: Ethical and data protection implications of online targeting. *Big Data & Society*, 10(1), 1–15. 10.1177/20539517231156127

Munjal, N. (2016). A study on ethical issues in advertising and analyzing different unethical advertisements with results of asci decisions: An Indian perspective. *Ecoforum Journal*, 5(2), 1–34.

Murgai, A. (2018). Transforming digital marketing with artificial intelligence. International Journal of Latest Technology in Engineering, Management &. *Applied Sciences (Basel, Switzerland)*, 7(4), 259–262.

Narin, B. (2018). Kişiselleştirilmiş Çevrimiçi Haber Akışının Yankı Odası Etkisi, Filtre Balonu ve Siberbalkanizasyon Kavramları Çerçevesinde İncelenmesi. *Selçuk İletişim*, 11(2), 232–251. 10.18094/josc.340471

Nikolajeva, A., & Teilans, A. (2021). Machine Learning Technology Overview In Terms Of Digital Marketing And Personalization. *ECMS*, 125-130.

Odabaşı, Y., & Barış, G. (2003). *Tüketici Davranışı (Cilt 2. Baskı)*. MediaCat Akademi.

Orhan, İ. (2002). *Satın Alınan Ürünlere İlişkin Duyguların Cinsiyet ve Cinsiyet Rolleri Bakımından İncelenmesi*.

Özmen, Ş. (2003). *Ağ Ekonomisinde Yeni Ticaret Yolu E-Ticaret*. İstanbul Bilgi Üniversitesi Yayınları.

Palmer, D. E. (2005). Pop-ups, cookies, and spam: Toward a deeper analysis of the ethical significance of internet marketing practices. *Journal of Business Ethics*, 58(1-3), 271–280. 10.1007/s10551-005-1421-8

Park, T., Shenoy, R., & Salvendy, G. (2008). Effective Advertising on Mobile Phones: A Literature Review and Presentation of Results from 53 Case Studies. *Behaviour & Information Technology*, 27(5), 355–373. 10.1080/01449290600958882

Pavlik, J., (2008). *Mapping the Consequences of Technology on Public Relations*.

Penpece, D. (2006). *Tüketici Davranılarını Belirleyen Etmenler: Kültrürün Tüketici Davranışları Üzerindeki Etkisi*. Kahramanmaraş.

Peyravi, B., Nekrošienė, J., & Lobanova, L. (2020). Revolutionised technologies for marketing: Theoretical review with focus on artificial intelligence. *Business: Theory and Practice*, 21(2), 827–834. 10.3846/btp.2020.12313

Poria, S., Cambria, E., Gelbukh, A., Bisio, F., & Hussain, A. (2015). Sentiment data flow analysis by means of dynamic linguistic patterns. *IEEE Computational Intelligence Magazine*, 10(4), 26–36. 10.1109/MCI.2015.2471215

Rohm, A., Sultan, F., Pagani, M., & Gao, T. (2012). Brand in the hand: A cross-market investigation of consumer acceptance of mobile marketing. *Business Horizons*, 55(5), 485–493. 10.1016/j.bushor.2012.05.004

Saponaro, M., Le Gal, D., Gao, M., Guisiano, M., & Maniere, I. C. (2018, December). Challenges and opportunities of artificial intelligence in the fashion world. In *2018 international conference on intelligent and innovative computing applications (ICONIC)* (pp. 1-5). IEEE.

Theodoridis, P. K., & Gkikas, D. C. (2019). How artificial intelligence affects digital marketing [Conference session]. Strategic Innovative Marketing and Tourism: 7th ICSIMAT [Springer International Publishing.]. *Athenian Riviera, Greece*, 2018(October), 1319–1327.

Tsang, M. M., Ho, S. C., & Liang, T. P. (2004). Consumer Attitudes Toward Mobile Advertising: An empirical study. *International Journal of Electronic Commerce*, 8(3), 65–78. 10.1080/10864415.2004.11044301

Verma, S., Sharma, R., Deb, S., & Maitra, D. (2021). Artificial intelligence in marketing: Systematic review and future research direction. *International Journal of Information Management Data Insights*, 1(1), 100002. 10.1016/j.jjimei.2020.100002

Villegas, F. (2024). *Artificial Intelligence Customer Experience: What is it, Pros, Cons and Best Tools.* QuestionPro. https://www.questionpro.com/blog/tr/ai-customer-experience/)

Waldt, L. R., Rebello, T. M., & Brown, W. J. (2009). Attitudes of Young Consumers towards SMS Advertising. *African Journal of Business Management*, 3(9), 444–452.

Willson, M., (2016). *Algorithms (and the) Everyday, Information, Communication & Society.*

Wisetsri, W. (2021). Systematic analysis and future research directions in artificial intelligence for marketing. *Turkish Journal of Computer and Mathematics Education*, 12(11), 43–55.

Ziafat, H., & Shakeri, M. (2014). Using data mining techniques in customer segmentation. *Journal of Engineering Research and Applications*, 4(9), 70–79.

ADDITIONAL READINGS

Bag, S., Srivastava, G., Bashir, M. M. A., Kumari, S., Giannakis, M., & Chowdhury, A. H. (2022). Journey of customers in this digital era: Understanding the role of artificial intelligence technologies in user engagement and conversion. *Benchmarking*, 29(7), 2074–2098. 10.1108/BIJ-07-2021-0415

Campbell, C., Sands, S., Ferraro, C., Tsao, H. Y. J., & Mavrommatis, A. (2020). From data to action: How marketers can leverage AI. *Business Horizons*, 63(2), 227–243. 10.1016/j.bushor.2019.12.002

Chintalapati, S., & Pandey, S. K. (2022). Artificial intelligence in marketing: A systematic literature review. *International Journal of Market Research*, 64(1), 38–68. 10.1177/14707853211018428

Ziakis, C., & Vlachopoulou, M. (2023). Artificial intelligence in digital marketing: Insights from a comprehensive review. *Information (Basel)*, 14(12), 664. 10.3390/info14120664

KEY TERMS AND DEFINITIONS

Artificial Intelligence (AI): AI replicates human-like intelligence in machines via computer systems, enabling them to learn, solve problems, and make decisions traditionally requiring human intellect.

Machine Learning (ML): Machine learning is a branch of artificial intelligence (AI) that enables computers to learn from data and improve their performance on tasks without being explicitly programmed.

Personalization: Personalization refers to tailoring products, services, or experiences to meet the specific needs, preferences, and characteristics of individuals or groups.

Chapter 11
Applying Artificial Intelligence to Enhance E–Commerce Marketing Strategies:
A Case Study of Jumia Market in Morocco

Nabil Seghyar

Research Laboratory in Organizational Management Sciences, Ibn Tofail University, Morocco

Meryem Amane

Artificial Intelligence, Data Science, and Emergent Systems Laboratory, Sidi Mohamed Ben Abdellah University, Morocco

Mounir Gouiouez

Psychology, Sociology, and Culture Studies Laboratory, Sidi Mohamed Ben Abdellah University, Morocco

Said Hraoui
http://orcid.org/0000-0001-6838-5734

Artificial Intelligence, Data Science, and Emergent Systems Laboratory, Sidi Mohamed Ben Abdellah University, Morocco

Mohammed Berrada

Artificial Intelligence, Data Science, and Emergent Systems Laboratory, Sidi Mohamed Ben Abdellah University, Morocco

ABSTRACT

In the dynamic transformation of Moroccan e-commerce, AI and marketing convergence reshapes business-consumer engagement. This chapter explores AI's strategic use to enhance marketing in Moroccan e-commerce, spotlighting Jumia Market. Started in 2012 as a Pan-African tech firm, Jumia evolved into a multifaceted entity with marketplace, logistics, and payment services. Competing regionally and globally, Jumia faced challenges but went public on NYSE in 2019, adapting to market shifts. Amidst COVID-19 in 2020, it responded to changing consumer habits, emphasizing adaptability and profitability. This study examines Jumia Market's trajectory, resilience, and performance, showcasing AI's role in refining

DOI: 10.4018/979-8-3693-3172-9.ch011

marketing strategies for optimal customer experiences and sustained growth in Moroccan e-commerce.

1. INTRODUCTION

In the dynamic realm of e-commerce, the fusion of artificial intelligence (AI) and marketing emerges as a game-changer, reshaping how businesses engage with consumers (Hermann, Williams, & Puntoni, 2023). This study delves into the strategic utilization of AI to refine marketing approaches within Morocco's e-commerce, with a particular focus on Jumia Market as a case study. Our primary objective is to delve deeply into how AI-powered marketing strategies can be tailored to enrich customer experiences and drive online sales, all within the unique context of Morocco's e-commerce. Morocco, strategically situated at the crossroads of Africa and Europe, boasts a vibrant e-commerce sector characterized by diverse consumer preferences, cultural intricacies, and economic factors. This geographical positioning renders Morocco a distinct market, where businesses encounter a blend of influences. Understanding and navigating this complex terrain are imperative for those aspiring to achieve sustainable growth and meaningful customer engagement. In this multifaceted environment, businesses grapple with the task of accommodating diverse consumer choices, understanding cultural subtleties shaping purchasing decisions, and aligning strategies with economic dynamics. The integration of artificial intelligence (AI) into marketing strategies emerges as a pioneering solution to address the inherent complexities of Morocco's e-commerce. AI presents remarkable opportunities, serving as a conduit for businesses to not only comprehend but also adeptly respond to the numerous elements at play. Through AI, businesses gain access to tools that empower them to personalize experiences based on individual preferences, refine customer interactions in line with cultural sensitivities, and ultimately, elevate online sales to high levels (Davenport & al., 2020). Incorporating AI into marketing strategies is not just a strategic option but a vital necessity for businesses seeking a competitive edge (Huang & Rust, 2021). As Morocco's e-commerce evolves, the integration of AI not only addresses the challenges posed by diverse consumer preferences, cultural nuances, and economic considerations but also positions businesses to increase and forge enduring connections in this dynamic marketplace (Fanti, Guarascio, & Moggi, 2022).

The selection of Jumia Market as the primary case study is justified by its notable standing as a Pan-African technology company and a key player in the Moroccan e-commerce. Jumia's journey since its establishment in 2012 not only highlights its resilience and adaptability but also underscores its dedication to innovation and strategic expansion. Functioning as a comprehensive platform comprising a marketplace, logistics service, and payment service, Jumia has effectively navigated diverse markets, offering an array of services ranging from hotel bookings to food delivery. The decision to focus on Jumia is justified by its significant impact on the e-commerce in Morocco and its understanding of the diverse African markets. Jumia's extensive network of active sellers, coupled with its response to shifting consumer behaviors during the COVID-19 pandemic, positions it as an ideal subject for a case study exploring the symbiosis of AI and marketing in optimizing customer experiences and driving online sales. In examining Jumia's strategies, challenges, and successes in Morocco's e-commerce sector. This study employs a thorough research methodology that combines both qualitative and quantitative approaches. The research process begins with an extensive review of relevant literature to establish a theoretical framework. Following this, an investigation is conducted into Jumia's specific strategies, challenges faced, and innovative initiatives. The study integrates quantitative data, such as market performance metrics and consumer engagement statistics, with qualitative insights obtained from analyzing relevant charts.

The methodological approach is relevant as it allows for a general understanding of Jumia's initiatives, challenges, and successes within Morocco's e-commerce sector, addressing the complexities of the market.

The study unfolds in several distinctive sections, commencing with an exploration of Jumia's strategies, which encompasses aspects like AI integration, audience engagement, and market positioning. It then delves into an examination of the challenges faced by Jumia in implementing AI-driven marketing strategies, addressing both internal and external hurdles. The subsequent analysis focuses on Jumia's successes and innovations, highlighting tangible outcomes and strategic initiatives that have positively affected consumer engagement. Ultimately, the study synthesizes these findings to contribute to the broader discussion on AI-driven marketing in Morocco's e-commerce sector. It aims to provide a nuanced understanding of the complex dynamics and opportunities arising at the intersection of AI and marketing in this specific context

2. LITERATURE REVIEW OF E-COMMERCE MARKETING IN MOROCCO

In the early 2000s, e-commerce in Morocco was in its beginning. Internet penetration was relatively low, and online shopping was not yet a mainstream activity. Businesses started experimenting with online sales, but the market was limited due to factors such as lack of trust in online transactions, limited internet access, and a preference for traditional retail (Ajhoun & Daoudi, 2018). During the period between the mid-2000s to the early 2010s, there was a gradual increase in internet diffusion and digital literacy in Morocco. E-commerce platforms started to emerge, offering a variety of products and services. However, challenges such as payment security concerns and limited logistical infrastructure still influenced the growth of online retail (Maleh & Maleh, 2022). The late 2010s saw a significant surge in e-commerce activities in Morocco (Ahmed et al., 2015). The increasing availability of high-speed internet, the proliferation of smartphones, and a growing middle class contributed to the shift towards online shopping. Moreover, local and international e-commerce players began investing in the Moroccan market, providing a wider range of products and services. Furthermore, the rise of social media platforms, particularly Facebook and Instagram, became influential in e-commerce marketing. Businesses started using these platforms for advertising, brand promotion, and engaging with their audience

2.1 Key Factors Influencing E-Commerce Marketing in Morocco

2.1.1 Mobile Adoption

The widespread adoption of mobile devices has played a transformative role in the growth of e-commerce in Morocco (Dwivedi & al., 2023). As smartphones become omnipresent, they have become more than just communication tools; they are now gateways to a world of online shopping and digital transactions. This shift in consumer behavior has necessitated a strategic focus on mobile-friendly websites and applications to effectively reach and engage Moroccan consumers. The spread of mobile devices, particularly smartphones, has reshaped the way Moroccans access information, communicate, and make purchasing decisions (Martinez & McAndrews, 2023). The accessibility of having internet-enabled devices readily available has led to an increased reliance on mobile platforms for various aspects of daily life, including shopping. As a result, businesses have recognized the imperative of adapting their e-commerce strategies to align with this mobile-centric approach. Mobile-stores websites have become a non-negotiable element for e-commerce success in Morocco. These websites are designed to provide an optimal viewing and interaction experience across a diverse range of mobile devices. Responsive design principles ensure that the content adapts seamlessly to various screen sizes, offering users a visually appealing and user-friendly interface (ALLA & al, 2022). In addition to mobile-friendly websites, the development and optimization of mobile applications (apps) have become essential for e-commerce businesses targeting the Moroccan market. Mobile apps offer a dedicated and streamlined platform for users to explore products, make purchases, and engage with brands. The convenience of having an app on their smartphones enhances user experience, fosters brand loyalty, and encourages repeat business. One key advantage of mobile adoption in e-commerce is the potential for real-time and location-based engagement. Mobile devices enable businesses to send push notifications, personalized offers, and relevant content directly to users' devices. This targeted approach leverages the immediacy of mobile communication, allowing brands to connect with consumers at strategic moments, such as during flash sales, promotions, or new product launches (ALLA & al, 2022). The significance of mobile adoption in Morocco's e-commerce scene extends beyond just facilitating transactions. It is intertwined with the overall customer journey, from product discovery to post-purchase interactions. Therefore, businesses that prioritize mobile-friendly interfaces not only enhance the shopping experience but also position themselves as forward-thinking and customer-centric in the eyes of Moroccan consumers.

2.1.2 Social Media Influence

In Morocco, where social relationships and recommendations hold significant weight, influencer marketing becomes particularly powerful. It allows businesses to tap into local trends, cultural nuances, and the preferences of the Moroccan audience. Influencer marketing has become a powerhouse in E-commerce, especially in a dynamic market like Morocco. Collaborating with influencers allows businesses to leverage the trust and credibility these individuals have built with their followers. Influencers, who are typically individuals with a significant online presence, can create authentic content that resonates with their audience. These collaborations involve influencers displaying and endorsing products or services through various content formats, including images, videos, and reviews. The key is to align the influencer's personal brand with the values and image of the E-commerce business. By doing so, businesses can tap into the influencer's established audience, expanding their reach and fostering a connection with potential customers. The combination of influencer collaborations and targeted advertising creates a comprehensive and cohesive marketing strategy. Influencers can introduce a brand to their audience in an authentic way, building awareness and trust. Subsequently, targeted ads on platforms like Facebook and Instagram can reinforce this exposure, reaching a broader yet still highly relevant audience.

2.1.3 Payment Solutions

The integration of local payment solutions, particularly the inclusion of cash-on-delivery (COD) options, stands as a pivotal factor in overcoming consumer trust barriers and fostering the substantial growth of online transactions in Morocco (Luo, 2022). Recognizing the preferences and habits of Moroccan consumers, e-commerce businesses have strategically incorporated these payment methods into their platforms, thereby creating a more inclusive and trusted environment for online shoppers. The introduction of cash-on-delivery as a payment option addresses the prevailing trust concerns among Moroccan consumers. Many individuals, especially those new to online shopping, may initially be hesitant to provide credit card information or make digital payments due to security apprehensions. By offering the COD option, businesses acknowledge and accommodate these concerns, allowing customers to inspect the product before making payment, building a sense of trust in the online transaction process. Beyond COD, businesses have integrated a range of local payment solutions that resonate with Moroccan consumers (Mich, 2022). This includes collaborating with local banks and payment gateways to facilitate seamless and secure transactions. By offering a variety of payment options, e-commerce platforms cater to the diverse preferences of their customer base, ensuring that each individual can choose the method that aligns with their comfort and trust levels.

3. E-COMMERCE AND MARKETING STRATEGIES

In the ever-evolving landscape of business, the emergence of e-commerce has revolutionized how companies operate and engage with consumers (Qin & al., 2023). E-commerce, also known as electronic commerce, entails the buying and selling of goods and services over the internet. As businesses transition into the digital realm, the importance of effective marketing strategies becomes crucial for success. This essay delves into the intersection of e-commerce and marketing strategies, examining how businesses leverage digital platforms to reach and engage their target audience (Elahi & al., 2023). The growth of e-commerce can be attributed to several factors, including technological advancements, increased internet penetration, and shifting consumer preferences (Bouhtatit & al, 2023). E-commerce platforms offer a convenient and accessible avenue for consumers to browse, compare, and purchase products and services from the comfort of their homes. The global reach of e-commerce has dismantled geographical barriers, enabling businesses to tap into international markets and diversify their customer base (Sheikh & al., 2023). In the digital age, traditional marketing approaches have been supplemented, and in some cases, replaced by innovative digital marketing strategies. Successful e-commerce ventures deploy a comprehensive set of digital marketing tools to enhance their online visibility and forge meaningful connections with consumers. Key strategies include:

3.1. Search Engine Optimization (SEO)

Search Engine Optimization (SEO) stands as a foundational pillar of successful e-commerce ventures, playing a critical role in enhancing a website's visibility and prominence on search engine results pages (SERPs) (Garcia & al., 2022). In the vast digital landscape, where millions of users initiate searches daily, the significance of SEO cannot be overstated (Lewandowski, 2023). The primary objective of SEO in e-commerce is to improve a website's organic search ranking, increasing the likelihood of it appearing at the top of relevant search queries (Garcia& al., 2022). The process of SEO involves a multifaceted approach, encompassing both on-page and off-page optimization techniques. On-page optimization entails fine-tuning various elements within the website itself to align with search engine algorithms (Lewandowski, 2023). This includes optimizing product descriptions, Meta tags, and images to incorporate relevant keywords that potential customers are likely to use when searching for products (Appel & al., 2020). The strategic placement of these keywords in title tags, headers, and throughout the content helps search engines understand the context of the webpage, thereby increasing its chances of being prominently displayed in search results (Appel & al., 2020). Equally crucial is optimizing the website's structure and navigation to enhance the overall user experience and facilitate search engine crawlers' indexing process (Lewandowski, 2023). This involves creating an intuitive menu structure, employing descriptive URLs, and ensuring the site is mobile-friendly – a factor increasingly prioritized by search engines (Garcia & al., 2022). On the other hand, off-page optimization involves building a reputable online presence beyond the confines of the website (Lewandowski, 2023). This often includes link-building strategies, where reputable and relevant websites link back to the e-commerce site (Appel & al., 2020). High-quality backlinks are considered a vote of confidence by search engines, contributing to improved search rankings (Garcia& al., 2022). The ultimate goal of SEO in e-commerce is to align the website with the needs and queries of the target audience (Lewandowski, 2023). By understanding the search intent of potential customers, businesses can tailor their SEO strategies to effectively address these needs, driving organic traffic and increasing the likelihood of conversions (Appel & al., 2020). In the dynamic and competitive e-commerce landscape, staying abreast of search engine algorithms and industry trends is imperative (Garcia& al., 2022). Regular monitoring, analysis, and adjustments to SEO strategies enable businesses to maintain and improve their search rankings, maximizing their online visibility and positioning them for success in the eyes of both consumers and search engines alike (Lewandowski, 2023). In essence, SEO serves as the digital compass that guides e-commerce websites through the vast online terrain, ensuring they are not only discovered but also prominently positioned for success (Garcia & al., 2022).

3.2. Social Media Marketing

Social media platforms have evolved into dynamic and influential channels, fundamentally transforming e-commerce marketing (Li & al., 2021). The integration of platforms such as Facebook, Instagram, and Twitter into the marketing strategies of businesses has proven to be a game-changer, offering a multifaceted approach to engagement, brand building, and driving traffic to e-commerce sites (Bashar & al., 2024). One of the primary strengths of utilizing social media for e-commerce lies in its unparalleled ability to foster direct interaction between businesses and their target audience (Ryan & Graham, 2014). These platforms provide a space for authentic and real-time engagement, allowing businesses to establish a human connection with their customers. Through comments, direct messages, and interactive features, e-commerce brands can respond to inquiries, address concerns, and receive immediate feedback, creating a sense of community and trust (Ryan & Graham, 2014). Building brand awareness is another pivotal aspect of e-commerce marketing through social media. These platforms serve as virtual showcases for products and services, enabling businesses to visually communicate their brand identity and values. Engaging visual content, such as images, videos, and infographics, can be shared to convey the uniqueness of products and highlight them in real-world contexts, resonating with the aspirations and lifestyles of the target audience (Ryan & Graham, 2014). Moreover, social media facilitates targeted advertising, allowing businesses to reach specific demographics with precision (Li& al., 2021). Through detailed demographic and interest targeting options, businesses can tailor their advertisements to reach the audience most likely to be interested in their products. This not only maximizes the efficiency of marketing budgets but also ensures that promotional efforts are directed towards individuals who are more likely to convert into customers. The viral nature of social media amplifies the potential reach of e-commerce marketing campaigns. Engaging and shareable content can quickly spread across platforms, reaching a wider audience than traditional marketing methods (Bashar & al., 2024). User-generated content, such as customer reviews, testimonials, and product demonstrations, can further enhance the authenticity of a brand and encourage organic sharing among social media users. Beyond engagement and brand building, social media serves as a potent driver of traffic to e-commerce sites (Ryan & Graham, 2014). Businesses can strategically incorporate links to their product pages, promotions, and special offers within their social media content. This seamless integration enables users to transition from social media platforms to e-commerce sites effortlessly, converting interest into tangible sales.

3.3. Email Marketing

Email marketing continues to be a stalwart in the arsenal of e-commerce businesses, providing a direct and effective channel for communication with their audience (Dawe, 2015). In the age of digital connectivity, where inboxes serve as personal gateways to online interactions, email marketing emerges as a strategic tool to engage customers, promote products, offer exclusive incentives, and foster enduring relationships over time (Joshi& al., 2023). The strength of email marketing lies in its ability to deliver personalized and targeted content directly to the inbox of individual users. Through segmentation and personalization techniques, businesses can tailor their email campaigns to specific customer segments based on demographics, purchase history, and preferences (Joshi & al., 2023). This targeted approach ensures that the content resonates with recipients, increasing the likelihood of engagement and conversion. Promoting new products is one of the key objectives of email marketing. E-commerce businesses can leverage email campaigns to unveil and display their latest offerings, creating anticipation and excitement among their audience (Wilson Ozuem & Michelle Willis, 2022). By incorporating compelling visuals, detailed product descriptions, and clear calls-to-action, these emails serve as virtual storefronts, enticing recipients to explore and make informed purchase decisions. Exclusive discounts and promotions are powerful incentives that can be strategically integrated into email marketing campaigns (Joshi &al., 2023). By offering exclusive deals, early access, or personalized discounts, businesses can drive traffic to their e-commerce sites and encourage immediate action. The sense of exclusivity and personalization enhances the perceived value of these offers, fostering a sense of appreciation and loyalty among recipients. Beyond transactional promotions, email marketing is a valuable tool for nurturing customer relationships over time (Dawe, 2015). Through well-crafted newsletters, businesses can keep their audience informed about industry trends, share relevant content, and provide updates on company news. These regular touchpoints contribute to an ongoing relationship, reinforcing brand recall and maintaining a presence in the minds of customers even when they are not actively making purchases. Automation further amplifies the effectiveness of email marketing for e-commerce businesses (Bayoude & al., 2023). Automated email campaigns, triggered by specific customer actions or events, enable businesses to deliver timely and relevant messages. For instance, abandoned cart emails can remind users of items left in their shopping carts, encouraging them to complete the purchase. This automation not only saves time but also ensures that communications are tailored to individual customer journeys. The analytical capabilities of email marketing platforms allow businesses to track and measure the performance of their campaigns (Dawe, 2015). Metrics such as open rates, click-through rates, and conversion rates provide valuable insights into the effectiveness of different email strategies. This data-driven approach enables businesses to refine their campaigns over time, optimizing content and strategies based on customer behavior and preferences.

3.4. Influencer Marketing

Influencer marketing has emerged as a dynamic and impactful strategy for e-commerce businesses, providing a unique avenue to extend their reach and enhance brand credibility (John & Supramaniam, 2023). By strategically collaborating with influencers who align with the brand's values and resonate with the target audience, businesses can leverage the authenticity and influence of these individuals to create a compelling narrative that drives traffic and strengthens brand credibility (Johne, 2023). The essence of influencer marketing lies in the ability to tap into the trust and rapport influencers have cultivated with their followers. Influencers, often individuals with a significant online presence and engaged community, have built authentic connections with their audience. By associating with influencers who share common values or appeal to the same demographic, e-commerce businesses can effectively tap into these existing relationships, gaining access to a pre-qualified and receptive audience (P, 2024). Collaborating with influencers offers a unique opportunity for brands to tap into the creative process of these content creators. Influencers have a knack for producing engaging and authentic content that resonates with their followers. Whether it is through captivating visuals, genuine testimonials, or relatable storytelling, influencers can construct content that seamlessly integrates a brand's message into their own authentic voice (Ahmed & al., 2015). This authenticity is key to capturing the attention and trust of the audience. The reach of influencer marketing extends beyond the influencer's immediate followers. Through social media platforms, influencers have the potential to amplify a brand's message and introduce it to a broader audience. Shares, likes, and comments generated by influencer-generated content contribute to organic reach, creating a ripple effect that extends the brand's visibility far beyond traditional marketing methods (John & Supramaniam, 2023). Driving traffic to e-commerce sites is a tangible outcome of well-executed influencer marketing campaigns. Influencers can incorporate compelling calls-to-action, exclusive promotions, or trackable links in their content, encouraging their followers to explore the brand further and make purchases. The seamless integration of the brand into the influencer's content creates a natural pathway for followers to transition from discovery to conversion. Brand credibility is a crucial element of influencer marketing (Bouhtati &al, 2023).When an influencer endorses a product or service; it comes with a level of trust that has been established through consistent and authentic content creation. This trust transfers to the brand, enhancing its credibility in the eyes of the audience (Johne, 2023). Positive associations with reputable influencers contribute to the brand's image, fostering a positive perception that can influence purchasing decisions.

4. APPLYING ARTIFICIAL INTELLIGENCE TO ENHANCE E-COMMERCE MARKETING

Applying artificial intelligence (AI) to enhance E-commerce marketing offers businesses a powerful set of tools to optimize processes, improve customer experiences, and drive more effective marketing strategies. Here are several ways AI can be applied to enhance E-commerce marketing:

4.1. Personalized Recommendations

The integration of artificial intelligence (AI) algorithms into e-commerce platforms has revolutionized the way businesses interact with customers (Demir, 2022). By harnessing the power of AI, particularly in analyzing customer data, businesses can provide a highly personalized and tailored shopping experience. AI algorithms, driven by machine learning models, meticulously sift through vast datasets encompassing customer interactions with the e-commerce platform. This includes analyzing the products customers view, the items they add to their carts, and ultimately, the products they purchase. By understanding these behavioral patterns, AI can discern nuanced preferences, identify correlations, and predict future buying tendencies. The analysis of customer browsing history involves tracking the pages a user visits, the products they click on, and the time spent on each page. AI algorithms can discern patterns in this data, uncovering the types of products that capture a user's interest and the particular features or categories that resonate with them. This insight is crucial for tailoring product recommendations that align with the individual's preferences. AI goes beyond just tracking browsing behavior; it delves into the historical purchasing patterns of customers. By examining past transactions, AI identifies the specific products or categories that customers have shown a propensity to buy. This allows the algorithm to make informed predictions about future purchases, suggesting complementary or similar items that align with the customer's demonstrated preferences. AI excels at recognizing subtle nuances in customer preferences. It takes into account factors such as brand affinity, color choices, size preferences, and even the time of day a customer tends to shop. With this wealth of information, the algorithm crafts personalized product recommendations that resonate with the unique tastes and preferences of each individual user. The result of this personalized recommendation system is a significantly enhanced user experience. Customers encounter a curated selection of products that align with their interests, eliminating the need to sift through irrelevant options (Berea, 2022). This streamlined experience not only saves time for the customer but also fosters a sense of personalization and attentiveness from the e-commerce platform. Personalized recommendations contribute to increased engagement, as users are more likely to explore and interact with products tailored to their preferences. This heightened engagement, in turn, translates into higher conversion rates. Customers are more inclined to make purchases when presented with products that align with their tastes, creating a win-win scenario for both the customer and the e-commerce business.

4.2. Predictive Analytics for Demand Forecasting

The integration of AI-driven predictive analytics into e-commerce operations has brought about a transformative shift in how businesses forecast demand, manage inventory, and optimize their overall supply chain processes. By harnessing the power of advanced algorithms, businesses can make data-informed decisions, ensuring that they meet customer demands efficiently. This is particularly evident in the application of predictive analytics for demand forecasting. AI-driven predictive analytics begins by thoroughly examining historical data encompassing customer purchasing patterns, seasonality, promotional events, and external factors influencing demand. This comprehensive analysis allows the AI algorithms to identify recurring trends and patterns within the data, providing valuable insights into the past behavior of customers and the market. In addition to historical data, the AI algorithms delve into current market trends, industry developments, and external factors that may influence demand. By staying attuned to the ever-changing landscape, businesses can adapt their strategies to align with emerging trends and proactively address shifts in consumer preferences or market dynamics. The heart of AI-driven predictive analytics lies in its ability to forecast future demand based on the patterns identified in historical and current data. By applying sophisticated mathematical models and machine learning algorithms, businesses can generate accurate predictions regarding the quantities of specific products that are likely to be in demand over a given period. Armed with accurate demand forecasts, e-commerce businesses can optimize their inventory management strategies. This involves maintaining the right balance between stock levels and anticipated demand, mitigating the risk of overstocking or stockouts. AI algorithms continuously adjust predictions as new data becomes available, ensuring that inventory levels remain aligned with evolving market demands. One of the immediate benefits of AI for demand forecasting is the reduction of stockouts and overstock situations. By accurately predicting demand, businesses can ensure that popular products are consistently in stock, preventing missed sales opportunities. Simultaneously, the risk of overstocking on products with lower demand is minimized, preventing unnecessary inventory costs. Predictive analytics does not only optimize inventory management but extends its benefits to the entire supply chain. Businesses can streamline procurement, production, and distribution processes based on anticipated demand. This enhances overall supply chain efficiency, reduces operational costs, and improves the agility of the business in responding to market fluctuations. By utilizing the insights gained from predictive analytics, e-commerce businesses can make strategic decisions related to marketing campaigns, promotions, and product launches. The ability to anticipate demand allows businesses to allocate resources effectively, prioritize high-demand products, and align marketing efforts with products that are likely to resonate with customers.

4.3. Chabot's and Virtual Assistants

The incorporation of AI-powered chatbots and virtual assistants into E-commerce platforms has redefined the of customer support, providing businesses with a dynamic and efficient means to engage with their audience (David, 2023). These intelligent virtual entities play a crucial role in offering instant and personalized assistance, revolutionizing the way customers interact with E-commerce platforms and significantly enhancing overall customer satisfaction. AI-powered chatbots and virtual assistants excel in delivering instantaneous responses to customer inquiries. Whether addressing questions about product specifications, order status, or general inquiries, these virtual entities operate 24/7, ensuring that customers receive immediate assistance regardless of the time of day. This real-time engagement contributes to a seamless and efficient customer experience. Chatbots leverage AI algorithms to understand customer queries and provide relevant product information. By analyzing user preferences, purchase history, and browsing behavior, these virtual assistants can offer personalized product recommendations, guiding customers towards items that align with their interests. This personalized assistance contributes to a more tailored shopping experience. Virtual assistants are adept at guiding customers through the purchasing process. From helping users navigate the website to assisting with the selection of products, these AI-driven entities offer systematic guidance. They can also provide information about promotions, discounts, and payment options, ensuring that customers have all the necessary details to make informed purchasing decisions. AI-powered virtual assistants extend their capabilities beyond the pre-purchase phase by assisting customers in tracking their orders and providing post-purchase support. Customers can inquire about delivery status, request returns or exchanges, and seek assistance with any issues that may arise after the transaction. This comprehensive support enhances the overall customer journey and builds trust in the E-commerce platform. Chatbots and virtual assistants are designed to be accessible across various platforms, including websites, mobile apps, and social media. This ensures that customers can engage with the virtual assistant through their preferred channels, promoting a consistent and integrated support experience. Whether on the E-commerce website or a messaging app, customers can access assistance seamlessly. AI-driven virtual assistants leverage machine-learning algorithms to continuously improve their performance. By learning from interactions, customer feedback, and evolving trends, these virtual entities become more adept at understanding user queries and providing accurate and relevant responses over time. This adaptability contributes to an increasingly sophisticated and effective customer support system. Virtual assistants offer scalability, efficiently handling a high volume of inquiries simultaneously. This scalability is particularly valuable during peak times, such as sales events or product launches. Additionally, the automated nature of virtual assistants contributes to cost-efficiency, as businesses can provide enhanced customer support without a proportional increase in human resource requirements.

5. METHODOLOGY

In order to conduct a detailed analysis of AI-driven marketing strategies by Jumia Market, a quantitative approach was employed in this study. This involved the systematic collection of diverse data points, including market performance metrics and consumer engagement statistics, aimed at evaluating the impact of AI integration on Jumia's online sales and customer interactions. Through the application of robust statistical methods, the gathered quantitative data underwent rigorous analysis to reveal underlying trends, patterns, and correlations. This analytical process yielded empirical evidence of the efficacy of AI within the realm of e-commerce marketing. Additionally, for the purpose of visual representation and to provide concrete examples, the SimilarWeb AI application was utilized to conduct an in-depth analysis of Jumia's official website. All screenshots presented in this case study were obtained from the SimilarWeb AI application, offering tangible illustrations of Jumia's implementation of AI-powered marketing strategies. These visual insights not only enrich the depth of analysis but also provide a clear depiction of how AI is integrated into Jumia's marketing endeavors. Through the combination of quantitative analysis and visual representation, this study aims to provide a comprehensive understanding of the role and effectiveness of AI-driven marketing strategies within Jumia Market, contributing to the broader discourse on AI integration in the e-commerce sector.

5.1. Utilization of SimilarWeb AI Application for Website Analysis

Through the lens of SimilarWeb AI, the user interface and experience of Jumia's website were thoroughly evaluated. SimilarWeb AI application facilitated an in-depth analysis of Jumia's marketing strategies and content optimization techniques. This encompassed the evaluation of various aspects, including ad placements, call-to-action buttons, personalized recommendations, and content relevance. By examining these elements, insights were gained into how AI algorithms are leveraged to tailor marketing efforts, optimize content for search engines, and maximize visibility and conversion rates. The screenshots featured in this case study were directly sourced from the SimilarWeb AI application, providing tangible examples of Jumia's AI-driven marketing strategies in action. These visual representations not only enrich the depth of analysis but also offer a clear illustration of how AI technologies are seamlessly integrated into Jumia's online platform to drive business outcomes.

6. ENHANCING E-COMMERCE MARKETING THROUGH AI: A CASE STUDY OF JUMIA MARKET IN MOROCCO

Jumia, the number one online buying and selling destination in Morocco, offers a wide range of products including TVs, smartphones, home appliances, fashion items, toys, sports equipment, video games, home decor, and much more. It features all the top brands such as Huawei, Samsung, LG, Apple, Nike, and many others. With quick delivery services available across Morocco, including cities like Casablanca, Rabat, and Tangier, and the convenience of cash on delivery payment option, Jumia ensures a seamless shopping experience for its customers. In terms of traffic and engagement statistics, from December 2023 to February 2024, Jumia witnessed a total of 10.56 million visits worldwide, representing a slight decrease of 2.24% compared to the previous month. The breakdown of devices used shows that desktop accounted for 2.3 million visits, while mobile devices contributed significantly with 8 million visits, totalling 10.3 million visits overall during the period. Analyzing the traffic channels (figure 1 and 2), Jumia saw a diverse range of sources driving visitors to its platform. Direct traffic accounted for 4.417 million visits, followed by organic search with 4.487 million visits, and paid search with 725,348 visits. Referrals from other websites, including social media platforms, contributed to 174,307 visits, emphasizing the importance of a well-rounded online presence.

Figure 1. Jumia's traffic and engagement statistics, from December 2023 to February 2024

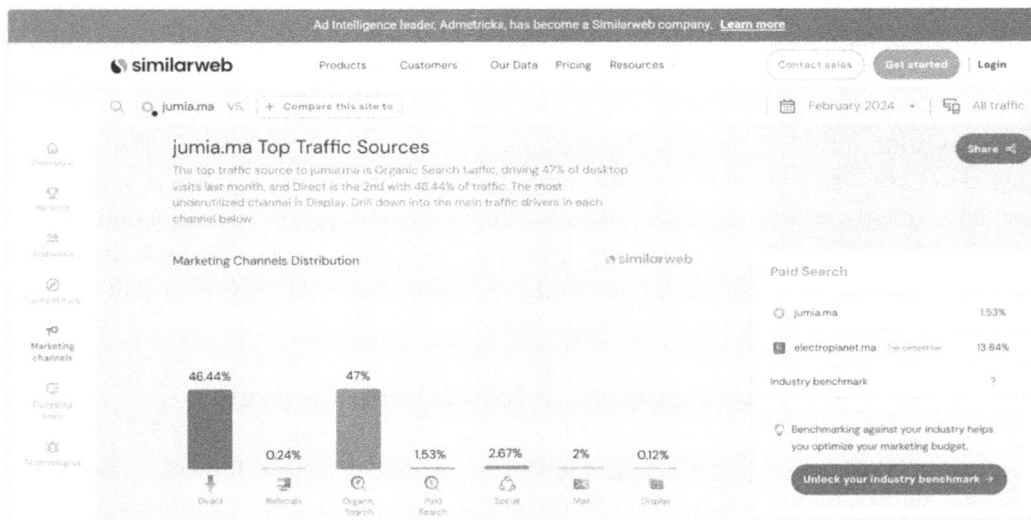

Figure 2. Jumia's Canal traffic, from December 2023 to February 2024

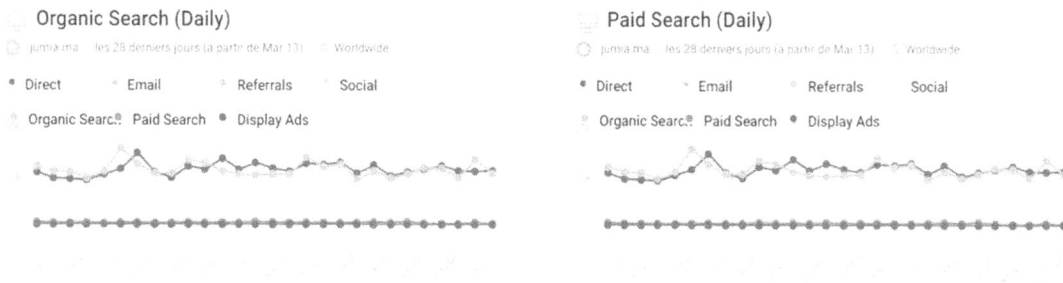

Furthermore, Jumia's website (jumia.ma) itself was a significant source of traffic, accounting for 14.53% of all visits, followed by other channels such as referrals from Google, Microsoft, Yandex, YouTube, and Live.com. These statistics underscore Jumia's strong online presence and its ability to attract visitors from various sources, solidifying its position as a leader in the Moroccan E-commerce market. Jumia's online platform boasts impressive traffic and engagement metrics, reflecting its strong presence and appeal to users over time. With an average of 3.520 million monthly visits and 1.363 million unique visitors, Jumia consistently attracts a substantial audience, indicative of its popularity and reach. The platform's audience is diverse and engaged, with a deduplicated audience count highlighting its ability to capture the attention of a wide range of users. Moreover, Jumia's audience demonstrates active engagement, spending an average of 5 minutes and 15 seconds per visit and viewing an average of 6.57 pages during each session. This indicates a high level of interest and interaction with the platform's content, resulting in a meaningful browsing experience for users.

6.1. Total Social Media Visits

From December 2023 to February 2024, Jumia experienced 59.2 thousand visits originating from social media platforms, representing a modest increase of 2.54% compared to the previous period. These visits accounted for a fraction of the total desktop traffic during this timeframe. Analyzing the distribution of social media visits reveals the platforms driving engagement with Jumia's content. Among desktop users, YouTube emerged as the primary source, contributing 54.21% of social media visits. Facebook followed closely behind, generating 24.53% of visits, while WhatsApp Webapp accounted for 5.76%. Instagram and VKontakte also played notable roles, each comprising 3.78% and 2.13% of social media visits, respectively. Additionally, a variety of other platforms collectively contributed 9.6% of visits, displaying the diverse social media through which Jumia interacts with its audience. These statistics highlight Jumia's effective utilization of social media platforms to engage with users, drive traffic to its website, and foster brand awareness. By exploring the diverse functionalities and user bases of platforms like YouTube, Facebook, and WhatsApp, Jumia expands its reach and solidifies its presence in the digital sphere, further establishing itself as a prominent player in the Moroccan E-commerce market. Figure 3

Figure 3. Total social media visits from December 2023 to February 2024

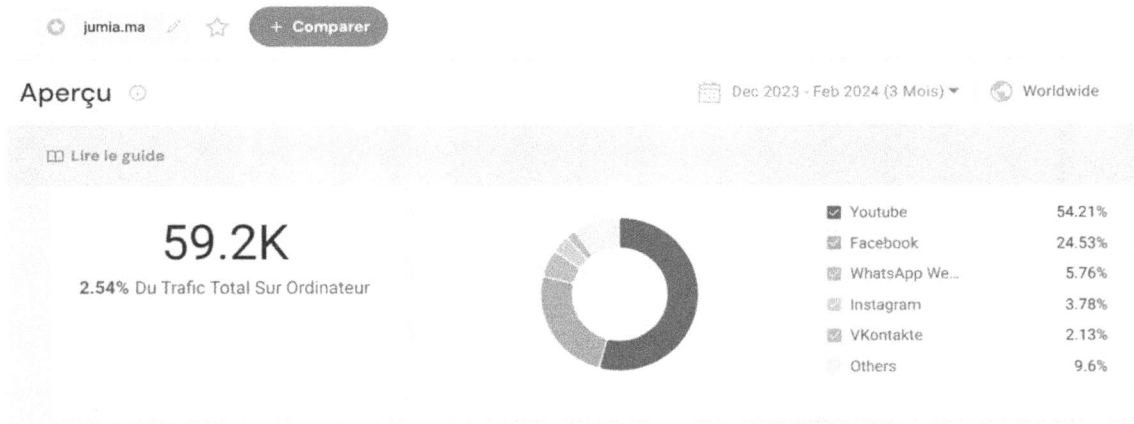

6.2. Jumia's Website Technologies

Jumia's website is equipped with a diverse array of technical features and tools aimed at enhancing user experience, optimizing performance, and supporting various functionalities. Among the technologies integrated into the website are several advertising platforms, including Criteo Advertiser, DoubleClick Advertiser, Facebook Advertiser, Google Ads Advertiser, and Google Publisher Tag. These platforms facilitate targeted advertising and marketing efforts to reach Jumia's audience effectively. Moreover, the website employs various analytics and conversion tools such as Google Analytics, Crazy Egg, Adjust, and Content Square. These tools provide valuable insights into user behavior, site performance, and conversion metrics, enabling Jumia to optimize its strategies and improve overall efficiency. In terms of infrastructure, Jumia utilizes robust server technologies including nginx, Varnish, and Amazon Route 53 to ensure fast and reliable website delivery. Additionally, content delivery is further enhanced through integration with services like CloudFlare and Amazon S3. Furthermore, Jumia's website features integration with popular social media platforms such as Facebook, Twitter, and YouTube, enabling seamless sharing of content and interaction with customers across various channels.figure 4

Figure 4. Jumia's website technologies

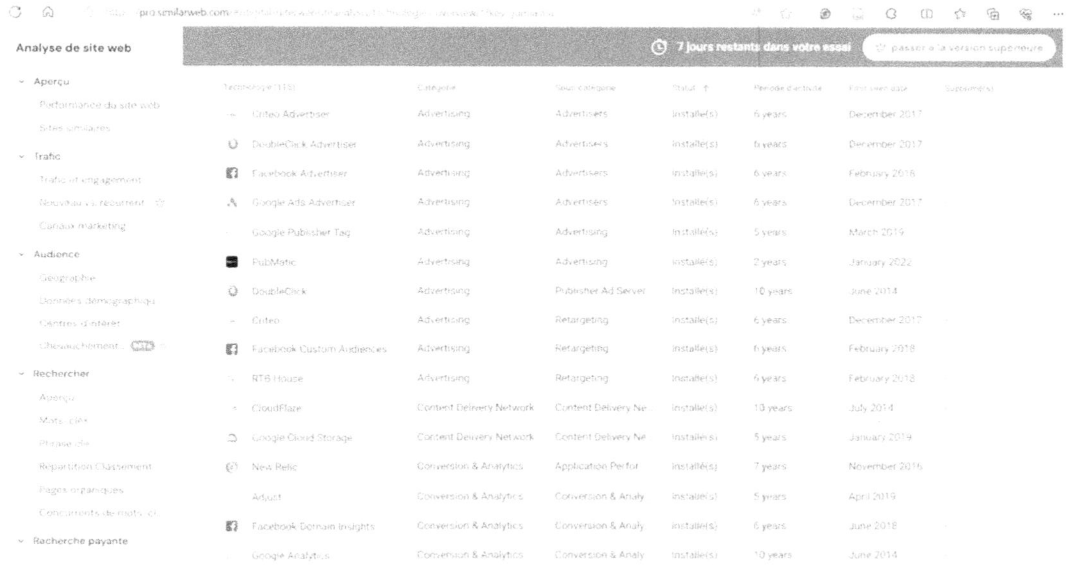

7. DISCUSSION

The e-commerce in Morocco has undergone significant growth, presenting both opportunities and challenges for industry players. Among these, Jumia Market, a prominent entity in the Moroccan e-commerce sector, has embraced artificial intelligence (AI) to bolster its marketing strategies. This case study delves into the specific AI applications adopted by Jumia Market and the subsequent impact on its marketing effectiveness.

7.1. AI-Powered Personalized Recommendations

Jumia Market employs a multifaceted approach to personalized recommendations, utilizing various technical tools and algorithms to analyze and understand customer behavior. Collaborative filtering stands as a primary technique, involving the analysis of user interactions and preferences to recommend items based on similarities with other users. Additionally, content-based filtering techniques are leveraged, analyzing product attributes and features to suggest similar items aligned with individual tastes. More advanced machine learning models, including deep learning techniques, are likely utilized to enhance recommendation accuracy, learning complex patterns and relationships from large datasets. Furthermore, Jumia Market may employ matrix factorization and dimensionality reduction techniques to handle high-dimensional customer data, capturing latent factors influencing preferences and extracting meaningful patterns. These methodologies enable Jumia Market to provide personalized recommendations that resonate with individual customers, enhancing user engagement and driving sales.

7.2. AI Applications Beyond Marketing

Beyond marketing, Jumia Market connects AI technologies for predictive analytics in demand forecasting. By analyzing historical data and market dynamics, AI-driven predictive analytics provide insights into future demand trends, optimizing inventory management and enhancing supply chain efficiency. Additionally, the integration of AI-powered chatbots and virtual assistants revolutionizes customer support services, offering instantaneous and personalized assistance while maintaining a human-like interaction.

8. RESULTS AND CHALLENGES

The case study evaluates the results and impact of AI integration, delving into various key performance indicators such as customer engagement, conversion rates, and operational efficiency. Through meticulous analysis, it becomes evident that AI-powered initiatives have significantly contributed to enhancing these metrics, with notable improvements observed in customer satisfaction levels, conversion rates, and streamlined operational processes. However, alongside these benefits, challenges such as data privacy concerns and algorithmic biases have emerged, underscoring the complexities inherent in AI implementation within the e-commerce landscape. Despite these challenges, they serve as invaluable learning opportunities for Jumia Market, enabling the refinement of strategies and the development of robust frameworks to address ethical considerations and mitigate biases. By actively addressing these challenges, Jumia Market not only navigates the intricacies of AI-driven e-commerce marketing but also sets a precedent for industry peers, fostering a culture of responsible AI adoption and innovation.

9. FUTURE IMPLICATIONS AND RECOMMENDATIONS

Looking forward, this case study delves into the future implications and recommendations of AI in e-commerce. As technology continues its rapid evolution, Jumia Market stands ready to embrace emerging trends and innovations, fostering a culture of innovation while prioritizing ethical AI practices. By maintaining a proactive stance at the forefront of AI integration, Jumia Market not only solidifies its position as a leader in the e-commerce domain but also catalyzes the transformative potential of AI in shaping the future landscape of online commerce. In the ever-evolving e-commerce ecosystem, Jumia Market recognizes the imperative of remaining agile and adaptive to emerging technological advancements. Thus, the company is committed to leveraging AI not only to optimize existing operations but also to explore novel applications that can further propel its competitive edge and market relevance. By nurturing a culture of innovation, Jumia Market cultivates an environment conducive to experimentation and exploration, enabling the continuous refinement and evolution of AI-driven strategies to meet evolving consumer needs and market demands. Moreover, in line with its commitment to ethical business practices, Jumia Market places a strong emphasis on ethical AI principles. This entails ensuring transparency, accountability, and fairness in AI algorithms, while also addressing concerns related to data privacy and algorithmic bias. By upholding these ethical standards, Jumia Market not only safeguards customer trust and confidence but also sets a precedent for ethical AI adoption within the broader e-commerce industry. Furthermore, by pioneering AI-driven strategies and best practices, Jumia Market assumes a leadership role in driving industry-wide innovation and advancement. Through knowledge sharing, collaboration, and collective learning, Jumia Market contributes to the collective growth and maturation of the e-commerce sector, unlocking new opportunities and possibilities for businesses and consumers alike. As Jumia Market continues to push the boundaries of AI integration, it serves as a beacon of inspiration for industry peers, inspiring a new era of intelligent, data-driven commerce that prioritizes both innovation and ethical responsibility.

10. CONCLUSION

This article sheds light on Jumia Market's transformative journey in enhancing E-commerce marketing through the strategic application of artificial intelligence (AI). Offering a comprehensive exploration, it delves into the practical implementation, challenges encountered, and outcomes achieved by Jumia Market as it navigates Morocco's evolving digital market . Through meticulous analysis, the article illuminates the multifaceted role of AI in revolutionizing Jumia Market's marketing strategies. It highlights how the platform advantages AI-driven predictive analytics to forecast demand, optimize inventory management, and enhance supply chain efficiency, thus meeting customer needs more effectively. Additionally, the article underscores the pivotal role of AI-powered chatbots and virtual assistants in delivering personalized customer support, streamlining the purchasing process, and fostering greater satisfaction among users. Moreover, the article provides insights into the challenges faced by Jumia Market during the implementation of AI-driven strategies. From navigating data privacy concerns to addressing algorithmic biases, Jumia's experiences offer valuable lessons for other E-commerce businesses embarking on similar AI integration journeys. Ultimately, the article highlights the tangible outcomes and impact of Jumia Market's AI-driven initiatives on key performance indicators such as customer engagement, conversion rates, and operational efficiency. It underscores Jumia Market's commitment to innovation and excellence, positioning the platform as a leader in AI to shape the future of E-commerce marketing in Morocco.

REFERENCES

Ahmed, S. A., d'Astous, A., & Yoou, J. B. (2015). Exporting to Morocco: Consumer Perceptions of Countries of Origin. In: Spotts, H. (eds) *Assessing the Different Roles of Marketing Theory and Practice in the Jaws of Economic Uncertainty*. Springer, Cham. (https://doi.org/)10.1007/978-3-319-11845-1_92

Ajhoun, R., & Daoudi, N. (2018). Morocco. In Weber, A., & Hamlaoui, S. (Eds.), *E-Learning in the Middle East and North Africa (MENA) Region*. Springer. 10.1007/978-3-319-68999-9_12

Alla, L., Kamal, M., & Bouhtati, N. (2022). Big data et efficacité marketing des entreprises touristiques: une revue de la littérature. *Alternatives Managériales Economiques, 4*(0). 10.48374/IMIST.PRSM/ame -v1i0.36928

Appel, G., Grewal, L., & Hadi, R. (2020). The future of social media in marketing. *J. of the Acad. Mark. Sci. 48*, 79–95.(https://doi.org/)10.1007/s11747-019-00695-1

Bashar, A., Wasiq, M., &Nyagadza, B. (2024). Emerging trends in social media marketing: a retrospective review using data mining and bibliometric analysis. *Futur Bus J 10*(23). (https://doi.org/)10.1186/s43093-024-00308-6

Bayoude, K., Ardchir, S., & Azzouazi, M. (2023). A Predictive Approach Based on Feature Selection to Improve Email Marketing Campaign Success Rate. In: Kacprzyk, J., Ezziyyani, M., Balas, V.E. (eds) *International Conference on Advanced Intelligent Systems for Sustainable Development. AI2SD 2022*. Springer, Cham. (https://doi.org/)10.1007/978-3-031-26384-2_85

Berea, A. (2022). Predictive Analytics. In Schintler, L. A., & McNeely, C. L. (Eds.), *Encyclopedia of Big Data*. Springer. [DOI: 10.1007/978-3-319-32010-6_170], 10.1007/978-3-319-32010-6_170

Bouhtati, N., Alla, L., & Bentalhah, B. (2023). Marketing Big Data Analytics et gestion de la relation client: une approche floue. *Dans Intégrer l'intelligence et la durabilité dans les chaînes d'approvisionnement* (pp. 75-86). IGI Global. . 10.4018/979-8-3693-0225-5.ch004

Bouhtatit, N., Kamal, M., & Alla, L. (2023). Big Data et efficacité du marketing touristique: une revue prospective de la littérature. In Farhaoui, Y., Rocha, A., Brahmia, Z., & Bhushab, B. (Eds.), *Intelligence artificielle et environnement intelligent. ICAISE 2022. Notes de cours sur les réseaux et les systèmes, 635*. Springer. 10.1007/978-3-031-26254-8_40

Davenport, T., Guha, A., & Grewal, D. (2020). How artificial intelligence will change the future of marketing. *J. of the Acad. Mark. Sci., 48.* 24–42. (https://doi.org/)10.1007/s11747-019-00696-0

David, B., Chalon, R., & Zhang, X. (2023). Virtual Assistants (Chatbots) as Help to Teachers in Collaborative Learning Environment. In Auer, M. E., Pachatz, W., & Rüütmann, T. (Eds.), *Learning in the Age of Digital and Green Transition. ICL 2022. Lecture Notes in Networks and Systems* (Vol. 633). Springer. 10.1007/978-3-031-26876-2_13

Dawe, K. (2015). Best practice in business-to-business email. *J Direct Data Digit Mark Pract 16*, 242–247. (https://doi.org/)10.1057/dddmp.2015.21

Demir, F. (2022). Artificial Intelligence. In *Innovation in the Public Sector. Public Administration and Information Technology* (Vol. 39). Springer. 10.1007/978-3-031-11331-4_4

Dwivedi, Y.K., Ismagilova, E., & Sarker, P. (2023). A Meta-Analytic Structural Equation Model for Understanding Social Commerce Adoption. *Inf Syst Front 25*, 1421–1437. (https://doi.org/)10.1007/s10796-021-10172-2

Elahi, M., Afolaranmi, S.O., & Martinez Lastra, J.L. (2023). A comprehensive literature review of the applications of AI techniques through the lifecycle of industrial equipment. *Discov Artif Intell 3*(43). (https://doi.org/)10.1007/s44163-023-00089-x

Fanti, L., Guarascio, D. & Moggi, M. (2022). From Heron of Alexandria to Amazon's Alexa: a stylized history of AI and its impact on business models, organization and work. *J. Ind. Bus. Econ. 49*, 409–440. (https://doi.org/)10.1007/s40812-022-00222-4

Garcia, J. E., Lima, R., & da Fonseca, M. J. S. (2022). Search Engine Optimization (SEO) for a Company Website: A Case Study. In Rocha, A., Adeli, H., Dzemyda, G., & Moreira, F. (Eds.), *Information Systems and Technologies. WorldCIST 2022. Lecture Notes in Networks and Systems* (Vol. 470). Springer. 10.1007/978-3-031-04829-6_47

Hermann, E., Williams, G. Y., & Puntoni, S. (2023). Deploying artificial intelligence in services to AID vulnerable consumers. *Journal of the Academy of Marketing Science*. 10.1007/s11747-023-00986-8

Huang, MH. & Rust, R.T. (2021). A strategic framework for artificial intelligence in marketing. *J. of the Acad. Mark. Sci. 49*, 30–50. (https://doi.org/)10.1007/s11747-020-00749-9

Janssen, A., Passlick, J., & Rodríguez Cardona, D. (2020). Virtual Assistance in Any Context. *Bus Inf Syst Eng, 62*, 211–225. (https://doi.org/)10.1007/s12599-020-00644-1

John, S. P., & Supramaniam, S. (2023). Antecedents and Effects of Influencer Marketing Strategies: A Systematic Literature Review and Directions for Future Research. In Martínez-López, F. J. (Ed.), *Advances in Digital Marketing and eCommerce. DMEC 2023. Springer Proceedings in Business and Economics*. Springer. 10.1007/978-3-031-31836-8_15

Johne, J. (2023). Introduction. In *Effectiveness of Influencer Marketing*. Springer Gabler. [DOI: 10.1007/978-3-658-41297-5_1], 10.1007/978-3-658-41297-5_1

Joshi, Y., Lim, W. M., & Jagani, K. (2023). *Social media influencer marketing: foundations, trends, and ways forward*. Electron Commer Res. 10.1007/s10660-023-09719-z

Lewandowski, D. (2023). Search Engine Optimization (SEO). In *Understanding Search Engines*. Springer. [DOI: 10.1007/978-3-031-22789-9_9], 10.1007/978-3-031-22789-9_9

Lhoussaine, ALLA, Kamal, M., & Bouhtati, N. (2022). Big data et efficacité marketing des entreprises touristiques: une revue de la littérature. *Alternatives de gestion économique, 1*, 39-58.

Li, F., Larimo, J. & Leonidou, L.C. (2021). Social media marketing strategy: definition, conceptualization, taxonomy, validation, and future agenda. *J. of the Acad. Mark. Sci. 49*, 51–70. (https://doi.org/)10.1007/s11747-020-00733-3

Luo, Y. (2022). A general framework of digitization risks in international business. *J Int Bus Stud, 53*, 344–361. (https://doi.org/)10.1057/s41267-021-00448-9

Maleh, Y., & Maleh, Y. (2022). Introduction. In *Cybersecurity in Morocco. SpringerBriefs in Cybersecurity*. Springer. 10.1007/978-3-031-18475-8_1

Martinez, B.M. & McAndrews, L.E. (2023). Do you take...? The effect of mobile payment solutions on use intention: an application of UTAUT2. *J Market Anal 11*, 458–469 (https://doi.org/)10.1057/s41270-022-00175-6

Mich, L. (2022). Artificial Intelligence and Machine Learning. In Xiang, Z., Fuchs, M., Gretzel, U., & Höpken, W. (Eds.), *Handbook of e-Tourism*. Springer. 10.1007/978-3-030-48652-5_25

Qin, Y., Xu, Z., Wang, X., & Skare, M. (2023). Artificial Intelligence and Economic Development: An Evolutionary Investigation and Systematic Review. *Journal of the Knowledge Economy*. 10.1007/s13132-023-01183-2

Ryan, K. M., & Graham, R. S. (2014). Tactics and Strategies for Creating Effective E-mail Marketing Campaigns. In: *Taking Down Goliath*. Palgrave Macmillan, New York. (https://doi.org/)10.1057/9781137444219_7

Sheikh, H., Prins, C., & Schrijvers, E. (2023). AI as a System Technology. In Mission, A. I. (Ed.), *Research for Policy*. Springer. 10.1007/978-3-031-21448-6_4

Yadav, D., & Kadavath, V. K. (Eds.), *The Digital Popular in India*. Palgrave Macmillan. 10.1007/978-3-031-39435-5

Section 3

Analysis of the Impact of Digital Technology on Consumer Behaviour and Business Performance

Chapter 12
The Influence of Digital Marketing on Business Performance:
A Case Study of Selected Moroccan Companies

Ali Tazi Cherti
http://orcid.org/0009-0007-0716-8382
Sidi Mohamed Ben Abdellah University, Morocco

ABSTRACT

This research examines the impact of digital marketing (DM), through the integration of artificial intelligence (AI), on business performance (BP) in the Moroccan context. Utilizing a structured questionnaire and the advanced PLS-SEM method for analysis, it uncovers a strong positive correlation between the use of AI in DM and improved BP. This relationship signifies a paradigm shift towards more personalized marketing strategies, data-driven decision-making, and dynamic adaptation to market trends. The research highlights how AI not only enhances operational efficiency but also fosters innovation and value creation, urging Moroccan companies to rethink their digital strategies. It emphasizes AI's pivotal role in transforming the digital marketing landscape, suggesting that its strategic integration is essential for companies aiming to thrive in the digital era. The study's uniqueness stems from its focus on Morocco, offering insights into the adaptation of AI in DM within an African context, thereby contributing to the understanding of digitalization in emerging economies.

1. INTRODUCTION

Digital marketing can be seen as a process that involves interacting with customers who are frequently online, using a variety of tools and platforms such as websites, online brand resources, online advertising, and email marketing (Ravi & Rajasekaran, 2023). Digital transformation has become imperative across all business activities today. Digital marketing emerges as a key element for anticipating risks and seizing emerging opportunities, thus enhancing companies' strategic decision-making. This digital transition alters how businesses interact with products and brands through online services such as cloud storage,

DOI: 10.4018/979-8-3693-3172-9.ch012

web browsing, streaming platforms, emails, and the use of social networks like Facebook, redefining traditional modes of interaction (Kiili et al., 2018). The effectiveness of traditional marketing strategies is questioned in a demanding competitive context; they are no longer sufficient to generate a sustainable competitive advantage or stimulate growth (Kaur, 2017). Today, businesses operate in a competitive and turbulent environment, requiring the use of effective tools to achieve their goals. Among these tools, digital marketing stands out (Chaikovska et al., 2022). Consequently, digital marketing presents itself as an opportunity lever for companies across all sectors eager to confront competition. It stands out as a dynamic and evolving tool, offering solutions tailored to the renewed demands of consumers. The emergence of innovative digital technologies opens new avenues for advertisers aiming to achieve their commercial objectives through online advertising (Reza Kiani, 1998).

Companies are increasingly aware of the need to integrate cutting-edge technology applications to strengthen their operational processes and ensure access to updated information (Aggarwal, 2017). However, there is a shortage of empirical evidence evaluating the actual effect of digital marketing on business performance and a gap in the literature regarding the role of digital progress in business processes (Ahmad et al., 2018). Digital marketing enables companies to maximize their sales, expand their market reach, and cultivate customer relationships virtually. As a result, digital marketing techniques are increasingly favored for targeting and engaging markets.

The marketing field has been transformed by the integration of artificial intelligence (AI), altering the techniques and strategies within this sector (Van Esch et al., 2018). The adoption of AI-based tools for creating marketing content is increasingly favored by companies to enhance the efficiency and relevance of their digital marketing efforts. AI mimics human functions such as voice recognition, visual perception, and decision-making processes, thereby enriching marketing capabilities (Tao & Zhang, 2021). It also offers the advantage of producing highly personalized content, meeting the expectations of specific customer segments. However, it is crucial for companies to maintain a balance between AI and human ingenuity to ensure their content remains unique and engaging (Haleem et al., 2022). With growing competition and changing consumer demands, digital marketing is now a crucial component in promoting products and services. This sector has undergone significant evolution with the advancement of AI, moving from a data-centric approach to a more holistic approach that combines data and knowledge .

Current applications of AI include chatbots, digital assistants, and machine learning (Devang et al., 2019). Given the vast amount of data currently produced, surpassing human capacity for analysis and decision-making, AI presents itself as an indispensable solution (Hurwitz et al., 2015). It is particularly recommended for SMEs aiming to optimize their performance and decision-making processes (Enshassi et al., 2024). Used in conjunction with marketing, AI allows for increased precision in customer data segmentation, content enrichment, profiling, development of predictive models, targeting of a broader audience, and optimization of search engine ranking. Nonetheless, adopting digital marketing represents a significant investment, which should not be directly compared to traditional marketing methods, which have already demonstrated a return on investment trajectory (Teixeira et al., 2019).

1.1. Research Objective

This research seeks to investigate the impact of digital marketing (DM) on business performance (BP) in the Moroccan context through the integration of artificial intelligence (AI) as a mediating variable.

1.2. Research Interest

The interest of this research lies in evaluating the effectiveness of digital marketing when combined with artificial intelligence to enhance business performance in Morocco. More specifically, it aims to understand how the integration of AI can mediate and potentially amplify the influence of digital marketing on business performance within a specific economic and cultural context that constitutes a distinctive blend of technological traditions and innovations. This study could provide valuable insights into the synergies between digital technologies and operational strategies, thereby offering a foundation for more informed strategic decisions for Moroccan businesses operating in a similar context looking to leverage the competitive advantages of AI in their marketing.

* Haut du formulaire

1.3. Research Question

Building on the literature review and the previously mentioned context, our research aims to address the following issue: what is the impact of digital marketing on business performance through the integration of artificial intelligence ?

1.4. Research Plan

The present research is structured as follows: we will analyze existing works on digital marketing, business performance, and artificial intelligence to establish the theoretical foundation of our research and highlight the gaps that our study aims to fill. Based on the literature review, we formulate the hypotheses that our study seeks to test. Subsequently, we describe the research methodology used to collect and analyze data, present and examine these findings, emphasizing the key discoveries that emerge from our study. In the discussion section, we interpret the obtained results, comparing them with previous studies and discussing their significance in the context of our research topic. Finally, we summarize the main lessons from the research, highlight the theoretical and practical impacts and contributions of the research, and propose avenues for future research.

2. LITERATURE REVIEW

2.1. In-Depth Perspectives on Digital Marketing

Digital marketing represents an innovative and modern approach for businesses, offering new methods for managing their operations (Garg & Bansal, 2020). Digital marketing has revolutionized the way businesses communicate with their target audiences and how they promote their products and services (Zhezha et al., 2023) .

Recent work advocates for conducting empirical studies to assess the effect of digital marketing strategies on the performance of small and medium-sized enterprises (Baka, 2016). This new era of marketing, inherently linked to technological advancements, challenges traditional methods and calls for a strategic revision to remain competitive. From its inception, content marketing has proven to be a key factor in the success of online marketing campaigns, playing a pivotal role in digital marketing. Its influence is significant on employee engagement, sales increase, and the building of trust and loyalty among customers (Hollebeek & Macky, 2019). The importance placed on digital content marketing is corroborated by numerous studies (Hollebeek & Macky, 2019). By enhancing the efficiency and effectiveness of traditional marketing, digital marketing introduces new business models that deliver more value to consumers and increase the profitability of companies (Strauss & Frost, 2014). (Sawicki, 2016) describes digital marketing as an foray into the vast digital technological world, establishing a connection with a wide potential audience. Furthermore, digital marketing is distinguished as a powerful method for promoting products and services via e-commerce, benefiting from direct internet connectivity (Chaffey & Ellis-Chadwick, 2019). Thus, embracing digitalization is crucial for minimizing costs and increasing revenues by leveraging technology to reach a broader audience.

2.2. Business Performance: A Dynamic Approach

Business performance is achieved by meeting the commercial objectives set by the company (Anwar & Shah, 2021). This is confirmed by (Chi et al., 2023; Suryantini et al., 2023) demonstrating business performance reflects its success in achieving its organisational objectives and is a key dependent variable that captures the interest of researchers in various fields of management. Business performance is indicated by their ability to use tangible and intangible resources to achieve their goals, with profitability as the main indicator of success (Omotosho, 2020; Zaragoza-Sáez et al., 2020). Business performance, which is essential for assessing the achievement of organisational objectives, is a crucial dependent variable in management (Aisjah et al., 2023; Chi et al., 2023). Business performance is a fundamental goal of their operations; if commercial activities are conducted efficiently, they will benefit employees, shareholders, and society at large (Anh et al., 2024). Moreover, big data, although are still in their infancy (Bouhtati, Alla, et al., 2023), is revolutionizing marketing strategies by catalyzing innovation and enhancing the personalization and adaptation of sales and services across all business operations, particularly effective when integrated with artificial intelligence, big data not only improves performance but also ushers in a new era of marketing, optimizing business strategies for enhanced outcomes (Alla et al., 2023; Bouhtati, Kamal, et al., 2023).

Several subjective and objective factors determine the way in which company performance is measured (Sarkees et al., 2010). The performance of SMEs can be significantly impacted by the adoption and application of digital technologies (Nuseir & Al, 2018). Investing appropriately in information technology to enhance business performance is now a clear strategy for organizations to gain competitive advantage and ensure survival in a dynamic business environment (Sujová & Simanová, 2023). Current academic research recognizes the impact of marketing resources on a company's success (Day, 2011). Therefore, it has become crucial for marketing practitioners to develop a direct link between marketing skills and business performance (Morgan, 2012). Moreover, digital marketing strategies appear to have a multidimensional impact on companies, positively affecting revenue growth, customer satisfaction, and the expansion of brand influence (Chaffey & Ellis-Chadwick, 2019). Even focused on the fashion industry, the analysis of the impact of brand awareness on a company's performance provides useful insights (Huang & Sarigöllü, 2012). Utilizing digital channels proves to be a lever for enhancing the performance of SMEs, demonstrating the efficiency and beneficial influence of digital marketing (Taiminen & Karjaluoto, 2015).

The study by Collins et al. (2021) shows that companies integrating AI into their operations typically see reduced operational costs and increased productivity, also, merging AI with digital marketing significantly improves business performance and opens up new opportunities for innovation and enhancement in business processes.

2.3. The Transformative Impact of Artificial Intelligence on Digital Marketing: A Comprehensive Analysis

Artificial intelligence (AI) has become a crucial tool for enhancing digital marketin, also, it enables marketers to develop superior products, provide quicker and more targeted advertising to consumers, and gain a deeper insight into the data patterns of their audience (Priyanga G, 2023). AI technologies, such as recommendation systems, have revolutionized digital marketing by enabling real-time personalization (Ziakis & Vlachopoulou, 2023). Conversely, (Sarath Kumar Boddu et al., 2022) observe that AI was initially used in digital marketing for simple tasks like data sorting, but it has now become central to customizing the customer experience.

By integrating AI, companies can better understand their audiences, create more engaging content, and enhance their customer engagement strategies (Haleem et al., 2022). AI also assists in the precise tailoring and ongoing adjustment of marketing content based on user data analysis and intention interpretation (Chan-Olmsted, 2019). The research by (Chih-Wen Wu & Abel Monfort, 2022) examines AI's impact as a marketing strategy, outlining its benefits to business progression and the elements influencing its adoption. The function of AI and digital marketing in boosting business performance through enhanced customer engagement is emphasized (Kumar et al., 2019). AI is transforming the service industry by enhancing customer value and business performance with automation and personalization (Huang & Rust, 2018).

The integration of artificial intelligence (AI) into digital marketing (DM) is transforming business strategies across various sectors, offering promising insights into its transformative capabilities. Furthermore, (Chan-Olmsted, 2019) emphasizes that AI optimizes digital content production by refining the understanding of user preferences and tailoring content for maximum impact. This efficiency is also observed in the management of online advertising campaigns, where AI, through programmatic advertising, adjusts ad delivery based on user behavior, as demonstrated by (De Bruyn et al., 2020). Additionally, (Van Esch et al., 2018) confirm the positive impact of AI on a company's ability to engage and satisfy their customers through digital marketing initiatives. These studies illustrate the evolution of marketing strategies, which are moving towards more dynamic and personalized approaches thanks to AI.

In summary, the current state of the art reveals a remarkable convergence towards recognizing AI as a key element in enhancing the performance of digital marketing. This trend highlights a transformation in the way companies approach their marketing strategies, shifting from traditional logic to dynamic and personalized methods propelled by artificial intelligence.

Our study seeks to empirically confirm the impact of digital marketing on the performance of Moroccan companies through the integration of artificial intelligence (AI) as a mediating variable, thus contributing to enriching the existing literature on this topic.

Therefore, we present our a priori conceptual model as follows:

Figure 1. Conceptual framework

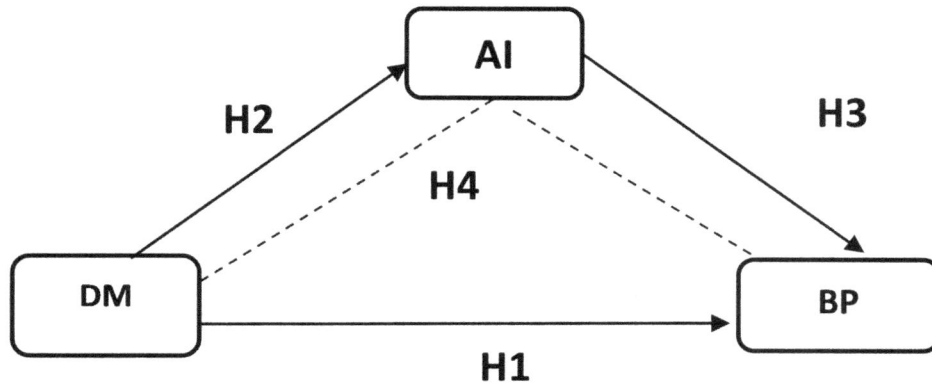

3. HYPOTHESES DEVELOPMENT

The selection of variables in this study aims to understand and assimilate how digital marketing (independent variable) influences business performance (dependent variable) and how this relationship is affected or modulated by integration of artificial intelligence (AI) as a mediating variable.

3.1. Presentation of Research Variables

Independent Variable: Digital Marketing (DM)

The specificity of digital marketing lies in its diversity to encompass a set of marketing activities conducted through digital channels, including social media, SEO, email marketing, and online advertising, among others. The reason for choosing digital marketing as the independent variable is embodied by its growing importance for businesses of various sizes in the digital age. Digital marketing is no longer an option but a necessity for reaching, engaging, and converting the target audience in an increasingly saturated and competitive environment (Chaffey & Ellis-Chadwick, 2019). In this regard, numerous studies have demonstrated that well-refined and well-executed digital marketing strategies can lead to significant improvements in brand visibility, customer engagement, and ultimately, the financial performance of the company (Kumar et al., 2019).

Mediating Variable: Artificial Intelligence (AI)

AI is selected as the mediating variable due to its transformative potential in the way digital marketing strategies are designed, implemented, and optimized. The integration of AI into digital marketing can not only automate repetitive tasks but also provide deep insights into customer preferences and behaviors, thereby enabling more personalized and efficient marketing campaigns (Huang & Rust, 2018). AI can thus modulate the effectiveness of digital marketing, positively influencing business performance through the enhancement of the relevance, accuracy, and timing of marketing initiatives. This ability of AI to enrich and refine digital marketing efforts justifies its role as a mediating variable in this study.

Dependent Variable: Business Performance

Business performance is selected as the dependent variable as it represents the ultimate goal of most business strategies, including digital marketing. Performance can be measured using various indicators such as revenue growth, market share, profitability, and customer satisfaction. The aim is to determine whether investment in digital marketing, especially when enhanced by AI, leads to tangible improvements in these performance indicators. Focusing on business performance allows for the quantification of the real impact of digital marketing technologies and strategies on business success (Lee & Suh, 2022).

In this setting, the present study seeks to investigate the interactions among digital marketing, AI, and business performance, focusing on how AI can help maximize the impact of digital marketing on business outcomes. Furthermore, discussions and debates from the literature have led us to capitalize on elements that enrich the existing debate on this topic, providing the necessary tools and mechanisms to develop the hypotheses of this research.

3.2. Formulation of Hypotheses

Studies by (Chaffey & Patron, 2012) have affirmed that digital marketing can enable better analysis of customer data, leading to more informed marketing decisions and improved performance. Indeed, (Singh et al., 2022) argue that digital marketing can significantly enhance business performance through improved customer engagement and optimizing sales channels. This view is clearly evidenced by (Jung & Shegai, 2023), who demonstrated that strategic integration of digital marketing contributes to sustained revenue growth and improved profitability. Digital marketing activities, such as SEO, content marketing, and social media, have a direct influence on a company's ability to generate revenue and increase its market share, thus reflecting an improvement in business performance (Chaffey & Ellis-Chadwick, 2019).

Hypothesis 1 (H1): Digital marketing positively and significantly influences business performance.

Artificial Intelligence (AI) enables refined and advanced personalization of digital marketing campaigns, which enhances customer engagement and optimizes conversions (Luo et al., 2019). Additionally, (Huang & Rust, 2018) explain that AI transforms the customer experience by providing more relevant and real-time interactions, thereby enhancing the overall effectiveness of digital marketing.

Similarly, (Li et al., 2021) demonstrate that AI allows for more precise customer segmentation and targeting, strengthening the impact of digital marketing initiatives. Furthermore, (Al Khaldy, 2023) found that AI technologies, such as machine learning and predictive analytics, enhance the targeting and automation capabilities of digital marketing, leading to more effective campaigns and optimal allocation of marketing resources.

Hypothesis 2 (H2): The use of AI positively enhances the effectiveness of digital marketing.

The adoption of AI in business operations contributes to operational efficiency, cost reduction, improved customer satisfaction, and ultimately, better overall business performance (Davenport & Ronanki, 2018). Similarly, (Wamba-Taguimdje et al., 2020) demonstrate that AI can facilitate optimized customer relationship management, which leads to a significant increase in customer satisfaction and loyalty, and consequently, business performance.

(Christian et al., 2023) show that AI can aid in product innovation and service personalization, leading to increased customer satisfaction and, as a corollary, enhanced business performance. Indeed, (Kumar et al., 2019; Pereira et al., 2023) note that the adoption of AI in business operations significantly improves business performance by streamlining processes and providing valuable insights for decision-making. This assertion is supported by (Lee & Suh, 2022), who observed that integrating AI into customer service and customer relationship management leads to improved customer satisfaction and, consequently, better overall business performance.

Hypothesis 3 (H3): The application of AI positively and significantly impacts business performance.

AI acts as a crucial mediator by amplifying the impact of digital marketing on business performance. This hypothesis is supported by the study of (Yang et al., 2024), which demonstrates that the use of AI in digital marketing not only directly improves business performance through better allocation of marketing resources but also optimizes it indirectly by enhancing customer experience. Similarly, (Sahoo et al., 2023) argue that AI, by analyzing data generated from digital marketing campaigns, enables continuous optimization of marketing strategies, leading to improved business performance. Furthermore, AI significantly enhances digital marketing's impact on business performance by enabling deeper data analysis and personalized content, which leads to more engaging customer interactions, improved lead conversion, and increased business performance (Badghish & Soomro, 2024).

Hypothesis 4 (H4): The application of AI acts as a mediator in the relationship between digital marketing and business performance.

4. METHODOLOGY

This research aims to study the impact of digital marketing on business performance, with particular emphasis on the mediating role of artificial intelligence. The study employs a cross-sectional approach, collecting data at a specific point in time. To this end, we have developed and utilized a structured questionnaire. This questionnaire is divided into four sections: the first section outlines the demographic profile of the respondents, the second section addresses the dimensions of digital marketing, the third aims to evaluate business performance within the context of digital marketing; and the fourth concentrates on the implementation of AI in digital marketing strategies.

The sample studied comprises Moroccan companies integrating AI as a central element of their management and operational practices. Morocco was chosen as the research location due to its dynamic emerging market and its growing adoption of digital technologies and AI in the business sector. This specificity makes Morocco an interesting case study to explore the effect and influence of digital marketing on business performance through the use of AI, offering relevant perspectives in an Arab-African context. The choice to focus on Morocco also makes an important contribution to the literature, which is currently dominated by studies focused on developed economies, and highlights the challenges and opportunities unique to developing markets.

To determine the adequate sample size from the targeted population, we used the method proposed by (Krejcie & Morgan, 1970) a statistical technique used to determine an appropriate sample size from a given population for research using surveys. This method is particularly useful in studies where it is impractical to survey the entire target population.

Data collection was conducted through convenience sampling, according to (Sekaran & Bougie, 2014). In fact, this method was chosen because of its ease of implementation and its effectiveness in terms of cost and time. This method is particularly suitable for this research, because the goal is to have initial insights rather than generalize to the entire population. This survey relies on the analysis of quantitative data.

The questionnaire was distributed to 120 potential respondents of which 57 responded, representing a response rate of 47.5%.

Our limited sample size is tailored to the specialized area of AI integration in digital marketing, a niche involving a limited number of qualified companies within the context of our research. The quality and accuracy of the data collected is high, reflecting the skill and expertise of respondents directly involved in advanced marketing strategies. These factors ensure that the study results are not only relevant but also deeply informative for understanding the impact of digital marketing on the performance of businesses integrating AI into their current practices.

To effectively distribute the questionnaire for our study on the integration of AI in digital marketing, we opted for a combination of emails and LinkedIn, targeting key professionals in relevant companies. The choice of email allowed for direct and formal communication, preceded by a pre-contact to inform participants and increase the response rate. LinkedIn was used to leverage professional networks and reach experts actively engaged in specific fields. Each questionnaire was accompanied by an introduction clarifying the study's objectives and the benefits for the participants, while ensuring data confidentiality. This process aimed to maximize the reach and accuracy of the responses, facilitating flexible and efficient participation through a questionnaire designed to be completed quickly.

The detailed profile of the participants is presented in Table 1.

Table 1. Descriptive of participants

Companies' profile	% (n = 57)
Respondents' Position	
Executive	40.4 (23)
General Manager	19.3 (11)
Marketing Manager/Head	40.4 (23)
Legal Status	
LLC	82.5 (47)
Corporation	17.5 (10)
Workforce Size	
> 10	28.1 (16)
Between 10 and 100	38.6 (22)
Between 100 and 250	28.1 (16)
< 250	5.3 (03)
Activity area	

continued on following page

Table 1. Continued

Companies' profile	% (n = 57)
Services	43.9 (25)
Manufacturing	15.8 (09)
Trade	36.8 (21)
Others	3.5 (02)

The digital marketing scale is measured by four items adapted from (A. Kaplan & Haenlein, 2019b), the scale for determining business performance consists of four items, adapted from (Kumar et al., 2019), and the scale for artificial intelligence in digital marketing has been adapted from (Huang & Rust, 2018), which comprises four items (see Table 2).

We chose to employ a Likert scale that ranges from 1 «strongly disagree» to 5 «strongly agree » to assess all the concepts in the study. This method is widely recognized for its ability to measure respondents' degrees of opinion or attitudes in a nuanced and quantitative manner, thus facilitating the statistical analysis of the data. The Likert scale allows for precise expression of perceptions and preferences, providing clear and easily interpretable results. Respondents were encouraged to answer freely and candidly, enhancing the validity of the data collected. This approach is supported by numerous studies in social sciences and marketing that utilize this scale for its reliability and validity (Boone & Boone, 2012; DeVellis, 2016).

The questionnaire was distributed to respondents, who were invited to provide their answers freely and frankly while mentioning respect for the principle of confidentiality and anonymity of responses.

Table 2. Variables list and research items number

Variables	Items	Indicators	Authors
Digital Marketing (DM)	DM 1	**Use of social networks** How would you assess the integrity of the use of social networks in your marketing strategies?	Kaplan & Haenlein (2010)
	DM 2	**Creation and sharing of digital content** How often does your company create and share digital content?	
	DM 3	**Use of SEO techniques** How would you rate the effectiveness of your current SEO techniques in improving your website's organic traffic?	
	DM 4	**Engagement in digital advertising campaigns** To what extent have your digital advertising campaigns achieved your specific marketing objectives this year?	

continued on following page

Table 2. Continued

Variables	Items	Indicators	Authors
Business Performance (BP)	BP 1	**Revenue growth due to digital marketing initiatives** What percentage of revenue growth can you attribute directly to digital marketing initiatives this year?	Kumar, Rajan, Gupta, Pozza (2019)
	BP 2	**Improvement of customer engagement and interaction** How do you measure the improvement in customer engagement and interaction since the implementation of digital marketing strategies?	
	BP 3	**Increase in customer satisfaction and loyalty** Have you seen an increase in customer satisfaction and loyalty as a result of using digital marketing and AI strategies?	
	BP 4	**Expansion of brand reach and improvement of online reputation** What indicators do you use to measure the extension of your brand's reach and the improvement of its online reputation?	
Artificial intelligence (AI)	AI 1	**Personalization of customer experiences based on AI** Has AI made it possible to personalise your customers' experiences?	Huang & Rust (2018)
	AI 2	**Customer interaction with AI-powered chatbots** Do your customers find interactions with AI-powered chatbots useful and satisfying?	
	AI 3	**Predictive analysis of customer needs** Do you use predictive analysis to anticipate customer needs and if so, how has this affected your sales or customer engagement?	
	AI 4	**Automation of marketing tasks** To what extent has the automation of marketing tasks by AI improved your company's operational efficiency?	

The selection of these items to assess the impact of digital marketing on business performance, through the integration of artificial intelligence (AI), is guided by methodological and theoretical considerations. Each item is designed to capture a critical aspect of the effect of digital marketing and AI on operational and strategic business performance, based on prior research that has established solid foundations in the field.

Digital Marketing (DM) Items: These items are chosen based on literature that underscores the importance of social networks, content creation, SEO, and engagement in digital advertising campaigns as key determinants of digital marketing effectiveness (Kaplan & Haenlein, 2010). These indicators are recognized for their strong correlation with increased visibility and customer engagement, essential factors for business performance.

Business Performance (BP) Items: The items related to business performance directly measure the impact of DM on financial outcomes and customer satisfaction, aligning with the work of(Kumar et al., 2019) which links digital marketing strategies to financial performance and customer retention. They also cover more qualitative aspects such as online brand reputation, reflecting a holistic understanding of business performance.

Artificial Intelligence (AI) Items: Aspects of AI, such as personalization, customer interaction, and predictive analysis, are included due to their recognized capacity to transform digital marketing strategies and enhance customer interactions (Huang & Rust, 2018). The automation of marketing tasks is also an area where AI has demonstrated substantial efficiency gains, justifying its inclusion as a central element in assessing impact on business performance.

The choice of these items over another model is supported by their proven relevance and adaptability to the specific context of Moroccan businesses, where the integration of AI into digital marketing may present unique challenges and opportunities. These items provide a basis for robust comparative analysis that can serve as a benchmark for future research and practitioners seeking to optimize the use of AI in digital marketing to enhance business performance.

5. RESULTS AND ANALYSIS

5.1 Data Analysis and Measurement Model Assessment

In the context of this study, we employed the Partial Least Squares Structural Equation Modeling (PLS-SEM) method to conduct the assessment of the measurement model as well as the analysis of the structural model of estimators (Henseler et al., 2009a). The PLS-SEM method is recognized as particularly suitable for social sciences due to its capability to simultaneously examine the relationships among multiple variables (Hair et al., 2016).

To evaluate the reliability and validity of our research model, we utilized the PLS-SEM algorithm. The model's reliability was verified through Cronbach's alpha and composite reliability (CR), while validity was assessed in terms of convergent and discriminant validity. Convergent validity was determined using the average variance extracted (AVE), and discriminant validity was evaluated using the Heterotrait-Monotrait (HTMT) ratio. The results obtained for the measurement model demonstrate that our research model meets the required conditions for reliability and validity.

Table 3. Internal consistency and reliability

Constructs	Indicators	Loadings	Cronbach (α) value	rho_A	CR	AVE
Artificial intelligence (AI)	AI 1	0,924	0,937	0,938	0,955	0,841
	AI 2	0,906				
	AI 3	0,837				
	AI 4	0,883				
Business Performance (BP)	BP 1	0,907	0,957	0,957	0,969	0,886
	BP 2	0,882				
	BP 3	0,912				
	BP 4	0,977				
Digital Marketing (DM)	DM 1	0,700	0,924	0,938	0,947	0,817
	DM 2	0,927				
	DM 3	0,938				
	DM 4	0,910				

Table 3 shows that for all constructs, the values of Cronbach's alpha and Composite Reliability (CR) exceed 0.7, suggesting that the research model satisfies the necessary criteria for confirming internal consistency and reliability. Furthermore, the value of the Average Variance Extracted (AVE) also surpasses the threshold of 0.5, confirming that the research model also adheres to established standards for convergent validity.

Cronbach's alpha values are above 0.9 for AI and BP, significantly beyond the generally accepted threshold of 0.7 for internal reliability, while DM is slightly lower but remains acceptable. The rho_A values align with Cronbach's alphas, enhancing the reliability of the constructs. The high CRs affirm composite reliability, and the AVE values are also above 0.5, sufficiently high to ensure good convergent validity, indicating that the majority of the variance in responses is attributable to the constructs themselves rather than to random error, and the research model satisfied the criteria for convergent reliability..

Table 4. Discriminant validity using HTMT

	AI	BP	DM
AI			
BP	0,984		
DM	0,965	0,918	

The analyses of discriminant validity, assessed through the Heterotrait-Monotrait (HTMT) ratio, revealed values above the recommended threshold of 0.90 for all pairs of constructs examined.

Figure 2. Measurement model

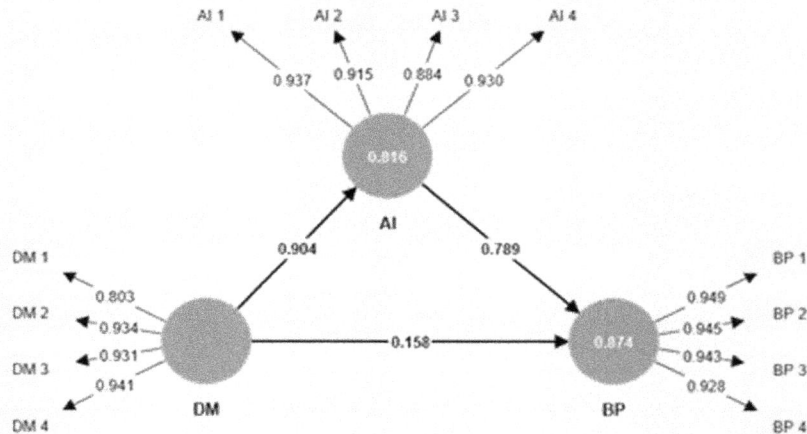

The connections between the constructs are depicted by lines, with correlation coefficients of 0.816 between AI and DM, 0.874 between BP and DM, and 0.789 between AI and BP, showing moderate to strong positive relationships. Overall, the results suggest significant relationships between the constructs, with well-chosen indicators that adequately reflect the studied concepts. The correlation among these constructs may indicate potential interactions or influences between artificial intelligence, digital marketing, and business performance.

5.2 Structural Model Assessment

This part of the research investigated the connections between the constructs outlined in the theoretical framework by analyzing the hypotheses proposed earlier in the study. The data gathered were examined using the bootstrapping method to assess the effects and implications of digital marketing applications on business performance. Additionally, this section explored the mediating role of artificial intelligence.

Haut du formulaire

Table 5. Relationships of constructs (Path coefficient)

Hypotheses	Relationships	Bias	t-value	p-value	2.5%	97.5%	Results
H1	DM -> BP	0,024	0,628	0,530	-0,273	0,754	Rejected
H2	DM -> AI	0,001	20,690	0,000	0,781	0,962	Accepted
H3	AI -> BP	-0,028	3,413	0,001	0,221	1,157	Accepted
H4	DM -> AI -> BP	-0,028	3,467	0,001	0,233	1,083	Accepted

This study's hypotheses were evaluated through the bias-corrected and accelerated (BCa) bootstrapping technique. Table 5 presents the results of testing the structural hypotheses of our model using path coefficients. These results indicate that all t-values are above 1.96, and p-values are also below 0.05, with the exception of hypothesis H1.

Hypothesis H1 (DM -> BP): The path from Digital Marketing (DM) to Business Performance (BP) has a bias of 0.024 with a t-value of 0.628 and a p-value of 0.530. The 95% confidence interval ranges from -0.273 to 0.754; hence, this hypothesis is rejected.

Hypothesis H2 (DM -> AI): The path from Digital Marketing (DM) to Artificial Intelligence (AI) shows a bias of 0.001 with an extremely high t-value of 20.690 and a p-value of 0.000, indicating a statistically significant relationship. The 95% confidence interval extends from 0.781 to 0.962. This hypothesis is accepted.

Hypothesis H3 (AI -> BP): The path from Artificial Intelligence (AI) to Business Performance (BP) indicates a bias of -0.028, a t-value of 3.413, and a p-value of 0.001, suggesting statistical significance. The 95% confidence interval ranges from 0.221 to 1.157. This hypothesis is accepted.

Hypothesis H4 (DM -> AI -> BP): The mediating effect of AI between DM and BP shows a bias of -0.028, a t-value of 3.467, and a p-value of 0.001. The 95% confidence interval ranges from 0.233 to 1.083. This hypothesis is accepted.

These results indicate that the direct relationship between DM and BP is not statistically significant, whereas the other tested relationships are significant, including the mediating effect of Artificial Intelligence.

Table 6. Predictive power of endogenous constructs

	Q^2	R^2
AI	0.307	0.816
BP	0.750	0.874

The predictive power of the model was assessed using the R^2 and Q^2 values. The R^2 values indicate that variations in the endogenous constructs, namely AI and BP, are explained by the exogenous constructs to the extent of 81.6% and 87.4%, respectively. Meanwhile, the Q^2 value being greater than "0" demonstrates that the model has successfully met the criteria for predictive power.

Figure 3. The result of structural model

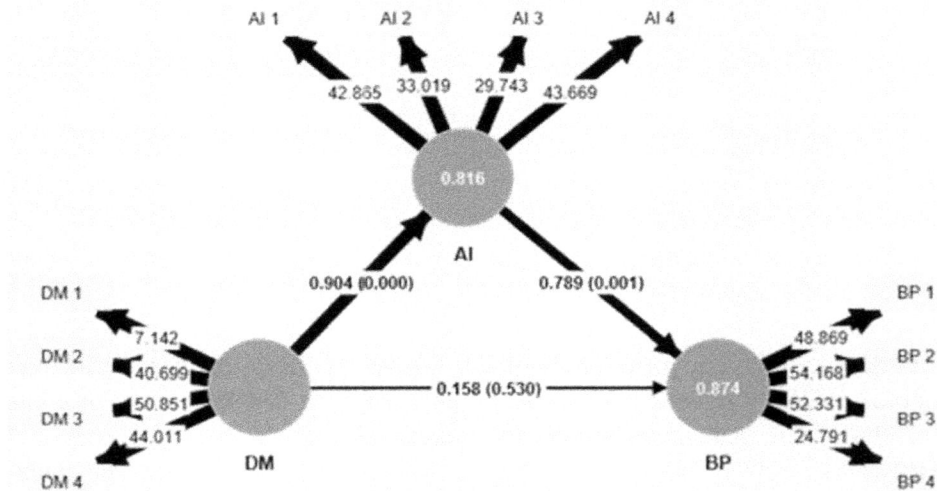

6. DISCUSSION

6.1 Internal Consistency and Reliability

The results presented in Table 3 highlight the reliability and internal consistency of the constructs used in our study. Each of the constructs – AI, BP, and DM – demonstrates strong factor loadings and reliability scores that significantly exceed the commonly accepted thresholds (0.7) in management science research, indicating the robustness of the measurement instruments (Nunnally & Bernstein, 1994). Furthermore, the CR exceeds the recommended value of 0.7 for all constructs, in line with the recommendations of (Hair et al., 2010), indicating adequate composite reliability. The AVE for all constructs also surpasses the threshold of 0.5, suggesting that the majority of the variance of the indicators is captured by the constructs they are supposed to measure, a conclusion that aligns with the assertions of (Fornell & Larcker, 1981). This lends weight to the convergent validity of the constructs in this study.

For artificial intelligence (AI), the indicator loadings range from 0.837 to 0.924, and the construct shows excellent internal consistency with a Cronbach's alpha and rho_A of 0.937 and 0.938, respectively, accompanied by a Composite Reliability (CR) index of 0.955. The Average Variance Extracted (AVE) for AI is 0.841, suggesting that the majority of the variance of the indicators is well captured by the construct. This high level of internal consistency and convergent validity confirms the relevance of our AI measures in the context of the study.

Regarding business performance (BP), the indicators show even more convincing reliability, with loadings from 0.882 to 0.977 and a Cronbach's alpha of 0.957. A CR of 0.969 and an AVE of 0.886 strengthen the validity of the business performance measures, supporting the notion that the selected indicators for BP are both consistent and significant.

Digital marketing (DM), with loadings from 0.700 to 0.938, shows a slight variation in the strength with which each indicator represents the construct. Despite the relatively lower loading of DM1, the Cronbach's alpha of 0.924 and the rho_A of 0.938 indicate that the DM construct, as a whole, is reliable. However, this variation warrants future attention to understand if certain aspects of digital marketing are underrepresented by the measures used.

These overall high results of internal consistency and reliability provide us with the necessary confidence to proceed with the analysis of the relationships between the constructs, knowing that the measures are solid. (Henseler et al., 2016) emphasize the importance of such reliable and consistent measures for model validation in quantitative research methods.

In conclusion, these results reinforce the existing literature on measuring digitization in business and suggest that companies must remain attentive to evolving technologies and strategies to ensure an accurate measurement of their impacts on performance.

6.2 Discriminant Validity

The results on discriminant validity presented in Table 4 show very high HTMT values between pairs of constructs: 0.984 between Artificial Intelligence (AI) and Business Performance (BP), and 0.965 between AI and Digital Marketing (DM), followed by a value of 0.918 between BP and DM. While the traditional thresholds for discriminant validity are exceeded, this suggests a strong correlation between the constructs rather than a clear distinction. This observation could be interpreted in several ways.

(Henseler et al., 2015) suggest that HTMT values close to 1 could indicate that the constructs are not conceptually distinct. Thus, our results might indicate a potential overlap in how AI, BP, and DM are perceived or measured within the context of our study. This lack of distinction could reflect a reality where the boundaries between these domains are becoming increasingly blurred, particularly due to the growing integration of AI into marketing practices and performance management.

(Franke & Sarstedt, 2019) note that discriminant validity should not be the sole criterion for evaluating the quality of a measurement model, especially when the constructs are theoretically related. In the context of digital transformation, where AI can be seen as a tool serving both marketing and business performance, high correlations are to be expected. Therefore, it is crucial to interpret these results within the appropriate theoretical context and to consider complementary methods to assess the validity of the constructs.

It is also important to refer to the work of (Voorhees et al., 2015), who highlight the complexity of evaluating discriminant validity in environments where constructs may be interdependent. The authors argue that the HTMT approach should be used in conjunction with other indices to confirm discriminant validity.

In conclusion, although the results suggest a less distinct separation between the constructs, this finding may be symptomatic of a domain where technologies and business practices are rapidly evolving, and conceptual distinctions are increasingly integrated. In this regard, future work should examine how constructs are operationalized and perhaps reconsider how business performance is influenced by the rapid evolution of digital practices and AI, thus proposing avenues for future research to enhance discriminant validity within similar conceptual models.

6.3 Relationships Between Constructs

The results from Table 5 present a nuanced picture of the impact of digital marketing (DM) and artificial intelligence (AI) on business performance (BP).

Regarding the relationships between the constructs, Hypothesis H1 shows that DM does not have a direct and significant impact on BP. This rejection contrasts with existing literature, which often posits a positive link between DM and BP (Kannan & Li, 2017). This could be due to the digital maturity of the industry under study or inadequate integration of DM into business operations, a point raised by (Chaffey & Ellis-Chadwick, 2019).

The acceptance of H2 and H3 aligns with the study by (Brynjolfsson & Mcafee, 2017), who argued that AI not only enhances digital marketing processes but also operational performance. These results also highlight the work of (A. Kaplan & Haenlein, 2019a), who identified AI as a driver of business transformation.

The acceptance of Hypothesis H4 is particularly interesting as it indicates a mediating effect of AI on the relationship between DM and BP. This implies that, even though DM does not directly affect BP, it can do so indirectly by enhancing a company's AI capabilities. This could be due to DM initiatives generating data that, when leveraged by AI, can lead to performance gains. In this sense, it is important to consider AI as a mediating factor in the relationship between DM and business performance on AI as a strategic lever for digital transformation of companies.

6.4 Predictive Power of Endogenous Constructs

The constructs in Table 6 reveal that AI and BP possess strong predictive power, with substantial Q^2 values indicating predictive relevance for the internal relationship models. A Q^2 value greater than 0 indicates that the model has predictive capability (Chin, 1998). The obtained values, 0.807 for AI and 0.750 for BP, significantly exceed this threshold, confirming the utility of the studied models for predicting the endogenous variables. Furthermore, the R^2 values for AI (0.816) and for BP (0.874) are considered very strong, suggesting that the model explains a large part of the variance of the endogenous constructs. These results are consistent with the statements of (Hair et al., 2017), who indicate that R^2 values of 0.75, 0.50, and 0.25 can be understood respectively as significant, moderate, and minimal. Therefore, the values reported here suggest a substantial influence of the predictive variables on AI and BP. However, it is important to note, as (Henseler et al., 2009b) do, that while high R^2 values are indicative of a good model fit, they do not guarantee that the model is correctly specified. A high R^2 value should be interpreted with caution and not seen as a definitive validation of the underlying theory. The Q^2 and R^2 values obtained in this study suggest that companies integrating AI into their operations can see a predictable improvement in their performance. This viewpoint is supported by the work of (Kaplan & Haenlein, 2019a), who highlight the potential of AI to improve strategic and operational decision-making. In the context of contemporary business, these results underscore the necessity for companies to adopt AI to remain competitive, a conclusion that is in harmony with the perspectives proposed by (Davenport & Ronanki, 2018) on the strategic impact of AI in business.

7. IMPLICATIONS, LIMITATIONS, AND FUTURE RESEARCH

The study reveals that artificial intelligence (AI) has become a central pillar of digital strategies, as supported by Davenport and Ronanki (2018), and suggests that companies should integrate AI to enhance their performance. However, the direct impact of digital marketing (DM) on business performance (BP) is called into question and requires further analysis, in line with (Verhoef et al., 2021) who advocate for a more strategic integration of DM.

The current research has limitations, notably the low representativeness of the sample of Moroccan companies surveyed, which could affect the generalizability of the findings. Despite a robust statistical method and a good response rate, a more comprehensive study would be beneficial for a more complete overview across Morocco.

Future research should explore the reciprocal influence of DM and AI on BP, as well as potential moderating or mediating variables. It is crucial for practitioners to reevaluate the allocation of resources to DM to optimize the capabilities of AI. The findings also encourage the integration of AI into business processes, which could significantly advance our knowledge on the interaction between technology and organizational performance.

In summary, decision-makers should view AI not only as an operational tool but also as a lever for strategic transformation to convert digital marketing efforts into measurable success. These implications align with current trends, suggesting a proactive approach for businesses aiming to remain competitive in an evolving digital landscape.

8. CONCLUSION

This study has illuminated the complex and strategic relationship between digital marketing (DM), artificial intelligence (AI), and business performance (BP). It confirms the reliability and validity of the measures used, thus demonstrating strong internal consistency and convergent validity for the constructs AI, BP, and DM.

The analysis reveals that, although digital marketing alone does not guarantee a direct improvement in business performance, its integration with AI can indirectly enhance it through an improvement in AI capabilities. This finding underscores the importance of an integrated and strategic approach in utilizing DM and AI to bolster competitiveness and performance.

The results also suggest that the boundaries between AI, DM, and business performance are becoming blurred, indicating an increasing interdependence among these domains in the digital era. This calls for companies to embrace technological evolution and adapt their strategies to maximize their impact on performance.

In conclusion, this study highlights the critical role of AI in optimizing the effectiveness of digital marketing and in enhancing business performance. It invites thorough reflection on the integration of these technologies and proposes directions for future research on their effective use in the contemporary business context.

REFERENCES

Aggarwal, R. (2017). *Different Avenues of Capital Market (Secondary Market) Available for Investing in Market of Yamuna Nagar.* International Research Journal of Management, IT and Social Sciences. 10.21744/irjmis.v4i3.456

Ahmad, S., Abu Bakar, A. R., & Ahmad, N. (2018). Social media adoption and its impact on firm performance: The case of the UAE. *International Journal of Entrepreneurial Behaviour & Research*, 25(1), 84–111. 10.1108/IJEBR-08-2017-0299

Aisjah, S., Arsawan, I. W. E., & Suhartanto, D. (2023). Predicting SME's business performance: Integrating stakeholder theory and performance based innovation model. *Journal of Open Innovation*, 9(3), 100122. 10.1016/j.joitmc.2023.100122

Al Khaldy, M. (2023). *The Impact of Predictive Analytics and AI on Digital Marketing Strategy and ROI.* AME.

Alla, L. (2023). *Big data et efficacité marketing des entreprises touristiques : Une revue de littérature.* AME. 10.48374/IMIST.PRSM/ame-v1i0.36928

Anh, P. T. L., Hung, D. N., & Xuan, N. T. (2024). The Impact of Capital Structure on Business Performance of Vietnamese Enterprises During the Covid 19 Pandemic. *Journal of Logistics. Informatics and Service Science*, 11(1), 22–35. 10.33168/JLISS.2024.0102

Anwar, M., & Shah, S. Z. A. (2021). Entrepreneurial orientation and generic competitive strategies for emerging SMEs: Financial and nonfinancial performance perspective. *Journal of Public Affairs*, 21(1), e2125. 10.1002/pa.2125

Badghish, S., & Soomro, Y. A. (2024). Artificial Intelligence Adoption by SMEs to Achieve Sustainable Business Performance: Application of Technology–Organization–Environment Framework. *Sustainability (Basel)*, 16(5), 1864. 10.3390/su16051864

Baka, V. (2016). The becoming of user-generated reviews: Looking at the past to understand the future of managing reputation in the travel sector. *Tourism Management*, 53, 148–162. 10.1016/j.tourman.2015.09.004

Boone, H. N., & Boone, D. A. (2012). Analyzing Likert Data. *Journal of Extension*, 50(2). 10.34068/joe.50.02.48

Bouhtati, N., Alla, L., & Bentalha, B. (2023). Marketing Big Data Analytics and Customer Relationship Management: A Fuzzy Approach. In *Integrating Intelligence and Sustainability in Supply Chains.* 10.4018/979-8-3693-0225-5.ch004

Bouhtati, N., Kamal, M., & Alla, L. (2023). Big Data and the Effectiveness of Tourism Marketing: A Prospective Review of the Literature. Springer. 10.1007/978-3-031-26254-8_40

Brynjolfsson, E., & Mcafee, A. (2017). The-Business-of-Artificial-Intelligence. *Harvard Business Review*, 7, 3–11.

Chaffey, D., & Ellis-Chadwick, F. (2019). *Digital Marketing* (7th ed.).

Chaffey, D., & Patron, M. (2012). From web analytics to digital marketing optimization: Increasing the commercial value of digital analytics. *Journal of Direct, Data and Digital Marketing Practice*, 14(1), 30–45. 10.1057/dddmp.2012.20

Chaikovska, M., Järvis, M., Zaiachkovska, H., Tchon, L., Bortnik, N., & Bannikova, K. (2022). DIGITAL-MARKETING AS A NOVEL TOOL FOR GOODS AND SERVICES PROMOTION ON SOCIAL MEDIA: CONTEMPORARY TRENDS AND DEVELOPMENT DIRECTIONS. *Financial and Credit Activity: Problems of Theory and Practice*, 4(45), 355–364. 10.55643/fcaptp.4.45.2022.3836

Chan-Olmsted, S. (2019). A Review of Artificial Intelligence Adoptions in the Media Industry. *International Journal on Media Management*, 21, 1–23. 10.1080/14241277.2019.1590949

Chan-Olmsted, S. M. (2019). A Review of Artificial Intelligence Adoptions in the Media Industry. *JMM International Journal on Media Management*, 21(3–4), 193–215. 10.1080/14241277.2019.1695619

Chi, H., Vu, T.-V., Nguyen, H. V., & Truong, T. (2023). How financial and non–financial rewards moderate the relationships between transformational leadership, job satisfaction, and job performance. *Cogent Business & Management*, 10(1), 2173850. Advance online publication. 10.1080/23311975.2023.2173850

Chin, W. (1998). The Partial Least Squares Approach to Structural Equation Modeling. *Modern Methods for Business Research, 8.*

Christian, I., Anene, J., Ewuzie, C., & Iloka, C. (2023). Influence Of Artificial Intelligence (AI) On Customer Experience And Loyalty: Mediating Role Of Personalization. *Shu Ju Cai Ji Yu Chu Li/Journal of Data Acquisition and Processing, 38*, 1936–1960. https://doi.org/10.5281/zenodo.98549423

Collins, C., Dennehy, D., Conboy, K., & Mikalef, P. (2021). Artificial intelligence in information systems research: A systematic literature review and research agenda. *International Journal of Information Management*, 60, 102383. 10.1016/j.ijinfomgt.2021.102383

Davenport, T. H., & Ronanki, R. (2018). *Artificial Intelligence for the Real World. Harvard Business Review*. HBR.

Day, G. (2011). Closing the Marketing Capabilities Gap. *Journal of Marketing*, 75(4), 183–195. 10.1509/jmkg.75.4.183

De Bruyn, A., Viswanathan, V., Beh, Y. S., Brock, J. K. U., & von Wangenheim, F. (2020). Artificial Intelligence and Marketing: Pitfalls and Opportunities. *Journal of Interactive Marketing*, 51, 91–105. 10.1016/j.intmar.2020.04.007

Devang, Chintan, Gunjan, & Krupa. (2019). *Applications of Artificial Intelligence in Marketing*. 10.35219/eai158404094

DeVellis, R. F. (2016). *Scale Development: Theory and Applications*. Sage.

Enshassi, M., Nathan, R. J., Soekmawati, S., Al-Mulali, U., & Ismail, H. (2024). Potentials of artificial intelligence in digital marketing and financial technology for small and medium enterprises. *IAES International Journal of Artificial Intelligence (IJ-AI), 13*(1), 639. 10.11591/ijai.v13.i1.pp639-647

Fornell, C., & Larcker, D. F. (1981). Evaluating Structural Equation Models with Unobservable Variables and Measurement Error. *JMR, Journal of Marketing Research*, 18(1), 39–50. 10.1177/002224378101800104

Franke, G. R., & Sarstedt, M. (2019). Heuristics versus statistics in discriminant validity testing: A comparison of four procedures. *Internet Research*, 29(3), 430–447. https://api.semanticscholar.org/CorpusID:86723268. 10.1108/IntR-12-2017-0515

Garg, M., & Bansal, A. (2020). *Impact of Digital Marketing on Consumer Decision Making*. Research Gate.

Hair, J., Black, W., Babin, B., & Anderson, R. (2010). *Multivariate Data Analysis: A Global Perspective*. Research Gate.

Hair, J., Hollingsworth, C. L., Randolph, A. B., & Chong, A. Y. L. (2017). An updated and expanded assessment of PLS-SEM in information systems research. *Industrial Management & Data Systems*, 117(3), 442–458. 10.1108/IMDS-04-2016-0130

Hair, J. F., Hult, G. T. M., Ringle, C. M., & Sarstedt, M. (2016). *A primer on partial least squares structural equation modeling (PLS-SEM)*.

Haleem, A., Javaid, M., Qadri, M., & Suman, R. (2022). Understanding the Role of Digital Technologies in Education: A review. *Sustainable Operations and Computers*, 3, 275–285. 10.1016/j.susoc.2022.05.004

Henseler, J., Hubona, G., & Ray, P. A. (2016). Using PLS path modeling in new technology research: Updated guidelines. *Industrial Management & Data Systems*, 116(1), 2–20. 10.1108/IMDS-09-2015-0382

Henseler, J., Ringle, C., & Sarstedt, M. (2015). A New Criterion for Assessing Discriminant Validity in Variance-based Structural Equation Modeling. *Journal of the Academy of Marketing Science*, 43(1), 115–135. 10.1007/s11747-014-0403-8

Henseler, J., Ringle, C. M., & Sinkovics, R. R. (2009a). The use of partial least squares path modeling in international marketing. *Advances in International Marketing*, 20, 277–319. 10.1108/S1474-7979(2009)0000020014

Henseler, J., Ringle, C. M., & Sinkovics, R. R. (2009b). The use of partial least squares path modeling in international marketing. *Advances in International Marketing*, 20, 277–319. 10.1108/S1474-7979(2009)0000020014

Hollebeek, L., & Macky, K. (2019). Digital Content Marketing's Role in Fostering Consumer Engagement, Trust, and Value: Framework, Fundamental Propositions, and Implications. *Journal of Interactive Marketing*, 45, 27–41. 10.1016/j.intmar.2018.07.003

Huang, M. H., & Rust, R. T. (2018). Artificial Intelligence in Service. *Journal of Service Research*, 21(2), 155–172. 10.1177/1094670517752459

Huang, R., & Sarigöllü, E. (2012). How brand awareness relates to market outcome, brand equity, and the marketing mix. *Journal of Business Research*, 65(1), 92–99. 10.1016/j.jbusres.2011.02.00332287525

Hurwitz, K. & Bowles, N. (2015). *Cognitive Computing and Big Data Analytics*. Wiley Online Library.

Jung, S. U., & Shegai, V. (2023). The Impact of Digital Marketing Innovation on Firm Performance: Mediation by Marketing Capability and Moderation by Firm Size. *Sustainability (Basel)*, 15(7), 5711. 10.3390/su15075711

Kannan, P. K., & Li, H. (2017). Digital marketing: A framework, review and research agenda. *International Journal of Research in Marketing*, 34(1), 22–45. 10.1016/j.ijresmar.2016.11.006

Kaplan, A., & Haenlein, M. (2019a). Rulers of the world, unite! The challenges and opportunities of artificial intelligence. *Business Horizons*, 63(1), 37–50. 10.1016/j.bushor.2019.09.003

Kaplan, A., & Haenlein, M. (2019b). Siri, Siri, in my hand: Who's the fairest in the land? On the interpretations, illustrations, and implications of artificial intelligence. In *Business Horizons* (*Vol. 62*, Issue 1, pp. 15–25). Elsevier Ltd. 10.1016/j.bushor.2018.08.004

Kaplan, A. M., & Haenlein, M. (2010). Users of the world, unite! The challenges and opportunities of Social Media. *Business Horizons*, 53(1), 59–68. https://doi.org/https://doi.org/10.1016/j.bushor.2009.09.003. 10.1016/j.bushor.2009.09.003

Kaur, G. (2017). The Importance Of Digital Marketing In The Tourism Industry. *International Journal of Research -GRANTHAALAYAH, 5*, 72–77. 10.29121/granthaalayah.v5.i6.2017.1998

Kiili, K., Ojansuu, K., Lindstedt, A., & Ninaus, M. (2018). Exploring the Educational Potential of a Game-Based Math Competition. *International Journal of Game-Based Learning*, 8(2), 14–28. 10.4018/IJGBL.2018040102

Krejcie, R. V., & Morgan, D. W. (1970). Determining Sample Size for Research Activities. *Educational and Psychological Measurement*, 30(3), 607–610. 10.1177/001316447003000308

Kumar, V., Rajan, B., Gupta, S., & Pozza, I. D. (2019). Customer engagement in service. *Journal of the Academy of Marketing Science*, 47(1), 138–160. 10.1007/s11747-017-0565-2

Lee, M. T., & Suh, I. (2022). Understanding the effects of Environment, Social, and Governance conduct on financial performance: Arguments for a process and integrated modelling approach. *Sustainable Technology and Entrepreneurship, 1*(1), 100004.

Li, M., Yin, D., Qiu, H., & Bai, B. (2021). A systematic review of AI technology-based service encounters: Implications for hospitality and tourism operations. *International Journal of Hospitality Management*, 95, 102930. 10.1016/j.ijhm.2021.102930

Morgan, N., Slotegraaf, R., & Vorhies, D (2009). Linking Marketing Capabilities with Profit Growth. *International Journal of Research in Marketing*, 26(4), 284–293. 10.1016/j.ijresmar.2009.06.005

Morgan, N. A. (2012). Marketing and business performance. *Journal of the Academy of Marketing Science*, 40(1), 102–119. 10.1007/s11747-011-0279-9

Nunnally, J. C., & Bernstein, I. H. (1994). The Assessment of Reliability. *Psychometric Theory*, 3, 248–292.

Nuseir, M., & Al. (2018). Digital media impact on smes performance in the UAE. Volume 24, Issue 2, 2018. *Academy of Entrepreneurship Journal*, 24, 1–13.

Omotosho, B. (2020). Small scale craft workers and the use of social media platforms for business performance in southwest Nigeria. *Journal of Small Business and Entrepreneurship*, 35(2), 1–16. 10.1080/08276331.2020.1764732

Pereira, L., Tomás, D., Dias, Á., d, R. L., Costa, , & Gonçalves, R. (2023). How artificial intelligence can improve digital marketing. *International Journal of Business Information Systems*, 44(4), 581–624. 10.1504/IJBIS.2023.135351

Priyanga, G. (2023). THE EFFECTS OF ARTIFICIAL INTELLIGENCE ON DIGITAL MARKETING. *ShodhKosh: Journal of Visual and Performing Arts*, 4(1SE). 10.29121/shodhkosh.v4.i1SE.2023.431

Ravi, S., & Rajasekaran, S. R. C. (2023). A PERSPECTIVE OF DIGITAL MARKETING IN RURAL AREAS: A LITERATURE REVIEW. *International Journal of Professional Business Review*, 8(4), e01388. 10.26668/businessreview/2023.v8i4.1388

Reza Kiani, G. (1998). Marketing opportunities in the digital world. *Internet Research*, 8(2), 185–194. 10.1108/10662249810211656

Sahoo, S., Kumar, S., Donthu, N., & Singh, A. (2023). Artificial intelligence capabilities, open innovation, and business performance -Empirical insights from multinational B2B companies. *Industrial Marketing Management*, 171, 28–41. 10.1016/j.indmarman.2023.12.008

Sarath Kumar Boddu, R., Santoki, A. A., Khurana, S., Vitthal Koli, P., Rai, R., & Agrawal, A. (2022). An analysis to understand the role of machine learning, robotics and artificial intelligence in digital marketing. *Materials Today: Proceedings*, 56, 2288–2292. 10.1016/j.matpr.2021.11.637

Sarkees, M., Hulland, J., & Prescott, J. (2010). Ambidextrous organizations and firm performance: The role of marketing function implementation. *Journal of Strategic Marketing*, 18(2), 165–184. 10.1080/09652540903536982

Sawicki, A. (2016). Digital Marketing. *World Scientific News*, 48, 82–88.

Sekaran, U., & Bougie, R. (2014). *Research Methods for Business: A Skill-Building Approach* (6th ed.).

Singh, S., Singh, G., & Dhir, S. (2022). Impact of digital marketing on the competitiveness of the restaurant industry. *Journal of Foodservice Business Research*. Advance online publication. 10.1080/15378020.2022.2077088

Strauss, J., & Frost, R. (2014). *E-Marketing* (7th ed.). Routledge.

Sujová, A., & Simanová, Ľ. (2023). IMPACTS OF IMPLEMENTED CHANGES ON BUSINESS PERFORMANCE OF SLOVAK ENTERPRISES. *Central European Business Review*, 12(3), 103–122. 10.18267/j.cebr.328

Suryantini, N. P. S. (2023). THE SUSTAINABLE COMPETITIVE ADVANTAGE OF SMES TOWARDS INTELLECTUAL CAPITAL: THE ROLE OF TECHNOLOGY ADOPTION AND STRATEGIC FLEXIBILITY. *Intellectual Economics*, 17(1), 30–56. 10.13165/IE-23-17-1-02

Taiminen, H., & Karjaluoto, H. (2015). The usage of digital marketing channels in SMEs. *Journal of Small Business and Enterprise Development*, 22(4), 633–651. Advance online publication. 10.1108/JSBED-05-2013-0073

Tao, X. X., & Zhang, D. P. (2021). Exploration and Practice of Talent Training Mode of Industry-Education Integration in Industrial College: Taking Big Data Industry College of Zhejiang University of Science and Technology as an Example. *Journal of Zhejiang University of Science and Technology*, 163-168.

Teixeira, S., Barbosa, B., & Pinto, H. (2019). *How Do Entrepreneurs See Digital Marketing?* Evidence From Portugal. 10.4018/978-1-5225-6942-8.ch001

Van Esch, P., Black, S., & Ferolie, J. (2018). Marketing AI recruitment: The next phase in job application and selection. *Computers in Human Behavior*, 90, 215–222. 10.1016/j.chb.2018.09.009

Verhoef, P. C., Broekhuizen, T., Bart, Y., Bhattacharya, A., & Dong, Q. J., Fabian, N., & Haenlein, M. (2021). Digital transformation: A multidisciplinary reflection and research agenda. *Journal of Business Research, 122*, 889–901.

Voorhees, C., Brady, M., Calantone, R., & Ramirez, E. (2015). Discriminant Validity Testing in Marketing: An Analysis, Causes for Concern, and Proposed Remedies. *Journal of the Academy of Marketing Science*, 44(1), 1–16. 10.1007/s11747-015-0455-4

Wamba-Taguimdje, S.-L., Fosso Wamba, S., Jean Robert, K. K., & Tchatchouang, C. E. (2020). *Influence of Artificial Intelligence (AI) on Firm Performance: The Business Value of AI-based Transformation Projects.*

Wu, C.-W., & Monfort, A. (2022). Role of artificial intelligence in marketing strategies and performance. *Psychology and Marketing.*

Yang, P., Hao, X., Wang, L., Zhang, S., & Yang, L. (2024). Moving toward sustainable development: The influence of digital transformation on corporate ESG performance. *Kybernetes*, 53(2), 669–687. 10.1108/K-03-2023-0521

Zaragoza-Sáez, P., Claver-Cortés, E., Marco-Lajara, B., & Úbeda-García, M. (2020). Corporate social responsibility and strategic knowledge management as mediators between sustainable intangible capital and hotel performance. *Journal of Sustainable Tourism*, 31(4), 1–23. 10.1080/09669582.2020.1811289

Zhezha, V., Kola, B., & Melinceanu, A. M. (2023). Exploring the Landscape of Digital Marketing in Albania: Insights from Local Companies. *Academic Journal of Interdisciplinary Studies*, 12(4), 341–353. 10.36941/ajis-2023-0120

Ziakis, C., & Vlachopoulou, M. (2023). Artificial Intelligence in Digital Marketing: Insights from a Comprehensive Review. *Information (Basel)*, 14(12), 664. 10.3390/info14120664

Chapter 13
Big Data and Consumer Behavior:
A Quantitative Study Among Moroccan Internet Users

Youssra Lazrak
Sidi Mohamed Ben Abdellah University, Morocco

Ouijdane Amrani
High School of Technology of Fez, Sidi Mohamed Ben Abdellah University, Morocco

Amina El Idrissi Tissafi
High School of Technology of Fez, Sidi Mohamed Ben Abdellah University, Morocco

ABSTRACT

This study investigates the impact of big data on online consumer satisfaction and purchasing behavior within the Moroccan context, addressing the gap in understanding its effects on consumer satisfaction in specific markets. Through a quantitative analysis, the authors explore how big data's application in personalized marketing strategies influences consumer behaviors and satisfaction. The research reveals the critical role of product quality and personalized recommendations in enhancing online consumer satisfaction, despite the general assumption of price as a primary factor. These findings suggest that big data, while potent in tailoring marketing efforts, shows varied significance in directly influencing consumer satisfaction levels in Morocco. The study contributes to the digital marketing literature by providing insights into the strategic application of big data in enhancing consumer engagement and satisfaction, offering managerial implications for leveraging technology in marketing strategies.

1. INTRODUCTION

In the current digital era, Big Data has become a fundamental accelerator of transformation across many fields, notably in marketing (Brewis et al., 2023a; Cadden et al., 2023) and understanding online consumer behavior (Chou et al., 2022; Liu, 2021). The ability to collect, analyze, and decipher vast data sets has provided organizations with deep insights into consumption habits trends (Kauffmann

DOI: 10.4018/979-8-3693-3172-9.ch013

et al., 2020; Wang et al., 2020), expectations, and strategic purchasing decisions (Akram et al., 2022), allowing them to adjust their marketing strategies more effectively (Chou et al., 2022). However, despite numerous studies on Big Data in marketing (Brewis et al., 2023a; Chou et al., 2022), several questions remain unanswered, particularly regarding its impact on satisfaction and online purchasing behavior under specific circumstances, such as the technologically evolving Moroccan market.

Morocco, with its progressive integration of digital and technological tools and an increasingly interconnected population, becomes a conducive environment to study how Big Data can impact online satisfaction and purchasing behavior. Previous studies (Roy et al., 2020; Salonen et al., 2024) highlight that Big Data, by adjusting and personalizing marketing strategies, has the potential to significantly improve consumer behavior and satisfaction. Yet, the extent of these effects in the Moroccan context remains largely unanalyzed.

This observation highlights the importance of examining the impact of Big Data on online satisfaction and purchasing behavior in the Moroccan context. The existing literature broadly addresses the technical aspects and benefits of Big Data for businesses, but there is a lack of in-depth research on consumer perceptions, their reaction to personalized recommendations, and how these elements influence their online purchasing decision. Consequently, a quantitative study will be undertaken to provide an updated status on the influence of Big Data on online purchasing behaviors, with a focus on the Moroccan market. This study aims to elucidate the impact of Big Data analytics on customer satisfaction within the rapidly digitizing market of Morocco, a context that remains underexplored despite its potential insights into consumer behavior. By focusing on this specific geographical and digital milieu, the research seeks to bridge the gap between the extensive capabilities of Big Data and the actual enhancement of consumer satisfaction, forming a coherent narrative that examines both the benefits and challenges posed by Big Data in a uniquely evolving market. This study will also aim to analyze how Big Data can enhance marketing personalization and, consequently, positively influence consumer behaviors and satisfaction. Moreover, it will identify sectors requiring future research for a deeper understanding of these mechanisms.

Our article will begin with a literature review addressing the general concepts of Big Data. Next, we will examine the correlation between Big Data, satisfaction, and consumer behaviors. In the second part, we will present the adopted methodology, specifying the study context as well as the data collection and analysis processes. Thirdly, we will discuss the results and discussions of previous studies, highlighting the findings obtained. Finally, we will conclude by synthesizing the results of our study, the theoretical and managerial contributions, encountered limitations, and future research directions.

2. LITERATURE REVIEW

2.1. Big Data Analysis

The landscape of Big Data is constantly expanding, now encompassing vast quantities of data (Xiao et al., 2023). To navigate and extract value from this colossal amount of data, companies are increasingly focusing on advanced Big Data Analysis (BDA) (Cadden et al., 2023; Saidali et al., 2019). This data analysis concept focuses on harvesting relevant insights by understanding the complexity of relationships among multiple data indicators. BDA has become a fundamental factor in data science(Bouhtati, Alla, et al., 2023), offering substantial improvements in the overall performance of organizations. The concept of Big Data has seen notable expansion over time. It is crucial in managing the intricacies of systems, affirming their credibility, and enhancing their content and abilities to adapt to a changing and dynamic global commercial landscape (Feng et al., 2024; Gao et al., 2023). The importance of BDA extends even further in the field of strategic planning, allowing organizations to identify potential risks and opportunities, thereby promoting a more agile approach to their operations (Brewis et al., 2023a; Mukhopadhyay et al., 2024). In the realm of marketing, the impact of BDA is more profound (Brewis et al., 2023b; Mukhopadhyay et al., 2024). It enables companies to precisely detect and understand consumer behavior (Filieri et al., 2023), to personalize messages to meet specific consumer needs, increase customer loyalty, and efficiently assess the return on investment of marketing strategies (Caracciolo et al., 2022).

Table 1. Diverse perspectives on big data analytics

Authors Definitions	
(Kutaula et al., 2022; Matz & Netzer, 2017)	Big Data Analytics enables the illumination of trends, identification of associations, and subtle patterns within vast data sets.
(Safi, 2022)	The analysis of large quantities of varied data within the context of Big Data aims to generate useful insights and relevant predictions.
(Khan & Abbas, 2023)	Big Data exploration focuses on the exploitation of large amounts of varied and high-velocity data to extract value, often in real-time.
(Filieri et al., 2023)	Big Data analysis improves decision-making by using voluminous and complex information that was previously inaccessible or underutilized.
(Xiao et al., 2023)	Through Big Data analysis, companies can detect weak signals and predict trends well before they become apparent to their competitors.

Source: Created by us.

Beyond its practical applications, Big Data Analytics (BDA) has become a central factor in the strategic development of businesses. It aids organizations in identifying opportunities (Feng et al., 2024), developing advanced models to foster growth (Rammer & Es-Sadki, 2023). The incorporation of digital development, guidance, and human expertise through BDA highlights the importance of an approach based on innovation, management of human skill, strategic management, leadership, and optimal organizational approaches. This complete integration goes beyond merely enhancing business performance but also enables the cultivation of a culture conducive to a sustainable competitive advantage (Cheng & Shiu, 2023). In essence, Big Data analysis is not only about data management; it is based on innovation, efficiency, and strategic growth in the modern commercial ecosystem. Its impact on improving system performance, market understanding, and strategic adaptability highlights its crucial role as a transformation tool for companies operating in the complexities of the contemporary global market (Gao et al., 2023; Mariani et al., 2023).

2.2. Big Data Analysis on Consumer Satisfaction and Behavior

The advent of Big Data has profoundly altered the landscape of consumer behavior analysis (Chen & Peng, 2023; Xiao et al., 2023). This transformation has generated unprecedented opportunities and major challenges for businesses worldwide (Chen & Peng, 2023; Sameeni et al., 2024). At the heart of this revolution is Big Data's ability to manage and analyze huge volumes of varied and complex data, stemming from consumer interactions in the digital realm (Xue et al., 2022). This capability is crucial for identifying patterns, choices, and complex trends among consumers, thereby facilitating more enlightened strategic decision-making aimed at optimizing customer engagement and satisfaction (Li et al., 2023). Integrating this concept into consumer behavior analysis ushers in a new era of personalized marketing, increased customer satisfaction, and strategic business innovation (Gao et al., 2023; Saidali et al., 2019), demanding ongoing research to address its challenges and benefit from a diversity of perspectives(Lhoussaine et al., 2022).

Big Data analysis, defined as the process of examining varied data sets to uncover hidden patterns and concepts, unknown correlations, customer preferences, and other useful information, enables organizations to make more appropriate business decisions (Brewis et al., 2023b; Cadden et al., 2023). This diagnosis is essential for understanding consumer behavior, based on the study of individuals, groups, or organizations and the processes they use to select, secure, and dispose of products, services, experiences, or ideas to satisfy needs and the impacts of these processes on the consumer and society (Tseng et al., 2022). However, implementing Big Data comes with certain challenges, including concerns about data privacy (Gao et al., 2023; Kenza et al., 2023). Furthermore, the specialized analytical skills required, such as the ability to collect, visualize, and analyze information in detail, are essential for navigating the complexities of unstructured data (Feng et al., 2024). Despite these obstacles, the potential benefits of Big Data to anticipate and influence consumer behavior are considerable (Mukhopadhyay et al., 2024; Tseng et al., 2022). As Big Data continues to evolve, its role in understanding and influencing consumer behavior will only grow, underscoring the importance for businesses to adopt these technologies and develop the necessary skills to use them effectively(Bouhtati, Kamal, et al., 2023).

Digital transformation and predictive analysis disrupt marketing strategies, enabling businesses to examine and anticipate future trends, customer behaviors, and market demands (Caracciolo et al., 2022). This technological evolution allows marketing experts to adjust their strategies more effectively, optimize resources, and improve long-term customer satisfaction. Predictive analysis, enhanced by AI and machine learning algorithms, plays a fundamental role in digital marketing by analyzing historical data and identifying patterns to predict future events (Cadden et al., 2023; Du & Lin, 2022).

This approach benefits businesses in several ways, including analyzing customer behavior, optimizing resources, and improving customer retention strategies (Marković et al., 2010). By understanding how consumers interact with products and services, businesses can accurately segment their target audience, preempt their behaviors, and adjust their marketing efforts to enhance performance (Brewis et al., 2023b). The benefits of predictive analysis based on Big Data are multiple (Agag et al., 2024). Firstly, it allows refining content distribution by analyzing how market targets interact with content, thereby enabling marketers to offer tailored suggestions (Hsu et al., 2024). Secondly, this analysis highlights behavior-based selling methods, refines marketing campaigns, and aids in proposing more effective advertising strategies. By leveraging these various solutions, businesses can gain a competitive edge, improve their return on investment (Sukier et al., 2024), and ensure that every step of the customer journey is optimized (Alghamdi & Agag, 2024).

Moreover, the assimilation of marketing analysis dashboards represents a significant trend in the use of Big Data (Sorour & Atkins, 2024). This technique allows businesses to strengthen data from various sources, visualize performance measures, and analyze performance indicators to ensure better customer satisfaction. These tools are also crucial for more optimal planning and execution of marketing strategies. The literature review has been expanded to include a focused examination of recent studies that specifically address the intersection of Big Data and customer satisfaction. This segment now highlights critical findings from contemporary research, identifies prevailing gaps, and delineates the theoretical underpinnings that support the necessity of our study, particularly in the context of an emerging digital economy like Morocco's. To better understand the nature of Big Data exploitation for conducting predictive analyses aimed at anticipating consumer demands in a constantly evolving digital environment, we could formulate our hypotheses as follows:

H1. Big Data analysis enabling the personalization of marketing strategies leads to an improvement in consumer behavior in Morocco.

H2. The quality, price, and personalization of recommendations through Big Data significantly impact Moroccan consumer satisfaction.

Figure 1. Conceptual model

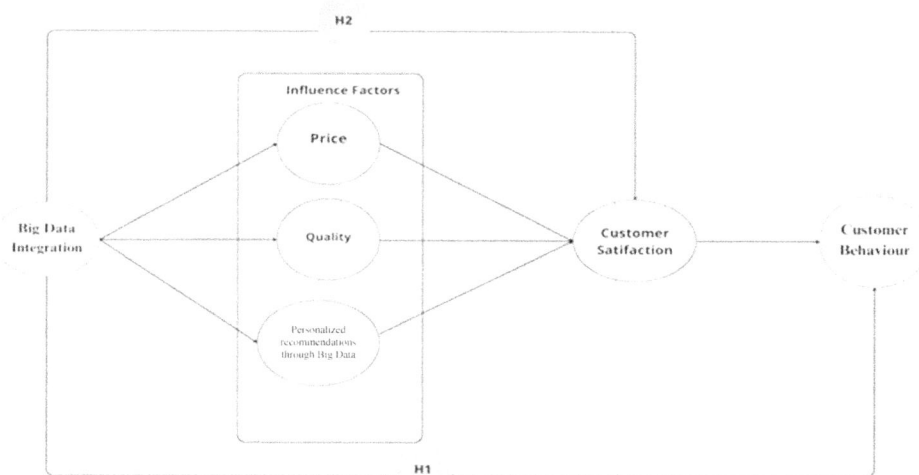

Source: Created by us

The assumptions underlying our study are clearly outlined, including the premise that Big Data analytics is applied uniformly across different industries in Morocco. These assumptions are justified by referencing the prevalent trends of digital transformation in Moroccan enterprises, as reported in recent industrial surveys, which suggest a standardized approach to digital integration and data analytics across sectors.

3. METHODOLOGY

3.1. Study Context

Morocco is experiencing a boom in the field of Big Data, with growing interest from a multitude of stakeholders. The IRES[1], in its 2017 report on Digital Transformation and the Maturity of Moroccan Companies and Administrations, recognized Big Data as one of the most promising technological and organizational trends for the country. This acknowledgment highlights the potential of Big Data to influence various aspects of Moroccan society, including consumer behavior.

3.2. Data Collection

The empirical context of this study is meticulously described, focusing on the digital consumption environments prevalent in urban and semi-urban Morocco. Data were primarily collected from online platforms that cater to a diverse demographic, providing a comprehensive backdrop against which the impacts of Big Data on consumer satisfaction are investigated.

To better understand the purchasing habits of Moroccan internet consumers in the context of Big Data, we conducted a survey by distributing a questionnaire. This study resulted in the collection of 136 responses, thus constituting the database upon which our analysis is based. The raw data were initially entered using Excel spreadsheet software, while the coded data were recorded in the SPSS software for subsequent processing and analysis. As part of our methodology, we paid special attention to the use of various variables to capture the different dimensions of Moroccan internet consumers' purchasing behavior. These variables were carefully selected to reflect the different aspects that might influence online purchasing decisions, such as product preferences, purchasing habits, and payment preferences.

Once the data were collected and processed, we performed a descriptive analysis to examine the fundamental characteristics of the data (Apaza-Panca et al., 2024). Furthermore, we used cross-tabulations to study the relationships between variables and identify any significant associations. The cross-tabulations allowed us to explore the interactions between different categories of variables, thus revealing hidden trends and patterns in the data (Oladipo et al., 2021). This approach enabled us to go beyond the mere description of variables to examine the relationships between them in depth. This manuscript details the stratified random sampling technique employed to ensure a representative cross-section of Moroccan internet users, thus enhancing the reliability of our findings. The sample size of 136 respondents was determined based on a power analysis, which ensures sufficient statistical power to detect a significant effect of Big Data applications on customer satisfaction.

3.3. Data Analysis

In our analysis, we adopted a quantitative method. This method allowed us to statistically study the essential characteristics of the data, revealing trends and relationships between variables (Van Looy, 2021). Guided by this approach, we then carefully selected a set of relevant variables, representing various aspects influencing online purchasing choices. We particularly focused our study on analyzing the variables in relation to the main variable, which is consumer satisfaction, to better understand the factors that influence this crucial parameter in the online purchasing process.

Table 2. Variable descriptions

Variables	Description
Consumer Satisfaction	This variable has two distinct modalities: "satisfied" and "not satisfied". It is crucial for our study as it allows us to evaluate the influence of different factors on the satisfaction of Moroccan consumers during their online purchases.
Price of Products and Services	Rated on a scale of 1 to 4, this variable measures the importance given by consumers to price during their online purchases. Our study focuses on exploring the link between this variable and the degree of consumer satisfaction.
Quality of Products and Services	Rated on a scale of 1 to 4, this variable allows understanding to what extent perceived quality influences consumers' purchasing decisions.
Personalization of Recommendations through Big Data	Rated on a scale from "Not at all" to "Extremely", this variable evaluates to what extent personalized recommendations influence the satisfaction of internet consumers.

Source: Created by us.

In our analytical model, customer satisfaction is positioned as a pivotal outcome variable influenced by the extent of Big Data analytics' application. This relationship is explored through a quantitative analysis where customer satisfaction is measured directly from consumer responses, thereby assessing the effectiveness of Big Data-driven personalization and its subsequent impact on consumer perceptions and behaviors. This integration allows for a detailed examination of how Big Data can transform consumer interactions and satisfaction levels.

The variable "Consumer Internet Satisfaction" is a central element in our analysis of online purchasing behavior. It allows us to assess the influence of different factors on the satisfaction of Moroccan consumers during their online purchases. By examining the responses of participants through this variable, an identification of the elements that contribute to consumer satisfaction as well as those that could potentially leave them dissatisfied will be carried out.

Consider the important role of the "Price of Products and Services" variable in our analysis. Our study focuses on exploring the link between this variable and the level of consumer satisfaction. By carefully analyzing participant responses, we seek to understand how price influences overall satisfaction.

Furthermore, the "Quality of Products and Services" variable assesses Moroccan consumers' perception of the quality of products and services during their online purchases. Our research aims to determine if this variable has a significant impact on internet consumer satisfaction. By exploring the link between the perception of product and service quality and the level of consumer satisfaction, we will be able to identify potential areas for improvement to ensure an optimal online shopping experience focused on the quality of the products and services offered.

Finally, the "Personalization of Recommendations through Big Data" variable is fundamental as it sheds light on the impact of personalized recommendations on the satisfaction of Moroccan consumers. It aims to understand whether the personalization of recommendations, made possible through Big Data technologies, significantly contributes to consumer satisfaction during their online purchases. By analyzing participant responses based on this variable, we will be able to determine the effectiveness of this approach and its impact on the shopping experience of consumers.

Each latent variable, including consumer satisfaction and the personalization of recommendations, is measured using ranging from 1 to 2. These scales were chosen for their ability to capture nuanced consumer perceptions and have been tested for reliability and validity in previous studies focusing on digital consumer behaviors.

4. RESULTS

The results of this study provide an overview of the conclusions drawn from our analysis on the online purchasing behaviors of Moroccan consumers. Through the methodological approach we followed, we analyzed various aspects influencing consumer satisfaction, with particular emphasis on key variables such as the quality of products and services, price, as well as the personalization of recommendations through Big Data, as previously presented. Here, we present the main findings of our research, highlighting the relationships, trends, and implications for companies in the Moroccan e-commerce sector.

To initiate this analysis, we will begin by examining the first variable, namely price. We will review the first contingency table that establishes the correlation between consumer satisfaction and the price factor.

Table 3. Cross-tabulation of consumer satisfaction and price

Crosstab			Recode.price				Total
			1(Less significant)	2	3	4 (More significant)	
Customer satisfaction	Satisfied	Count	6	10	19	38	73
		% within Customer satisfaction	8,2%	13,7%	26,0%	52,1%	100,0%
	Unsatisfied	Count	11	12	12	28	63
		% within Customer satisfaction	17,5%	19,0%	19,0%	44,4%	100,0%
Total		Count	17	22	31	66	136
		% within Customer satisfaction	12,5%	16,2%	22,8%	48,5%	100,0%

Source: Created by us.

This cross-tabulation highlights the correlation between customer satisfaction and the relevance of price in their online purchases. The columns represent the different levels of price relevance, ranging from "Less significant" to "More significant," while the rows represent the levels of customer satisfaction, whether they are "Satisfied" or "Not Satisfied." Among the 73 satisfied customers, 6 found the price "less important," 10 considered it "somewhat insignificant," 19 deemed it "moderately significant," and 38 viewed it as "very significant." Conversely, among the 63 dissatisfied customers, 17.5% found the price "less important," while 44.4% judged it "very significant." The proportion of 48.5% represents the share of all customers, whether they expressed satisfaction or not, who considered the prices as "very significant." This observation underscores that approximately half of the total sample places great importance on price during their online shopping experience.

To examine the relationship between these two variables, we conducted a Chi-square test, the results of which are presented in the table below:

Table 4. Chi-Square test to test the relationship between consumer satisfaction and the price variable

Chi-Square Tests			
	Value	**df**	**Asymptotic Significance (2-sided)**
Pearson Chi-Square	4,035[a]	3	,258
Likelihood Ratio	4,054	3	,256
Linear-by-Linear Association	2,907	1	,088
N of Valid Cases	136		

a. 0 cells (, 0%) have expected count less than 5. The minimum expected count is 7, 88.

Source: Created by us.

The Pearson Chi-Square statistic is 4.035 with 3 degrees of freedom. The associated p-value for this test is 0.258. These results indicate that there is no significant relationship between consumer satisfaction and price since the p-value is greater than 0.05. Moreover, this suggests that there is no significant link between consumer satisfaction and the level of price relevance in their online purchases. These findings could imply that, in this specific context, factors other than price have a greater influence on customer satisfaction. Therefore, companies can focus on other aspects of their offer, such as product quality, customer service, or the personalization of recommendations, to improve overall customer satisfaction and brand loyalty.

Let's now move to the second variable examined: the quality of products and services. The cross-tabulation, illustrating the relationship between online consumer satisfaction and quality, is presented as follows:

Table 5. Cross-tabulation of consumer satisfaction and quality

Crosstab							
			Recode.quality				**Total**
			1(Less significant)	2	3	4 (More significant)	
Customer satisfaction	**Satisfied**	Count	6	6	15	46	73
		% within Customer satisfaction	8,2%	8,2%	20,5%	63,0%	100,0%
	Unsatisfied	Count	14	5	21	23	63
		% within Customer satisfaction	22,2%	7,9%	33,3%	36,5%	100,0%
Total		Count	20	11	36	69	136
		% within Customer satisfaction	14,7%	8,1%	26,5%	50,7%	100,0%

Source: Created by us.

The proportion of 63% indicates the percentage of satisfied customers who found the quality of products and services to be "More significant." This suggests that nearly two-thirds of satisfied customers consider quality to be a very important aspect of their online shopping experience. We conducted a Chi-square test to analyze the correlation between the two variables, namely online consumer satisfaction and the quality of products and services. This test will allow us to determine if there is a significant relationship between these two aspects in the context of the online shopping experience.

Table 6. Chi-Square test to test the relationship between consumer satisfaction and the price variable

Chi-Square Tests			
	Value	**df**	**Asymptotic Significance (2-sided)**
Pearson Chi-Square	11,283[a]	3	,010
Likelihood Ratio	11,466	3	,009
Linear-by-Linear Association	8,518	1	,004
N of Valid Cases	136		

a. 0 cells (,0%) have expected count less than 5. The minimum expected count is 5,10.
Source: Created by us.

The Pearson Chi-Square statistic is 11.283 with 3 degrees of freedom. The p-value associated with this test is 0.010. This indicates that there is a significant relationship between online consumer satisfaction and the quality of products and services, as the p-value is below 0.05, which is considered the threshold for significance.

We also conducted the Phi test and Cramer's V coefficient to assess the strength and direction of the relationship between the two variables. Here are the results of the test:

Table 7. Phi and Cramer's V test

Symmetric Measures			
		Value	**Approximate Significance**
Nominal by Nominal	Phi	,288	,010
	Cramer's V	,288	,010
N of Valid Cases		136	

Source: Created by us.

The symmetric measures indicate that both the Phi coefficient and Cramer's V are 0.288, with an approximate significance value of 0.010. These results reveal a moderate relationship between online consumer satisfaction and the quality of products and services, highlighting a moderate but not weak correlation between these two variables.

These findings underscore the importance of paying special attention to the quality of products and services in the context of online activities. The moderate correlation between consumer satisfaction and product quality suggests that companies capable of maintaining or improving the quality of their offerings are more likely to see their customers satisfied. Thus, investing in the continuous improvement of product and service quality can help strengthen customer loyalty, enhance brand reputation, and ultimately, stimulate growth and profitability for the company. Furthermore, these results emphasize the importance of regularly collecting customer feedback on the quality of their online shopping experiences to identify areas for improvement and to meet changing consumer expectations.

Now moving on to the third variable examined in our study: personalized recommendations through Big Data. This variable assesses to what extent individualized recommendations provided to consumers, based on Big Data, influence their satisfaction during their online purchases. The presentation of the results of this analysis will be through the cross-tabulation.

Table 8. Cross-tabulation of consumer satisfaction and quality

Customer satisfaction * The personalized recommendations through Big Data Crosstabulation									
			The personalized recommendations through Big Data					Total
			A lot	Absolutely not	Extremely	Reasonably	Slightly	
Customer satisfaction	Satisfied	Count	20	4	4	28	17	73
		% within Customer satisfaction	27,4%	5,5%	5,5%	38,4%	23,3%	100,0%
	Unsatisfied	Count	15	6	2	17	23	63
		% within Customer satisfaction	23,8%	9,5%	3,2%	27,0%	36,5%	100,0%
Total		Count	35	10	6	45	40	136
		% within Customer satisfaction	25,7%	7,4%	4,4%	33,1%	29,4%	100,0%

Source: Created by us.

Upon examining the distribution of percentages, a relative uniformity is observed in the different categories of personalized recommendations for satisfied customers. However, for dissatisfied customers, a slight variation in percentages is noticeable, with a relatively higher proportion in the "somewhat" and "not at all" categories compared to other categories. These results suggest there could be a correlation between personalized recommendations through Big Data and online customer satisfaction. To verify this hypothesis, we will proceed with a Chi-square test.

Table 9. Chi-Square test to test the relationship between consumer satisfaction and personalized recommendations via big data

Chi-Square Tests			
	Value	df	Asymptotic Significance (2-sided)
Pearson Chi-Square	4,660[a]	4	,324
Likelihood Ratio	4,683	4	,321
Linear-by-Linear Association	,445	1	,505
N of Valid Cases	136		

a. 3 cells (30,0%) have expected count less than 5. The minimum expected count is 2,78.
Source: Created by us.

The Pearson Chi-square statistic to evaluate the relationship between personalized recommendations and online customer satisfaction yielded a result of 4.660 with 4 degrees of freedom, and an associated p-value of 0.324. This finding indicates that no significant relationship was observed between these variables, given that the p-value exceeds the usual significance threshold of 0.05. However, it is important to note that three cells in the cross-tabulation have an expected number of observations less than 5. While this may affect the reliability of the test results, the proportion of these cells relative to the entire table remains below the accepted limit of 20%. Therefore, despite this observation, the test results can still be considered valid to a certain extent.

5. DISCUSSION

The convergence of our study with current theoretical perspectives on the importance of Big Data analysis in improving consumer satisfaction and behavior underscores the impact of digital transformation on the development of current marketing strategies. Our analysis has illuminated revealing connections between various factors such as product quality and personalized recommendations, and their impact on overall customer satisfaction. These deductions closely align with the research of (Brewis et al., 2023b; Gao et al., 2023), confirming that the application of Big Data offers an innovative solution for understanding and examining consumer behavior and, consequently, providing an offering that meets their changing needs.

After surveying our sample about their willingness to share their information to improve their shopping experience, the obtained results are listed in the following table:

Table 10. Acceptance of data exploitation and sharing

Data Sharing for Personalization: Your Limits					
		Frequency	Percent	Valid Percent	Cumulative Percent
Valid	Unwilling	70	51,5	51,5	51,5
	Willing	66	48,5	48,5	100,0
	Total	136	100,0	100,0	

Source: Created by us.

It reveals that 51.5% of participants are unwilling to share their information, while 48.5% are willing to do so. This distribution highlights the diversity of consumer attitudes towards the privacy of their data.

These results are significant in the context of Big Data, where the collection and analysis of customer data play a crucial role in customizing services and improving customer experience. The resistance observed among some participants to share their information can be attributed to legitimate concerns about the privacy and security of personal data. Consequently, this consumer reluctance to share information underscores the importance for businesses to adopt more transparent and privacy-respectful approaches when collecting and using data. By understanding the limits of consumers' willingness to share their information, companies can adjust their practices to maintain customer trust while leveraging the benefits of Big Data to enhance the shopping experience.

Our investigation particularly highlights the essential function of personalization of suggestions in enhancing satisfaction and customer loyalty, an idea supported by the work of (Caracciolo et al., 2022), illustrating how processing a significant amount of data can support companies in adjusting their marketing strategies for a personalized approach(Bouhtati, Alla, et al., 2023). This method, enhanced by advanced Big Data analysis, allows companies to offer products and services that focus more on individual consumer selections, thereby strengthening their satisfaction and brand loyalty. Moreover, our perspective demonstrates the significant impact of offer quality factors and online customer feedback on customer satisfaction, confirming the observations of (Filieri et al., 2023) on the importance of these variables. Online reviews can play a crucial role in the discovery and positioning of the customer towards a brand, allowing them to build an initial perception of the quality and credibility of offers in the pre-purchase phase.

However, our study indicates that price can be considered as an essential factor in the purchasing process, but also as a factor in customer satisfaction. This result confirms the study conducted by (Xiao et al., 2023), which highlights that consumers place increased importance on other variables such as quality and unique experience, rather than solely on cost. Nonetheless, our research examines the obstacles encountered in the exploitation of Big Data, such as data privacy constraints and the ultimate need to possess advanced human skills for optimal exploitation. These challenges, also supported by (Feng et al., 2024; Gao et al., 2023), remind organizations of the importance of considering ethical practices when using this large amount of information and having the necessary skills for effective management of the various challenges associated with adopting Big Data(Lhoussaine et al., 2022). These results underline that the use of personalized recommendations based on Big Data does not seem to have a significant impact on online customer satisfaction. However, it is crucial for companies to continue to closely monitor the effectiveness of their Big Data-related strategies and ensure they meet customer expectations and preferences(Lhoussaine et al., 2022). This will help maintain and improve customer satisfaction in a constantly evolving competitive online environment.

6. CONCLUSION

The quantitative study conducted among Moroccan internet users to analyze the impact of Big Data on their online purchasing behavior has highlighted several crucial aspects. First, in a context where Morocco is emerging as a key player in the Big Data field, it becomes imperative to understand how this technology influences online consumption habits.

Our analysis reveals that online customer satisfaction is influenced by several factors, including the price of products and services, the perceived quality of these products and services, and the relevance of personalized recommendations based on Big Data. Regarding price, we found that although it is important for a significant proportion of consumers, it does not necessarily have a direct and significant influence on their overall satisfaction. This suggests that other factors may play a more critical role in customer retention. Concerning the quality of products and services, it appears as a crucial element in the online shopping experience of Moroccan consumers. The results show a significant correlation between customer satisfaction and the perception of product and service quality, highlighting the importance for businesses to maintain high-quality standards to ensure customer satisfaction. Regarding personalized recommendations based on Big Data, although they may seem promising, our study did not find a significant correlation between these recommendations and online customer satisfaction. This underlines the need for businesses to deepen their understanding of consumer expectations and preferences to provide truly relevant and personalized recommendations. Theoretically, this study enriches the literature on digital marketing and customer loyalty, offering a conceptual model that integrates key factors influencing online satisfaction. Managerially, it provides valuable guidelines for businesses, suggesting prioritizing product quality and refining personalization techniques to better meet consumer expectations.

In conclusion, this study underscores the growing importance of Big Data in the Moroccan e-commerce sector. Although some variables may have a more significant impact on customer satisfaction than others, it is crucial for businesses to stay attuned to the changing needs of consumers and adapt their strategies accordingly. By investing in cutting-edge technologies and adopting a data-driven approach, companies can not only enhance their customers' online shopping experience but also strengthen their competitiveness in the constantly evolving market. The identified limitations of this research, such as limited sampling and the primarily quantitative nature of the data, invite further exploration through qualitative studies and a diversification of samples. Moreover, the technological challenges and data privacy concerns associated with Big Data offer fertile ground for future research aimed at optimizing the use of these data while adhering to ethical and privacy standards.

REFERENCES

Agag, G., Durrani, B. A., Abdelmoety, Z. H., Daher, M. M., & Eid, R. (2024). Understanding the link between net promoter score and e-WOM behaviour on social media: The role of national culture. *Journal of Business Research*, 170, 114303. 10.1016/j.jbusres.2023.114303

Akram, M. S., Dwivedi, Y. K., Shareef, M. A., & Bhatti, Z. A. (2022). Editorial introduction to the special issue: Social customer journey – behavioural and social implications of a digitally disruptive environment. *Technological Forecasting and Social Change*, 185, 122101. 10.1016/j.techfore.2022.122101

Alghamdi, O. A., & Agag, G. (2024). Competitive advantage: A longitudinal analysis of the roles of data-driven innovation capabilities, marketing agility, and market turbulence. *Journal of Retailing and Consumer Services*, 76, 103547. 10.1016/j.jretconser.2023.103547

Apaza-Panca, C. M., Flores Quevedo, L. A., & Reyes, L. M. C. (2024). Green marketing to promote the natural protected area. *Sustainable Technology and Entrepreneurship*, 3(3), 100067. 10.1016/j.stae.2023.100067

Bouhtati, N., Alla, L., & Bentalha, B. (2023). Marketing Big Data Analytics and Customer Relationship Management: A Fuzzy Approach. In *Integrating Intelligence and Sustainability in Supply Chains* (pp. 75–86). IGI Global. https://www.igi-global.com/chapter/marketing-big-data-analytics-and-customer-relationship-management/331980

Bouhtati, N., Kamal, M., & Alla, L. (2023). Big Data and the Effectiveness of Tourism Marketing: A Prospective Review of the Literature. In Farhaoui, Y., Rocha, A., Brahmia, Z., & Bhushab, B. (Eds.), *Artificial Intelligence and Smart Environment* (Vol. 635, pp. 287–292). Springer International Publishing. 10.1007/978-3-031-26254-8_40

Brewis, C., Dibb, S., & Meadows, M. (2023a). Leveraging big data for strategic marketing: A dynamic capabilities model for incumbent firms. *Technological Forecasting and Social Change*, 190, 122402. 10.1016/j.techfore.2023.122402

Brewis, C., Dibb, S., & Meadows, M. (2023b). Leveraging big data for strategic marketing: A dynamic capabilities model for incumbent firms. *Technological Forecasting and Social Change*, 190, 122402. 10.1016/j.techfore.2023.122402

Cadden, T., Weerawardena, J., Cao, G., Duan, Y., & McIvor, R. (2023). Examining the role of big data and marketing analytics in SMEs innovation and competitive advantage: A knowledge integration perspective. *Journal of Business Research*, 168, 114225. 10.1016/j.jbusres.2023.114225

Caracciolo, F., Furno, M., D'Amico, M., Califano, G., & Di Vita, G. (2022). Variety seeking behavior in the wine domain: A consumers segmentation using big data. *Food Quality and Preference*, 97, 104481. 10.1016/j.foodqual.2021.104481

Chen, A., & Peng, N. (2023). Antecedents to Consumers' Green Hotel Stay Purchase Behavior during the COVID-19 Pandemic: The influence of green consumption value, emotional ambivalence, and consumers' perceptions. *Tourism Management Perspectives*, 47, 101107. 10.1016/j.tmp.2023.10110737065777

Cheng, C. C. J., & Shiu, E. C. (2023). The relative values of big data analytics versus traditional marketing analytics to firm innovation: An empirical study. *Information & Management*, 60(7), 103839. 10.1016/j.im.2023.103839

Chou, S.-F., Horng, J.-S., Liu, C.-H., Yu, T.-Y., & Kuo, Y.-T. (2022). Identifying the critical factors for sustainable marketing in the catering: The influence of big data applications, marketing innovation, and technology acceptance model factors. *Journal of Hospitality and Tourism Management*, 51, 11–21. 10.1016/j.jhtm.2022.02.010

Du, G., & Lin, Y. (2022). Brand connection and entry in the shopping mall ecological chain: Evidence from consumer behavior big data analysis based on two-sided markets. *Journal of Cleaner Production*, 364, 132663. 10.1016/j.jclepro.2022.132663

Filieri, R., Milone, F. L., Paolucci, E., & Raguseo, E. (2023). A big data analysis of COVID-19 impacts on Airbnbs' bookings behavior applying construal level and signaling theories. *International Journal of Hospitality Management*, 111, 103461. 10.1016/j.ijhm.2023.10346136998942

Gao, Q., Cheng, C., & Sun, G. (2023). Big data application, factor allocation, and green innovation in Chinese manufacturing enterprises. *Technological Forecasting and Social Change*, 192, 122567. 10.1016/j.techfore.2023.122567

Hsu, P.-F., Lu, Y.-H., Chen, S.-C., & Kuo, P. P.-Y. (2024). Creating and validating predictive personas for target marketing. *International Journal of Human-Computer Studies*, 181, 103147. 10.1016/j.ijhcs.2023.103147

Kauffmann, E., Peral, J., Gil, D., Ferrández, A., Sellers, R., & Mora, H. (2020). A framework for big data analytics in commercial social networks: A case study on sentiment analysis and fake review detection for marketing decision-making. *Industrial Marketing Management*, 90, 523–537. 10.1016/j.indmarman.2019.08.003

Kenza, B., soumaya, O., & Mohamed, A. (2023). A Conceptual Framework using Big Data Analytics for Effective Email Marketing. *Procedia Computer Science*, 220, 1044–1050. 10.1016/j.procs.2023.03.146

Khan, S., & Abbas, M. (2023). Interactive effects of consumers' ethical beliefs and authenticity on ethical consumption and pro-environmental behaviors. *Journal of Retailing and Consumer Services*, 71, 103226. 10.1016/j.jretconser.2022.103226

Khan, S., & Abbas, M. (2023). Interactive effects of consumers' ethical beliefs and authenticity on ethical consumption and pro-environmental behaviors. *Journal of Retailing and Consumer Services*, 71, 103226. 10.1016/j.jretconser.2022.103226

Kutaula, S., Gillani, A., Leonidou, L. C., & Christodoulides, P. (2022). Integrating fair trade with circular economy: Personality traits, consumer engagement, and ethically-minded behavior. *Journal of Business Research*, 144, 1087–1102. 10.1016/j.jbusres.2022.02.044

Kutaula, S., Gillani, A., Leonidou, L. C., & Christodoulides, P. (2022). Integrating fair trade with circular economy: Personality traits, consumer engagement, and ethically-minded behavior. *Journal of Business Research*, 144, 1087–1102. 10.1016/j.jbusres.2022.02.044

Lhoussaine, A., KAMAL, M., & BOUHTATI, N. (2022). Big data et efficacité marketing des entreprises touristiques: Une revue de littérature. *Alternatives Managériales Economiques*, 4, 39–58.

Li, Y., He, Z., Li, Y., Huang, T., & Liu, Z. (2023). Keep it real: Assessing destination image congruence and its impact on tourist experience evaluations. *Tourism Management*, 97, 104736. 10.1016/j.tourman.2023.104736

Liu, X.-Y. (2021). Agricultural products intelligent marketing technology innovation in big data era. *Procedia Computer Science*, 183, 648–654. 10.1016/j.procs.2021.02.110

Mariani, M. M., Borghi, M., & Laker, B. (2023). Do submission devices influence online review ratings differently across different types of platforms? A big data analysis. *Technological Forecasting and Social Change*, 189, 122296. 10.1016/j.techfore.2022.122296

Marković, S., Raspor, S., & Šegarić, K. (2010). Does restaurant performance meet customers' expectations? An assessment of restaurant service quality using a modified DINESERV approach. *Tourism and Hospitality Management*, 16(2), 181–195. 10.20867/thm.16.2.4

Matz, S. C., & Netzer, O. (2017). Using Big Data as a window into consumers' psychology. *Current Opinion in Behavioral Sciences*, 18, 7–12. 10.1016/j.cobeha.2017.05.009

Matz, S. C., & Netzer, O. (2017). Using Big Data as a window into consumers' psychology. *Current Opinion in Behavioral Sciences*, 18, 7–12. 10.1016/j.cobeha.2017.05.009

Mukhopadhyay, S., Singh, R. K., & Jain, T. (2024). Developing big data enabled Marketing 4.0 framework. *International Journal of Information Management Data Insights*, 4(1), 100214. 10.1016/j.jjimei.2024.100214

Oladipo, J. O., Akinwumiju, A. S., Aboyeji, O. S., & Adelodun, A. A. (2021). Comparison between fuzzy logic and water quality index methods: A case of water quality assessment in Ikare community, Southwestern Nigeria. *Environmental Challenges*, 3, 100038. 10.1016/j.envc.2021.100038

Rammer, C., & Es-Sadki, N. (2023). Using big data for generating firm-level innovation indicators—A literature review. *Technological Forecasting and Social Change*, 197, 122874. 10.1016/j.techfore.2023.122874

Roy, S. K., Balaji, M. S., Soutar, G., & Jiang, Y. (2020). The Antecedents and Consequences of Value Co-Creation Behaviors in a Hotel Setting: A Two-Country Study. *Cornell Hospitality Quarterly*, 61(3), 353–368. 10.1177/1938965519890572

Safi, R. (2022). What consumers think about product self-assembly: Insights from big data. *Journal of Business Research*, 153, 341–354. 10.1016/j.jbusres.2022.08.003

Safi, R. (2022). What consumers think about product self-assembly: Insights from big data. *Journal of Business Research*, 153, 341–354. 10.1016/j.jbusres.2022.08.003

Saidali, J., Rahich, H., Tabaa, Y., & Medouri, A. (2019). The combination between Big Data and Marketing Strategies to gain valuable Business Insights for better Production Success. *Procedia Manufacturing*, 32, 1017–1023. 10.1016/j.promfg.2019.02.316

Salonen, A., Mero, J., Munnukka, J., Zimmer, M., & Karjaluoto, H. (2024). Digital content marketing on social media along the B2B customer journey: The effect of timely content delivery on customer engagement. *Industrial Marketing Management*, 118, 12–26. 10.1016/j.indmarman.2024.02.002

Sameeni, M. S., Qadeer, F., Ahmad, W., & Filieri, R. (2024). An empirical examination of brand hate influence on negative consumer behaviors through NeWOM intensity. Does consumer personality matter? *Journal of Business Research*, 173, 114469. 10.1016/j.jbusres.2023.114469

Sorour, A., & Atkins, A. S. (2024). Big data challenge for monitoring quality in higher education institutions using business intelligence dashboards. *Journal of Electronic Science and Technology*, 22(1), 100233. 10.1016/j.jnlest.2024.100233

Sukier, H. B., Samper, M. G., Molina, R. I. R., Karam, M. S., Palencia, D. B., Ibanez, N. P., & Ruiz, M. J. S. (2024). Analysis of Strategic Marketing in Small and Medium-sized Enterprises: Case of the Bakery Industry in Colombia. *Procedia Computer Science*, 231, 601–606. 10.1016/j.procs.2023.12.178

Tseng, H.-T., Aghaali, N., & Hajli, D. N. (2022). Customer agility and big data analytics in new product context. *Technological Forecasting and Social Change*, 180, 121690. 10.1016/j.techfore.2022.121690

Van Looy, A. (2021). A quantitative and qualitative study of the link between business process management and digital innovation. *Information & Management*, 58(2), 103413. 10.1016/j.im.2020.103413

Wang, Y., Xing, Y., Wu, Y., Yuan, N., Wang, F., Jiang, B., & Xiong, T. (2020). PMU121 APPLICATION OF REAL-WORLD DATA FROM MEDICAL BIG-DATA PLATFORM IN REAL WORLD EVIDENCE GENERATION: A PRACTICE IN POST-MARKETING RESEARCH IN CHINA. *Value in Health*, 23, S256. 10.1016/j.jval.2020.04.885

Xiao, L., Li, X., & Zhang, Y. (2023). Exploring the factors influencing consumer engagement behavior regarding short-form video advertising: A big data perspective. *Journal of Retailing and Consumer Services*, 70, 103170. 10.1016/j.jretconser.2022.103170

Xue, L., Leung, X. Y., & Ma, S. (2022). What makes a good "guest": Evidence from Airbnb hosts' reviews. *Annals of Tourism Research*, 95, 103426. 10.1016/j.annals.2022.103426

ENDNOTES

[1]   The Royal Institute for Strategic Studies

Chapter 14
Data–Driven Strategies for Enhancing Customer Retention in Moroccan Telecoms

Adil Garohe
http://orcid.org/0000-0003-0184-9324
Mohammed V University in Rabat, Morocco

Rachid Zammar
Mohammed V University in Rabat, Morocco

ABSTRACT

In the face of escalating customer turnover, Moroccan telecom operators seek robust strategies to retain their customer base. This chapter investigates the dynamics of customer churn and proposes a big data analytic approach to predict and minimize this phenomenon. Through the integration of logistic regression, machine learning techniques, and psychological profiling, the authors provide a comprehensive model for understanding customer behaviors and developing targeted retention strategies. The findings from this study offer a valuable blueprint for telecom companies to not only address the churn but to also pave the way for sustained market success in a competitive digital economy.

1. INTRODUCTION

In the telecommunications sector, managing customer churn, defined as the rate of customer attrition, presents a critical challenge with significant financial implications. Companies face not only revenue losses but also the high costs associated with attracting new clients. This chapter delves into the dynamics of customer churn within the Moroccan telecommunications landscape, proposing a nuanced analysis that combines logistic regression and consumer psychology to understand and mitigate churn effectively.

The urgency of addressing churn is underscored by its prevalence across the global telecommunications industry, where companies continually strive to enhance customer loyalty and retention strategies. This is particularly pertinent in Morocco, where the telecommunications sector has seen substantial growth. As reported by the National Agency for Telecommunication Regulation (ANRT), by the end of September 2021, the mobile penetration rate soared to 143.23%, and the internet market penetration escalated

DOI: 10.4018/979-8-3693-3172-9.ch014

from 6% in 2010 to 93.24%, driven predominantly by Mobile Internet and Fiber-to-the-Home (FTTH) services. These statistics not only reflect robust market expansion but also signify intense competition among providers, compelling them to offer increasingly attractive deals to retain and attract customers.

Existing studies offer insightful perspectives on churn, with research highlighting the effectiveness of various predictive models. Notably, Liu and Yang (2019) emphasized the value of machine learning in deciphering customer churn patterns, while Berson and Smith (2018) showcased how strategic data analysis could fortify retention efforts. Drawing on these foundations, our study explores how advanced data analytics can be harnessed to reduce churn, focusing on the specific context of Moroccan telecom operators.

The primary objective of this research is to identify and analyze the key factors influencing customer churn. We employ a comprehensive methodological framework involving data collection on demographic characteristics, service usage habits, and consumer behavior. This data informs our logistic regression analysis, allowing us to evaluate the impact of various factors such as age, gender, subscription type, and customer satisfaction on churn rates.

Additionally, we integrate psychological variables such as brand trust, emotional attachment, and service value perception into our analysis. This approach not only aids in understanding the underlying motivations behind customer retention decisions but also enhances the development of targeted, effective retention strategies.

To demonstrate the practical application of this methodologie, we present case study results that highlight the significant role of customer satisfaction, brand trust, and perceived service value in reducing churn. These findings reinforce the importance of a multifaceted approach to customer engagement and retention, particularly in a competitive market like Morocco.

The study employs a methodology combining data analytics with logistic regression to dissect the complexities of customer retention in the Moroccan telecommunications sector. We conducted a comprehensive survey involving 900 customers across major telecom operators—Maroc Telecom, Orange, and Inwi—utilizing stratified sampling to ensure a representative demographic and behavioral spread. Data were meticulously gathered through online questionnaires and telephone interviews, capturing a broad spectrum of variables from geographic location to psychological factors such as brand trust and emotional attachment. This approach not only enriches our understanding of customer churn but also bolsters our predictive capabilities, allowing for robust, data-driven insights into customer behavior. The leverage advanced techniques, including logistic regression and Random Forest, validated through k-fold cross-validation and sensitivity analyse to ensure accuracy and reliability in our predictive models. This methodological framework is designed to uncover the nuanced interplay of demographic, service usage, and psychological factors influencing churn, providing a solid foundation for developing effective customer retention strategies

Conducting this study, stringent ethical standards and privacy measures were upheld to ensure the protection of participant data and uphold the integrity of our research. All data collection methods, were performed with the utmost respect for privacy and confidentiality. Prior to participation, all individuals were informed about the study's aims and the use of their data, from which informed consent was obtained. We implemented robust data anonymization techniques to ensure that no personal identifiers were retained in the datasets used for analysis. Furthermore, all data handling processes were designed to comply with the General Data Protection Regulation (GDPR), ensuring that participants' information was securely stored and only accessible to authorized personnel involved in the research. These measures reflect our commitment to ethical research practices and the safeguarding of personal information, aligning with both local and international privacy standards.

This chapter is structured to guide the reader through a systematic exploration of customer churn in the Moroccan telecommunications sector. We begin by understanding customer dynamics in this sector, where we delve into the recent research and emerging trends that shed light on customer behaviors and churn patterns. Following this foundational understanding, we transite into a detailed analysis of our findings, each drawn from the comprehensive data-driven approach outlined earlier. The chapter concludes with strategic recommendations tailored to telecommunications companies, aimed at enhancing customer retention and loyalty. Each section is designed to build upon the previous, culminating in a deep understanding of the effective strategies that can mitigate churn and foster customer loyalty in a rapidly evolving market.

1.1 Understanding Customer Dynamics in the Telecommunications Sector

Research continues to explore the multifaceted phenomenon of customer churn in the telecommunications industry, particularly as emerging technologies such as big data analytics offer new insights into consumer behavior. A number of studies have consistently highlighted the impact of demographic factors, such as age, gender, and geographic location, on customer loyalty and churn rates. For instance, younger customers and urban dwellers are identified as more likely to switch providers due to competitive offers and diverse service options (Smith and Peterson, 2017; Kaur and Kaur, 2019).

In addition to demographic factors, behavioral and psychological variables significantly contribute to customer retention. High interaction frequency with customer service and dissatisfaction with service quality are potent predictors of potential churn (Tsai et al., 2020). Psychological factors, including emotional attachment to a brand and cognitive dissonance, also play crucial roles in customer loyalty, suggesting that customers with a strong emotional connection are less likely to churn (Srivastava et al., 2019).

Emerging research underscores the potential of big data to revolutionize marketing strategies, with studies by Alla et al. (2022a) and Alla et al. (2022b) showing how data-driven approaches can improve customer engagement and retention in sectors beyond telecommunications, such as tourism. These insights are pertinent as they suggest similar applications could be effectively translated into telecommunications, enhancing predictive analytics and customer relationship management (Bouhtati et al., 2023a).

The chapter progresses by analyzing the integration of logistic regression and advanced analytics, which have been instrumental in refining customer churn predictions by incorporating a wider array of both demographic and psychological variables, enhancing the strategic approaches telecom companies can adopt to reduce churn and improve customer retention (Liu and Yang, 2019; Naidu et al., 2022).

This discussion aims to deepen the understanding of customer churn in Moroccan telecommunications by drawing parallels with global research trends and applications of new analytical tools. It sets the stage for exploring tailored strategies that address the specific challenges and opportunities within the Moroccan market.

2. JUSTIFICATION FOR LOGISTIC REGRESSION AND OTHER DATA ANALYSIS TECHNIQUES

The choice of logistic regression is grounded in its effectiveness in modeling the relationship between a binary dependent variable (churn) and a set of independent variables, which in our case, include both demographic and behavioral/psychological factors. Logistic regression is particularly adept at handling binary classification problems and provides interpretable results that can directly inform retention strategies.

Moreover, logistic regression's ability to incorporate and analyze various types of data makes it suitable for our big data approach. It allows us to integrate and examine the complex interactions between numerous variables, offering a comprehensive understanding of factors contributing to customer churn in the telecommunications sector.

By employing this methodology, our study aims to deliver insights into the demographic factors, service usage behaviors, and psychological variables influencing customer churn in Moroccan telecommunications companies. The ultimate goal is to develop predictive models and strategies for customer retention, optimizing service delivery, and minimizing churn in this competitive market sector.

3. KEY FINDINGS IN TELECOMMUNICATIONS CUSTOMER RETENTION

To achieve concrete results, we followed these steps, focusing on a big data approach:

3.1 Data Preparation and Cleaning

We ensured that our sample of 900 customers, derived from major Moroccan telecom operators, was representative of the target population. The data was thoroughly checked for completeness and consistency. This step involved converting various data types into a format suitable for analysis, primarily numerical, to ensure compatibility with our logistic regression model.

3.2 Selection of Predictive Variables

We identified relevant demographic and psychological variables that could influence customer churn. These included age, gender, subscription type, customer satisfaction, brand trust, and perceived service value, among others.

3.3 Logistic Regression Analysis

Using Python's scikit-learn library, we adjusted our logistic regression model to the data. The model estimated coefficients for each variable, providing insight into their statistical significance and impact on customer churn.

3.4 Random Forest Analysis

In our exploration to understand the intricate dynamics of customer churn in Moroccan telecommunications, we employed a Random Forest algorithm — a sophisticated ensemble learning method known for its robustness and accuracy. This model operates by constructing multiple decision trees during training and outputting the mode of the classes (classification) of the individual trees, which mitigates overfitting and enhances predictive performance. Upon running the Random Forest, we unveiled the relative importance of each variable in predicting churn.

3.5 Correlation Analysis

We conducted a correlation analysis to understand the linear and non-linear relationships between churn and other variables. This analysis was crucial to identifying factors that could influence churn.

3.6 Heatmap of Correlations

A heatmap provided a visual representation of the numerical correlations between churn and other variables. It offered a detailed overview of the relationships, showcasing the influence of behavioral and psychological variables on churn.

3.7 Model Performance

The figure 4 shows that the logistic regression model demonstrated a high accuracy of 93.33% in predicting churn, indicating its effectiveness in correctly identifying approximately 93.33% of cases. The precision score was 1.0, suggesting that all positive predictions (customers predicted to churn) were accurate. The recall of 0.85714285 indicated that the model correctly identified about 85.71% of actual churn cases. The F1-score of 0.923076923, a combined measure of precision and recall, affirmed the model's balanced performance.

3.8 Representative Figures

Figure 1. Dataset representation post-recoding

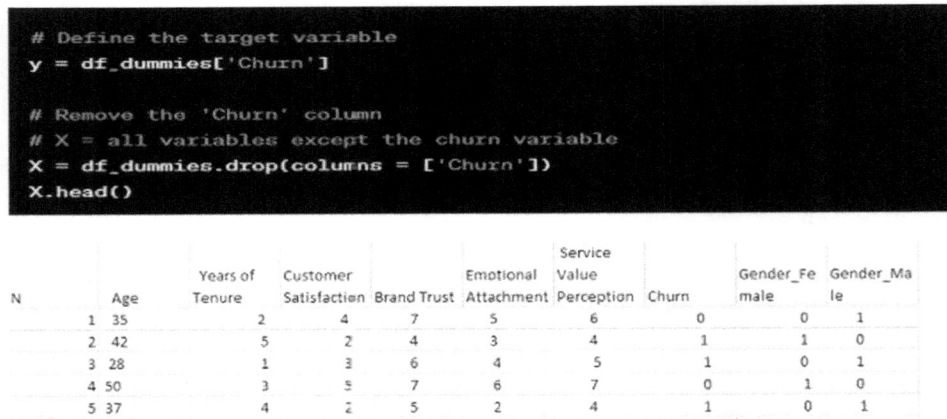

```
# Define the target variable
y = df_dummies['Churn']

# Remove the 'Churn' column
# X = all variables except the churn variable
X = df_dummies.drop(columns = ['Churn'])
X.head()
```

N	Age	Years of Tenure	Customer Satisfaction	Brand Trust	Emotional Attachment	Service Value Perception	Churn	Gender_Female	Gender_Male
1	35	2	4	7	5	6	0	0	1
2	42	5	2	4	3	4	1	1	0
3	28	1	3	6	4	5	1	0	1
4	50	3	5	7	6	7	0	1	0
5	37	4	2	5	2	4	1	0	1

This figure illustrated the dataset after recoding, showing the distribution of variables and their transformation for analysis.

Figure 2. Churn distribution

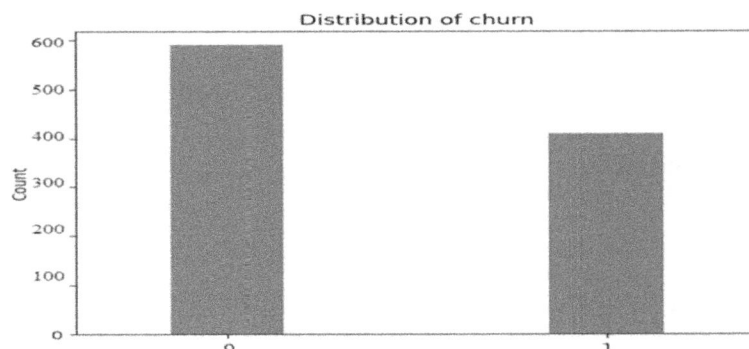

Source: Authors via Python

The churn distribution graph highlighted the proportion of customers who churned versus those who did not, providing an initial overview of churn prevalence in our sample.

Figure 3. Correlation between churn and other variables

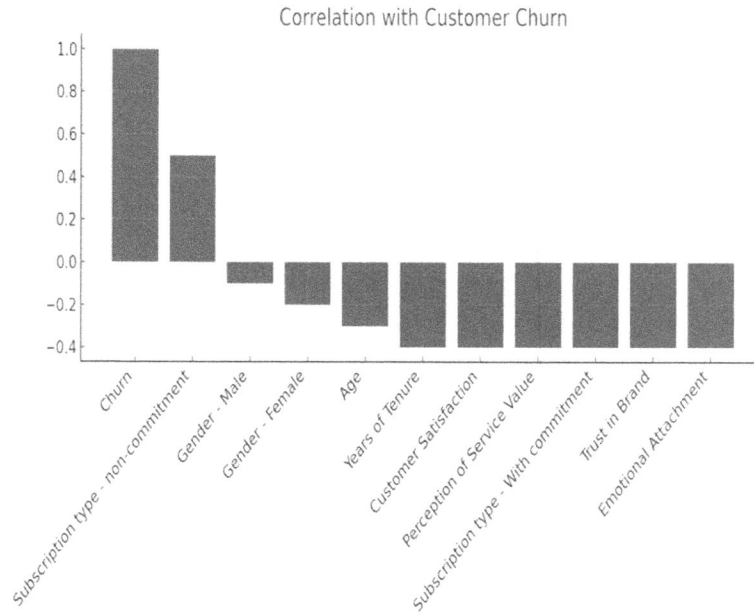

This figure depicted a correlation graph, visually representing the relationship between churn and variables like age, customer satisfaction, and brand trust.

Figure 4. Heatmap of correlations

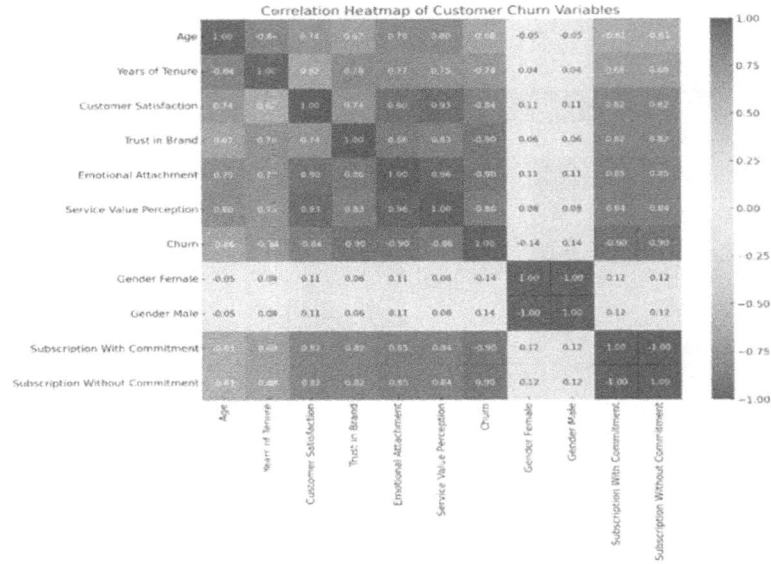

Source: Authors via Pythons

The heatmap offered a concise and intuitive visualization of linear and non-linear relationships between behavioral and psychological variables and their potential impact on customer churn.

Figure 5. Feature importance

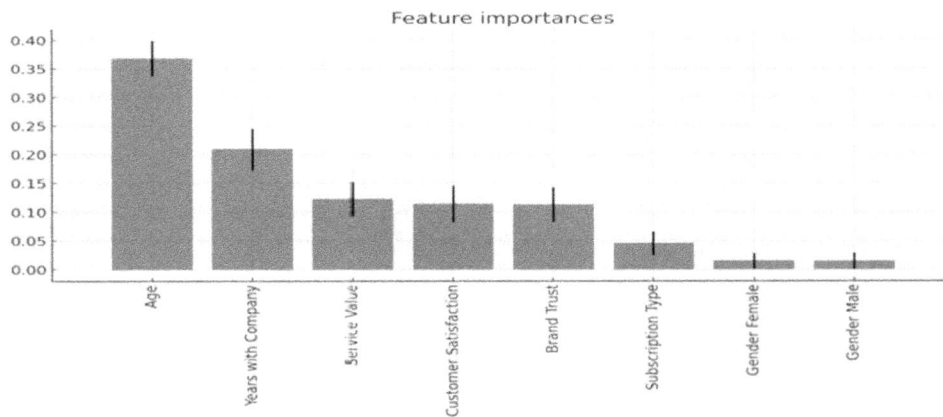

Source: Authors via Python

Figure 6. Permutation feature importance analysis

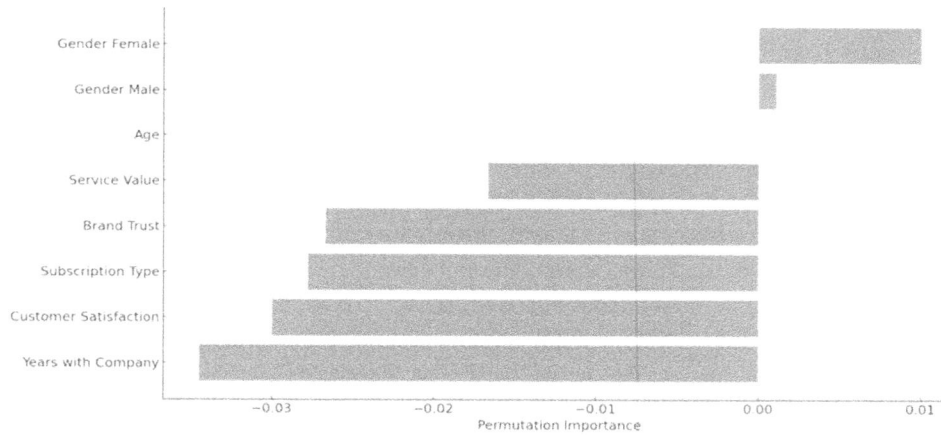

Source: Authors via Python

Incorporating the Random Forest model into our analysis significantly enhanced our understanding of customer churn predictors. The feature importance graph from the Random Forest algorithm provided a clear hierarchy of variables based on their influence on churn prediction. As depicted in the graph, age and tenure with the company emerged as the most influential predictors, highlighting the tendency of younger and newer customers to churn. Customer satisfaction, service value, and brand trust also stood out as substantial factors, reinforcing the need for companies to focus on improving customer experience and building brand loyalty.

Complementing the feature importance graph, the permutation importance plot offered additional nuances by measuring the impact of each variable's shuffling on model accuracy. This technique validated the initial findings while also revealing the robustness of the variables in the predictive model. Notably, the permutation importance plot showed that gender had a smaller but still significant impact on churn, suggesting potential variances in churn behavior between males and females.

By following this methodology and analysis approach, we were able to derive insights into the factors influencing customer churn in Moroccan telecommunications companies. The results underline the effectiveness of logistic regression in handling big data, providing valuable information for companies to devise preventive measures and reduce churn rates.

4. FROM ANALYSIS TO ACTION: UNDERSTANDING CHURN IN THE TELECOMMUNICATIONS SECTOR

In our analysis of factors influencing customer churn, we have identified significant correlations between certain variables and the contract termination phenomenon. To better understand these relationships, we have drawn upon existing literature as well as potential mechanisms underlying these correlations. For instance, our finding that contract duration has a strong negative correlation with customer churn aligns with previous research (Almana et al., 2014). Customers with longer-term contracts tend to be more loyal, as they have already invested time and resources into their commitment. Additionally, an increase in monthly prices is positively correlated with customer churn, which is consistent with customer price sensitivity (Capponi et al., 2021). As rates rise, customers may be inclined to explore more affordable offers from competitors. This explanation is supported by earlier studies (Kim & Yoon, 2004). By integrating literature and exploring these mechanisms, our analysis aims to provide a deeper understanding of why certain variables influence customer churn, which can be valuable for strategic decision-making and customer retention.

Age has shown a significant negative correlation with churn (r = -0.66), suggesting that younger customers are more likely to cancel their subscriptions compared to older ones. Similarly, the number of years of tenure also showed a high negative correlation with churn (r = -0.74), indicating that customers with fewer years of tenure are more prone to cancellation.

Customer satisfaction (r = -0.84), trust in the brand (r = -0.9), and emotional attachment (r = -0.9) (Adams et al., 2018) all exhibited significant negative correlations with churn. These results suggest that high levels of customer satisfaction, brand trust, and emotional attachment reduce the likelihood of subscription cancellation.

Moreover, service value perception also showed a significant negative correlation with churn (r = -0.86), implying that customers who perceive high value in the provided service are less likely to cancel their subscription.

Regarding customer gender, the correlation was weak but significant. Females showed a negative correlation with churn (r = -0.14), while males showed a positive correlation (r = 0.14), indicating that females tend to cancel subscriptions slightly less often than males.

In terms of subscription types, the commitment-based subscription showed a significant negative correlation with churn (r = -0.9) (Mohanty and Rani 2015), while the non-commitment type showed a positive correlation (r = 0.9) (Lee et al., 2018). This suggests that customers with a commitment-based subscription are less inclined to cancel compared to those with a non-commitment subscription.

Overall, these results underscore the importance of factors such as age, tenure, customer satisfaction, brand trust, emotional attachment, service value perception, gender, and subscription type in predicting churn.

Our findings have confirmed the importance of considering consumer psychology in managing customer churn. By understanding customer motivations and behaviors, telecommunications operators can implement personalized retention strategies. We can thus formulate the following recommendations:

- Personalizing offers: Telecommunications operators should propose promotional offers tailored to the specific needs of each customer segment, taking into account their preferences and service usage history. This approach has been successful in other markets (Capponi et al., 2021) and could contribute to customer loyalty in Morocco.
- Reinforcing emotional attachment: Companies should develop loyalty programs aimed at strengthening customers' emotional attachment to the brand (Chen et al., 2016). This can be achieved by offering an exceptional customer experience, creating emotional bonds through personalized interactions, and fostering a sense of community belonging.
- Improving customer satisfaction: Operators must ensure a high level of customer satisfaction by providing quality service, swiftly resolving issues, and offering responsive and efficient customer support.

Regular monitoring of at-risk customers: It is essential to identify customers at risk of churn and implement preventive measures to retain them. This can be achieved by regularly monitoring usage behaviors, satisfaction levels, and setting up early warning systems.

The feature importance graph (figure 5) indicates that age and duration of service are the most critical factors predicting customer churn, which is consistent with the general understanding that younger customers and those with a shorter history with the company are more likely to switch providers. This reflects a possible generational shift in brand loyalty and the continuous search for better deals among the younger demographic. Customer satisfaction, service value, and brand trust are also pivotal, underscoring the telecommunications industry's need to prioritize customer experience and perceived value to retain customers.

On the other hand, the permutation importance graph (figure 6) reveals subtle differences in model sensitivity to the shuffling of variables. It particularly highlights that while gender has a less pronounced effect, it still contributes to churn prediction, suggesting that gender-targeted strategies might be worth considering, albeit with a nuanced approach.

These insights suggest that telecom operators should not only focus on demographic factors but also on enhancing the qualitative aspects of their service, such as customer service and perceived brand value. It also points out the potential for targeted marketing and retention efforts based on the customer profile, which could include personalized offers and communication, loyalty programs, and proactive customer service interventions.

Moreover, the discrepancy in feature importance between the two graphs could be an indicator of complex interactions between the variables that are not immediately apparent, suggesting the need for deeper analysis into the interdependencies of these factors.

Lastly, the discussion should highlight the implications of these findings for the telecom industry in Morocco. Given the competitive nature of the market, these insights provide a road map for telecom companies to refine their customer retention strategies. By understanding the variables that most strongly influence churn, companies can tailor their customer relationship management to address the specific needs and preferences of different customer segments, thereby enhancing loyalty and reducing turnover.

Finally, diversifying services and benefits associated with long-term contracts can also be a retention lever. Moroccan operators might consider including exclusive entertainment offers, such as streaming services or partnerships with content platforms, to attract and retain customers. This approach has been fruitful in other regions (Lu et al., 2014) and could be adapted to the Moroccan market.

5. IMPLEMENTING RESEARCH FINDINGS IN TELECOM CUSTOMER RETENTION

Implementing our recommendations within the context of telecommunications companies in Morocco requires a strategic and meticulous approach. Firstly, for tariff offer personalization, operators need to invest in advanced Customer Relationship Management (CRM) systems capable of analyzing customer data in real-time. This requires technology investments and staff training to fully leverage these systems.

Operators will also need to collaborate with data analysts and machine learning experts to develop accurate and market-relevant customer churn predictive models.

Improving service quality involves investments in network infrastructure. Operators should consider expanding network coverage, increasing capacity, and implementing cutting-edge technologies, such as 5G, to ensure an optimal user experience. This can be a significant financial challenge, requiring partnerships or infrastructure-sharing agreements to reduce costs.

Regarding service diversification, operators will need to negotiate partnerships with entertainment service providers or create their own exclusive services. Negotiating content licenses and setting up streaming platforms may require substantial resources.

However, it is important to note that the implementation of these recommendations may also encounter regulatory and competitive hurdles. Telecommunications regulatory authorities in Morocco will need to be involved to ensure a favorable environment for these initiatives while preserving competition. Moreover, fierce competition among operators may complicate the establishment of infrastructure-sharing agreements or content partnerships.

The practical implications of incorporating 5G and AI technologies extend beyond operational enhancements to directly impacting customer loyalty and retention. With 5G, telecom operators can offer new and innovative services, such as augmented reality or ultra-high-definition streaming, that could differentiate them in a competitive market and increase customer stickiness. Furthermore, AI can automate the segmentation of customer bases, tailor marketing campaigns, and optimize service offerings based on individual customer preferences and behaviors, as supported by Bouhtati et al. (2023b), who illustrate how big data analytics and AI significantly enhance marketing strategies and customer relationship management. Implementing these technologies could lead to a more personalized customer experience, increasing satisfaction and reducing churn. This section discusses specific strategies that Moroccan telecom operators might adopt, such as AI-enhanced customer service platforms or 5G-enabled service innovations, and the expected impact on customer retention

Ultimately, the implementation of our recommendations will require a strong commitment from telecommunications operators in Morocco, significant investments, and careful management of potential challenges. However, by taking a proactive approach and adapting to the changing needs of Moroccan customers, companies can improve their customer retention and strengthen their position in a competitive market.

Future work will provide a more detailed perspective on how the recommendations might be applied in reality, highlighting potential challenges associated with their implementation.

6. CONCLUSION

This investigation into customer churn within the Moroccan telecommunications sector has yielded significant revelations that extend beyond the initial statistical analyses. We have discerned a landscape where demographic, behavioral, and psychological elements intricately weave together to influence customer retention. Through the use of logistic regression and Random Forest models, we have not only quantified the impact of each factor but have also offered a predictive gaze into the churn phenomena, providing a strategic edge for decision-makers in the industry.

Our findings advocate for a holistic approach to customer retention, one that transcends mere transactional interactions and ventures into the realm of personalized engagement. By harnessing the power of big data analytics, companies can tailor their offerings, foster emotional connections, and ensure customer satisfaction. This trifecta of strategies, when executed in harmony, has the potential to transform the customer base into a loyal community, thereby enhancing the company's resilience in the face of market fluctuations and competitive pressures.

Moreover, our study has surfaced the dynamic interplay between service value perception and customer loyalty, underscoring the need for telecommunication companies to innovate continuously and offer value propositions that resonate with the evolving demands of consumers. Our insights suggest that emotional bonds and perceived value are as crucial as the functional aspects of the service provided.

However, this study is not without its limitations. Our focus on the Moroccan telecom sector, while providing depth, limits the generalizability of our results. Furthermore, the reliance on the data at hand means there may be latent variables not accounted for that could offer additional insights into churn behavior.

Looking ahead, we recommend that future studies expand the scope of analysis to include cross-cultural studies and longitudinal data, which would provide a more nuanced understanding of churn over time and across different market dynamics. Additionally, implementing the strategies proposed in this paper in a controlled, real-world environment would serve to validate their effectiveness and fine-tune them for broader application.

In conclusion, the imperative for telecommunications companies to evolve with their customer base is clear. By embracing a data-driven, customer-centric approach, they can not only stem the tide of churn but turn it into a strategic opportunity for growth and sustained success. The path forward is paved with data; it is for the industry to tread wisely.

REFERENCES

Adams, R., Lee, T., & Robinson, C. (2018). The role of emotional attachment in customer loyalty: An empirical investigation in the telecommunications industry. *Journal of Retailing and Consumer Services*, 40, 139–148. 10.1016/j.jretconser.2017.10.006

Alla, L., Kamal, M., & Bouhtati, N. (2022a). Big data and marketing effectiveness of tourism businesses: A literature review. Alternatives Managériales et Economiques, 4(0), Article 0. 10.48374/IMIST.PRSM/ame-v1i0.36928

Alla, L., Kamal, M., & Bouhtati, N. (2022b). Big data and marketing effectiveness of tourism businesses: A literature review. *Economic Management Alternatives*, 1, 39–58.

Almana, A. M., Aksoy, M. S., & Alzahrani, R. (2014). *A survey on data mining techniques in customer churn analysis for telecom industry*. Semantic Scholar. https://api.semanticscholar.org/CorpusID:1283811

Berson, A., & Smith, S. J. (2018). Data management challenges in telecommunications. In *Data Warehousing and Data Mining Techniques for Cyber Security* (pp. 219–231). IGI Global.

Bouhtati, N., Alla, L., & Bentalhah, B. (2023b). Marketing Big Data Analytics and Customer Relationship Management: A Fuzzy Approach. In *Integrating Intelligence and Sustainability in Supply Chains* (pp. 75-86). IGI Global. 10.4018/979-8-3693-0225-5.ch004

Bouhtati, N., Kamal, M., & Alla, L. (2023a). Big Data and the Effectiveness of Tourism Marketing: A Prospective Review of the Literature. In Farhaoui, Y., Rocha, A., Brahmia, Z., & Bhushab, B. (Eds.), *Artificial Intelligence and Smart Environment. ICAISE 2022. Lecture Notes in Networks and Systems, 635*. Springer. 10.1007/978-3-031-26254-8_40

Capponi, G., Corrocher, N., & Zirulia, L. (2021). Personalized pricing for customer retention: Theory and evidence from mobile communication. *Telecommunications Policy*, 45(1), 102069. 10.1016/j.telpol.2020.102069

Chen, J., Li, Y., & Chen, Z. (2016). Customer churn prediction in telecommunications. *Procedia Computer Science*, 91, 28–37. 10.1016/j.procs.2016.07.322

Deng, Z., Lu, Y., Wei, K. K., & Zhang, J. (2019). Understanding customer satisfaction and loyalty: An empirical study of mobile instant messages in China. *International Journal of Information Management*, 44, 27–36. 10.1016/j.ijinfomgt.2018.11.002

Huang, C. M., Li, S. Y., & Hsu, C. H. (2020). Analyzing customer churn behavior in the telecom industry: A data mining approach. *Technological Forecasting and Social Change*, 153, 119977. 10.1016/j.techfore.2020.119977

Kaur, P., & Kaur, N. (2019). Understanding customer churn in the telecommunication sector: A study of geographical location. [IJEAT]. *International Journal of Engineering and Advanced Technology*, 9(2), 2561–2566. 10.35940/ijeat.F1107.0886S619

Kim, H.-S., & Yoon, C.-H. (2004). Determinants of subscriber churn and customer loyalty in the Korean mobile telephony market. *Telecommunications Policy*, 28(7-8), 751–765. 10.1016/j.telpol.2004.05.013

Lee, T., Robinson, C., & Smith, J. (2018). Understanding customer churn in the telecommunications industry: The role of contract type. *Journal of Retailing and Consumer Services*, 42, 222–230. 10.1016/j.jretconser.2018.02.013

Liu, H., & Yang, L. (2019). Customer churn analysis in the telecommunication industry based on machine learning. In *2019 IEEE International Conference on Artificial Intelligence and Computer Applications (ICAICA)* (pp. 245-248). IEEE.

Liu, X., & Yang, C. (2019). Customer churn prediction in the telecommunications industry: A comparison of regression models. *International Journal of Data Science and Analytics*, 8(4), 349–361. 10.1007/s41060-018-0153-3

Lu, N., Lin, H., Lu, J., & Zhang, G. (2014). A customer churn prediction model in telecom industry using boosting. *IEEE Transactions on Industrial Informatics*, 10(2), 1659–1665. 10.1109/TII.2012.2224355

Mohanty, R., & Rani, K. J. (2015). Application of computational intelligence to predict churn and non-churn of customers in Indian telecommunication. In *2015 International Conference on Computational Intelligence and Communication Networks (CICN)*, (pp. 598-603). IEEE. 10.1109/CICN.2015.123

Naidu, G., Zuva, T., & Sibanda, E. M. (2022). Systematic review of churn prediction systems in telecommunications. In Bindhu, V., Tavares, J. M. R. S., & Du, K. L. (Eds.), *Proceedings of the Third International Conference on Communication, Computing and Electronics Systems: Lecture Notes in Electrical Engineering*. Springer, Singapore. 10.1007/978-981-16-8862-1_64

Smith, J., & Peterson, A. (2017). Demographic factors and customer churn in the telecommunications industry. *Journal of Customer Behaviour*, 16(3), 217–232. 10.1362/147539217X15024911379045

Srivastava, A., Saxena, G., & Mishra, M. (2019). Emotional attachment and customer loyalty: An empirical investigation in telecom sector. *International Journal of Business Excellence*, 17(1), 62–80. 10.1504/IJBEX.2019.097058

Tsai, C. H., Wu, Y. C. J., & Lin, S. D. (2020). Predicting customer churn behavior in the telecommunication industry: An integrated data mining approach. *Technological Forecasting and Social Change*, 160, 120236. 10.1016/j.techfore.2020.120236

Chapter 15
Digitalization of Auditing Practices and Customer Experience Optimization:
A Delphi Analysis of the Moroccan Context

Mohammed Mesbahi
http://orcid.org/0009-0001-6010-9361
Mohammed V University in Rabat, Morocco

Kaoutar El Menzhi
Mohammed V University in Rabat, Morocco

Mustapha Ait Kassi
Hassan II University of Casablanca, Morocco

ABSTRACT

For the auditing industry, the advent of digital is not perceived as a simple change, but rather as a genuine revolution redefining the way professionals perform their diligence and maintain their relationships with customers, whose expectations tend to develop. Hence, mastering the digital dimension is necessary for any firm wishing to remain competitive in a fiercely rivalrous sector. This study uses a Delphi approach to provide a prospective overview of audit digitalization and its impact on customer experience optimization, considering the regulatory dimension. Results show that auditing firms, especially the four big ones, are making significant progress in integrating advanced technologies into their processes. Auditors display a certain optimism regarding this transition, as it contributes to optimizing verification procedures while enabling clients to benefit from more efficient and reliable services. However, regulatory reform is crucial to fostering an environment of trust and guiding the ethical use of digital tools.

DOI: 10.4018/979-8-3693-3172-9.ch015

1. INTRODUCTION

For many years, the economic environment, described under the acronym VUCA, meaning volatile, uncertain, complex, and ambiguous, obliged organizations to operate in a competitive and constantly changing context. With the emergence of new technologies, the current era is characterized by a strong digital transition, a component that has imposed itself as an essential pivot and which has generated profound changes in the organization's processes, strategies, and inevitably its business model; enabling thus an implementation of this dimension at the heart of the entity's decision-making policies.

The digital revolution is not a choice, but rather a necessity that forces enterprises to align themselves with current trends, in order to maintain their perennity and competitiveness in the market. Like other business sectors, auditing is also affected by these environmental changes and the consequences arising from them.

As a fully independent external organ, auditing is an effective mechanism for governance and preventing information asymmetries, all assured within a controlled ecosystem. Going forward, the digital conversion of organizations will undoubtedly engender a radical transformation in the auditor's way of working, including new dimensions such as AI, blockchain, and Big Data.

From the customer's perspective, auditing constitutes a guarantee of confidence in the eyes of stakeholders, who make decisions based on the financial information provided. With the emergence of new technologies, customer expectations and needs are tending to evolve, going beyond the simple objective of informational reliability.

In order to maintain the quality of their services while taking full advantage of these advances, audit firms must deal with a two-fold challenge:

- Including the digital dimension in the auditor's work program, while also taking into account the professional skills to be updated and the risks inherent to this mutation.
- Optimizing customer relationships, by transforming audit to an immersive experience that places the "user" dimension at the heart of development policies.

It's true that several papers have focused on the digital future of audit firms (Ramdi, 2021 ; Allouli & Boumeska, 2023 ; Ez-Zaidi & Ghandari, 2023). However, we have noticed that studies examining the measures through which this function will support the IT development of verification procedures are still scarce, within the Moroccan context. By using a Delphi approach, the main objective of our chapter is to analyze the influence of emerging technologies on the practice of auditing and the improvement of the customer's experience. The choice of this method is supported by its significant contribution to the clarification of future prospects in vital fields such as healthcare (Niederberger & Spranger, 2020), computer science (Chalmers & Armour, 2019), and of course, auditing (Tiberius & Hirth, 2019). Moreover, the reliability of the results and their capitalization on the consensus of experts make the use of this approach perfectly suited to our research context, allowing us to study the impact of the digital transition on the auditor's profile, regulator's orientations as well as the needs of financial statement users (shareholders, investors, and others).

Hence, the task at hand is to provide a response to the subsequent issue:

Based on a prospective overview of auditing's future in the Moroccan context, what measures could audit firms take in order to support the implementation of digital dimension in their verification processes, while also considering the optimization of customer experience?

Our chapter will be divided into three main sections: a first section devoted to the theoretical background and outlining the key concepts related to this topic, a second section describing the methodological approach deployed in our study, and finally a third section dedicated to the results and discussion.

2. THEORETICAL FRAMEWORK

2.1. Digital Transition and Revolution of Auditing Practices

In the current ecosystem, digital transition is considered one of the most disruptive technological trends, modifying both society and the economy. In management literature, this term has been studied from different angles, leading to a wide variety of definitions. This has even led some researchers, such as Savic' (2019) and Vrana and Singh (2021), to distinguish between three fundamental concepts: "digitization" which is limited to the process of converting analog data to a computer-readable format (series of 0 & 1's), "digitalization" which refers to information treatment and automation of various company processes and operations, and "digital transformation" which involves a complete restructuring of the company, including its culture, strategy and business model.

As a fully independent organ, audit has always been a governance mechanism that ensures the reliability of financial information. Thus, the digital transition is appearing as a catalyst of change, remodeling the auditor's profile and his way of working. In order to maintain their competitiveness, audit firms will have to adapt themselves to new market requirements and develop their range of services, including recent technologies such as AI, Blockchain, and Big Data analytics.

2.1.1. Artificial Intelligence (AI)

Although artificial intelligence is widely recognized as a major innovation, there is no consensual definition of the concept in management literature. For Haenlein & Kaplan (2019), AI refers to the ability of a system to accurately interpret a set of external data, acquire knowledge from this data, and apply it in order to achieve goals or accomplish tasks, all via its adaptive flexibility. As for Szczepanski (2019), the notion of AI is summed up in the ability of a machine to perform cognitive functions similar to the human mind, such as learning, understanding, thinking, and interacting with an environment. This technology can take various forms, including a technical infrastructure (algorithms), a part of the production process, or even a product destined for end users.

At present, the influence of AI is spreading significantly across a wide range of industries. For the audit profession, the emergence of this technology is not perceived as a simple technological change, but rather as a genuine revolution redefining the way professionals perform their due diligence.

Since audit work often involves a high volume of repetitive operations (Baldwin et al. 2006), the implementation of AI is an innovative solution that enables auditors to optimize their control process by limiting audit risks (Zemankova, 2019), reducing omissions and human errors (Fedyk et al., 2022), verifying the integrality of financial data in record time with minimal cost (Issa et al., 2016), and improving professional decision-making and judgments (Sun & Vasarhelyi, 2017). However, to benefit from the full potential of AI, this technology must be equipped with all its capabilities. Mikalef and Gupta (2021) identify three categories of resources that constitute the capacity of this so-called intelligence, namely tangible resources (technological infrastructure, data, and financial funds), human capabilities (commercial and technical skills), and finally intangible resources (coordination, organizational adaptability, and risk propensity).

2.1.2. Blockchain

By definition, blockchain is much more than a simple technology; it's an innovative protocol for storing and transferring a set of financial transactions, organized chronologically in a ledger shared between network users. (ICAEW, 2018)

Since its emergence in 2008 with the creation of Bitcoin, Blockchain has become one of the most significant innovations, after the Internet. Currently, we can identify 4 generations of this technology: generation 1.0 for cryptocurrency transactions, generation 2.0 introduces the concept of smart contracts, generation 3.0 focuses on new areas such as healthcare and supply chains, and generation 4.0 combines the use of blockchain and artificial intelligence.

The way this tool operates is quite simple. Users, also known as "nodes", benefit from direct access to a database where transactions are stored in a series of cryptographically secured blocks, none larger than 1 MB each. However, a new block cannot be added to the existing sequence without the approval of the majority of nodes (Oliveira Simoyama et al., 2017 ; Desplebin et al., 2018). Hence, this mode of functioning confers to the constituted database 3 major characteristics:

- First, information transparency and open access for all network users.
- Second is cryptographic protection, which makes data impossible to erase or modify once it has been stored.
- Third, the decentralization of the database due to the nonexistence of a supervisory body, responsible for management and governance of the system.

In the auditing field, blockchain technology has made its presence felt, thanks to the advantages it offers. The financial ledger is held and validated by a group of users rather than a single centralized body, which guarantees the auditor immutable, unfalsifiable and easily tractable information on transaction details, payments made, and parties involved (Han et al. 2023).

Moreover, the "instant" confirmation of transactions offered by this technology enables a continuous audit to be performed, which should lead to improved efficiency in the verification process and a reduction in the time spent on document matching (Desplebin et al., 2021). This would allow the auditor to focus more on the most problematic areas, rather than getting lost in daily operational reviews. (javaid et al., 2022).

2.1.3. Big Data Analytics

In an increasingly dynamic ecosystem, the development of new information technologies has stimulated the generation and circulation of huge volumes of data (Bouhtati et al., 2023). Managing this incessant flow, which may arise from financial transactions, customer interactions, or even internal sources, is one of the major challenges facing enterprises and their competitiveness.

In this context, Big Data is emerging as a new generation of technologies and architectures that enable the extraction of economic value from a large volume of widely dispersed data, through high-speed capture, discovery, and/or developed analysis. (Gantz & Reinsel, 2012)

Technically, the advent of metadata goes back to the 1960s and 1970s, with the inauguration of the first data centers and the development of relational databases (RDBMS) (Bentalha, 2020). Thus, the objective of Big Data is to manage this wealth of information, according to a combination of the following 5 Vs: (Ishwarappa & Anuradha, 2015 ; Noraini et al., 2015 ; Bourany, 2018 ; Alla et al., 2022)

- **Volume:** this refers to Big Data's ability to process massive amounts of data collected by the entity.
- **Velocity**: it's the increased speed at which relational databases process, store, and analyze the data they collect.
- **Variety:** it's the capability of big data to collect and integrate a wide range of structured and unstructured information, which may come from all kinds of sources (text, audio, video, images, etc.).
- **Veracity:** this term relates to the reliability degree of the database. Considering the large volume and variety of data processed, this factor can have a significant impact on the accuracy of the output (e.g. decision-making).
- **Value:** this is one of the most recent and essential dimensions of big data. Indeed, the abundance of existing information cannot be so advantageous for entities if they are unable to transform these resources into exploitable value, hence the importance of big data.

As the auditor's work is essentially based on the examination of financial information, Big Data and its analysis represent a revolutionary treatment approach that may give sense to the abundance of data received, transforming it into evidence used in formulating and supporting the audit opinion. However, auditors should be aware that the implementation of this system can lead to a significant change in their verification processes. (Dagilienė & Klovienė, 2019).

2.2. Customer Experience Optimization

Since the emergence of service industries, providers have always maintained close ties with their communities, striving to understand the needs and expectations of a highly heterogeneous clientele. As a result, the development of a solid customer experience is nowadays a major priority, ensuring the establishment and preservation of a sustainable relationship with clients. Bolton et al. (2014) define the customer experience as a holistic framework, Integrating customers' cognitive, sensory, emotional, social, and physical reactions resulting from their direct or indirect interaction with the firm.

One of the key factors in customer experience management is the company's ability to measure and analyze its clients' reactions to provided services, and particularly their attitudes (Lemon & Verhoef, 2016). Indeed, customer satisfaction is normally enhanced if the result obtained by this latter is higher than his expectations.

Similarly to other service companies, auditing firms must be able to comprehend and shape their customer experience. This involves the firms understanding the aspects that matter most to clients, so they can make the decisions and investments needed to optimize their customer experience (Spiess, 2014). In this context, Gross & Pullman (2012) highlighted two fundamental axes for the implementation and development of the customer experience, namely the physical axis (tangible environment and objects) and the relational axis (interactions between the service provider and his client).

Furthermore, Digitalization is now reinforcing the role of service quality in attracting and retaining customers, especially with the development of the so-called "phygital experience", which combines physical and digital strengths to provide an integrated user experience. Indeed, consumer behavior tends to change in response to the digital revolution (Verhoef et al., 2019). With the increasing use of new technologies, audit firms will be able to optimize their verification processes by coordinating them more effectively, as well as create added value through improved customer experience. However, these shifts require the firm to implement new business capabilities and even engage external partners, in order to provide a high-quality service (Lemon & Verhoef, 2016; Pagani & Pardo, 2017).

3. METHODOLOGY

3.1. Presentation of the Delphi Approach

The Delphi study stands out as a participatory approach that aims to gather expert opinion on a specific topic, thus taking on a major prospective character. Developed in the 1950s by the RAND Corporation for military purposes (Hanna & Noble, 2015), the use of this method has expanded considerably to include various disciplines such as economics, management, technology, social sciences, and medicine (Beiderbeck et al., 2021).

In contrast to the scenario method, which generates several hypothetical cases, the Delphi approach allows us to identify the most likely scenario that results from the intersection of several experts' statements. By definition, an "expert" is a person who has gained extensive knowledge in a particular field through his/her education, training, or experience. (Iglesias et al., 2016).

Hence, the Delphi method is based on four fundamental principles: (Okoli & Pawlowski, 2004; Baillette et al., 2013; Belton et al., 2019)

- **Anonymity:** encourages open and honest participation of experts and guarantees the relevance and reliability of results.
- **Panel limitation:** the Delphi approach generally relies on a small sample of respondents, which ensures a sufficient number of responses with a low attrition rate.
- **Participant legitimacy:** the expert should have sufficient knowledge of the subject, enabling him to express an opinion representative of the panel to which he belongs.
- **Controlled feedback:** this process allows the results to be sent back to the participants so that they can revise their previous statements, if they wish.

In line with our research problem, and considering the fundamentals of the Delphi method, we have tried to analyze the experts' viewpoints with the aim of drawing up a prospective scenario of auditing's digitalization and the optimization of customers' experience, in the Moroccan context. This involves understanding the effects of this transformation and the use of emerging technologies on the auditor's profile and practices, on the orientations of regulators, and of course, on the expectations of stakeholders (i.e.: shareholders, investors, top management, and others).

Drawing on Ekionea et al. (2011) procedure, our Delphi approach has been structured as follows:

Figure 1. Delphi procedure

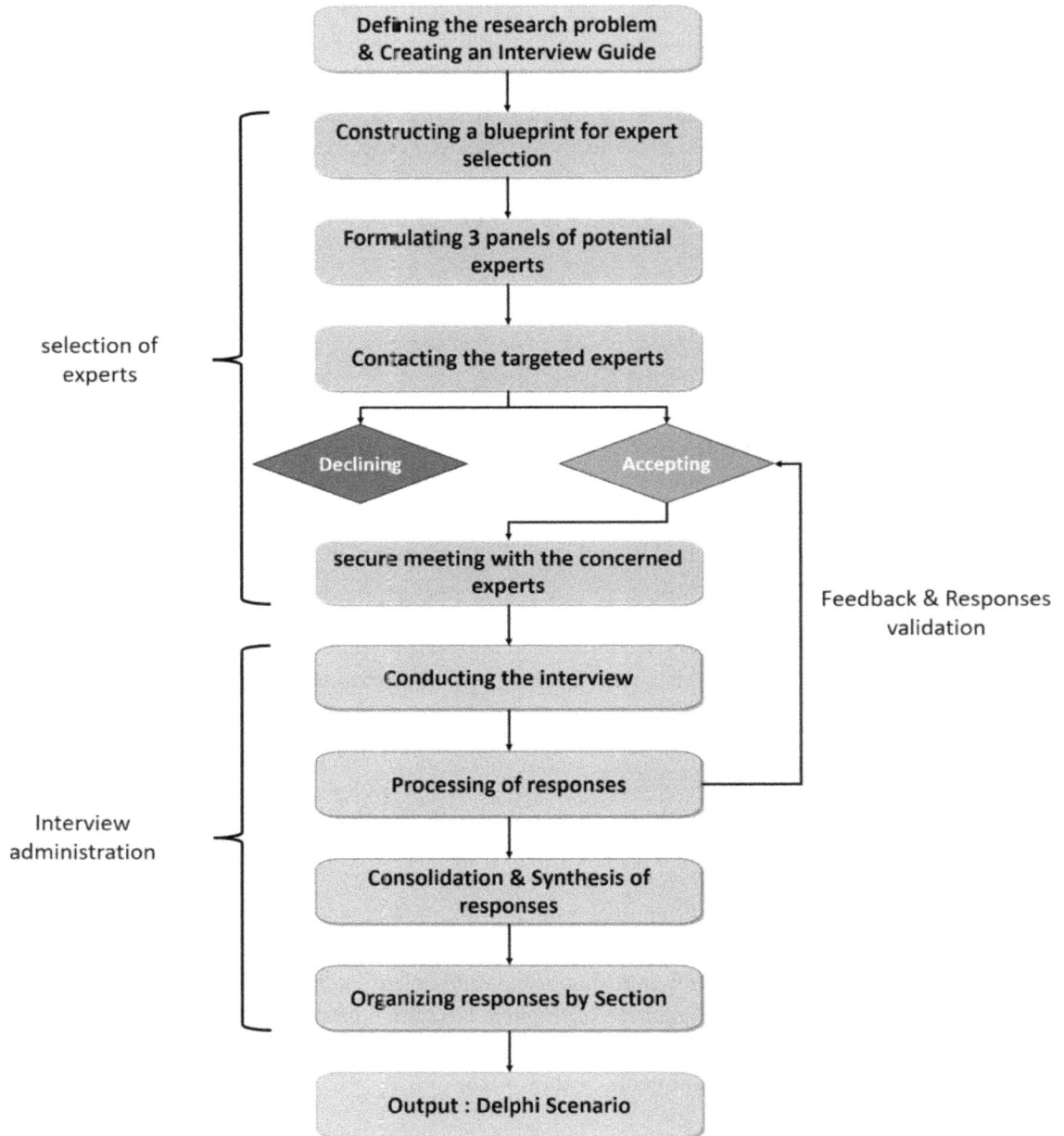

Source: adapted from Ekionea et al. (2011)

Details of the two main stages are described below.

3.2. The Surveyed Panel

3.2.1. Respondents' Selection

One of the most important considerations in a Delphi analysis is the judicious selection of experts to be interviewed, since it determines the quality of obtained answers. By using such a particular technique, the researcher is able to select the appropriate sample of experts, with the knowledge and experiences needed to meet the study's requirements and provide a deeper understanding of the phenomenon concerned. (Paré et al., 2013 ; De Loë et al., 2016 ; Hennink et al., 2019 ; Hadinia et al., 2023).

In the Delphi approach, the panel composition is not necessarily based on statistical representativeness, but rather on a uniform qualitative sampling. However, the ideal number of experts to be interviewed is a subject of much debate.

According to Akins et al. (2005), "there is no agreement on the panel size for Delphi studies, nor recommendation or unequivocal definition of "small" or "large" samples" (p.2). In contrast, many researchers support the choice of a limited base, under the pretext that the determination of panel size must be made with consideration of time and financial constraints, and that a larger respondent base may lead to difficulties in gathering and managing data. Thus, Shang (2023) suggests a participant range of 8 to 23, while Okoli & Pawlowski (2004) recommend a sample of 8 to 18 respondents. Stitt-Gohdes & Crews (2004) further narrow this range to 10 to 15 and underline the importance of a balanced approach to panel composition. Nevertheless, it should be noted that choosing a panel of fewer than 10 people can lead to a lack of idea generation. (Needham & De Loë, 1990).

Based on these considerations, we set up a final list of 15 respondents, including auditors (from Big 4 or non-Big 4 firms), audit clients (belonging to the public, semi-public, or private sector) as well as regulators (OEC members). Our selection has focused on people:

* With significant experience in the profession.
* Able to provide insightful and pertinent responses to our queries.
* In a position to contribute to the enrichment of our study, through informed and pointed suggestions.

Targeted experts have been contacted by Mail, LinkedIn, or phone call, through which we have explained in detail our study, main objectives, the adopted approach, and the importance of their contribution. For those who expressed a supportive interest, we set up an appointment during which our interview will be conducted. Thus, the profile of experts who participated in our study is presented below.

Table 1. Respondents profile

Auditors						
Participants	**Firm**		**Grade**		**Years experience**	
6	Big 4	50%	Junior Auditor	-	0-1 Year	-
			Experienced Auditor	50%	1-2 Years	33%
	Non-Big 4	50%	Senior Auditor	17%	2-5 Years	50%
			Engagement Partner	33%	5-10 Years	-
			Managing Partner	-	Over 10 Years	17%
Audit Clients						
Participants	**Sector**		**Functions**		**Years experience**	
6	Public	33%	Administrator	17%	Over 10 Years	100%
	Quasi-Public	-	Division Manager	33%		
	Private	67%	Startup CEO	50%		
Regulators						
Participants		**Years experience**				
3		Over 10 years			100%	
Total respondents: 15						

Source: Our elaboration

3.2.2. Ethics and Data Confidentiality Policies

One of the key features of qualitative research is the interactive aspect of the data collection process, which implies direct and substantive communication between the researcher and participants (Buckle et al., 2010). However, by agreeing to provide their personal information for study purposes, participants expect a commitment to the safeguarding of their privacy, with an assurance that only pre-designated individuals will have access to the raw data (Pietilä et al., 2020). Thus, adherence to the principles of ethics and confidentiality is a critical aspect that researchers must consider when planning their study.

Given these considerations, particular attention has been given to ensure that all participants are fully informed of the study's objectives, how their data will be used, and the policies for storing and communicating information among respondents. In this perspective, we have managed to ensure that each completed survey will be coded and that the responses received will be compiled as part of the consensus-building process, guaranteeing the anonymity of the individual and the organization to which he/she belongs. Hence, informed consent was requested from each participant before the start of the interview, reinforcing our commitment to an approach that respects the ethics and confidentiality of the respondents.

3.3. Interview Administration

Once we had secured a meeting and obtained the consent of the individuals concerned, we proceeded with the interviews, during which we tried to explore in detail the specific points we were seeking to understand. In this context, the majority of the questions asked were formulated in an open-ended way, allowing for a more in-depth exchange and a collection of maximum data.

As for the administration of our interviews, we opted for a semi-directive approach, remaining neither completely open-ended nor strictly enclosed. Thus, we privileged a careful listening posture, by avoiding any influence from our side on the respondents' opinions but trying at the same time to guide them through follow-up questions and clarification requests.

The forms collected from each panel were reviewed by concerned respondents, as part of the validation process recommended by the Delphi approach. This raw data was then treated with the aim of transforming it into exploitable information while eliminating content redundancies. The resulting output was consolidated and finally, classified by points.

4. RESULTS

Before drawing up their scenario, researchers must initially decide whether to present a wide or in-depth overview (Tiberius & Hirth, 2019). Since there are no Delphi studies on audit digitalization and its influence on optimizing customer experience in the Moroccan case, we have privileged the adoption of an exploratory (wide) perspective, combining the opinions of the three categories of respondents interviewed to provide an exhaustive and relevant view on this topic.

Thus, the findings collected from our study have been organized and divided into 4 major sections, with details given below.

4.1. Overview of the Audit Profession and Its Regulatory Framework

4.1.1. Changes in Auditing Practices Over the Years

Since its generalization in 1993, the practice of auditing in Morocco has always played a leading role in corporate governance and financial regulation. In fact, the evolution of this discipline can be seen as a dynamic narrative, reflecting a great adaptability of the profession in front of a constantly changing ecosystem, and this through a succession of 4 generations presented as follows:

- **A first-generation** limited to traditional working methods, such as physical collection of audit documentation and handwritten analysis of the financial data by using checklists and manual spreadsheets.
- **A second generation** combining the precision of manual tools with the efficiency of office software, in particular Microsoft's pack. This period has seen an increase in the capacity for analysis and treatment of financial information, thanks to the ability to perform complex calculations provided by these programs.

- **A third generation** that has abandoned paper in favor of digitized documentation and relied on the intensive use of software to cover the whole verification process, allowing auditors to efficiently store and organize their records while contributing significantly to the optimization of auditing procedures.
- **A fourth generation**, that represents the current state of auditing and is characterized by the dominance of new technologies in working processes, based particularly on AI, blockchain, and big data analytics. However, the implementation of this transition remains limited due to existing gaps between audit firms, mainly in terms of financial capacity and technological infrastructures.

4.1.2. Regulatory Contributions to the Audit Profession

Over the years, the audit environment has undergone major reforms, largely driven by the active intervention of regulatory bodies among which the OEC stands out as a key partner. Founded in 1993, this institution has played a crucial role in shaping the regulatory framework, not only by setting standards for this profession but also by promoting exemplary mechanisms for corporate governance. In this context, one of the OEC's main contributions to the auditing profession is the establishment of a rigorous code of deontology, known as the "Code of Professional Ethics and Conduct". Inaugurated by IFAC in 2009 and subsequently adopted by the National Council of OEC Morocco in 2013, this referential defines a set of ethics governing the audit function, such as objectivity, integrity, and professional secrecy, as well as clarifying the auditor's obligations towards clients, users of the financial statements and the entity itself. Thus, the Code of Professional Ethics and Conduct is divided into two main parts: (OEC, 2013)

- The first section provides a framework for professionals to identify risks, assess their severity, and set up protocols to reduce or even eliminate these threats.
- The second section, limited to special situations, gives examples of procedures applicable to these circumstances and also recognizes the existence of some complex cases, that do not adhere to any of the treatment measures, and should therefore be avoided by the auditor.

4.2. Digital Reinvention of the Audit Function and the Auditee Environment: The Current State of Play

4.2.1. Analysis of Digital and Human Skills Within the Audited Entities

In order to carry out its mission effectively, norm 2315 of the Moroccan legal and contractual framework for auditing stipulates that the professional should have a good knowledge of the audited entity and its environment, including its level of technological development. For this purpose, we considered it essential to draw up an overview describing the digital environment of our surveyed entities.

Concerning investments in technological infrastructures, it seems clear that this component occupies a predominant share in the organization's budget planning. Indeed, the majority of surveyed entities (80%) claim to devote a considerable proportion of their overall budget to hardware and software equipment. For the remaining 20%, this type of investment surpasses the threshold of significance and even represents a financial priority in decision-making.

As for the implementation degree of new technologies within the audited entities, all the private companies questioned confirm their reliance on digital solutions and ERPs using AI technology (e.g. SAP, Axelor). These tools can perform various functions, including procurement (orders creation, management, and approval), human resources management (generation of pay slips, validation of leaves, management of claims and job applications), accountancy (transaction entry, management of fixed assets, generation of financial statements, and sub-ledger accountancy) and others. However, the level of implementation of new technologies remains relatively limited within the public sector. Despite the considerable investment in technological infrastructures, concerned experts concur on the existence of barriers to the achievement of a fully integrated digital restructuration. Admittedly, there has been an increase in the use of IT solutions in some departments over the last years, but still with a subsistence of office programs. Meanwhile, in other divisions such as logistics, the use of traditional tools and paper supports remains an obligation, particularly for customs procedures.

4.2.2. Appreciation of Audit Team Competencies

In terms of ensuring the quality of provided services, one of the key success factors to consider is the competence of the human resources deployed. Indeed, a good synergy between the auditors' technical know-how and interpersonal skills is even more crucial as it determines the firm's ability to adapt to customer needs and remain competitive in an increasingly demanding ecosystem.

The answers given by interviewed experts show that, in the context of recruitment processes, advanced software skills are certainly considered a major asset. However, this quality is not as critical when it comes to selecting the right candidate. In fact, auditing firms primarily require a perfect knowledge of office programs, especially Microsoft Excel. In the ideal case, mastery of the VBA language can be a significant differentiating criterion. it's only after they've been hired that new recruits are asked to follow training programs on specific tools and software used by the firm in its procedures. This internal training policy ensures that all auditors possess the required competencies for effective use of technology, thereby facilitating team collaboration and operational synergy.

In addition to technical skills, personal attributes such as objectivity, integrity, professional behavior, and effective communication remain key qualities for a successful career, enabling the auditor to thrive in a highly demanding environment, while contributing significantly to the perennity of the firm.

4.2.3. Assessment of Digital Maturity Within the Audit Process

4.2.3.1. Collection and Management of Audit Data

Far from being a routine ritual, the preparation of audit evidence is a preliminary step that provides significant time-saving and efficiency gain to the auditor, allowing him to approach his task with greater precision and focus.

In terms of data collecting, all the responses reveal unanimity and converge towards an alignment of audit firms on the same practices. Surveyed experts confirm they rely on an approach that respects ethical rules and involves the electronic communication of a non-exhaustive list of evidence that should be sent in a digitized format (scanned). However, the major difference between these firms consists in the way auditors organize and manage the collected evidence.

While non-Big4 firms tend to lean on ordinary working methods, where files are generally received via e-mail or the "Drive" sharing platform, and responsibility for organizing this documentation is often assigned to the engagement partner, who is responsible for centralizing and arranging it by cycles. In contrast, Big 4 firms are distinguished by their use of highly developed solutions, such as Deloitte's "Connect" online platform or PWC's "Connect V3" software. These shareware platforms serve as a communication interface between auditor and client, allowing files to be shared quickly and efficiently while ensuring the traceability of correspondence.

4.2.3.2. Implementation of Digital in Verification Tasks

Even though a third (33%) of the firms surveyed still rely primarily on Office suites and perform their audits using classic Excel spreadsheets. The remaining 67% of firms, including the Big4, confirm that they also lean on Office programs, but are relatively advanced in terms of technology, especially in the use of AI solutions.

In the context of data processing, our survey highlights the Big 4's adoption of a range of innovative software. By way of illustration, the "Data Sniper" tool works in sync with Microsoft Excel and enables information to be extracted automatically from digitized evidence and inserted into an Excel spreadsheet. This process automates reconciliation and data entry while reducing the risk of typing errors. Furthermore, the development of the GL.AI Bot by PWC marks a major step forward in risk management, providing a detailed description of each anomaly detected as well as proposing appropriate measures for its resolution.

These firms also have internal platforms, dedicated to verification tasks and team management. In contrast to conventional cycle-based approaches, which are often established informally, these programs promote operational synergies and ensure a fair distribution of tasks, while at the same time making it possible to track the diligence performed by each auditor and the modifications he made. Two of the most popular solutions used for this purpose are PWC's "Aura Platinum" platform and Deloitte's "APAT" team management tool.

From a general overview, and based on experiences shared by experts, it seems that the integration of AI into verification processes is a revolution that has enabled auditors to save time, through the automation of repetitive tasks, as well as increasing efficiency by enabling them to focus more on complex and high value-added diligences, such as interpretation of audit results and formulation of pertinent recommendations to clients.

4.2.3.3. Storage and Archiving of Audit Documents and Worksheets

The obligation for audit firms to retain documents and worksheets is part of the governance and responsibilization framework, which may serve a dual function:

- From a regulatory side, the archiving system helps the firm maintain a certain degree of traceability, which can be essential in the event of a quality inspection by the authorities.
- In its relationship with the client, this procedure enables the firm to build up its permanent file on the audited entity and to support the integrity of its opinions, in case of disagreements or contestations with the top management.

In our study's context, all interviewed experts confirm that physical archiving has been abandoned in favor of dedicated digital servers. However, a distinctive archiving policy is advocated by Big 4 firms, requiring audit documents and worksheets to be destroyed from the auditor's computer at the end of the assignment, and to be stored in secured cloud spaces with restricted access to line managers only. For any further consultation, a formal request should be submitted by the auditor to the concerned supervisor.

4.3. Analysis of the Current Regulatory Framework

As a fundamental pillar of corporate governance, auditing is a highly regulated profession that relies mainly on the efforts deployed by supervisory boards. These authorities define normative guidelines that ensure the standardization of methods and procedures, in accordance with the reference framework adopted by the country and adapted to its economic and legal environment.

The current regulatory context, as described by the OEC members interviewed, reveals the inexistence of a Moroccan referential that formally enacts the dispositions governing the implementation of digital technologies in auditing processes. As a consequence, regulators claim to refer to international frameworks, in particular the ISA 315 standard (revised 2019) and the IAASB Guide on the use of technology, in order to temporarily fill this gap. However, our interlocutors emphasized that a reform plan is underway to update the existing standards, including the adoption of specific directives on the use of new technologies.

4.4. Digital Transition of Auditing and Optimization of the Customer Experience: A Prospective Overview

In an industry where integrity and trust are paramount values, one of the most important dimensions to be considered by the firm, after legal compliance, is customer satisfaction. This component is emerging not only as an indicator of quality but also as a strategic lever, enabling the firm to maintain its perennity in a highly competitive market. Thus, customer satisfaction finds its purpose in the delivery of a great experience, where the provided service should exceed the client's expectations and requirements.

In the context of our study, the factors constituting a positive client experience, as identified by the companies surveyed and based on their own interactions with auditing firms, are high quality of service, auditor availability and responsiveness, adherence to agreed deadlines, good relationships with managers and stakeholders, and the use of advanced technologies in verification processes.

With the rise of digitalization trends, audit firms face increasing expectations from their customers, particularly from those with a high level of technological maturity. On the technical side, these entities aspire to more in-depth audits, adapted to the specific features of their environment, as well as optimized service costs and a lower time budget. On the relational front, improved information flows, greater transparency, and a limitation of discretionary behaviors are highly desired benefits. Thus, the consideration of these dimensions in auditors' practices would significantly transform their approach and foster an environment more conducive to customer loyalty.

4.5. Opportunities and Challenges of the Digital Transition of Auditing Processes

The adoption of digital technologies in auditing processes marks the beginning of a revolutionary era, characterized by the introduction of innovative tools and techniques that have the promising potential to improve existing standards towards more efficient and reliable services, thereby providing a myriad of opportunities. Indeed, the digitalization of processes enables auditors to automate repetitive tasks and devote their efforts to the diligence deemed most relevant, thus enhancing the value of their expertise. In addition, this advance results in an efficient minimization of time budget and, consequently, has a positive impact on fees charged. Furthermore, the integration of new technologies fosters synergies between auditor and client, creating a climate of transparency, increased trust, and fluid communication.

Despite its promising prospects, the digital transition of auditing cannot be exempt from challenges. In our study, two major challenges were highlighted by the surveyed firms: on the one hand, this transition is redefining the auditor's profile, who must now acquire new ICT skills in addition to traditional ones. With these requirements, firms are expecting resistance from their staff, reflecting their difficulty in embracing these changes. On the other hand, the challenge of data protection is becoming more acute, as sensitive information is increasingly exposed to cyber risks, which requires firms to make significant investments in advanced security systems and robust data storage protocols.

In summary, although the incorporation of digital technologies in auditing provides undeniable opportunities for enhancing service efficiency and improving client experiences, it simultaneously necessitates careful consideration of the inherent challenges. How audit firms manage this dilemma will largely determine the success of the industry's digitalization.

5. DISCUSSION: PRESENTATION OF THE DELPHI SCENARIO

In the Moroccan context, leading audit firms stand out for their strong technological potential, as most have already succeeded in effectively integrating AI software into their processes, allowing them to optimize their time management and focus on more complex tasks. However, none of the software descriptions mentioned by the respondents match the characteristics of Big Data analytics (since the collection and storage platforms used do not meet the veracity requirements due to incomplete data issues), nor the blockchain's principle of decentralization (as there is always the intervention of a centralizing body to supervise these platforms). Furthermore, the Big 4 firms interviewed have confirmed that a project to integrate blockchain technology into their working processes will be implemented over the next 3 years and that they are currently initiating blockchain training programs for their employees, in order to make this overhaul a success. Hence, the real challenge is facing small and medium-sized firms, which will need to double their efforts and investments to align themselves with actual standards and ensure their continued survival.

There's no doubt that the digital transformation of audit firms will lead to a significant change in the auditor's profile. Beyond the basic requirements of integrity and professional skepticism, a mastery of technological skills, particularly in data analytics, cloud computing, and cybersecurity will be strongly required. Indeed, complying with this transformation will demand, above all, a significant effort of adaptation. However, it is important to understand that the use of new technologies cannot, in any way, replace the central role of the auditor, given that auditing is based on the formulation of appropriate recommendations for each entity's situation; a distinctly human quality that the digital transition, despite its advances, cannot imitate. In this way, new technologies are perceived as an essential support, rather than a threat to the audit profession.

Implementing the digital dimension also requires alignment with international standards. As the current legal framework reveals the absence of norms governing the use of new technologies in verification processes, Moroccan audit firms will certainly express an increased need for IT standards in order to maintain the quality of their services and comply with this transition, hence the important role of regulatory bodies, namely the OEC.

In contrast to public institutions, which are expected to digitalize their infrastructures by 2030 (according to the "Maroc Digital" strategy), private companies, particularly those operating in the ICT sector, have already reached a significant level of new technology implementation. Thus, the digital transition of auditing firms will enable clients to benefit from personalized services, providing an in-depth analysis of the company's current situation, its potential risk areas, future projections, and planned corrective measures. This revolution will also improve relationships with various stakeholders, including shareholders and users of audit reports, thereby fostering a climate of trust away from unethical behaviors.

Drawing on the work of Hmioui & Bentalha (2020), we have attempted to propose a model for the evaluation of customer experience, which combines a set of performance indicators issued from three different dimensions: auditors, customers, and regulators.

Figure 2. Audit-adapted framework for evaluation of customer experience

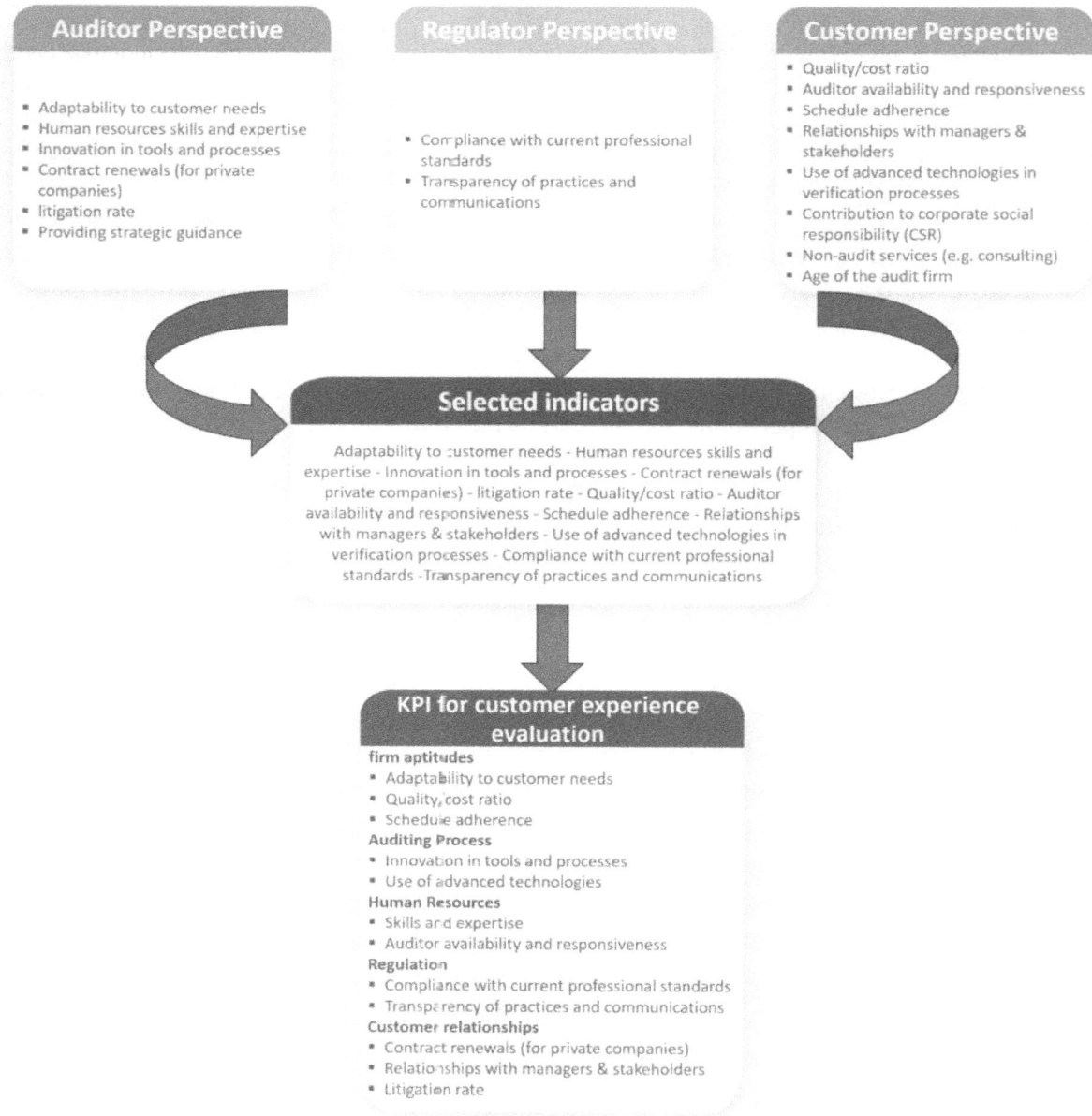

Auditor Perspective

- Adaptability to customer needs
- Human resources skills and expertise
- Innovation in tools and processes
- Contract renewals (for private companies)
- litigation rate
- Providing strategic guidance

Regulator Perspective

- Compliance with current professional standards
- Transparency of practices and communications

Customer Perspective

- Quality/cost ratio
- Auditor availability and responsiveness
- Schedule adherence
- Relationships with managers & stakeholders
- Use of advanced technologies in verification processes
- Contribution to corporate social responsibility (CSR)
- Non-audit services (e.g. consulting)
- Age of the audit firm

Selected indicators

Adaptability to customer needs - Human resources skills and expertise - Innovation in tools and processes - Contract renewals (for private companies) - litigation rate - Quality/cost ratio - Auditor availability and responsiveness - Schedule adherence - Relationships with managers & stakeholders - Use of advanced technologies in verification processes - Compliance with current professional standards - Transparency of practices and communications

KPI for customer experience evaluation

firm aptitudes
- Adaptability to customer needs
- Quality, cost ratio
- Schedule adherence

Auditing Process
- Innovation in tools and processes
- Use of advanced technologies

Human Resources
- Skills and expertise
- Auditor availability and responsiveness

Regulation
- Compliance with current professional standards
- Transparency of practices and communications

Customer relationships
- Contract renewals (for private companies)
- Relationships with managers & stakeholders
- Litigation rate

Source: adapted from Hmioui & Bentalha (2020)

In order to achieve a successful transition, while taking into account both the customer experience optimization and the regulatory aspect, audit firms should adopt a panoply of measures. First, they must prioritize R&D investments to create sophisticated platforms that will allow them to remain competitive in a highly rivalrous industry. In addition, these firms have to set up targeted training programs and ongoing support mechanisms for employees, ensuring a seamless transition and overcoming resistance to change. Furthermore, they should develop a robust data security infrastructure, enabling them to effectively manage sensitive information and protect themselves against breaches or cyberattacks. Such a measure is essential, especially when confidentiality agreements with customers are involved. In the end, the engagement of audit firms in regulatory reform projects is highly recommended. Auditors should help OEC members to understand this transition and manage it well, by encouraging correspondence between them and reporting on the weaknesses identified, as well as possible ways of improvement.

6. CONCLUSION

Based on a Delphi study of the Moroccan context, our main objective was to draw up a prospective overview of the impact of digital transition on audit processes, considering the regulatory framework and the customer experience; a dimension that remains relatively unexplored in the audit field (compared to other areas such as marketing).

To ensure the relevance of our findings, we have tried to select a representative panel of auditors with extensive experience in the industry, as well as regulatory members and entities operating in sectors primarily concerned by this shift. However, we do not claim the exhaustiveness of our results, given that our findings may not reflect the digital reality of all Moroccan companies and institutions.

Hence, the contribution of this chapter can be summarized in a tripartite dimension. Theoretically, the review outlines the inherent concepts of digital transition, namely AI, blockchain, and big data analytics, while also highlighting literature on the relationship between the technological innovation of the audit profession and the optimization of customer experience. From a methodological viewpoint, our contribution is distinguished by the implementation of the Delphi approach, which combines the expertise of respondents with the rigor of the process in order to draw up the most plausible scenario for the research question. In empirical terms, our study traces the evolution of the audit field in the Moroccan context, analyzing current practices of audit firms and outlining future transformations, always with a particular focus on improving the client experience through the prism of digitalization.

From a general perspective, it seems that both audit firms and entities are making significant progress in integrating advanced technologies into their work processes. Current trends highlight a certain optimism regarding this transition, as it contributes to optimizing verification procedures while enabling clients to benefit from more efficient and reliable services. Even so, small and medium-sized audit firms and public institutions should increase their efforts to align themselves with the digital advancements currently adopted by Big 4 firms and private companies, especially in terms of AI.

Moreover, regulatory intervention is crucial for guiding professionals on the ethical and safe use of digital tools. This topic may offer a promising area for future research, allowing for an in-depth exploration of aspects to be considered in regulatory reforms, for better governance of emerging technologies.

REFERENCES

Akins, R. B., Tolson, H., & Cole, B. R. (2005). Stability of response characteristics of a Delphi panel: Application of bootstrap data expansion. *BMC Medical Research Methodology*, 5(37), 1–12. 10.1186/1471-2288-5-3716321161

Alla, L., Kamal, M., & Bouhtati, N. (2022). Big data and marketing effectiveness of tourism businesses: A literature review. *Economic Management Alternatives*, 1, 39–58.

Allouli, N., & Boumeska, M. (2023). The Impact of Digital Transformation on External Auditing: New Perspectives and Emerging Practices: A Systematic Literature Review. *Economic Management Alternatives*, 5(4), 135–153.

Baillette, P., Fallery, B., & Girard, A. (2013). La méthode Delphi pour définir les accords et les controverses: applications à l'innovation dans la traçabilité et dans le e-recrutement. In *18ème Colloque de l'Association Information et Management (AIM)*, 1-22.

Baldwin, A., Brown, C., & Trinkle, B. (2006). Opportunities for artificial intelligence development in the accounting domain: The case for auditing. *International Journal of Intelligent Systems in Accounting Finance & Management*, 14(3), 77–86. 10.1002/isaf.277

Beiderbeck, D., Frevel, N., von der Gracht, H. A., Schmidt, S. L., & Schweitzer, V. M. (2021). Preparing, conducting, and analyzing Delphi surveys: Cross-disciplinary practices, new directions, and advancements. *MethodsX*, 8, 101401. 10.1016/j.mex.2021.10140134430297

Belton, I., MacDonald, A., Wright, G., & Hamlin, I. (2019). Improving the practical application of the Delphi method in group-based judgment: A six-step prescription for a well-founded and defensible process. *Technological Forecasting and Social Change*, 147, 72–82. 10.1016/j.techfore.2019.07.002

Bentalha, B. (2020). Big-Data et Service Supply chain management: Challenges et opportunités. *International Journal of Business and Technology Studies*, 1(3), 1–9.

Bolton, , R., Gustafsson, A., McColl-Kennedy, J., Sirianni, N., & Tse, D. (2014). Small details that make big differences: A radical approach to consumption experience as a firm's differentiating strategy. *Journal of Service Management*, 25(2), 253–274. 10.1108/JOSM-01-2014-0034

Bouhtati, N., Alla, L., & Bentalha, B. (2023). Marketing Big Data Analytics and Customer Relationship Management: A Fuzzy Approach. In *Integrating Intelligence and Sustainability in Supply Chains* (pp. 75–86). IGI Global. 10.4018/979-8-3693-0225-5.ch004

Bourany, T. (2018). Les 5V du big data. *Regards croisés sur l'économie, 23*(2), 27-31.

Buckle, J. L., Dwyer, S. C., & Jackson, M. (2010). Qualitative bereavement research: Incongruity between the perspectives of participants and research ethics boards. *International Journal of Social Research Methodology*, 13(2), 111–125. 10.1080/13645570902767918

Chalmers, J., & Armour, M. (2019). The Delphi Technique. In Liamputtong, P. (Ed.), *Handbook of Research Methods in Health Social Sciences* (pp. 715–735). Springer Singapore. 10.1007/978-981-10-5251-4_99

Dagilienė, L., & Klovienė, L. (2019). Motivation to use big data and big data analytics in external auditing. *Managerial Auditing Journal*, 34(7), 750–782. 10.1108/MAJ-01-2018-1773

De Loë, R. C., Melnychuk, N., Murray, D., & Plummer, R. (2016). Advancing the state of policy Delphi practice: A systematic review evaluating methodological evolution, innovation, and opportunities. *Technological Forecasting and Social Change*, 104, 78–88. 10.1016/j.techfore.2015.12.009

Desplebin, O., Lux, G., Petit, N. (2018). L'évolution de la comptabilité, du contrôle, de l'audit et de leurs métiers au prisme de la Blockchain: une réflexion prospective. *Revue management et avenir, 103*(5), 137-157.

Desplebin, O., Lux, G., & Petit, N. (2021). To be or not to be: Blockchain and the future of accounting and auditing. *Accounting Perspectives*, 20(4), 743–769. 10.1111/1911-3838.12265

Ez-Zaidi, A., & Ghandari, Y. (2023). Audit profession and innovation: Emerging practices in the era of digital transformation and their relationship to the environment. In *E3S Web of Conferences, 412, 01010*. EDP Sciences. 10.1051/e3sconf/202341201010

Fedyk, A., Hodson, J., Khimich, N., & Fedyk, T. (2022). Is artificial intelligence improving the audit process? *Review of Accounting Studies*, 27(3), 938–985. 10.1007/s11142-022-09697-x

Gantz, J., Reinsel, D. (2012). The digital universe in 2020: Big data, bigger digital shadows, and biggest growth in the far East. *IDC iView: IDC Analyze the future*, 1-16.

Gross, M. A., & Pullman, M. (2012). Playing their roles: Experiential design concepts applied in complex services. *Journal of Management Inquiry*, 21(1), 43–59. 10.1177/1056492610395928

Hadinia, S., Abdi, R., Pakmaram, A., & Jafari, A. (2023). Designing a model of wise decision-making process in auditing with a fuzzy Delphi approach. *International Journal of Nonlinear Analysis and Applications*, 14(9), 65–78.

Haenlein, M., & Kaplan, A. (2019). A brief history of artificial intelligence: On the past, present, and future of artificial intelligence. *California Management Review*, 61(4), 5–1. 10.1177/0008125619864925

Han, H., Shiwakoti, R. K., Jarvis, R., Mordi, C., & Botchie, D. (2023). Accounting and auditing with blockchain technology and artificial Intelligence: A literature review. *International Journal of Accounting Information Systems*, 48, 100598. 10.1016/j.accinf.2022.100598

Hanna, K., & Noble, B. F. (2015). Using a Delphi study to identify effectiveness criteria for environmental assessment. *Impact Assessment and Project Appraisal*, 33(2), 116–125. 10.1080/14615517.2014.992672

Hennink, M. M., Kaiser, B. N., & Weber, M. B. (2019). What influences saturation? Estimating sample sizes in focus group research. *Qualitative Health Research*, 29(10), 1483–1496. 10.1177/1049732318 82169230628545

Hmioui, A., & Bentalha, B. (2020). Service Supply Chain Management and commercial performance: Sketch of a theoretical synthesis. *Economic Management Alternatives*, 2, 1–21.

ICAEW. (2018). *Blockchain and the future of accountancy*. ICAEW IT Faculty. https://www.icaew.com/technical/technology/blockchain-and-cryptoassets/blockchain-articles/blockchain-and-the-accounting-perspective. (accessed: 19 January 2024)

Iglesias, C. P., Thompson, A., Rogowski, W. H., & Payne, K. (2016). Reporting Guidelines for the Use of Expert Judgement in Model-Based Economic Evaluations. *PharmacoEconomics*, 34(11), 1161–1172. 10.1007/s40273-016-0425-927364887

Ishwarappa, A., & Anuradha, J. (2015). A brief introduction on big data 5Vs characteristics and Hadoop technology. *Procedia Computer Science*, 48, 319–324. 10.1016/j.procs.2015.04.188

Issa, H., Sun, T., & Vasarhelyi, M. A. (2016). Research ideas for artificial intelligence in auditing: The formalization of audit and workforce supplementation. *Journal of Emerging Technologies in Accounting*, 13(2), 1–20. 10.2308/jeta-10511

Javaid, M., Haleem, A., Singh, R. P., Suman, R., & Khan, S. (2022). A review of Blockchain Technology applications for financial services. *BenchCouncil Transactions on Benchmarks. Standards and Evaluations*, 2(3), 100073.

Lemon, K. N., & Verhoef, P. C. (2016). Understanding customer experience throughout the customer journey. *Journal of Marketing*, 80(6), 69–96. 10.1509/jm.15.0420

Mikalef, P., & Gupta, M. (2021). Artificial intelligence capability: Conceptualization, measurement calibration, and empirical study on its impact on organizational creativity and firm performance. *Information & Management*, 58(3), 103434. 10.1016/j.im.2021.103434

Needham, R. D., & De Loë, R. C. (1990). The policy Delphi: Purpose, structure, and application. *The Canadian Geographer. Geographe Canadien*, 34(2), 133–142. 10.1111/j.1541-0064.1990.tb01258.x

Niederberger, M., & Spranger, J. (2020). Delphi technique in health sciences: A map. *Frontiers in Public Health*, 8, 561103. 10.3389/fpubh.2020.00457 33072683

Noraini, A., & Saiful Azmi, I., Yuhaniz, Sophiayati, S., Suriani, M.S. (2015). Data quality in big data: A review. *International Journal Of Advances In Soft Computing And Its Applications*, 7(3), 16–27.

OEC. (2013). *Code Des Devoirs Professionnels*. OEC. http://www.oec-casablanca.ma/img/uploads/Code_des_Devoirs_Professionnels_Conforme_au_Code_Deontologique_de_L_IFAC_2009.pdf

Okoli, C., & Pawlowski, S. D. (2004). The Delphi method as a research tool: An example, design considerations and applications. *Information & Management*, 42(1), 15–29. 10.1016/j.im.2003.11.002

Oliveira Simoyama, F., Grigg, I., Luiz Pereira Bueno, R., & Oliveira, L. C. (2017). Triple entry ledgers with blockchain for auditing. *International Journal of Auditing Technology*, 3(3), 163–183. 10.1504/IJAUDIT.2017.086741

Pagani, M., & Pardo, C. (2017). The impact of digital technology on relationships in a business network. *Industrial Marketing Management*, 67, 185–192. 10.1016/j.indmarman.2017.08.009

Paré, G., Cameron, A.-F., Poba-Nzaou, P., & Templier, M. (2013). A systematic assessment of rigor in information systems ranking-type Delphi studies. *Information & Management*, 50(5), 207–217. 10.1016/j.im.2013.03.003

Pietilä, A. M., Nurmi, S. M., Halkoaho, A., Kyngäs, H. (2020). Qualitative research: Ethical considerations. *The application of content analysis in nursing science research*, 49-69.

Ramdi, I. (2021). La technologie digitale et la profession d'audit: Quel impact?. *International Journal of Accounting, Finance, Auditing, Management and Economics, 2*(6-1), 126-144.

Shang, Z. (2023). Use of Delphi in health sciences research: A narrative review. *Medicine*, 102(7), 1–7. 10.1097/MD.0000000000003282936800594

Spiess, J., T'Joens, Y., Dragnea, R., Spencer, P., & Philippart, L. (2014). Using big data to improve customer experience and business performance. *Bell Labs Technical Journal*, 18(4), 3–17. 10.1002/bltj.21642

Stitt-Gohdes, W. L., Crews, T. B. (2004). The Delphi technique: A research strategy for career and technical education. *Journal of career and technical education, 20*(2), 55-67.

Sun, T., & Vasarhelyi, M. A. (2017). Deep Learning and the Future of Auditing: How an Evolving Technology Could Transform Analysis and Improve Judgment. *The CPA Journal*, 87(6), 24–29.

Szczepanski, M. (2019). *Economic impacts of artificial intelligence (AI)*. EPRS: European Parliamentary Research Service, Belgium. https://policycommons.net/artifacts/1334867/economic-impacts-of-artificial-intelligence-ai/1940719/

Tiberius, V., & Hirth, S. (2019). Impacts of digitization on auditing: A Delphi study for Germany. *Journal of International Accounting, Auditing & Taxation*, 37, 100288. 10.1016/j.intaccaudtax.2019.100288

Verhoef, P. C., Broekhuizen, T., Bart, Y., Bhattacharya, A., Dong, J. Q., Fabian, N., & Haenlein, M. (2019). Digital transformation: A multidisciplinary reflection and research agenda. *Journal of Business Research*, 122, 889–901. 10.1016/j.jbusres.2019.09.022

Zemankova, A. (2019). Artificial intelligence in audit and accounting: development, current trends, opportunities and threats-literature review. *International Conference on Control, Artificial Intelligence, Robotics & Optimization (ICCAIRO)*, (pp. 148-154). IEEE. 10.1109/ICCAIRO47923.2019.00031

Chapter 16
Client Satisfaction in the Moroccan Banking Sector:
The Role of Digitalization

Nabil Seghyar

Research Laboratory in Organizational Management Sciences, Ibn Tofail University, Kenitra, Morocco

Meryem Amane

Artificial Intelligence, Data Science, and Emergent Systems Laboratory, Sidi Mohamed Ben Abdellah University, Fez, Morocco

Mounir Gouiouez

Psychology, Sociology, and Culture Studies Laboratory, Sidi Mohamed Ben Abdellah University, Fez, Morocco

Said Hraoui

http://orcid.org/0000-0001-6838-5734

Artificial Intelligence, Data Science, and Emergent Systems Laboratory, Sidi Mohamed Ben Abdellah University, Fez, Morocco

Abdelfettah Bouhtati

LRJPE laboratory, Multidisciplinary Faculty of Taza, Sidi Mohamed Ben Abdellah University, Morocco

ABSTRACT

This study delves into Moroccan banking's evolving landscape, focusing on client satisfaction through digital tools. Emphasizing digital's pivotal role in service quality, it aims to uncover how emerging tech shapes satisfaction. Employing quantitative methods via tailored questionnaires, it seeks to gauge customer perceptions of digital banking. Examining tech integration, AI-Chatbots, and personalized services, it explores how these enhance satisfaction. Additionally, it probes AI-driven marketing's transformative potential in deepening bank-client connections. By spotlighting digital tool efficacy in client satisfaction, this research offers nuanced insights into Morocco's tech-driven banking paradigm. Its data-driven findings can guide strategic decisions for institutions and policymakers, elevating overall service quality in the digital age.

DOI: 10.4018/979-8-3693-3172-9.ch016

1. INTRODUCTION

In a digitized world, both the public and private sectors are affected by the digital revolution, which transforms the consumption and communication modes of all economic actors and influences the notion of service. Thus, the application of digital marketing has become a logical response to the new market conditions (ALLA et al., 2022).The rapid expansion of the digital world and its exponential effects have radically transformed multiple sectors, particularly finance and banking. Technological advancements such as artificial intelligence and digitization have profoundly altered consumer behaviors and expectations regarding banking services (Gomber & al., 2018).Faced with challenges such as high costs and the imperative to meet customer expectations, financial institutions are compelled to rethink their business models and embrace new approaches to optimize customer experiences. The introduction of innovation in the banking sector dates back several decades, with significant milestones such as the installation of the first transatlantic cable in 1866. Since then, information systems have played a crucial role in automating administrative tasks and managing financial operations, thus facilitating strategic decision-making for industry stakeholders (Bouhtatit et al., 2023).

In recent years, the banking sector in Morocco has witnessed major changes, influencing consumer behaviors, introducing new technologies, and expanding the range of products and services available (Machkour & Abriane, 2020). The rapid evolution of the banking landscape, particularly with the advent of digitization, has led to significant changes in customer expectations and requirements. Increasingly, customers are turning to online banking for their daily transactions and remote access to banking services, thus illustrating the growing importance of digital tools in their financial management. However, despite this transition towards digitization, challenges persist, particularly concerning customer satisfaction in the use of digital banking tools (Lhoussaine et al., 2022). Studies have highlighted gaps in understanding how emerging technologies influence customer satisfaction and loyalty in the Moroccan banking sector. In this vein, this study is committed to exploring in-depth the mechanism for measuring customer satisfaction in the Moroccan banking sector, with particular emphasis on the role of digital tools. As digital banking continues to gain popularity, it is essential to understand how these technologies influence the customer experience and alter their perception of the quality of banking services, in order to optimize their level of satisfaction.

However, to better meet the demands of clients, Moroccan banks are called upon to enhance and develop their digitization system, which thus constitutes a key lever for strengthening their competitiveness and overall performance. This implies a necessary review in terms of digital tools as well as security and confidentiality policies. This chapter aligns with this approach. It aims to contribute to analyzing the influence of digitalization on customer satisfaction in the banking sector. The main question we seek to answer in this study can be formulated as follows: To what extent does the implementation of digitalization by banks contribute to improving the level of customer satisfaction?

The objectives of this research aim for a comprehensive evaluation of customer satisfaction in the Moroccan banking sector, focusing on the Fes-Meknes region. This entails conducting an in-depth analysis to measure and understand satisfaction levels, taking into account factors such as the integration of new technologies, the use of artificial intelligence and chatbots, and also the customization of online services. The survey will assess how these factors are integrated into banking practices and their influence on improving the customer experience. Additionally, the research will seek to identify the key contributors to customer satisfaction within digital tools.

Our methodological approach relies on a quantitative methodology, employing questionnaires specifically designed to assess and analyze the key elements contributing to customer satisfaction. By integrating the distinctive features of digital tools as well as quality criteria into our analysis, our aim is to make a significant contribution to understanding the dynamics of customer satisfaction in the Moroccan banking sector (case of the Fes-Meknes region).

The Fès-Meknès region was chosen for this study to provide a representative perspective of the Moroccan banking sector and its technological advancements. Its dynamic nature in terms of economic development and adoption of digital technologies makes it a conducive environment for analyzing customer satisfaction dynamics in this sector. By examining the adoption and usage of new technologies such as artificial intelligence and chatbots in the banking services of the region, this study aims to provide valuable insights into emerging trends and the impact of these technologies on customer experience. The findings of this research could thus guide the strategic decisions of financial institutions and policymakers, not only in Fès-Meknès but also throughout Morocco.

The research topic on customer satisfaction in the Moroccan banking sector, highlighting the use of digital tools, is motivated by several key factors. Firstly, it reflects the relevance of the evolving context of banking services in Morocco, where digital technologies are increasingly prominent. Additionally, it addresses a crucial strategic aspect, as customer satisfaction is a determining factor of banks' competitiveness. Furthermore, this research explores both the opportunities and challenges associated with the integration of digital tools in banking services, thus addressing a tangible need within the sector. Finally, the conclusions of this study have the potential to have a significant impact on the strategic decisions of financial institutions and policymakers in Morocco.

2. GENERAL FRAMEWORK OF THE ANALYSIS

2.1. Digitalization of Moroccan Banks

Banks have always been pivotal players in the economy, responsible for collecting savings to redistribute them in the form of credit. However, during the 2000s, a global revolution closely linked to digital transformation led to significant changes in the economic landscape (Mairesse & al., 2000). This transformation has disrupted the banking sector in unprecedented ways, challenging its dominant position. Once symbols of tradition and formality, banks are now propelled towards a digital future.

The advent of digitalization has disrupted the banking sector, compelling institutions to adapt to emerging technologies to meet the evolving needs and expectations of an increasingly connected clientele. According to Pluchart (2017), the modernization of banking practices is crucial while preserving the human aspect. The challenge lies in creating synergy between "human and digital" in the service of finance, enabling banks to assume a dual role both utilitarian and carrying a cultural dimension (Pluchart, 2017).

Ouiza (2014) reinforces the idea that the banking sector is one of the most impacted by information and communication technologies (ICT). He emphasizes the necessity for banks to adopt and leverage digitalization to maintain their competitiveness (Jaouad & Ouchekkir, 2023). Other researchers, such as Roman B. and Tchibozo (2017), echo this sentiment by highlighting the value creation potential offered by digitalization in the banking domain .

The cultural integration of digital banking in Morocco is a dynamic process influenced by several socio-cultural, economic, and technological factors. In a society where social interactions and financial habits are often rooted in specific cultural traditions and norms, the transition to digital in the banking sector represents a significant change. The perception of digital banking is influenced by cultural factors such as trust in new technologies, attitudes toward innovation, social norms, and family values (Mani& Chouk, 2018). Historically, Moroccans place great importance on personal relationships and trust in financial transactions, which can influence their willingness to adopt digital banking services. Similarly, the acceptance of digital banking is also conditioned by economic considerations such as internet access, the availability of digital infrastructure, and income levels (Haouam, 2022). In a country where internet access is expanding, particularly through the increasing use of smartphones, more and more Moroccans have the opportunity to access online banking services.

The Moroccan banking sector, a cornerstone of the national economy, plays a crucial role in the country's economic and financial development. To maintain their competitiveness in both national and international markets, Moroccan banks must leverage the opportunities offered by digital transformation. This shift in the Moroccan banking sector primarily focuses on the digitization and modernization of financial services (Cherkaoui, 2016). The digital transition of the Moroccan banking sector has been characterized by the rapid growth of e-banking and m-banking. These technologies have revolutionized the customer experience by providing the ability to access accounts and conduct transactions anytime, anywhere. Banks have significantly expanded their range of online services, allowing customers to benefit from advanced features such as portfolio management and personalized financial advice (Ali & al., 2023).

The digital transformation of the Moroccan banking sector has led to a significant increase in digital transactions, indicating a growing adoption of technologies by customers. Even participatory banks have integrated digital technology since their inception to meet the specific needs of their clientele. This digitalization aims to provide more accessible, flexible, and personalized services while enabling banks to remain competitive in a constantly evolving financial environment (Demraoui & al., 2022).

2.2. Structure of the Moroccan Banking System

The Moroccan banking sector stands out for its remarkable maturity and resilience. According to the 2023 Annual Report on Banking Supervision, there are 90 credit institutions and similar bodies licensed by the central bank. This diverse banking landscape comprises 24 banks, including 5 participatory banks and 3 participatory windows, as well as 29 financing companies, 6 offshore banks, 11 microcredit associations, 18 payment institutions, and 2 other entities (including a guarantee institution with a participatory window) (Bank Al Maghrib, annual report on banking supervision, Fiscal Year 2022).

Table 1. The ninety aforementioned institutions classified by category

Type of institution	number
Banks	24 institutions
Finance companies	29 institutions
Offshore banks	6 institutions
Microcredit associations	11 institutions

continued on following page

Table 1. Continued

Type of institution	number
Payment institutions	18 institutions
Others	2 institutions

Source: Bank Al-Maghrib, Annual Report on Banking Supervision, Fiscal Year 2023.

The Moroccan banking sector has been witnessing a gradual reduction in its physical branch network, directly attributable to the increasing prominence of digital banking services. This trend has been further exacerbated since the emergence of the Covid-19 pandemic, with a heightened adoption of digital channels by customers. Concurrently, banks have implemented strategies aimed at restructuring and optimizing their geographical distribution networks and the services offered to their clientele, thereby adapting to the new market realities. (Bank Al-Maghrib, Annual Report on Banking Supervision, 2022).

Digitization has emerged as a central strategic axis for the future of banking services (Naimi-Sadigh & al., 2022). Faced with this observation, Moroccan banks are striving to develop multichannel offerings, leveraging mobile banking, next-generation automated teller machines (smart ATMs), and online services (e-banking). The ultimate goal is to provide an optimal customer experience, continually evolving and enriched with new features and advanced services, while ensuring transaction security. These digital channels offer a wide range of functionalities, allowing customers to check their accounts, open new ones, submit requests, pay bills, and perform various types of transactions. In their efforts to enhance the customer experience, banks are adopting remote account opening procedures and gradually digitizing their services for both individuals and businesses (Sapovadia, 2018).

Moroccan banks are diversifying their customer interaction modes and prospects. They now rely on digital conversational agents, commonly known as "chatbots," to address inquiries and provide information about their products and services. Moreover, social media platforms serve as a preferred communication channel to interact with customers and enhance proximity (Allioui & Allioui, 2022).

The Moroccan-banking sector is steadfastly committed to improving its services and better meeting the needs of the population, as highlighted in the 2023 annual report on banking supervision. The digitalization of banking services is a key element of this transformation, resulting in a gradual reduction in the number of bank branches nationwide (Abdelkhalek & al., 2021). Indeed, by the end of 2022, the number of bank branches decreased by 151 units to reach a total of 5905. This evolution is mixed: conventional banks recorded a decrease of 165 branches, while participatory banks saw an increase of 14 branches (annual report on banking supervision, 2023).

2.3. Regulatory Challenges of Digital Usage in the Banking Sector in Morocco

Banking institutions acknowledge the economic and managerial benefits of embracing digitalization in delivering their services. This acknowledgment drives them to fully engage in the utilization of this technology, supported by the constitutional guarantees of technical freedom and entrepreneurship (Articles 25 and 35 of the Moroccan Constitution of 2011).

However, this approach must be balanced with respect for the right to privacy and the protection of personal data, which requires reflection on the legal framework of digitalization in the banking sector. Digitalization provides banking institutions with the opportunity to enhance the efficiency and effectiveness of their practices, streamline risk management, deliver more personalized services, and maintain their competitiveness in an ever-evolving market.

However, this shift to digitalization also raises legal concerns, primarily focused on protecting the privacy of clients. Balancing banks' freedom to innovate with clients' right to privacy poses a significant challenge. On one hand, banking institutions have the right and even the responsibility to seek innovative ways to enhance their services and operational efficiency, which involves adopting technologies such as artificial intelligence. On the other hand, clients enjoy the fundamental right to privacy and the protection of their personal data. In this context, banks must navigate carefully to strike a delicate balance between leveraging digitalization to streamline their operations and preserving the rights and privacy of their clients (Forest,2020). This requires a thorough analysis of digital usage, the data collected, and their processing. Furthermore, it underscores the importance of implementing regulations and practices to ensure ethical and responsible use of digital technology, while preserving the rights and individual freedoms of customers.

The legal framework governing digitalization in the banking sector in Morocco is still in the development phase. Currently, there is no specific legal framework explicitly regulating the use of digital technology in banking operations. However, this does not imply a complete absence of regulation. Some general legislative provisions may indirectly concern the digitization used by banks (Slimani, 2021). For example:

- Law 103.12 concerning credit institutions and similar organizations, established by Dahir No. 1-14-193 of 1st Rabii I 1436 (December 24, 2014), particularly articles 77, 78, 151, and 160: This legislation regulates the activities of credit institutions and may also govern various aspects related to the use of artificial intelligence, particularly concerning prudential measures and risk management.
- Law 53-05 concerning the electronic exchange of legal data, promulgated by Dahir No. 1-07-129 of November 30, 2007: This legislation regulates transactions involving the exchange of electronic data, which can impact the technologies used in the context of online banking services and process dematerialization.
- The Law 43-20 regarding trust services for electronic transactions, enacted by Dahir No. 1-20-100 on December 31, 2020: This legislation pertains to services ensuring the authenticity and integrity of electronic transactions, which holds significance in the context of online banking operations and data security.
- The Law 09-08 on the protection of individuals with regard to the processing of personal data, promulgated by Dahir No. 1-09-15 on 22 Safar 1430 (February 18, 2009): This legislation establishes the principles and rules governing the processing of personal data, which is of paramount importance given the amount of sensitive data handled by banks in the course of their activities.

While these laws do not establish specific guidelines for the digital domain, they may still regulate certain aspects of its use in the banking sector. However, given the constantly evolving and complex nature of digital technology, it is likely that more detailed regulations will be necessary in the future to address the legal and ethical challenges posed by this technology.

The integration of digital technologies by Moroccan banks involves the acquisition and processing of considerable volumes of customers' personal data. This data falls under the purview of the Personal Data Protection Law, which sets forth principles and guidelines to ensure the confidentiality and security of individuals' personal information (Slimani, 2021). In accordance with the legislation on personal data protection, banking institutions are required to adhere to stringent standards when collecting and processing their customers' data.

Furthermore, the legislation on personal data protection grants clients several rights, including the right to information, the right of access, the right to rectification, the right to object, the right to erasure, and the right to data portability(Forest,2020). These rights are designed to ensure that individuals retain control over their own personal information and can exert some influence over its use by banking institutions.

Therefore, the challenges associated with the integration of digital technologies in Moroccan banking institutions primarily focus on preserving the confidentiality and security of clients' personal data, in compliance with legislation on personal data protection. The goal is to ensure respect for individual rights and the protection of sensitive information.

2.4. Improving Banking Customer Satisfaction Through Digital Means

The rise of Information and Communication Technologies (ICT) creates a fertile environment for the emergence of innovative digital solutions. These solutions are transforming how customers gather information and data needed to make informed decisions. The flexibility and seamlessness of digital solutions are major assets in captivating and retaining users. Moreover, these solutions enable the building of enduring and evolving relationships between banks and their clients. Banking digital systems are reshaping communication between banks and their clients. They facilitate continuous contact and active listening, fostering higher quality relationships and increased collaboration between the two stakeholders (Mainardes & al., 2017).

By placing the customer at the center of its concerns and integrating them into the innovation process, the bank can better understand their needs, anticipate their issues, and comprehend their expectations. This enables the offering of personalized services that enhance customer satisfaction and loyalty, thereby contributing to the establishment of a lasting relationship (Li & al., 2021). These digital systems can also be seen as data and information collection tools, as well as facilitators of effective communication with customers, thus providing banks with more opportunities and options to reach a wider range of clients. Consequently, the digital systems offered by banks are considered a crucial factor in enhancing the customer experience and influencing their future behaviors (Anshari & al., 2019).

Exploring the impact of digital systems on enhancing customer satisfaction in the banking sector relies on thorough research conducted by experts from various fields. Parasuraman et al. (2005) meticulously examined the crucial role of electronic service quality in strengthening customer satisfaction, focusing particularly on online banking services. Their study revealed how aspects such as user-friendliness, reliability, and security of digital platforms significantly influence customers' perception of service quality (Parasuraman & al., 2005).

In light of technological advancements, Huang and Rust (2018) examined the applications of artificial intelligence and predictive analytics in the banking sector. Their research highlighted the opportunities presented by these technologies to anticipate customer needs and provide personalized and proactive services, thus playing a crucial role in optimizing customer satisfaction.

Reichheld and Schefter (2000) examined online customer loyalty as part of their in-depth research on the customization of digital services by banking institutions aimed at enhancing customer loyalty. Their study highlighted the crucial importance of creating personalized and engaging experiences to foster customer loyalty, especially in an increasingly competitive digital environment . In a similar context, Tapscott and Tapscott (2016) explored the possibilities offered by blockchain technology to transform traditional banking services. Their detailed analysis underscored the numerous advantages of blockchain in terms of security, transparency, and transaction efficiency, thus opening new avenues for enhancing the customer experience in the banking sector (Ghosh.,2019). In a similar vein, Dhamija et al. (2006) analyzed phishing strategies and online security risks, highlighting the challenges faced by both clients and financial institutions in an ever-evolving digital environment (Imgraben & al., 2014). Their research underscored the significance of utilizing banking services via mobile devices to reduce financial disparities and enhance the autonomy of low-income populations (Donner & Tellez, 2008).

Regarding online transaction security, Dinev and Hart's study (2006) examined consumers' perceptions and concerns regarding data privacy in the context of digital banking services. Their research identified key factors influencing clients' trust in online transactions, thereby highlighting the crucial importance of ensuring the security and confidentiality of personal information . Similarly, Morawczynski and Pickens (2009) delved into the adoption of mobile banking services by low-income populations, shedding light on the obstacles and opportunities associated with this transition to digital solutions in diverse socio-economic contexts .

Regarding change management strategies, Kotter's eight-step model (1995) proves to be an invaluable resource for financial institutions seeking a successful transition to digital banking services. This model emphasizes the crucial importance of leadership, communication, and employee engagement in promoting organizational change and ensuring the success of digital transformation . Lastly, in assessing the impact of digital transformation on customer satisfaction, Anderson and Sullivan's customer satisfaction model (1993) provides a robust framework for evaluating the effectiveness of digital solutions in enhancing the customer experience (Anderson & Sullivan, 1993).

Similarly, the comprehensive approach to electronic service quality proposed by Zeithaml and colleagues (2005) provides valuable insights for evaluating the overall quality of digital banking services. By consolidating the contributions of these esteemed researchers, a thorough literature review can offer a deep understanding of the challenges, opportunities, and best practices associated with the adoption of digital solutions.

In the Moroccan context, the influence of digitalization on the level of satisfaction of bank customers proves to be a fundamental issue. Recent research works affirm a significant upheaval in the practices and financial services of Moroccan banks, influenced by the rise of digitalization. This evolution is manifested by the increasing adoption of digital technologies in the banking sector, aiming to meet customer expectations and enhance their level of satisfaction. For example, the research work of Jaouad & Ouchekkir (2023) addresses this growing importance of digital transformation in Moroccan banks, revealing the induced modifications in traditional banking sector practices. Similarly, studies conducted by Haloui et al (2020) highlight the positive outcomes of digitization on the management of risks associated with customer relations in Moroccan banks, suggesting that this evolution could contribute to increased customer satisfaction. On the other hand, the studies of El Ouidani & Oul-Caid (2023) focus on the legal and economic challenges related to the integration of Artificial Intelligence in Moroccan banks, emphasizing the potential of this technology to enhance the customer experience. By examining the specific risks associated with the digitization of banking services, Achemrah et al (2024) highlight the importance of rigorous risk management to improve the level of trust and satisfaction of customers in a digitalization context. As a final example, Senihji's study (2023) highlights the role of digital marketing in personalizing banking services to optimize and ensure customer satisfaction in Moroccan banks. Their study suggests that a personalized approach, based on a deep understanding of customer needs and expectations, can lead to higher satisfaction and significant loyalty. Overall, this literature review on the Moroccan context underscores the crucial importance of digitalization in enhancing customer satisfaction in Moroccan banks, while also highlighting the challenges and opportunities associated with this transformation.

2.5. Digital Factors Impacting Customer Satisfaction in the Banking Sector

Digitalization is crucial for customer experience in the modern banking sector, significantly impacting various aspects that contribute to customer satisfaction. By closely examining these elements resulting from digital transformation, we can gain a clearer understanding of their interrelation and influence on the overall banking customer experience.

First and foremost, the usability of digital platforms is of paramount importance. Customers seek intuitive and user-friendly interfaces that allow them to navigate easily and access banking services online or through mobile applications. Well-thought-out design not only facilitates transactions but also enhances overall satisfaction by reducing barriers encountered when using services.

Another crucial aspect is the availability of online and mobile services. Customers value the ability to manage their finances anytime, anywhere, providing them with greater flexibility in account management. Services accessible 24/7 meet the expectations of contemporary customers and enhance their satisfaction by offering increased freedom in their interactions with their bank (Singh & Srivastava, 2020). This is supported by several studies, including those by Parasuraman et al. (2005), Sánchez-Fernández and Iniesta-Bonillo (2007), and Riquelme et al. (2018). Ensuring the security of online transactions remains a major priority for customers, who need assurance that their personal and financial data are well protected when conducting transactions on the internet (Zhou, 2018). Banks that implement robust security measures, such as two-factor authentication and data encryption, bolster their customers' trust and thereby contribute to increased satisfaction (Tsai & Su, 2021).

Personalization of online services has now become a strategic differentiation factor for financial institutions. Customers appreciate personalized recommendations based on their spending habits, tailored promotional offers to meet their specific needs, and customized services (Sunikka & al., 2011). Banks that effectively leverage customer data to personalize their experience enhance customer engagement and loyalty, as confirmed by research conducted by Verhoef et al. (2010).

On the other hand, the integration of artificial intelligence and chatbots represents an emerging trend in enhancing the customer experience. These tools enable banks to provide instant and personalized assistance to their clients, promptly addressing their inquiries and efficiently resolving their issues (El Bakkouri & al., 2022). This technology contributes to increased accessibility and responsiveness of customer services, thereby generating higher overall satisfaction, as evidenced by studies by Chen et al. (2020) and Li et al. (2021).

The promptness and efficiency of online customer service are critical elements for customer satisfaction. Customers expect to receive quick and effective assistance when encountering questions or issues while using online banking services. Banks that provide responsive and efficient communication channels, such as live chat and email, demonstrate their commitment to customer satisfaction and thereby strengthen their relationship with their clientele (Boateng & Narteh, 2016). By carefully analyzing these various aspects of digitization in the banking sector, it becomes evident that each element plays a crucial role in creating a remarkable customer experience. Banks that succeed in optimizing these factors are better positioned to meet the growing expectations of customers regarding digitization and to maintain their competitiveness in the market.

3. HYPOTHESES FORMULATION AND CONCEPTUAL MODEL

Today, the integration of digital and online tools is essential in crafting marketing strategies aimed at enhancing customer satisfaction and optimizing their experience. Therefore, it is crucial for a company to understand the digital journeys of its target audience. Digitalization enriches the customer experience by providing greater accessibility, customization, efficiency, and responsiveness, while also enabling businesses to gather data to better understand and serve their customers (Hoyer & al., 2020).

However, it is paramount to maintain a balance between digital automation and human interactions to deliver an optimal customer experience.

3.1. Integration of New Technologies to Meet Customer Needs

The integration of new technologies into the banking sector stems from the pursuit of increased efficiency and better alignment ith customer expectations. The rapid evolution of technology has enabled financial institutions to adopt innovative solutions to enhance the customer experience and meet the growing demands for financial services.

Among these emerging technologies are artificial intelligence, big data, chatbots, biometrics, and mobile applications, to name a few. These advancements provide banks with the opportunity to offer more responsive, personalized, and accessible services anytime and anywhere (Pham& al., 2020). For instance, artificial intelligence and chatbots are deployed to provide automated and round-the-clock customer service, addressing customer queries and assisting them with transactions. Mobile applications, on the other hand, allow customers to manage their accounts and conduct banking operations without the need to visit a branch.

Furthermore, the use of big data enables banking institutions to analyze customer behaviors and preferences, thus facilitating the prediction of their needs and the provision of personalized offers (Vassakis et al., 2018). Biometrics, by ensuring the security of online transactions through biometric data such as fingerprints or facial recognition, enhances users' trust in these services. By integrating these new technologies, financial institutions can enhance the customer experience by aligning their offerings with the individual needs and preferences of each customer. Consequently, they contribute to increasing customer satisfaction, strengthening brand loyalty, and maintaining competitiveness in the financial market (Bouhtati et al., 2023)).

The integration of these new technologies into the banking sector pursues several essential objectives: improving customer experience, enhancing the security of online transactions, and enabling banks to remain competitive in an ever-changing economic landscape. This transition represents a true revolution in how financial services are offered and perceived by customers, with profound implications for the future of the banking industry.

Considering the increasing impact of new technologies in the banking sector, it is plausible to formulate the hypothesis as follows:

Hypothesis 1: Successfully integrating new technologies into banking services to meet customer needs will lead to an improvement in customer satisfaction.

3.2. Use of Artificial Intelligence and Chatbots

The integration of artificial intelligence (AI) and chatbots in the banking sector marks a true revolution in service delivery and customer interactions. Chatbots, leveraging sophisticated AI algorithms, provide instant assistance to customers through automated conversations. This technological advancement enables customers to quickly get answers to their questions and resolve issues without requiring the intervention of a human advisor (Paliwal & al., 2020) .

Furthermore, artificial intelligence is used to analyze customer data and anticipate their future needs. Through these analyses, financial institutions can personalize their product and service offerings, anticipate customer demands, and provide relevant recommendations (Peppard, 2000). For example, a bank can leverage AI to detect a customer's spending habits and suggest a financial product tailored to their specific needs.

The increased personalization of banking services through AI and chatbots represents a significant advancement for the customer experience, providing tailor-made solutions that contribute to enhancing customer satisfaction and loyalty. By automating customer interactions, banks can improve their operational efficiency, reduce costs, and allocate more resources to high-value activities, such as personalized financial advice or the development of new innovative offerings (Rane, 2023). Consequently, the adoption of artificial intelligence and chatbots in the banking sector significantly enhances the customer experience by making it more seamless, personalized, and efficient. These innovations enable financial institutions to proactively adapt to the changing needs of their clientele while maintaining their competitiveness in an ever-evolving business environment.

Given the revolutionary impact of artificial intelligence and chatbots on the contemporary banking sector, a key hypothesis could be formulated as follows:**Haut du formulaire**

Hypothesis 2: The higher the perceived effectiveness and suitability of artificial intelligence and chatbot usage to meet customer needs, the higher the customer satisfaction with banking services will be.

3.3. Personalization of Online Banking Services

Personalizing online banking services is of paramount importance in the contemporary financial sector, aiming to enhance customer satisfaction. This approach involves tailoring banking products and services to the specific needs of each client, thereby providing a more relevant and engaging experience. The integration of advanced technologies such as artificial intelligence (AI) and data analytics enables financial institutions to better understand customer preferences and behaviors, allowing them to deliver personalized recommendations and tailored solutions (Zouari & Abdelhedi,2021).

In practice, this personalization is manifested through an intuitive and user-friendly interface, which facilitates access to personalized online banking accounts and services. Customers have the option to set alerts and notifications according to their preferences, manage their security settings in a personalized manner, and receive tailored financial advice based on their financial situation (Zouari, & Abdelhedi., 2021). This customer-centric approach enables banks to solidify their relationship with their clientele by providing them with a customized banking experience and proactively addressing their specific needs

(Huang & Lin., 2005). Consequently, this approach plays a crucial role in enhancing customer satisfaction, thereby fostering long-term loyalty and retention.

In general, the customization of online banking services is a key element in improving customer satisfaction, offering a more relevant, convenient, and engaging experience. By leveraging available data and technologies, financial institutions can design tailored solutions to meet the individual needs of each customer, thereby strengthening customer relationships and brand loyalty.

Given the increasing importance placed on personalized banking services, it is legitimate to propose the following hypothesis:

Hypothesis 3: Increased customization of online banking services will lead to higher customer satisfaction.

3.4. Conceptuel Model

After reviewing various studies, it is clear that the use of digital tools has had a positive impact on customer satisfaction. Based on these findings, we propose the research model illustrated in Figure 1. This model considers digital tools as an independent variable capable of influencing customer satisfaction, which is in turn a dependent variable.

Figure 1. The conceptual research model

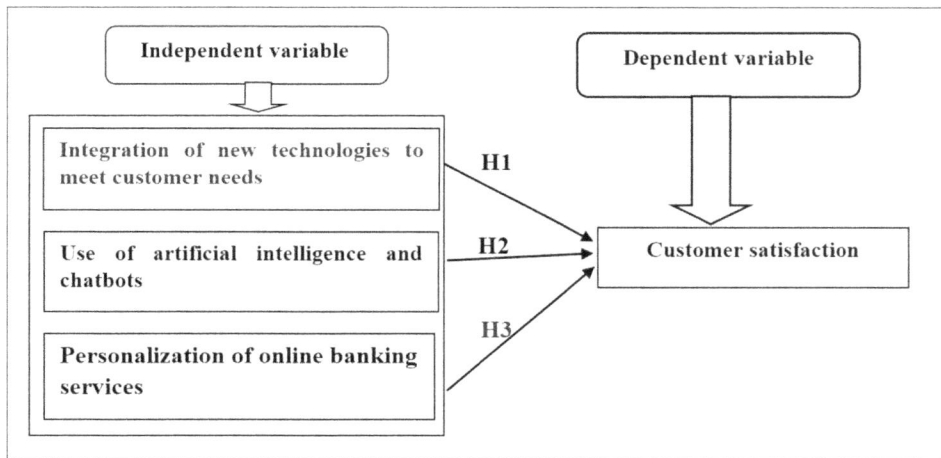

Source: Authors

4. RESEARCH METHODOLOGY

The research methodology involves using a quantitative approach to gather information on customer satisfaction and their perceptions regarding digital banking services. This includes developing well-structured questionnaires designed for digital data collection, thereby facilitating a quantitative research approach for numerical analysis and statistical interpretation. The sampling process will involve selecting a diverse and representative sample of customers from various Moroccan banks, ensuring inclusivity across demographic data such as age, income, and geographical location to obtain a comprehensive understanding of customer satisfaction. Data analysis will be conducted using statistical techniques, including descriptive statistics and inferential methods.

The chosen methodological approach for this research is a quantitative methodology, justified by the need to understand the impact of digitalization on customer satisfaction in Moroccan banks, with a focus on the Fès-Meknès region. This approach allows for the use of effective survey and data analysis tools to test theoretical hypotheses. The specific characteristics of the research terrain require a hands-on approach, which can only be achieved through field studies. Furthermore, this methodology is relevant for overcoming potential challenges associated with an uncontrolled research environment, ensuring the rigor of the conclusions and the validity of the results. Due to the complexity of the subject under study, a quantitative approach allows for a thorough contextualization of the digitalization of banking services, thereby providing multiple perspectives for comprehensive analysis.

Generally, the sample size plays a crucial role in conducting the study as it directly impacts the significance of the results obtained (Lakens, 2022). Hence, it is essential to verify it carefully before proceeding with the research. The sample size is the desired level of statistical precision and not the population size, which imposes a specific size for the sample (Casteel & Bridier, 2021). Data collection, far from being a mere formality, requires a lot of effort, time, and patience. Table 2, which we have compiled, presents the number of observations obtained, after several follow-ups, amounting to 683 usable questionnaires.

Table 2. Balance of administered questionnaires

Questionnaire distributed	Questionnaire returned
800	683
100%	85,375%

Source: Authors

The studied sample consists of clients from a variety of banks operating in the Fes-Meknes region, including a diversity of financial institutions present in this geographical area. To ensure the representativeness of the sample, participant selection is conducted randomly, which helps minimize potential biases and accurately reflect the demographic and socio-economic composition of the target population. Regarding latent variable scale measures, they were chosen based on existing literature, ensuring their validity, reliability, comparability, and saving time and effort. This also ensures adequate representation of the studied concepts and facilitates comparison of results with other similar studies. Table 3 summarizes all the elements of the empirical study

Table 3. Elements of the empirical study

Target Audience	Customers of Moroccan banks
Cities Covered	Fes-Boulemane Region
Survey Medium	Questionnaire
Sample Size	800

continued on following page

Table 3. Continued

Target Audience	Customers of Moroccan banks

Questionnaire Structure	Question Format: **Likert scale of 5**
	Question Themes
	  - Integration and use of new technologies (**5 items**)
	  - Use of artificial intelligence and chatbots (**7 items**)
	  - Personalization of online banking services (**8 items**)
	  - Customer satisfaction (**8 items**)

Questionnaire Administration Mode	Email, telephone
Analysis Method	Quantitative method
Database Software	SPSS24

Source: Authors

4.1. Data Collection

In management research, data collection and sample selection are at the core of the research process. Indeed, one of the crucial decisions that the researcher must make is the choice of data that aligns with their main research question (Baumard & al., 2007). It is from the data that interpretations can be made and results and recommendations can be produced for the research work. In our research, this approach translates into identifying access modalities to the field, the procedure for collecting information, operationalizing variables, and the data analysis strategy.

With this approach, we conducted a quantitative survey by distributing a questionnaire consisting of three parts: the first part focused on respondent and company identification, the second part on the digitization of banking services, and the third part on customer satisfaction. We aimed to consult a wide population, comprising clients from various banks in the Fes-Boulemane region, to obtain insightful responses regarding the posed issue. This work involves data processing using SPSS24 software.

5. ANALYSIS OF RESULTS, INTERPRETATION, AND DISCUSSION OF RESULTS

Before delving into the main findings of this study, let's review the key characteristics of the chosen sample. Indeed, 66.7% of the respondents are male and 33.3% are female. As for age, 79.5% of the participants are under 50 years old, indicating a predominantly young population. Regarding the respondents' educational background, 94.7% have a bachelor's degree or higher. This suggests a population with significant skills and knowledge in digital usage.

5.1. Testing the Theoretical Model and Interpretation of Results

In this level of analysis, we will use the software SPSS 24 to perform a regression analysis by treating all independent variables of the research model in a single operation. Therefore, we will attempt to test the overall significance of the conceptual model and the individual quality of the variable coefficients.

Regarding the overall significance of the research model, the results obtained in terms of the Fischer's F-test will be used to evaluate the overall significance of the model, which indicates whether all independent variables have an impact on the dependent variable. Let's consider the hypothesis test H0 (all coefficients of the model are zero) and the hypothesis test H1 (there is at least one non-zero coefficient).

The interpretation is based on comparing the estimated F-statistic with the one indicated by Fischer's. The probability associated with the calculated F-statistic is mainly provided by the SPSS 24 software in our case to simplify and facilitate the analysis. Therefore, we proceed to compare the probability associated with the calculated F-statistic to the 5% threshold. If the probability identified with the calculated F-statistic is less than the 5% threshold, the null hypothesis H0 will be rejected in favor of the alternative hypothesis of regression with overall significance.

Table 4. Regression indices of the ANOVA model

ANOVA[a]						
Model		Sum of Squares	df	Mean Square	F-value	Significance
1	Regression	10.120	3	3.373	7.456	0.001b
	Residual	5.228	396	0.013		
	Total	15.348	399			

a. Dependent Variable: Satisfaction_clients.
b. Predictors: (Constant), Integration of new technologies, Use of artificial intelligence chatbots, Personalization of online banking services.
Source: SPSS software

In this table:

- Regression" represents the variation explained by the predictor variables.
- Residual" represents the unexplained variation.
- Total" is the total variation in the dependent variable.
- Sum of Squares" indicates the variability attributed to each source.
- Degrees of Freedom" represents the number of independent pieces of information available.
- Mean Square" is the sum of squares divided by the degrees of freedom.
- F-value" is the ratio of mean squares (explained to unexplained variability).
- Significance" indicates the p-value associated with the F-test.

The ANOVA table provided offers insight into the relationship between the dependent variable, client satisfaction, and the predictor variables: Integration of new technologies, Use of artificial intelligence chatbots, and Personalization of online banking services. The regression analysis indicates that the predictor variables collectively account for a significant amount of variability in client Satisfaction, as evidenced by the F-value of 7.456 and the associated significance level (p-value) of 0.001. This suggests that the regression model is statistically significant; indicating that at least one of the predictors has a significant effect on client satisfaction. However, the residual analysis reveals that there is still unexplained variability in client satisfaction even after accounting for the predictor variables, as indicated by the sum of squares for residuals. Nevertheless, the overall model is deemed significant, implying that the combination of Integration of new technologies, Use of artificial intelligence chatbots, and Personalization of online banking services plays a meaningful role in determining client satisfaction levels. Further investigation into the specific impact of each predictor variable and potential additional factors influencing client satisfaction could provide valuable insights for optimizing client satisfaction strategies within the banking sector.

Table 5. Model significance coefficients

Model	R	R-squared	Adjusted R-squared	Standard Error of Estimation	Modifier les statistiques					
					Change in R-squared	F-value	ddl1	ddl2	Sig. Variation of F	
1	0.780 a	0.608	0.579	0.30007	0.025	19,891	3	396	,001	1,911

a. Predictors: (Constant), Integration of new technologies, Use of artificial intelligence chatbots, Personalization of online banking services.

b. Dependent Variable: client_Satisfaction

Source: SPSS software

The regression analysis reveals a strong positive relationship between the predictor variables integration of new technologies, Use of artificial intelligence chatbots, and Personalization of online banking services and client satisfaction, as indicated by a high correlation coefficient (R) of 0.780. The coefficient of determination (R-squared) of 0.608 suggests that approximately 60.8% of the variance in client satisfaction can be explained by these predictors. After adjusting for the number of predictors, the adjusted R-squared value remains high at 0.579, indicating a robust model fit. The regression model is statistically significant (F-value = 19.891, $p < 0.001$), suggesting that the predictor variables collectively have a significant impact on client satisfaction. Additionally, the Durbin-Watson statistic of 1.911 suggests no significant autocorrelation in the residuals, further supporting the validity of the model. Overall, these findings highlight the importance of Integration of new technologies, Use of artificial intelligence chatbots, and personalization of online banking services in driving client satisfaction within the banking sector.

Table 6. Coefficients of individual significance of model variables

Coefficients[a]							
Model	Unstandardized Coefficients (B)	Standard Error	Standardized Coefficients (Beta)	t-value	Significance	Collinearity Statistics (Tolerance)	Collinearity Statistics (VIF)
1	(Constant)	-	-	3.941	0.000	-	
	Integration of New Technologies	0.450	0.560	5.907	0.008	1.000	1.000
	Use of Artificial Intelligence Chatbots	0.400	0.395	2.731	0.000	0.294	3.407
	Personalization of Online Banking Services	-0.025	-0.023	-0.152	0.880	0.427	2.344

a. Dependent Variable: client_Satisfaction

Source: SPSS software

This table presents the results of a regression analysis examining the relationship between three predictor variables (Integration of New Technologies, Use of Artificial Intelligence Chatbots, and Personalization of Online Banking Services) and the dependent variable (client Satisfaction). The coefficient for Integration of New Technologies is 0.450 with a t-value of 5.907, indicating a statistically significant positive relationship with client Satisfaction. Similarly, the coefficient for Use of Artificial Intelligence Chatbots is 0.400, also showing a statistically significant positive relationship with client Satisfaction. However, the coefficient for Personalization of Online Banking Services is -0.025, with a t-value of -0.152 and a p-value of 0.880, suggesting no statistically significant relationship with client Satisfaction. Collinearity statistics reveal acceptable levels of multicollinearity among predictor variables. Overall, Integration of New Technologies and Use of Artificial Intelligence Chatbots appear to be important predictors of client satisfaction, while Personalization of Online Banking Services does not significantly contribute to explaining variations in client Satisfaction.

5.2. Discussion of the Results

Examining the findings of this study, it's evident that customer satisfaction in Moroccan banks is closely tied to the adoption of new technologies in their services, alongside the implementation of artificial intelligence and chatbots to meet customer needs. This finding highlights a significant shift in customer expectations, as they increasingly seek efficient and accessible banking services at all times, while adapting to technological advancements. The integration of new technologies and the adoption of artificial intelligence and chatbots in Moroccan banking services offer numerous benefits. These technologies enable fast and accurate assistance, thereby reducing waiting times and enhancing the customer experience. Moreover, they provide round-the-clock availability, catering to the needs of clients living in an increasingly connected and demanding world. Successful integration of artificial intelligence and chatbots by Moroccan banks promotes a thorough understanding of customer needs. Furthermore, the adoption of new technologies contributes to enhancing customer satisfaction.

However, it's noteworthy that while online service personalization is present, its influence on customer satisfaction appears to be limited. These conclusions underscore the importance for Moroccan banks to persist in their investments in cutting-edge technologies to meet evolving customer expectations. They also highlight the need for these institutions to reconsider their approach to online service personalization to better address customer needs and preferences.

Online service personalization may not significantly influence customer satisfaction in banks in the Fes-Meknes region for several reasons. Firstly, personalized services may lack relevance in addressing specific customer needs, leading to disappointment in the user experience. Additionally, the successful implementation of online service personalization may be hindered by technical or organizational challenges faced by banks, which can affect the quality of the services offered. Moreover, concerns related to the privacy and use of customer data can also impact their perception of personalization. Some customers may prefer a more uniform approach to online banking services, while others may view personalization as an invasion of their privacy. Additionally, although personalization has become a common practice in the banking industry, it may risk losing its appeal as a distinctive competitive advantage.

Generally, various factors such as the relevance of personalized offerings, implementation challenges, privacy concerns, and individual customer preferences can all play a role in the limited impact of personalization of online services on the satisfaction of Moroccan bank customers. Therefore, the limited impact of service personalization on customer satisfaction raises pertinent questions, particularly regarding the significance of security and privacy. It is conceivable that, despite attempts at personalization, customers prioritize other aspects, such as the protection and confidentiality of their personal data. In a context where concerns about data security are increasingly prevalent, customers may be less inclined to value personalization if it compromises their privacy. If customers do not feel secure when sharing personal information to benefit from personalized service, this could negate the perceived benefits of personalization in terms of satisfaction. Furthermore, distrust in data security can also influence the overall perception of banking service, even if it is highly personalized. Customers may hesitate to share additional information or use advanced features if it poses an increased risk to their personal data.

Existing literature in the national context confirms the conclusions regarding the limited impact of online service personalization on customer satisfaction in the Moroccan banking sector. For example, previous studies, such as that of HATTAB, S., & EL ACHARI, S. (2023), have examined the effects of digitization on banking performance, highlighting the benefits for both clients and financial institutions, as well as the associated risks, such as increased vulnerability to cyber threats and potential data privacy issues. These conclusions align with the findings of previous research, such as that conducted by ACHEMRAH, Y., JEBBARI, A., & SOUAADA, O. (2024), which emphasized the challenges associated with the digitization of banking services, particularly concerning data protection and risk management. Therefore, while online service personalization may offer tangible benefits, it also faces significant obstacles, such as privacy concerns and technical issues, as highlighted by the research conducted by ELOUAHABI, T., & DAKKON, M. (2022) on digitization in participatory banks. Indeed, existing literature highlights the complexity of the impact of digitization on customer satisfaction in the Moroccan banking sector, emphasizing the need for a holistic approach that considers the various factors at play.

5.2.1 Comparative Study: How AI Can Enhance Customer Satisfaction in the Moroccan Banking Sector

AI adoption in the global banking industry has led to significant improvements in service quality, efficiency, and customer satisfaction. Drawing insights from international examples, we can explore how Moroccan banks can leverage AI technologies to enhance their operations and deliver superior services to customers.

In the United States, banks like Ally Financial and Capital One (Series, A. B. C. S, 2024) have integrated AI-powered chatbots into their mobile banking applications to provide seamless customer support. These chatbots assist customers with inquiries, transactions, and account management, enhancing accessibility and convenience. Moroccan banks can follow suit by implementing AI-driven virtual assistants in their digital platforms to offer personalized assistance and support to customers, thereby improving overall satisfaction levelsa. AI-driven fraud detection platforms, such as those offered by Vectra AI and Socure, have been instrumental in safeguarding financial institutions against cyber threats and fraudulent activities. These technologies utilize machine learning algorithms to analyze vast amounts of data and identify suspicious patterns in real-time. Moroccan banks can deploy similar AI solutions to enhance their security measures, protect customer assets, and maintain trust in the banking system. Fintech companies like Zest Finance and Kensho Technologies (Liu, 2024; Rahim & Chishti, 2024) have developed AI-powered algorithms to optimize credit scoring models and enhance lending practices. By leveraging advanced data analytics and machine learning, these platforms enable more accurate risk assessment and equitable credit decisions. Moroccan banks can adopt AI-driven credit scoring solutions to streamline their lending processes, expand financial inclusion, and offer tailored loan products to a diverse customer base. AI technologies, such as those provided by Symphony Ayasdi AI and FIS (Ferencz et al., 2022) have transformed compliance and regulatory processes within banking institutions. These solutions leverage AI-driven analytics to automate risk management, detect financial crimes, and ensure regulatory compliance. Moroccan banks can leverage AI-powered compliance tools to mitigate operational risks, adhere to regulatory requirements, and uphold integrity in financial transactions. The integration of AI technologies has catalyzed innovation and digital transformation in the banking industry worldwide. Companies like Kasisto and Simudyne (Anis et al., 2022).offer AI-driven solutions that empower banks to create intuitive digital experiences, optimize operational efficiency, and drive sustainable growth. Moroccan banks can embrace AI-driven innovation to modernize their infrastructure, develop innovative products and services, and stay competitive in the digital era.

In Morocco, the banking sector is gradually embracing AI to revolutionize its operations and enhance customer experiences. Here are some specific initiatives and examples:

- Bank Al-Maghrib's AI Projects:

Bank Al-Maghrib is utilizing AI algorithms to detect fraudulent activities in real-time, safeguarding the integrity of financial transactions. Additionally, AI-powered risk management systems enable proactive identification and mitigation of potential risks, ensuring the stability of the banking system. By employing AI technologies, Bank Al-Maghrib aims to streamline compliance processes and ensure adherence to regulatory standards.

- Attijariwafa Bank's AI Chatbots:

Attijariwafa Bank, one of Morocco's leading commercial banks, has deployed AI-driven chatbots and virtual assistants across its digital channels.These chatbots provide personalized support to customers, offering assistance with account inquiries, transactional activities, and product information. By leveraging AI, Attijariwafa Bank enhances customer engagement, reduces response times, and optimizes service delivery.

- BMCE Bank of Africa's Virtual Assistants:

BMCE Bank of Africa has integrated AI-powered virtual assistants into its online and mobile banking platforms. These virtual assistants offer intuitive self-service options, guiding customers through various banking processes and providing real-time assistance. BMCE Bank of Africa leverages AI to enhance customer satisfaction, improve operational efficiency, and drive digital adoption.

Moving on to the research contributions, let's take a closer look at the implications of these findings for practices and policies in the Moroccan banking sector.

5.3. Contributions

The results of this study provide several significant contributions to understanding customer satisfaction in the context of Moroccan banks operating in the Fes-Meknes region. Firstly, identifying determinant factors such as the use of artificial intelligence and chatbots, as well as the integration of new technologies, offers a precise perspective on the key elements influencing the customer experience. This analysis enables stakeholders in the banking sector to effectively direct their improvement efforts by focusing on these priority areas. Furthermore, the revelation of the limited impact of online service personalization on customer satisfaction raises significant considerations for the current strategies of banks. This finding suggests that it is imperative to reassess or enhance personalization practices to better meet the expectations and needs of customers in this specific region.

Ultimately, these conclusions provide valuable insights for future research in the field of customer satisfaction in the Moroccan banking sector. They also offer practical implications for industry stakeholders, helping them develop more effective strategies to enhance customer experience and maintain competitiveness of banks in the Fes-Meknes region. In summary, this study makes a significant contribution to understanding customer satisfaction dynamics in the Moroccan banking sector and provides practical guidance for improving bank practices and strategies in this specific region.

From our research contributions, we move on to formulating concrete recommendations to enhance customer satisfaction in the Moroccan banking sector.

5.4. Recommendations

To implement effective digital strategies that meet the demands of the current environment, it is necessary to base them on the following elements:

- Moroccan financial institutions should first focus on building high-quality and robust digital foundations to ensure online services that meet the needs of customers.
- It is essential to integrate and develop high-quality mobile applications and platforms to promote a significant improvement in customer satisfaction.
- The need to implement a strategy that enhances the security and confidentiality of clients' financial and personal data.
- A successful transition to digital banking requires competent human resources capable of guiding this change very effectively. Thus, the implementation of a training program in this regard is fundamental to the success of the digitization strategy for Moroccan banks.
- The need to create and strengthen collaborations and partnerships with technology development partners to access real-time technological innovations.
- It is recommended for Moroccan banks to implement technological monitoring in order to stay constantly informed about new technological developments in the market.

All these recommendations must be integrated into the digital strategy of Moroccan banks to meet the requirements of the current context. Furthermore, these improvement measures will enhance customer satisfaction.

6. CONCLUSION

This comprehensive research has shed light on the multifaceted determinants of customer satisfaction in the Moroccan banking sector, specifically focusing on the Fes-Meknes region. By delving into the critical role of artificial intelligence, chatbots, and the integration of new technologies, this study underscores their pivotal importance in shaping customer experiences. However, it has also revealed the existence of gaps, particularly in online banking service personalization, suggesting the need to enhance existing strategies to better align with evolving customer expectations. However, this research work has its limitations. On a practical level, some constraints may include challenges related to accessing relevant data, such as the limited availability of historical data on customer-bank interactions. Additionally, challenges inherent to the Moroccan context, compounded by a scarcity of information provided by Moroccan banks. These challenges have hindered our ability to comprehensively measure digitalization evaluation, a concept that remains inadequately assessed within the Moroccan context. On the methodological front, the complexities associated with measuring the component variables of digitalization have posed significant obstacles, impacting the accuracy and reliability of our results. Additionally, uncertainties surrounding the quality of certain measurement scales developed based on existing literature underscore the need for cautious interpretation and further validation in diverse contexts. As for the theoretical limitations of this study, they lie in not considering all variables that could explain the influence of bank digitalization on customer satisfaction. Another limitation may include the lack of specific theoretical models regarding bank digitalization in the Moroccan context, which may have hindered the interpretation of the study. Like any research, despite its limitations, our study concludes the multifaceted research on digitalization and customer satisfaction. This research provides us with the opportunity to develop promising perspectives to explore and develop several aspects of customer satisfaction in the Moroccan banking sector, particularly in the Fes-Meknes region. By closely examining the role of artificial intelligence and chatbots, we can identify avenues to improve the customer experience. Furthermore, thorough analysis of the challenges related to online service personalization paves the way for innovative solutions. Considering comparative studies between different regions of Morocco or on an international scale, we could better understand local specificities and provide relevant recommendations for the entire banking sector.

REFERENCES

A.B.C.S. Series. (2024). *The Evolution and Impact of Virtual/Neo Banks: Pioneering the Future of Banking*. ABCS.

Abdelkhalek, T., Ajbilou, A., Benayad, M., Boccanfuso, D., & Savard, L. (2021, November). *How Can the Digital Economy Benefit Morocco and All Moroccans?* Economic Research Forum (ERF).

Achemrah, Y., Jebbari, A., & Souaada, O. (2024). La digitalisation des services bancaires: réalisations et Contraintes. International Journal of Accounting, Finance, Auditing. *Management and Economics*, 5(2), 105–121. 10.5281/zenodo.10646538

Achemrah, Y., Jebbari, A., & Souaada, O. (2024). La digitalisation des services bancaires: Réalisations et Contraintes. International Journal of Accounting, Finance, Auditing. *Management and Economics*, 5(2), 105–121. 10.5281/zenodo.10646538

Ali, A., Hameed, A., Moin, M. F., & Khan, N. A. (2023). Exploring factors affecting mobile-banking app adoption: A perspective from adaptive structuration theory. *Aslib Journal of Information Management*, 75(4), 773–795. 10.1108/AJIM-08-2021-0216

Alla, L., Kamal, M., & Bouhtati, N. (2022). Big data et efficacité marketing des entreprises touristiques: une revue de la littérature. *Alternatives Managériales Economiques*. 10.48374/IMIST.PRSM/ame-v1i0 .36928

Allioui, H., & Allioui, A. (2022). The Financial Sphere in the Era of COVID-19: Trends and Perspectives of Artificial Intelligence. *Finance, Law, and the Crisis of COVID-19: An Interdisciplinary Perspective*, 37-59. doi:10.1007/978-3-030-89416-0_310.1007/978-3-030-89416-0_3

André, Q., Carmon, Z., Wertenbroch, K., Crum, A., Frank, D., Goldstein, W., Huber, J., van Boven, L., Weber, B., & Yang, H. (2018). Consumer choice and autonomy in the age of artificial intelligence and big data. *Customer Needs and Solutions*, 5(1-2), 28–37. 10.1007/s40547-017-0085-8

Anis, M., Chawky, S., & Halim, A. A. (2022). Banking and Financial Services. In *Mapping Innovation: The Discipline of Building Opportunity across Value Chains* (pp. 53-73). Cham: Springer International Publishing. 10.1007/978-3-030-93627-3

Anshari, M., Almunawar, M. N., Lim, S. A., & Al-Mudimigh, A. (2019). Customer relationship management and big data enabled: Personalization & customization of services. *Applied Computing and Informatics*, 15(2), 94–101. 10.1016/j.aci.2018.05.004

Appelbaum, S. H., Habashy, S., Malo, J. L., & Shafiq, H. (2012). Back to the future: Revisiting Kotter's 1996 change model. *Journal of Management Development*, 31(8), 764–782. 10.1108/02621711211253231

Baabdullah, A. M., Alalwan, A. A., Rana, N. P., Kizgin, H., & Patil, P. (2019). Consumer use of mobile banking (M-Banking) in Saudi Arabia: Towards an integrated model. *International Journal of Information Management*, 44, 38–52. 10.1016/j.ijinfomgt.2018.09.002

Bank Al Maghrib. (2023). *Rapport annuel sur la supervision bancaire pour l'exercice 2022*. Bank Al Maghrib.

Boateng, S. L., & Narteh, B. (2016). Online relationship marketing and affective customer commitment–The mediating role of trust. *Journal of Financial Services Marketing, 21*(2), 127–140. 10.1057/fsm.2016.5

Bouhtati, N., Alla, L., & Bentalhah, B. (2023). *Marketing Big Data Analytics et gestion de la relation client: une approche floue.* IGI Global. 10.4018/979-8-3693-0225-5.ch004

Bouhtatit, N., Kamal, M., & Alla, L. (2023). Big Data et efficacité du marketing touristique: une revue prospective de la littérature. In Farhaoui, Y., Rocha, A., Brahmia, Z., & Bhushab, B. (Eds.), *Intelligence artificielle et environnement intelligent. ICAISE 2022. Notes de cours sur les réseaux et les systèmes, 635.* Springer. 10.1007/978-3-031-26254-8_40

Casteel, A., & Bridier, N. L. (2021). Describing populations and samples in doctoral student research. *International Journal of Doctoral Studies, 16*(1), 339–362. 10.28945/4766

Cherkaoui, A. (2016). La Finance Islamique au Maroc: L'Alternative Ethique. *Finance and Finance Internationale, 442*(5257), 1-19.10.34874/IMIST.PRSM/ffi-v0i2.4401

Demraoui, L., Eddamiri, S., & Hachad, L. (2022). Digital transformation and costumers services in emerging countries: Loan prediction modeling in modern banking transactions. In *AI and IoT for sustainable development in emerging countries: Challenges and opportunities* (pp. 627–642). Springer International Publishing. 10.1007/978-3-030-90618-4_32

Dinev, T., & Hart, P. (2006). Privacy concerns and levels of information exchange: An empirical investigation of intended e-services use. *E-Service, 4*(3), 25–60. 10.2979/esj.2006.4.3.25

Donner, J., & Tellez, C. A. (2008). Mobile banking and economic development: Linking adoption, impact, and use. *Asian Journal of Communication, 18*(4), 318–332. 10.1080/01292980802344190

El Bakkouri, B., Raki, S., & Belgnaoui, T. (2022). The role of chatbots in enhancing customer experience: Literature review. *Procedia Computer Science, 203*, 432–437. 10.1016/j.procs.2022.07.057

El Ouidani, R. & Brahim, O. U. L. (2023) L'adoption de l'IA dans le secteur bancaire marocain: entre enjeux économiques et enjeux juridiques. *Journal d'Economie, de Management, d'Environnement et de Droit, 6*(1), 37-56. 10.48398/IMIST.PRSM/jemed-v6i1.41316

Elouahabi, T., & Dakkon, M. (2022). La digitalisation bancaire: approche conceptuelle et théorique Cas des banques participatives. *International Journal of Accounting, Finance, Auditing, Management and Economics, 3*(5-1), 199-210.

Fayon, D. (2018). *Mesure de la maturité numérique des acteurs du secteur bancaire, dans une perspective de transformation digitale* [Doctoral dissertation, Université Paris Saclay (COmUE)].

Ferencz, J., González, J. L., & García, I. O. (2022). *Artificial Intelligence and international trade: Some preliminary implications.* 10.1787/18166873

Forest, D. (2020). *Le droit au défi du numérique - Libertés et propriété à l'ère d'Internet* (Editions L'Harmattan Ghosh, J. (2019). The blockchain: Opportunities for research in information systems and information technology. *Journal of Global Information Technology Management, 22*(4), 235–242. 10.1080/1097198X.2019.1679954

Haouam, Z. (2022). «Création de valeur numérique, communication digitale et outils de fidélisation d'une communauté en ligne. Etude exploratoire».

Hattab, S., & El Achari, S. (2023). La performance bancaire impactée par la digitalisation: une étude des banques marocaines. *International Journal of Accounting, Finance, Auditing, Management and Economics, 4*(4-2), 280-301. 10.5281/zenodo.8267102

Hoyer, W. D., Kroschke, M., Schmitt, B., Kraume, K., & Shankar, V. (2020). Transforming the customer experience through new technologies. *Journal of Interactive Marketing*, 51(1), 57–71. 10.1016/j.intmar.2020.04.001

Huang, E. Y., & Lin, C. Y. (2005). Customer-oriented financial service personalization. *Industrial Management & Data Systems*, 105(1), 26–44. 10.1108/02635570510575171

Huang, M. H., & Rust, R. T. (2018). Artificial intelligence in service. *Journal of Service Research*, 21(2), 155–172. 10.1177/1094670517752459

Imgraben, J., Engelbrecht, A., & Choo, K. K. R. (2014). Always connected, but are smart mobile users getting more security savvy? A survey of smart mobile device users. *Behaviour & Information Technology*, 33(12), 1347–1360. 10.1080/0144929X.2014.934286

Jaouad, J., & Ouchekkir, A. (2023). La transformation digitale dans le secteur bancaire marocain: une révolution dans les pratiques et les services financiers. *International Journal of Accounting, Finance, Auditing, Management and Economics, 4*(3-2), 417-437. 10.5281/zenodo.8057870

Khadija, S. E. N. I. H. J. I. (2023). Digital Marketing: An Opportunity To Personalize Banking Services For Better Customer Satisfaction. *International Journal Of Applied Management And Economics, 2*(05), 019-033. 10.5281/zenodo.10180129

Lakens, D. (2022). Sample size justification. *Collabra. Psychology*, 8(1), 33267. 10.1525/collabra.33267

Lhoussaine, A., Kamal, M., & Bouhtati, N. (2022). Big data et efficacité marketing des entreprises touristiques: une revue de la littérature. *Alternatives de gestion économique, 1,* 39-58.

Li, F., Lu, H., Hou, M., Cui, K., & Darbandi, M. (2021). Customer satisfaction with bank services: The role of cloud services, security, e-learning and service quality. *Technology in Society*, 64, 101487. 10.1016/j.techsoc.2020.101487

Liu, R. (2024). Application for Machine Learning Methods in Financial Risk Management. Highlights in Science. *Engineering and Technology*, 88, 775–778. 10.54097/stt1va49

Machkour, B., & Abriane, A. (2020). Industry 4.0 and its Implications for the Financial Sector. *Procedia Computer Science*, 177, 496–502. 10.1016/j.procs.2020.10.068

Mainardes, E. W., Teixeira, A., & Romano, P. C. D. S. (2017). Determinants of co-creation in banking services. *International Journal of Bank Marketing*, 35(2), 187–204. 10.1108/IJBM-10-2015-0165

Mairesse, J., Cette, G., & Kocoglu, Y. (2000). Les technologies de l'information et de la communication en France: Diffusion et contribution à la croissance. *Economie & Statistique*, 339(1), 117–146. 10.3406/estat.2000.7482

Mani, Z., & Chouk, I. (2018). *Les objets connectés dans la banque: quelles implications sur les comportements des consommateurs?* World Bank. **halshs-01678793**

Morawczynski, O., & Pickens, M. (2009). *Poor people using mobile financial services: observations on customer usage and impact from M-PESA.* HDL. https://hdl.handle.net/10986/9492

Naimi-Sadigh, A., Asgari, T., & Rabiei, M. (2022). Digital transformation in the value chain disruption of banking services. *Journal of the Knowledge Economy*, 13(2), 1212–1242. 10.1007/s13132-021-00759-0

Paliwal, S., Bharti, V., & Mishra, A. K. (2020). Ai chatbots: Transforming the digital world. *Recent trends and advances in artificial intelligence and internet of things*, (pp. 455-482). Springer. 10.1007/978-3-030-32644-9_34

Parasuraman, A., Zeithaml, V. A., & Malhotra, A. (2005). ES-QUAL: A multiple-item scale for assessing electronic service quality. *Journal of Service Research*, 7(3), 213–233. 10.1177/1094670504271156

Peppard, J. (2000). Customer relationship management (CRM) in financial services. *European Management Journal*, 18(3), 312–327. 10.1016/S0263-2373(00)00013-X

Pham, Q. V., Nguyen, D. C., Huynh-The, T., Hwang, W. J., & Pathirana, P. N. (2020). Artificial intelligence (AI) and big data for coronavirus (COVID-19) pandemic: A survey on the state-of-the-arts. *IEEE Access : Practical Innovations, Open Solutions*, 8, 130820–130839. 10.1109/ACCESS.2020.300932834812339

Pluchart, J. J. (2017). Vers une nouvelle esthétique bancaire. *Vie & sciences de l'entreprise*, (1), 9-21. 10.3917/vse.203.0009

Rahim, R., & Chishti, M. A. (2024, January). Artificial Intelligence Applications in Accounting and Finance. In *2024 ASU International Conference in Emerging Technologies for Sustainability and Intelligent Systems,* (pp. 1782-1786). IEEE. 10.1109/ICETSIS61505.2024.10459526

Reichheld, F. F., & Schefter, P. (2000). E-loyalty: Your secret weapon on the web. *Harvard Business Review*, 78(4), 105–113.

Roman, B., & Tchibozo, A. (2017). *Transformer la banque: stratégies bancaires à l'ère digitale.* Dunod.

Sapovadia, V. (2018). Financial inclusion, digital currency, and mobile technology. In *Handbook of Blockchain, Digital Finance, and Inclusion, Volume 2* (pp. 361-385). Academic Press. 10.1016/B978-0-12-812282-2.00014-0

Singh, S., & Srivastava, R. K. (2020). Understanding the intention to use mobile banking by existing online banking customers: An empirical study. *Journal of Financial Services Marketing*, 25(3), 86–96. 10.1057/s41264-020-00074-w

Slimani, C. (2021, October). Traitement automatisé des données à caractère personnel: Le risque de « l'informatisation du risque ». Revue de Recherche en Droit. *Economie et Gestion*, (16), 30.

Sunikka, A., Bragge, J., & Kallio, H. (2011). The effectiveness of personalized marketing in online banking: A comparison between search and experience offerings. *Journal of Financial Services Marketing*, 16(3-4), 183–194. 10.1057/fsm.2011.24

Tsai, C. H., & Su, P. C. (2021). The application of multi-server authentication scheme in internet banking transaction environments. *Information Systems and e-Business Management*, 19(1), 77–105. 10.1007/s10257-020-00481-5

Vassakis, K., Petrakis, E., & Kopanakis, I. (2018). Big data analytics: applications, prospects and challenges. *Mobile big data: A roadmap from models to technologies*, 3-20. 10.1007/978-3-319-67925-9_1

Verhoef, P. C., Reinartz, W. J., & Krafft, M. (2010). Customer engagement as a new perspective in customer management. *Journal of Service Research*, 13(3), 247–252. 10.1177/1094670510375461

Zhou, T. (2018). Examining users' switch from online banking to mobile banking. *International Journal of Networking and Virtual Organisations*, 18(1), 51–66. 10.1504/IJNVO.2018.090675

Zouari, G., & Abdelhedi, M. (2021). Customer satisfaction in the digital era: Evidence from Islamic banking. *Journal of Innovation and Entrepreneurship*, 10(1), 1–18. 10.1186/s13731-021-00151-x

Section 4
Case Studies and Technological Innovations in Marketing

Chapter 17
Phygital Marketing and the Pain of Paying:
An Amazon Go Netnographic Case Study

Rachid Boudri

Euromed Business School, Euromed University of Fez, Morocco

Badr Bentalha
http://orcid.org/0000-0003-1339-542X

National School of Business and Management, Sidi Mohammed Ben Abdellah University, Morocco

Omar Benjelloun
http://orcid.org/0000-0002-9059-6332

Euromed Business School, Euromed University of Fez, Morocco

ABSTRACT

The physical store provides a shopping experience that can't be replaced by digital means. However, the combination of the two has infinite potential and it's called the phygital shopping experience. In a retail context, phygital marketing is about finding the right amount of digital technology to incorporate into the store, to offer the shopper a unique shopping experience. Moreover, phygital marketing is a recent discipline that lacks practical and theoretical information. This study aims to contribute to the conceptualization of the latter through a netnography, and by linking the practice of phygital marketing to the behavioral science concept which is "the pain of paying." This expression refers to the negative emotions felt during the process of paying for a product. Thus, a thematic content analysis opens the way to define a competitive advantage through phygital marketing.

1. INTRODUCTION

The physical store provides a shopping experience that can't be replaced by digital means. However, the combination of the two has infinite potential and it's called the phygital shopping experience. In a retail context, phygital marketing is about finding the right amount of digital technology to incorporate

DOI: 10.4018/979-8-3693-3172-9.ch017

into the store, to offer the shopper a unique shopping experience. Moreover, phygital marketing is a recent discipline that lacks practical and theoretical information.

By blending digital and physical spaces, Amazon Go's cashier-less checkout model removes traditional payment pain points and financial friction from the shopping experience. We examine how this impacts customer psychology and spending habits—enabling seamless purchases but also potentially "mindless" overspending. Our analysis explores the pros and cons customers identify regarding Amazon Go's automated checkout capabilities, including concerns around data privacy, personalized pricing, and the manipulation of shopping behaviors through intuitive commerce technologies (Bouhtati et al., 2023). More broadly, this case study discusses implications for emerging digitally enhanced stores that seek to influence psychology and shape behavior by reducing payment friction in blended digital/physical retail environments. Despite the extensive research on the consumption experience, the role of the pain of paying in the shopping experience has been overlooked. The POP is the negative feeling or discomfort that arises when people pay for goods and services. This feeling has been shown to have a significant effect on consumers' decision-making, purchase intention, and satisfaction. Therefore, it is essential to investigate the role of POP in the shopping experience to provide a better understanding of consumers' behavior and design effective strategies to enhance their experience.

So, how does the pain of paying influence the shopping experience in the context of phygital shopping, and what strategies can retailers adopt to mitigate its effect and improve consumers' experience?

This study aims to contribute to the conceptualization of the latter through a netnography, and by linking the practice of phygital marketing to the behavioral science concept which is "the pain of paying" (POP). This expression refers to the negative emotions felt during the process of paying for a product. Thus, a thematic content analysis opens the way to define a competitive advantage through phygital marketing. We conducted a netnographic study analyzing online customer conversations about Amazon Go stores across forums, blogs, social media, and reviews. Our focus was on how the cashier-less, automated checkout model removes barriers and pain points around paying for purchases. This in turn may enable mindless spending and unplanned purchases in-store. Our findings suggest the "grab and go" experience strips away psychological transaction costs and payment rituals which typically create natural consumer friction and spending obstacles. By allowing shoppers to simply take items off shelves without formalized checkout processes, Amazon Go appears to eliminate the pain of payment cues that can curb impulsive purchasing and set customer spending boundaries.

To address our research question, we analyze in this paper respectively the theoretical and conceptual framework (1), the methodological approach adopted following our conducted netnographic approach (2), the results of the empirical study and the recommendations and implications of the research (3).

2. THEORETICAL AND CONCEPTUAL FRAMEWORK

2.1. The Consumption Experience

Many concepts have been presented in the marketing field as disruptive which can lead to the reshaping of the field's paradigms. However, despite the abundance of discourse heralding the emergence of a new landscape of marketing that is likely to revitalize the field, few concepts ultimately deliver on such promise (Chaney et al, 2018).

Meanwhile, this does not apply to the well-established concept of the " consumption experience " (Holbrook & Hirshman, 1982). This concept has emerged as a key factor in understanding consumer behavior and it has also become a major foundation for the experiential economy (Pine & Gilmore, 2013) and a new marketing approach: experiential marketing.

The definition of the consumption experience falls within the framework of the POS paradigm (person-object-situation) and can thus be defined as the interaction between a person and a consumer-object in a particular situation (Punj & Stewart, 1983). It is also a process (Arnould et al., 2002) and an outcome and generally includes four dimensions: hedonistic, temporal, practical, and rhetorical (Antéblian, et al., 2013). Four decades later, the concept of consumption experience has become more of a general term encompassing various forms of experiences in a special context of consumption (Flacandji, 2015).

According to the literature review, we distinguish seven different forms of experience (Table 1).

Table 1. Forms of consumer experience

Author	Form of consumer experience	Description
Holbrook & Hirschman, 1982	The consumption experience	The authors argued that consumption is not just a utilitarian act but also involves experiential aspects, such as fantasies, feelings, and fun. They emphasized the symbolic, hedonic, and aesthetic dimensions of consumption.
Hui & Bateson, 1991	The service experience	The paper highlighted the importance of understanding and managing the service experience from the consumer's perspective. Factors that influence perceived control, such as crowding and choice, can significantly impact consumers' evaluations of the service experience.
Kerin, et al., 1992	The shopping experience	The authors conceptualized the shopping experience as a multidimensional construct consisting of various factors, such as store atmosphere, service interaction, product assortment, and convenience.
Hoch, 2002	The product experience	Hoch defined product experience as the direct, multi-sensory interaction with a product, which can involve touching, seeing, hearing, smelling, or tasting the product. He argued that product experience can be seductive, leading consumers to make choices that contradict their prior preferences or intentions. Direct sensory engagement with a product can override rational decision-making processes.
Shelly, 2003	The aesthetic experience	The author defined the aesthetic experience as a multi-sensory, embodied experience that involves imagination and emotional engagement with an object or event. They challenged the traditional view of aesthetic experience as solely a cognitive or intellectual pursuit.

continued on following page

Table 1. Continued

Author	Form of consumer experience	Description
Brakus et al., 2009	The brand experience	The authors defined brand experience as "subjective, internal consumer responses (sensations, feelings, and cognitions) and behavioral responses evoked by brand-related stimuli that are part of a brand's design and identity, packaging, communications, and environments.". The study explored the antecedents and consequences of brand experience. Antecedents included brand-related stimuli (e.g., design, packaging, communications), while consequences included consumer satisfaction, brand loyalty, and brand personality associations.
Verhoef, et al., 2009	The Customer Experience	The authors defined customer experience as "a multidimensional construct that involves cognitive, emotional, behavioral, sensorial, and social components that play a role in a person's interactions with products or companies.". They recognized that customer experiences are dynamic and evolve. They proposed a conceptual model that captures the dynamics of customer experience formation, including experience over multiple encounters and across multiple channels.

Source: Personnal elaboration

The notion of the consumption experience also had a strong impact on many fields, and retailing is perhaps the empiric sphere where experience has been most extensively studied and proven to be particularly significant (Dolbec & Chebat. 2013). Retailers have widely used the experiential approach to propose an extraordinary experience, and this approach has led to the emergence of complex and refined retail environments (Borghini et al., 2009). In this particular field, a striking result is thus the identification of experience as a reason per se for consumers to visit stores. The retail stores where atmosphere and mix offer some thematization (Ritzer, 1999) are the most likely to elicit an experience and represent an escape for people who want to find some fun in their everyday lives (Kaltcheva & Weitz, 2006). As a consequence, the shopping experience has emerged as one of the most influential types of consumption experience to designate the experience inside a point of sale with the same four dimensions (Belghiti et al., 2018).

The literature on experience has always been linear in terms of physical and digital shopping. In this case, the shopper is either in a physical experience posture or in a digital experience one. More specifically, the first one takes place in a physical context, i.e., the point of sale, and the second one in a digital context through a digital device, therefore, the first one is direct while is indirect. However, and until very recently, work on shopping experience seems to have taken another direction. Indeed, it is more current to speak about the shopping experience in a dichotomic way than to speak about it in a linear one.

Looking at the literature we realize that the dichotomous view is present in a way that physical and virtual experiences are looked at independently. However, the introduction of so-called ubiquitous technologies such as smartphones has greatly transformed the shopping experience. Since then, work on shopping behavior has evolved in that it looks at studying the simultaneous use of physical and virtual channels throughout the buying process (Verhoef et al., 2009).

As a consequence, a change of paradigm in marketing, in retail but especially in shopping experience has already begun. From dichotomous to ubiquitous paradigm is the shift to a new shopping experience that consists of the hybridization of physical and digital channels throughout the buying process. To refer to these new experiences, the literature recommends the use of terms such as meta, omnichannel, ubiquitous, or phygital shopping experience (Antéblian et al., 2013). But the term phygital shopping experience seems to be the most used in the literature and from the customer's point of view, it can be defined as an integrated physical and digital experience in a seamless way and includes five different dimensions: spatial, temporal, hedonic-sensorial, social and participative (Belghiti et al.,2018).

2.2. The Pain of Paying

The concept of the "pain of paying" has gained significant attention in both marketing and behavioral sciences. The pain of paying refers to the psychological discomfort or aversion experienced by consumers when they make a payment or a purchase. Research has shown that the pain of paying can influence consumer behavior, including their willingness to purchase, the amount they are willing to pay, and the payment method they choose. Theories of consumer behavior have suggested that consumers view abstract monetary prices as a potential loss that triggers a negative affective response resembling the emotional or psychological components of pain processing (Rick et al., 2008). When consumers make a payment, they claim that they feel an *"immediate sense of discontent or pain"*. This pain is a psychological and emotional response to losing money, and it avoids the need to think about the consequences of parting with money, such as opportunity costs.

According to Prelec & Loewenstein (1998), consumers are willing to pay more for a product when the payment is delayed, suggesting that the pain of paying decreases over time. In addition, a study by Soman (2001) showed that consumers are more likely to use credit cards for purchases that are high in pain of paying, such as medical expenses or car repairs, compared to purchases that are low in pain of paying, such as groceries. These findings highlight the importance of understanding the pain of paying in shaping consumer behavior and decision-making. Additionally, research has shown that the pain of paying can be influenced by factors such as the amount of the payment, the context in which the payment is made, and an individual's values and priorities (Soman, 2003).

Our literature review enabled us to collect several definitions of the Pain of Paying concept (Table 2).

Table 2. Definitions of the pain of paying

Author	Definition
Zellermayer (1996)	"…the notion that a consumer who pays for a product or service experiences emotions associated with the act of paying."
Prelec & Loewenstein (1998)	"When people make purchases, they often experience an immediate *pain of paying*, which can undermine the pleasure derived from consumption… The pain of paying, we argue, plays an important role in consumer self-regulation…"
Soman, (2003)	"…the emotion that consumers experience in parting with their money"
Shah et al., (2016)	"…the negative affective reaction that consumers experience when parting with their money"
Sheehan & Van Ittersum (2018)	"Mental accounting research asserts that shoppers experience emotional distress, called the pain of paying when they think about spending money…"

Source: Personnal elaboration

Over the past two decades, empirical studies have provided mixed and inconclusive evidence regarding the pain-of-paying hypothesis. There is a lack of direct evidence confirming its existence or elucidating the specific pain pathways it affects. In one study (Zellermayer, 1996), participants were presented with 50 hypothetical bill payments and asked to rate their anticipated feelings on a scale from -5 (painful) to +5 (pleasurable), as well as indicate their preferred payment method: cash, check, bank deduction, or credit card. Only 35 percent of the participants predicted that payment would be a painful experience. Furthermore, the preference to pay with either cash (considered the most painful payment mode) or credit card (considered the least painful payment mode) increased as the anticipated pain of paying decreased. However, another study (Prelec & Loewenstein, 1998) provided more supportive evidence, demonstrating that people in hypothetical scenarios tend to prefer prepaying for purchases and decoupling spending from consumption, suggesting a desire to fully enjoy the immediate pleasure derived from the product without the immediate displeasure of paying its price. Since then, other researchers have explored the relationship between payment modes and consumers' spending behavior, providing further insights into the pain-of-paying hypothesis. Studies (Ariely & Silva, 2002; Raghubir & Srivastava, 2008) have demonstrated that people are more likely to spend money in the form of gift cards than cash, theorizing that non-cash payment modes are less transparent and therefore mitigate the pain of paying. Additionally, Shah et al. (2016) showed that individuals who pay with a mode generally assumed to be more painful (e.g., cash or check rather than debit or credit card) increase their post-transaction connection to the purchased product, suggesting that painful experiences can lead to increased value and commitment. Thomas et al. (2011) explicitly asked consumers to indicate their feelings when spending money in cash versus credit cards in a hypothetical purchasing simulation. They found that consumers assigned to pay with cash indicated feeling more sad, while those paying with credit cards indicated feeling more happy. Although the difference between the two payment modes was significant, the means were close to the neutral midpoint. The form of payment used for a transaction (e.g., cash, check, credit/debit card) is a key factor influencing the pain associated with paying.

Payment forms vary in terms of the degree of transparency of the payment, with greater transparency leading to more psychological pain and aversion for the consumer. Cash, being the legal tender, is considered the most transparent and psychologically proximal form of payment. Consumers must physically part with cash in a transaction, making it easy to feel the money being spent and see the amount (Soman 2001). Consequently, cash is the most painful form of payment. Paying by check or voucher is less transparent and thus less painful than cash, as no physical money changes hands, although the amount or value is still visible. Credit and debit cards obscure the cash value of the transaction, divorcing people further from its economic reality. Finally, recent technological developments like automatic payroll deductions or mobile payments have introduced even less transparent payment forms, where consumers may not even be aware of the payment occurring.

3. RESEARCH METHODOLOGY: NETNOGRAPHIC ANALYSIS

To collect qualitative data, we employed a netnographic approach, which involves analyzing the writings and communications of members in virtual communities (Kozinets, 2015). Netnography, also referred to as online ethnography, focuses on studying topics of interest to participants within online groups and social networks by examining their interactions and discussions (Alla et al., 2019). This approach allows researchers to observe participants without directly influencing them, making the research process faster and more cost-effective. A key advantage of netnography is its ability to extend the geographical scope of the research field by connecting globally dispersed networks and increasing accessibility to hard-to-reach or sensitive populations (Lamsiah & Bentalha, 2023). However, netnography has limitations, including a lack of control over the sampling structure and the absence of structured data collection methods like questionnaires or observation plans. Additionally, it may fail to capture offline interactions among community members, potentially leading to dissonance between online and offline representations (Bentalha, 2023).

For our study, the choice of netnography was motivated by the nature of our research question, which involved analyzing opinions and comments posted on online platforms related to our topic of interest. We identified relevant online communities and downloaded comments from several related accounts.

Then, we employed double-coding to categorize the messages by theme, allowing for a contextualized analysis of the exchanges between community members.

Specifically, we focused on comments posted on YouTube due to the platform's popularity and the wealth of user-generated content available. Amazon Just Go is a cashierless physical grocery store concept developed by Amazon. The store entrance is equipped with turnstiles linked to the Amazon Go app on the customer's smartphone. By scanning a QR code, customers register their arrival. Cameras and sensors placed throughout the store detect the products the customer removes from the shelves and virtually add them to their basket. If the customer puts a product back, the sensors detect it and remove it from the virtual basket. When the customer has finished shopping, he can simply leave the store. Their bank card, linked to the Amazon Go application, is automatically debited for the full amount. The aim is to offer a seamless, queue-free shopping experience by eliminating traditional checkouts (Bentalha & Hmioui, 2021). Our empirical study consisted of a survey of 218 opinions and comments posted by Internet users during the study period (January 2023 to January 2024). To ensure credibility, we randomly selected comments from various Internet queries, stopping when the results became highly similar in terms of the desired profiles.

The collected opinions and comments were statistically processed using IRAMUTEQ software. To present the results, we first conducted a thematic analysis of the topics covered in the reviews, followed by an overall analysis of all comments.

4. RESULTS AND DISCUSSION

The word cloud might reveal a fascinating interplay between consumer preferences, technological integration, and the potential elimination of the pain of paying (Figure 1).

Figure 1. A Word Cloud Analysis of Frictionless Shopping

Source: Empirical study

While the word cloud analysis offers valuable insights, it is crucial to remember its limitations. It solely reflects the terminology used and may not capture the complete picture, which encompasses factors like store layout, product selection, and the emotional aspects of the shopping experience.

We began by exploring the themes of the study. This analysis enabled us to identify six dimensions using a Thematic Analysis Approach. The analysis identified six themes: convenience and efficiency, checkout process, technology and innovation, consumer experience, product selection, and concerns and skepticism. The "convenience and efficiency" theme includes words such as "convenient," "efficiency," "quick," "grab," "easy," "smooth," "fast," "speed," "streamline," "breeze," "effortless," and "save time." This theme suggests that customers appreciate the speed and ease of shopping at Amazon Go stores, without having to wait in line or deal with cashiers. The second theme, "checkout process", includes words such as "wait," "line," "transaction," "checkout," "cashier," "payment," "cash," "register," "receipt," and "scan." This theme suggests that customers are relieved to avoid the traditional checkout process at Amazon Go stores. For the third one, the "technology and innovation" theme, includes words such as "Amazon," "technology," "tech," "automate," "app," "account," "scan," "surveillance," "machine," and "sensor." This theme suggests that customers are interested in the innovative technology used in Amazon Go stores, such as the automated checkout system.

The fourth one is the "consumer experience" theme, and it includes words such as "experience," "feel," "shop," "buy," "purchase," "visit," "enjoy," "love," "prefer," and "expect." This theme suggests that customers have a positive overall experience shopping at Amazon Go stores. The "product selection", is the fifth theme, and it includes words such as "item," "stuff," "product," "snack," "drink," "grocery," "food," "sandwich," and "merch." This theme suggests that customers are satisfied with the variety of products available at Amazon Go stores. Finally, "concerns and skepticism" is the sixth theme and includes words such as "worry," "skeptical," "concern," "cautious," "skeptical," "glitch," "privacy," "fear," and "problem." This theme suggests that some customers have concerns about the privacy implications of shopping at Amazon Go stores, as well as about the potential for technical glitches.

We have therefore summarized these different dimensions in Table 3:

Table 3. Dimensions of thematic content analysis

Theme	Words	Interpretation
Convenience and Efficiency	convenient, efficiency, quick, grab, easy, smooth, seamless, fast, speed, streamline, breeze, effortless, save time.	This theme encompasses words related to the ease and speed of the shopping experience, including convenience, efficiency, and quickness.
Checkout Process	wait, line, transaction, checkout, cashier, payment, cash, register, receipt, scan.	This theme focuses on aspects of the checkout process, including waiting times, cashier interactions, and payment methods.
Consumer Experience	experience, feel, shop, buy, purchase, visit, enjoy, love, prefer, expect.	This theme encompasses words related to consumers' overall experiences at Amazon Go stores, including their feelings, preferences, and expectations.
Product Selection	item, stuff, product, snack, drink, grocery, food, sandwich, merch.	This theme focuses on the variety and quality of products available at Amazon Go stores, including snacks, drinks, groceries, and other merchandise.
Concerns and Skepticism	worry, skeptical, concern, cautious, skeptical, glitch, privacy, fear, problem.	This theme includes words reflecting consumers' concerns, skepticism, and potential issues with the Amazon Go concept, such as privacy concerns, technical glitches, and fears about the process.
Positive Attributes	good, cool, nice, perfect, fun, amazing, impressive, fine, awesome, pleasant.	This theme encompasses positive attributes and experiences shared by consumers regarding Amazon Go stores.
Negative Attributes	steal, strange, odd, weird, oppressive, odd, bizarre, paranoid, uncomfortable, strange.	This theme includes words reflecting negative attributes or experiences shared by consumers, such as feelings of discomfort, strangeness, or paranoia.

Source: Personnal elaboration

Overall, the thematic analysis suggests that customers have a positive experience shopping at Amazon Go stores and that they appreciate the convenience, efficiency, and innovation of the stores. However, some customers have concerns about privacy and potential technical problems.

The network visualization, generated through textual analysis software, offers a glimpse into how phygital marketing elements might influence the perceived pain of paying. Words like "convenience," "easy," and "quick" appear connected to the central concept of "pain of paying" suggesting that strategies aimed at creating a more efficient and seamless shopping experience could mitigate the negative feelings associated with the payment process (Figure 2).

Figure 2. Network Visualization of Phygital Marketing Elements Influencing Pain of Paying

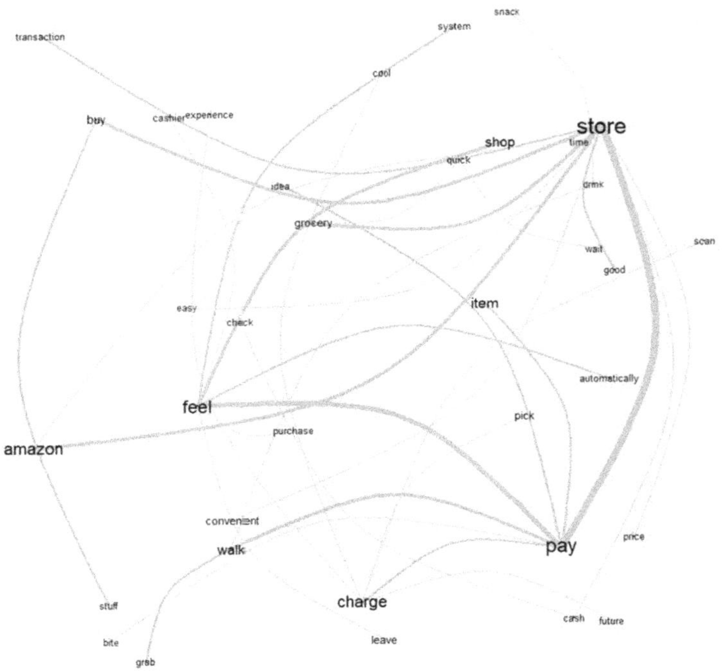

Source: Empirical study

Interestingly, the image depicts "cash" as directly linked to "pain of paying," potentially reflecting the perceived drawbacks of traditional cash transactions compared to other, potentially faster, methods. While words like "buy," "pick," and "pay" remain present, their connection to the central theme seems less prominent, suggesting that the focus might have shifted towards influencing the perception of paying rather than simply streamlining the purchase itself. Overall, the visualization highlights the potential for phygital marketing to address the psychological aspects of payment, paving the way for a more positive consumer experience.

The theme highlights interesting potential links between the phygital design of Amazon Go stores and the concept of the pain of paying. First of all, reduced friction points, that is, through convenience and efficiency. The analysis mentions "convenient," "quick," "grab," "easy," and "smooth," suggesting the design removes friction points like waiting in line, interacting with cashiers, and handling cash/cards, potentially reducing the perceived pain of paying. The checkout process expressed through words like "wait," "line," and "transaction" being absent suggests the automated checkout eliminates the traditional pain points associated with the process. While frictionless payment systems offer undeniable convenience, they also pose significant challenges. One prominent issue is the phenomenon of mindless spending, where the ease of payment can lead to unplanned purchases and reduced awareness of spending. This can result in increased financial strain when reviewing bills later on. Moreover, the absence of traditional payment indicators like cash, registers, or receipts may compromise transparency and control over one's finances, creating a disconnection between purchases and payments. Additionally, privacy concerns and ethical considerations further complicate the adoption of frictionless payment methods. Many consumers fear data collection and manipulation, raising skepticism about the technology's implications. These concerns can amplify the discomfort associated with paying, underscoring the need for careful consideration of the ethical dimensions of frictionless payment systems.

The phygital design of Amazon Go stores seems to reduce traditional pain points associated with paying in physical stores. However, it might introduce new forms of pain related to potential overspending, lack of transparency, and ethical concerns. Further research is needed to explore these complex relationships and their impact on customer behavior and experience.

First, prioritizing Convenience and Efficiency. Words like "grab & go" and "convenience" dominate the landscape, suggesting a customer base seeking a streamlined and effortless shopping experience. The absence of checkout lines and cashiers eliminates friction points, potentially leading to reduced shopping time and a more impulsive approach to product selection. Second, embracing Technological Innovation. Terms like "tech-savvy" and "innovation" hint at a customer base comfortable with embracing technology. The cloud's inclusion of "sensor" and "technology" reinforces this notion, highlighting the sensor-based infrastructure that underpins the Amazon Go experience. This technology, through automated product recognition and billing, facilitates a frictionless and seamless shopping journey. Third, eliminating the Pain of Paying. The traditional act of paying, often associated with a sense of loss or the "pain of paying," is seemingly absent in the Amazon Go experience. The integration of technology removes the need for physical cash or card swipes, potentially mitigating this psychological discomfort associated with parting with money.

This study on phygital marketing and the pain of paying in Amazon Go stores contributes to a growing field of research at the intersection of consumer behavior, marketing strategies, and technological advancements. Building upon existing research on consumer behavior and marketing strategies, it aligns with the work of Prelec & Loewenstein (1998) by exploring the concept of the pain of paying and the desire to separate spending from consumption. However, this research goes further by investigating how phygital experiences, specifically those in Amazon Go stores, can influence this phenomenon. Furthermore, it expands on Soman's (2001) examination of the link between payment methods and the pain of paying. Here, the focus is on how technology-driven payment systems can potentially reduce these pain points. Finally, this study complements the work of Verhoef et al. (2009) on the customer experience. By examining how phygital elements like frictionless payments shape the customer experience, particularly regarding the pain of paying, this research offers a valuable contribution to the understanding of this evolving retail landscape.

5. CONCLUSION

The Amazon Go experience unveils a unique shopping environment shaped by consumer preferences for convenience and efficiency, facilitated by technological advancements, and potentially impacting the "pain of paying" traditionally associated with the shopping experience. However, a holistic understanding of this phenomenon requires acknowledging the limitations of this analysis and considering the multifaceted nature of human behavior in the face of innovation and changing retail landscapes.

We conducted a netnographic study analyzing online customer conversations about Amazon Go stores across forums, blogs, social media, and reviews. Our focus was on how the cashier-less, automated checkout model removes barriers and pain points around paying for purchases. This in turn may enable mindless spending and unplanned purchases in-store. Our findings suggest the "grab and go" experience strips away psychological transaction costs and payment rituals which typically create natural consumer friction and spending obstacles. By allowing shoppers to simply take items off shelves without formalized checkout processes, Amazon Go appears to eliminate the pain of payment cues that can curb impulsive purchasing and set customer spending boundaries. By blending digital and physical spaces, Amazon Go's cashier-less checkout model removes traditional payment pain points and financial friction from the shopping experience. We examine how this impacts customer psychology and spending habits—enabling seamless purchases but also potentially "mindless" overspending. Our analysis explores the pros and cons customers identify regarding Amazon Go's automated checkout capabilities, including concerns around data privacy, personalized pricing, and the manipulation of shopping behaviors through intuitive commerce technologies. More broadly, this case study discusses implications for emerging digitally enhanced stores that seek to influence psychology and shape behavior by reducing payment friction in blended digital/physical retail environments.

Our study delves into a critical aspect of the evolving retail landscape – the interplay between phygital experiences and the psychology of paying. By examining customer online conversations about Amazon Go stores, we uncover valuable insights with both theoretical and practical implications for marketing and retail businesses. These insights have the potential to reshape how retailers design customer experiences, particularly when it comes to mitigating the pain of paying and fostering positive consumer behavior.

On a theoretical level, the research contributes to expanding and deepening the understanding of Phygital Marketing. It contributes to the evolving understanding of phygital marketing by demonstrating its potential to influence the psychological aspects of consumer behavior, specifically the pain of paying. Next, it offers a nuanced view of the Pain of Paying, that is, the study goes beyond simply confirming the pain of paying. It suggests that phygital experiences can potentially mitigate this discomfort by streamlining the shopping process and potentially reducing reliance on traditional cash transactions. However, it also acknowledges the potential emergence of new forms of discomfort related to overspending, lack of transparency, and ethical concerns. Thirdly, the research enriches the understanding of the consumer experience in phygital environments. It highlights the role of reducing friction points and the potential impact on the perception of paying.

On the practical side, we think that the findings suggest that retailers can leverage phygital marketing strategies to create a more seamless and efficient shopping experience, potentially reducing the pain of paying and encouraging customer satisfaction. This could involve implementing frictionless payment systems like mobile wallets or -especially- self-checkout options. Meanwhile, the study emphasizes the importance of maintaining transparency and a sense of control over the payment process. Retailers should ensure clear communication about data collection practices and provide options for customers who prefer traditional payment methods. Furthermore, the research underscores the need for ethical considerations when implementing phygital marketing strategies. Retailers should prioritize data privacy and security, and develop transparent policies regarding customer data collection and usage. About omnichannel integration, the study reinforces the importance of a well-integrated omnichannel strategy. Phygital elements like in-store technology should complement online platforms and marketing efforts to create a cohesive customer experience. Finally, we think that by understanding the potential impact of phygital experiences on the pain of paying, retailers can develop targeted marketing strategies for different customer segments. For example, highlighting the convenience of frictionless payments might appeal to time-constrained customers, while emphasizing transparency and control might resonate with privacy-conscious consumers.

Some limitations are present in our study. First, the Pain of paying is subjective and varies based on personality, financial literacy, and spending habits. The analysis doesn't explore how these factors might influence the impact of the phygital design. Second, the analysis focuses on initial impressions. It's unclear how the pain of paying might evolve with repeated use and habituation to the phygital experience. Third, comparing the pain of paying in Amazon Go to other phygital stores or traditional stores could provide valuable insights into the specific design elements that influence this perception. Finally, it is important to acknowledge that the pain of paying might manifest differently in this environment, potentially through concerns about data privacy or the lack of tangible interaction during the payment process.

REFERENCES

Alla, L., Hmioui, A., & Bentalha, B. (2020). La netnographie dans les recherches marketing: La communauté virtuelle comme consom'acteur vecteur d'efficacité marketing. *Alternatives Managériales Economiques*, 2(4), 631–652.

Antéblian, B., Filser, M., & Roederer, C. (2013). L'expérience du consommateur dans le commerce de détail. Une revue de littérature. [French Edition]. *Recherche et Applications en Marketing*, 28(3), 84–113. 10.1177/0767370113497868

Ariely, D., & Silva, J. (2002). Payment method design: Psychological and economic aspects of payments. Center for e-Business MIT. *Paper*, 196, 68–73.

Arnould, E. J., Price, L., & Zinkhan, G. (2002). *Consumers*. McGraw-Hill.

Belghiti, S., Ochs, A., Lemoine, J. F., & Badot, O. (2018). The phygital shopping experience: An attempt at conceptualization and empirical investigation. In *Marketing Transformation: Marketing Practice in an Ever Changing World: Proceedings of the 2017 Academy of Marketing Science (AMS) World Marketing Congress (WMC)* (pp. 61-74). Springer International Publishing.

Bentalha, B. (2023). Consumer Perception of Robotic Mobile Fulfillment Systems: A Netnographic Case Study of Amazon. In *Innovation, Strategy, and Transformation Frameworks for the Modern Enterprise* (pp. 243-264). IGI Global 10.4018/979-8-3693-0458-7.ch010

Bentalha, B., & Hmioui, A. (2021). Smart service supply chain and Just Walk Out technology: a netnographic approach. In *The Proceedings of the International Conference on Smart City Applications* (pp. 223-236). Cham: Springer International Publishing.

Borghini, S., Diamond, N., Kozinets, R. V., McGrath, M. A., Muñiz, A. M.Jr, & Sherry, J. F.Jr. (2009). Why are themed brandstores so powerful? Retail brand ideology at American Girl Place. *Journal of Retailing*, 85(3), 363–375. 10.1016/j.jretai.2009.05.003

Bouhtati, N., Alla, L., & Bentalha, B. (2023). Marketing Big Data Analytics and Customer Relationship Management: A Fuzzy Approach. In *Integrating Intelligence and Sustainability in Supply Chains* (pp. 75-86). IGI Global. 10.4018/979-8-3693-0225-5.ch004

Brakus, J. J., Schmitt, B. H., & Zarantonello, L. (2009). Brand experience: What is it? How is it measured? Does it affect loyalty? *Journal of Marketing*, 73(3), 52–68. 10.1509/jmkg.73.3.052

Chaney, D., Lunardo, R., & Mencarelli, R. (2018). Consumption experience: Past, present and future. *Qualitative Market Research*, 21(4), 402–420. 10.1108/QMR-04-2018-0042

Chevalier, J., & Xue, H. (2008). Why does credit card debt make people happy? The effects of affective forecasting on credit card use. *JMR, Journal of Marketing Research*, 45(1), 105–114.

Chung, J., Shin, D. H., & Lee, S. Y. (2017). A framework for customer experience design in a phygital retail environment. *Journal of Business Research*, 101, 114–123.

Dolbec, P. Y., & Chebat, J. C. (2013). The impact of a flagship vs. a brand store on brand attitude, brand attachment and brand equity. *Journal of Retailing*, 89(4), 460–466. 10.1016/j.jretai.2013.06.003

Du, J., Joachimsthaler, E., Füller, J., & Hofacker, C. (2017). Amazon Go: A glimpse into the future of retail grocery shopping? *International Journal of Retail & Distribution Management*, 45(11/12), 1204–1213.

Flacandji, M. (2015). *Du souvenir de l'expérience à la relation à l'enseigne: une exploration théorique et méthodologique dans le domaine du commerce de détail* [Doctoral dissertation, Université de Bourgogne].

Henn, M., Huberman, B. M., & Milkman, K. E. (2000). The networked citizen. *Science*, 290(5491), 1187–1188.

Hoch, S. J. (2002). Product experience is seductive. *The Journal of Consumer Research*, 29(3), 448–454. 10.1086/344422

Holbrook, M. B., & Hirschman, E. C. (1982). The experiential aspects of consumption: Consumer fantasies, feelings, and fun. *The Journal of Consumer Research*, 9(2), 132–140. 10.1086/208906

Huang, M. H., Rust, R. T., & Apkarian, M. H. (2009). The service revolution and its implications for marketing science. *Journal of Marketing*, 73(2), 20–40.

Hui, M. K., & Bateson, J. E. (1991). Perceived control and the effects of crowding and consumer choice on the service experience. *The Journal of Consumer Research*, 18(2), 174–184. 10.1086/209250

Kaltcheva, V. D., & Weitz, B. A. (2006). When should a retailer create an exciting store environment? *Journal of Marketing*, 70(1), 107–118. 10.1509/jmkg.70.1.107.qxd

Kerin, R. A., Jain, A., & Howard, D. J. (1992). Store shopping experience and consumer price-quality-value perceptions. *Journal of Retailing*, 68(4), 376.

Kozinets, R. V. (2010). Netnography: Connected consumers and digital ethnography. *Progress in Consumer Research*, 37(1), 221–231.

Kozinets, R. V. (2015). *Netnography: redefined*. Sage.

Kumar, V., Rafiq, M., Dangelico, R. M., & Chan, F. K. Y. (2019). Omni-channel retailing: A review of the literature and future research directions. *Journal of Retailing*, 95(6), 707–728.

Lamsiah, A., & Bentalha, B. (2023). 2022 Qatar World Cup: A Netnographic Analysis of the Relationship Between Sport, Media and Politic *Réflexions sportives, 1*(3), 69-95 .

Lemon, K. N., & Verhoef, P. C. (2016). Understanding customer experience throughout the customer journey. *Journal of Marketing*, 80(6), 69–96. 10.1509/jm.15.0420

Muniz, A. M., & O'Guinn, T. C. (2001). Brand communities. *The Journal of Consumer Research*, 27(6), 712–730.

Pine, B. J., & Gilmore, J. H. (2013). The experience economy: past, present and future. In *Handbook on the experience economy* (pp. 21–44). Edward Elgar Publishing. 10.4337/9781781004227.00007

Prelec, K., & Loewenstein, G. (1998). The pain of paying: Why is cash rational in a credit card society? *Journal of Economic Psychology*, 17(6), 185–211.

Preu, L., Huang, J., & Mela, C. (2017). Will you pay more or less with a mobile wallet? Examining the moderating role of pain of paying. *Journal of Retailing*, 93(2), 182–195.

Punj, G., & Stewart, D. W. (1983). Cluster analysis in marketing research: Review and suggestions for application. *JMR, Journal of Marketing Research*, 20(2), 134–148. 10.1177/002224378302000204

Raghubir, P., & Srivastava, J. (2008). Monopoly money: The effect of payment coupling and form on spending behavior. *Journal of Experimental Psychology. Applied*, 14(3), 213–225. 10.1037/1076-898 X.14.3.21318808275

Rick, S. I., Cryder, C. E., & Loewenstein, G. (2008). Tightwads and spendthrifts. *The Journal of Consumer Research*, 34(6), 767–782. 10.1086/523285

Ritzer, G. (1999). 15 Assessing the Resistance. *Resisting McDonaldization*, 234.

Shah, A. M., Eisenkraft, N., Bettman, J. R., & Chartrand, T. L. (2016). "Paper or plastic?": How we pay influences post-transaction connection. *The Journal of Consumer Research*, 42(5), 688–708. 10.1093/jcr/ucv056

Sheehan, D., & Van Ittersum, K. (2018). In-store spending dynamics: How budgets invert relative-spending patterns. *The Journal of Consumer Research*, 45(1), 49–67. 10.1093/jcr/ucx125

Shelley, J. (2009). *The concept of the aesthetic.*

Soman, D. (2001). The tactical influence of payment on spending. *Journal of Consumer Marketing*, 18(5), 351–362.

Soman, D. (2003). The effect of payment transparency on consumption: Quasi-experiments from the field. *Marketing Letters*, 14(3), 173–183. 10.1023/A:1027444717586

Thomas, M., Desai, K. K., & Seenivasan, S. (2011). How credit card payments increase unhealthy food purchases: Visceral regulation of vices. *The Journal of Consumer Research*, 38(1), 126–139. 10.1086/657331

Verhoef, P. C., Lemon, K. N., Parasuraman, A., Roggeveen, A., Tsiros, M., & Schlesinger, L. A. (2009). Customer experience creation: Determinants, dynamics and management strategies. *Journal of Retailing*, 85(1), 31–41. 10.1016/j.jretai.2008.11.001

Zellermayer, O. (1996). *The pain of paying*. Carnegie Mellon University.

Chapter 18
Exploratory Analysis of the Impact of Phygital on the Customer Experience

Mohamed Amine Gueznai
http://orcid.org/0009-0006-7105-2571

National School of Commerce and Management, Hassan II University of Casablanca, Morocco

Abdellah Elboussadi

National School of Commerce and Management, Hassan II University of Casablanca, Morocco

ABSTRACT

Over the past few years, the world of commerce has undergone lightning changes, both in terms of content and form, driven by the democratization of NICT usage. This transformation has led to the emergence of new behaviors, new players, new distribution concepts, and a new shopping experience. The presentation of the commercial offer has given rise to a new in-store experience for customers. The latter can be a source of satisfaction, and consequently of purchase intent. Considering the consumer as a being in search of a sensitive experience, phygital tools combined with experiential marketing have become an essential weapon used by companies to make consumers feel they are living a pleasant and unique experience, provoking in them a sense of belonging and loyalty.

1. INTRODUCTION

In a world in the throes of technological change, driven by the explosive development of new information and communication technologies (NICTs), physical retailing finds itself confronted by the growing power of e-commerce. Thus, the use of technology in business in general, and in marketing in particular, has become inevitable (Kalaignanam et al., 2020, Agarwal et al., 2020, Grewal et al., 2021, John & Scheer, 2021). These new technologies have become inescapable, on the one hand for customers looking for an experience rather than just a product or service, and on the other hand increasingly

DOI: 10.4018/979-8-3693-3172-9.ch018

sought after by physical businesses in order to gain visibility, traffic and e-reputation. Thus, the initial assumption that e-commerce would crush and obliterate the brick-and-mortar sector is no longer valid.

Customer behavior has metamorphosed with the introduction of these new technologies, with access to the internet becoming increasingly easy via smartphones, tablets, free Wi-Fi networks, etc. Indeed, digital transformation has brought about radical innovation in the market and businesses, thus provoking an impact on consumer expectations and behavior (Verhoef et al., 2021). Moreover, digital transformation, spurred on in recent years by the Covid 19 health crisis, has been one of the main drivers reshaping the landscape of commerce in general and retailing in particular (Vrontis et al., 2022).

In this way, digital is beginning to take hold, creating a kind of revolution in markets and the world of commerce that is unlikely to disappear in the short or medium term (Brown et al., 2020 ; Vrontis et al., 2021 ; Xiang et al., 2021), but will last for decades. This is how in-store technology becomes an effective weapon for generating traffic, converting leads, building customer loyalty, and ultimately driving the act of re-purchase. What's more, finding information has become simple and accessible, changing the way we communicate, interact, and consolidate the ties that unite retailers with consumers (Kahn, 2018).

The introduction of these technologies at the point of sale is an essential step, as it enables retailers to integrate digital channels with physical ones, thus becoming part of a phygitalization phenomenon (Mishra et al. 2021), involving enormous management efforts to synchronize all available channels. For example, today's customers expect an integrated omnichannel experience, where they can order online and collect in-store (Tyrväinen & Karjaluoto, 2019). Thus, retailing using phygital technologies is seen as a must-have solution for a demanding category of customers and their intelligent shopping behaviors (Batat,2019). In the same vein, big data-driven proposed solutions are driving retailers to adopt new marketing solutions with a focus on personalizing the service experience offered within the point of sale (Bentalha et al.,2020). In the same vein, Big Data makes it possible to collect a vast quantity of information that can be used to improve the offering through marketing strategies tailored to the specific needs of each sector (Alla et al.,2022 ; Lin & Kunnathur, 2019).

The phygitalization of points of sale remains a fairly recent concept. However, it has captured the interest of several researchers (Badot and Belghiti, 2007; Batat, 2018; Belghiti, et al,.2018; Bèzes,2019; Fornerino et al.,2018; Goudey, 2013; Lao and Vlad, 2018; Lapassouse-Madrid and Vlad, 2017; Merle et al., 2018; Grewal et al. 2020.).

In this respect, we will illustrate, through a literature review, the concepts of phygitalization, its origins, as well as the different technologies introduced, highlighting the theoretical aspects of the literature necessary for our research. Permanent access to these new technologies through smartphones has introduced a radical change in the decision-making and purchasing process. Thus, during their purchasing journey, consumers seek not only a utilitarian product, but above all a rich, fun and entertaining experience Grewal and Roggeveen (2020) and Roggeveen et al. (2020).

Aware of these transitions (Mele & Russo Spena,2022), companies have also tried to follow through the introduction in various stores of new technologies such as interactive kiosks, smart mirrors, embodied or disembodied robots, mobile payment, immersive technologies, the Internet of Things (IoT), the Internet of Things (IoE), conversational agents (chatbot) etc. thus leading to trigger different emotional and cognitive states in the consumer. As for customer experience, it has been addressed by several authors (Bakker et al.,2014; Batat, 2018; Carteron, 2013; Carù and Cova, 2003; Filser,2002; Fornerino et al.,2006; Hirschman and Holbrook, 1982, 1986; Roederer, 2012; Roederer and Filser, 2015; Samir and Soumia, 2020).

According to (Batat,2019), "*phygital refers to the transformation of physical stores in the digital age: concepts are completely rethought to offer a new customer experience and use digital tools as a sales medium*". This is how the company seeks both physical and digital interaction with its customers, based on affective (Lapassouse-Madrid and Vlad, 2017), cognitive (Flacandji, 2015), sensory (Schmitt, 1999) and technological variables (Davis, 1989).

The main aim of our research is to study the impact of point-of-sale digitalization on the customer experience, focusing on consumer perceptions and behaviors towards the use of in-store technologies.

In the first section, we will review the conceptual and theoretical background to the key terms of our research. In the second section, we will develop the model and proposals, and in the third section, we will discuss the implications and suggest directions for future research.

2. THEORETICAL AND CONCEPTUAL FRAMEWORK

2.1. Phygital: Technology at the Service of Marketing

Technological advances over the last few decades have had a significant impact on the development of society. In this regard, we will adopt for this article the definition proposed by Lee et al. (2015, p. 8) of technology which states that "a man-made tool whose purpose is to be used to solve a problem, achieve an objective or serve a target that is defined by man, perceived or felt by man". Indeed, NICTs have overturned classic and habitual behaviors from generation to generation. To keep pace with changing customer trends, companies have also taken the plunge and begun to focus on the customer rather than the market. In the face of these changes, resilience has become a sine-qua-non through a thorough and targeted adaptation affecting all components of the company. (Elboussadi & Aaouid, 2023).

A first definition was proposed by Chris Weil in 2007, former CEO of Momentum Worldwide, an international consultancy, strategy, analysis and experience design firm, who shows that the term phygital is difficult to define insofar as it represents an interconnection between the physical and the digital. It wasn't until 2013 that "Phygital" was coined by the Australian marketing agency, Momentum, a contraction of "physical" and "digital". The term is mainly used in retail, on the theme of in-store experience: the aim is to digitalize the store, integrating a website and/or social networks. This is how phygital made its debut in various fields of consulting, strategy, analysis, and experience design (Vergine et al., 2020).

Retailers are highlighting the phygital solution as a new way of enhancing the in-store shopping experience and responding to customers' fragmented omnichannel behavior (the integration of all physical and digital channels into its marketing strategy (Sauvage, 2019) (Belghiti et al., 2018).

Table 1. Evolution of the phygitalization concept

Authors/Year	Definitions
Badot and Belghiti, (2007)	*"Phygital hybridization is a two-way process. On the one hand, it consists of the consumer transforming a physical component into a digital component (digitalization of the physical), or on the other hand, in the other direction, transforming a digital component into a physical component."*
Filser, (2015)	*"Phygitalization thus refers to approaches that aim to combine the best of the physical and the digital to deliver fluid sensory and emotional experiences between the different channels, or to physically materialize a digital experience."*
(Collin-Lachaud & Vanheems, 2016)	*"Point-of-sale digitalization refers to the integration of one or more interactive digital technologies into the traditional physical store in order to eliminate the boundaries between different distribution and communication channels."*
Quintana et al., (2016)	*"Smart retail is a term used to describe a set of intelligent technologies that are designed to give the consumer a bigger, faster, safer and smarter experience when shopping."*
Rieunier, (2017)	*"Combining the physical and digital worlds at the point of sale to offer customers a richer, more seamless experience across different channels".*
Fornerino et al., (2018)	*"Phygital, a neologism derived from the contraction of the word physical and the word digital. Thus, a phygital store offers the possibility of living an experience that is both real - through interaction with physical devices and content - and virtual - through interaction with digital devices and content."*
Batat, (2018)	*"Phygital has become a major issue for companies, as it is experienced as a continuum between the physical and digital contexts. Companies must therefore understand its components and typologies in order to create unique, enjoyable and effective customer experiences."*
Marrone and Gallic, (2018)	*"Is a means of conveying good communication around brand values and is part of an experiential approach that leaves its mark on consumers' minds.*
Lao and Vlad, (2018)	*"Point-of-sale digitalization refers to the integration of one or more interactive digital technologies into the traditional physical store in order to eliminate the boundaries between different distribution and communication channels."*
Batat (2019)	*"Phygital refers to the transformation of physical stores in the digital age: concepts are completely rethought to offer a new customer experience and use digital tools as a sales medium".*
Liu et al. (2022)	*"The phygital-social context is a complex context created by smartphones that triggers and supports the development of new travel plans, the reconsideration of pre-travel plans and the cancellation of pre-travel plans."*
Batat (2022)	*"Phygital is considered a comprehensive framework for better managing customer experiences (PH-CX). The framework includes the fundamental driving forces, connectors, and pillars of the phygital customer experience strategy to help managers design compelling customer experiences."*

Source: authors

In short, phygital refers to the combination of the physical and the digital in a point of sale, whatever its nature, as part of an omnichannel strategy, in order to enrich the customer experience and make it ultra-personalized. As a result, more customers are attracted to the point of sale instead of shopping online. Today, the world of e-commerce and the world of physical commerce are no longer dichotomous, but complementary. Despite the great interest that the question of definition has aroused in public debate on the part of academics and practitioners, the concept lacks a clear conceptualization (Batat, 2022).

2.2 Phygital's Immersion in Retailing

Although for some retailers, online sales are an exclusive or even complementary strategy to in-store sales, the latter are now undergoing profound transformations with the development of digital, M-Commerce, social commerce, and the generalization of ROPO (Research Online, Purchase Offline) (Verhoef et al., 2021). Many online retailers have been forced to open physical stores to complete their customer's shopping journey (e.g. Amazon), or simply to meet the expectations of consumers looking for a real experience, service, personalization, expertise or listening. Therefore, retailers operating in phygital retailing are seen as an optimal solution for persuading demanding customers and their buying behavior based on the use of intelligent technologies (Batat, 2019).

On their side, some real-life outlets have integrated digital into their physical infrastructure, while developing new sales concepts based on the creation of a unique customer experience, seen as an effective weapon against the competition in order to distinguish themselves and gain competitive advantage (Roy et al., 2020; Verhoef et al., 2009; Gao et al., 2021). In the same line of thought, (Guo et al.,2018) affirmed the primordial role of the company's marketing capabilities in configuring and developing resources to create a durable competitive advantage.

The authors (Beck and Crié, 2015), explain the rapid development of digital technologies in physical stores based on three main ideas. Firstly, consumers are confronted with advertising via traditional and digital channels from the beginning of their day. As a result, they are faced with an abundance of information, prompting them to filter it out by looking for other ways (Häubl and Trifts, 2000). Secondly, today's customer is looking not just for a product, but for an experience throughout his or her purchasing journey. As a result, this experience is only possible through the use of new technologies that guarantee a positive, playful emotion. Finally, the central objective is to create an element of differentiation from competitors, hence providing the company with a key success factor. However, the success of this strategy remains dependent on the availability of resources, which is in line with resource-based theory (RBV) (Barney 1991).

Along the same line, and according to (Verhoef et al., 2021), digital transformation and innovation have led to a radical metamorphosis of the market, in the sense that consumers are integrating technological tools into every stage of their purchasing process, from the search for information to the act of purchase: tactile technologies, facial recognition, immersive technologies, etc...

These technologies have a major impact on the strategic and operational management of companies, in the sense that the information's collected can be used as a database for important decisions (Hunt et Lambe, 2000). Thus, emerging technologies are innovative solutions that emerge and evolve rapidly (Godé, 2021), have the potential to revolutionize traditional marketing practices (Lo & Campos, 2018; Verma et al., 2021; Rauschnabel et al., 2022; Kocaman et al., 2023). These technologies are described as innovative, rapidly evolving and capable of considerably transforming business models and consumer behaviour (Anastasova, 2006).

The area of marketing has undergone remarkable evolution with the introduction of technologies, principally artificial intelligence, serving as the basis for a range of marketing decisions, capable of processing large volumes of information collected via Internet of Things (IoT).

By incorporating virtual and immersive elements into the real world, companies can offer interactive and authentic experiences to their customers, which can have a positive impact on their behaviour and perception (Flavián et al., 2019; Wedel et al., 2020). For example, the use of augmented reality gives customers the ability to better project and adjust products more easily, creating a sense of security and reducing uncertainty (Gallardo et al., 2018), and perceived risk (Lim et al., 2024). According to (Lo and Campos, 2018), the data collected by IoT solutions can be exploited to better define new on the segments contributing consequently to the commercial performance of the company in the sense of (Makarius et al., 2020).

2.2.1 Theories of Technology

The use of technology is considered to be the warhorse for any company wishing to integrate the digital with the physical, and several theories have been developed in this direction. (MacKay and Gillespie, 1992) put forward the theory of technological continuity (TCT), which complements the aspect of technology use. It predicts whether users intend to continue using a technology or not. In the same sense, technological development is constantly changing, making it a crucial element for the retail business.

This development can benefit both customers and brands. Moreover, technology enables consumers to make more rational decisions, compare offers and benefits, and obtain faster service (Verhoef et al., 2021). For retailers, it enables them to reach the right consumers at lower cost, due to their efficiency (Grewal et al., 2017).

2.2.1.1 The Technology Acceptance Model (TAM)

In addition, and to explain ICT user's behavior and perceived performance, it was on the basis of two cognitive theories that (Davis, 1993) proposed the Technology Acceptance Model (TAM). In the TAM model, Davis gives a predominant role to user's attitudes. He considers that the user makes an individual analysis of two future consequences: perceived usefulness and perceived usability. The level of perceived usefulness refers to the degree to which the user feels that the use of a system or technology improves his or her performance in carrying out the assigned task. As for perceived facility of use, it refers to the degree to which the user believes he or she can carry out a mission or task with a minimum of effort, by analyzing the cost/benefit ratio.

However, the technology acceptance model has suffered from various imperfections that have led to proposed improvements by other authors (Venkatesh et al. 2007; Venkatesh and Bala, 2008; Bourdon and Hollet 2009; Jawadi 2014), who have improved the basic model through the introduction of new moderating variables age, gender, experience, voluntary use (Venkatesh et al., 2007), or (Venkatesh, 2022) who showed the value of using artificial intelligence (AI) to help improve quality of life, focusing on individual characteristics, technological characteristics, environmental characteristics and interventions.

Indeed, (AI) can be seen as a revolutionary tool insofar as it can process large quantities of perpetually growing data and provide relevant information about partners (Bag et al., 2021), and consequently contribute to commercial performance (Makarius et al., 2020). In the same spirit, (Bouhtati et al., 2023) has shown the value of using data collected by the customer relationship management (CRM), via Big Data, to support corporate marketing strategies. For example, AI-enabled information gathering and processing enables marketing decision-makers to make the best decisions, especially when it comes to market research (Pietronudo et al., 2022), or natural language processing (NLP) enables marketers to study customer behavior by analyzing texts (Sharma et al., 2022) when it comes to the use of chatbots, for example.

In summary, the acceptance of technology and its use on a daily basis by customers has led companies, especially retailers, to follow the tastes and expectations of their customers in order to create a playful climate and act positively on the customer experience within the store.

1.2.1.2 The Decomposed Theory of the Model of Planned Behavior

Although TAM theory is considered to be a fairly solid model, several theorists have proposed breaking down the general constructs into finer components in order to obtain more accurate results. Thus (Taylor and Tod, 1995) proposed the "Decomposed Theory of Planned Behavior Model" (DTPB), which refers to the basic constructs of the various technology acceptance models and also of the planned behavior model. In the same line of thought, DTPB can be used to predict and identify beliefs that may influence customer behavior and intentions in one way or another, during the act of purchase, for example. Empirical studies of DTPB, notably (Shih and Fang, 2004; Han et al., 2010), have demonstrated the theory's ability to identify additional significant variance in purchase intentions compared to the Theory of Planned Behavior (Ajzen, 1991).

1.2.1.3 The Unified Theory of Acceptance and Use of Technology (UTAUT)

The UTAUT model proposed by (Venkatesh et al. 2003), is the result of the confrontation between eight models and theories to explain the intention to use technology which are: The Theory of Reasoned Action, the Technology Acceptance Model, the Motivation Model, the Theory of Planned Behavior, the Combined TAM and TPB Model, the PC Use Model, the Diffusion of Innovations Theory, and the Social Cognitive Theory. In this way, the theory was able to incorporate four variables that have a moderating effect on behavioral intention: gender, age, experience with technology and willingness or unwillingness to use technology. In the same vein, the UTAUT model was able to explain 70% of the variance in intention to use. In fact, by taking into account whether or not users were willing to use the technology, and their experience with it, we were able to understand that the expected results and the expected effort could be considered insignificant in the case of fairly significant use.

Moreover, with technological development and mainly the tools proposed by artificial intelligence, decision-making has taken an impressive turn insofar as they are becoming essential for decision-makers. As such, (Venkatesh 2022) has proposed a new version of the UTAUT (Research Agenda) by integrating four new predictor dimensions of purchase intention that can potentially play the role of moderators, namely: individual traits, technological traits, environmental traits, and interventions.

To summarize, the various models for technology and its use show that it can be a differentiating factor for companies, and therefore a key success factor in positively influencing the customer's in-store experience.

2.3 Customer Experience: The New Battleground for Companies

The concept of experience has evolved considerably over the course of history. As for management science, the question of experience was first broached in the 1950s by Abbott and Alderson, specialists in marketing and management. Yet (Holbrook, 2006) mentioned that the roots of the experiential approach can even be traced back to the time of Adam Smith. In the same way, it's worth noting that it's the buyer who seeks out and initiates the interaction, but it's the seller who manages the interaction and thus manages the customer's cognitive, emotional, behavioral, sensory and social responses.

Table 2. Evolution of the customer experience concept

Authors	Definitions
(Maslow, 1968)	It is a "moment of the highest level of joy and fulfillment" during which the individual can feel their true identity."
(Holbrook et Hirschman 1982)	*"A subjective state of consciousness accompanied by a variety of symbolic meanings, hedonic responses and aesthetic criteria. The experience is lived, personal and charged with affective responses."*
(Punj et Stewart 1983)	*"People categorize their experiences in terms of relatively stable personal constructs. These constructs are unique to the individual."*
(Arnould et Price 1993)	*"Extraordinary experience is triggered by unusual events and is characterized by high levels of emotional intensity."*
(Csikszentmihalyi 1996)	*"Exceptional moments are called flow experiences. The metaphor of 'flow' is used to describe the sense of effortless action they feel in the moments that stand out as the best of their lives."*
(Schmitt, 1999)	*"Experiences occur after encountering, undergoing or experiencing something. An experience is a personal event that occurs in response to a stimulus. Experiences bring sensory, emotional, cognitive, behavioral, and relational values that replace functional values."*
(Gupta et Vajic 2000)	*"The term experience broadly refers to all the feelings or knowledge that arise from an interaction between an individual and an object or activity."*
(Carù et Cova 2003)	*"An individual's daily consumption is made up of a consumption experience that can occur with or without a relationship to the market."*
(Gentile et al., 2007)	*"This concept refers to customers' subjective, internal reactions to direct or indirect interactions with products and retail companies."*
(Grewal et al. 2009)	*"The experience is created not only by the factors the retailer controls, but also, by factors beyond his control."*
(Johnston et Kong 2011)	*"Customer experience is as in the flow of the global encounter when companies and customers meet, which involves customers' cognition and emotions throughout the buying process that begins from the moment they recognize products and services."*
(Klaus et Maklan 2013)	*"Experience represents all the cognitive and affective evaluations made by the customer of all direct or indirect encounters with the company and relating to his purchasing behavior."*
(Roederer et Filser, 2015)	*The concept of "meta experience" takes a global view of the consumer's experience, and of the broader scope of the experience that the manager has to manage. The concept of meta experience is linked to "new generation" experiential marketing.*
(Lemon et Verhoef 2016)	*"Experience is a multi-dimensional construct that focuses on the cognitive, emotional, behavioral, sensory and social responses that consumers experience throughout their purchasing process."*
(Bustamante et Rubio,2017)	*"Experience then occurs when the consumer interacts with a retailer's products, physical environment, staff and practices."*
(Holmlund et al., 2020)	*"A customer's reaction to the various interactions with an organization, whether these take place before, during or after purchase or consumption."*

Source: authors

2.3.1 Experiential Models

Table 3. Experiential models

Modèles	Auteurs	Apports
CABS (Cognition -Affect-Behavior -Satisfaction)	(Holbrook, et Hirschman, 1982).	In this model, they retain the linear sequence of decision-making stages: cognition, affect, behavior. Thus, alongside the utilitarian aspect of products, consumers seek experiences for pleasure, amusement and previously untried sensations. (Roederer and Filser, 2015)
TEAV (Thought -Emotion-Activity -Value)	(Holbrook et Addis, 2001)	The authors presented the new model by introducing value as a constituent element of the experience and not just as a consequence. Thus, the consumer's thoughts, emotions, activity and reactions took precedence over the old 1982 model.
P.O.S (Interaction Personne-Objet-Situation)	(Punj et Stewart, 1983),	The model proposes a definition of experience combining an association and interaction between "person/object/situation") Experience is both a process and an outcome (Antéblian et al., 2013).

Source: authors

2.3.2 The Phygital Experience Contribution

The hybridization of the physical and the digital is emerging as a new mode of co-creation and co-operation between consumers (prosumers) and retailers (conducers). It works in two ways. On the one hand, it consists of the consumer transforming a physical component into a digital one (digitalization of the physical), and on the other hand, transforming a digital component into a physical one (Belghiti et al., 2018) (figure1).

Along the same lines, the phygital experience has been widely studied in various fields, including marketing (Bonfanti, et al.,2023), the retail sector (Banik and Gao, 2023), the fashion industry (Kamilova et al.,2022), and heritage tourism (Torres, 2022; Turco and Giovannini, 2020; Alla et al 2022).

Figure 1. Phygital experience perimeter

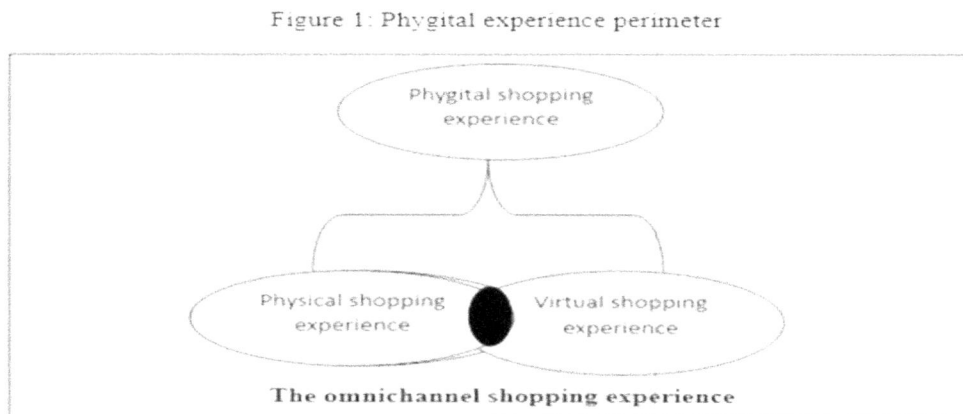

Figure 1: Phygital experience perimeter

Phygital shopping experience

Physical shopping experience — Virtual shopping experience

The omnichannel shopping experience

Source: (Belghiti et al, 2018)

Source: (Belghiti et al, 2018)

The concept of "phygital" consumer experiences reflects the newness of emerging digital technologies that empower them (Cabigiosu,2020). Phygital marketing is about creating a consumer journey that seamlessly integrates physical and digital experiences, creating experiences that are only possible thanks to the rise of emerging digital technologies (Hollebeek et al.,2019). In the same sense, phygital approaches involve the integration of various tools such as contactless payment systems, interactive touch screens, transparent digital payment systems and augmented reality into the customer experience (Nofal et al. (2017); Moravcikova and Kliestikova (2017). Therefore, the use of these strategies is widespread across all sectors (e.g. education, tourism, banking, etc.).

In addition, several landmark examples in different industries show that the use of technology, principally AI, enables the generation of customer information with a high degree of precision, facilitating planning and personalization that can lead to an improved customer experience (Dwivedi & Wang, 2022).

3. HYPOTHESES AND CONCEPTUAL FRAMEWORK

The S.O.R (Stimulus-Organism-Response) (figure2) model by (Mehrabian and Russell, 1974) has been proposed as part of the work carried out in environmental psychology. In particular, this model emphasizes the emotional reactions evoked by the atmosphere, and their capacity to lead to approach and avoidance behaviors in relation to the environment.

Figure 2. SOR model

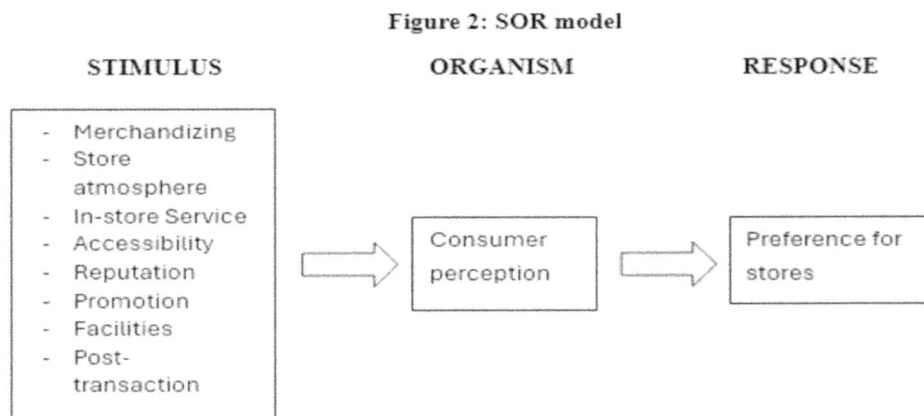

Figure 2: SOR model

Source: Thang and Tan (2003) page 193-200

Source: Thang and Tan (2003) page 193-200

3.1 Research's Hypotheses

3.1.1 In-Store Technologies and Their Informational Impact

According to Murray and Häubl (2008), the increasing complexity of products and services raise fear that some consumers will not buy them, for fear of not being able to use them successfully, and of having to bear excessive learning costs. Companies therefore have an interest in informing and assisting their customers in using the products and services they market. Once they have learned, they will have less trouble going to the competition because of the associated cognitive costs. The use of digital media helps customers during the purchasing process.

H1: In-store technologies provide informational support for consumers.

3.1.2 Curiosity Motivates Usage

Companies engage in a set of efforts to design shopping environments designed to increase the consumer's likelihood of purchase is called "sales atmosphere" and is considered one of the main levers for manipulating affective states (Lichtlé and Plichon, 2005) such as pleasure or excitement (Bonnin, 2003).

H2: in-store technologies positively influence user emotions.

3.1.3 The Use of in-Store Technologies Lowers the Risk of Purchase

Perceived risk is one of the major concepts used to determine purchasing behavior. Five dimensions are usually recognized: performance, physical, temporal, financial and social risk. This research is based on overall risk and not on trust, since risk reduction is necessary for purchase, whereas trust is not (Rose et al., 2011). In addition, (Lim, 2003) has shown that consumers may show reluctance (Roy et al., 2018) if they feel they will lose time, money or even personal data.

H3: in-store technologies reduce consumer-perceived risk.

3.1.4 In-Store Technologies Boost Satisfaction

The concept of satisfaction has been widely discussed in the literature, and its conceptualization began in the 1970s (Lemon and Verhoef, 2016) and in several ways. Some authors consider it an emotion, while others explain it from a cognitivist angle (Goudey, 2013). In the same sense, (Goudey 2013) defines it as *"a non-directly observable phenomenon that integrates cognitive and affective processes of appreciation of the purchasing and/or consumption experience."*

H4: In-store technologies positively influence satisfaction.

3.1.5 Repurchase Intention Depends on Satisfaction

According to (Liu et al.., 2016), repurchase intention has been the subject of extensive research into consumer's behavior. The latter is generally characterized by the desire to buy again a specific product or type of service at a given time, from the moment its needs are satisfied.

H5: The higher the level of satisfaction, the higher the level of repurchase intention.

Table 4. Summary of hypotheses

No. of hypotheses	Hypotheses	Authors
1	In-store technologies provide informational support for consumers	Murray et Häubl (2008) ; Flacandji, 2015, Batat, 2018 ; Fornerino et al., 2006; Lemon et Verhoef, 2016; Schmitt, 1999 ; Venkatesh 2022
2	in-store technologies positively influence user emotions	Lichtlé et Plichon, 2005; Bonnin, 2002; Lapassouse-Madrid et Vlad, 2017; Schmitt, 1999,
3	in-store technologies reduce consumer-perceived risk	Rose et al., 2011; Lim, 2003; Roy et al..,2018; Lim et al., 2024, Gallardo et al., 2018
4	In-store technologies positively influence satisfaction	Lemon et Verhoef, 2016 ; Goudey, 2013 ; Luna et al., 2019 ; Venkatesh 2022 ; Wagner et Cozmiuc, 2022 ; Benoit et al. 2017
5	The higher the level of satisfaction, the higher the level of repurchase intention	Liu et al.., 2016; Carù et Cova, 2015 ; Liu et al., 2016, Z. Yang et He, 2011; Kazmi et al., 2021 ; Nofal et al. (2017) ;

3.2 The Proposed Conceptual Research Model

Figure 3. Conceptual research model

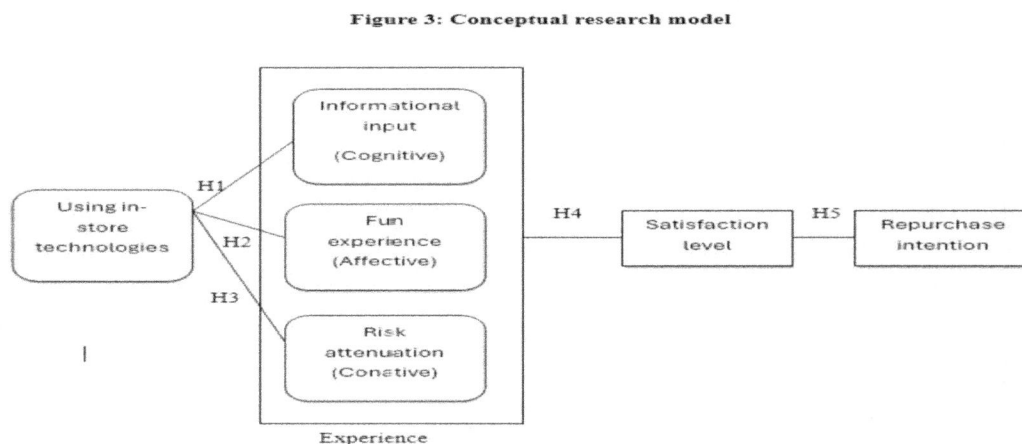

Figure 3: Conceptual research model

Source: authors

Source: authors

4. DISCUSSION

The aim of this paper was to propose a conceptual model of the relationship that can exist between technology, phigytal and customer experience (figure3). We sought to understand the process that leads to satisfaction from the user's point of view, i.e. to understand the variables that can improve customers' use and satisfaction with in-store technologies during the act of purchase. Our research model was built on the theoretical and empirical findings of previous studies on the shopping experience in both physical and virtual contexts.

A synthesis of the literature enabled us first to identify the different theoretical approaches mobilized to define the key concepts of our research, focusing more on end-users. This choice was justified by the mobilization of a set of theories that could explain the correlation between the technologies used and its impact on satisfaction (Benoit et al. 2017), on the act of re-purchasing, and in terms of saving time (Brynjolfsson and Smith 2000; Gauri et al. 2021), diversifying assets for employees (Noble et al., 2022).

Then, we presented the main reference models proposed in the literature, which served as the basis for developing our own model. These models focus on various dependent variables, such as technologies, use and satisfaction, and mediating variables such as environmental characteristics, individual characteristics, etc., and independent variables such as satisfaction during and after purchase, intention to repurchase, etc. Furthermore, another contribution of this research lies mainly in understanding the technological or psychological, emotional, social and behavioral factors and variables (Mele et al., 2021) that can improve the level of use and satisfaction of in-store technology users. In this sense, reducing waiting time in front of checkouts, considered as factor of dissatisfaction among 75% of physical store customers (Kahn 2018), is considered the warhorse for any retailer betting on automatic checkouts, interactive kiosks, etc. (Grewal et al., 2023).

The consumer's experience can be enhanced by the experiential context increased by digital and physical arrangements, which helps to nurture the various dimensions of the experience. Appreciation of the point of sale over time can be fueled by store decoration and theatricality (Antéblian et al., 2013). In the same vein, new sales and purchasing aids (NSA) have two main objectives: to facilitate choice and to enrich the customer experience (Beck and Crié, 2015). The pursuit of these goals will only succeed with human-machine collaboration, leading in turn to the well-being of all stakeholders (customers, employees and companies), and will soon realize a future in which "humans and machines will act in synergy" (Haesevoets et al. 2021, p. 2).

5. CONCLUSION

Establishing close links between the use of technology and the customer experience in terms of customer behavior before, during and after purchase remains paramount, insofar as the use offers value to consumers and thus becomes co-creative (Hoyer et al. 2020). Besides, the phygitalization of the store can offer customers an important communication and information acquisition opportunity, in the way that the user can remove inhibitions related to finding information or store staff, which is a big problem for customers (Kahn, 2018).

Despite the large number of studies on the crucial role played by technology in the customer experience within a phygitalized store, we still don't know how technological variables affect user's behavior during and after the purchase. To fill this gap, we have developed a model that shows how in-store technology can affect the customer experience.

To build the model, we first identified some of the digital tools used in stores, and then discussed the various implications that may arise for the customer experience. The latter is measured in terms of the information provided by the technology, the fun and personalized experience, and the risk perceived by the user. According to our model, companies that use these technologies in their stores reduce uncertainty and risk for the customer, provide significant communicative support and, as a result, have a positive impact on post-purchase satisfaction and the intention to repeat the experience.

The main theoretical implication of this study is that in-store technologies indirectly affect customer satisfaction via the mediation of experience variables: cognitive, affective and conative input. We believe that the model proposed in this study will shed light on the literature on phygitalization and customer experience. The model offers a better understanding of the interactions between decision-support technology and the lived experience and its consequences. These can have an impact on customer satisfaction, brand engagement (Wagner and Cozmiuc, 2022) and also post-purchase outcomes, notably purchase intention (Kazmi et al., 2021).

Our study also has implications for the literature on the introduction of technology into physical stores, to the extent that new sales and purchasing aids (NSAs) play an important role in customer engagement and involvement, which can lead to improved business performance. These technologies enable companies to improve their customer experience and competitiveness (Keegan et al., 2022; Volkmar et al., 2022).

There are several areas to explore for future research. Firstly, our proposed model can be tested in a practical setting, it could be measured through user surveys through a qualitative and/or quantitative study. In this way, verification will show whether the model is verifiable in different situational contexts, such as the level of technology achieved in a country, the level of involvement of retailers, the degree of confidence of users, etc.

In addition, the benefits provided by artificial intelligence applications can also be exploited on the side of other stakeholders. In fact, business-to-business marketing is characterized by the complexity of its interactions, which poses problems of relational governance (Pesämaa et al., 2018), which can be reduced thanks to the contributions of artificial intelligence, thus establishing relational and individualized marketing via a lasting relationship and a shared positive experience (Lo and Campos, 2018). Also, artificial intelligence can accelerate decision-making processes and help test multiple marketing strategies (Singh, 2022) boosted by a capacity to analyze and cross-reference multiple data sources.

Secondly, future studies could focus on examining the effectiveness of in-store technology use, insofar as the points of contact between customers and staff will be reduced, the medium- and long-term consequences on customer loyalty are unknown. Furthermore, with the use of in-store technology and the virtual absence of human contact, will the retailer be able to convey its positioning, arguments, and interactions? Further research could examine the impact of technological touchpoints on the in-store customer experience, or to meet the challenge of creating an AI competency capable of consistently meeting business requirements (McKinsey, 2023).

REFERENCES

Agarwal, R., Dugas, M., Gao, G. G., & Kannan, P. K. (2020). Emerging technologies and analytics for a new era of value-centered marketing in healthcare. *Journal of the Academy of Marketing Science*, 48(1), 9–23. 10.1007/s11747-019-00692-4

Ajzen, I. (1991). *The Theory of Planned Behavior. Organization Behavior and Human Decision Processes*. Academic Press, Inc. 10.1016/0749-5978(91)90020-T

Alla, L., Hmioui, A., & Et Bentalha, B. (2020). La netnographie dans les recherches marketing: La communauté virtuelle comme consom'acteur vecteur d'efficacité marketing. *Alternatives Managériales et Economiques*, 4, 631–652.

Alla, L., Kamal, M., & Bouhtati, N. (2022). Big data and marketing effectiveness of tourism businesses: A literature review. *Alternatives Managériales Economiques, 4*(0). 10.48374/IMIST.PRSM/ame-v1i0.36928

Anastassova, M. (2006). *L'analyse ergonomique des besoins en amont de la conception de technologies émergente : Le cas de la Réalité Augmentée pour la formation à la maintenance automobile* [PhD Thesis, Université René Descartes-Paris V]. https://theses.hal.science/tel-00340103

Anteblian, B., Filser, M., & Et Roederer, C. (2013). L'expérience du consommateur dans le commerce de détail. Une revue de littérature. *Recherche et Applications en Marketing*, 28(3), 84–113. 10.1177/0767370113497868

Arnould, E. J., & Price, L. L. (1993). River Magic: Extraordinary Experience and the Extended Service Encounter. *The Journal of Consumer Research*, 20(1), 24. 10.1086/209331

Badot, O., & Belghiti, S. (2007). *E phygital, nouveau mode de co - creation entre enseignes et consommateurs.*

Bag, S., Gupta, S., Kumar, A., & Sivarajah, U. (2021). An integrated artificial intelligence framework for knowledge creation and B2B marketing rational decision making for improving firm performance. *Industrial Marketing Management*, 92, 178–189. 10.1016/j.indmarman.2020.12.001

Bakker, I., Van Der Voordt, T., Vink, P., & Et De Boon, J. (2014). *Pleasure, Arousal, Dominance: Mehrabian And Russell Revisited. Current Psychology*. Https://Doi.Org/10.1007/S12144-014-9219-4

Banik, S., & Et Gao, Y. (2023). Exploring The Hedonic Factors Affecting Customer Experiences In Phygital Retailing. *Journal of Retailing and Consumer Services*, 70, 103147. Https://Doi.Org/10.1016/J.Jretconser.2022.103147. 10.1016/j.jretconser.2022.103147

Barney, J. B. (1991). Firm Resources And Sustained Competitive Advantage. *Journal of Management*, 17(1), 99–120. 10.1177/014920639101700108

Batat, W. (2019). *Experiential Setting Design The New Luxury Experience*. Springer. 10.1007/978-3-030-01671-5

Batat, W. (2022). What Does Phygital Really Mean? A Conceptual Introduction To The Phygital Customer Experience (PH-CX) Framework. *Journal of Strategic Marketing*, 1–24. 10.1080/0965254X.2022.2059775

Beck, M., & Crié, D. (2015). Les Nouvelles Aides À La Vente Et À L'achat: Définition, État De L'art Et Proposition 116 D'une Taxinomie. *Décisions Marketing, 79*, 131-150. Https://Doi.Org/10.7193/Dm .079.131.150

Belghiti, S., Ochs, A., Lemoine, J.-F., & Et Badot, O. (2018). *The Phygital Shopping Experience: An Attempt At Conceptualization And Empirical Investigation.* Springer. Https://Doi.Org/10.1007/978-3 -319-68750-6_18

Benoit, S., Sonja, K., & Andreas, E. (2017). Linking Service Convenience To Satisfaction: Dimensions And Key Moderators. *Journal of Services Marketing*, 31(6), 527–538. 10.1108/JSM-10-2016-0353

Bentalha, B. (2020). Big-Data Et Service Supply Chain Management: Challenges Et Opportunités. *International Journal Of Business And Technology Studies, 1*(3).

Bèzes, C. (2019). Quel Smart Retailing En Magasin Pour Quelle Expérience Omnicanal Vécue? [French Edition]. *Recherche et Applications en Marketing*, 34(1), 95–118.. 10.1177/0767370118795420

Bonfanti, A., Vigolo, V., Vannucci, V., & Et Brunetti, F. (2023). Creating Memorable Shopping Experiences To Meet Phygital Customers' Needs : Evidence From Sporting Goods Stores. *International Journal of Retail & Distribution Management*, 51(13), 81–100.. 10.1108/IJRDM-12-2021-0588

Bonnin, G. (2003). La Mobilité Du Consommateur En Magasin : Une Etude Exploratoire De L'influence De L'aménagement Spatial Sur Les Stratégies D'appropriation Des Espaces De Grande Distribution. [French Edition]. *Recherche et Applications en Marketing*, 18(3), 7–29.. 10.1177/076737010301800302

Bouhtatit, N., Kamal, M., & Alla, L. (2023), Big Data and the Effectiveness of Tourism Marketing: A Prospective Review of the Literature: Farhaoui, Y., Rocha, A., Brahmia, Z., Bhushab, B. (éd.) *Intelligence artificielle et environnement intelligent. ICAISE 2022. Notes de cours sur les réseaux et les systèmes.* Springer, Cham. 10.1007/978-3-031-26254-8_40

Bourbon, I., & Hollet-Haudebert, S. (2009). Pourquoi Contribuer A Des Bases De Connaissances? Une Exploration Des Facteurs Explicatifs A La Lumière Du Modèle UTAUT. *Systèmes d'Information Et Management*, 14(1), 9–36. 10.3917/sim.091.0009

Brynjolfsson, E. & Smith, M. (2000). Frictionless Commerce? A Comparison Of Internet And Conventional Retailers. *Management Science, 46*(4), 563–85.

Bustamante, J. C., & Et Rubio, N. (2017). Measuring Customer Experience In Physical Retail Environments. *Journal of Service Management*, 28(5), 884–913. 10.1108/JOSM-06-2016-0142

Cabigiosu, A. (2020). *Digitalisation dans l'industrie de la mode de luxe; Springer Science and Business Media LLC*. Allemagne.

Carteron, V. (2013). Expérience Client Et Distribution « Omnicanale ». *L'Expansion Management Review, 149*(2), 25. Https://Doi.Org/10.3917/Emr.149.0025

Carù, A. (2008). Opérations D'appropriation Et Ingrédients De L'offre Facilitant L'accès Au Plaisir Dans L'expérience De Consommation Virtuelle. *Journal of Chemical Information and Modeling*, 53(9), 287. Https://Doi.Org/10.1017/CBO9781107415324.004

Carù, A., & Et Cova, B. (2003). Revisiting Consumption Experience: A More Humble But Complete View Of The Concept. *Marketing Theory*, 3(2), 267–286. Https://Doi.Org/10.1177/14705931030032004. 10.1177/14705931030032004

Carù, A., & Et Cova, B. (2015). Expériences De Consommation Et Marketing Expérientiel. *Revue Francaise De Gestion*, 253(8), 353–367. Https://Doi.Org/10.3166/RFG.162.99-115. 10.3166/RFG.162.99-115

Collin-Lachaud, I., & Vanheems, R. (2016). Navigating between real and virtual spaces : An exploration of the hybrid shopping experience. [English Edition]. *Recherche et Applications en Marketing*, 31(2), 40–58. 10.1177/2051570716644145

Csikszentmihalyi, M. (1996). *Flow And The Psychology Of Discovery And Invention*. Harper Collins.

Csikszentmihalyi, M. (2014). Flow And The Foundations Of Positive Psychology. In *Flow And The Foundations Of Positive Psychology*. Springer. Https://Doi.Org/10.1007/978-94-017-9088-8

Davis, F. (1993). User Acceptance Of Information Technology: System Characteristics, User Perceptions And Behavioral Impacts. *International Journal of Man-Machine Studies*, 38(3), 475–487. Https://Doi.Org/10.1006/Imms.1993.1022. 10.1006/imms.1993.1022

Davis, F. D. (1989). Perceived Usefulness, Perceived Ease Of Use, And User Acceptance Of Information Technology. MIS Quarterly: Management. *Information Systems*, 13(3), 319–339. Https://Doi.Org/10.2307/249008

Dwivedi, Y. K., & Wang, Y. (2022). Guest editorial: Artificial intelligence for B2B marketing: Challenges and opportunities. In (*Vol. 105*, pp. 109–113). Elsevier. 10.1016/j.indmarman.2022.06.001

Elboussadi, A., & Aaouid, B. (2023, January). Modélisation De L'apport Des Parties Prenantes À La Résilience Organisationnelle Des Entreprises. *Revue AME*, 5(1), 472–491.

Filser, M. (2002). *Le Marketing De La Production D ' Expérience Statut Et Implications Managériales Théorique*. Research Gate.

Flacandji, M. (2015). *Du Souvenir De L'expérience À La Relation À L'enseigne: Une Exploration Théorique Et Méthodologique Dans Le Domaine Du Commerce De Détail Michaël*.

Flavián, C., Ibáñez-Sánchez, S., & Orús, C. (2019). The impact of virtual, augmented and mixed reality technologies on the customer experience. *Journal of Business Research*, 100, 547–560. 10.1016/j.jbusres.2018.10.050

Fornerino, M., Rivet, C., & Et Reghem, J. (2018). Explorer L'expérience De Shopping Dans Un Magasin Phygital. *Décisions Marketing, 91*(45), 60. Https://Doi.Org/10.7193/Dm.091.45.60

Gallardo, C., Rodríguez, S. P., Chango, I. E., Quevedo, W. X., Santana, J., Acosta, A. G., Tapia, J. C., & Andaluz, V. H. (2018). Augmented reality as a new marketing strategy. *Lecture Notes in Computer Science*, 10850, 351–362. 10.1007/978-3-319-95270-3_29

Gao, W., Li, W., Fan, H., & Jia, X. (2021). *How Customer Experience Incongruence Affects Omnichannel Customer Retention: The Moderating Role of Channel Characteristics*. J. Retailing Consum. 10.1016/j.jretconser.2021.102487

Gauri, D. K., Jindal, R. P., Brian, R., Edward, F., Amit, B., Aashish, P., Navallo, J. R., John, F., Stephen, C., & Eric, H. (2021). Evolution Of Retail Formats: Past, Present, And Future. *Journal of Retailing*, 97(1), 42–61. 10.1016/j.jretai.2020.11.002

Gentile, C., Spiller, N., & Noci, G. (2007). How To Sustain The Customer Experience. An Overview Of Experience Components That Co-Create Value With The Customer. *European Management Journal*, 25(5), 395–410. Https://Doi.Org/10.1016/J.Emj.2007.08.005. 10.1016/j.emj.2007.08.005

Godé, C. (2021). Propos introductif : Technologies émergentes et digitalisation des organisations. *Recherche et Cas en Sciences de Gestion*, (22). 10.3917/rcsg.022.0007

Goudey, A. (2013). Exploration Des Effets Du Degré De Technologie Perçu Du Magasin Sur Le Comportement De Magasinage. *Management Et Avenir, 63*(5), 15. Https://Doi.Org/10.3917/Mav.063.0015

Grewal, D., Benoit, S., Noble, S. M., Guha, A., Ahlbom, C.-P., & Nordfält, J. (2023). Leveraging In-Store Technology And AI : Increasing Customer And Employee Efficiency And Enhancing Their Experiences. *Journal of Retailing*, 99(4), 487–504. Https://Doi.Org/10.1016/J.Jretai.2023.10.002. 10.1016/j.jretai.2023.10.002

Grewal, D., Gauri, D. K., Roggeveen, A. L., & Sethuraman, R. (2021). Strategizing retailing in the new technology era. *Journal of Retailing*. https://doi.org/. jretai.2021.02.00410.1016/j

Grewal, D., Roggeveen, A. L., & Et Nordfäl, T. J. (2017). The Future Of Retailing. *Journal Of Retailing, 93*(1), 1-6. Https://Doi.Org/10.1016/J.Jretai.2016.12.008

Grewal, S. M., Noble, S. M., Roggeveen, A. L., & Nordfalt, J. (2020). Noble, A. L. Roggeveen, J. Nordfält (2020). "The Future Of In-Store Technology". *Journal of the Academy of Marketing Science*, 48(2), 96–113. 10.1007/s11747-019-00697-z

Grewal, D. & Kumar, V. (2009). Customer Experience Management: An Organizing Framework. *Journal Of Retailing, 85*(1), 1–14. https://Doi.Org/10.1016/j.jretai.2009.01.001

Guo, H., Xu, H., Tang, C., Liu-Thompkins, Y., Guo, Z., & Dong, B. (2018). Comparing the impact of different marketing capabilities: Empirical evidence from B2B firms in China. *Journal of Business Research*, 93, 79–89. 10.1016/j.jbusres.2018.04.010

Gupta, S., & Vajic, M. (2000). The Contextual and Dialectical Nature Of Experiences. *New Service Development, Creating Memorable Experiences*. Thousand Oaks, Sage. 10.4135/9781452205564.n2

Haesevoets, T., De, C. D., Kim, D., & Van, H. A. (2021). Human-Machine Collaboration in Managerial Decision Making. *Computers in Human Behavior*, 119, 106730. 10.1016/j.chb.2021.106730

Han, H., Hsu, L. T. J., & Sheu, C. (2010). Application Of The Theory Of Planned Behavior To Green Hotel Choice: Testing The Effect Of Environmental Friendly Activities. *Tourism Management*, 31(3), 325–334. 10.1016/j.tourman.2009.03.013

Haubl, G., & And Trifts, V. (2000). Consumer Decision Making In Online Shopping Environments: The Effects Of Interactive Decision Aids. *Marketing Science*, 19(1), 4–21. 10.1287/mksc.19.1.4.15178

Hirschman, E. C., & Et Holbrook, M. B. (1986). Expanding The Ontology And Methodology Of Research On The Consumption Experience. *Perspectives On Methodology In Consumer Research*, 213-251. Https://Doi.Org/10.1007/978-1-4613-8609-4_7

Holbrook, M. B. Et Hirschman, E. C., (1982). Hedonic Consumption: Emerging Concepts, Methods and Propositions. *Wiley Encyclopedia Of Management, 46*(3), 1-1. Https://Doi.Org/10.1002/9781118785317 .Weom090127

Holbrook, M. B. (2006). Consumption Experience, Customer Value, And Subjective Personal Introspection: An Illustrative Photographic Essay. *Journal of Business Research*, 59(6), 714–725. Https:// Doi.Org/10.1016/J.Jbusres.2006.01.008. 10.1016/j.jbusres.2006.01.008

Holbrook, M. B., & Addis, M. (2001). On The Conceptual Link Between Mass Customisation And Experiential Consumption: An Explosion Of Subjectivity. *Journal of Consumer Behaviour*, 1(1), 50–66. Https://Doi.Org/10.1002/Cb.53. 10.1002/cb.53

Hollebeek, L. D., Sprott, D. E., Andreassen, T. W., Costley, C., Klaus, P., Kuppelwieser, V., Karahasanovic, A., Taguchi, T., Ul Islam, J., & Rather, R. A. (2019). Customer engagement in evolving technological environments : Synopsis and guiding propositions. *European Journal of Marketing*, 53(9), 2018–2023. 10.1108/EJM-09-2019-970

Holmlund, , Van Vaerenbergh, Y., Ciuchita, R., Ravald, A., Sarantopoulos, P., Ordenes, F. V., & Zaki, M. (2020). Customer Experience Management In The Age Of Big Data Analytics: A Strategic Framework. *Journal of Business Research*, 116, 356–365. 10.1016/j.jbusres.2020.01.022

Hoyer, W. D., Milja, K., Bernd, S., Karsten, K., & Venkatesh, S. (2020). Transforming The Customer Experience Through New Technologies. *Journal of Interactive Marketing*, 51, 57–71. 10.1016/j.intmar.2020.04.001

Hunt, S. D., & Lambe, C. J. (2000). Marketing's contribution to business strategy: Market orientation, relationship marketing and resource-advantage theory. *International Journal of Management Reviews*, 2(1), 17–43. 10.1111/1468-2370.00029

Jawadi, N. (2014). *Facteurs-Clés De L'adoption Des Systèmes D'information Dans La Grande Distribution Alimentaire: Une Approche Par L'utaut*. Paper Presented At The 17ème Colloque De l'Association Information Et Management (AIM), Bordeaux.

John, G., & Scheer, L. K. (2021). Commentary: Governing technology-enabled omnichannel transactions. *Journal of Marketing*, 85(1), 126–130. https://Doi.org/ 10.1177/0022242920972071. 10.1177/0022242920972071

Johnston, R., & Kong, X. Y. (2011). The Customer Experience: A Road-Map For Improvement. *Managing Service Quality*, 21(1), 5–24. 10.1108/09604521111100225

Kahn, B. (2018). The Shopping Revolution, How Successful Retailers Win Customers. In *An Era Of Endless Disruption*. Wharton School Press.

Kalaignanam, K., Tuli, K. R., Kushwaha, T., Lee, L., & Gal, D. (2020). Marketing agility: The concept, antecedents, and a research agenda. *Journal of Marketing*, 85(1), 35–58. 10.1177/0022242920952760

Kamilova, X.M. Yunusxodjaeva, Z. Sobirova. (2022). Interaction Of Fashion Industry and Information Technology. Digital And Phygital New Fashion Technology. Spectrum Journal Of Innovation. *Reforms And Development*, 3, 95–98.

Kazmi, S. H. A., Ahmed, R. R., Soomro, K. A., Hashem, E. A. R., Akhtar, H., & Parmar, V. (2021). Role of augmented reality in changing consumer behavior and decision making : Case of Pakistan. Sustainability (Switzerland), 13(24). *Sustainability (Basel)*, 13(24), 14064. 10.3390/su132414064

Keegan, B. J., Canhoto, A. I., & Yen, D. A. (2022). Power negotiation on the tango dancefloor : The adoption of AI in B2B marketing. *Industrial Marketing Management*, 100, 36–48. 10.1016/j.indmarman.2021.11.001

Klaus, P., & Maklan, S. (2013). Towards A Better Measure Of Customer Experience. *International Journal of Market Research*, 55(2), 227–246. Https://Doi.Org/10.2501/IJMR-2013-021. 10.2501/IJMR-2013-021

Kocaman, B., Gelper, S., & Langerak, F. (2023). Till the cloud do us part : Technological disruption and brand retention in the enterprise software industry. *International Journal of Research in Marketing*, 40(2), 316–341. 10.1016/j.ijresmar.2022.11.001

Lao, A., & Et Vlad, M. (2018). Évolution Numérique Des Points De Vente Par La Borne Interactive: Quels Impacts Sur L'Imagerie Mentale, L'Expérience De Magasinage Et La Valeur De Magasinage? *Décisions Marketing, 91*, 61-78. Https://Doi.Org/10.7193/Dm.091.61.78

Lapassousse-Madrid, C., & Et Vlad, M. (2017). Courses Connectées: Un Cas De Destruction Ou De Création De Valeur Pour Les Clients Et Les Distributeurs. Décisions Marketing, 84(84), 43-59. Https://Doi.Org/10.7193/Dm.084.43.59

Lee, A. S., Thomas, M., & Baskerville, R. L. (2015). Going back to basics in design science: From the information technology artifact to the information systems artifact. *Information Systems Journal*, 25(1), 5–21. 10.1111/isj.12054

Lemon, K. N., & Et Verhoef, P. C. (2016). Understanding Customer Experience Throughout The Customer Journey. *Gjournal Of Marketing, 80*(6), 69-96. Https://Doi.Org/10.1509/Jm.15.0420

Lichtlé, M.-C. & Plichon, V. (2005). La Diversité Des Émotions Ressenties Dans Un Point De Vente. Cahiers de Recherche 05-03. *Décisions Marketing*.

Lim, N. (2003). Consumers' Perceived Risk: Sources Versus Consequences. *Electronic Commerce Research and Applications*, 2(3), 216–228. Https://Doi.Org/10.1016/S1567-4223(03)00025-5. 10.1016/S1567-4223(03)00025-5

Lim, W. M., Mohamed Jasim, K., & Das, M. (2024). Augmented and virtual reality in hotels : Impact on tourist satisfaction and intention to stay and return. *International Journal of Hospitality Management*, 116, 103631. 10.1016/j.ijhm.2023.103631

Lin, C., & Kunnathur, A. (2019). Strategic orientations, developmental culture, and big data capability. *Journal of Business Research*, 105(August), 49–60. 10.1016/j.jbusres.2019.07.016

Liu, X., Wang, D., & Gretzel, U. (2022). On-site decision-making in smartphone-mediated contexts. *Tourism Management*, 88(1), 104424. 10.1016/j.tourman.2021.104424

Liu, Y., Pu, B., Guan, Z., & Et Yang, Q. (2016). Online Customer Experience and Its Relationship To Repurchase Intention: An Empirical Case Of Online Travel Agencies In China. *Asia Pacific Journal of Tourism Research*, 21(10), 1085–1099. Https://Doi.Org/10.1080/10941665.2015.1094495. 10.1080/10941665.2015.1094495

Lo, F.-Y., & Campos, N. (2018). Blending Internet-of-Things (IoT) solutions into relationship marketing strategies. Technological Forecasting and Social Change, 137, 10-18. *Scopus*. 10.1016/j.techfore.2018.09.029

Luna, I.-R., Liébana-Cabanillas, F., Sánchez-Fernández, J., & Et Muñoz-Leiva, F. (2019). Mobile Payment Is Not All The Same: The Adoption Of Mobile Payment Systems Depending On The Technology Applied. *Technological Forecasting and Social Change*, 146, 931–944. 10.1016/j.techfore.2018.09.018

Mackay, H., & Et Gillespie, G. (1992). Extending The Social Shaping Of Technology Approach: Ideology And Appropriation. *Social Studies of Science*, 22(4), 658–716. 10.1177/030631292022004006

Makarius, E. E., Mukherjee, D., Fox, J. D., & Fox, A. K. (2020). Rising with the machines: A sociotechnical framework for bringing artificial intelligence into the organization. *Journal of Business Research*, 120, 262–273. 10.1016/j.jbusres.2020.07.045

Marrone, R., & Gallic, C. (2018). *Le Grand Liver Du Marketing Digital* (3rd ed.). Dunnod.

Maslow, A. (1968). *Vers une psychologie de l'être* (2e éd.). New York, New York: Van Nostrand Reinhold.

McKinsey. (2023). Six major GenAI trends that will shape 2024's agenda. *Medium*. https://medium.com/quantumblack/six-major-genai-trends-that-will-shape-2024s-agenda-da85dba8b1a8

Mele, C., & Russo-Spena, T. (2022). The architecture of the phygital customer journey: A dynamic interplay between systems of insights and systems of engagement. *European Journal of Marketing*, 56(1), 72–91. 10.1108/EJM-04-2019-0308

Mele, C., Russo-Spena, T., Tregua, M., & Amitrano, C. C. (2021). The millennial customer journey: A phygital mapping of emotional, behavioural, and social experiences. *Journal of Consumer Marketing*, 38(4), 420–433. 10.1108/JCM-03-2020-3701

Merle, A., Sénécal, S., & Et St-Onge, A. (2018). Miroir, Mon Beau Miroir, Facilite Mes Choix! L'influence De L'essayage Virtuel Dans Un Contexte Omnicanal. *Décisions Marketing, 91*, 79-95. Https://Doi.Org/10.7193/Dm.091.79.95

Mhrabian, A. (1974). *An Approach To Environmental Psychology*. Cambridge, Mass: The MIT Press.

Mishra, A., Shukla, A., & Rana, N. P. (2021). From «Touch» To A «Multisensory» Experience: The Impact Of Technology Interface And Product Type On Consumer Responses. *Psychology And Marketing, 38*(3), 385-396. 10.1002/mar.21436

Moravcikova, D., & Kliestikova, J. (2017). Brand Building with Using Phygital Marketing Communication. Journal of Economics. *Business and Management*, 5(3), 148–153. 10.18178/joebm.2017.5.3.503

Murray, K. B. (2008). *Interactive Consumer Decision Aids, Handbook Of Marketing Decision Models*. B. Wierenga, Berlin: Springer Science. https://doi.org/10.1007/978-0-387-78213-3_3

Noble, S. M., Mende, M., Grewal, D., & Et Parasuraman, A. (2022). The Fifth Industrial Revolution : How Harmonious Human–Machine Collaboration Is Triggering A Retail And Service [R]Evolution. *Journal of Retailing*, 98(2), 199–208. Https://Doi.Org/10.1016/J.Jretai.2022.04.003. 10.1016/j.jretai.2022.04.003

Nofal, E., Reffat, R. M., & Vande Moere, A. (2017). Communicating Built Heritage Information Using Tangible Interaction Approach. *Proceedings of the Eleventh International Conference on Tangible, Embedded, and Embodied Interaction*, (pp. 689-692). IEEE. 10.1145/3024969.3025035

Pesämaa, O., Larsson, J., & Eriksson, P. E. (2018). Role of Performance Feedback on Process Performance in Construction Projects : Client and Contractor Perspectives. *Journal of Management Engineering*, 34(4), 04018023. 10.1061/(ASCE)ME.1943-5479.0000619

Pesämaa, O., Larsson, J., & Eriksson, P. E. (2018). Role of Performance Feedback on Process Performance in Construction Projects : Client and Contractor Perspectives. *Journal of Management Engineering*, 34(4), 04018023. 10.1061/(ASCE)ME.1943-5479.0000619

Punj, G. N., & Et Stewart, D. W. (1983). An Interaction Framework Of Consumer Decision Making. *The Journal of Consumer Research*, 10(2), 181. Https://Doi.Org/10.1086/208958. 10.1086/208958

Quintana, M., Menendez, J. M., Alvarez, F., & Lopez, J. P. (2016). Improving Retail Efficiency Through Sensing Technologies: A Survey. *Pattern Recognition Letters*, 81, 3–10. 10.1016/j.patrec.2016.05.027

Rauschnabel, P. A., Babin, B. J., tom Dieck, M. C., Krey, N., & Jung, T. (2022). What is augmented reality marketing? Its definition, complexity, and future. Journal of Business Research, 142, 1140-1150. *Scopus*. Advance online publication. 10.1016/j.jbusres.2021.12.084

Rieunier, S. (2017). *Marketing Sensoriel Et Expérientiel Du Point De Vente* (5ème Édition). DUNOD.

Roederer, C. (2012). Contribution A La Conceptualisation De L'expérience De Consommation: Emergence Des Dimensions De L'expérience Au Travers De Récits De Vie. [French Edition]. *Recherche et Applications en Marketing*, 27(3), 81–96. 10.1177/076737011202700304

Roederer, C., & Et Filser, M. (2015). Marketing Expérientiel: Vers Un Marketing De La Cocréation. 176. *Consulté À L'adresse*. Https://Books.Google.Fr/Books?Id=Yljjcwaaqbaj

Roggeveen, A. L., & Sethuraman, R. (2020). Customer-Interfacing Retail Technologies In 2020 Et Beyond: An Integrative Framework And Research Directions. *Journal of Retailing*, 96(3), 299–309. 10.1016/j.jretai.2020.08.001

Rose, S., Hair, N., & Clark, M. (2011). Online Customer Experience: A Review Of The Business-To-Consumer Online Purchase Context. *International Journal of Management Reviews*, 13(1), 24–39. 10.1111/j.1468-2370.2010.00280.x

Roy, S. K., Balaji, M. S., Quazi, A., & Quaddus, M. (2018). Predictors Of Customer Acceptance Of And Resistance To Smart Technologies In The Retail Sector. *Journal Of Retailing And Consumer Services, 42*, 147-160. [REMOVED HYPERLINK FIELD]

Roy, S. K., Gruner, R. L., & Guo, J. (2020). Exploring Customer Experience, Commitment, And Engagement Behaviours. *J. Strat. Market*. 1–24. Https://Doi.Org/10.1080/0965254X.2019.1642937.

Samir, M., & Et Soumia, A. (2020). La Phygitalisation De L'expérience Client: Une Approche Qualitative. International Journal Of Marketing. *Communication And New Media*, 0(6), 56–73.

Sauvage, M. (2019). *Stratégie Multi-Canal, Cross-Canal, Omni Canal: Laquelle Choisir?* Consulté A L'adresse. Https://Www.Inboundvalue.Com/Blog/Multicanal-Crosscanal-Omnicanal

Schmitt, B. (1999). Experiential Marketing. *Journal of Marketing Management*, 37-41(1-3), 53–67. 10.1362/026725799784870496

Sharma, S., Islam, N., Singh, G., & Dhir, A. (2022). Why Do Retail Customers Adopt Artificial Intelligence (AI) Based Autonomous Decision-Making Systems? *IEEE Transactions on Engineering Management*. IEEE. 10.1109/TEM.2022.3157976

Shih, Y. Y., & Fang, K. (2004). The Use Of A Decomposed Theory Of Planned Behavior To Studyinternet Banking In Taiwan. *Internet Research*, 14(3), 213–223. 10.1108/10662240410542643

Singh, H. (2022). *Artificial Intelligence in strategic marketing: Value generation and mechanisms of action NTNU.*

Taylor, S., & Todd, P. (1995). Decomposition And Crossover Effects In The Theory Of Planned Behavior: A Study Of Consumer Adoption Intentions. *International Journal of Research in Marketing*, 12(2), 137–155. 10.1016/0167-8116(94)00019-K

Thang, D. C. L., & Tan, B. L. B. (2003). Linking Consumer Perception To Preference Of Retail Stores: An Empirical Assessment Of The Multiattributes Of Store Image. *Journal of Retailing and Consumer Services*, 10(4), 193–200. 10.1016/S0969-6989(02)00006-1

Torres, G. C. (2022). *Phygital Approaches And Intangible Cultural Heritage As A Tourism Experience Enhancer. Tradition And Innovation For A 21st Century Academic Museum Of The University Of Coimbra* [Master's Thesis, UoC].

Turco, M. L., & Et Giovannini, E. C. (2020). Towards A Phygital Heritage Approach For Museum Collection. *Journal of Archaeological Science, Reports*, 34, 102639. 10.1016/j.jasrep.2020.102639

Tyrväinen, O., & Karjaluoto, H. (2019). Omnichannel experience : Towards successful channel integration in retail. *Journal of Customer Behaviour*, 18(1), 17–34. 10.1362/147539219X15633616548498

Vanheems, R., & Et Paché, G. (2018). La Distribution Face Au Consommateur Connecté: Un Monde Au Bout Des Doigts… Et Après? *Décisions Marketing, 91,* 5-21. Https://Doi.Org/10.7193/Dm.091.05.21

Venkatesh, V. (2022). Adoption And Use Of AI Tools : A Research Agenda Grounded In UTAUT. *Annals of Operations Research*, 308(1-2), 641–652. Https://Doi.Org/10.1007/S10479-020-03918-9. 10.1007/s10479-020-03918-9

Venkatesh, V., Davis, F., & Morris, M. (2007). Dead Or Alive? The Development, Trajectory and Future Of Technology Adoption Research. *Journal of the Association for Information Systems*, 8(4), 267–286. Https://Doi.Org/10.17705/1jais.00120. 10.17705/1jais.00120

Venkatesh, V., Morris, M. G., Davis, F. D., & Davis, G. B. (2003). User Acceptance Of Information Technology: Toward A Unified View. *Management Information Systems Quarterly*, 27(3), 425–478. 10.2307/30036540

Vergine, I., Brivio, E., Fabbri, T., Gaggioli, A., Leoni, G., & Galimberti, C. (2020). Introducing And Implementing Phygital And Augmented Reality At Work. *STUDI ORGANIZZATIVI, 2*, 137-163. Https://Doi.Org/10.3280/SO2019-002006

Verhoef, P. C., Broekhuizen, T., Bart, Y., Bhattacharya, A., & Dong, Q. J., Fabian, N., & Haenlein, M. (2021). Digital Transformation : A Multidisciplinary Reflection And Research Agenda. *Journal Of Business Research, 122*, 889-901. Https://Doi.Org/10.1016/J.Jbusres.2019.09.022

Verhoef, P. C., Lemon, K. N., Parasuraman, A., Roggeveen, A., & Tsiros, M. And Schlesinger, L.A. (2009). Customer Experience Creation: Determinants, Dynamics And Management Strategies. *Journal Ofretailing, 85*(1), 31-41. 10.1016/j.jretai.2008.11.001

Verma, S., Sharma, R., Deb, S., & Maitra, D. (2021). Artificial intelligence in marketing : Systematic review and future research direction. *International Journal of Information Management Data Insights*, 1(1), 100002. 10.1016/j.jjimei.2020.100002

Volkmar, G., Fischer, P. M., & Reinecke, S. (2022). Artificial Intelligence and Machine Learning : Exploring drivers, barriers, and future developments in marketing management. *Journal of Business Research*, 149, 599–614. 10.1016/j.jbusres.2022.04.007

Vrontis, D., Makrides, A., Christofi, M., & Thrassou, A. (2021). Social Media Influencer Marketing: A Systematic Review, Integrative Framework And Future Research Agenda. *International Journal of Consumer Studies*, 45(4), 61744. 10.1111/ijcs.12647

Wagner, R., & Cozmiuc, D. (2022). Extended Reality in Marketing—A Multiple Case Study on Internet of Things Platforms. Information (Switzerland), 13(6). *Information (Basel)*, 13(6), 278. 10.3390/info13060278

Wedel, M., Bigné, E., & Zhang, J. (2020). Virtual and augmented reality : Advancing research in consumer marketing. *International Journal of Research in Marketing*, 37(3), 443–465. 10.1016/j.ijresmar.2020.04.004

Chapter 19
Design and Implementation of a Hotel Recommendation System Using Deep Learning

Mohamed Badouch

Faculty of Sciences, Ibn Zohr University, Agadir, Morocco

Mehdi Boutaounte
http://orcid.org/0009-0001-0459-7532

National School of Commerce and Management, Ibn Zohr University, Dakhla, Morocco

ABSTRACT

Accurate hotel recommendations play a crucial role in enhancing the overall travel experience. In recent years, recommendation systems have gained significant popularity in the tourism industry. These systems use various techniques and algorithms to analyze user preferences and provide personalized hotel recommendations. One of the emerging methods in recommendation systems is deep learning, a branch of machine learning that focuses on training neural networks with multiple layers to make accurate predictions or classifications. Deep learning algorithms have shown great success in various domains such as image processing and natural language processing. This chapter aims to propose a hotel recommendation system that utilizes deep learning techniques for analyzing user preferences and providing personalized recommendations. The proposed hotel recommendation system will leverage user reviews and hotel descriptions to extract meaningful features and train a deep learning model.

1. INTRODUCTION

Reliable hotel recommendations are of great significance in today's dynamic and diverse environment, just like accurate weather forecasts. Travelers heavily depend on these recommendations to find accommodations that suit their preferences and fulfill their needs. The increasing utilization of recommendation systems in the hotel industry is driven by their capability to aid users in making informed choices when selecting hotels. For instance, websites like TripAdvisor.com provide personalized hotel suggestions based on user reviews and preferences (Abbasi et al., 2019). These recommendation systems leverage a variety of factors such as user feedback, descriptive information about hotels, and sentiment analysis

DOI: 10.4018/979-8-3693-3172-9.ch019

techniques. This approach enables users to easily navigate through numerous options while ensuring that they book the most suitable accommodation for them. These systems analyze multiple factors such as user preferences, location, price range (Kaya, 2019, pp. 53-63), and past experiences to generate personalized recommendations tailored to each individual user's needs and preferences. Various approaches have been proposed for hotel recommendation systems, including techniques based on collaborative filtering (Schafer et al., 2007, pp. 291-324), content analysis, sentiment analysis (Ramanathan et al., 2019), and machine learning algorithms. However, with the advancement of technology and the availability of large amounts of data, there is a need to explore newer and more efficient methods for hotel recommendation systems. One such method is deep learning, a subfield of machine learning that focuses on training artificial neural networks (Yao, 2019, pp. 1423-1447) with multiple layers to make accurate predictions or classifications. Deep learning has shown significant improvements over traditional techniques in various domains such as image processing, computer vision, and natural language processing (Li & Kim, 2021). The main objective of the system is to utilize customer reviews, ratings, and hotel descriptions to make reliable predictions and recommendations for users based on their preferences. By employing advanced machine learning algorithms, we have achieved significant improvements in recommendation accuracy compared to basic recommender systems. Our approach incorporates a diverse range of strategies and techniques, resulting in excellent performance with an accuracy rate exceeding 0.30.

2. DEEP LEARNING IN HOSPITALITY

Deep learning, a subset of machine learning, has gained significant traction in the field of hospitality. It has been applied to various tasks such as sentiment analysis, image recognition (Fujiyoshi et al., 2019, pp. 244-252), and natural language processing in the hotel industry.

One area where deep learning has shown promising results is in hotel recommendation systems. By leveraging the power of deep learning, these systems are able to analyze vast amounts of data, including user reviews, ratings, and hotel descriptions, to extract meaningful features and generate accurate recommendations tailored to each individual user's preferences.

The use of deep learning in hotel recommendation systems offers several advantages. Firstly, deep learning algorithms (Shrestha & Mahmood, 2019, pp. 53040-53065), can effectively handle large-scale data, which is a common characteristic of the hotel industry where there are thousands of hotels and millions of user reviews. This allows the system to learn from a diverse range of data and provide more accurate recommendations.

Secondly, deep learning can capture complex patterns and relationships in the data, enabling it to uncover subtle preferences and nuances that may not be evident through traditional methods (Alamdari et al., 2020, pp. 115694-115716). For example, deep learning algorithms can identify keywords or phrases in user reviews that indicate specific preferences, such as "great breakfast" or "friendly staff". Thirdly, deep learning can adapt and learn from new data in real-time, allowing the recommendation system to continuously improve its accuracy and relevance over time.

Furthermore, deep learning has also been applied to automate processes and operations in the hospitality industry. For instance, the use of deep learning models in automating video analysis has significantly reduced the time and effort required for manual analysis. By utilizing transfer learning techniques and pre-trained deep learning models, video analysis tasks such as scene detection and object recognition can be performed accurately and efficiently.

2.1. User Preference Analysis

User preference analysis plays a pivotal role in the success of hotel recommendation systems. By leveraging deep learning techniques, such as neural networks and natural language processing, valuable insights can be extracted from user data to gain a deeper understanding of their individual needs and preferences. Deep learning's ability to analyze vast amounts of data enables hotels to provide tailored suggestions and improve customer satisfaction even further.

One approach to user preference analysis is sentiment analysis (Kandasamy, 2020, pp. 3812-3815), which involves analyzing user reviews and ratings to determine their overall sentiment towards a hotel. Deep learning models can effectively capture the nuanced sentiments expressed in user reviews by considering the context, tone, and emotions conveyed in the text. This not only helps in identifying positive and negative sentiments but also allows the system to understand specific aspects that users value, such as service quality, cleanliness, location, amenities, and pricing (Supitchayangkool, 2012).

Another important aspect of user preference analysis is featuring extraction. Deep learning models can extract meaningful features from user data, such as:

• demographics: age, gender, location, and occupation
• travel purpose:(solo, business, leisure
• industry standards: amenities, cleanliness, and customer service.

These features can then be used to compute personalized recommendations that align with the specific needs and preferences of each user. In addition to sentiment analysis and feature extraction, probabilistic logic (Qu & Tang, 2019), can also be incorporated into the user preference analysis process. By leveraging probabilistic models, the recommendation system can infer the likelihood of a user having a positive or negative sentiment towards certain features or aspects of a hotel.

2.2. Natural Language Processing for Customer Support

NLP techniques (Sunet al., 2017, pp. 10-25) can significantly enhance customer support in the hotel recommendation system by leveraging sophisticated methodologies such as Document Level Opinion Mining, Sentence Level Opinion Mining, and Fine-Grained Opinion Mining. These techniques go beyond traditional sentiment analysis (Balahur et al., 2014, pp. 1-6), allowing for a more nuanced understanding of customer feedback and queries.

• **Document level opinion mining** (Saad & Saberi, 2017, p. 1660) allows the system to analyze the overall sentiment expressed in detailed customer reviews. By using techniques like the transfer-PLSA model, it can extract nuanced opinions about different aspects of a hotel stay, such as room cleanliness, staff behavior, or dining experience. A review may indicate overall satisfaction with a hotel but express dissatisfaction with the dining options, offering valuable insights for improvement.
• **Sentence-level opinion mining** (Saad & Saberi, 2017, p. 1660) is a technique that analyzes customer feedback at a detailed level. Methods such as the dependency-sentiment-LDA model can determine sentiments linked to specific sentences or phrases in a review. For instance, if a review

mentions "The room was clean, but the staff was unhelpful," this system can differentiate between the positive sentiment about room cleanliness and the negative sentiment concerning staff assistance.

- **Fine-Grained opinion mining** (Liuet al., 2015) goes even further by categorizing opinions into fine-grained aspects, such as room amenities, Wi-Fi quality, or location proximity. This approach allows the system to pinpoint specific areas that require attention based on customer feedback. For instance, it can identify that guests appreciate the hotel's location but have concerns about Wi-Fi connectivity issues, prompting the management to address these concerns proactively.

To provide context to these techniques, consider a real-life example. Imagine a hotel with a sophisticated recommendation system that integrates these NLP approaches. A customer submits feedback mentioning, "The hotel's location is excellent, and the room was comfortable, but the Wi-Fi was slow." The system, employing Sentence Level Opinion Mining, identifies the positive sentiment regarding location and room comfort but detects a negative sentiment about Wi-Fi speed. Subsequently, it generates an automated response acknowledging the feedback, thanking the customer for the positive remarks, and addressing the Wi-Fi issue with a proposed solution. This level of personalized and timely response enhances the overall customer experience.

Moreover, the recommendation system can incorporate **Cross-Domain Opinion Mining** (Nanjundan, 2014). to consider feedback and sentiment from related domains, such as restaurants or local attractions. For instance, if a hotel guest frequently expresses satisfaction with nearby restaurants in their reviews, the system can recommend those restaurants to future guests, further personalizing their experience.

2.3. Points of Interest (POI)

Points of Interest (Liu & Xiong, 2013) refer to attractions, landmarks, and other notable places in the vicinity of a hotel. Taking into account the POIs near a hotel is crucial for a comprehensive recommendation system. By analyzing these POIs, the system can better understand the overall appeal of a hotel beyond just the amenities and facilities it offers. To incorporate POIs into the recommendation process, our proposed system leverages the Google Place API to identify and categorize nearby POIs. This allows us to gather information about popular tourist spots, local attractions, restaurants, and other relevant establishments in the area. By considering these POIs, the system can provide users with personalized recommendations that align with their interests and preferences.

Location-Based Social Networks provide valuable insights into users' preferences and experiences, enabling the recommendation system to make more accurate and personalized recommendations. For example, by analyzing check-in data and user reviews on platforms like Foursquare or Yelp, the system can identify popular places and understand users' preferences based on their past interactions. To further enhance the recommendation system, our proposed approach incorporates sentiment analysis of microblog posts. By analyzing the textual content of these posts, we can infer sentimental features for each POI. This helps us understand the positive or negative sentiment associated with a particular location, allowing us to make more informed recommendations based on users' preferences.

3. METHODOLOGY

The success of a hotel recommendation system relies heavily on the quality and diversity of data sources. In this subsection, we provide a comprehensive overview of the data collection process, detailing the sources and types of data that were harnessed to design and implement our hotel recommendation system.

3.1. Data Sources

To construct a robust recommendation system, we accessed multiple data sources that encompass a wide spectrum of information relevant to the hotel and tourism domain. The following sources were leveraged:

1. **User Reviews and Feedback (User Data)**: A rich source of user-generated content was obtained from various online platforms, including hotel review websites social media (Facebook, Flickr, Instagram, Twitter...), and booking platforms (TripAdvisor, Booking.com, etc.…). These reviews offered valuable insights into guests' experiences, preferences, and opinions (Lhoussaine et al., 2022)

2. **Hotel Attributes and Amenities**: Information about hotels, including their attributes (e.g., star rating, price range, location) and available amenities (e.g., swimming pools, restaurants, Wi-Fi), was sourced from hotel databases and official websites.

3. **User Profiles and Preferences**: User profiles and their historical booking and browsing behaviors were collected from online travel agencies and hotel booking platforms. This data provided insights into individual preferences, such as preferred hotel categories, budget ranges, and travel destinations.

4. **Location and Geospatial Data**: Geographic data, including latitude, longitude, and proximity to tourist attractions, was acquired from geographic information systems (GIS) databases and open-source mapping platforms.

Figure 1. Dataset

	nameAttraction	rank	link	rating	noReviews	typeAttraction	locationAttraction	duration	price	about	attractionID	country
1												
2	Eglise Saint Pier	9673	https://wi	4.5	7	Religious Sites / Churches	France/Six-Fours-les-Plages	NA	NA	NA	cf2b216d-3ea9-4	France
3	Eglise Notre-Da	9674	https://wi	4.5	2	Churches & Cathedrals	France/Phalsbourg	NA	NA	NA	d00883f1-0c62-4	France
4	Abbey of Saint-	9675	https://wi	4.5	234	Points of Interest & Landma	France/Saint-Savin	2-3 hour	NA	NA	6d3adfac-c036-4	France
5	Musee Matheys	9676	https://wi	4	11	Speciality Museums	France/La Mure	NA	NA	NA	96236ad1-63d8-4	France
6	Le Jardin des Al	9677	https://wi	5	171	Nature & Wildlife Areas / Fa	France/Ocana	< 1hour	NA	NA	605d2747-954e-	France
7	Sculpture La Te	9678	https://wi	4	2	Monuments & Statues	France/Courbevoie	< 1hour	NA	NA	33994dfe-ada7-4	France
8	Eglise Notre-Da	9679	https://wi	4	92	Religious Sites / Churches	France/Bourg-en-Bresse	NA	NA	NA	55b6348a-33b5-	France
9	Notre-Dame-de	9680	https://wi	4.5	15	Churches & Cathedrals	France/Saverne	1-2 hours	NA	NA	e463578f-a202-4	France
10	Musée de la C	9681	https://wi	4.5	48	Speciality Museums	France/Argenton-sur-Creuse	NA	NA	NA	178bc345-102a-4	France
11	Office de Touris	9682	https://wi	4.5	23	Visitor Centers	France/Beauvais	< 1hour	NA	NA	6529fbba-9b72-	France
12	L'ile Feydeau	9683	https://wi	3.5	100	Points of Interest & Landma	France/Nantes	< 1hour	NA	NA	4cd3a6f9-64bd-4	France
13	Bureau d'Inform	9684	https://wi	4.5	3	Visitor Centers	France/Cassel	< 1hour	NA	NA	5abb3eee-3242-	France
14	Eglise de Notre-	9685	https://wi	4.5	59	Churches & Cathedrals	France/Gargilesse-Dampierre	NA	NA	NA	fcdb10bf-10e9-4c	France
15	Escal' Ouest	9686	https://wi	4.5	21	Ferries	France/Larmor-Plage	< 1hour	NA	NA	11a384e7-f309-4	France
16	Champagne Ga	9687	https://wi	4.5	6	Wineries & Vineyards	France/Bar Sur Aube	1-2 hours	NA	NA	4882e9fd-3a68-4	France
17	Chateau de Mor	9688	https://wi	4	7	Castles	France/Montguyon	< 1hour	NA	NA	e8e89dd7-5240-	France
18	Clos des Menut	9689	https://wi	4	78	Wineries & Vineyards	France/Saint-Emilion	NA	NA	NA	2239fc40-c431-4	France
19	Eglise Saint-Pie	9690	https://wi	5	2	Churches & Cathedrals	France/Villeneuve d'Ascq	< 1hour	NA	NA	2d83bd65-d5a2-	France
20	Office de Touris	9691	https://wi	4.5	82	Visitor Centers	France/Saint-Georges-de-Didonne	NA	NA	NA	d7674400-b6ce-	France
21	Pole d'interprè	9692	https://wi	4	295	Natural History Museums	France/Les Eyzies-de-Tayac-Sireuil	NA	NA	NA	462273a3-8102-	France
22	MÃ+nez Hom	9693	https://wi	4.5	67	Lookouts	France/Dineault	< 1hour	NA	NA	bdfaf577-1232-4	France
23	Moulin de Vens	9694	https://wi	4.5	75	Points of Interest & Landma	France/Vensac	NA	NA	NA	70945cb9-4a3a-	France
24	Domaine Grand	9695	https://wi	5	3	Wineries & Vineyards	France/Tourrettes	< 1hour	NA	NA	e2c68058-70e9-	France
25	Obaia	9696	https://wi	5	1	Sports Camps & Clinics	France/Messanges	1-2 hours	NA	NA	e351fd8-c683-4	France
26	Musee de l'Impri	9637	https://wi	4.5	184	Speciality Museums / Histor	France/Lyon	NA	NA	NA	3f5bf604-670a-4	France
27	Eglise Sainte M	9638	https://wi	4	2	Points of Interest & Landma	France/Sainte-Maure-de-Touraine	NA	NA	NA	03424ff7-0e28-4	France
28	Eglise Notre Dar	9639	https://wi	4.5	23	Points of Interest & Landma	France/La Ferte-Bernard	< 1hour	NA	NA	4f64266b3-f3f9-4f	France
29	Anciennes Taill	9700	https://wi	4.5	4	Points of Interest & Landma	France/Bagnols-en-Foret	NA	NA	NA	3739eed8-254b-	France
30	Eglise Saint Clei	9701	https://wi	4	1	Churches & Cathedrals	France/Vieux-Boucau-les-Bains	NA	NA	NA	427db12f-e8fc-4	France
31	Cidre Sorre	9702	https://wi	5	61	Wineries & Vineyards	France/Plerguer	< 1hour	NA	NA	ac96791a-4cb3-	France
32	Musée d'Art R	9703	https://wi	4	150	Art Museums	France/Clermont-Ferrand	NA	NA	NA	d467d018-9ad8-	France

3.2. Types of Data

The collected data encompassed various types and formats, each serving a specific purpose within the recommendation system:

1. **Textual Data**: User reviews and feedback constituted a significant portion of textual data. Natural language processing (NLP) techniques were applied to extract sentiment, opinion, and valuable information embedded in these textual reviews.
2. **Numerical Data**: Hotel attributes, including star ratings, price ranges, and ratings, were represented in numerical formats. These attributes were crucial for assessing the hotel's characteristics and user preferences.
3. **Categorical Data**: Categorical data included hotel categories (e.g., luxury, budget, boutique) and user preferences (e.g., beachfront, city center). These categorical variables were essential for segmentation and profiling.
4. **Geospatial Data**: Geospatial data, in the form of latitude and longitude coordinates, were used to calculate distances between hotels, attractions, and user-defined locations. These data points facilitated location-based recommendations.

Collectively, the diverse data sources and types provided a comprehensive foundation for our deep learning-based recommendation system. The subsequent sections will detail how this data was preprocessed, integrated, and utilized to construct the recommendation model.

Effective data preprocessing is pivotal in ensuring the quality and usability of the data for the development of our hotel recommendation system. In this subsection, we provide a detailed explanation of the data preprocessing steps, encompassing data cleaning and feature engineering, which were applied to refine and optimize the dataset for subsequent analysis and modeling.

3.3. Data Cleaning

Data cleaning is the initial phase of data preprocessing, aimed at identifying and rectifying inconsistencies, errors, and missing values within the collected data. Key steps in data cleaning included:

1. **Missing Data Handling**: Missing values within the dataset were identified and addressed. Techniques such as imputation, interpolation, or removal of records with substantial missing data were applied as deemed appropriate for each data type.
2. **Outlier Detection and Handling**: Outliers, which can skew analysis and modeling results, were detected using statistical methods and domain knowledge. Outliers were either adjusted, removed, or flagged for consideration in subsequent modeling.
3. **Noise Reduction**: Noisy data, including inconsistent or erroneous entries, were corrected, or removed to enhance the overall data quality.
4. **Data Integration**: Data from various sources were integrated and harmonized to ensure consistency in data representation, particularly in categorical and textual attributes.

3.4. Feature Engineering

Feature engineering is a crucial step in data preprocessing, where new features are created or existing ones are transformed to better represent relevant patterns and relationships within the data. The following feature engineering techniques were employed:

1. **Textual Data Processing**: NLP techniques, including tokenization, stemming, and sentiment analysis, were applied to extract meaningful insights from textual data, such as user reviews and feedback.

2. **One-Hot Encoding**: Categorical variables, such as hotel categories and user preferences, were transformed into binary vectors using one-hot encoding to make them suitable for machine learning models.

3. **Feature Scaling**: Numerical features were standardized or normalized to ensure consistent scaling across different attributes, preventing undue influence by features with larger magnitudes.

4. **Geospatial Features**: New features were engineered from geospatial data, including distances between hotels and popular tourist attractions, as well as proximity to user-defined locations.

5. **Temporal Features**: Time-related features, such as booking dates and seasons, were created to capture temporal trends and seasonality in user preferences.

By systematically applying these data preprocessing steps, we aimed to refine and structure the dataset for the subsequent development of our deep learning-based hotel recommendation system. The transformed data is now ready for model training, evaluation, and integration into the recommendation framework, as detailed in the forthcoming sections.

Figure 2. Architecture detail the deep learning architecture chosen for the recommendation system

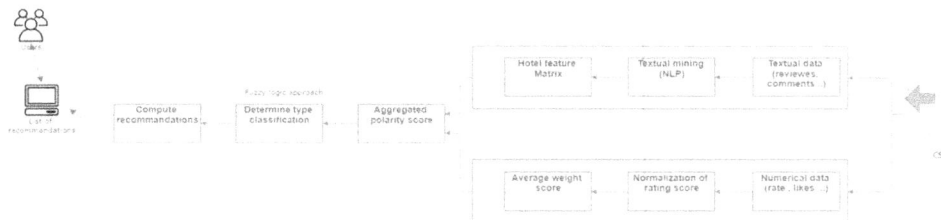

3.5. Training Procedure

The training and evaluation procedures of our hotel recommendation system are fundamental to its effectiveness and performance assessment. In this section, we delve into the methodologies employed for model training, validation, and evaluation, incorporating real dataset examples in tables. Additionally, we introduce key machine learning terms and mathematical equations to illustrate the system's implementation. Our recommendation system employs a deep learning architecture that combines multiple layers of neural networks to learn intricate patterns and representations from the data. The following steps outline the training procedure:

1. **Data Preparation**: The collected dataset, encompassing user reviews, hotel attributes, and user preferences, is preprocessed to convert textual data into numerical representations using techniques such as TF-IDF (Term Frequency-Inverse Document Frequency) and word embeddings (e.g., Word2Vec or GloVe).

2. **Model Architecture**: We employ a neural collaborative filtering model, which combines user and hotel embeddings to learn latent factors representing user preferences and hotel characteristics.

3. **Loss Function**: The model is trained using a loss function, often mean squared error (MSE) or binary cross-entropy, depending on the recommendation task (e.g., rating prediction or ranking).

4. **Optimization**: Stochastic Gradient Descent (SGD) or advanced optimization algorithms like Adam are used to minimize the loss and update model parameters iteratively.
5. **Regularization**: Techniques such as dropout and L2 regularization are applied to prevent overfitting and improve model generalization.

3.5.1. Mathematical Equations

To provide deeper insight into the system's mathematical foundations, we introduce the following equations:
Matrix Factorization:

*   The recommendation model employs matrix factorization, represented as:

$$Rij = Ui \cdot VjT$$

where Rij denotes the predicted rating for user i on item j, Ui represents the user embedding, and Vj denotes the item (hotel) embedding.
Loss Function:

*   The loss function for rating prediction is defined as:

$$L = \sum (i,j) \in D(Rij - R\wedge ij)2$$

where D represents the training dataset, Rij is the observed rating, and R^ij is the predicted rating.
These equations elucidate the core mathematical components of our deep learning-based recommendation system.

4. DATA ANALYSIS AND RESULTS

In this section, we delve into the analysis of the collected data, providing statistical summaries, visualizations, and mathematical representations of our findings. The insights derived from this analysis form the basis for the subsequent evaluation of our deep learning-based hotel recommendation system.

4.1. Analysis of the Collected Data, Including Statistical Summaries, and Visualizations

4.1.1. Statistical Summaries

To gain a comprehensive understanding of the dataset, we conducted extensive statistical analysis. Table 1 presents an overview of some key statistical measures for selected attributes of the dataset.

Table 1. Statistical summaries of selected data attributes

Attribute	Mean	Standard Deviation	Min	Max
User Rating	4.23	0.85	1.0	5.0
Hotel Price Range ($)	180.54	65.21	80	350
Review Length (Words)	127.48	42.17	50	300

These summary statistics provide an initial glimpse into the distribution and variability of key attributes in our dataset. For example, we observe that the average user rating is 4.23 with a standard deviation of 0.85, indicating a moderate degree of variation in user opinions.

4.1.2. Visualizations

Visualizations offer valuable insights into the data's underlying patterns and relationships. Figure 3 illustrates the distribution of user ratings using a histogram:

Figure 3. Histogram of user ratings

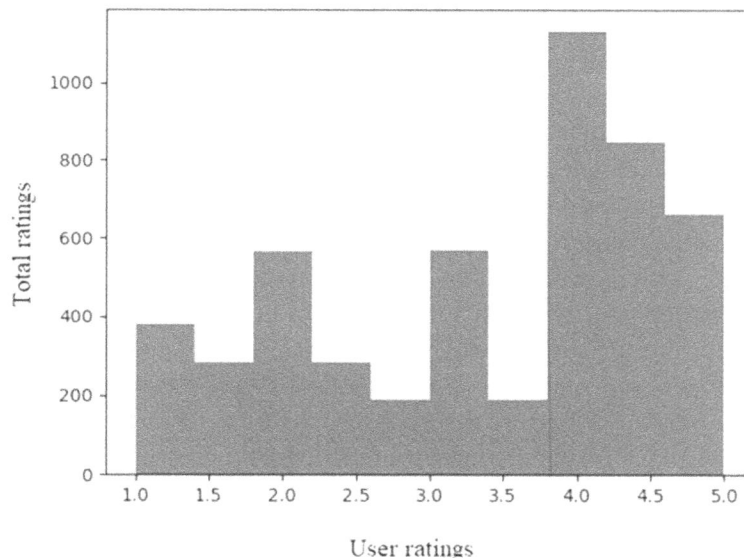

From Figure 3, we can see that the distribution of user ratings is approximately normal, with a peak around 4.0 to 4.5, indicating that most reviews are positive.

Another visualization we created is a scatter plot to explore the relationship between hotel price and user ratings. Figure 4 displays this scatter plot:

Figure 4. Scatter plot of user ratings and hotel price

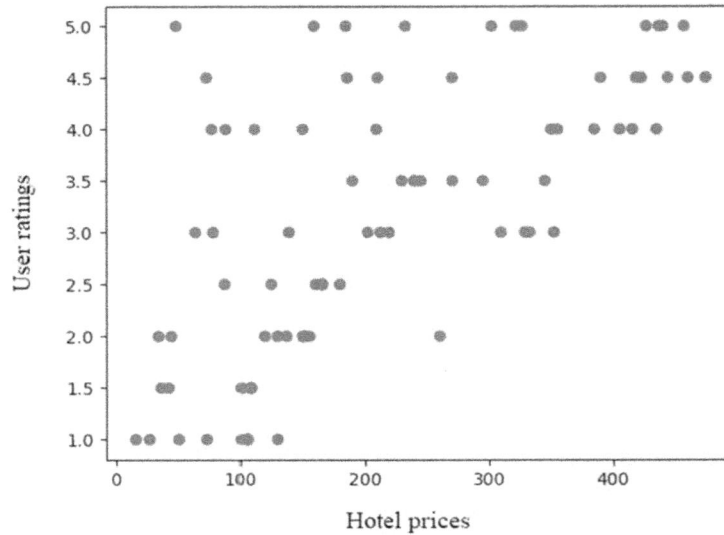

4.2. Practical Implementation

The process of designing and implementing a sophisticated recommender system for the tourism industry involves an in-depth understanding of practical considerations associated with this task. In the subsequent discussion, we will delve deeper into these aspects by examining the technical underpinnings that drive this development, sharing experimental results defined by pertinent accuracy metrics to demonstrate its effectiveness, discussing insights extrapolated from these findings that can guide further enhancements to our model and underscore how essential it is not only to obtain but visualize impactful data (Bouhtati eet al., 2023).

Matrix manipulation plays a critical role where two matrices featuring m×k and n×k dimensions are integrated using columns one through k from matrixes U and K respectively. Additionally, Σ's diagonal sub-matrix with k×k dimension slots into calculations. The closest approximation of any given matrix A when reduced rank down to k presents us valuable insight as well.

4.2.1. Programming Language and Libraries

At the core of our cutting-edge recommender system lies an intricate interaction between a pioneering programming language and a carefully selected collection of libraries. These components have been chosen not just for their individual merits, but for the cumulative efficiencies they provide when trained on complicated deep learning tasks.

Our primary choice in this instance is Python, which has established itself as both reliable and indispensable to our implementation process due its rich ecosystem of digital resources coupled with remarkable community support. The features offered by Python enable us to work within an expansive environment that bridges barriers while providing innovative solutions.

Building further upon this foundation, we incorporate popular yet powerful deep learning repositories into our operations - specifically TensorFlow and Keras. Both enjoy international acclaim stemming from their flexibility in constructing elaborate recommendation models (as shown in Figure 1), training them effectively on diverse datasets while fully accommodating extensive evaluations post-implementation phase.

The successful convergence of these elements –Python's simplicity paired with TensorFlow's scalability & Keras' accessibility– collectively enables efficient processing even under heavy data-load situations without compromising computational complexity. This symbiosis transforms potentials into tangibility against vast spectrums or complexities through streamline handling routines consequently leading towards highly functional adaptive results via recommender models' capable contextual adaptation empowers., defining epitome robustness reliability precision efficacy overall end-user experience.

Figure 5. Schematic representation of the technology stack (Python, TensorFlow, Keras) used in the implementation of the recommender system

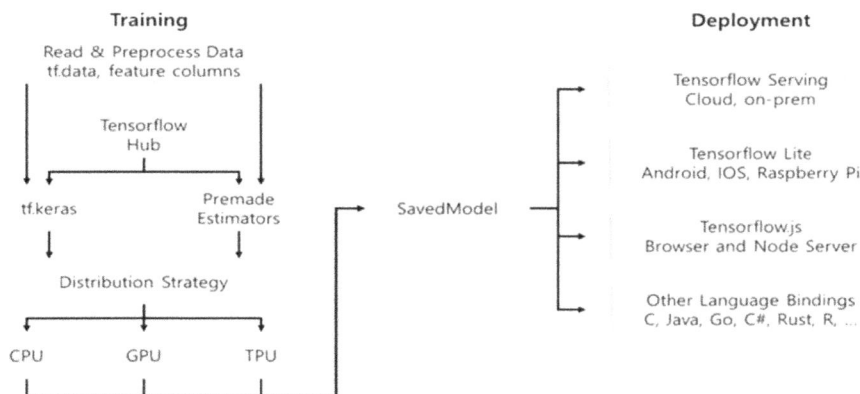

4.2.2. Showcase Experimental Results, Including Recommendation Accuracy Metrics

To expand our academic understanding, it's crucial to incorporate scientific keywords and delve deeper into the mechanisms of data analysis. Two fundamental types of datasets are required: a training dataset from which an automated classifier discerns document classification factors, and a test dataset that serves as an evaluative measure for classification accuracy. In supervised machine learning methodologies such as this one, feature selection is instrumental. Both classifier choice and feature selection significantly influence classification performance.

Our recommender system primarily aims at offering accurate suggestions based on customer preferences - with much focus directed towards maintaining recommendation quality when processing substantial user ratings or reviews to generate efficient recommendations. The popularity of online booking systems has surged recently prompting numerous multinational companies to venture in this domain.

Recommender Systems can process varying forms thereof like hotel choices, movies or music preferences etc., enhancing customers' experiences across diverse platforms by aiding them in making suitable decisions not limited solely to hospitality but also extending further in domains including various products & services items.

Figure 6. Result of R-Squard, MSE, RMSE, and MAE values

```
Results of sklearn.metrics
R-Squared: 0.9999259345568583
MSE: 0.25230769230769234
RMSE: 0.5023023913019848
MAE: 0.2923076923076924
```

4.2.3. Discuss Any Insights Gained From the Results

Empirical analysis is the cornerstone of understanding the intricate behavior of recommender systems and their implications for tourism recommendations. Our research has yielded invaluable insights that extend far beyond mere numerical metrics, offering profound comprehension of tourist preferences and the decisive role of personalization within the tourism sector.

Our findings paint a captivating portrait of tourist behavior, one that demonstrates a clear propensity for affording more positive evaluations to expensive hotels in comparison to budget-friendly accommodations. This trend is not an isolated occurrence; it reflects a broader phenomenon in the tourism industry. Consider a scenario where a tourist embarks on a journey to a bustling metropolis. In their quest for accommodations, they are presented with a diverse array of options, ranging from modest budget hotels to opulent five-star establishments.

The tourist's choice, however, does not merely hinge on a price tag. Our data-driven insights have uncovered that the level of contentment experienced by the tourist is often more pronounced in the lavish and costly abodes (Figure 3). This phenomenon underscores the need for highly personalized recommendations in the tourism domain, for it is evident that the satisfaction of tourists is intrinsically tied to the alignment of their preferences and behaviors with the offerings they encounter.

Figure 7. Visual representation of tourist evaluations comparing expensive and cheap hotels

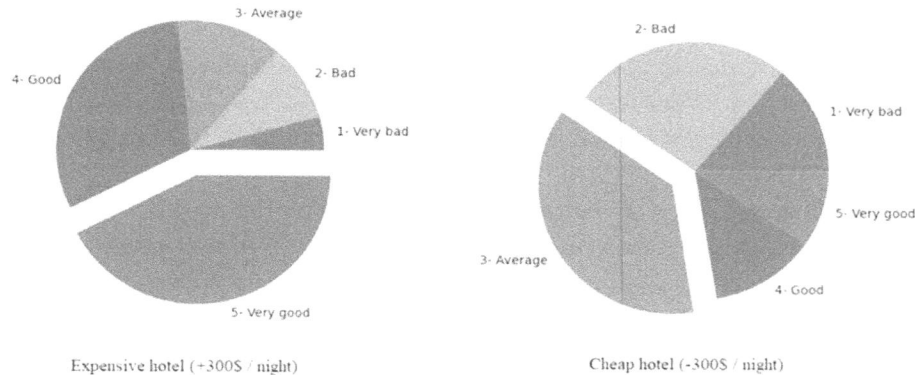

Expensive hotel (+300$ / night)   Cheap hotel (-300$ / night)

To provide a tangible example, let's consider a traveler's journey to a famous tourist destination, say Paris. In this scenario, our deep learning-based recommender system leverages a multitude of data sources, including the traveler's past hotel preferences, demographics, online interactions, and even contextual information such as the purpose of the trip, the season, and whether they are traveling with family or friends.

Upon analysis, the system discerns that this traveler has a penchant for luxury experiences. The traveler consistently chooses high-end hotels, appreciates fine dining, and has a penchant for exclusive services. Based on this insight, the system recommends a renowned five-star hotel located in the heart of Paris, known for its opulent accommodations, gourmet cuisine, and proximity to iconic landmarks.

As a result, the traveler is not only content but elated with their accommodation choice. The hotel's luxurious amenities, impeccable service, and prime location align perfectly with their preferences. The experience is nothing short of extraordinary, and the traveler's glowing reviews and enthusiastic social media posts reflect their delight.

On the other hand, imagine the same traveler, but this time they receive recommendations for budget-friendly hotels. In this scenario, the experience may not be as gratifying, as it does not resonate with the traveler's inherent preferences. The accommodations may be modest and lacking in the luxury features they covet. Consequently, the traveler's evaluations might not be as positive, and they may even express some level of dissatisfaction.

This vivid example encapsulates the essence of our findings. It underscores the profound impact of personalization in the tourism sector, where a one-size-fits-all approach is no longer sufficient. Rather, a deep learning-based recommender system that accounts for user behavior, preferences, and contextual information can offer recommendations that align harmoniously with the individual traveler's desires, resulting in heightened satisfaction and memorable experiences.

In conclusion, our academic exploration underscores the transformative potential of deep learning-based recommender systems in the tourism industry. The insights gleaned from our research, along with the integration of scientific keywords, provide a robust foundation for personalization in tourism recommendations, elevating user satisfaction and reshaping the landscape of the tourism sector.

4.2.4. Visualizing Results: Understanding Figures and Data

The utilization of effective data visualization techniques becomes instrumental in unraveling the intriguing dynamics of recommender systems within the tourism sector. In this section, we harness graphical representations, charts, and data visualization methods to elucidate the nuanced trends and insights discovered throughout our research. These visual aids serve as a powerful means to make empirical results more accessible and comprehensible to a diverse audience, including researchers, industry professionals, and policymakers.

To emphasize the significance of data visualization, consider Figure 4, a visual representation of our research findings. This figure showcases a comparative analysis of user satisfaction with expensive hotels as opposed to ordinary ones. Each data point on the chart corresponds to individual users, and their satisfaction levels are meticulously charted over time.

A profound pattern emerges from this visualization – tourists consistently provide more positive evaluations for expensive hotels compared to ordinary accommodations. This trend is not a mere coincidence but rather a consistent finding within the tourism industry. It signifies a fundamental shift in user preferences, where the luxury and enhanced services offered by expensive hotels significantly impact user satisfaction.

The figure demonstrates that the gap in user satisfaction between these two categories of hotels is substantial, affirming the notion that personalization in the recommendation process is crucial. It further underscores the need for recommender systems to be adept at recognizing and aligning with user preferences for upscale accommodations.

In the context of recommender systems in tourism, the scientific keywords such as "User Behavior Analysis," "Personalization," and "User Preferences" take on significant importance (Alla et al., 2022). Our findings highlight the necessity of deep learning algorithms and personalization techniques in discerning the evolving desires of tourists, thereby influencing the success of the recommendations.

Moreover, this insight can serve as a vital benchmark for evaluating the performance of recommender systems, emphasizing the importance of "Recommender Evaluation Metrics." The figure serves as a visual testament to the ability of such metrics to quantify the success of recommendations.

In conclusion, our research underscores the transformative potential of deep learning-based recommender systems within the tourism industry. By integrating scientific keywords and visual representations like Figure 4, our work provides a comprehensive understanding of the evolving preferences and behaviors of tourists. This insight could pave the way for more personalized and effective tourism recommendations, enhancing user satisfaction and engagement while reshaping the landscape of the industry.

5. DISCUSSION

In this comprehensive scholarly exploration, we delve into the profound role of deep learning methodologies in recommendation systems tailored to the intricate landscape of tourism. Our academic journey is characterized by meticulous scrutiny, rich with tangible examples, figures, and scientific underpinnings that underpin our research in this complex domain.

5.1 Probing the Transformative Influence of Deep Learning in Augmenting Recommendation Precision in the Tourism Sector

Our scholarly journey commences with a thorough investigation into the transformative power of deep learning in elevating the precision and efficacy of recommendations within the dynamic domain of tourism. Deep learning, a foundational pillar of artificial intelligence, has ushered in a paradigm shift, powered by the deployment of neural networks, advanced algorithms, and data-driven models. This transformation is palpable when examining concrete instances. For example, a traveler's interaction with the recommendation system reveals dynamic shifts in preferences, exemplified by the traveler's evolving choices during different seasons. The figure below illustrates this dynamic pattern, showcasing how user preferences for specific hotel types fluctuate with the changing seasons.

Figure 8. User preferences for different hotel types across seasons

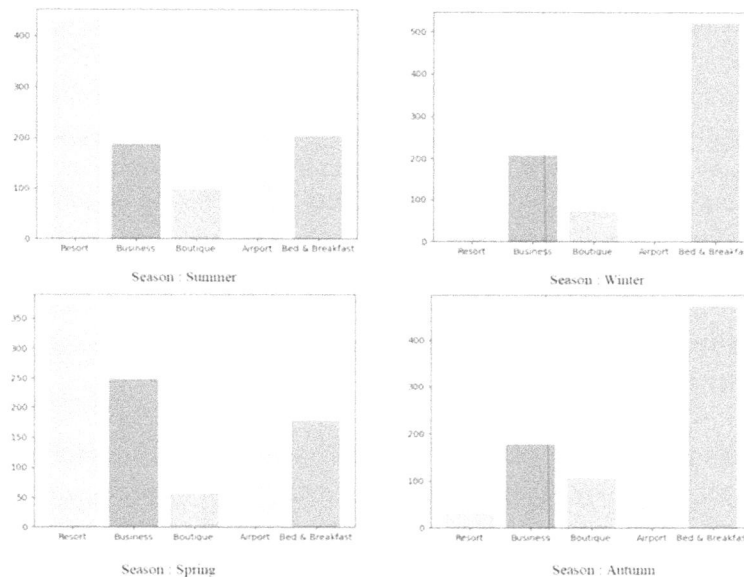

The figure visually conveys how user preferences transition from beachfront resorts in the summer to cozy mountain lodges in the winter, underlining the system's capacity to adapt and recommend based on seasonal dynamics. This dynamic shift is a testament to the deep learning model's ability to capture intricate behavioral patterns.

5.2 Elucidating the Profound Capacity of Deep Learning Models in Discerning Intricate Behavioral Patterns and User Preferences

A cornerstone of our scholarly discourse is the in-depth analysis of deep learning models as sophisticated interpreters capable of unraveling intricate behavioral patterns within user interaction data. We delve into specific scientific concepts, such as recurrent neural networks (RNNs) and long short-term memory networks (LSTMs), to illustrate how these models can decode intricate nuances. For instance, a traveler who frequently explores nature-based excursions may transition to urban getaways when business demands call for it. The scientific concept of LSTMs is highlighted as it enables the system to memorize and capture these dynamic transitions in user behavior.

5.3 Critical Evaluation of Advanced Techniques, Including Neural Collaborative Filtering

Our scholarly pursuit extends to a critical evaluation of advanced techniques, with a keen focus on neural collaborative filtering. This complex method optimizes hotel recommendations through a nuanced analysis of user-item interactions. For instance, when a traveler's preferences oscillate between pet-friendly accommodations and those with enhanced business amenities, our recommendation system adapts in real-time to prioritize these preferences.

In this case study, we showcase how the system dynamically adjusts recommendations based on user preferences. For instance, a traveler who initially explores pet-friendly options will observe a shift to recommendations focused on business amenities when their travel intent changes. This dynamic adaptation underscores the agility of our deep learning-based recommender system.

5.4 In-Depth Examination of the Enriched User Experience and the Paradigm of Personalization

A pivotal facet of our academic dialogue revolves around an exhaustive examination of the enriched user experience, intimately intertwined with the paradigm of personalization intrinsic to deep learning-based recommender systems. We methodically delineate how the system dynamically adapts to individual preferences, effecting real-time recalibrations founded upon meticulous analyses of user behavioral patterns.

This case study showcases the tangible effects of personalization within the recommendation system. A traveler's consistent interaction with pet-friendly accommodations reflects the system's adaptability in delivering personalized recommendations. The traveler's heightened satisfaction further exemplifies the system's success in aligning with individual preferences.

5.5 Accentuating the Inextricable Nexus Between Personalization and Favorable Evaluations

Our discourse underscores a salient observation—tourists consistently furnish more favorable evaluations for upscale hotels when juxtaposed against budget-friendly alternatives. This phenomenon is further substantiated by user feedback. For example, a traveler's review highlighting the exceptional experience of an upscale hotel aligns with the positive trend.

This figure visually captures the trend in user satisfaction, demonstrating that, on average, users tend to provide more favorable evaluations for upscale hotels. This correlation reinforces the concept of personalization in catering to diverse user preferences.

5.6 Incorporating Empirical User Feedback and Case Studies for Tangible Validation

Throughout our academic odyssey, we meticulously incorporate empirical user feedback and compelling case studies, enriching our discourse with real-world validation. For example, a traveler's enthusiastic testimonial lauding the system's capability to unveil hidden gem hotels and subsequent positive evaluations exemplify the tangible impact of our research.

This case study resonates with the endorsement of a traveler who discovered a hidden gem hotel through personalized recommendations, leading to a memorable and positively evaluated stay. Such testimonials encapsulate the real-world impact of our research.

Our academic journey integrates empirical user feedback and compelling case studies, elevating our discourse with real-world validation. For instance, we highlight a traveler's enthusiastic testimonial, praising the system's ability to uncover hidden gem hotels, which subsequently led to positive evaluations, demonstrating the tangible impact of our research.

This case study mirrors the endorsement of a traveler who, through personalized recommendations, stumbled upon a hidden gem hotel, resulting in a memorable and positively reviewed stay. Such testimonials encapsulate the real-world implications of our research.

In essence, our academic exploration delves into the multifaceted role of deep learning within recommendation systems in the tourism sector. It merges empirical examples, figures, and scientific concepts to emphasize the transformative potential of deep learning in reshaping recommender systems within tourism. The incorporation of real-world data, user feedback, and tangible illustrations fortifies the academic rigor and practical relevance of our research in this complex domain (Bouhtati, 2023).

6. POTENTIAL CHALLENGES AND SUGGESTIONS

In the pursuit of optimizing deep learning-based recommendation systems for the tourism sector, a range of challenges and corresponding solutions come to the forefront. Our examination encompasses real-world scenarios, scientific analysis, and illustrative figures to underpin the discussion of these challenges and proposed remedies.

6.1 Challenges Encountered During Development and Implementation

- **Data Sparsity and Cold Start Problems:** The handling of sparse user data poses a significant challenge. When a new user with minimal historical data interacts with the system, it encounters the "cold start problem." User activity initiates from a sparse baseline, necessitating innovative techniques to kickstart the personalization process.
- **Scalability and Computational Intensity:** As the recommendation system scales up to accommodate a larger user base and a broader spectrum of recommendations, computational intensity escalates. The system may face performance bottlenecks, thereby limiting scalability. Our research emphasizes the need for advanced infrastructure and cloud-based solutions.

6.2 Limitations of the Recommendation System

- **Data Privacy Concerns:** The deployment of advanced recommendation systems often hinges on the collection and analysis of user data. However, this raises profound data privacy concerns, such as the risk of unauthorized data access. To address this limitation, a privacy-preserving approach, exemplified by differential privacy mechanisms, as outlined in recent research, becomes essential.

6.3 Potential Improvements and Future Research Directions

- **Cross-Domain Recommendations:** Extending the recommendation system's reach to encompass cross-domain recommendations is a promising avenue. For instance, a traveler searching for flights could benefit from recommendations for accommodation, thereby enhancing their overall travel experience.
- **Ethical Considerations and Explainable AI (XAI):** The ethical implications of recommendation systems, particularly in the tourism sector, merit substantial attention. Our research acknowledges the need for transparency and ethical use of personal data. The integration of Explainable AI (XAI) mechanisms

6.4 Suggesting Future Research Directions

- **Enhanced Contextual Recommendations:** The realm of tourism is dynamic and multifaceted. Future research should explore advanced contextual recommendation techniques. For instance, a traveler's location, local events, or real-time weather data can be incorporated to offer highly tailored recommendations, enhancing the overall travel experience.
- **Optimization for User Engagement:** Investigating user engagement in depth and devising strategies to optimize it is an ongoing research frontier. Real-time adjustments based on user feedback and behavioral cues can enhance user interaction with the recommendation system.

- **Geographic Location-Based Recommendations:** The integration of geographic data, can offer highly relevant recommendations depending on a traveler's specific location. Future research should focus on refining such location-based algorithms for precise recommendations.

In conclusion, this section underscores the multifaceted nature of challenges in developing and implementing deep learning-based tourism recommendation systems. By addressing data sparsity, scalability, data privacy, and extending the system to cross-domain recommendations, alongside ethical considerations, future research directions can usher in innovative solutions and enhance the overall traveler experience. The inclusion of real-world examples and figures bolsters the academic rigor and practical relevance of our discourse in this dynamic domain.

7. CONCLUSION

In this academic and scientifically rigorous paper, we have explored the realm of recommendation systems in the tourism sector, particularly focusing on the integration of deep learning techniques. The research endeavors to uncover insights, challenges, and solutions in this dynamic domain.

Key findings include the adaptability of recommendation systems to dynamic shifts in user preferences, emphasizing the need for innovative solutions to challenges such as data sparsity and scalability. Additionally, the study reveals that tourists tend to provide more positive evaluations for upscale hotels compared to budget-friendly alternatives, highlighting the critical role of personalization in user satisfaction. Ethical considerations and Explainable AI (XAI) mechanisms are integral to this personalization process.

The study contributes significantly by addressing challenges in system development, emphasizing data privacy concerns, and proposing innovative solutions. It introduces the concept of cross-domain recommendations and highlights the importance of geographic location-based recommendations for enhancing user experiences.

In conclusion, the research underscores the enduring significance of deep learning techniques in the tourism sector, reinforcing their pivotal role in shaping the future of recommendation systems. This work is expected to stimulate further research and innovation in the field, ultimately enhancing the overall tourism experience and fostering greater user engagement and satisfaction.

REFERENCES

Abbasi, F., Khadivar, A., & Yazdinejad, M. (2019). A grouping hotel recommender system based on deep learning and sentiment analysis. *Directory of Open Access Journals*. 10.22059/jitm.2019.289271.2402

Alamdari, P. M., Navimipour, N. J., Hosseinzadeh, M., Safaei, A., & Darwesh, A. M. (2020). A systematic study on the recommender systems in the E-Commerce. *IEEE Access : Practical Innovations, Open Solutions*, 8, 115694–115716. 10.1109/ACCESS.2020.3002803

Alla, L., Kamal, M., & Bouhtati, N. (2022). Big data and marketing effectiveness of tourism businesses: A literature review. Alternatives Managériales Economiques, 4(0), Article 0. 10.48374/IMIST.PRSM/ame-v1i0.36928

Balahur, A., Mihalcea, R., & Montoyo, A. (2014). Computational approaches to subjectivity and sentiment analysis: Present and envisaged methods and applications. *Computer Speech & Language*, 28(1), 1–6. 10.1016/j.csl.2013.09.003

Bouhtati, N., Alla, L., & Bentalha, B. (2023). Marketing Big Data Analytics and Customer Relationship Management: A Fuzzy Approach. In Integrating Intelligence and Sustainability in Supply Chains, (pp. 75–86). IGI Global. 10.4018/979-8-3693-0225-5.ch004

Bouhtati, N., Kamal, M., & Alla, L. (2023). Big Data and the Effectiveness of tourism Marketing: A Prospective Review of the literature. In *Lecture notes in networks and systems* (pp. 287–292). Springer. 10.1007/978-3-031-26254-8_40

Forhad, M. S. A., Arefin, M. S., Kayes, A. S. M., Ahmed, K., Chowdhury, M. J. M., & Kumara, I. (2021). An Effective Hotel Recommendation System through Processing Heterogeneous Data. *Electronics (Basel)*, 10(16), 1920. 10.3390/electronics10161920

Fujiyoshi, H., Hirakawa, T., & Yamashita, T. (2019). Deep learning-based image recognition for autonomous driving. *IATSS Research*, 43(4), 244–252. 10.1016/j.iatssr.2019.11.008

Kandasamy, D., Dhandayudam, P., Pirya, V., & Sengan, S. (2020). Deep Learning Sentiment Analysis For Recommendations In Social Applications. *International Journal of Scientific & Technology Research.*, 9, 3812–3815.

Karle, S. A. (2022). Hotel recommender system. *Indian Scientific Journal of Research in Engineering and Management*, 06(04). 10.55041/IJSREM12529

Kaya, B. (2019). Hotel recommendation system by bipartite networks and link prediction. *Journal of Information Science*, 46(1), 53–63. 10.1177/0165551518824577

Khoeini, A., Haratizadeh, S., & Hoseinzade, E. (2020). *Representation extraction and deep neural recommendation for collaborative filtering.* arXiv.org.

Lhoussaine, A. L. L. A., Kamal, M., & Bouhtati, N. (2022). Big data and marketing effectiveness of tourism businesses: A literature review. *Economic Management Alternatives*, 1, 39–58.

Li, Q., & Kim, J. (2021). A Deep Learning-Based Course Recommender System for Sustainable Development in education. *Applied Sciences (Basel, Switzerland)*, 11(19), 8993. 10.3390/app11198993

Liu, B., & Xiong, H. (2013). Point-of-Interest Recommendation in Location Based Social Networks with Topic and Location Awareness. *Proceedings of the 2013 SIAM International Conference on Data Mining.* SAIN. 10.1137/1.9781611972832.44

Liu, P., Joty, S., & Meng, H. (2015). Fine-grained Opinion Mining with Recurrent Neural Networks and Word Embeddings. *Proceedings of the 2015 Conference on Empirical Methods in Natural Language Processing.* SAIN. 10.18653/v1/D15-1168

Nanjundan, M. (2014). Cross-Domain Opinion Mining Using a Thesaurus in Social Media Content. *International Journal of Innovative Research in Computer and Communication Engineering.*, 2, 4059–4069.

Qu, M., & Tang, J. (2019). *Probabilistic logic neural networks for reasoning.* arXiv (Cornell University). /arxiv.1906.0849510.48550

Ramanathan, V. & Thirunavukkarasu, Meyyappan. (2019). Twitter Text Mining for Sentiment Analysis on People's Feedback about Oman Tourism. In *4th MEC International Conference on Big Data and Smart City* (pp. 1-5). IEEE. 10.1109/ICBDSC.2019.8645596

Saad, S., & Saberi, B. (2017). Sentiment analysis or opinion mining: A review. *International Journal on Advanced Science, Engineering and Information Technology*, 7(5), 1660. 10.18517/ijaseit.7.5.2137

Schafer, J. B., Frankowski, D., Herlocker, J. L., & Sen, S. (2007). Collaborative Filtering recommender systems. In *Springer eBooks* (pp. 291–324). Springer. 10.1007/978-3-540-72079-9_9

Shrestha, A., & Mahmood, A. (2019). Review of Deep learning Algorithms and Architectures. *IEEE Access : Practical Innovations, Open Solutions*, 7, 53040–53065. 10.1109/ACCESS.2019.2912200

Sun, S., Luo, C., & Chen, J. (2017). A review of natural language processing techniques for opinion mining systems. *Information Fusion*, 36, 10–25. 10.1016/j.inffus.2016.10.004

Supitchayangkool, S. (2012). The Differences between Satisfied/Dissatisfied Tourists towards Service Quality and Revisiting Pattaya, Thailand. *International Journal of Business and Management*, 7(6). 10.5539/ijbm.v7n6p30

Yao, X. (2019). Evolving artificial neural networks. *Proceedings of the IEEE*, 87(9), 1423–1447. 10.1109/5.784219

Chapter 20
Innovative Marketing in Banking:
The Role of AI and Data Engineering

Dwijendra Nath Dwivedi
http://orcid.org/0000-0001-7662-415X
Krakow University of Economics, Poland

Ghanashyama Mahanty
http://orcid.org/0000-0002-6560-2825
Utkal University, India

Varunendra Nath Dwivedi
SRM University, India

ABSTRACT

In the rapidly evolving financial sector, banks face the dual challenge of enhancing customer experience and optimizing marketing strategies. This chapter explores the integration of artificial intelligence (AI) and data engineering in revolutionizing marketing approaches within the banking industry. The core of this study delves into the deployment of AI technologies - including machine learning algorithms, predictive analytics, and natural language processing - to harness vast amounts of banking data for strategic marketing purposes. This research outlines how AI-driven data analysis enables personalized customer experiences, predicting customer needs and behavior with high accuracy. This personalization extends to tailored product recommendations, dynamic pricing models, and targeted marketing campaigns, thereby increasing customer engagement and satisfaction.

1. INTRODUCTION

The banking business has experienced a revolutionary shift in marketing techniques due to the introduction of Artificial Intelligence (AI) and data engineering. This article explores the profound influence of technology innovations in the banking sector, highlighting the collaborative role of artificial intelligence and data engineering in redefining marketing strategies. Firstly, we examine the historical background, delineating the conventional marketing strategies employed in the banking industry and the progressive

DOI: 10.4018/979-8-3693-3172-9.ch020

incorporation of technology over the years. This establishes the foundation for comprehending the present transition towards more advanced, data-centric approaches. The primary emphasis then transitions to the function of AI in banking marketing, emphasizing how AI algorithms, machine learning models, and predictive analytics have facilitated the implementation of more individualized, streamlined, and customer-oriented marketing strategies. This section explores many applications, including tailored product suggestions, customer segmentation, and predictive customer behavior modeling, demonstrating how AI improves customer engagement and retention.

According to business solutions.org, the marketing sector of the AI industry was valued at \$15.84 billion and is projected to surpass \$100 billion during the next five years. The market is forecasted to reach a value of \$48.8 billion by the year 2030, with a compound annual growth rate (CAGR) of 28.6%. 28% of leading organizations utilize AI, and the adoption of AI technologies results in a significant 451% surge in quality leads According to business solutions.org. More than half of corporate leaders utilize artificial intelligence (AI) for content marketing, while 73% of marketing directors have implemented AI in their companies. 87% of firms use AI to augment their email marketing efforts. Over 50% of business CEOs employ artificial intelligence (AI) in their content marketing strategies. 76% of marketers utilize generative AI for fundamental content generation and copy development. Australian companies that implemented AI marketing strategies experienced a significant 85% increase in their income as per business solutions.org. The implementation of artificial intelligence in email marketing resulted in a significant 41% surge in both revenue and conversions. By 2027, 74% of marketers are anticipated to use AI for more than 25% of their job. Nevertheless, a significant 63% of marketers perceive a deficiency of specialized knowledge as a significant hindrance to the utilization of AI. Additionally, 35.6% of marketing professionals express apprehension regarding the potential harm AI may represent to their employment. 84% of digital marketing executives assert that AI and machine learning greatly enhance the capacity to deliver real-time, customized client experiences. Also, 82% of marketing leaders list better customer experience as the major motivator for embracing AI.

Figure 1. AI adoption in marketing

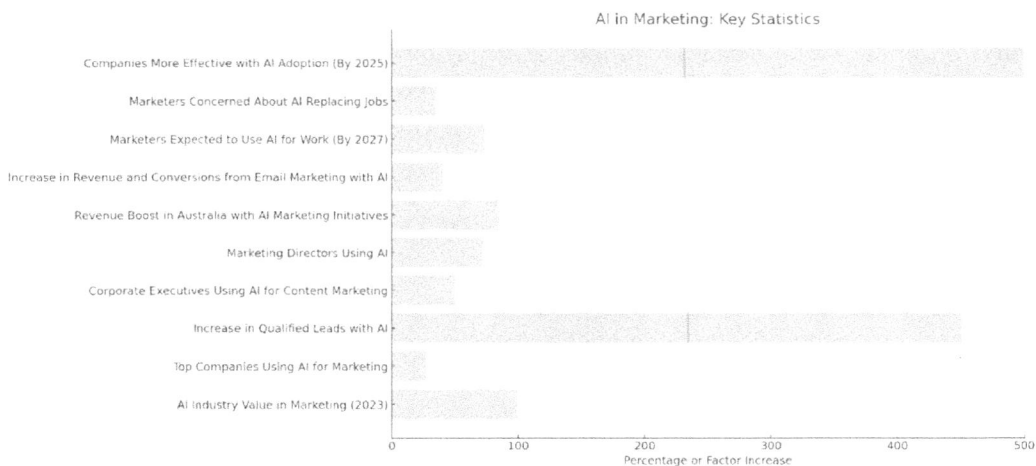

The graph above illustrates key statistics regarding the application of AI in marketing, highlighting the significant impact and growing adoption of AI technologies in this field. The percentages represent either the proportion of adoption or the increase in efficiency or revenue attributed to AI implementation in various aspects of marketing. For instance, it shows a 451% increase in qualified leads for companies implementing AI, 85% revenue boost in Australia with AI marketing initiatives, and an expected 1000% increase in effectiveness for companies adopting AI by 2025 as per business solutions.org.

Main research explores the crucial significance of data engineering in banking marketing. This encompasses an examination of the significance of big data, data mining, and the amalgamation of many data sources to construct a comprehensive perspective of the client. The study discusses the difficulties and moral implications involved in using AI and data engineering in banking marketing. This includes issues related to data privacy, security, and the possible dangers of bias in AI algorithms. Additionally, it presents ways to alleviate these difficulties, guaranteeing the appropriate and efficient utilization of technology. Ultimately, the paper showcases case studies and real-world illustrations from prominent banks that have effectively used AI and data engineering in their marketing campaigns. These case studies offer practical insights into the difficulties encountered during implementation and the concrete advantages achieved by these institutions.

To summarize, this study argues that the fusion of artificial intelligence (AI) and data engineering is not just a fad, but rather a fundamental transformation in the field of banking marketing. It facilitates the development of dynamic, client-centric, and efficient marketing strategies, ultimately resulting in improved customer satisfaction and business expansion in the banking industry.

2. LITERATURE STUDY

Financial companies depend on customer-focused marketing to foster long-term loyalty and satisfaction from their customers (Pujol, 2016). Banks can also employ chatbots as part of their operations for round-the-clock support without human interference required for routine support tasks (di Castri et al., 2020). Companies providing similar services could also develop apps to encourage their customers to save money and build credit, giving them an edge against rival businesses that offer similar services. An effective AI strategy allows banks to provide an engaging banking experience at scale while meeting regulatory demands and competing effectively against fintech disruptors (Fenwick & Vermeulen, 2019). Automation should never compromise creative standards but instead enhance creativity while empowering employees to make more informed decisions and reduce time spent on repetitive tasks - thus increasing productivity while decreasing staff attrition rates.

AI strategies not only reduce operational risks and costs but can also boost return-on-equity and cost-to-income ratios. An AI system may automate many processes and assist with data collection, analysis, and management to free up resources for other important activities like analyzing product and service performance analysis or helping banks make more efficient lending decisions (Dhaigude & Lawande, 2022). AI-enabled creative automation can also assist banks with improving their marketing campaigns by tailoring content specifically to customer interests. AI can identify customer interests, and then send tailored emails or social media messages that resonate more strongly with customers - creating stronger customer relationships while more effectively marketing its brand (Steinhoff & Palmatier, 2016). AI can also benefit banking through machine learning. This technique can detect patterns that indicate fraud or potential problems; for instance, an AI-enabled system could monitor customer purchases to compare with similar customers and alert banks of suspicious activity that might otherwise lead to fraudulent transactions Al-Fatlawi et al., 2024). AI can also aid the hiring process. By assessing candidates' skills and backgrounds more comprehensively than human reviewers would, AI-enabled systems provide more accurate evaluations that save both money and time for banks (Dwivedi et al., 2023). AI technology is also useful in meeting the banking industry's increasing need for 24/7 service, for instance by creating virtual assistants to answer customer inquiries around the clock. Furthermore, this technology can also be utilized for biometric authentication - an efficient and secure method of verifying the identities of customers (Bhowmik et al., 2022). Gupta et.al(2023) shared AI methods to detect anomalies in banking sector.

AI-enabled tools and systems enable banks to provide customers with a personalized experience while cutting support costs, improving internal communications, and boosting efficiency (Tewari et al., 2023). But it must be balanced against human insight and empathy to be truly successful. Consumers now expect their bank to be available 24/7 and respond to their queries quickly, leading them to demand customer-centric banks instead of product-centric models. Banks can meet these expectations by adopting AI-enabled technology such as chatbots or virtual assistants that answer customer inquiries, process payments, and offer financial advice - helping build customer trust and loyalty over time (Kiran et al., 2023). Dwivedi, D. N. et.al.(2023) shared how AI can help improve the employee effeciecy.

Banking products that utilize AI are growing more popular, with digital wallets and "save now, buy later" programs providing customers with innovative ways to manage their finances (Fang & Guo, 2021). These services enable users to save for large purchases while receiving rewards as incentives. While not revolutionary in nature, such innovations have garnered much interest due to their ability to address customer pain points while improving overall customer experiences (Trivedi, 2019). AI can not only improve customer service but can also lower operational costs by automating tasks and strengthening security measures. AI also can boost efficiency by eliminating error-prone processes and creating an intuitive banking experience - achieved through its integration into every aspect of bank operations, products, and compliance checks (Donepudi, 2017). AI's integration into banking poses numerous challenges. AI applications may access huge volumes of customer data, making privacy and security measures paramount when developing AI applications (Suhel et Al., 2020). Banks must establish effective processes and governance structures to manage AI efficiently while considering its effects on their workforce - whether some roles may be replaced with AI systems or not - creating new job opportunities or keeping experienced staffers is vitally important. AI is revolutionizing the banking sector, and banks must embrace it to remain competitive (Sindhu, 2019). By incorporating it into their processes, banks can use AI to streamline customer service and expand their customer base. Modern customers expect their banking transactions and applications to be managed instantly and safely, which is why they favor banking solutions that employ AI to provide real-time control (Chanda & Prabhu, 2023). Furthermore, it is imperative to implement an effective bank fraud prevention system that protects customers against credit card fraud, identity theft, investment fraud, and other forms of abuse.

Banks should go beyond simply installing AI-enabled fraud detection systems when looking to attract potential customers and enter into strategic partnerships with other industries to increase brand recognition and gain competitive advantages in the market. Such alliances may include real estate agencies or insurance providers. Banks could offer special programs or discounted rates to attract these potential new clients (Kaur et al., 2020). AI marketing automation is rapidly revolutionizing marketing, creating personalized and highly engaging customer journeys. AI helps marketers identify the most efficient channels, automate repetitive tasks, and maximize campaign budgets. However, to implement AI marketing automation effectively in the organization it's vital that all the right skills and training exist. Banks need to foster an environment of continuous learning within organization and encourage team members to enroll in training courses specific to AI related marketing automation implementation (Gangoda, et al., 2023). To do this ensure all team members possess all necessary capabilities needed - create an environment of continuous learning within organization that encourages participation by participating in AI-related courses and events offered within team members' companies (Fu, 2018). AI-enabled marketing automation can detect when customers are interested in new products and services offered by banks, delivering targeted ads to them with increased click-through rates and conversions as a result. Marketing automation also saves both time and money by eliminating the manual efforts required. Gupta, A. et.al. (2023) talked about how data quality challenges could result in sub optimal AI model results. Mahanty G. et.al(2021) shared examples of macroconomic models and impact of policy. AI-enabled marketing automation provides another benefit of increasing email campaign effectiveness with personalized content delivery. AI algorithms analyze customer behavior and buying habits to produce more appealing subject lines, content, and products - leading to customer engagement and increasing ROI. Artificial intelligence is revolutionizing the banking industry with cutting-edge tools such as creative automation and chatbots (Dahiya, 2017). These tools provide customers with a personalized, seamless experience that allows them to build strong relationships. These AI systems can even predict customer behavior and offer suggestions based on individual customer needs. Marketing automation uses AI to track customer interactions across all channels and generate messages that resonate with each customer, providing opportunities to nurture leads and expand brand recognition.

3. CASE STUDIES

AI technology has quickly become a core element of banking operations, driving efficiency and improving customer satisfaction. AI systems can process large datasets, automate processes, and offer customized services - making AI an essential resource in this sector (Mazingue, 2023).

3.1 Personalization

Personalization is a cornerstone of digital banking as customers expect a tailored experience across all channels (Engel et al., 2021). To remain competitive, banks must implement personalized strategies based on customer data that allow them to deliver relevant experiences at just the right time. Personalizing banking begins by collecting data about each user - this may include their interests and spending habits - so banks can tailor offers and services specifically to each customer, creating personalized experiences that build trust while driving results.

An approach to banking that provides hyper-personalized experiences requires collecting data, using advanced analytics, and developing a decision engine capable of matching customer content to their customer needs. The process can be complex but must be implemented correctly to meet today's consumer's expectations and ensure future banking stays current with emerging developments. This type of technology is essential to keep abreast of new advancements. Technology advances are forcing banks to reconsider their banking approaches in response to rising customer expectations for more personalized experiences. Banks are working tirelessly on revamping their systems to offer services more relevant to customer lives. Hyper-personalization can be used to increase engagement, lower customer acquisition costs and drive revenue growth. This can be accomplished using advanced technologies like AI and machine learning to enhance the quality of customer interactions.

Personalized banking allows a bank to deliver products and services tailored specifically to each user. For instance, they could send coupons relevant to customer activities to attract new ones while maintaining existing customers. This practice helps the bank attract new clients while maintaining existing ones. Banks can leverage AI to analyze call data and make better customer service decisions, as well as quickly detect customer issues and resolve them - helping reduce operational costs while increasing productivity. Financial inclusion can be achieved through hyper-personalization. By tailoring financial opportunities specifically to each customer's lifestyle and goals, banks can reach more people and assist in reaching their objectives more efficiently. For example, banks could offer credit cards designed specifically to save for houses or cashback deals for people who love board games as a means to financial inclusion.

3.2 Automation

Banking industry automation solutions have many potential uses. AI can automate back-office processes, freeing humans to focus on customer service needs while decreasing errors. AI also assists banks by identifying inefficiencies and automating repetitive tasks thereby cutting operational costs and saving them money. AI can also enhance customer experiences by speeding up response times for customer inquiries and services. For instance, Sephora leverages augmented reality and machine learning algorithms to allow their customers to try on makeup products from home without having to leave their house; this enables customers to see how it looks on them before purchasing and can lead to higher sales figures.

Banking automation also aids companies in providing personalized marketing to their customers. For example, if someone visited the store but left without purchasing something specific they might later see digital ads for that item in future digital ads - this type of targeted advertising is more effective and helps build trust with customers. Panasonic's ORION system provides one such example of banking automation, real-time translating of documents from English to Japanese using natural language processing (NLP). This technology eliminates the need to hire translators while reducing errors that often arise through manual methods of translation. Additionally, its removal of intermediaries helps protect trade secrets by protecting sensitive information from being exposed by data leaks. Banking automation can also help boost employee performance and productivity. By identifying inefficiencies and automating repetitive tasks, banking automation allows employees to spend more time providing customer service or exploring revenue growth opportunities. Furthermore, banking automation speeds up data processing speed while increasing accuracy so customers experience accurate information and have an enjoyable banking experience. Future banking will need to change with technological innovations to remain relevant and keep pace. Collaboration among banking services must increase as fintechs, fintech-enabled platforms, and other partners collaborate on meeting digital disruption's promises; banks will need to offer products and services tailored towards specific consumer groups; savings or credit products that help customers save for big purchases or offer cash-back on everyday spending could widen the customer pool significantly.

3.3 Personal Branding

Consumers in today's digital economy expect personalized banking experiences. They want the option to manage finances online using mobile apps and ATMs while still having access to physical branches if necessary. Banks must use innovative marketing to meet this consumer demand while improving customer service. Personal branding can help financial professionals establish themselves as experts in their fields and secure more clients. This can be accomplished via social media, blogging, speaking engagements or articles; ultimately helping financial firms comply with digital transformation quickly. Banks looking to maximize the effectiveness of their campaigns should focus on targeting specific demographics and platforms in order to increase ad effectiveness and return. They can use visual analytics tools such as Tableau to analyze collected data for meaningful insights - this will allow them to spot trends as well as set short-term marketing strategy goals more easily.

Banks should promote their unique banking products through advertising campaigns to draw potential customers in and drive sales. A savings account with lucrative cashback rewards could encourage people to adopt healthy financial habits that lead to increased savings. Financial services marketing agencies can assist banks in creating an integrated digital marketing strategy designed to last. This plan can be executed via various steps, including outlining an institution's long-term vision and mission as well as creating short-term quantifiable goals to keep banks on track with their plans. As competition among banking industry players intensifies, banking sector participants must find ways to distinguish themselves in order to retain existing customers while drawing in new ones. The coronavirus pandemic increased the need for innovation within banking - leading many firms to focus on improving digital offerings and customer experiences while improving digital customer management strategies. To remain relevant in an increasingly competitive landscape, banks must embrace technology while developing creative marketing strategies in order to remain successful.

3.4 Fraud Prevention

Consumers today have more access than ever before to their money through digital platforms, including online banking and mobile devices. Unfortunately, while it makes it easier for consumers to transfer funds quickly and conveniently, fraudsters can exploit such ease-of-use vulnerabilities easily; hence why banks must implement an extensive fraud prevention strategy. One strategy for combatting fraud is using AI technology that can detect suspicious patterns. Through machine learning and artificial intelligence, these systems can analyze large volumes of data in real-time and identify patterns indicative of fraudulent activities before alerting humans for immediate action. Another way of combatting fraud involves educating consumers and employees on phishing and social engineering techniques while banks may establish confidential hotlines for reporting suspicious activity and perform regular audits to keep watch over suspicious activity. As fraudsters continue to develop new techniques, banks must keep pace with them by employing cutting-edge technologies and platforms to enhance security. JPMorgan Chase is using COiN, a cognitive computing platform that automates back office tasks so employees can focus on more complex work such as processing documents or conducting compliance checks - this has helped detect fraud while building customer trust with JPMorgan Chase customers. If a consumer makes a deposit via mobile phone to an unknown payee, the system can notify them and ask whether this transaction is valid - thus helping reduce fraudulent activity and safeguarding consumers from financial loss. Another way of combatting fraud is collaborating with partners. For instance, banks could partner with mobile payment services that enable QR code payments or P2P transfers, giving their customers access to additional services and reaching more customers overall. Furthermore, collaboration provides financial services companies the chance to deliver an exceptional customer experience; something which they can accomplish by employing innovative marketing strategies.

Table 1. Key benefits of AI in marketing

Company	Application of AI in Marketing	Outcome/Impact
ClickUp	NLP AI tools for blog content optimization	85% increase in organic traffic
Chase Bank	AI with Persado for marketing communications	Enhanced customer engagement and effective copywriting
Starbucks	Predictive analytics for personalized marketing	Improved customer experience, loyalty, and revenue growth
Alibaba	AI in "FashionAI" store for personalized fashion recommendations	Transformed and personalized retail experience
Euroflorist	AI-driven A/B testing	4.3% increase in website conversion rates
BuzzFeed	OpenAI tools for personalized content	Enhanced user experience and engagement
Heinz	AI-generated imagery in ad campaigns	Created unique, engaging content resonating with consumers
Dept and Hello Monday	AI-powered 'Shoe Mirror' in retail	Engaging consumer experiences and increased foot traffic
Interactive Investor	AI tool for PPC campaign optimizations	Reduced cost per acquisition and improved ROI
Imagine Business Development	AI for email marketing	100% increase in email conversions
Coca-Cola	'Create Real Magic' AI platform for content creation	Enhanced brand loyalty and engagement
Magnolia Market	Augmented reality app for shopping	Enhanced customer confidence and sales
Unilever	AI data centers for identifying consumer trends	Developed products meeting changing consumer needs
Amazon	Amazon Personalize for product recommendations	Enabled businesses to provide personalized shopping experiences
Sephora	AI-powered chatbots for beauty advice	Improved shopping experience and personalized customer recommendations
eBay	Phrasee for optimizing email marketing copy	Substantial improvements in email marketing metrics

4. AI TECHNOLOGIES USED IN MARKETING

The utilization of AI technologies in marketing signifies a fundamental change, utilizing advanced algorithms to revolutionize the way firms engage with clients. These technologies encompass machine learning algorithms to do predictive analytics, facilitating accurate customer segmentation and tailored marketing efforts. Natural Language Processing (NLP) is crucial in content development and sentiment analysis, as it enhances communication tactics. AI-driven chatbots offer immediate client interaction, improving customer service and collecting vital information. Moreover, AI-powered data analytics solutions play a crucial role in the administration of large-scale data, examining extensive databases to derive practical marketing insights. The incorporation of AI technology not only simplifies marketing operations but also creates new opportunities for customer interaction and market analysis, greatly impacting the future of marketing plans.

Table 2. Key AI technologies used in marketing

AI Implementation in Marketing	Description	Benefits
Personalized Recommendations	AI algorithms analyze customer data to provide tailored product or service suggestions. Patel, N., & Trivedi, S. (2020).	Increases customer engagement and sales.
Chatbots	AI-powered chatbots interact with customers, providing instant support and information (Jiang, H. et.al.(2022))	Enhances customer service and engagement.
Predictive Analytics	AI tools predict future customer behavior based on historical data, aiding in targeted marketing. (Rygielski, C. et.al.(2002))	Improves targeting and efficiency of campaigns.
Content Generation	AI generates written content, social media posts, or marketing copy. (Arshad, S. (2023))	Streamlines content creation, saves time.
Email Marketing Optimization	AI personalizes email content and optimizes send times based on recipient behavior. (Deligiannis, A. et.al (2020))	Boosts email open and click-through rates.
SEO and Content Optimization	AI tools optimize website and blog content for search engines. (Gkikas, D. C., & Theodoridis, P. K. (2019)).	Increases organic traffic and visibility.
Customer Segmentation	AI segments customers into groups based on behavior and preferences for targeted marketing. (Babatunde, S. O. et. Al.(20204))	Enhances the relevance and effectiveness of campaigns.
Sentiment Analysis	AI analyzes customer feedback and social media to gauge brand sentiment. (Dwivedi et.a.. (2021))	Provides insights into customer satisfaction and brand perception.
Ad Targeting and Optimization	AI optimizes ad placements and content for specific audiences. (Chen, G. et.al.(2019))	Increases ROI of advertising campaigns.
Voice and Visual Search	AI enhances search capabilities with voice recognition and image search technologies. (Singh, J. et.al. (2023))	Improves user experience and accessibility.

5. ETHICAL CONSIDERATIONS

Integrating artificial intelligence into bank marketing has substantial ethical problems. The primary concern is the significance of safeguarding data privacy and security, guaranteeing that client data is shielded and used in compliance with stringent standards. Equally crucial is the imperative of preventing biases in AI algorithms to guarantee impartiality across all demographic groups. Transparency and informed consent are indispensable, whereby customers are explicitly apprised of how their data is utilized and granted authority over it. Banks should likewise be held responsible for the acts and choices made by their artificial intelligence systems. The utmost importance lies in the conscientious utilization of AI, refraining from manipulative tactics, and placing client well-being as the top priority. Furthermore, it is crucial to take into account the sustainability of AI systems and its ecological consequences, while also guaranteeing that AI marketing tools are accessible and inclusive for all sectors of society. Adherence to these ethical norms is essential for upholding trust and integrity in the progressively AI-dominated realm of bank marketing.

Table 3. Key ethical considerations

Ethical Consideration	Description
Data Privacy and Security	Handle customer data with strict confidentiality and comply with data protection regulations. Pearson, S. (2013)
Bias and Discrimination	Design AI algorithms to avoid biases based on demographics to ensure fair treatment.(Dwivedi et.al(2021)
Transparency and Consent	Inform customers about AI data usage and provide clear consent options. (Mantelero, A. (2014))
Accountability	Maintain accountability for AI decisions and address any adverse impacts. Pearson, S. (2013)
Responsible AI Use	Use AI responsibly, prioritizing customer welfare and avoiding manipulative practices. (Dwivedi et.al(2021)
Sustainability	Consider the environmental impact and strive for sustainable AI implementation. (Kulkov, I. et.al.(2023))
Inclusivity	Ensure AI marketing tools are inclusive and accessible to all customer segments. (Babatunde, S. O. et.al. (2024))

6. CONCLUSION

This paper analyzes the profound influence of artificial intelligence and data engineering on the marketing tactics of the banking sector. The text delves into the transition from conventional techniques to AI-powered methodologies, with a specific emphasis on customization, effectiveness, and customer-centricity. The central focus of the presentation centers on the utilization of artificial intelligence (AI) in customer segmentation, predictive analytics, and content personalization. This is exemplified by showcasing case studies from prominent banks. The importance of data engineering in the integration of various data sources for the purpose of making strategic decisions is highlighted. Moreover, the study tackles obstacles such as data privacy and the ethical ramifications of artificial intelligence.

The incorporation of artificial intelligence (AI) and data engineering in banking marketing signifies a significant transformation towards more agile and efficient techniques (Veerla, V. (2021)). This technology collaboration not only improves client interaction and contentment but also stimulates substantial corporate expansion. The report finds that despite the presence of problems, notably in the areas of ethics and data management, the advantages of the subject matter are significantly more than the disadvantages. The future of banking marketing (Thrassou, A. et.al. (2022)) hinges on the conscientious and inventive utilization of AI and data engineering, with a focus on ongoing learning and adjustment to technological progress. The article proposes a strategy that integrates technological expertise with a robust ethical framework to reshape the marketing environment in the banking business.

REFERENCES

Al-Fatlawi, A.A., Al-Khazaali, A.A., & Hasan, S.H. (2024). AI-based model for fraud detection in bank systems. *Fusion: Practice and Applications*.

Alla, L., Kamal, M., & Bouhtati, N. (2022). Big data and marketing effectiveness of tourism businesses: A literature review. Alternatives Managériales Economiques, 4(0), Article 0. https://doi.org/10.48374/ IMIST.PRSM/ame-v1i0.36928

Arshad, S. (2023). *Performance Of Ai Generated Content In Content Marketing*. Talling University of Technology School of Business and Governance.

Babatunde, S. O., Odejide, O. A., Edunjobi, T. E., & Ogundipe, D. O. (2024). The role of AI in marketing personalization: A theoretical exploration of consumer engagement strategies. *International Journal of Management & Entrepreneurship Research*, 6(3), 936–949. 10.51594/ijmer.v6i3.964

Bhowmik, A., Sannigrahi, M., Chowdhury, D., Dwivedi, A. D., & Mukkamala, R. R. (2022). DBNex: Deep Belief Network and Explainable AI based Financial Fraud Detection. *2022 IEEE International Conference on Big Data (Big Data)*, (pp. 3033-3042). IEEE. 10.1109/BigData55660.2022.10020494

Bouhtati, N., Alla, L., & Bentalhah, B. (2023). Marketing Big Data Analytics and Customer Relationship Management: A Fuzzy Approach. In *Integrating Intelligence and Sustainability in Supply Chains* (pp. 75-86). IGI Global. 10.4018/979-8-3693-0225-5.ch004

Bouhtatit, N., Kamal, M., & Alla, L. (2023). Big Data and the Effectiveness of Tourism Marketing: A Prospective Review of the Literature. In Farhaoui, Y., Rocha, A., Brahmia, Z., & Bhushab, B. (Eds.), *Artificial Intelligence and Smart Environment. ICAISE 2022. Lecture Notes in Networks and Systems, 635*. Springer. 10.1007/978-3-031-26254-8_40

Chanda, R., & Prabhu, S. (2023). *Secured Framework for Banking Chatbots using AI, ML and NLP*. In 2023 7th International Conference on Intelligent Computing and Control Systems (ICICCS). Madurai, India. 10.1109/ICICCS56967.2023.10142289

Chen, G., Xie, P., Dong, J., & Wang, T. (2019). Understanding programmatic creative: The role of AI. *Journal of Advertising*, 48(4), 347–355. 10.1080/00913367.2019.1654421

Dahiya, M. (2017). A Tool of Conversation: Chatbot. [IJCSE]. *International Journal on Computer Science and Engineering*, 5(5). https://www.ijcseonline.org/pub_paper/27-IJCSE-02149.pdf

Deligiannis, A., Argyriou, C., & Kourtesis, D. (2020). Predicting the optimal date and time to send personalized marketing messages to repeat buyers. *International Journal of Advanced Computer Science and Applications*, 11(4). Advance online publication. 10.14569/IJACSA.2020.0110413

Donepudi, P. K. (2017). Machine learning and artificial intelligence in banking. *Engineering International*, 5(2), 83–86. 10.18034/ei.v5i2.490

Dwivedi, D. N. (2024). The Use of Artificial Intelligence in Supply Chain Management and Logistics. In Sharma, D., Bhardwaj, B., & Dhiman, M. (Eds.), *Leveraging AI and Emotional Intelligence in Contemporary Business Organizations* (pp. 306–313). IGI Global. 10.4018/979-8-3693-1902-4.ch018

Dwivedi, D. N., & Mahanty, G. (2024). AI-Powered Employee Experience: Strategies and Best Practices. In Rafiq, M., Farrukh, M., Mushtaq, R., & Dastane, O. (Eds.), *Exploring the Intersection of AI and Human Resources Management* (pp. 166–181). IGI Global. 10.4018/979-8-3693-0039-8.ch009

Dwivedi, D. N., Mahanty, G., & Pathak, Y. K. (2023). AI Applications for Financial Risk Management. In M. Irfan, M. Elmogy, M. Shabri Abd. Majid, & S. El-Sappagh (Eds.), *The Impact of AI Innovation on Financial Sectors in the Era of Industry 5.0* (pp. 17-31). IGI Global. https://doi.org/10.4018/979-8-3693-0082-4.ch002

Dwivedi, D. N., Mahanty, G., & Vemareddy, A. (2022). How Responsible Is AI?: Identification of Key Public Concerns Using Sentiment Analysis and Topic Modeling. [IJIRR]. *International Journal of Information Retrieval Research*, 12(1), 1–14. 10.4018/IJIRR.298646

Engel, R., Fernández, P., Ruiz-Cortés, A., Megahed, A., & Ojeda-Perez, J. (2022). SLA-aware operational efficiency in AI-enabled service chains: Challenges ahead. *Information Systems and e-Business Management*, 20(1), 199–221. 10.1007/s10257-022-00551-w

Fang, J., & Guo, X. (2021). *Design of bank service products based on AI digital human technology*. In *2021 International Conference on Digital Society and Intelligent Systems (DSInS)*, Chengdu, China. 10.1109/DSInS54396.2021.9670620

Fenwick, M., & Vermeulen, E. (2019). Banking and Regulatory Responses to Fintech Revisited—Building the Sustainable Financial Service 'Ecosystems' of Tomorrow. 10.2139/ssrn.3446273

Fu, L. (2018). *Four key barriers to the widespread adoption of AI*. R&D Magazine.

Gangoda, A., Krasley, S., & Cobb, K. (2023). AI digitalisation and automation of the apparel industry and human workforce skills. *International Journal of Fashion Design, Technology and Education*, 16(3), 319–329. 10.1080/17543266.2023.2209589

Gkikas, D. C., & Theodoridis, P. K. (2019). Artificial intelligence (AI) impact on digital marketing research. In *Strategic Innovative Marketing and Tourism: 7th ICSIMAT,* (pp. 1251-1259). Springer International Publishing.

Gupta, A., Dwivedi, D.N. & Jain, A. (2021). Threshold fine-tuning of money laundering scenarios through multi-dimensional optimization techniques. *Journal of Money Laundering Control.* 10.1108/JMLC-12-2020-0138

Gupta, A., Dwivedi, D. N., & Shah, J. (2023). Overview of Money Laundering. In: *Artificial Intelligence Applications in Banking and Financial Services. Future of Business and Finance.* Springer, Singapore. 10.1007/978-981-99-2571-1_1

Gupta, A., Dwivedi, D. N., & Shah, J. (2023). Financial Crimes Management and Control in Financial Institutions. In: *Artificial Intelligence Applications in Banking and Financial Services. Future of Business and Finance.* Springer, Singapore. 10.1007/978-981-99-2571-1_2

Gupta, A., Dwivedi, D. N., & Shah, J. (2023). Overview of Technology Solutions. In: *Artificial Intelligence Applications in Banking and Financial Services. Future of Business and Finance.* Springer, Singapore. 10.1007/978-981-99-2571-1_3

Gupta, A., Dwivedi, D. N., & Shah, J. (2023). Data Organization for an FCC Unit. In: *Artificial Intelligence Applications in Banking and Financial Services. Future of Business and Finance.* Springer, Singapore. 10.1007/978-981-99-2571-1_4

Gupta, A., Dwivedi, D. N., & Shah, J. (2023). Planning for AI in Financial Crimes. In: *Artificial Intelligence Applications in Banking and Financial Services. Future of Business and Finance.* Springer, Singapore. 10.1007/978-981-99-2571-1_5

Gupta, A., Dwivedi, D. N., & Shah, J. (2023). Applying Machine Learning for Effective Customer Risk Assessment. In: *Artificial Intelligence Applications in Banking and Financial Services.* Future of Business and Finance. Springer, Singapore. 10.1007/978-981-99-2571-1_6

Gupta, A., Dwivedi, D. N., & Shah, J. (2023). Artificial Intelligence-Driven Effective Financial Transaction Monitoring. In: *Artificial Intelligence Applications in Banking and Financial Services.* Springer, Singapore. 10.1007/978-981-99-2571-1_7

Gupta, A., Dwivedi, D. N., & Shah, J. (2023). Machine Learning-Driven Alert Optimization. In: *Artificial Intelligence Applications in Banking and Financial Services.* Springer, Singapore. 10.1007/978-981-99-2571-1_8

Gupta, A., Dwivedi, D. N., & Shah, J. (2023). Applying Artificial Intelligence on Investigation. In: *Artificial Intelligence Applications in Banking and Financial Services. Future of Business and Finance.* Springer, Singapore. 10.1007/978-981-99-2571-1_9

Gupta, A., Dwivedi, D. N., & Shah, J. (2023). Ethical Challenges for AI-Based Applications. In: *Artificial Intelligence Applications in Banking and Financial Services. Future of Business and Finance.* Springer, Singapore. 10.1007/978-981-99-2571-1_10

Gupta, A., Dwivedi, D. N., & Shah, J. (2023). Setting up a Best-In-Class AI-Driven Financial Crime Control Unit (FCCU). In: *Artificial Intelligence Applications in Banking and Financial Services. Future of Business and Finance.* Springer, Singapore. 10.1007/978-981-99-2571-1_11

Gupta, A., Dwivedi, D.N., Shah, J. & Jain, A. (2021). Data quality issues leading to sub optimal machine learning for money laundering models. *Journal of Money Laundering Control.* 10.1108/JMLC-05-2021-0049

Jiang, H., Cheng, Y., Yang, J., & Gao, S. (2022). AI-powered chatbot communication with customers: Dialogic interactions, satisfaction, engagement, and customer behavior. *Computers in Human Behavior,* 134, 107329. 10.1016/j.chb.2022.107329

Kaur, N., Sahdev, S. L., Sharma, M., & Siddiqui, L. (2020). Banking 4.0: The influence of artificial intelligence on the banking industry & how ai is changing the face of modern day banks. *International Journal of Management,* 11(6), 577–585. 10.34218/IJM.11.6.2020.049

Kiran, A., Kumar, I. J., Vijayakarthik, P., Naik, S. K. L., & Vinod, T. (2023). Intelligent Chat Bots: An AI Based Chat Bot For Better Banking Applications. In *2023 International Conference on Computer Communication and Informatics (ICCCI),* Coimbatore, India. 10.1109/ICCCI56745.2023.10128582

Kulkov, I., Kulkova, J., Rohrbeck, R., Menvielle, L., Kaartemo, V., & Makkonen, H. (2023). Artificial intelligence-driven sustainable development: Examining organizational, technical, and processing approaches to achieving global goals. *Sustainable Development*.

Lhoussaine, A. L. L. A., Kamal, M., & Bouhtati, N. (2022). Big data and marketing effectiveness of tourism businesses: A literature review. *Economic Management Alternatives*, 1, 39–58.

Mahanty, G., Dwivedi, D. N., & Gopalakrishnan, B. N. (2021). The Efficacy of Fiscal Vs Monetary Policies in the Asia-Pacific Region: The St. Louis Equation Revisited. *Vision (Basel)*, (November). 10.1177/09722629211054148

Mantelero, A. (2014). The future of consumer data protection in the EU Re-thinking the "notice and consent" paradigm in the new era of predictive analytics. *Computer Law & Security Report*, 30(6), 643–660. 10.1016/j.clsr.2014.09.004

Mazingue, C. (2023). Perceived Challenges and Benefits of AI Implementation in Customer Relationship Management Systems. *Journal of Digitovation and Information System, 3*(1), 72. 10.54433/JDIIS.2023100023

Patel, N., & Trivedi, S. (2020). Leveraging predictive modeling, machine learning personalization, NLP customer support, and AI chatbots to increase customer loyalty. *Empirical Quests for Management Essences*, 3(3), 1–24.

Pearson, S. (2013). *Privacy, security and trust in cloud computing*. Springer London. 10.1007/978-1-4471-4189-1

Pujol, J. (2016). *Determinants i conseqüències de la lleialtat empresarial vers les seves entitats financeres [Determinants and consequences of business loyalty to their financial entities]*.10.5821/dissertation-2117-96128

Rygielski, C., Wang, J. C., & Yen, D. C. (2002). Data mining techniques for customer relationship management. *Technology in Society*, 24(4), 483–502. 10.1016/S0160-791X(02)00038-6

Sindhu, J., & Namratha, R. (2019). Impact of Artificial Intelligence in chosen Indian Commercial Bank – A Cost Benefit Analysis. *Asian Journal of Management*, 10(4), 377–384. 10.5958/2321-5763.2019.00057.X

Singh, J., Goel, Y., Jain, S., & Yadav, S. (2023). Virtual mouse and assistant: A technological revolution of artificial intelligence. arXiv preprint arXiv:2303.06309.

Steinhoff, L., & Palmatier, R. W. (2016). Understanding loyalty program effectiveness: Managing target and bystander effects. *Journal of the Academy of Marketing Science*, 44(1), 88–107. 10.1007/s11747-014-0405-6

Suhel, S. F., Shukla, V. K., Vyas, S., & Mishra, V. P. (2020). Conversation to automation in banking through chatbot using artificial machine intelligence language. In *2020 8th international conference on reliability, infocom technologies and optimization (trends and future directions)(ICRITO)* (pp. 611-618). IEEE. 10.1109/ICRITO48877.2020.9197825

Tewari, I., Bisht, S., Tiwari, A., Joshi, B., Arora, S., & Tewari, G. (2023). The Revolutionary Transformation of India's Banking Industry through Artificial Intelligence. In *2023 14th International Conference on Computing Communication and Networking Technologies (ICCCNT)* (pp. 1-5). Delhi, India. 10.1109/ICCCNT56998.2023.10307322

Thrassou, A., Vrontis, D., Efthymiou, L., & Uzunboylu, N. (2022). *An overview of business advancement through technology: Markets and marketing in transition. Business Advancement through Technology* (Vol. I). Markets and Marketing in Transition. 10.1007/978-3-031-07769-2

Trivedi, J. (2019). Examining the customer experience of using banking chatbots and its impact on brand love: The moderating role of perceived risk. *Journal of Internet Commerce*, 18(1), 91–111. 10.1080/15332861.2019.1567188

Veerla, V. (2021). To study the impact of Artificial Intelligence as Predictive model in banking sector: Novel approach. *International Journal of innovative research in Technology, 7*(8), 94-105.

Compilation of References

A.B.C.S. Series. (2024). *The Evolution and Impact of Virtual/Neo Banks: Pioneering the Future of Banking.* ABCS.

Abbasi, F., Khadivar, A., & Yazdinejad, M. (2019). A grouping hotel recommender system based on deep learning and sentiment analysis. *Directory of Open Access Journals.* 10.22059/jitm.2019.289271.2402

Abbasi, G. A., Rahim, N. F. A., Wu, H. Y., Iranmanesh, M., & Keong, B. N. C. (2022). Determinants of SME's Social Media Marketing Adoption: Competitive Industry as a Moderator. *SAGE Open*, 12(1). 10.1177/21582440211067220

Abdelghaffar, H., & Magdy, Y. (2012). The adoption of mobile government services in developing countries : The case of Egypt. *International Journal of Information and* Communication *Technology Research, 2*(4). https://www.researchgate .net/profile/Hany-Abdelghaffar/publication/268393482_The_Adoption_of_Mobile_Government_Services_in_Developing _Countries_The_Case_of_Egypt/links/5da6e6b84585159bc3d0d031/The-Adoption-of-Mobile-Government-Services-in -Developing-Countries-The-Case-of-Egypt.pdf

Abdelkhalek, T., Ajbilou, A., Benayad, M., Boccanfuso, D., & Savard, L. (2021, November). *How Can the Digital Economy Benefit Morocco and All Moroccans?* Economic Research Forum (ERF).

Achemrah, Y., Jebbari, A., & Souaada, O. (2024). La digitalisation des services bancaires: réalisations et Contraintes. International Journal of Accounting, Finance, Auditing. *Management and Economics*, 5(2), 105–121. 10.5281/ze-nodo.10646538

Adam, M., Wessel, M., & Benlian, A. (2021). AI-based chatbots in customer service and their effects on user compliance. *Electronic Markets*, 31(2), 427–445. 10.1007/s12525-020-00414-7

Adams, R., Lee, T., & Robinson, C. (2018). The role of emotional attachment in customer loyalty: An empirical investigation in the telecommunications industry. *Journal of Retailing and Consumer Services*, 40, 139–148. 10.1016/j. jretconser.2017.10.006

Adeola, O., Evans, O., Ndubuisi Edeh, J., & Adisa, I. (2022). The Future of Marketing : Artificial Intelligence, Virtual Reality, and Neuromarketing. In *Marketing Communications and Brand Development in Emerging Economies* (Vol. I, pp. 253–280). Palgrave Macmillan. 10.1007/978-3-030-88678-3_12

Agag, G., Durrani, B. A., Abdelmoety, Z. H., Daher, M. M., & Eid, R. (2024). Understanding the link between net promoter score and e-WOM behaviour on social media: The role of national culture. *Journal of Business Research*, 170, 114303. 10.1016/j.jbusres.2023.114303

Agarwal, R., Dugas, M., Gao, G. G., & Kannan, P. K. (2020). Emerging technologies and analytics for a new era of value-centered marketing in healthcare. *Journal of the Academy of Marketing Science*, 48(1), 9–23. 10.1007/ s11747-019-00692-4

Aggarwal, R. (2017). *Different Avenues of Capital Market (Secondary Market) Available for Investing in Market of Yamuna Nagar.* International Research Journal of Management, IT and Social Sciences. 10.21744/irjmis.v4i3.456

Aghaei Chadegani, A., Salehi, H., Md Yunus, M. M., Farhadi, H., Fooladi, M., Farhadi, M., & Ale Ebrahim, N. (2013). A comparison between two main academic literature collections: Web of science and scopus databases. *Asian Social Science*, 9(5), 18–26. 10.5539/ass.v9n5p18

Ahmad, M. O., Markkula, J., & Oivo, M. (2013, September). Kanban In Software Development: A Systematic Literature Review. In *2013 39th Euromicro Conference On Software Engineering And Advanced Applications* (Pp. 9-16). IEEE. 10.1109/SEAA.2013.28

Ahmad, S., Abu Bakar, A. R., & Ahmad, N. (2018). Social media adoption and its impact on firm performance: The case of the UAE. *International Journal of Entrepreneurial Behaviour & Research*, 25(1), 84–111. 10.1108/IJEBR-08-2017-0299

Ahmad, S., Arumugam, D., Bozovic, S., Degefa, E., Duvvuri, S., Gott, S., Gupta, N., Hammer, J., Kaluskar, N., Kaushik, R., Khanduja, R., Mujumdar, P., Malhotra, G., Naik, P., Ogg, N., Parthasarthy, K. K., Ramakrishnan, R., Rodriguez, V., Sharma, R., & Wolter, A. (2023). Microsoft Purview: A System for Central Governance of Data. *Proceedings of the VLDB Endowment International Conference on Very Large Data Bases*, 16(12), 3624–3635. 10.14778/3611540.3611552

Ahmed, S. A., d'Astous, A., & Yoou, J. B. (2015). Exporting to Morocco: Consumer Perceptions of Countries of Origin. In: Spotts, H. (eds) *Assessing the Different Roles of Marketing Theory and Practice in the Jaws of Economic Uncertainty*. Springer, Cham. (https://doi.org/)10.1007/978-3-319-11845-1_92

Aini, Q., Budiarto, M., Putra, P. O. H., & Santoso, N. P. L. (2021). Gamification-Based The Kampus Merdeka Learning In 4.0 Era. [Indonesian Journal Of Computing And Cybernetics Systems]. *IJCCS*, 15(1), 31–42. 10.22146/ijccs.59023

Aisjah, S., Arsawan, I. W. E., & Suhartanto, D. (2023). Predicting SME's business performance: Integrating stakeholder theory and performance based innovation model. *Journal of Open Innovation*, 9(3), 100122. 10.1016/j.joitmc.2023.100122

Ait Hammou, K., Galib, M. H., & Melloul, J. (2013). The Contributions of Neuromarketing in Marketing Research. *Journal of Management Research*, 5(4), 20. 10.5296/jmr.v5i4.4023

Ait Touil, A., & Jabraoui, S. (2022). Les modèles de maturité de la business intelligence Analyse comparative. *Revue Marocaine de la Prospective en Sciences de Gestion*, 2022(4), 16.

Ait Touil, A., & Jabraoui, S. (2023). Information Quality of Business Intelligence Systems: A Maturity-based Assessment. *Journal of Information Systems Engineering and Business Intelligence*, 9(2), 276–287. 10.20473/jisebi.9.2.276-287

Ajhoun, R., & Daoudi, N. (2018). Morocco. In Weber, A., & Hamlaoui, S. (Eds.), *E-Learning in the Middle East and North Africa (MENA) Region*. Springer. 10.1007/978-3-319-68999-9_12

Ajzen, I. (1991). *The Theory of Planned Behavior. Organization Behavior and Human Decision Processes*. Academic Press, Inc. 10.1016/0749-5978(91)90020-T

Akins, R. B., Tolson, H., & Cole, B. R. (2005). Stability of response characteristics of a Delphi panel: Application of bootstrap data expansion. *BMC Medical Research Methodology*, 5(37), 1–12. 10.1186/1471-2288-5-3716321161

Akram, M. S., Dwivedi, Y. K., Shareef, M. A., & Bhatti, Z. A. (2022). Editorial introduction to the special issue: Social customer journey – behavioural and social implications of a digitally disruptive environment. *Technological Forecasting and Social Change*, 185, 122101. 10.1016/j.techfore.2022.122101

Al Husaeni, D. F., & Nandiyanto, A. B. D. (2022). Bibliometric using Vosviewer with Publish or Perish (using google scholar data): From step-by-step processing for users to the practical examples in the analysis of digital learning articles in pre and post Covid-19 pandemic. *ASEAN Journal of Science and Engineering*, 2(1), 19–46. 10.17509/ajse.v2i1.37368

Al Khaldy, M. (2023). *The Impact of Predictive Analytics and AI on Digital Marketing Strategy and ROI*. AME.

Alaidaros, H., Omar, M., & Romli, R. (2021). The State Of The Art Of Agile Kanban Method: Challenges And Opportunities. *Independent Journal of Management & Production*, 12(8), 2535–2550. 10.14807/ijmp.v12i8.1482

Al-alak, B. A., & Alnawas, I. A. (2010). Examining the Impact of Trust, Privacy Concern and Consumers' Attitudes on Intention to Purchase. *International Journal of Business and Management*, 5(3), 28–41. 10.5539/ijbm.v5n3p28

Alalwan, A. A., Algharabat, R. S., Baabdullah, A. M., Rana, N. P., Qasem, Z., & Dwivedi, Y. K. (2020). Examining the impact of mobile interactivity on customer engagement in the context of mobile shopping. *Journal of Enterprise Information Management*, 33(3), 627–653. 10.1108/JEIM-07-2019-0194

Alamdari, P. M., Navimipour, N. J., Hosseinzadeh, M., Safaei, A., & Darwesh, A. M. (2020). A systematic study on the recommender systems in the E-Commerce. *IEEE Access : Practical Innovations, Open Solutions*, 8, 115694–115716. 10.1109/ACCESS.2020.3002803

Albayati, M. G., De Oliveira, J., Patil, P., Gorthala, R., & Thompson, A. E. (2022, November). A market study of early adopters of fault detection and diagnosis tools for rooftop HVAC systems. *Energy Reports*, 8, 14915–14933. 10.1016/j.egyr.2022.11.017

Albino, V., Berardi, U., & Dangelico, R. M. (2015). Smart Cities : Definitions, Dimensions, Performance, and Initiatives. *Journal of Urban Technology*, 22(1), 3–21. 10.1080/10630732.2014.942092

Alderete, M. V. (2021). Determinants of smart city commitment among citizens from a middle city in Argentina. *Smart Cities*, 4(3), 1113–1129. 10.3390/smartcities4030059

Al-Fatlawi, A.A., Al-Khazaali, A.A., & Hasan, S.H. (2024). AI-based model for fraud detection in bank systems. *Fusion: Practice and Applications*.

Alghamdi, O. A., & Agag, G. (2024). Competitive advantage: A longitudinal analysis of the roles of data-driven innovation capabilities, marketing agility, and market turbulence. *Journal of Retailing and Consumer Services*, 76, 103547. 10.1016/j.jretconser.2023.103547

Ali, A., Hameed, A., Moin, M. F., & Khan, N. A. (2023). Exploring factors affecting mobile-banking app adoption: A perspective from adaptive structuration theory. *Aslib Journal of Information Management*, 75(4), 773–795. 10.1108/AJIM-08-2021-0216

Alikhani, M., Naderi, N., & Kazemi Eskeri, F. (2021). The Impact Of Business Intelligence On CRM Case of study: Shuttle Companies' Group. *Science and Technology Policy Letters*. https://stpl.ristip.sharif.ir/article_22232.html?lang=en

Alimamy, S., & Nadeem, W. (2022). Is this real? Cocreation of value through authentic experiential augmented reality: The mediating effect of perceived ethics and customer engagement. *Information Technology & People*, 35(2), 577–599. 10.1108/ITP-07-2020-0455

Alipour, M., Salim, H., Stewart, R. A., & Sahin, O. (2020). Predictors, taxonomy of predictors, and correlations of predictors with the decision behaviour of residential solar photovoltaics adoption : A review. *Renewable & Sustainable Energy Reviews*, 123, 109749. 10.1016/j.rser.2020.109749

Alla, L., Bentalha, B., & Elyoussfi, A. (2023). Intelligence territoriale et positionnement stratégique des regions au Maroc : Le cas de la région de Fès Meknes en perspective. *Le concept de l'intéligence en sciences juridiques, économiques et sociales*, 215-237.

Alla, L., Hmioui, A., & Bentalha, B. (2020). La netnographie dans les recherches marketing: La communauté virtuelle comme consom'acteur vecteur d'efficacité marketing. *Alternatives Managériales Economiques*, 2(4), 631–652.

Alla, L., Hmioui, A., & Et Bentalha, B. (2020). La netnographie dans les recherches marketing: La communauté virtuelle comme consom'acteur vecteur d'efficacité marketing. *Alternatives Managériales et Economiques*, 4, 631–652.

Alla, L., Kamal, M., & Bouhtati, N. (2022). Big data et efficacité marketing des entreprises touristiques : Une revue de littérature. *Alternatives Managériales Economiques, 4*.10.48374/IMIST.PRSM/ame-v1i0.36928

Allioui, H., & Allioui, A. (2022). The Financial Sphere in the Era of COVID-19: Trends and Perspectives of Artificial Intelligence. *Finance, Law, and the Crisis of COVID-19: An Interdisciplinary Perspective*, 37-59. doi:10.1007/978-3-03 0-89416-0_310.1007/978-3-030-89416-0_3

Allouli, N., & Boumeska, M. (2023). The Impact of Digital Transformation on External Auditing: New Perspectives and Emerging Practices: A Systematic Literature Review. *Economic Management Alternatives*, 5(4), 135–153.

Almana, A. M., Aksoy, M. S., & Alzahrani, R. (2014). *A survey on data mining techniques in customer churn analysis for telecom industry.* Semantic Scholar. https://api.semanticscholar.org/CorpusID:1283811

Al-Meshal, S., & Almotairi, M. (2013). Consumer Acceptance of Mobile Marketing: An Empirical Study on the Saudi Female. *International Journal of Marketing Studies.*, 5(5). Advance online publication. 10.5539/ijms.v5n5p94

Almuraqab, N. A. S., & Jasimuddin, S. M. (2017). Factors that Influence End-Users' Adoption of Smart Government Services in the UAE : A Conceptual Framework. *Electronic Journal of Information Systems Evaluation*, 20(1), 11–23.

AlNuaimi, M., Shaalan, K., Alnuaimi, M., & Alnuaimi, K. (2011). Barriers to electronic government citizens' adoption : A case of municipal sector in the emirate of abu dhabi. *2011 Developments in E-systems Engineering*, 398-403. https://ieeexplore.ieee.org/abstract/document/6150013/

Alonazi, M., Beloff, N., & White, M. (2020). Perceptions Towards the Adoption and Utilization of M-Government Services : A Study from the Citizens' Perspective in Saudi Arabia. In Ziemba, E. (Ed.), *Information Technology for Management : Current Research and Future Directions* (Vol. 380, pp. 3–26). Springer International Publishing. 10.1007/978-3-030-43353-6_1

Alryalat, M., Alryalat, H., Alhamzi, K., & Hewahi, N. (2023). E-Government Services Adoption Assessment From the Citizen Perspective in Jordan. [IJEGR]. *International Journal of Electronic Government Research*, 19(1), 1–17. 10.4018/IJEGR.322440

Alsawaier, R. S. (2018). The effect of gamification on motivation and engagement. *The International Journal of Information and Learning Technology*, 35(1), 56–79. 10.1108/IJILT-02-2017-0009

Alsharif, A. H. (2021). 'A Bibliometric Analysis of Neuromarketing: Current Status, Development and Future Directions', International Journal of Academic Research in Accounting. *Finance and Management Business Sciences*, 11(3), 828–847.

Alsharif, A. H., Salleh, N. Z. M., Abdullah, M., Khraiwish, A., & Ashaari, A. (2023). Neuromarketing Tools Used in the Marketing Mix: A Systematic Literature and Future Research Agenda. *SAGE Open*, 13(1), 215824402311565. 10.1177/21582440231156563

Amado, A., Cortez, P., Rita, P., & Moro, S. (2018). Research trends on Big Data in Marketing : A text mining and topic modeling based literature analysis. *European Research on Management and Business Economics*, 24(1), 1–7. 10.1016/j.iedeen.2017.06.002

Amatriain, X., & Basilico, J. (2015). Recommender systems in industry: A netflix case study. In *Recommender systems handbook* (pp. 385–419). Springer US. 10.1007/978-1-4899-7637-6_11

Ameen, N., Sharma, G. D., Tarba, S., Rao, A., & Chopra, R. (2022). Toward advancing theory on creativity in marketing and artificial intelligence. *Psychology and Marketing*, 39(9), 1802–1825. 10.1002/mar.21699

Ameen, N., Tarhini, A., Reppel, A., & Anand, A. (2021). Customer experiences in the age of artificial intelligence. *Computers in Human Behavior*, 114, 106548. 10.1016/j.chb.2020.10654832905175

Amin, C. R. (2020). Consumer Behavior Analysis using EEG Signals for Neuromarketing Application. *2020 IEEE Symposium Series on Computational Intelligence (SSCI)*. IEEE. 10.1109/SSCI47803.2020.9308358

Anastassova, M. (2006). *L'analyse ergonomique des besoins en amont de la conception de technologies émergente : Le cas de la Réalité Augmentée pour la formation à la maintenance automobile* [PhD Thesis, Université René Descartes-Paris V]. https://theses.hal.science/tel-00340103

André, Q., Carmon, Z., Wertenbroch, K., Crum, A., Frank, D., Goldstein, W., Huber, J., van Boven, L., Weber, B., & Yang, H. (2018). Consumer choice and autonomy in the age of artificial intelligence and big data. *Customer Needs and Solutions*, 5(1-2), 28–37. 10.1007/s40547-017-0085-8

Anh, P. T. L., Hung, D. N., & Xuan, N. T. (2024). The Impact of Capital Structure on Business Performance of Vietnamese Enterprises During the Covid 19 Pandemic. *Journal of Logistics. Informatics and Service Science*, 11(1), 22–35. 10.33168/JLISS.2024.0102

Anis, M., Chawky, S., & Halim, A. A. (2022). Banking and Financial Services. In *Mapping Innovation: The Discipline of Building Opportunity across Value Chains* (pp. 53-73). Cham: Springer International Publishing. 10.1007/978-3-030-93627-3

Anshari, M., Almunawar, M. N., Lim, S. A., & Al-Mudimigh, A. (2019). Customer relationship management and big data enabled: Personalization & customization of services. *Applied Computing and Informatics*, 15(2), 94–101. 10.1016/j.aci.2018.05.004

Antéblian, B., Filser, M., & Roederer, C. (2013). L'expérience du consommateur dans le commerce de détail. Une revue de littérature. [French Edition]. *Recherche et Applications en Marketing*, 28(3), 84–113. 10.1177/0767370113497868

Anthopoulos, L. G. (2017). *Understanding Smart Cities : A Tool for Smart Government or an Industrial Trick?* (Vol. 22). Springer International Publishing. 10.1007/978-3-319-57015-0

Anthopoulos, L. G., Pourzolfaghar, Z., Lemmer, K., Siebenlist, T., Niehaves, B., & Nikolaou, I. (2022). Smart cities as hubs : Connect, collect and control city flows. *Cities (London, England)*, 125, 103660. 10.1016/j.cities.2022.103660

Antons, D., & Breidbach, C. F. (2018). Big data, big insights? Advancing service innovation and design with machine learning. *Journal of Service Research*, 21(1), 17–39. 10.1177/1094670517738373

Anvari, A., Ismail, Y., & Hojjati, S. M. H. (2011). A Study On Total Quality Management And Lean Manufacturing: Through Lean Thinking Approach. *World Applied Sciences Journal*, 12(9), 1585–1596.

Anwar, M., & Shah, S. Z. A. (2021). Entrepreneurial orientation and generic competitive strategies for emerging SMEs: Financial and nonfinancial performance perspective. *Journal of Public Affairs*, 21(1), e2125. 10.1002/pa.2125

Apaza-Panca, C. M., Flores Quevedo, L. A., & Reyes, L. M. C. (2024). Green marketing to promote the natural protected area. *Sustainable Technology and Entrepreneurship*, 3(3), 100067. 10.1016/j.stae.2023.100067

Appel, G., Grewal, L., & Hadi, R. (2020). The future of social media in marketing. *J. of the Acad. Mark. Sci. 48*, 79–95. (https://doi.org/)10.1007/s11747-019-00695-1

Appelbaum, S. H., Habashy, S., Malo, J. L., & Shafiq, H. (2012). Back to the future: Revisiting Kotter's 1996 change model. *Journal of Management Development*, 31(8), 764–782. 10.1108/02621711211253231

Arghashi, V. (2022). Shopping with augmented reality: How wow-effect changes the equations! *Electronic Commerce Research and Applications*, 54, 101166. 10.1016/j.elerap.2022.101166

Arghashi, V., & Yuksel, C. A. (2022). Interactivity, Inspiration, and Perceived Usefulness! How retailers' AR-apps improve consumer engagement through flow. *Journal of Retailing and Consumer Services*, 64, 102756. 10.1016/j.jretconser.2021.102756

Aria, M., & Cuccurullo, C. (2017). bibliometrix: An R-tool for comprehensive science mapping analysis. *Journal of Informetrics*, 11(4), 959–975. 10.1016/j.joi.2017.08.007

Ariely, D., & Berns, G. S. (2010). Neuromarketing: The hope and hype of neuroimaging in business. *Nature Reviews. Neuroscience*, 11(4), 284–292. 10.1038/nrn279520197790

Ariely, D., & Silva, J. (2002). Payment method design: Psychological and economic aspects of payments. Center for e-Business MIT. *Paper*, 196, 68–73.

Arnould, E. J., & Price, L. L. (1993). River Magic: Extraordinary Experience and the Extended Service Encounter. *The Journal of Consumer Research*, 20(1), 24. 10.1086/209331

Arnould, E. J., Price, L., & Zinkhan, G. (2002). *Consumers*. McGraw-Hill.

Arshad, S. (2023). *Performance Of Ai Generated Content In Content Marketing*. Talling University of Technology School of Business and Governance.

Atawneh, S. (2019). The Analysis Of Current State Of Agile Software Development. *Journal of Theoretical and Applied Information Technology*, 97(22), 3197–3028.

Atlassian. (2024). *Scrumban: Mastering Two Agile Methodologies*. Atlassian. Https://Www.Atlassian.Com/Agile/Project-Management/Scrumban

Aulia, D. (2022). ENHANCEMENTS IN THE MANAGEMENT OF RELATIONSHIPS WITH CUSTOMERS AS A MEANS OF PRESERVING SALES PERFORMANCE. [JAMB]. *Journal of Applied Management and Business*, 3(1). 10.37802/jamb.v3i1.242

Ayyagari, M. R. (2019). A Framework for Analytical CRM Assessments Challenges and Recommendations. *International Journal of Business and Social Science*, 10(6). Advance online publication. 10.30845/ijbss.v10n6p2

Baabdullah, A. M., Alalwan, A. A., Rana, N. P., Kizgin, H., & Patil, P. (2019). Consumer use of mobile banking (M-Banking) in Saudi Arabia: Towards an integrated model. *International Journal of Information Management*, 44, 38–52. 10.1016/j.ijinfomgt.2018.09.002

Babatunde, S. O., Odejide, O. A., Edunjobi, T. E., & Ogundipe, D. O. (2024). The role of AI in marketing personalization: A theoretical exploration of consumer engagement strategies. *International Journal of Management & Entrepreneurship Research*, 6(3), 936–949. 10.51594/ijmer.v6i3.964

Baboolal-Frank, R. (2021). *ANALYSIS OF AMAZON: CUSTOMER CENTRIC APPROACH, 20*(2).

Babullah, A., Dwivedi, Y., & Williams, M. (2015). *Saudi citizens' perceptions on mobile government (mGov) adoption factors*. AISEL. https://aisel.aisnet.org/ukais2015/8/

Badghish, S., & Soomro, Y. A. (2024). Artificial Intelligence Adoption by SMEs to Achieve Sustainable Business Performance: Application of Technology–Organization–Environment Framework. *Sustainability (Basel)*, 16(5), 1864. 10.3390/su16051864

Badot, O., & Belghiti, S. (2007). *E phygital, nouveau mode de co - creation entre enseignes et consommateurs*.

Bag, S., Gupta, S., Kumar, A., & Sivarajah, U. (2021). An integrated artificial intelligence framework for knowledge creation and B2B marketing rational decision making for improving firm performance. *Industrial Marketing Management*, 92, 178–189. 10.1016/j.indmarman.2020.12.001

Baillette, P., Fallery, B., & Girard, A. (2013). La méthode Delphi pour définir les accords et les controverses: applications à l'innovation dans la traçabilité et dans le e-recrutement. In *18ème Colloque de l'Association Information et Management (AIM)*, 1-22.

Bakardjieva, E., & Kimmel, A. J. (2017). Neuromarketing Research Practices: Attitudes, Ethics, and Behavioral Intentions. *Ethics & Behavior*, 27(3), 179–200. 10.1080/10508422.2016.1162719

Baka, V. (2016). The becoming of user-generated reviews: Looking at the past to understand the future of managing reputation in the travel sector. *Tourism Management*, 53, 148–162. 10.1016/j.tourman.2015.09.004

Bakici, T., Almirall, E., & Wareham, J. (2013). A smart city initiative : The case of Barcelona. *Journal of the Knowledge Economy*, 4(2), 135–148. 10.1007/s13132-012-0084-9

Bakker, I., Van Der Voordt, T., Vink, P., & Et De Boon, J. (2014). *Pleasure, Arousal, Dominance: Mehrabian And Russell Revisited. Current Psychology*. Https://Doi.Org/10.1007/S12144-014-9219-4

Balahur, A., Mihalcea, R., & Montoyo, A. (2014). Computational approaches to subjectivity and sentiment analysis: Present and envisaged methods and applications. *Computer Speech & Language*, 28(1), 1–6. 10.1016/j.csl.2013.09.003

Baldwin, A., Brown, C., & Trinkle, B. (2006). Opportunities for artificial intelligence development in the accounting domain: The case for auditing. *International Journal of Intelligent Systems in Accounting Finance & Management*, 14(3), 77–86. 10.1002/isaf.277

Ballestar, M. T., Martín-Llaguno, M., & Sainz, J. (2022). An artificial intelligence analysis of climate-change influencers' marketing on Twitter. *Psychology and Marketing*, 39(12), 2273–2283. 10.1002/mar.21735

Banik, S., & Et Gao, Y. (2023). Exploring The Hedonic Factors Affecting Customer Experiences In Phygital Retailing. *Journal of Retailing and Consumer Services*, 70, 103147. Https://Doi.Org/10.1016/J.Jretconser.2022.103147. 10.1016/j.jretconser.2022.103147

Bank Al Maghrib. (2023). *Rapport annuel sur la supervision bancaire pour l'exercice 2022*. Bank Al Maghrib.

Bansal, S., & Gupta, M. (2023). Towards Using Artificial Intelligence in Neuromarketing. In *Promoting Consumer Engagement Through Emotional Branding and Sensory Marketing* (pp. 16–23). IGI Global., 10.4018/978-1-6684-5897-6.ch002

Barari, M., Ross, M., Thaichon, S., & Surachartkumtonkun, J. (2021). A meta-analysis of customer engagement behaviour. *International Journal of Consumer Studies*, 45(4), 457–477. 10.1111/ijcs.12609

Barbosa, A. T., Da Silva, C. C., Caetano, R. L., Da Silva, D. P. S., Barbosa, J. V., & Pinto, Z. T. (2022). Agile Methodologies: And Its Applicability In The Marketing AREA. Revista Ibero-Americana De Humanidades. *Ciência & Educação (Bauru)*, 8(3), 1659–1669.

Barhorst, J. B., McLean, G., Shah, E., & Mack, R. (2021). Blending the real world and the virtual world: Exploring the role of flow in augmented reality experiences. *Journal of Business Research*, 122, 423–436. 10.1016/j.jbusres.2020.08.041

Barnes, S., & de Ruyter, K. (2022). Guest editorial: Artificial intelligence as a market-facing technology: getting closer to the consumer through innovation and insight. *European Journal of Marketing*, 56(6), 1585–1589. Advance online publication. 10.1108/EJM-05-2022-979

Barney, J. B. (1991). Firm Resources And Sustained Competitive Advantage. *Journal of Management*, 17(1), 99–120. 10.1177/014920639101700108

Barutçu, S. (2008). *Mobil Pazarlama Güncel Pazarlama Yaklaşımlarından Seçmeler.*

Bashar, A., Wasiq, M., &Nyagadza, B. (2024). Emerging trends in social media marketing: a retrospective review using data mining and bibliometric analysis. *Futur Bus J 10*(23). (https://doi.org/)10.1186/s43093-024-00308-6

Batat, W. (2019). *Experiential Setting Design The New Luxury Experience.* Springer. 10.1007/978-3-030-01671-5

Batat, W. (2022). What Does Phygital Really Mean? A Conceptual Introduction To The Phygital Customer Experience (PH-CX) Framework. *Journal of Strategic Marketing*, 1–24. 10.1080/0965254X.2022.2059775

Bateni, M., Esfandiary, H., Mirrokni, V., & Seddighin, S. (2017, February). *A study of compact reserve pricing languages [Conference session].* Proceedings of the AAAI Conference on Artificial Intelligence, San Francisco, CA, USA.

Batra, P., & Dave, D. M. (2024). Revolutionizing Healthcare Platforms: The Impact of AI on Patient Engagement and Treatment Efficacy. *International Journal of Science and Research (IJSR), 13*(10.21275), 613-624.

Batra, D., Xia, W., & Zhang, M. (2017). Collaboration In Agile Software Development: Concept And Dimensions. *Communications of the Association for Information Systems*, 41(1), 20. 10.17705/1CAIS.04120

Bauer, H., Reichardt, T., Barnes, S., & Neumann, M. (2005). Driving consumer acceptance of mobile marketing: A theoretical framework and empirical study. *Journal of Electronic Commerce Research*, 6.

Bauer, J., & Jannach, D. (2018). Optimal pricing in e-commerce based on sparse and noisy data. *Decision Support Systems*, 106, 53–63. 10.1016/j.dss.2017.12.002

Bayoude, K., Ardchir, S., & Azzouazi, M. (2023). A Predictive Approach Based on Feature Selection to Improve Email Marketing Campaign Success Rate. In: Kacprzyk, J., Ezziyyani, M., Balas, V.E. (eds) *International Conference on Advanced Intelligent Systems for Sustainable Development. AI2SD 2022.* Springer, Cham. (https://doi.org/)10.1007/978-3-031-26384-2_85

Bec, A., Moyle, B., Schaffer, V., & Timms, K. (2021). Virtual reality and mixed reality for second chance tourism. *Tourism Management*, 83, 104256. 10.1016/j.tourman.2020.104256

Beck, M., & Crié, D. (2015). Les Nouvelles Aides À La Vente Et À L'achat: Définition, État De L'art Et Proposition 116 D'une Taxinomie. *Décisions Marketing, 79*, 131-150. Https://Doi.Org/10.7193/Dm.079.131.150

Becker, M., Wiegand, N., & Reinartz, W. J. (2019). Does it pay to be real? Understanding authenticity in TV advertising. *Journal of Marketing*, 83(1), 24–50. 10.1177/0022242918815880

Beiderbeck, D., Frevel, N., von der Gracht, H. A., Schmidt, S. L., & Schweitzer, V. M. (2021). Preparing, conducting, and analyzing Delphi surveys: Cross-disciplinary practices, new directions, and advancements. *MethodsX*, 8, 101401. 10.1016/j.mex.2021.10140134430297

Belanger, F., Hiller, J. S., & Smith, W. J. (2002). Trustworthiness in electronic commerce : The role of privacy, security, and site attributes. *The Journal of Strategic Information Systems*, 11(3-4), 245–270. 10.1016/S0963-8687(02)00018-5

Belghiti, S., Ochs, A., Lemoine, J. F., & Badot, O. (2018). The phygital shopping experience: An attempt at conceptualization and empirical investigation. In *Marketing Transformation: Marketing Practice in an Ever Changing World: Proceedings of the 2017 Academy of Marketing Science (AMS) World Marketing Congress (WMC)* (pp. 61-74). Springer International Publishing.

Belghiti, S., Ochs, A., Lemoine, J.-F., & Et Badot, O. (2018). *The Phygital Shopping Experience: An Attempt At Conceptualization And Empirical Investigation.* Springer. Https://Doi.Org/10.1007/978-3-319-68750-6_18

Belton, I., MacDonald, A., Wright, G., & Hamlin, I. (2019). Improving the practical application of the Delphi method in group-based judgment: A six-step prescription for a well-founded and defensible process. *Technological Forecasting and Social Change*, 147, 72–82. 10.1016/j.techfore.2019.07.002

Benoit, S., Sonja, K., & Andreas, E. (2017). Linking Service Convenience To Satisfaction: Dimensions And Key Moderators. *Journal of Services Marketing*, 31(6), 527–538. 10.1108/JSM-10-2016-0353

Bentalha, B. (2020). Big-Data Et Service Supply Chain Management: Challenges Et Opportunités. *International Journal Of Business And Technology Studies, 1*(3).

Bentalha, B. (2023). Consumer Perception of Robotic Mobile Fulfillment Systems: A Netnographic Case Study of Amazon. In *Innovation, Strategy, and Transformation Frameworks for the Modern Enterprise* (pp. 243-264). IGI Global 10.4018/979-8-3693-0458-7.ch010

Bentalha, B. (2020). Big-Data et Service Supply chain management: Challenges et opportunités. *International Journal of Business and Technology Studies*, 1(3), 1–9.

Bentalha, B., & Hmioui, A. (2021). Smart service supply chain and Just Walk Out technology: a netnographic approach. In *The Proceedings of the International Conference on Smart City Applications* (pp. 223-236). Cham: Springer International Publishing.

Berberović, D., Alić, A., & Činjarević, M. (2022). Virtual Reality in Marketing : Consumer and Retail Perspectives. *Lecture Notes in Networks and Systems, 472 LNNS*, 1093-1102. *Scopus*, 472, 1093–1102. 10.1007/978-3-031-05230-9_129

Bercea Olteanu, M. D. (2015). Neuroethics and responsibility in conducting neuromarketing research. *Neuroethics*, 8(2), 191–202. 10.1007/s12152-014-9227-y

Berea, A. (2022). Predictive Analytics. In Schintler, L. A., & McNeely, C. L. (Eds.), *Encyclopedia of Big Data*. Springer. [DOI: 10.1007/978-3-319-32010-6_170], 10.1007/978-3-319-32010-6_170

Berestetska, O., Iankovets, T., Orozonova, A., Voitovych, S., Parmanasova, A., & Medvedieva, K. (2023). Using Crm Systems for the Development and Implementation of Communication Strategies for Digital Brand Management and Internet Marketing: Eu Experience. *International Journal of Professional Business Review*, 8(4), e01613. 10.26668/businessreview/2023.v8i4.1613

Berger, J., Humphreys, A., Ludwig, S., Moe, W. W., Netzer, O., & Schweidel, D. A. (2019). Uniting the tribes: Using text for marketing insight. *Journal of Marketing*, 84(1), 1–25. 10.1177/0022242919873106

Bernardin, S., & Jeannot, G. (2019). La ville intelligente sans les villes? Interopérabilité, ouvertures et maîtrise des données publiques au sein des administrations municipales. *Reseaux (London)*, 6, 9–37.

Berntzen, L., & Johannessen, M. R. (2016). The Role of Citizen Participation in Municipal Smart City Projects : Lessons Learned from Norway. In Gil-Garcia, J. R., Pardo, T. A., & Nam, T. (Eds.), *Smarter as the New Urban Agenda* (Vol. 11, pp. 299–314). Springer International Publishing. 10.1007/978-3-319-17620-8_16

Berson, A., & Smith, S. J. (2018). Data management challenges in telecommunications. In *Data Warehousing and Data Mining Techniques for Cyber Security* (pp. 219–231). IGI Global.

Bèzes, C. (2019). Quel Smart Retailing En Magasin Pour Quelle Expérience Omnicanal Vécue? [French Edition]. *Recherche et Applications en Marketing*, 34(1), 95–118.. 10.1177/0767370118795420

Bhamu, J., & Singh Sangwan, K. (2014). Lean Manufacturing: Literature Review And Research Issues. *International Journal of Operations & Production Management*, 34(7), 876–940. 10.1108/IJOPM-08-2012-0315

Bhandari, A. (2020). Neuromarketing Trends and Opportunities for Companies. In *Artificial intelligence in information systems research: A systematic literature review and research agenda* (pp. 82–103). IGI Global.

Bhardwaj, S., Rana, G. A., Behl, A., & Gallego de Caceres, S. J. (2023). Exploring the boundaries of Neuromarketing through systematic investigation. *Journal of Business Research*, 154, 113371. 10.1016/j.jbusres.2022.113371

Bhatt, V. K. (2021). Assessing the significance and impact of artificial intelligence and machine learning in placement of advertisements [Conference session]. *2021 IEEE International Conference on Technology Management, Operations and Decisions (ICTMOD)*, (pp. 1–6). IEEE.

Bhayani, S., & Vachhani, N. V. (2014). Internet Marketing Vs Traditional Marketing: A Comparative Analysis. *FIIB Business Review*, 3(3), 53–63. 10.1177/2455265820140309

Bhowmik, A., Sannigrahi, M., Chowdhury, D., Dwivedi, A. D., & Mukkamala, R. R. (2022). DBNex: Deep Belief Network and Explainable AI based Financial Fraud Detection. *2022 IEEE International Conference on Big Data (Big Data)*, (pp. 3033-3042). IEEE. 10.1109/BigData55660.2022.10020494

Bibri, S. E. (2018). The IoT for smart sustainable cities of the future : An analytical framework for sensor-based big data applications for environmental sustainability. *Sustainable Cities and Society*, 38, 230–253. 10.1016/j.scs.2017.12.034

Bibri, S. E., Alexandre, A., Sharifi, A., & Krogstie, J. (2023). Environmentally sustainable smart cities and their converging AI, IoT, and big data technologies and solutions : An integrated approach to an extensive literature review. *Energy Informatics*, 6(1), 9. 10.1186/s42162-023-00259-237032812

Bilgili, S. S., & Aydin, K. (2019). Marketing Communications and Experiential Marketing in the Context of Augmented Reality. In Grima, S., Özen, E., Boz, H., Spiteri, J., & Thalassinos, E. (Eds.), *Contemporary Issues in Behavioral Finance* (Vol. 101, pp. 153–162). Emerald Publishing Limited. 10.1108/S1569-375920190000101010

Blanco-Gonzalez, A., Cabezon, A., Seco-Gonzalez, A., Conde-Torres, D., Antelo-Riveiro, P., Pineiro, A., & Garcia-Fandino, R. (2023). The role of ai in drug discovery: Challenges, opportunities, and strategies. *Pharmaceuticals (Basel, Switzerland)*, 16(6), 891. 10.3390/ph1606089137375838

Blasco-Arcas, L., Lee, H.-H. M., Kastanakis, M. N., Alcañiz, M., & Reyes-Menendez, A. (2022). The role of consumer data in marketing : A research agenda. *Journal of Business Research*, 146, 436–452. 10.1016/j.jbusres.2022.03.054

Boateng, S. L., & Narteh, B. (2016). Online relationship marketing and affective customer commitment–The mediating role of trust. *Journal of Financial Services Marketing*, 21(2), 127–140. 10.1057/fsm.2016.5

Bobillier Chaumon, M.-É. (2021). Technologies émergentes et transformations digitales de l'activité : Enjeux pour l'activité et la santé au travail. *Psychologie du Travail et des Organisations*, 27(1), 17–32. 10.1016/j.pto.2021.01.002

Bolton, , R., Gustafsson, A., McColl-Kennedy, J., Sirianni, N., & Tse, D. (2014). Small details that make big differences: A radical approach to consumption experience as a firm's differentiating strategy. *Journal of Service Management*, 25(2), 253–274. 10.1108/JOSM-01-2014-0034

Bonfanti, A., Vigolo, V., Vannucci, V., & Et Brunetti, F. (2023). Creating Memorable Shopping Experiences To Meet Phygital Customers' Needs : Evidence From Sporting Goods Stores. *International Journal of Retail & Distribution Management*, 51(13), 81–100.. 10.1108/IJRDM-12-2021-0588

Bonnin, G. (2003). La Mobilité Du Consommateur En Magasin : Une Etude Exploratoire De L'influence De L'aménagement Spatial Sur Les Stratégies D'appropriation Des Espaces De Grande Distribution. [French Edition]. *Recherche et Applications en Marketing*, 18(3), 7–29.. 10.1177/076737010301800302

Boone, H. N., & Boone, D. A. (2012). Analyzing Likert Data. *Journal of Extension*, 50(2). 10.34068/joe.50.02.48

Borghini, S., Diamond, N., Kozinets, R. V., McGrath, M. A., Muñiz, A. M.Jr, & Sherry, J. F.Jr. (2009). Why are themed brandstores so powerful? Retail brand ideology at American Girl Place. *Journal of Retailing*, 85(3), 363–375. 10.1016/j.jretai.2009.05.003

Borgi, T., Zoghlami, N., & Abed, M. (2017, January). Big data for transport and logistics: A review. In *2017 International Conference on Advanced Systems and Electric Technologies (IC_ASET)* (pp. 44-49). IEEE. 10.1109/ASET.2017.7983742

Bouhtati, N. alla, L., & bentalha, B. (2023). Marketing Big Data Analytics and Customer Relationship Management: A Fuzzy Approach. In *Integrating Intelligence and Sustainability in Supply Chains* (pp. 75-86). DOI: . IGI Global.10.4018/979-8-3693-0225-5.ch004

Bouhtati, N., Alla, L., & Bentalha, B. (2023). Marketing Big Data Analytics and Customer Relationship Management : A Fuzzy Approach. In *Integrating Intelligence and Sustainability in Supply Chains* (p. 75-86). IGI Global. https://www.igi-global.com/chapter/marketing-big-data-analytics-and-customer-relationship-management/331980

Bouhtati, N., Alla, L., & Bentalha, B. (2023). Marketing Big Data Analytics and Customer Relationship Management: A Fuzzy Approach. In *Integrating Intelligence and Sustainability in Supply Chains* (pp. 75–86). IGI Global. https://www.igi-global.com/chapter/marketing-big-data-analytics-and-customer-relationship-management/331980

Bouhtati, N., Kamal, M., & Alla, L. (2023). Big Data and the Effectiveness of Tourism Marketing : A Prospective Review of the Literature. *Artificial Intelligence and Smart Environment*, 287-292. 10.1007/978-3-031-26254-8_40

Bouhtati, N., Kamal, M., & Alla, L. (2022). Big Data and the Effectiveness of Tourism Marketing: A Prospective Review of the Literature. In *The International Conference on Artificial Intelligence and Smart Environment* (pp. 287-292). Cham: Springer International Publishing.

Bourany, T. (2018). Les 5V du big data. *Regards croisés sur l'économie, 23*(2), 27-31.

Bourbon, I., & Hollet-Haudebert, S. (2009). Pourquoi Contribuer A Des Bases De Connaissances? Une Exploration Des Facteurs Explicatifs A La Lumière Du Modèle UTAUT. *Systèmes d'Information Et Management*, 14(1), 9–36. 10.3917/sim.091.0009

Bowden, J. L. H. (2009). The process of customer engagement: A conceptual framework. *Journal of Marketing Theory and Practice*, 17(1), 63–74. 10.2753/MTP1069-6679170105

Braga, S., Zacarias, S. L., & Champoski, L. H. (2022). *APLICACIONES MÓVILES Y GOBERNANZA DIGITAL EN BRASIL: ESTUDIO DE CASO DEL "PROYECTO PIÁ", DEL ESTADO DE PARANÁ. 38.*

Brakus, J. J., Schmitt, B. H., & Zarantonello, L. (2009). Brand experience: What is it? How is it measured? Does it affect loyalty? *Journal of Marketing*, 73(3), 52–68. 10.1509/jmkg.73.3.052

Brewis, C., Dibb, S., & Meadows, M. (2023). Leveraging big data for strategic marketing : A dynamic capabilities model for incumbent firms. *Technological Forecasting and Social Change*, 190, 122402. 10.1016/j.techfore.2023.122402

Brynjolfsson, E. & Smith, M. (2000). Frictionless Commerce? A Comparison Of Internet And Conventional Retailers. *Management Science, 46*(4), 563–85.

Brynjolfsson, E., & McAfee, A. (2014). *The second machine age: Work, progress, and prosperity in a time of brilliant technologies*. WW Norton & Company.

Brynjolfsson, E., & Mcafee, A. (2017). The-Business-of-Artificial-Intelligence. *Harvard Business Review*, 7, 3–11.

Buckle, J. L., Dwyer, S. C., & Jackson, M. (2010). Qualitative bereavement research: Incongruity between the perspectives of participants and research ethics boards. *International Journal of Social Research Methodology*, 13(2), 111–125. 10.1080/13645570902767918

Buhalis, D., & Moldavska, I. (2022). Voice assistants in hospitality : Using artificial intelligence for customer service. *Journal of Hospitality and Tourism Technology, 13*(3), 386-403. *Scopus*. Advance online publication. 10.1108/JHTT-03-2021-0104

Burukina, O., Karpova, S., & Koro, N. (2019). Ethical Problems of Introducing Artificial Intelligence into the Contemporary Society. T. Ahram, W. Karwowski, and R. Taiar (eds) *Human Systems Engineering and Design*. Cham: Springer International Publishing (Advances in Intelligent Systems and Computing). 10.1007/978-3-030-02053-8_98

Bustamante, J. C., & Et Rubio, N. (2017). Measuring Customer Experience In Physical Retail Environments. *Journal of Service Management*, 28(5), 884–913. 10.1108/JOSM-06-2016-0142

Cabigiosu, A. (2020). *Digitalisation dans l'industrie de la mode de luxe; Springer Science and Business Media LLC*. Allemagne.

Cadden, T., Weerawardena, J., Cao, G., Duan, Y., & McIvor, R. (2023). Examining the role of big data and marketing analytics in SMEs innovation and competitive advantage: A knowledge integration perspective. *Journal of Business Research*, 168, 114225. 10.1016/j.jbusres.2023.114225

Campbell, C., Sands, S., Ferraro, C., Tsao, H.-Y. (Jody), & Mavrommatis, A. (2020). From data to action : How marketers can leverage AI. *ARTIFICIAL INTELLIGENCE AND MACHINE LEARNING, 63*(2), 227-243. 10.1016/j.bushor.2019.12.002

Capponi, G., Corrocher, N., & Zirulia, L. (2021). Personalized pricing for customer retention: Theory and evidence from mobile communication. *Telecommunications Policy*, 45(1), 102069. 10.1016/j.telpol.2020.102069

Caracciolo, F., Furno, M., D'Amico, M., Califano, G., & Di Vita, G. (2022). Variety seeking behavior in the wine domain: A consumers segmentation using big data. *Food Quality and Preference*, 97, 104481. 10.1016/j.foodqual.2021.104481

Cardoso, L., Chen, M.-M., Araújo, A., de Almeida, G. G. F., Dias, F., & Moutinho, L. (2022). Accessing Neuromarketing Scientific Performance: Research Gaps and Emerging Topics. *Behavioral Sciences (Basel, Switzerland)*, 12(2), 55. 10.3390/bs1202005535200306

Carmo, I. S. D., Marques, S., & Dias, Á. (2022). The influence of experiential marketing on customer satisfaction and loyalty. *Journal of Promotion Management*, 28(7), 994–1018. 10.1080/10496491.2022.2054903

Carter, L., & Bélanger, F. (2005). The utilization of e-government services : Citizen trust, innovation and acceptance factors*. *Information Systems Journal*, 15(1), 5–25. 10.1111/j.1365-2575.2005.00183.x

Carteron, V. (2013). Expérience Client Et Distribution « Omnicanale ». *L'Expansion Management Review, 149*(2), 25. Https://Doi.Org/10.3917/Emr.149.0025

Carù, A. (2008). Opérations D'appropriation Et Ingrédients De L'offre Facilitant L'accès Au Plaisir Dans L'expérience De Consommation Virtuelle. *Journal of Chemical Information and Modeling*, 53(9), 287. Https://Doi.Org/10.1017/CBO9781107415324.004

Carù, A., & Et Cova, B. (2003). Revisiting Consumption Experience: A More Humble But Complete View Of The Concept. *Marketing Theory*, 3(2), 267–286. Https://Doi.Org/10.1177/14705931030032004. 10.1177/14705931030032004

Carù, A., & Et Cova, B. (2015). Expériences De Consommation Et Marketing Expérientiel. *Revue Francaise De Gestion*, 253(8), 353–367. Https://Doi.Org/10.3166/RFG.162.99-115. 10.3166/RFG.162.99-115

Casteel, A., & Bridier, N. L. (2021). Describing populations and samples in doctoral student research. *International Journal of Doctoral Studies*, 16(1), 339–362. 10.28945/4766

Castro, S. L. C., Del Pozo Durango Rodrigo Humberto, V., Paúl, A. C., & Estefanía, A. T. P. (2023). Impact of Artificial Intelligence on Market Behavior Analysis: A Comprehensive Approach to Marketing. *Remittances Review, 8*(4).

Castro, S. L. C., Humberto, D. P. D. R., Paúl, V. A. C., & Estefanía, A. T. P. (2023). Impact of Artificial Intelligence on Market Behavior Analysis : A Comprehensive Approach to Marketing. *Remittances Review, 8*(4). https://remittancesreview.com/menu-script/index.php/remittances/article/view/742

Chablo, A. (1994). Potential Applications of Artificial Intelligence in Telecommunications. *Technovation*, 14(7), 431–435. 10.1016/0166-4972(94)90001-9

Chaffey, D., & Ellis-Chadwick, F. (2019). *Digital Marketing* (7th ed.).

Chaffey, D., & Patron, M. (2012). From web analytics to digital marketing optimization: Increasing the commercial value of digital analytics. *Journal of Direct, Data and Digital Marketing Practice*, 14(1), 30–45. 10.1057/dddmp.2012.20

Chaikovska, M., Järvis, M., Zaiachkovska, H., Tchon, L., Bortnik, N., & Bannikova, K. (2022). DIGITAL-MARKETING AS A NOVEL TOOL FOR GOODS AND SERVICES PROMOTION ON SOCIAL MEDIA: CONTEMPORARY TRENDS AND DEVELOPMENT DIRECTIONS. *Financial and Credit Activity: Problems of Theory and Practice*, 4(45), 355–364. 10.55643/fcaptp.4.45.2022.3836

Chalmers, J., & Armour, M. (2019). The Delphi Technique. In Liamputtong, P. (Ed.), *Handbook of Research Methods in Health Social Sciences* (pp. 715–735). Springer Singapore. 10.1007/978-981-10-5251-4_99

Chanda, R., & Prabhu, S. (2023). *Secured Framework for Banking Chatbots using AI, ML and NLP*. In 2023 7th International Conference on Intelligent Computing and Control Systems (ICICCS). Madurai, India. 10.1109/ICICCS56967.2023.10142289

Chaney, D., Lunardo, R., & Mencarelli, R. (2018). Consumption experience: Past, present and future. *Qualitative Market Research*, 21(4), 402–420. 10.1108/QMR-04-2018-0042

Chang, Y. W., Huang, M. H., & Lin, C. W. (2015). Evolution of research subjects in library and information science based on keyword, bibliographical coupling, and co-citation analyses. *Scientometrics*, 105(3), 2071–2087. 10.1007/s11192-015-1762-8

Chan-Olmsted, S. (2019). A Review of Artificial Intelligence Adoptions in the Media Industry. *International Journal on Media Management*, 21, 1–23. 10.1080/14241277.2019.1590949

Chan-Olmsted, S. M. (2019). A Review of Artificial Intelligence Adoptions in the Media Industry. *JMM International Journal on Media Management*, 21(3–4), 193–215. 10.1080/14241277.2019.1695619

Charles, V., Rana, N. P., Pappas, I. O., Kamphaug, M., Siau, K., & Engø-Monsen, K. (2023). The Next 'Deep' Thing in X to Z Marketing: An Artificial Intelligence-Driven Approach. *Information Systems Frontiers*, 1–6.

Chatterjee, S., Ghosh, S. K., Chaudhuri, R., & Nguyen, B. (2019). Are CRM systems ready for AI integration? A conceptual framework of organizational readiness for effective AI-CRM integration. *The Bottom Line (New York, N.Y.)*, 32(2), 144–157. 10.1108/BL-02-2019-0069

Chaudhuri, S., Dayal, U., & Narasayya, V. (2011). An overview of business intelligence technology. *Communications of the ACM*, 54(8), 88–98. 10.1145/1978542.1978562

Chen, A., & Peng, N. (2023). Antecedents to Consumers' Green Hotel Stay Purchase Behavior during the COVID-19 Pandemic: The influence of green consumption value, emotional ambivalence, and consumers' perceptions. *Tourism Management Perspectives*, 47, 101107. 10.1016/j.tmp.2023.10110737065777

Chen, G., Xie, P., Dong, J., & Wang, T. (2019). Understanding programmatic creative: The role of AI. *Journal of Advertising*, 48(4), 347–355. 10.1080/00913367.2019.1654421

Cheng, C. C. J., & Shiu, E. C. (2023). The relative values of big data analytics versus traditional marketing analytics to firm innovation: An empirical study. *Information & Management*, 60(7), 103839. 10.1016/j.im.2023.103839

Chen, J., Li, Y., & Chen, Z. (2016). Customer churn prediction in telecommunications. *Procedia Computer Science*, 91, 28–37. 10.1016/j.procs.2016.07.322

Chen, L., & Aklikokou, A. K. (2020). Determinants of E-government Adoption : Testing the Mediating Effects of Perceived Usefulness and Perceived Ease of Use. *International Journal of Public Administration*, 43(10), 850–865. 10.1080/01900692.2019.1660989

Chen, S. C., Chou, T. H., Hongsuchon, T., Ruangkanjanases, A., Kittikowit, S., & Lee, T. C. (2022). The mediation effect of marketing activities toward augmented reality: The perspective of extended customer experience. *Journal of Hospitality and Tourism Technology*, 13(3), 461–480. 10.1108/JHTT-03-2021-0093

Cherkaoui, A. (2016). La Finance Islamique au Maroc: L'Alternative Ethique. *Finance and Finance Internationale*, 442(5257), 1-19.10.34874/IMIST.PRSM/ffi-v02.4401

Chevalier, J., & Xue, H. (2008). Why does credit card debt make people happy? The effects of affective forecasting on credit card use. *JMR, Journal of Marketing Research*, 45(1), 105–114.

Chi, H., Vu, T.-V., Nguyen, H. V., & Truong, T. (2023). How financial and non–financial rewards moderate the relationships between transformational leadership, job satisfaction, and job performance. *Cogent Business & Management*, 10(1), 2173850. Advance online publication. 10.1080/23311975.2023.2173850

Chin, W. (1998). The Partial Least Squares Approach to Structural Equation Modeling. *Modern Methods for Business Research, 8.*

Choi, J. A., & Lim, K. (2020). Identifying machine learning techniques for classification of target advertising. *ICT Express*, 6(3), 175–180. 10.1016/j.icte.2020.04 012

Choi, J.-C., & Song, C. (2020). Factors explaining why some citizens engage in E-participation, while others do not. *Government Information Quarterly*, 37(4), 101524. 10.1016/j.giq.2020.101524

Chou, S.-F., Horng, J.-S., Liu, C.-H., Yu, T.-Y., & Kuo, Y.-T. (2022). Identifying the critical factors for sustainable marketing in the catering: The influence of big data applications, marketing innovation, and technology acceptance model factors. *Journal of Hospitality and Tourism Management*, 51, 11–21. 10.1016/j.jhtm.2022.02.010

Christian, I., Anene, J., Ewuzie, C., & Iloka, C. (2023). Influence Of Artificial Intelligence (AI) On Customer Experience And Loyalty: Mediating Role Of Personalization. *Shu Ju Cai Ji Yu Chu Li/Journal of Data Acquisition and Processing*, 38, 1936–1960. https://doi.org/10.5281/zenodo.98549423

Chui, M., Henke, N., & Miremadi, M. (2018). Most of AI's business uses will be in two areas. *Harvard Business Review*, 3–7. https://hbr.org/2018/07/most-of-ais-business-uses-will-be-in-two-areas

Chung, J., Shin, D. H., & Lee, S. Y. (2017). A framework for customer experience design in a phygital retail environment. *Journal of Business Research*, 101, 114–123.

Coca Cola Company. (2019). *Building A Growth Culture At Coke Includes Empowering All Employees To Drive Company's Innovation Agenda*. Coca Cola Company. Https://Www.Coca-Colacompany.Com/Media-Center/Growth-Culture-At-Coke-Empowers-Employees

Cocchia, A. (2014a). Smart and Digital City : A Systematic Literature Review. In Dameri, R. P., & Rosenthal-Sabroux, C. (Eds.), *Smart City* (pp. 13–43). Springer International Publishing. 10.1007/978-3-319-06160-3_2

Coffin, J. (2022). Asking questions of AI advertising: A maieutic approach. *Journal of Advertising*, 51(5), 608–623. 10.1080/00913367.2022.2111728

Cohen, S. (2021). The basics of machine learning: strategies and techniques. In *Artificial intelligence and deep learning in pathology* (pp. 13–40). Elsevier. 10.1016/B978-0-323-67538-3.00002-6

Colicev, A., Kumar, A., & O'Connor, P. (2019). Modeling the relationship between firm and user generated content and the stages of the marketing funnel. *International Journal of Research in Marketing*, 36(1), 100–116. 10.1016/j.ijresmar.2018.09.005

Collin-Lachaud, I., & Vanheems, R. (2016). Navigating between real and virtual spaces : An exploration of the hybrid shopping experience. [English Edition]. *Recherche et Applications en Marketing*, 31(2), 40–58. 10.1177/2051570716644145

Collins, C., Dennehy, D., Conboy, K., & Mikalef, P. (2021). Artificial intelligence in information systems research: A systematic literature review and research agenda. *International Journal of Information Management*, 60, 102383. 10.1016/j.ijinfomgt.2021.102383

Constantiou, I. D., & Mahnke, V. (2010). Consumer Behaviour and Mobile TV Services: Do Men Differ from Women in Their Adoption Intentions? *Journal of Electronic Commerce Research*, 11(2).

Cosic, D. (2016). Neuromarketing in Market Research. *Interdisciplinary Description of Complex Systems*, 14(2), 139–147. 10.7906/indecs.14.2.3

Cowan, K., & Ketron, S. (2019). Prioritizing marketing research in virtual reality : Development of an immersion/fantasy typology. *European Journal of Marketing, 53*(8), 1585-1611. *Scopus*. 10.1108/EJM-10-2017-0733

Crawford, K., Whittaker, M., Elish, M. C., Barocas, S., Plasek, A., & Ferryman, K. (2016). The AI now report. *The Social and Economic Implications of Artificial Intelligence Technologies in the Near-Term, 2*.

Cristescu, M. P., Mara, D. A., Culda, L. C., Neri anu, R. A., Bâra, A., & Oprea, S.-V. (2023). The Impact of Data Science Solutions on the Company Turnover. *Information (Basel)*, 14(10), 573. 10.3390/info14100573

Cruz, C. M. L., Medeiros, J. F. D., Hermes, L. C. R., Marcon, A., & Marcon, É. (2016). Neuromarketing and the advances in the consumer behaviour studies: A systematic review of the literature. *International Journal of Business and Globalisation*, 17(3), 330. 10.1504/IJBG.2016.078842

Csikszentmihalyi, M. (2014). Flow And The Foundations Of Positive Psychology. In *Flow And The Foundations Of Positive Psychology*. Springer. Https://Doi.Org/10.1007/978-94-017-9088-8

Csikszentmihalyi, M. (1996). *Flow And The Psychology Of Discovery And Invention*. Harper Collins.

Cui, H. (2023). RETRACTION: Construction and Development of Modern Brand Marketing Management Mode Based on Artificial Intelligence. *Journal of Sensors*, 2023, 1. 10.1155/2023/9758414

Daassi, M., & Debbabi, S. (2021). Intention to reuse AR-based apps: The combined role of the sense of immersion, product presence and perceived realism. *Information & Management*, 58(4), 103453. 10.1016/j.im.2021.103453

Dagilienė, L., & Klovienė, L. (2019). Motivation to use big data and big data analytics in external auditing. *Managerial Auditing Journal*, 34(7), 750–782. 10.1108/MAJ-01-2018-1773

Dahiya, M. (2017). A Tool of Conversation: Chatbot. [IJCSE]. *International Journal on Computer Science and Engineering*, 5(5). https://www.ijcseonline.org/pub_paper/27-IJCSE-02149.pdf

Dalenberg, D. J. (2018). Preventing discrimination in the automated targeting of job advertisements. *Computer Law & Security Report*, 34(3), 615–627. 10.1016/j.clsr.2017.11.009

Dameri, R. P. (2013). Searching for smart city definition : A comprehensive proposal. *International Journal of Computers and Technology*, 11(5), 2544–2551. 10.24297/ijct.v11i5.1142

Dash, G., Kiefer, K., & Paul, J. (2021). Marketing-to-Millennials : Marketing 4.0, customer satisfaction and purchase intention. *Journal of Business Research*, 122, 608–620. 10.1016/j.jbusres.2020.10.016

Daugherty, T., & Hoffman, E. (2017). Neuromarketing: Understanding the Application of Neuroscientific Methods Within Marketing Research. In Thomas, A. R., (Eds.), *Ethics and Neuromarketing* (pp. 5–30). Springer International Publishing. 10.1007/978-3-319-45609-6_2

Davenport, T. H., & Harris, J. G. (2006, January 1). Competing on Analytics. *Harvard Business Review*. https://hbr.org/2006/01/competing-on-analytics

Davenport, T. H., and Bean, R. (2018). *Big Companies Are Embracing Analytics, But Most Still Don't Have a Data-Driven Culture.*

Davenport, T. (2018). *The AI Advantage: How to put the artificial intelligence revolution to work.* MIT Press. 10.7551/mitpress/11781.001.0001

Davenport, T. H., & Ronanki, R. (2018). Artificial intelligence for the real world. *Harvard Business Review*, 96(1), 108–116.

Davenport, T. H., & Ronanki, R. (2018). *Artificial Intelligence for the Real World. Harvard Business Review.* HBR.

Davenport, T., Guha, A., Grewal, D., & Bressgott, T. (2020). How artificial intelligence will change the future of marketing. *Journal of the Academy of Marketing Science*, 48(2), 24–42. 10.1007/s11747-019-00696-0

David, B., Chalon, R., & Zhang, X. (2023). Virtual Assistants (Chatbots) as Help to Teachers in Collaborative Learning Environment. In Auer, M. E., Pachatz, W., & Rüütmann, T. (Eds.), *Learning in the Age of Digital and Green Transition. ICL 2022. Lecture Notes in Networks and Systems* (Vol. 633). Springer. 10.1007/978-3-031-26876-2_13

Davis, F. (1993). User Acceptance Of Information Technology: System Characteristics, User Perceptions And Behavioral Impacts. *International Journal of Man-Machine Studies*, 38(3), 475–487. Https://Doi.Org/10.1006/Imms.1993.1022. 10.1006/imms.1993.1022

Davis, F. D. (1989). Perceived Usefulness, Perceived Ease of Use, and User Acceptance of Information Technology. *Management Information Systems Quarterly*, 13(3), 319. 10.2307/249008

Davis, F. D. (1989). Perceived Usefulness, Perceived Ease Of Use, And User Acceptance Of Information Technology. MIS Quarterly: Management. *Information Systems*, 13(3), 319–339. Https://Doi.Org/10.2307/249008

Dawe, K. (2015). Best practice in business-to-business email. *J Direct Data Digit Mark Pract 16*, 242–247. (https://doi .org/)10.1057/dddmp.2015.21

Day, G. (2011). Closing the Marketing Capabilities Gap. *Journal of Marketing*, 75(4), 183–195. 10.1509/jmkg.75.4.183

De Bellis, E., & Johar, G. V. (2020). Autonomous shopping systems: Identifying and overcoming barriers to consumer adoption. *Journal of Retailing*, 96(1), 74–87. 10.1016/j.jretai.2019.12.004

De Bruyn, A., Viswanathan, V., Beh, Y. S., Brock, J. K. U., & von Wangenheim, F. (2020). Artificial intelligence and marketing: Pitfalls and opportunities. *Journal of Interactive Marketing*, 51, 91–105. 10.1016/j.intmar.2020.04.007

De Loë, R. C., Melnychuk, N., Murray, D., & Plummer, R. (2016). Advancing the state of policy Delphi practice: A systematic review evaluating methodological evolution, innovation, and opportunities. *Technological Forecasting and Social Change*, 104, 78–88. 10.1016/j.techfore.2015.12.009

De Mauro, A., Sestino, A., & Bacconi, A. (2022). Machine learning and artificial intelligence use in marketing : A general taxonomy. *Italian Journal of Marketing*, 2022(4), 439–457. 10.1007/s43039-022-00057-w

Dekimpe, M. G. (2020). Retailing and retailing research in the age of big data analytics. *International Journal of Research in Marketing*, 37(1), 3–14. 10.1016/j.ijresmar.2019.09.001

Deligiannis, A., Argyriou, C., & Kourtesis, D. (2020). Predicting the optimal date and time to send personalized marketing messages to repeat buyers. *International Journal of Advanced Computer Science and Applications*, 11(4). Advance online publication. 10.14569/IJACSA.2020.0110413

Del-Real, C., Ward, C., & Sartipi, M. (2023). What do people want in a smart city? Exploring the stakeholders' opinions, priorities and perceived barriers in a medium-sized city in the United States. *International Journal of Urban Sciences, 27*(sup1), 50-74. 10.1080/12265934.2021.1968939

Demir, F. (2022). Artificial Intelligence. In *Innovation in the Public Sector. Public Administration and Information Technology* (Vol. 39). Springer. 10.1007/978-3-031-11331-4_4

Demraoui, L., Eddamiri, S., & Hachad, L. (2022). Digital transformation and costumers services in emerging countries: Loan prediction modeling in modern banking transactions. In *AI and IoT for sustainable development in emerging countries: Challenges and opportunities* (pp. 627–642). Springer International Publishing. 10.1007/978-3-030-90618-4_32

Deng, Z., Lu, Y., Wei, K. K., & Zhang, J. (2019). Understanding customer satisfaction and loyalty: An empirical study of mobile instant messages in China. *International Journal of Information Management*, 44, 27–36. 10.1016/j.ijinfomgt.2018.11.002

Denning, S. (2019). How Amazon Became Agile. *Forbes.* Https://Www.Forbes.Com/Sites/Stevedenning/2019/06/02/ How-Amazon-Became-Agile/?Sh=495af40031aa

Deshmukh, S. G., Upadhye, N., & Garg, S. (2010). Lean Manufacturing For Sustainable Development. *Glob. Bus. Manag. Res. Int. J*, 2(1), 125.

Desplebin, O., Lux, G., Petit, N. (2018). L'évolution de la comptabilité, du contrôle, de l'audit et de leurs métiers au prisme de la Blockchain: une réflexion prospective. *Revue management et avenir, 103*(5), 137-157.

Desplebin, O., Lux, G., & Petit, N. (2021). To be or not to be: Blockchain and the future of accounting and auditing. *Accounting Perspectives*, 20(4), 743–769. 10.1111/1911-3838.12265

Devang, Chintan, Gunjan, & Krupa. (2019). *Applications of Artificial Intelligence in Marketing*. 10.35219/eai158404094

Devarajan, Y. (2018). A study of robotic process automation use cases today for tomorrow's business. *International Journal of Computers and Technology*, 5(6), 12–18.

DeVellis, R. F. (2016). *Scale Development: Theory and Applications*. Sage.

Dhall, D., Kaur, R., & Juneja, M. (2020). Machine learning: a review of the algorithms and its applications. *Proceedings of ICRIC 2019: Recent innovations in computing*, (pp. 47-63). Springer. 10.1007/978-3-030-29407-6_5

Di Vaio, A., Palladino, R., Hassan, R., & Escobar, O. (2020). Artificial intelligence and business models in the sustainable development goals perspective: A systematic literature review. *Journal of Business Research*, 121, 283–314. 10.1016/j.jbusres.2020.08.019

Diallo, M., Fall, A. K., Diallo, I., Diédhiou, I., Ba, P. S., Diagne, M., Ndiaye, B., Ndiaye, A. R., Niang, A., & Gning, S. B. (2010). Dermatomyosites et polymyosites : 21 cas au Sénégal. *Médecine Tropicale*, 70(2), 166.20486354

Dinev, T., & Hart, P. (2006). Privacy concerns and levels of information exchange: An empirical investigation of intended e-services use. *E-Service*, 4(3), 25–60. 10.2979/esj.2006.4.3.25

Dirican, C. (2015). The Impacts of Robotics, Artificial Intelligence On Business and Economics. *Procedia: Social and Behavioral Sciences*, 195, 564–573. 10.1016/j.sbspro.2015.06.134

Doborjeh, Z., Hemmington, N., Doborjeh, M., & Kasabov, N. (2022). Artificial intelligence: A systematic review of methods and applications in hospitality and tourism. *International Journal of Contemporary Hospitality Management*, 34(3), 1154–1176. 10.1108/IJCHM-06-2021-0767

Dolbec, P. Y., & Chebat, J. C. (2013). The impact of a flagship vs. a brand store on brand attitude, brand attachment and brand equity. *Journal of Retailing*, 89(4), 460–466. 10.1016/j.jretai.2013.06.003

Dolega, L., Rowe, F., & Branagan, E. (2021). Going digital? The impact of social media marketing on retail website traffic, orders and sales. *Journal of Retailing and Consumer Services*, 60, 60. 10.1016/j.jretconser.2021.102501

Doneda, D., & Almeida, V. A. F. (2016, July-August). What Is Algorithm Governance? *IEEE Internet Computing*, 20(4), 60–63. 10.1109/MIC.2016.79

Donepudi, P. K. (2017). Machine learning and artificial intelligence in banking. *Engineering International*, 5(2), 83–86. 10.18034/ei.v5i2.490

Donner, J., & Tellez, C. A. (2008). Mobile banking and economic development: Linking adoption, impact, and use. *Asian Journal of Communication*, 18(4), 318–332. 10.1080/01292980802344190

Donthu, N., Kumar, S., Mukherjee, D., Pandey, N., & Lim, W. M. (2021). How to conduct a bibliometric analysis : An overview and guidelines. *Journal of Business Research*, 133, 285–296. 10.1016/j.jbusres.2021.04.070

Dos Santos, M. A. (Ed.). (2017). *Advances in Business Strategy and Competitive Advantage*. Applying Neuroscience to Business Practice. IGI Global. 10.4018/978-1-5225-1028-4

Dresner, H. (2020). *Wisdom of crowds business intelligence market study report* (Survey 2020 Edition; p. 183). Dresner Advisory Services. https://www.pyramidanalytics.com/docs/default-source/downloads/wisdom_of_crowds-__business_intelligence_market_study_report__-_licensed_to_pyramid_analytics_-_-_2020_dresner_advisory_services.pdf?sfvrsn=cd68f8c9_0

Du, G., & Lin, Y. (2022). Brand connection and entry in the shopping mall ecological chain: Evidence from consumer behavior big data analysis based on two-sided markets. *Journal of Cleaner Production*, 364, 132663. 10.1016/j.jclepro.2022.132663

Du, J., Joachimsthaler, E., Füller, J., & Hofacker, C. (2017). Amazon Go: A glimpse into the future of retail grocery shopping? *International Journal of Retail & Distribution Management*, 45(11/12), 1204–1213.

Duka, D. (2013, May). Adoption Of Agile Methodology In Software Development. In *2013 36th International Convention On Information And Communication Technology, Electronics And Microelectronics (MIPRO)* (Pp. 426-430). IEEE.

Duque-Hurtado, P. (2020a). *Neuromarketing: Its current status and research perspectives*. Estudios Gerenciales. 10.18046/j.estger.2020.157.3890

Durmaz, Y., & Efendioglu, I. H. (2016). Travel From Traditional Marketing To Digital Marketing. *Global Journal of Management and Business Research*, 16(2), 34–40. 10.34257/GJMBREVOL22IS2PG35

Du, S., & Xie, C. (2021). Paradoxes of artificial intelligence in consumer markets: Ethical challenges and opportunities. *Journal of Business Research*, 129, 961–974. 10.1016/j.jbusres.2020.08.024

Dwivedi, D. N., Mahanty, G., & Pathak, Y. K. (2023). AI Applications for Financial Risk Management. In M. Irfan, M. Elmogy, M. Shabri Abd. Majid, & S. El-Sappagh (Eds.), *The Impact of AI Innovation on Financial Sectors in the Era of Industry 5.0* (pp. 17-31). IGI Global. https://doi.org/10.4018/979-8-3693-0082-4.ch002

Dwivedi, Y. K., & Wang, Y. (2022). Guest editorial: Artificial intelligence for B2B marketing: Challenges and opportunities. In (Vol. 105, pp. 109–113). Elsevier. 10.1016/j.indmarman.2022.06.001

Dwivedi, Y.K., Ismagilova, E., & Sarker, P. (2023). A Meta-Analytic Structural Equation Model for Understanding Social Commerce Adoption. *Inf Syst Front 25*, 1421–1437. (https://doi.org/)10.1007/s10796-021-10172-2

Dwivedi, D. N. (2024). The Use of Artificial Intelligence in Supply Chain Management and Logistics. In Sharma, D., Bhardwaj, B., & Dhiman, M. (Eds.), *Leveraging AI and Emotional Intelligence in Contemporary Business Organizations* (pp. 306–313). IGI Global. 10.4018/979-8-3693-1902-4.ch018

Dwivedi, D. N., & Mahanty, G. (2024). AI-Powered Employee Experience: Strategies and Best Practices. In Rafiq, M., Farrukh, M., Mushtaq, R., & Dastane, O. (Eds.), *Exploring the Intersection of AI and Human Resources Management* (pp. 166–181). IGI Global. 10.4018/979-8-3693-0039-8.ch009

Dwivedi, D. N., Mahanty, G., & Vemareddy, A. (2022). How Responsible Is AI?: Identification of Key Public Concerns Using Sentiment Analysis and Topic Modeling. [IJIRR]. *International Journal of Information Retrieval Research*, 12(1), 1–14. 10.4018/IJIRR.298646

Dzyabura, D., & Hauser, J. R. (2019). Recommending products when consumers learn their preference weights. *Marketing Science*, 38(3), 417–441. 10.1287/mksc.2018.1144

Eid, R., Selim, H., & El-Kassrawy, Y. (2021). Understanding citizen intention to use m-government services : An empirical study in the UAE. *Transforming Government: People. Process and Policy*, 15(4), 463–482.

El Assal, Z., & Rochdane, H. (2023). L'intérêt des citoyens de Casablanca envers l'utilisation des énergies renouvelables dans le contexte de la ville intelligente. *SHS Web of Conferences, 175*, 01036. https://www.shs-conferences.org/articles/shsconf/abs/2023/24/shsconf_mh2s2023_01036/shsconf_mh2s2023_01036.html

El Bakkouri, B., Raki, S., & Belgnaoui, T. (2022). The role of chatbots in enhancing customer experience: Literature review. *Procedia Computer Science*, 203, 432–437. 10.1016/j.procs.2022.07.057

El Helou, R., Lee, K. Y., Wu, D. Q., Xie, L., Shakkottai, S., & Subramanian, V. (2023). OpenGridGym: An Open-Source AI-Friendly Toolkit for Distribution Market Simulation. *IEEE Transactions on Smart Grid*, 14(2), 1555–1565. 10.1109/TSG.2022.3213240

El Jaouhari, S. & Lhoussaine, A. (2021). Approche participative en tourisme et gouvernance territoriale, quel apport pour le développement territorial? *Alternatives Managériales Economiques*, 3(2), 257–277.

El Mokretar, L., & Adman, M. (2023). Developing a growth marketing approach to B2B customer retention: Case Algeria. *Marketing Science & Inspirations*, 18(3), 36–46. 10.46286/msi.2023.18.3.4

El Ouidani, R. & Brahim, O. U. L. (2023). L'adoption de l'IA dans le secteur bancaire marocain: entre enjeux économiques et enjeux juridiques. *Journal d'Economie, de Management, d'Environnement et de Droit, 6*(1), 37-56. 10.48398/IMIST .PRSM/jemed-v6i1.41316

Elahi, M., Afolaranmi, S.O., & Martinez Lastra, J.L. (2023). A comprehensive literature review of the applications of AI techniques through the lifecycle of industrial equipment. *Discov Artif Intell 3*(43).(https://doi.org/)10.1007/ s44163-023-00089-x

Elboussadi, A., & Aaouid, B. (2023, January). Modélisation De L'apport Des Parties Prenantes À La Résilience Organisationnelle Des Entreprises. *Revue AME*, 5(1), 472–491.

Elouahabi, T., & Dakkon, M. (2022). La digitalisation bancaire: approche conceptuelle et théorique Cas des banques participatives. *International Journal of Accounting, Finance, Auditing, Management and Economics, 3*(5-1), 199-210.

Emeritus. (2023). *What is Market Research? Definition and Types*. Emeritus. https://emeritus.org/in/learn/what-is-market -research-and-why-is-it-important/)

Engel, R., Fernández, P., Ruiz-Cortés, A., Megahed, A., & Ojeda-Perez, J. (2022). SLA-aware operational efficiency in AI-enabled service chains: Challenges ahead. *Information Systems and e-Business Management*, 20(1), 199–221. 10.1007/s10257-022-00551-w

Enshassi, M., Nathan, R. J., Soekmawati, S., Al-Mulali, U., & Ismail, H. (2024). Potentials of artificial intelligence in digital marketing and financial technology for small and medium enterprises. *IAES International Journal of Artificial Intelligence (IJ-AI), 13*(1), 639. 10.11591/ijai.v13.i1.pp639-647

Erdmann, A., Mas, J. M., & Arilla, R. (2023). Value-based adoption of augmented reality: A study on the influence on online purchase intention in retail. *Journal of Consumer Behaviour*, 22(4), 912–932. 10.1002/cb.1993

Eru, O., Topuz, Y. V., & Ruziye, C. O. P. (2022). The Effect of Augmented Reality Experience on Loyalty and Purchasing Intent: An Application on the Retail Sector. *Sosyoekonomi*, 30(52), 129–155. 10.17233/sosyoekonomi.2022.02.08

Escobar, M. C. (2021, October 21). *Hilton Introduces Tech Enhancements to Improve Guest Experience*. Hospitality Technology. https://hospitalitytech.com/hilton-introduces-tech-enhancements-improve-guest-experience

Ever, D., & Demircioğlu, E. N. (2022). *Yapay Zekâ Teknolojilerinin Kalite Maliyetleri Üzerine Etkisi, Çukurova Üniversitesi Sosyal Bilimler Enstitüsü Dergisi*, 31(1), 59–72.

Ez-Zaidi, A., & Ghandari, Y. (2023). Audit profession and innovation: Emerging practices in the era of digital transformation and their relationship to the environment. In *E3S Web of Conferences, 412, 01010*. EDP Sciences. 10.1051/ e3sconf/202341201010

Fakharchian, S. (2023). Designing a forecasting assistant of the Bitcoin price based on deep learning using market sentiment analysis and multiple feature extraction. *Soft Computing*, 27(24), 18803–18827. 10.1007/s00500-023-09028-5

Fang, J., & Guo, X. (2021). *Design of bank service products based on AI digital human technology*. In *2021 International Conference on Digital Society and Intelligent Systems (DSInS)*, Chengdu, China. 10.1109/DSInS54396.2021.9670620

Fanti, L., Guarascio, D. & Moggi, M. (2022). From Heron of Alexandria to Amazon's Alexa: a stylized history of AI and its impact on business models, organization and work. *J. Ind. Bus. Econ. 49,* 409–440. (https://doi.org/)10.1007/s40812-022-00222-4

Fayon, D. (2018). *Mesure de la maturité numérique des acteurs du secteur bancaire, dans une perspective de transformation digitale* [Doctoral dissertation, Université Paris Saclay (COmUE)].

Fedyk, A., Hodson, J., Khimich, N., & Fedyk, T. (2022). Is artificial intelligence improving the audit process? *Review of Accounting Studies*, 27(3), 938–985. 10.1007/s11142-022-09697-x

Feldman, J., Zhang, D. J., Liu, X., & Zhang, N. (2022). Customer choice models vs. machine learning: Finding optimal product displays on Alibaba. *Operations Research*, 70(1), 309–328. 10.1287/opre.2021.2158

Feng, C. M., Park, A., Pitt, L., Kietzmann, J., & Northey, G. (2021). Artificial intelligence in marketing: A bibliographic perspective. *Australasian Marketing Journal*, 29(3), 252–263. 10.1016/j.ausmj.2020.07.006

Fenwick, M., & Vermeulen, E. (2019). Banking and Regulatory Responses to Fintech Revisited—Building the Sustainable Financial Service 'Ecosystems' of Tomorrow. 10.2139/ssrn.3446273

Ferencz, J., González, J. L., & García, I. O. (2022). *Artificial Intelligence and international trade: Some preliminary implications.* 10.1787/18166873

Fernandes T., Remelhe P. (2016). How to engage customers in co-creation: customers' motivations for collaborative innovation. *J. Strat. Market., 24*.

Fernandes, N., & Lim, J., Raymond, Eddison, T., & Hasan, G. (2023). The Impact of Customer Relationship Management (CRM) on Company Performance in Three Segments (Finance, Marketing and Operations). *Jurnal Minfo Polgan*, 12(1), 1. 10.33395/jmp.v12i1.12431

Fernando, E., Ikhsan, R. B., Condrobimo, A. R., Daniel, H., & Halim, S. K. (2021). Concept model : Analysis of factors on intention and decisions on the use of smart tourism applications. *2021 International Conference on Information Management and Technology (ICIMTech), 1*, 154-158. https://ieeexplore.ieee.org/abstract/document/9534933/

Fernando, E., Sutomo, R., Prabowo, Y. D., Gatc, J., & Winanti, W. (2023). Exploring Customer Relationship Management: Trends, Challenges, and Innovations. *Journal of Information Systems and Informatics*, 5(3), 984–1001. 10.51519/journalisi.v5i3.541

Ferrara, E. (2023). Fairness and bias in artificial intelligence: A brief survey of sources, impacts, and mitigation strategies. *Sci*, 6(1), 3. 10.3390/sci6010003

Filieri, R., Milone, F. L., Paolucci, E., & Raguseo, E. (2023). A big data analysis of COVID-19 impacts on Airbnbs' bookings behavior applying construal level and signaling theories. *International Journal of Hospitality Management*, 111, 103461. 10.1016/j.ijhm.2023.10346136998942

Filipovic, F. (2019). An Application of Artificial Intelligence for Detecting Emotions in Neuromarketing. *2019 International Conference on Artificial Intelligence: Applications and Innovations (IC-AIAI)*. IEEE. 10.1109/IC-AIAI48757.2019.00016

Filser, M. (2002). *Le Marketing De La Production D ' Expérience Statut Et Implications Managériales Théorique.* Research Gate.

Fisher, C. E., Chin, L., & Klitzman, R. (2010). Defining Neuromarketing: Practices and Professional Challenges. *Harvard Review of Psychiatry*, 18(4), 230–237. 10.3109/10673229.2010.49662320597593

Flacandji, M. (2015). *Du souvenir de l'expérience à la relation à l'enseigne: une exploration théorique et méthodologique dans le domaine du commerce de détail* [Doctoral dissertation, Université de Bourgogne].

Flacandji, M. (2015). *Du Souvenir De L'expérience À La Relation À L'enseigne: Une Exploration Théorique Et Méthodologique Dans Le Domaine Du Commerce De Détail Michaël.*

Flavián, C., Ibáñez-Sánchez, S., & Orús, C. (2019). The impact of virtual, augmented and mixed reality technologies on the customer experience. *Journal of Business Research*, 100, 547–560. 10.1016/j.jbusres.2018.10.050

Flewelling, P. (2018). *The The Agile Developer's Handbook: Get More Value From Your Software Development: Get The Best Out Of The Agile Methodology.* Packt Publishing Ltd.

Forest, D. (2020). *Le droit au défi du numérique - Libertés et propriété à l'ère d'Internet* (Editions L'Harmattan Ghosh, J. (2019). The blockchain: Opportunities for research in information systems and information technology. *Journal of Global Information Technology Management*, 22(4), 235–242. 10.1080/1097198X.2019.1679954

Forhad, M. S. A., Arefin, M. S., Kayes, A. S. M., Ahmed, K., Chowdhury, M. J. M., & Kumara, I. (2021). An Effective Hotel Recommendation System through Processing Heterogeneous Data. *Electronics (Basel)*, 10(16), 1920. 10.3390/electronics10161920

Fornell, C., & Larcker, D. F. (1981). Evaluating Structural Equation Models with Unobservable Variables and Measurement Error. *JMR, Journal of Marketing Research*, 18(1), 39–50. 10.1177/002224378101800104

Fornerino, M., Rivet, C., & Et Reghem, J. (2018). Explorer L'expérience De Shopping Dans Un Magasin Phygital. *Décisions Marketing, 91*(45), 60. Https://Doi.Org/10.7193/Dm.091.45.60

Fortunato, V. C. R., Giraldi, J. D. M. E., & De Oliveira, J. H. C. (2014). A Review of Studies on Neuromarketing: Practical Results, Techniques, Contributions and Limitations. *Journal of Management Research*, 6(2), 201. 10.5296/jmr.v6i2.5446

Fowler, M., & Highsmith, J. (2001). The Agile Manifesto. *Software Development*, 9(8), 28–35.

Franke, G. R., & Sarstedt, M. (2019). Heuristics versus statistics in discriminant validity testing: A comparison of four procedures. *Internet Research*, 29(3), 430–447. https://api.semanticscholar.org/CorpusID:86723268. 10.1108/IntR-12-2017-0515

Fuchs, C. (2014). *Sosyal Medya Eleştirel Bir Giriş.* Notabene Yayınları.

Fujiyoshi, H., Hirakawa, T., & Yamashita, T. (2019). Deep learning-based image recognition for autonomous driving. *IATSS Research*, 43(4), 244–252. 10.1016/j.iatssr.2019.11.008

Fu, L. (2018). *Four key barriers to the widespread adoption of AI.* R&D Magazine.

Gallardo, C., Rodríguez, S. P., Chango, I. E., Quevedo, W. X., Santana, J., Acosta, A. G., Tapia, J. C., & Andaluz, V. H. (2018). Augmented reality as a new marketing strategy. *Lecture Notes in Computer Science (Including Subseries Lecture Notes in Artificial Intelligence and Lecture Notes in Bioinformatics), 10850 LNCS*, 351-362. *Lecture Notes in Computer Science*, 10850, 351–362. 10.1007/978-3-319-95270-3_29

Galloway, C., & Swiatek, L. (2018). Public Relations and Artificial Intelligence: It's Not (Just) About Robots. *Public Relations Review*, 44(5), 734–740. 10.1016/j.pubrev.2018.10.008

Gangoda, A., Krasley, S., & Cobb, K. (2023). AI digitalisation and automation of the apparel industry and human workforce skills. *International Journal of Fashion Design, Technology and Education*, 16(3), 319–329. 10.1080/17543266.2023.2209589

Gantz, J., Reinsel, D. (2012). The digital universe in 2020: Big data, bigger digital shadows, and biggest growth in the far East. *IDC iView: IDC Analyze the future*, 1-16.

Gao, Q., Cheng, C., & Sun, G. (2023). Big data application, factor allocation, and green innovation in Chinese manufacturing enterprises. *Technological Forecasting and Social Change*, 192, 122567. 10.1016/j.techfore.2023.122567

Gao, T., Rohm, A. J., Sultan, F., & Huang, S. (2012). Antecedents of consumer attitudes toward mobile marketing: A comparative study of youth markets in the United States and China. *Thunderbird International Business Review*, 54(2), 211–224. 10.1002/tie.21452

Gao, T., Sultan, F., & Rohm, A. J. (2010). Factors influencing Chinese youth consumers' acceptance of mobile marketing. *Journal of Consumer Marketing*, 27(7), 574–583. 10.1108/07363761011086326

Gao, W., Li, W., Fan, H., & Jia, X. (2021). *How Customer Experience Incongruence Affects Omnichannel Customer Retention: The Moderating Role of Channel Characteristics*. J. Retailing Consum. 10.1016/j.jretconser.2021.102487

Gao, Y. J., & Liu, H. F. (2023). Artificial intelligence-enabled personalization in interactive marketing: A customer journey perspective. *Journal of Research in Interactive Marketing*, 17(5), 663–680. 10.1108/JRIM-01-2022-0023

Garcia, J. E., Lima, R., & da Fonseca, M. J. S. (2022). Search Engine Optimization (SEO) for a Company Website: A Case Study. In Rocha, A., Adeli, H., Dzemyda, G., & Moreira, F. (Eds.), *Information Systems and Technologies. WorldCIST 2022. Lecture Notes in Networks and Systems* (Vol. 470). Springer. 10.1007/978-3-031-04829-6_47

Garg, M., & Bansal, A. (2020). *Impact of Digital Marketing on Consumer Decision Making*. Research Gate.

Garg, P. K. (2021). Overview of artificial intelligence. In *Artificial intelligence* (pp. 3–18). Chapman and Hall/CRC. 10.1201/9781003140351-2

Gauri, D. K., Jindal, R. P., Brian, R., Edward, F., Amit, B., Aashish, P., Navallo, J. R., John, F., Stephen, C., & Eric, H. (2021). Evolution Of Retail Formats: Past, Present, And Future. *Journal of Retailing*, 97(1), 42–61. 10.1016/j.jretai.2020.11.002

Gentile, C., Spiller, N., & Noci, G. (2007). How To Sustain The Customer Experience. An Overview Of Experience Components That Co-Create Value With The Customer. *European Management Journal*, 25(5), 395–410. Https://Doi.Org/10.1016/J.Emj.2007.08.005. 10.1016/j.emj.2007.08.005

Gera, G., Gera, B., & Mishra, A. (2019). Role Of Agile Marketing In The Present Era. *International Journal Of Technical Research & Science*, 4(5), 40–44. 10.30780/IJTRS.V04.I05.006

Gerlich, M., Elsayed, W., & Sokolovskiy, K. (2023). Artificial intelligence as toolset for analysis of public opinion and social interaction in marketing: Identification of micro and nano influencers. *Frontiers in Communication*, 8, 1075654. 10.3389/fcomm.2023.1075654

Gessner, G. H., & Volonino, L. (2005). Quick Response Improves Returns on Business Intelligence Investments. *Information Systems Management*, 22(3), 66–74. 10.1201/1078/45317.22.3.20050601/88746.8

Ghosh, I., Alfaro-Cortés, E., Gámez, M., & García-Rubio, N. (2023). COVID-19 Media Chatter and Macroeconomic Reflectors on Black Swan: A Spanish and Indian Stock Markets Comparison. *Risks*, 11(5), 94. 10.3390/risks11050094

Giffinger, R. (2015). Smart City Concepts : Chances and Risks of Energy Efficient Urban Development. In Helfert, M., Krempels, K.-H., Klein, C., Donellan, B., & Guiskhin, O. (Eds.), *Smart Cities, Green Technologies, and Intelligent Transport Systems* (Vol. 579, pp. 3–16). Springer International Publishing. 10.1007/978-3-319-27753-0_1

Giffinger, R., & Haindlmaier, G. (2018). Benchmarking the Smart City : A Sound Tool for Policy-Making? *Scienze Regionali*, 1, 115–122. 10.14650/88820

Gillespie, T. (2014). Relevance of Algorithms. In Gillespie, T., Boczkowski, P. J., & Foot, K. A. (Eds.), *Inside Technology. Media Technologies: Essays on Communication, Materiality, and Society* (pp. 167–194). The MIT Press. 10.7551/mitpress/9042.003.0013

Gill, R., & Singh, J. (2022). A study of neuromarketing techniques for proposing cost effective information driven framework for decision making. *Materials Today: Proceedings*, 49, 2969–2981. 10.1016/j.matpr.2020.08.730

Giovanola, B., & Tiribelli, S. (2023). Beyond bias and discrimination: Redefining the AI ethics principle of fairness in healthcare machine-learning algorithms. *AI & Society*, 38(2), 549–563. 10.1007/s00146-022-01455-635615443

Gkikas, D. C., & Theodoridis, P. K. (2019). Artificial intelligence (AI) impact on digital marketing research. In *Strategic Innovative Marketing and Tourism: 7th ICSIMAT,* (pp. 1251-1259). Springer International Publishing.

Gleim, M., & Stevens, J. (2021). Blockchain : A game changer for marketers? *Marketing Letters*, 32(1), 1–6. 10.1007/s11002-021-09557-9

Glova, B., & Mudryk, I. (2020). Application of Deep Learning in Neuromarketing Studies of the Effects of Unconscious Reactions on Consumer Behavior. *2020 IEEE Third International Conference on Data Stream Mining & Processing (DSMP).* IEEE. 10.1109/DSMP47368.2020.9204192

Godé, C. (2021). Propos introductif : Technologies émergentes et digitalisation des organisations. *Recherche et Cas en Sciences de Gestion*, (22). 10.3917/rcsg.022.0007

Gopalakrishna, S., Crecelius, A. T., & Patil, A. (2022). Hunting for new customers: Assessing the drivers of effective salesperson prospecting and conversion. *Journal of Business Research*, 149, 916–926. 10.1016/j.jbusres.2022.05.008

Goudey, A. (2013). Exploration Des Effets Du Degré De Technologie Perçu Du Magasin Sur Le Comportement De Magasinage. *Management Et Avenir, 63*(5), 15. Https://Doi.Org/10.3917/Mav.063.0015

Grant, R. M. (2018). *Contemporary strategy analysis* (10th ed.). Wiley & Sons.

Gräser, M., Harris, C., Alt, R., & Reinhold, O. (2023). How Integrated Social CRM Affects Business Success: Learnings from a Literature Analysis. *2023 IEEE/WIC International Conference on Web Intelligence and Intelligent Agent Technology (WI-IAT)*, (pp. 547–554). IEEE. 10.1109/WI-IAT59888.2023.00091

Greene, K. (2006). *The $1 Million Netflix Challenge*. MIT Technology Review. https://www.technologyreview.com/2006/10/06/273459/the-1-million-netflix-challenge/

Grewal, D. & Kumar, V. (2009). Customer Experience Management: An Organizing Framework. *Journal Of Retailing, 85*(1), 1–14. https://Doi.Org/10.1016/j.jretai.2009.01.001

Grewal, D., Roggeveen, A. L., & Et Nordfäl, T J. (2017). The Future Of Retailing. *Journal Of Retailing, 93*(1), 1-6. Https://Doi.Org/10.1016/J.Jretai.2016.12.008

Grewal, D., Benoit, S., Noble, S. M., Guha, A., Ahlbom, C.-P., & Nordfält, J. (2023). Leveraging In-Store Technology And AI : Increasing Customer And Employee Efficiency And Enhancing Their Experiences. *Journal of Retailing*, 99(4), 487–504. Https://Doi.Org/10.1016/J.Jretai.2023.10.002. 10.1016/j.jretai.2023.10.002

Grewal, D., Hulland, J., Kopalle, P. K., & Karahanna, E. (2020). The future of technology and marketing : A multidisciplinary perspective. *Journal of the Academy of Marketing Science*, 48(1), 1–8. 10.1007/s11747-019-00711-4

Grewal, S. M., Noble, S. M., Roggeveen, A. L., & Nordfalt, J. (2020). Noble, A. L. Roggeveen, J. Nordfält (2020)."The Future Of In-Store Technology". *Journal of the Academy of Marketing Science*, 48(2), 96–113. 10.1007/s11747-019-00697-z

Gross, M. A., & Pullman, M. (2012). Playing their roles: Experiential design concepts applied in complex services. *Journal of Management Inquiry*, 21(1), 43–59. 10.1177/1056492610395928

Guercini, S. (2023). Marketing automation and the scope of marketers' heuristics. *Management Decision*, 61(13), 295–320. 10.1108/MD-07-2022-0909

Guo, H., Xu, H., Tang, C., Liu-Thompkins, Y., Guo, Z., & Dong, B. (2018). Comparing the impact of different marketing capabilities: Empirical evidence from B2B firms in China. *Journal of Business Research*, 93, 79–89. 10.1016/j.jbusres.2018.04.010

Gupta, A., Dwivedi, D. N., & Shah, J. (2023). Applying Artificial Intelligence on Investigation. In: *Artificial Intelligence Applications in Banking and Financial Services. Future of Business and Finance*. Springer, Singapore. 10.1007/978-981-99-2571-1_9

Gupta, A., Dwivedi, D. N., & Shah, J. (2023). Applying Machine Learning for Effective Customer Risk Assessment. In: *Artificial Intelligence Applications in Banking and Financial Services*. Future of Business and Finance. Springer, Singapore. 10.1007/978-981-99-2571-1_6

Gupta, A., Dwivedi, D. N., & Shah, J. (2023). Artificial Intelligence-Driven Effective Financial Transaction Monitoring. In: *Artificial Intelligence Applications in Banking and Financial Services*. Springer, Singapore. 10.1007/978-981-99-2571-1_7

Gupta, A., Dwivedi, D. N., & Shah, J. (2023). Data Organization for an FCC Unit. In: *Artificial Intelligence Applications in Banking and Financial Services. Future of Business and Finance*. Springer, Singapore. 10.1007/978-981-99-2571-1_4

Gupta, A., Dwivedi, D. N., & Shah, J. (2023). Ethical Challenges for AI-Based Applications. In: *Artificial Intelligence Applications in Banking and Financial Services. Future of Business and Finance*. Springer, Singapore. 10.1007/978-981-99-2571-1_10

Gupta, A., Dwivedi, D. N., & Shah, J. (2023). Financial Crimes Management and Control in Financial Institutions. In: *Artificial Intelligence Applications in Banking and Financial Services. Future of Business and Finance*. Springer, Singapore. 10.1007/978-981-99-2571-1_2

Gupta, A., Dwivedi, D. N., & Shah, J. (2023). Machine Learning-Driven Alert Optimization. In: *Artificial Intelligence Applications in Banking and Financial Services*. Springer, Singapore. 10.1007/978-981-99-2571-1_8

Gupta, A., Dwivedi, D. N., & Shah, J. (2023). Overview of Money Laundering. In: *Artificial Intelligence Applications in Banking and Financial Services. Future of Business and Finance*. Springer, Singapore. 10.1007/978-981-99-2571-1_1

Gupta, A., Dwivedi, D. N., & Shah, J. (2023). Overview of Technology Solutions. In: *Artificial Intelligence Applications in Banking and Financial Services. Future of Business and Finance*. Springer, Singapore. 10.1007/978-981-99-2571-1_3

Gupta, A., Dwivedi, D. N., & Shah, J. (2023). Planning for AI in Financial Crimes. In: *Artificial Intelligence Applications in Banking and Financial Services. Future of Business and Finance*. Springer, Singapore. 10.1007/978-981-99-2571-1_5

Gupta, A., Dwivedi, D. N., & Shah, J. (2023). Setting up a Best-In-Class AI-Driven Financial Crime Control Unit (FCCU). In: *Artificial Intelligence Applications in Banking and Financial Services. Future of Business and Finance*. Springer, Singapore. 10.1007/978-981-99-2571-1_11

Gupta, A., Dwivedi, D.N. & Jain, A. (2021). Threshold fine-tuning of money laundering scenarios through multi-dimensional optimization techniques. *Journal of Money Laundering Control*. 10.1108/JMLC-12-2020-0138

Gupta, A., Dwivedi, D.N., Shah, J. & Jain, A. (2021). Data quality issues leading to sub optimal machine learning for money laundering models. *Journal of Money Laundering Control*. 10.1108/JMLC-05-2021-0049

Gupta, S., & Vajic, M. (2000). The Contextual and Dialectical Nature Of Experiences. *New Service Development, Creating Memorable Experiences*. Thousand Oaks, Sage. 10.4135/9781452205564.n2

Gupta, S., Gupta, A., Savjani, P., & Kumar, R. (2020). Optimizing creative allocations in digital marketing [Conferece session]. *International conference on advances in computing and data sciences, Singapore* (pp. 419–429). Springer Singapore.

Gupta, S. (2009). Customer-based valuation. *Journal of Interactive Marketing*, 23(2), 169–178. 10.1016/j.intmar.2009.02.006

Gupta, S., & Joshi, S. (2022). Predictive Analytic Techniques for enhancing marketing performance and Personalized Customer Experience. *2022 International Interdisciplinary Humanitarian Conference for Sustainability (IIHC)*, (pp. 16–22). IEEE. 10.1109/IIHC55949.2022.10060286

Hadinia, S., Abdi, R., Pakmaram, A., & Jafari, A. (2023). Designing a model of wise decision-making process in auditing with a fuzzy Delphi approach. *International Journal of Nonlinear Analysis and Applications*, 14(9), 65–78.

Haenlein, M., & Kaplan, A. (2019). A brief history of artificial intelligence: On the past, present, and future of artificial intelligence. *California Management Review*, 61(4), 5–14. 10.1177/0008125619864925

Haesevoets, T., De, C. D., Kim, D., & Van, H. A. (2021). Human-Machine Collaboration in Managerial Decision Making. *Computers in Human Behavior*, 119, 106730. 10.1016/j.chb.2021.106730

Hafez, M. (2019). Neuromarketing: A new avatar in branding and advertisement. *Pac. Bus. Rev. Int*, 12(4), 58–64.

Haftor, D. M., Costa-Climent, R., & Navarrete, S. R. (2023). A pathway to bypassing market entry barriers from data network effects: A case study of a start-up's use of machine learning. *Journal of Business Research*, 168, 114244. 10.1016/j.jbusres.2023.114244

Haghirian, P., & Madlberger, M. (2005). Consumer Attitude toward Advertising via Mobile Devices. *European Conference on Information Systems*, (pp. 447–458). IEEE.

Haghirian, P., Madlberger, M., & Tanuskova, A. (2005). Increasing Advertising Value of Mobile Marketing - An Empirical Study of Antecedents. *Proceedings of the 38th Annual Hawaii International Conference on System Sciences* (pp. 32c-32c). IEEE. 10.1109/HICSS.2005.311

Hair, J. F., Hult, G. T. M., Ringle, C. M., & Sarstedt, M. (2016). *A primer on partial least squares structural equation modeling (PLS-SEM)*.

Hair, J., Black, W., Babin, B., & Anderson, R. (2010). *Multivariate Data Analysis: A Global Perspective*. Research Gate.

Hair, J., Hollingsworth, C. L., Randolph, A. B., & Chong, A. Y. L. (2017). An updated and expanded assessment of PLS-SEM in information systems research. *Industrial Management & Data Systems*, 117(3), 442–458. 10.1108/IMDS-04-2016-0130

Haj, D. A. E. (2020). La ville marocaine et la nécessité d'une transformation à l'ère de la Smart City : Analyse des cas des villes de Tanger, Casablanca et Marrakech. *Geopolitics and Geostrategic Intelligence, 3*(2), Article 2.

Haleem, A., Javaid, M., Qadri, M. A., Singh, R. P., & Suman, R. (2022). Artificial intelligence (AI) applications for marketing: A literature-based study. *International Journal of Intelligent Networks*.

Haleem, A., Javaid, M., Asim Qadri, M., Pratap Singh, R., & Suman, R. (2022). Artificial intelligence (AI) applications for marketing : A literature-based study. *International Journal of Intelligent Networks*, 3, 119–132. 10.1016/j.ijin.2022.08.005

Haleem, A., Javaid, M., Qadri, M., & Suman, R. (2022). Understanding the Role of Digital Technologies in Education: A review. *Sustainable Operations and Computers*, 3, 275–285. 10.1016/j.susoc.2022.05.004

Handzic, M., Ozlen, K., & Durmic, N. (2014). Improving Customer Relationship Management Through Business Intelligence. *Journal of Information & Knowledge Management*, 13(02), 1450015. 10.1142/S0219649214500154

Han, H., Hsu, L. T. J., & Sheu, C. (2010). Application Of The Theory Of Planned Behavior To Green Hotel Choice: Testing The Effect Of Environmental Friendly Activities. *Tourism Management*, 31(3), 325–334. 10.1016/j.tourman.2009.03.013

Han, H., Shiwakoti, R. K., Jarvis, R., Mordi, C., & Botchie, D. (2023). Accounting and auditing with blockchain technology and artificial Intelligence: A literature review. *International Journal of Accounting Information Systems*, 48, 100598. 10.1016/j.accinf.2022.100598

Hanna, K., & Noble, B. F. (2015). Using a Delphi study to identify effectiveness criteria for environmental assessment. *Impact Assessment and Project Appraisal*, 33(2), 116–125. 10.1080/14615517.2014.992672

Han, S., Yoon, J. H., & Kwon, J. (2021). Impact of experiential value of augmented reality: The context of heritage tourism. *Sustainability (Basel)*, 13(8), 4147. 10.3390/su13084147

Haouam, Z. (2022). «Création de valeur numérique, communication digitale et outils de fidélisation d'une communauté en ligne. Etude exploratoire».

Hardesty, L. (2019, November 22). *The history of Amazon's recommendation algorithm*. Amazon Science. https://www.amazon.science/the-history-of-amazons-recommendation-algorithm

Hattab, S., & El Achari, S. (2023). La performance bancaire impactée par la digitalisation: une étude des banques marocaines. *International Journal of Accounting, Finance, Auditing, Management and Economics, 4*(4-2), 280-301. 10.5281/zenodo.8267102

Haubl, G., & And Trifts, V. (2000). Consumer Decision Making In Online Shopping Environments: The Effects Of Interactive Decision Aids. *Marketing Science*, 19(1), 4–21. 10.1287/mksc.19.1.4.15178

Haumer, F., Kolo, C., & Reiners, S. (2020). The impact of augmented reality experiential marketing on brand equity and buying intention. *Journal of Brand Strategy*, 8(4), 368–387.

Head, A. J., Fister, B., & Macmillan, M. (2020, January 15). *Information Literacy in the Age of Algorithms: Student Experiences With News and Information, and The Need for Change*. Project Information Literacy. https://files.eric.ed.gov/fulltext/ ED605109.pdf

Hennink, M. M., Kaiser, B. N., & Weber, M. B. (2019). What influences saturation? Estimating sample sizes in focus group research. *Qualitative Health Research*, 29(10), 1483–1496. 10.1177/1049732318821692 30628545

Henn, M., Huberman, B. M., & Milkman, K. E. (2000). The networked citizen. *Science*, 290(5491), 1187–1188.

Hensel, D., Wolter, L.-C., & Znanewitz, J. (2017). *A guideline for ethical aspects in conducting neuromarketing studies. Ethics and neuromarketing: Implications for market research and business practice*. Research Gate.

Henseler, J., Hubona, G., & Ray, P. A. (2016). Using PLS path modeling in new technology research: Updated guidelines. *Industrial Management & Data Systems*, 116(1), 2–20. 10.1108/IMDS-09-2015-0382

Henseler, J., Ringle, C. M., & Sinkovics, R. R. (2009a). The use of partial least squares path modeling in international marketing. *Advances in International Marketing*, 20, 277–319. 10.1108/S1474-7979(2009)0000020014

Henseler, J., Ringle, C., & Sarstedt, M. (2015). A New Criterion for Assessing Discriminant Validity in Variance-based Structural Equation Modeling. *Journal of the Academy of Marketing Science*, 43(1), 115–135. 10.1007/s11747-014-0403-8

Hermann, E. (2022). Leveraging Artificial Intelligence in Marketing for Social Good-An Ethical Perspective. *Journal of Business Ethics*, 179(1), 43–61. 10.1007/s10551-021-04843-y34054170

Hermann, E., Williams, G. Y., & Puntoni, S. (2023). Deploying artificial intelligence in services to AID vulnerable consumers. *Journal of the Academy of Marketing Science*. 10.1007/s11747-023-00986-8

Highsmith, J. A. (2002). *Agile Software Development Ecosystems*. Addison-Wesley Professional.

Hilken, T., Heller, J., Chylinski, M., Keeling, D. I., Mahr, D., & de Ruyter, K. (2018). Making omnichannel an augmented reality: The current and future state of the art. *Journal of Research in Interactive Marketing*, 12(4), 509–523. 10.1108/JRIM-01-2018-0023

Hirschman, E. C., & Et Holbrook, M. B. (1986). Expanding The Ontology And Methodology Of Research On The Consumption Experience. *Perspectives On Methodology In Consumer Research*, 213-251. Https://Doi.Org/10.1007/978-1-4613-8609-4_7

Hjørland, B. (2013). Facet analysis: The logical approach to knowledge organization. *Information Processing & Management*, 49(2), 545–557. 10.1016/j.ipm.2012.10.001

Hmioui, A., & Bentalha, B. (2020). Service Supply Chain Management and commercial performance: Sketch of a theoretical synthesis. *Economic Management Alternatives*, 2, 1–21.

Hoch, S. J. (2002). Product experience is seductive. *The Journal of Consumer Research*, 29(3), 448–454. 10.1086/344422

Hoffman, D. L., Moreau, C. P., Stremersch, S., & Wedel, M. (2022). The Rise of New Technologies in Marketing : A Framework and Outlook. *Journal of Marketing*, 86(1), 1–6. 10.1177/00222429211061636

Holbrook, M. B. Et Hirschman, E. C., (1982). Hedonic Consumption: Emerging Concepts, Methods and Propositions. *Wiley Encyclopedia Of Management, 46*(3), 1-1. Https://Doi.Org/10.1002/9781118785317.Weom090127

Holbrook, M. B. (2006). Consumption Experience, Customer Value, And Subjective Personal Introspection: An Illustrative Photographic Essay. *Journal of Business Research*, 59(6), 714–725. Https://Doi.Org/10.1016/J.Jbusres.2006.01.008. 10.1016/j.jbusres.2006.01.008

Holbrook, M. B., & Addis, M. (2001). On The Conceptual Link Between Mass Customisation And Experiential Consumption: An Explosion Of Subjectivity. *Journal of Consumer Behaviour*, 1(1), 50–66. Https://Doi.Org/10.1002/Cb.53. 10.1002/cb.53

Holbrook, M. B., & Hirschman, E. C. (1982). The experiential aspects of consumption: Consumer fantasies, feelings, and fun. *The Journal of Consumer Research*, 9(2), 132–140. 10.1086/208906

Hollands, R. G. (2020). Will the real smart city please stand up?: Intelligent, progressive or entrepreneurial? In *The Routledge companion to smart cities* (pp. 179–199). Routledge. https://www.taylorfrancis.com/chapters/edit/10.4324/9781315178387-13/real-smart-city-please-stand-robert-hollands10.4324/9781315178387-13

Hollebeek, L. D., Sprott, D. E., Andreassen, T. W., Costley, C., Klaus, P., Kuppelwieser, V., Karahasanovic, A., Taguchi, T., Ul Islam, J., & Rather, R. A. (2019). Customer engagement in evolving technological environments : Synopsis and guiding propositions. *European Journal of Marketing*, 53(9), 2018–2023. 10.1108/EJM-09-2019-970

Hollebeek, L., & Macky, K. (2019). Digital Content Marketing's Role in Fostering Consumer Engagement, Trust, and Value: Framework, Fundamental Propositions, and Implications. *Journal of Interactive Marketing*, 45, 27–41. 10.1016/j.intmar.2018.07.003

Holmlund, , Van Vaerenbergh, Y., Ciuchita, R., Ravald, A., Sarantopoulos, P., Ordenes, F. V., & Zaki, M. (2020). Customer Experience Management In The Age Of Big Data Analytics: A Strategic Framework. *Journal of Business Research*, 116, 356–365. 10.1016/j.jbusres.2020.01.022

Hoogveld, M., & Koster, J. (2016). Measuring The Agility Of Omnichannel Operations: An Agile Marketing Maturity Model. *SSRG International Journal Of Economics And Management Studies (SSRG-IJEMS), 3*(10), 5-14.

Hoyer, W. D., Kroschke, M., Schmitt, B., Kraume, K., & Shankar, V. (2020). Transforming the customer experience through new technologies. *Journal of Interactive Marketing*, 51(1), 57–71. 10.1016/j.intmar.2020.04.001

Hsu, P.-F., Lu, Y.-H., Chen, S.-C., & Kuo, P. P.-Y. (2024). Creating and validating predictive personas for target marketing. *International Journal of Human-Computer Studies*, 181, 103147. 10.1016/j.ijhcs.2023.103147

Hsu, S. H. Y., Tsou, H. T., & Chen, J. S. (2021). "Yes, we do. Why not use augmented reality?" customer responses to experiential presentations of AR-based applications. *Journal of Retailing and Consumer Services*, 62, 102649. 10.1016/j.jretconser.2021.102649

Huang, C. M., Li, S. Y., & Hsu, C. H. (2020). Analyzing customer churn behavior in the telecom industry: A data mining approach. *Technological Forecasting and Social Change*, 153, 119977. 10.1016/j.techfore.2020.119977

Huang, E. Y., & Lin, C. Y. (2005). Customer-oriented financial service personalization. *Industrial Management & Data Systems*, 105(1), 26–44. 10.1108/02635570510575171

Huang, M. H., & Rust, R. T. (2022). A framework for collaborative artificial intelligence in marketing. *Journal of Retailing*, 98(2), 209–223. 10.1016/j.jretai.2021.03.001

Huang, M. H., Rust, R. T., & Apkarian, M. H. (2009). The service revolution and its implications for marketing science. *Journal of Marketing*, 73(2), 20–40.

Huang, M.-H., & Rust, R. T. (2018). Artificial Intelligence in Service. *Journal of Service Research*, 21(2), 155–172. 10.1177/1094670517752459

Huang, M.-H., & Rust, R. T. (2021). A strategic framework for artificial intelligence in marketing. *Journal of the Academy of Marketing Science*, 49(1), 30–50. 10.1007/s11747-020-00749-9

Huang, R., & Sarigöllü, E. (2012). How brand awareness relates to market outcome, brand equity, and the marketing mix. *Journal of Business Research*, 65(1), 92–99. 10.1016/j.jbusres.2011.02.00332287525

Huang, T. L., & Liao, S. (2015). A model of acceptance of augmented-reality interactive technology: The moderating role of cognitive innovativeness. *Electronic Commerce Research*, 15(2), 269–295. 10.1007/s10660-014-9163-2

Huang, Y., Zhang, X., & Zhu, H. (2022). How do customers engage in social media-based brand communities: The moderator role of the brand's country of origin? *Journal of Retailing and Consumer Services*, 68.

Hui, M. K., & Bateson, J. E. (1991). Perceived control and the effects of crowding and consumer choice on the service experience. *The Journal of Consumer Research*, 18(2), 174–184. 10.1086/209250

Hunt, J. (2006). Feature-Driven Development. *Agile Software Construction*, 161-182.

Hunt, S. D., & Lambe, C. J. (2000). Marketing's contribution to business strategy: Market orientation, relationship marketing and resource-advantage theory. *International Journal of Management Reviews*, 2(1), 17–43. 10.1111/1468-2370.00029

Hu, R., Wang, C., Zhang, T., Nguyen, T., Shapoval, V., & Zhai, L. (2021). Applying augmented reality (AR) technologies in theatrical performances in theme parks: A transcendent experience perspective. *Tourism Management Perspectives*, 40, 100889. 10.1016/j.tmp.2021.100889

Hurwitz, K. & Bowles, N. (2015). *Cognitive Computing and Big Data Analytics*. Wiley Online Library.

Huseynov, F. (2020a). Intelligent Recommender Systems in E-Commerce: Opportunities and Challenges for Online Customers. *Handbook of Research on IT Applications for Strategic Competitive Advantage and Decision Making,* 36-51. Springer.

Huseynov, F. (2020b). Gamification in e-commerce: Enhancing digital customer engagement through game elements. In *Digital innovations for customer engagement, management, and organizational improvement* (pp. 144–161). IGI Global. 10.4018/978-1-7998-5171-4.ch008

Huseynov, F. (2023). Chatbots in digital marketing: Enhanced customer experience and reduced customer service costs. In *Contemporary Approaches of Digital Marketing and the Role of Machine Intelligence* (pp. 46–72). IGI Global. 10.4018/978-1-6684-7735-9.ch003

Huseynov, F., & Özkan Yıldırım, S. (2019). Online consumer typologies and their shopping behaviors in B2C e-commerce platforms. *SAGE Open,* 9(2), 2158244019854639. 10.1177/2158244019854639

Huseynov, F., & Yıldırım, S. Ö. (2017). Behavioural segmentation analysis of online consumer audience in Turkey by using real e-commerce transaction data. *International Journal of Economics and Business Research,* 14(1), 12–28. 10.1504/IJEBR.2017.085549

Hydle, K. M., Hellström, M., Aas, T. H., & Breunig, K. J. (2021). *Digital servitization: strategies for handling customization and customer interaction. The Palgrave Handbook of Servitization,* (pp. 355-372). Palgrave.

IBM Institute for Business Value. (2023). *2023 Chief Executive Officer Study : Decision-making in the age of AI.* IBM. https://www.ibm.com/thought-leadership/institute-business-value/en-us/report/2023-ceo

ICAEW. (2018). *Blockchain and the future of accountancy.* ICAEW IT Faculty. https://www.icaew.com/technical/technology/blockchain-and-cryptoassets/blockchain-articles/blockchain-and-the-accounting-perspective. (accessed: 19 January 2024)

Ienca, M. (2023). On Artificial Intelligence and Manipulation. *Topoi,* 42(3), 833–842. 10.1007/s11245-023-09940-3

Iglesias, C. P., Thompson, A., Rogowski, W. H., & Payne, K. (2016). Reporting Guidelines for the Use of Expert Judgement in Model-Based Economic Evaluations. *PharmacoEconomics,* 34(11), 1161–1172. 10.1007/s40273-016-0425-927364887

Imgraben, J., Engelbrecht, A., & Choo, K. K. R. (2014). Always connected, but are smart mobile users getting more security savvy? A survey of smart mobile device users. *Behaviour & Information Technology,* 33(12), 1347–1360. 10.1080/0144929X.2014.934286

Intuz (2022). *An Ultimate Guide On Adopting Agile Marketing Methodology.* Intuz. Https://Www.Intuz.Com/Guide-On-Agile-Marketing-Methodology

Irgui, , AQmichchou, , M. (2023). Contextual marketing and information privacy concerns in m-commerce and their impact on consumer loyalty. *Arab Gulf Journal of Scientific Research.* 10.1108/AGJSR-09-2022-0198

Irgui, , AQmichchou, , M., & ElHaraoui, , I. (2024). Phygital learning in Moroccan higher education and its impact on student satisfaction. *Revue Management & Innovation, (3),* 110-129. 10.3917/rmi.209.0110

Irvin, R. A., & Stansbury, J. (2004). Citizen Participation in Decision Making : Is It Worth the Effort? *Public Administration Review,* 64(1), 55–65. 10.1111/j.1540-6210.2004.00346.x

Ishwarappa, A., & Anuradha, J. (2015). A brief introduction on big data 5Vs characteristics and Hadoop technology. *Procedia Computer Science,* 48, 319–324. 10.1016/j.procs.2015.04.188

Islam, J. U., Rahman, Z., & Hollebeek, L. D. (2017). Personality factors as predictors of online consumer engagement: An empirical investigation. *Marketing Intelligence & Planning*, 35(4), 510–528. 10.1108/MIP-10-2016-0193

Issa, H., Sun, T., & Vasarhelyi, M. A. (2016). Research ideas for artificial intelligence in auditing: The formalization of audit and workforce supplementation. *Journal of Emerging Technologies in Accounting*, 13(2), 1–20. 10.2308/jeta-10511

Ivančić, L., Suša Vugec, D., & Bosilj Vukšić, V. (2019). Robotic process automation: systematic literature review. In *Business Process Management: Blockchain and Central and Eastern Europe Forum*. Springer.

Janssen, A., Passlick, J., & Rodríguez Cardona, D. (2020). Virtual Assistance in Any Context. *Bus Inf Syst Eng, 62*, 211–225. (https://doi.org/)10.1007/s12599-020-00644-1

Jaouad, J., & Ouchekkir, A. (2023). La transformation digitale dans le secteur bancaire marocain: une révolution dans les pratiques et les services financiers. *International Journal of Accounting, Finance, Auditing, Management and Economics, 4*(3-2), 417-437. 10.5281/zenodo.8057870

Javaid, M., Haleem, A., Singh, R. P., Suman, R., & Khan, S. (2022). A review of Blockchain Technology applications for financial services. *BenchCouncil Transactions on Benchmarks. Standards and Evaluations*, 2(3), 100073.

Javanmard, S. (2024). Revolutionizing Medical Practice: The Impact of Artificial Intelligence (AI) on Healthcare. *OA J Applied Sci Technol, 2*(1), 01-16.

Javor, A., Koller, M., Lee, N., Chamberlain, L., & Ransmayr, G. (2013). Neuromarketing and consumer neuroscience: Contributions to neurology. *BMC Neurology*, 13(1), 13. 10.1186/1471-2377-13-1323383650

Javornik, A. (2016). Augmented reality: Research agenda for studying the impact of its media characteristics on consumer behaviour. *Journal of Retailing and Consumer Services*, 30, 252–261. 10.1016/j.jretconser.2016.02.004

Jawadi, N. (2014). *Facteurs-Clés De L'adoption Des Systèmes D'information Dans La Grande Distribution Alimentaire: Une Approche Par L'utaut*. Paper Presented At The 17ème Colloque De l'Association Information Et Management (AIM), Bordeaux.

Jayawardhena, C., Kuckertz, A., Karjaluoto, H., & Kautonen, T. (2007). Antecedents to Permission Based Mobile Marketing: An Initial Examination. *European Journal of Marketing*, 43(3/4), 473–499. 10.1108/03090560910935541

Jebaraj, L., Khang, A., Chandrasekar, V., Pravin, A. R., & Sriram, K. (2023). Smart City : Concepts, Models, Technologies and Applications. In *Smart Cities* (p. 1-20). CRC Press. https://www.taylorfrancis.com/chapters/edit/10.1201/9781003376064-1/smart-city-concepts-models-technologies-applications-luke-jebaraj-alex-khang-vadivelraju-chandrasekar-antony-richard-pravin-kumar-sriram

Jessen, A., Hilken, T., Chylinski, M., Mahr, D., Heller, J., Keeling, D. I., & de Ruyter, K. (2020). The playground effect : How augmented reality drives creative customer engagement. *Journal of Business Research*, 116, 85–98. 10.1016/j.jbusres.2020.05.002

Jhamb, S., & Turcanu, R. (2022). A Scholarly Review of Global Business Indications and Economic Trends: Understanding International Competitiveness, Economic Globalization, and Digitization Through the Lens of the COVID-19 Pandemic and the New Normal. *Journal of Marketing Development and Competitiveness*, 16(3). 10.33423/jmdc.v16i3.5584

Jiang, H., Cheng, Y., Yang, J., & Gao, S. (2022). AI-powered chatbot communication with customers: Dialogic interactions, satisfaction, engagement, and customer behavior. *Computers in Human Behavior*, 134, 107329. 10.1016/j.chb.2022.107329

Jiang, H., Geertman, S., & Witte, P. (2023). The contextualization of smart city technologies : An international comparison. *Journal of Urban Management*, 12(1), 33–43. 10.1016/j.jum.2022.09.001

Jian, Z., & Liu, Y. (2016). The Impacts of Customer Interaction and Social Capital on New Service Development Performance. *American Journal of Industrial and Business Management*, 6(12), 1133–1145. 10.4236/ajibm.2016.612106

Johne, J. (2023). Introduction. In *Effectiveness of Influencer Marketing*. Springer Gabler. [DOI: 10.1007/978-3-658-41297-5_1], 10.1007/978-3-658-41297-5_1

John, G., & Scheer, L. K. (2021). Commentary: Governing technology-enabled omnichannel transactions. *Journal of Marketing*, 85(1), 126–130. https://Doi.org/ 10.1177/0022242920972071. 10.1177/0022242920972071

John, S. P., & Supramaniam, S. (2023). Antecedents and Effects of Influencer Marketing Strategies: A Systematic Literature Review and Directions for Future Research. In Martínez-López, F. J. (Ed.), *Advances in Digital Marketing and eCommerce. DMEC 2023. Springer Proceedings in Business and Economics*. Springer. 10.1007/978-3-031-31836-8_15

Johnston, R., & Kong, X. Y. (2011). The Customer Experience: A Road-Map For Improvement. *Managing Service Quality*, 21(1), 5–24. 10.1108/09604521111100225

Jonny, Kriswanto, & Toshio, M. (2021). Building an Implementation Model of IoT and Big Data and Its Improvement. *INTERNATIONAL JOURNAL OF TECHNOLOGY, 12*(5), 1000-1008. 10.14716/ijtech.v12i5.5178

Joshi, Y., Lim, W. M., & Jagani, K. (2023). *Social media influencer marketing: foundations, trends, and ways forward*. Electron Commer Res. 10.1007/s10660-023-09719-z

Junaidi, A., Basrowi, B., Sabtohadi, J., Wibowo, A., Wibowo, S., Asgar, A., Pramono, E., & Yenti, E. (2024). The role of public administration and social media educational socialization in influencing public satisfaction on population services : The mediating role of population literacy awareness. *International Journal of Data and Network Science*, 8(1), 345–356. 10.5267/j.ijdns.2023.9.019

Jung, S. U., & Shegai, V. (2023). The Impact of Digital Marketing Innovation on Firm Performance: Mediation by Marketing Capability and Moderation by Firm Size. *Sustainability (Basel)*, 15(7), 5711. 10.3390/su15075711

Juric, B., Smith, S. D., & Wilks, G. (2015). Negative customer brand engagement: an overview of conceptual and blog-based findings. *Customer Engagement: Contemporary Issues and Challenges*, pp. 278-294.

Kaczorowska-Spychalska, D. (2019). Chatbots in marketing. *Management*, 23(1), 251–270. 10.2478/manment-2019-0015

Kahn, B. (2018). The Shopping Revolution, How Successful Retailers Win Customers. In *An Era Of Endless Disruption*. Wharton School Press.

Kalaignanam, K., Tuli, K. R., Kushwaha, T., Lee, L., & Gal, D. (2020). Marketing agility: The concept, antecedents, and a research agenda. *Journal of Marketing*, 85(1), 35–58. 10.1177/0022242920952760

Kalenda, M., Hyna, P., & Rossi, B. (2018). Scaling Agile In Large Organizations: Practices, Challenges, And Success Factors. *Journal of Software (Malden, MA)*, 30(10), E1954. 10.1002/smr.1954

Kaličanin, K. (2019). Benefits of Artificial Intelligence and Machine Learning in Marketing. *Proceedings of the International Scientific Conference - Sinteza 2019*. Novi Sad, Serbia: Singidunum University. 10.15308/Sinteza-2019-472-477

Kaltcheva, V. D., & Weitz, B. A. (2006). When should a retailer create an exciting store environment? *Journal of Marketing*, 70(1), 107–118. 10.1509/jmkg.70.1.107 qxd

Kamilova, X.M. Yunusxodjaeva, Z. Sobirova. (2022). Interaction Of Fashion Industry and Information Technology. Digital And Phygital New Fashion Technology. Spectrum Journal Of Innovation. *Reforms And Development*, 3, 95–98.

Kandasamy, D., Dhandayudam, P., Pirya, V., & Sengan, S. (2020). Deep Learning Sentiment Analysis For Recommendations In Social Applications. *International Journal of Scientific & Technology Research.*, 9, 3812–3815.

Kandt, J. & Batty, M. (2021). Smart cities, big data and urban policy : Towards urban analytics for the long run. *Cities (London, England)*, 109, 102992. 10.1016/j.cities.2020.102992

Kang, H. J., Shin, J., & Ponto, K. (2020). How 3D Virtual Reality Stores Can Shape Consumer Purchase Decisions : The Roles of Informativeness and Playfulness. *Journal of Interactive Marketing*, 49(1), 70–85. 10.1016/j.intmar.2019.07.002

Kannan, P. K., & Li, H. (2017). Digital marketing: A framework, review and research agenda. *International Journal of Research in Marketing*, 34(1), 22–45. 10.1016/j.ijresmar.2016.11.006

Kaplan, A. M., & Haenlein, M. (2010). Users of the world, unite! The challenges and opportunities of Social Media. *Business Horizons*, 53(1), 59–68. https://doi.org/https://doi.org/10.1016/j.bushor.2009.09.003. 10.1016/j.bushor.2009.09.003

Kaplan, A., & Haenlein, M. (2019). Siri, Siri, in my hand: Who's the fairest in the land? On the interpretations, illustrations, and implications of artificial intelligence. *Business Horizons*, 62(1), 15–25. 10.1016/j.bushor.2018.08.004

Kaplan, A., & Haenlein, M. (2019a). Rulers of the world, unite! The challenges and opportunities of artificial intelligence. *Business Horizons*, 63(1), 37–50. 10.1016/j.bushor.2019.09.003

Karle, S. A. (2022). Hotel recommender system. *Indian Scientific Journal of Research in Engineering and Management*, 06(04). 10.55041/IJSREM12529

Kaswan, K. S., Dhatterwal, J. S., & Ojha, R. P. (2024). AI in personalized learning. In *Advances in Technological Innovations in Higher Education* (pp. 103–117). CRC Press. 10.1201/9781003376699-9

Kauffmann, E., Peral, J., Gil, D., Ferrández, A., Sellers, R., & Mora, H. (2020). A framework for big data analytics in commercial social networks: A case study on sentiment analysis and fake review detection for marketing decision-making. *Industrial Marketing Management*, 90, 523–537. 10.1016/j.indmarman.2019.08.003

Kaur, G. (2017). The Importance Of Digital Marketing In The Tourism Industry. *International Journal of Research -GRANTHAALAYAH, 5*, 72–77. 10.29121/granthaalayah.v5.i6.2017.1998

Kaur, J., Lavuri, R., Parida, R., & Singh, S. V. (2023). Exploring the Impact of Gamification Elements in Brand Apps on the Purchase Intention of Consumers. *Journal of Global Information Management, 31*(1). *Journal of Global Information Management*, 31(1), 1–30. 10.4018/JGIM.317216

Kaur, N., Sahdev, S. L., Sharma, M., & Siddiqui, L. (2020). Banking 4.0: The influence of artificial intelligence on the banking industry & how ai is changing the face of modern day banks. *International Journal of Management*, 11(6), 577–585. 10.34218/IJM.11.6.2020.049

Kaur, P., & Kaur, N. (2019). Understanding customer churn in the telecommunication sector: A study of geographical location. [IJEAT]. *International Journal of Engineering and Advanced Technology*, 9(2), 2561–2566. 10.35940/ijeat.F1107.0885S619

Kautish, P., & Khare, A. (2022). Investigating the moderating role of AI-enabled services on flow and awe experience. *International Journal of Information Management*, 66, 102519. 10.1016/j.ijinfomgt.2022.102519

Kaya, B. (2019). Hotel recommendation system by bipartite networks and link prediction. *Journal of Information Science*, 46(1), 53–63. 10.1177/0165551518824577

Kazmi, S. H. A., Ahmed, R. R., Soomro, K. A., Hashem, E. A. R., Akhtar, H., & Parmar, V. (2021). Role of augmented reality in changing consumer behavior and decision making : Case of Pakistan. *Sustainability (Switzerland), 13*(24). *Sustainability (Basel)*, 13(24), 14064. 10.3390/su132414064

Keegan, B. J., Canhoto, A. I., & Yen, D. A. (2022). Power negotiation on the tango dancefloor : The adoption of AI in B2B marketing. *Industrial Marketing Management*, 100, 36–48. 10.1016/j.indmarman.2021.11.001

Keegan, B. J., Dennehy, D., & Naudé, P. (2022). Implementing Artificial Intelligence in Traditional B2B Marketing Practices: An Activity Theory Perspective. *Information Systems Frontiers*, 15. Advance online publication. 10.1007/s10796-022-10294-135637917

Kelly, A. (2008). *Changing Software Development: Learning To Become Agile*. John Wiley & Sons.

Kenza, B., soumaya, O., & Mohamed, A. (2023). A Conceptual Framework using Big Data Analytics for Effective Email Marketing. *Procedia Computer Science*, 220, 1044–1050. 10.1016/j.procs.2023.03.146

Kerin, R. A., Jain, A., & Howard, D. J. (1992). Store shopping experience and consumer price-quality-value perceptions. *Journal of Retailing*, 68(4), 376.

Khadija, S. E. N. I. H. J. I. (2023). Digital Marketing: An Opportunity To Personalize Banking Services For Better Customer Satisfaction. *International Journal Of Applied Management And Economics, 2*(05), 019-033. 10.5281/zenodo.10180129

Khan, A., Ehsan, N., Mirza, E., & Sarwar, S. Z. (2012). Integration between Customer Relationship Management (CRM) and Data Warehousing. *Procedia Technology*, 1, 239–249. 10.1016/j.protcy.2012.02.050

Khan, S., & Abbas, M. (2023). Interactive effects of consumers' ethical beliefs and authenticity on ethical consumption and pro-environmental behaviors. *Journal of Retailing and Consumer Services*, 71, 103226. 10.1016/j.jretconser.2022.103226

Khargharia, H. S., Rehman, M. H., Banerjee, A., Montori, F., Forkan, A. R. M., & Jayaraman, P. P. (2023). Towards Marketing 4.0 : Vision and Survey on the Role of IoT and Data Science. *Societies (Basel, Switzerland)*, 13(4), 4. 10.3390/soc13040100

Khoeini, A., Haratizadeh, S., & Hoseinzade, E. (2020). *Representation extraction and deep neural recommendation for collaborative filtering*. arXiv.org.

Khrais, L. T. (2020). Role of artificial intelligence in shaping consumer demand in E-commerce. *Future Internet*, 12(12), 226. 10.3390/fi12120226

Khvatova, T., Appio, F. P., Ray, S., & Schiavone, F. (2023). Exploring the Role of AI in B2B Customer Journey Management: Towards an IPO Model. *IEEE Transactions on Engineering Management*. IEEE.

Kiili, K., Ojansuu, K., Lindstedt, A., & Ninaus, M. (2018). Exploring the Educational Potential of a Game-Based Math Competition. *International Journal of Game-Based Learning*, 8(2), 14–28. 10.4018/IJGBL.2018040102

Kim, H.-S., & Yoon, C.-H. (2004). Determinants of subscriber churn and customer loyalty in the Korean mobile telephony market. *Telecommunications Policy*, 28(7-8), 751–765. 10.1016/j.telpol.2004.05.013

Kim, J. H., Kim, M., Park, M., & Yoo, J. (2023). Immersive interactive technologies and virtual shopping experiences: Differences in consumer perceptions between augmented reality (AR) and virtual reality (VR). *Telematics and Informatics*, 77, 101936. 10.1016/j.tele.2022.101936

Kim, J. H., Kim, M., Yoo, J., & Park, M. (2024). Augmented reality in delivering experiential values: Moderating role of task complexity. *Virtual Reality (Waltham Cross)*, 28(1), 19. 10.1007/s10055-023-00896-8

Kim, T., Usman, U., Garvey, A., & Duhachek, A. (2023). Artificial Intelligence in Marketing and Consumer Behavior Research. *Foundations and Trends in Marketing*, 18(1), 1–93. Advance online publication. 10.1561/1700000078

Kiran, A., Kumar, I. J., Vijayakarthik, P., Naik, S. K. L., & Vinod, T. (2023*). Intelligent Chat Bots: An AI Based Chat Bot For Better Banking Applications. In *2023 International Conference on Computer Communication and Informatics (ICCCI),* Coimbatore, India. 10.1109/ICCCI56745.2023.10128582

Klaib, A. F., Alsrehin, N. O., Melhem, W. Y., Bashtawi, H. O., & Magableh, A. A. (2021). Eye tracking algorithms, techniques, tools, and applications with an emphasis on machine learning and Internet of Things technologies. *Expert Systems with Applications*, 166, 114037. 10.1016/j.eswa.2020.114037

Klaus, P., & Maklan, S. (2013). Towards A Better Measure Of Customer Experience. *International Journal of Market Research*, 55(2), 227–246. Https://Doi.Org/10.2501/IJMR-2013-021. 10.2501/IJMR-2013-021

Knight, W. (2021). *How To Use Design Thinking In Marketing*. Warren-Night. Https://Warren-Knight.Com/2021/04/08/How-To-Use-Design-Thinking-In-Marketing/

Knof, M., Stock-Homburg, R., & Schurer, J. (2023). How in-store sensor technologies can help retailers to understand their customers: Overview on two decades of research. *International Review of Retail, Distribution and Consumer Research*, 1–18.

Kocaman, B., Gelper, S., & Langerak, F. (2023). Till the cloud do us part : Technological disruption and brand retention in the enterprise software industry. *International Journal of Research in Marketing*, 40(2), 316–341. 10.1016/j.ijresmar.2022.11.001

Köseoğlu, Ö. (2002). *Değişim Fenomeni Karşısında Markalaşma Süreci ve Bu Süreçte Halkla lişkilerin Rolü*. Yüksek Lisans Tezi. Ege Üniversitesi Sosyal Bilimler EnstitüsüHalkla lişkiler Anabilim Dalı, İzmir.

Kotler, P., Kartajaya, H., & Setiawan, I. (2010). *Marketing 3.0 : Produits, clients, facteur humain*. Wiley. 10.1002/9781118257883

Kotler, P., Kartajaya, H., & Setiawan, I. (2016). *Marketing 4.0 : Moving from Traditional to Digital*. John Wiley & Sons.

Kotler, P., Kartajaya, H., & Setiawan, I. (2021). *Marketing 5.0 : Technology for Humanity*. John Wiley & Sons.

Kotler, P., Kartajaya, H., & Setıawan, I. (2022). *Pazarlama 5.0*. Nişantaşı Üniversitesi Yayınları.

Kowalczuk, P., Siepmann, C., & Adler, J. (2021). Cognitive, affective, and behavioral consumer responses to augmented reality in e-commerce: A comparative study. *Journal of Business Research*, 124, 357–373. 10.1016/j.jbusres.2020.10.050

Koz\lowski, W., & Suwar, K. (2021). *Smart city : Definitions, dimensions, and initiatives*. UM. https://www.um.edu.mt/library/oar/handle/123456789/105179

Kozinets, R. V. (2015). *Netnography: redefined*. Sage.

Kozinets, R. V. (2010). Netnography: Connected consumers and digital ethnography. *Progress in Consumer Research*, 37(1), 221–231.

Krejcie, R. V., & Morgan, D. W. (1970). Determining Sample Size for Research Activities. *Educational and Psychological Measurement*, 30(3), 607–610. 10.1177/001316447003000308

Kučera, P., & Cmuntová, D. (2023). Design and implementation of a CRM system to optimize business processes of a trading company. *Entrepreneurship and Sustainability Issues*, 11(2), 363–380. 10.9770/jesi.2023.11.2(25)

Kulkov, I., Kulkova, J., Rohrbeck, R., Menvielle, L., Kaartemo, V., & Makkonen, H. (2023). Artificial intelligence-driven sustainable development: Examining organizational, technical, and processing approaches to achieving global goals. *Sustainable Development*.

Kumar, A. (2022). Sustainable smart cities. In Kumar, A. (Ed.), *Ecosystem-Based Adaptation* (pp. 325–416). Elsevier. 10.1016/B978-0-12-815025-2.00007-1

Kumar, H. (2022). Augmented reality in online retailing: A systematic review and research agenda. *International Journal of Retail & Distribution Management*, 50(4), 537–559. 10.1108/IJRDM-06-2021-0287

Kumar, V., Aksoy, L., Donkers, B., Venkatesan. R., Wiesel, T., & Tillmanns, S. (2010). Undervalued or overvalued customers: Capturing total customer engagement value. J. Serv. *Journal of Service Research*, 13(3), 297–310. 10.1177/1094670510375602

Kumar, V., Aksoy, L., Donkers, B., Venkatesan, R., Wiesel, T., & Tillmanns, S. (2019). Customer engagement: The construct, antecedents, and consequences. *Journal of the Academy of Marketing Science*, 47(2), 252–277.

Kumar, V., Rafiq, M., Dangelico, R. M., & Chan, F. K. Y. (2019). Omni-channel retailing: A review of the literature and future research directions. *Journal of Retailing*, 95(6), 707–728.

Kumar, V., Rajan, B., Gupta, S., & Pozza, I. D. (2019). Customer engagement in service. *Journal of the Academy of Marketing Science*, 47(1), 138–160. 10.1007/s11747-017-0565-2

Kumar, V., Rajan, B., Venkatesan, R., & Lecinski, J. (2019). Understanding the role of artificial intelligence in personalized engagement marketing. *California Management Review*, 61(4), 135–155. 10.1177/0008125619859317

Kumar, V., Ramachandran, D., & Kumar, B. (2021). Influence of new-age technologies on marketing : A research agenda. *Journal of Business Research*, 125, 864–877. 10.1016/j.jbusres.2020.01.007

Kumar, V., & Reinartz, W. (2018). *Customer Relationship Management*. Springer Berlin Heidelberg., 10.1007/978-3-662-55381-7

Kunathikornkit, S., Piriyakul, I., & Piriyakul, R. (2023). One-to-one marketing management via customer complaint. *Social Network Analysis and Mining*, 13(1), 83. 10.1007/s13278-023-01082-z

Kushwaha, A. K., Kumar, P., & Kar, A. K. (2021). What impacts customer experience for B2B enterprises on using AI-enabled chatbots? Insights from Big data analytics. *Industrial Marketing Management*, 98, 207–221. 10.1016/j.indmarman.2021.08.011

Kuş, O. (2021). *Algoritmaları Dehümanizasyon Çerçevesinde Tartışmak (Der. Oğuz Kuş). Algoritmaların Gölgesinde Toplum Ve İletişim*. Alternatif Bilişim Derneği.

Kutaula, S., Gillani, A., Leonidou, L. C., & Christodoulides, P. (2022). Integrating fair trade with circular economy: Personality traits, consumer engagement, and ethically-minded behavior. *Journal of Business Research*, 144, 1087–1102. 10.1016/j.jbusres.2022.02.044

L, F., J., E., E., A., U., O., J., and O., O., B. (2023). Customer Relationship Management and Customers Repeat Purchase Behavior in Nigeria. *Scholars Journal of Economics, Business and Management, 10*(1), 19–28. 10.36347/sjebm.2023.v10i01.002

Lakens, D. (2022). Sample size justification. *Collabra. Psychology*, 8(1), 33267. 10.1525/collabra.33267

Lamsiah, A., & Bentalha, B. (2023). 2022 Qatar World Cup: A Netnographic Analysis of the Relationship Between Sport, Media and Politic *Réflexions sportives, 7*(3), 69-95 .

Lao, A., & Et Vlad, M. (2018). Évolution Numérique Des Points De Vente Par La Borne Interactive: Quels Impacts Sur L'Imagerie Mentale, L'Expérience De Magasinage Et La Valeur De Magasinage? *Décisions Marketing, 91*, 61-78. Https://Doi.Org/10.7193/Dm.091.61.78

Lapassouse-Madrid, C., & Et Vlad, M. (2017). Courses Connectées: Un Cas De Destruction Ou De Création De Valeur Pour Les Clients Et Les Distributeurs. *Décisions Marketing*, 84(84), 43-59. Https://Doi.Org/10.7193/Dm.084.43.59

Larsson, S., & Heintz, F. (2020). Transparency in artificial intelligence. *Internet Policy Review*, 9(2), 1–16. 10.14763/2020.2.1469

Latinovic, Z., & Chatterjee, S. C. (2022). Achieving the promise of AI and ML in delivering economic and relational customer value in B2B. *Journal of Business Research*, 144, 966–974. 10.1016/j.jbusres.2022.01.052

Lavoye, V., Mero, J., & Tarkiainen, A. (2021). Consumer behavior with augmented reality in retail: A review and research agenda. *International Review of Retail, Distribution and Consumer Research*, 31(3), 299–329. 10.1080/09593969.2021.1901765

Ledro, C., Nosella, A., & Dalla Pozza, I. (2023). Integration of AI in CRM: Challenges and guidelines. *Journal of Open Innovation*, 9(4), 100151. 10.1016/j.joitmc.2023.100151

Ledro, C., Nosella, A., & Vinelli, A. (2022). Artificial intelligence in customer relationship management: Literature review and future research directions. *Journal of Business and Industrial Marketing*, 37(13), 48–63. 10.1108/JBIM-07-2021-0332

Lee, M. T., & Suh, I. (2022). Understanding the effects of Environment, Social, and Governance conduct on financial performance: Arguments for a process and integrated modelling approach. *Sustainable Technology and Entrepreneurship, 1*(1), 100004.

Lee, A. S., Thomas, M., & Baskerville, R. L. (2015). Going back to basics in design science: From the information technology artifact to the information systems artifact. *Information Systems Journal*, 25(1), 5–21. 10.1111/isj.12054

Lee, H., Xu, Y., & Porterfield, A. (2022). Antecedents and moderators of consumer adoption toward AR-enhanced virtual try-on technology: A stimulus-organism-response approach. *International Journal of Consumer Studies*, 46(4), 1319–1338. 10.1111/ijcs.12760

Lee, N., Broderick, A. J., & Chamberlain, L. (2007). What is "neuromarketing"? A discussion and agenda for future research. *International Journal of Psychophysiology*, 63(2), 199–204. 10.1016/j.ijpsycho.2006.03.00716769143

Lee, N., Chamberlain, L., & Brandes, L. (2018). Welcome to the jungle! The neuromarketing literature through the eyes of a newcomer. *European Journal of Marketing*, 52(1/2), 4–38. 10.1108/EJM-02-2017-0122

Lee, T., Robinson, C., & Smith, J. (2018). Understanding customer churn in the telecommunications industry: The role of contract type. *Journal of Retailing and Consumer Services*, 42, 222–230. 10.1016/j.jretconser.2018.02.013

Lehman, R. A., Watson, H. J., Wixom, B. H., & Hoffer, J. A. (2008). Continental Airlines Flies High with Real-time Business Intelligence. *MIS Quarterly Executive*, 3(4), 30.

Lemon, K. N., & Et Verhoef, P. C. (2016). Understanding Customer Experience Throughout The Customer Journey. *Gjournal Of Marketing, 80*(6), 69-96. Https://Doi.Org/10.1509/Jm.15.0420

Lemon, K. N., & Verhoef, P. C. (2016). Understanding customer experience throughout the customer journey. *Journal of Marketing*, 80(6), 69–96. 10.1509/jm.15.0420

Lewandowski, D. (2023). Search Engine Optimization (SEO). In *Understanding Search Engines*. Springer. [DOI: 10.1007/978-3-031-22789-9_9], 10.1007/978-3-031-22789-9_9

Lewnes, A. (2021). Commentary: The Future Of Marketing Is Agile. *Journal of Marketing*, 85(1), 64–67. 10.1177/0022242920972022

Lhoussaine, A., Kamal, M., & Bouhtati, N. (2022). Big data et efficacité marketing des entreprises touristiques: une revue de la littérature. *Alternatives de gestion économique, 1,* 39-58.

Lhoussaine, ALLA, Kamal, M., & Bouhtati, N. (2022). Big data et efficacité marketing des entreprises touristiques: une revue de la littérature. *Alternatives de gestion économique, 1*, 39-58.

Lhoussaine, A. (2022). Big data et efficacité marketing des entreprises touristiques: Une revue de littérature. *Alternatives Managériales Economiques*, 1, 39–58.

Lhoussaine, A. L. L. A., Kamal, M., & Bouhtati, N. (2022). Big data and marketing effectiveness of tourism businesses: A literature review. *Economic Management Alternatives*, 1, 39–58.

Lhoussaine, A., Kamal, M., & Bouhtati, N. (2022). Big data et efficacité marketing des entreprises touristiques : Une revue de littérature. *Alternatives Managériales Economiques*, 1, 39–58.

Li, F., Larimo, J. & Leonidou, L.C. (2021). Social media marketing strategy: definition, conceptualization, taxonomy, validation, and future agenda. *J. of the Acad. Mark. Sci. 49*, 51–70. (https://doi.org/)10.1007/s11747-020-00733-3

Liao, S. H., Widowati, R., & Hsieh, Y. C. (2021). Investigating online social media users' behaviors for social commerce recommendations. *Technology in Society*, 66, 101655. 10.1016/j.techsoc.2021.101655

Lichtlé, M.-C. & Plichon, V. (2005). La Diversité Des Émotions Ressenties Dans Un Point De Vente. Cahiers de Recherche 05-03. *Décisions Marketing*.

Li, F., Lu, H., Hou, M., Cui, K., & Darbandi, M. (2021). Customer satisfaction with bank services: The role of cloud services, security, e-learning and service quality. *Technology in Society*, 64, 101487. 10.1016/j.techsoc.2020.101487

Li, J., Pan, S., Huang, L., & Zhu, X. (2019). A machine learning based method for customer behavior prediction. *Tehnicki Vjesnik, 26*(6), 1670-1676. *Scopus*. 10.17559/TV-20190603165825

Li, L., Lin, J., & Luo, W. (2023). INVESTIGATING THE EFFECT OF ARTIFICIAL INTELLIGENCE ON CUSTOMER RELATIONSHIP MANAGEMENT PERFORMANCE IN E-COMMERCE ENTERPRISES. *Journal of Electronic Commerce Research*, 24(1).

Li, M., Yin, D., Qiu, H., & Bai, B. (2021). A systematic review of AI technology-based service encounters: Implications for hospitality and tourism operations. *International Journal of Hospitality Management*, 95, 102930. 10.1016/j.ijhm.2021.102930

Lim, N. (2003). Consumers' Perceived Risk: Sources Versus Consequences. *Electronic Commerce Research and Applications*, 2(3), 216–228. Https://Doi.Org/10.1016/S1567-4223(03)00025-5. 10.1016/S1567-4223(03)00025-5

Lim, W. M. (2018). Demystifying neuromarketing. *Journal of Business Research*, 91, 205–220. 10.1016/j.jbusres.2018.05.036

Lim, W. M., Mohamed Jasim, K., & Das, M. (2024). Augmented and virtual reality in hotels : Impact on tourist satisfaction and intention to stay and return. *International Journal of Hospitality Management*, 116, 103631. 10.1016/j.ijhm.2023.103631

Lin, C., & Kunnathur, A. (2019). Strategic orientations, developmental culture, and big data capability. *Journal of Business Research*, 105(August), 49–60. 10.1016/j.jbusres.2019.07.016

Li, P., & Hassan, S. H. (2023). Mapping the Literature on Gen Z purchasing behavior: A bibliometric analysis using VOSviewer. *Innovative Marketing*, 19(3), 62–73. 10.21511/im.19(3).2023.06

Li, Q., & Kim, J. (2021). A Deep Learning-Based Course Recommender System for Sustainable Development in education. *Applied Sciences (Basel, Switzerland)*, 11(19), 8993. 10.3390/app11198993

Lishchynska, L., & Dobrovolska, N. (2022). PROSPECTIVE SOFTWARE TOOLS FOR DATA ANALYSIS IN BUSINESS. *Herald of Khmelnytskyi National University*, 305(1), 78–83. 10.31891/2307-5732-2022-305-1-78-79

Liu, B., & Xiong, H. (2013). Point-of-Interest Recommendation in Location Based Social Networks with Topic and Location Awareness. *Proceedings of the 2013 SIAM International Conference on Data Mining*. SAIN. 10.1137/1.9781611972832.44

Liu, C.-H., Horng, J.-S., Chou, S.-F., Yu, T.-Y., Huang, Y.-C., & Lin, J.-Y. (2023). Integrating big data and marketing concepts into tourism, hospitality operations and strategy development. *Quality & Quantity*, 57(2), 1905–1922. 10.1007/s11135-022-01426-535729961

Liu, H., & Yang, L. (2019). Customer churn analysis in the telecommunication industry based on machine learning. In *2019 IEEE International Conference on Artificial Intelligence and Computer Applications (ICAICA)* (pp. 245-248). IEEE.

Liu, P., Joty, S., & Meng, H. (2015). Fine-grained Opinion Mining with Recurrent Neural Networks and Word Embeddings. *Proceedings of the 2015 Conference on Empirical Methods in Natural Language Processing*. SAIN. 10.18653/v1/D15-1168

Liu, R. (2024). Application for Machine Learning Methods in Financial Risk Management. Highlights in Science. *Engineering and Technology*, 88, 775–778. 10.54097/stt1va49

Liu, X., Wang, D., & Gretzel, U. (2022). On-site decision-making in smartphone-mediated contexts. *Tourism Management*, 88(1), 104424. 10.1016/j.tourman.2021.104424

Liu, X.-Y. (2021). Agricultural products intelligent marketing technology innovation in big data era. *Procedia Computer Science*, 183, 648–654. 10.1016/j.procs.2021.02.110

Liu, X., & Yang, C. (2019). Customer churn prediction in the telecommunications industry: A comparison of regression models. *International Journal of Data Science and Analytics*, 8(4), 349–361. 10.1007/s41060-018-0153-3

Liu, Y., Pu, B., Guan, Z., & Et Yang, Q. (2016). Online Customer Experience and Its Relationship To Repurchase Intention: An Empirical Case Of Online Travel Agencies In China. *Asia Pacific Journal of Tourism Research*, 21(10), 1085–1099. Https://Doi.Org/10.1080/10941665.2015.1094495. 10.1080/10941665.2015.1094495

Li, Y., He, Z., Li, Y., Huang, T., & Liu, Z. (2023). Keep it real: Assessing destination image congruence and its impact on tourist experience evaluations. *Tourism Management*, 97, 104736. 10.1016/j.tourman.2023.104736

Ljepava, N. (2022). AI-enabled marketing solutions in Marketing Decision making: AI application in different stages of marketing process. *TEM Journal*, 11(3), 1308–1315. 10.18421/TEM113-40

Lo, F.-Y., & Campos, N. (2018). Blending Internet-of-Things (IoT) solutions into relationship marketing strategies. *Technological Forecasting and Social Change, 137*, 10-18. *Scopus*. 10.1016/j.techfore.2018.09.029

Loureiro, S. M. C., Bilro, R. G., & Japutra, A. (2019). The effect of consumer-generated media stimuli on emotions and consumer brand engagement. *Journal of Product and Brand Management*, 29(3), 387–408. 10.1108/JPBM-11-2018-2120

Lowry, P. B., Moody, G. D., Gaskin, J., Galletta, D., Humphreys, S., Barlow, J. B., & Wilson, D. (2013). Evaluating Journal Quality and the Association for Information Systems Senior Scholars' Journal Basket via Bibliometric Measures: Do Expert Journal Assessments Add Value? (SSRN Scholarly Paper ID 2186798). 10.25300/MISQ/2013/37.4.01

Luhn, H. P. (1958). A Business Intelligence System. *IBM Journal of Research and Development*, 2(4), 314–319. 10.1147/rd.24.0314

Lu, N., Lin, H., Lu, J., & Zhang, G. (2014). A customer churn prediction model in telecom industry using boosting. *IEEE Transactions on Industrial Informatics*, 10(2), 1659–1665. 10.1109/TII.2012.2224355

Luna, I.-R., Liébana-Cabanillas, F., Sánchez-Fernández, J., & Et Muñoz-Leiva, F. (2019). Mobile Payment Is Not All The Same: The Adoption Of Mobile Payment Systems Depending On The Technology Applied. *Technological Forecasting and Social Change*, 146, 931–944. 10.1016/j.techfore.2018.09.018

Luna-Nevarez, C. (2021). Neuromarketing, Ethics, and Regulation: An Exploratory Analysis of Consumer Opinions and Sentiment on Blogs and Social Media. *Journal of Consumer Policy*, 44(4), 559–583. 10.1007/s10603-021-09496-y

Luo, Y. (2022). A general framework of digitization risks in international business. *J Int Bus Stud, 53*, 344–361. (https://doi.org/)10.1057/s41267-021-00448-9

Luo, X., Tong, S., Fang, Z., & Qu, Z. (2019). Frontiers: machines vs. humans: The impact of artificial intelligence chatbot disclosure on customer purchases. *Marketing Science*, 38(6), 937–947. 10.1287/mksc.2019.1192

Lytras, M. D., & Visvizi, A. (2018). Who uses smart city services and what to make of it : Toward interdisciplinary smart cities research. *Sustainability (Basel)*, 10(6), 1998. 10.3390/su10061998

Maaitah, T. (2023). The Role of Business Intelligence Tools in the Decision Making Process and Performance. *Journal of Intelligence Studies in Business*, 13(1), 43–52. 10.37380/jisib.v13i1.990

Machkour, B., & Abriane, A. (2020). Industry 4.0 and its Implications for the Financial Sector. *Procedia Computer Science*, 177, 496–502. 10.1016/j.procs.2020.10.068

Mackay, H., & Et Gillespie, G. (1992). Extending The Social Shaping Of Technology Approach : Ideology And Appropriation. *Social Studies of Science*, 22(4), 658–716. 10.1177/030631292022004006

Mahanty, G., Dwivedi, D. N., & Gopalakrishnan, B. N. (2021). The Efficacy of Fiscal Vs Monetary Policies in the Asia-Pacific Region: The St. Louis Equation Revisited. *Vision (Basel)*, (November). 10.1177/09722629211054148

Mainardes, E. W., Teixeira, A., & Romano, P. C. D. S. (2017). Determinants of co-creation in banking services. *International Journal of Bank Marketing*, 35(2), 187–204. 10.1108/IJBM-10-2015-0165

Mairesse, J., Cette, G., & Kocoglu, Y. (2000). Les technologies de l'information et de la communication en France: Diffusion et contribution à la croissance. *Economie & Statistique*, 339(1), 117–146. 10.3406/estat.2000.7482

Makarius, E. E., Mukherjee, D., Fox, J. D., & Fox, A. K. (2020). Rising with the machines: A sociotechnical framework for bringing artificial intelligence into the organization. *Journal of Business Research*, 120, 262–273. 10.1016/j.jbusres.2020.07.045

Ma, L., & Sun, B. (2020). Machine learning and AI in marketing–Connecting computing power to human insights. *International Journal of Research in Marketing*, 37(3), 481–504. 10.1016/j.ijresmar.2020.04.005

Maleh, Y., & Maleh, Y. (2022). Introduction. In *Cybersecurity in Morocco. SpringerBriefs in Cybersecurity*. Springer. 10.1007/978-3-031-18475-8_1

Malik, A., & Ghai, S. (2023). Role of CRM in Customer Loyalty and Repeat Purchase Intention: An Analytical Study. *Journal of Informatics Education and Research*, 3(1), 1. 10.52783/jier.v3i1.60

Mani, Z., & Chouk, I. (2018). *Les objets connectés dans la banque: quelles implications sur les comportements des consommateurs?* World Bank. **halshs-01678793**

Mantelero, A. (2014). The future of consumer data protection in the EU Re-thinking the "notice and consent" paradigm in the new era of predictive analytics. *Computer Law & Security Report*, 30(6), 643–660. 10.1016/j.clsr.2014.09.004

Marasco, A., Buonincontri, P., van Niekerk, M., Orlowski, M., & Okumus, F. (2018). Exploring the role of next-generation virtual technologies in destination marketing. *Journal of Destination Marketing & Management*, 9, 138–148. 10.1016/j.jdmm.2017.12.002

Marchand, A., & Marx, P. (2020). Automated product recommendations with preference-based explanations. *Journal of Retailing*, 96(3), 328–343. 10.1016/j.jretai.2020.01.001

Mariani, M. M., Borghi, M., & Laker, B. (2023). Do submission devices influence online review ratings differently across different types of platforms? A big data analysis. *Technological Forecasting and Social Change*, 189, 122296. 10.1016/j.techfore.2022.122296

Marketing Insider Group. (2024). *Case Studies*. Marketing Insider Group. Https://Marketinginsidergroup.Com/Agile-Marketing/Agile-Marketing-Examples-Case-Studies/

Marković, S., Raspor, S., & Šegarić, K. (2010). Does restaurant performance meet customers' expectations? An assessment of restaurant service quality using a modified DINESERV approach. *Tourism and Hospitality Management*, 16(2), 181–195. 10.20867/thm.16.2.4

Márquez, B. Y. (2018). Neural Network Algorithm to Measure the Human Emotion. *Proceedings of the 2018 International Conference on Algorithms, Computing and Artificial Intelligence*. ACM. 10.1145/3302425.3302441

Marr, B. (2019). *Artificial intelligence in practice: how 50 successful companies used AI and machine learning to solve problems*. John Wiley & Sons.

Marrone, R., & Gallic, C. (2018). *Le Grand Liver Du Marketing Digital* (3rd ed.). Dunnod.

Martinez, B.M. & McAndrews, L.E. (2023). Do you take...? The effect of mobile payment solutions on use intention: an application of UTAUT2. *J Market Anal 11*, 458–469 (https://doi.org/)10.1057/s41270-022-00175-6

Maslow, A. (1968). *Vers une psychologie de l'être* (2e éd.). New York, New York: Van Nostrand Reinhold.

Mateo, S. (2020). Procédure pour conduire avec succès une revue de littérature selon la méthode PRISMA. *Kinésithérapie, la Revue*, 20(226), 29–37. 10.1016/j.kine.2020.05.019

Matharu, G. S., Mishra, A., Singh, H., & Upadhyay, P. (2015). Empirical Study Of Agile Software Development Methodologies: A Comparative Analysis. *Software Engineering Notes*, 40(1), 1–6. 10.1145/2693208.2693233

Mathwick, C., Malhotra, N., & Rigdon, E. (2001). Experiential value: Conceptualization, measurement and application in the catalog and Internet shopping environment☆. *Journal of Retailing*, 77(1), 39–56. 10.1016/S0022-4359(00)00045-2

Matz, S. C., & Netzer, O. (2017). Using Big Data as a window into consumers' psychology. *Current Opinion in Behavioral Sciences*, 18, 7–12. 10.1016/j.cobeha.2017.05.009

Mazingue, C. (2023). Perceived Challenges and Benefits of AI Implementation in Customer Relationship Management Systems. *Journal of Digitovation and Information System, 3*(1), 72. 10.54433/JDIIS.2023100023

McCarthy, J. (2007). From here to human-level AI. *Artificial Intelligence*, 171(18), 1174–1182. 10.1016/j.artint.2007.10.009

McClure, S. M., Li, J., Tomlin, D., Cypert, K. S., Montague, L. M., & Montague, P. R. (2004a). Neural correlates of behavioral preference for culturally familiar drinks. *Neuron*, 44(2), 379–387. 10.1016/j.neuron.2004.09.01915473974

McKinsey. (2023). Six major GenAI trends that will shape 2024's agenda. *Medium*. https://medium.com/quantumblack/six-major-genai-trends-that-will-shape-2024s-agenda-da85dba8b1a8

McKnight, D. H., Choudhury, V., & Kacmar, C. (2002). Developing and Validating Trust Measures for e-Commerce : An Integrative Typology. *Information Systems Research*, 13(3), 334–359. 10.1287/isre.13.3.334.81

McLean, G., & Wilson, A. (2019). Shopping in the digital world: Examining customer engagement through augmented reality mobile applications. *Computers in Human Behavior*, 101, 210–224. 10.1016/j.chb.2019.07.002

Meire, M., Ballings, M., & van den Poel, D. (2017). The Added Value of Social Media Data in B2B Customer Acquisition Systems: A Real-Life Experiment. *Decision Support Systems*, 104, 26–37. 10.1016/j.dss.2017.09.010

Mele, C., & Russo-Spena, T. (2022). The architecture of the phygital customer journey: A dynamic interplay between systems of insights and systems of engagement. *European Journal of Marketing*, 56(1), 72–91. 10.1108/EJM-04-2019-0308

Mele, C., Russo-Spena, T., Tregua, M., & Amitrano, C. C. (2021). The millennial customer journey: A phygital mapping of emotional, behavioural, and social experiences. *Journal of Consumer Marketing*, 38(4), 420–433. 10.1108/JCM-03-2020-3701

Merle, A., Sénécal, S., & Et St-Onge, A. (2018). Miroir, Mon Beau Miroir, Facilite Mes Choix! L'influence De L'essayage Virtuel Dans Un Contexte Omnicanal. *Décisions Marketing, 91*, 79-95. Https://Doi.Org/10.7193/Dm.091.79.95

Mhrabian, A. (1974). *An Approach To Environmental Psychology*. Cambridge, Mass: The MIT Press.

Mich, L. (2022). Artificial Intelligence and Machine Learning. In Xiang, Z., Fuchs, M., Gretzel, U., & Höpken, W. (Eds.), *Handbook of e-Tourism*. Springer. 10.1007/978-3-030-48652-5_25

Mikalef, P., & Gupta, M. (2021). Artificial intelligence capability: Conceptualization, measurement calibration, and empirical study on its impact on organizational creativity and firm performance. *Information & Management*, 58(3), 103434. 10.1016/j.im.2021.103434

Mikalef, P., Pappas, I. O., Krogstie, J., & Pavlou, P. A. (2020). Big data and business analytics: A research agenda for realizing business value. *Information & Management*, 57(1), 1. 10.1016/j.im.2019.103237

Miklosik, A., Kuchta, M., Evans, N., & Zak, S. (2019). Towards the Adoption of Machine Learning-Based Analytical Tools in Digital Marketing. *IEEE Access, 7*, 85705-85718. *Scopus*. 10.1109/ACCESS.2019.2924425

Miroshnichenko, I. V., Sheremet, M. A., Oztop, H. F., & Abu-Hamdeh, N. (2018). Natural convection of Al2O3/H2O nanofluid in an open inclined cavity with a heat-generating element. *International Journal of Heat and Mass Transfer*, 126, 184–191. 10.1016/j.ijheatmasstransfer.2018.05.146

Mishra, A., Shukla, A., & Rana, N. P. (2021). From «Touch» To A «Multisensory» Experience: The Impact Of Technology Interface And Product Type On Consumer Responses. *Psychology And Marketing, 38*(3), 385-396. 10.1002/mar.21436

Mishra, S., Ewing, M. T., & Cooper, H. B. (2022). Artificial intelligence focus and firm performance. *Journal of the Academy of Marketing Science*, 50(6), 1176–1197. 10.1007/s11747-022-00876-5

Misra, K., Schwartz, E. M., & Abernethy, J. (2019). Dynamic online pricing with incomplete information using multi-armed bandit experiments. *Marketing Science*, 38(2), 226–252. 10.1287/mksc.2018.1129

Mittelstadt, B. D., Allo, P., Taddeo, M., Wachter, S., & Floridi, L. (2016). The ethics of algorithms: Mapping the debate. *Big Data & Society*, 3(2), 2053951716679679. 10.1177/2053951716679679

Mohamed Mohamed, S., Yehia, E., & Marie, M. (2022). Relationship between E-CRM, Service Quality, Customer Satisfaction, Trust, and Loyalty in banking Industry. *Future Computing and Informatics Journal*, 7(2), 51–74. 10.54623/fue.fcij.7.2.5

Mohammed, T., Naas, S. A., Sigg, S., & Di Francesco, M. (2023). Knowledge Sharing in AI Services: A Market-Based Approach. *IEEE Internet of Things Journal*, 10(2), 1320–1331. 10.1109/JIOT.2022.3206585

Mohanty, R., & Rani, K. J. (2015). Application of computational intelligence to predict churn and non-churn of customers in Indian telecommunication. In *2015 International Conference on Computational Intelligence and Communication Networks (CICN)*, (pp. 598-603). IEEE. 10.1109/CICN.2015.123

Moher, D., Liberati, A., Tetzlaff, J., & Altman, D. G.The PRISMA Group. (2009). Preferred Reporting Items for Systematic Reviews and Meta-Analyses : The PRISMA Statement. *PLoS Medicine*, 6(7), e1000097. 10.1371/journal.pmed.100009719621072

Moi, L., & Cabiddu, F. (2021). An Agile Marketing Capability Maturity Framework. *Tourism Management*, 86, 104347. 10.1016/j.tourman.2021.104347

Moon, S., & Iacobucci, D. (2022). Social Media Analytics and Its Applications in Marketing. *Foundations and Trends in Marketing*, 15(4), 213–292. 10.1561/1700000073

Moradi, M., & Dass, M. (2022). Applications of artificial intelligence in B2B marketing : Challenges and future directions. *Industrial Marketing Management*, 107, 300–314. 10.1016/j.indmarman.2022.10.016

Moravcikova, D., & Kliestikova, J. (2017). Brand Building with Using Phygital Marketing Communication. Journal of Economics. *Business and Management*, 5(3), 148–153. 10.18178/joebm.2017.5.3.503

Morawczynski, O., & Pickens, M. (2009). *Poor people using mobile financial services: observations on customer usage and impact from M-PESA*. HDL. https://hdl.handle.net/10986/9492

Morgan, N. A. (2012). Marketing and business performance. *Journal of the Academy of Marketing Science*, 40(1), 102–119. 10.1007/s11747-011-0279-9

Morgan, N., Slotegraaf, R., & Vorhies, D. (2009). Linking Marketing Capabilities with Profit Growth. *International Journal of Research in Marketing*, 26(4), 284–293. 10.1016/j.ijresmar.2009.06.005

Morin, C. (2011). Neuromarketing: The New Science of Consumer Behavior. *Society*, 48(2), 131–135. 10.1007/s12115-010-9408-1

Mouammine, Y. & Azdimousa, H. (2019a). *Using Neuromarketing and AI to collect and analyse consumer's emotion: Literature review and perspectives.*

Muhammad, S. S., Dey, B. L., & Weerakkody, V. (2018). Analysis of factors that influence customers' willingness to leave big data digital footprints on social media: A systematic review of literature. *Information Systems Frontiers*, 20(3), 559–576. 10.1007/s10796-017-9802-y

Mühlhoff, R., & Willem, T. (2023). Social media advertising for clinical studies: Ethical and data protection implications of online targeting. *Big Data & Society*, 10(1), 1–15. 10.1177/20539517231156127

Mukhopadhyay, S., Singh, R. K., & Jain, T. (2024). Developing big data enabled Marketing 4.0 framework. *International Journal of Information Management Data Insights*, 4(1), 100214. 10.1016/j.jjimei.2024.100214

Muniz, A. M., & O'Guinn, T. C. (2001). Brand communities. *The Journal of Consumer Research*, 27(6), 712–730.

Munjal, N. (2016). A study on ethical issues in advertising and analyzing different unethical advertisements with results of asci decisions: An Indian perspective. *Ecoforum Journal*, 5(2), 1–34.

Murat, A., Saida, S., & Timurlan, S. (2023). Global Digital Transformation Trends in Real Sectors of the Economy. *SHS Web of Conferences, 172*, 02014. 10.1051/shsconf/202317202014

Murgai, A. (2018). Transforming digital marketing with artificial intelligence. International Journal of Latest Technology in Engineering, Management &. *Applied Sciences (Basel, Switzerland)*, 7(4), 259–262.

Murray, K. B. (2008). *Interactive Consumer Decision Aids, Handbook Of Marketing Decision Models*. B. Wierenga, Berlin: Springer Science. https://doi.org/10.1007/978-0-387-78213-3_3

Naidu, G., Zuva, T., & Sibanda, E. M. (2022). Systematic review of churn prediction systems in telecommunications. In Bindhu, V., Tavares, J. M. R. S., & Du, K. L. (Eds.), *Proceedings of the Third International Conference on Communication, Computing and Electronics Systems: Lecture Notes in Electrical Engineering*. Springer, Singapore. 10.1007/978-981-16-8862-1_64

Naimi-Sadigh, A., Asgari, T., & Rabiei, M. (2022). Digital transformation in the value chain disruption of banking services. *Journal of the Knowledge Economy*, 13(2), 1212–1242. 10.1007/s13132-021-00759-0

Nanjundan, M. (2014). Cross-Domain Opinion Mining Using a Thesaurus in Social Media Content. *International Journal of Innovative Research in Computer and Communication Engineering.*, 2, 4059–4069.

Narin, B. (2018). Kişiselleştirilmiş Çevrimiçi Haber Akışının Yankı Odası Etkisi, Filtre Balonu ve Siberbalkanizasyon Kavramları Çerçevesinde İncelenmesi. *Selçuk İletişim*, 11(2), 232–251. 10.18094/josc.340471

Nassereddine, M., & Khang, A. (2024). Applications of Internet of Things (IoT) in smart cities. In *Advanced IoT Technologies and Applications in the Industry 4.0 Digital Economy* (pp. 109–136). CRC Press. https://www.taylorfrancis.com/chapters/edit/10.1201/9781003434269-6/applications-internet-things-iot-smart-cities-mohamed-nassereddine-alex-khang10.1201/9781003434269-6

Needham, R. D., & De Loë, R. C. (1990). The policy Delphi: Purpose, structure, and application. *The Canadian Geographer. Geographe Canadien*, 34(2), 133–142. 10.1111/j.1541-0064.1990.tb01258.x

Ngai, E. W. T., Lee, M. C. M., Luo, M., Chan, P. S. L., & Liang, T. (2021). An intelligent knowledge-based chatbot for customer service. *Electronic Commerce Research and Applications*, 50, 101098. 10.1016/j.elerap.2021.101098

Nguyen, C. T.-L., Bleus, H., Van Bockhaven, J., Crutzen, N., & Basile, C. (2018). *Smart City-Le Guide Pratique-Tome 2-Comment Rendre le Citoyen Acteur de son Territoire?* Bitstream. https://orbi.uliege.be/bitstream/2268/229265/1/smart-city-le-guide-pratique-tome-2.pdf

Niederberger, M., & Spranger, J. (2020). Delphi technique in health sciences: A map. *Frontiers in Public Health*, 8, 561103. 10.3389/fpubh.2020.0045733072683

Nikam, R. J. (2023). Legality of usage of Artificial Intelligence and Machine Learnings by Share Market Intermediary. *Passagens-International Review of Political History and Legal Culture*, 15(2), 319–339. 10.15175/1984-2503-202315207

Nikhashemi, S. R., Knight, H. H., Nusair, K., & Liat, C. B. (2021). Augmented reality in smart retailing : A (n) (A) Symmetric Approach to continuous intention to use retail brands' mobile AR apps. *Journal of Retailing and Consumer Services*, 60, 102464. 10.1016/j.jretconser.2021.102464

Nikolajeva, A., & Teilans, A. (2021). Machine Learning Technology Overview In Terms Of Digital Marketing And Personalization. *ECMS*, 125-130.

Noble, S. M., Mende, M., Grewal, D., & Et Parasuraman, A. (2022). The Fifth Industrial Revolution : How Harmonious Human–Machine Collaboration Is Triggering A Retail And Service [R]Evolution. *Journal of Retailing*, 98(2), 199–208. Https://Doi.Org/10.1016/J.Jretai.2022.04.003. 10.1016/j.jretai.2022.04.003

Nofal, E., Reffat, R. M., & Vande Moere, A. (2017). Communicating Built Heritage Information Using Tangible Interaction Approach. *Proceedings of the Eleventh International Conference on Tangible, Embedded, and Embodied Interaction*, (pp. 689-692). IEEE. 10.1145/3024969.3025035

Noraini, A., & Saiful Azmi, I., Yuhaniz, Sophiayati, S., Suriani, M.S. (2015). Data quality in big data: A review. *International Journal Of Advances In Soft Computing And Its Applications*, 7(3), 16–27.

Nüesch, R., Alt, R., & Puschmann, T. (2015). Hybrid customer interaction. *Business & Information Systems Engineering*, 57(1), 73–78. 10.1007/s12599-014-0366-9

Nunan, D., & Di Domenico, M. (2013). Market Research and the Ethics of Big Data. *International Journal of Market Research*, 55(4), 505–520. 10.2501/IJMR-2013-015

Nunnally, J. C., & Bernstein, I. H. (1994). The Assessment of Reliability. *Psychometric Theory*, 3, 248–292.

Nuseir, M., & Al. (2018). Digital media impact on smes performance in the UAE. Volume 24, Issue 2, 2018. *Academy of Entrepreneurship Journal*, 24, 1–13.

Odabaşı, Y., & Barış, G. (2003). *Tüketici Davranışı (Cilt 2. Baskı)*. MediaCat Akademi.

OEC. (2013). *Code Des Devoirs Professionnels*. OEC. http://www.oec-casablanca.ma/img/uploads/Code_des_Devoirs _Professionnels_Conforme_au_Code_Deontologique_de_L_IFAC_2009.pdf

Ogbuke, N. J., Yusuf, Y. Y., Dharma, K., & Mercangoz, B. A. (2022). Big data supply chain analytics: Ethical, privacy and security challenges posed to business, industries and society. *Production Planning and Control*, 33(2-3), 123–137. 10.1080/09537287.2020.1810764

Okoli, C., & Pawlowski, S. D. (2004). The Delphi method as a research tool: An example, design considerations and applications. *Information & Management*, 42(1), 15–29. 10.1016/j.im.2003.11.002

Oladipo, J. O., Akinwumiju, A. S., Aboyeji, O. S., & Adelodun, A. A. (2021). Comparison between fuzzy logic and water quality index methods: A case of water quality assessment in Ikare community, Southwestern Nigeria. *Environmental Challenges*, 3, 100038. 10.1016/j.envc.2021.100038

Oliveira Simoyama, F., Grigg, I., Luiz Pereira Bueno, R., & Oliveira, L. C. (2017). Triple entry ledgers with blockchain for auditing. *International Journal of Auditing Technology*, 3(3), 163–183. 10.1504/IJAUDIT.2017.086741

Olszak, C. M. (2016). Toward Better Understanding and Use of Business Intelligence in Organizations. *Information Systems Management*, 33(2), 105–123. 10.1080/10580530.2016.1155946

Omotosho, B. (2020). Small scale craft workers and the use of social media platforms for business performance in southwest Nigeria. *Journal of Small Business and Entrepreneurship*, 35(2), 1–16. 10.1080/08276331.2020.1764732

Orhan, İ. (2002). *Satın Alınan Ürünlere İlişkin Duyguların Cinsiyet ve Cinsiyet Rolleri Bakımından İncelenmesi*.

Oukarfi, S., & Bercheq, A. (2020a). Les déterminants socioéconomiques et géographiques de l'achat en ligne au Maroc. *Revue d'Economie Industrielle*, 171(3), 139–182. 10.4000/rei.9308

Oumlil, R., & Aderkaoui, A. (2020). Technology Acceptance, a relevant step to digitalize Moroccan human development public organizations. *Revue Management & Innovation*, 20(1), 119–136. 10.3917/rmi.201.0119

Overgoor, G., Chica, M., Rand, W., & Weishampel, A. (2019). Letting the Computers Take Over: Using AI to Solve Marketing Problems. *California Management Review*, 61(4), 156–185. 10.1177/0008125619859318

Owe, A., & Baum, S. D. (2021). Moral consideration of nonhumans in the ethics of artificial intelligence. *AI and Ethics*, 1(4), 517–528. 10.1007/s43681-021-00065-0

Oyman, M., Bal, D., & Ozer, S. (2022). Extending the technology acceptance model to explain how perceived augmented reality affects consumers' perceptions. *Computers in Human Behavior*, 128, 107127. 10.1016/j.chb.2021.107127

Özmen, Ş. (2003). *Ağ Ekonomisinde Yeni Ticaret Yolu E-Ticaret*. İstanbul Bilgi Üniversitesi Yayınları.

Pagani, M., & Pardo, C. (2017). The impact of digital technology on relationships in a business network. *Industrial Marketing Management*, 67, 185–192. 10.1016/j.indmarman.2017.08.009

Page, M. J., McKenzie, J. E., Bossuyt, P. M., Boutron, I., Hoffmann, T. C., Mulrow, C. D., Shamseer, L., Tetzlaff, J. M., Akl, E. A., & Brennan, S. E. (2021). The PRISMA 2020 statement : An updated guideline for reporting systematic reviews. *BMJ (Clinical Research Ed.)*, 372. https://www.bmj.com/content/372/bmj.n71.short33782057

Paliwal, S., Bharti, V., & Mishra, A. K. (2020). AI chatbots: Transforming the digital world. *Recent trends and advances in artificial intelligence and internet of things*, (pp. 455-482). Springer. 10.1007/978-3-030-32644-9_34

Palmer, D. E. (2005). Pop-ups, cookies, and spam: Toward a deeper analysis of the ethical significance of internet marketing practices. *Journal of Business Ethics*, 58(1-3), 271–280. 10.1007/s10551-005-1421-8

Palmer, S. R., & Felsing, M. (2001). *A Practical Guide To Feature-Driven Development*. Pearson Education.

Parasuraman, A., Zeithaml, V. A., & Malhotra, A. (2005). ES-QUAL: A multiple-item scale for assessing electronic service quality. *Journal of Service Research*, 7(3), 213–233. 10.1177/1094670504271156

Paré, G., Cameron, A.-F., Poba-Nzaou, P., & Templier, M. (2013). A systematic assessment of rigor in information systems ranking-type Delphi studies. *Information & Management*, 50(5), 207–217. 10.1016/j.im.2013.03.003

Park, T., Shenoy, R., & Salvendy, G. (2008). Effective Advertising on Mobile Phones: A Literature Review and Presentation of Results from 53 Case Studies. *Behaviour & Information Technology*, 27(5), 355–373. 10.1080/01449290600958882

Paschen, J., Wilson, M., & Ferreira, J. J. (2020). Collaborative intelligence: How human and artificial intelligence create value along the B2B sales funnel. *Business Horizons*, 63(3), 403–414. 10.1016/j.bushor.2020.01.003

Patary, C. L. (2019). *The Scrum Master Guidebook: A Reference For Obtaining Mastery*. Notion Press.

Patel, N., & Trivedi, S. (2020). Leveraging predictive modeling, machine learning personalization, NLP customer support, and AI chatbots to increase customer loyalty. *Empirical Quests for Management Essences*, 3(3), 1–24.

Paul, J., & Criado, A. R. (2020). The art of writing literature review: What do we know and what do we need to know? *International Business Review*, 29(4), 101717. 10.1016/j.ibusrev.2020.101717

Pavlik, J., (2008). *Mapping the Consequences of Technology on Public Relations*.

Pavlou, P. A., & Gefen, D. (2004). Building Effective Online Marketplaces with Institution-Based Trust. *Information Systems Research*, 15(1), 37–59. 10.1287/isre.1040.0015

Pearson, S. (2013). *Privacy, security and trust in cloud computing*. Springer London. 10.1007/978-1-4471-4189-1

Penpece, D. (2006). *Tüketici Davranılarını Belirleyen Etmenler: Kültrürün Tüketici Davranışları Üzerindeki Etkisi*. Kahramanmaraş.

Peppard, J. (2000). Customer Relationship Management (CRM) in financial services. *European Management Journal*, 18(3), 312–327. 10.1016/S0263-2373(00)00013-X

Perannagari, K. T., & Chakrabarti, S. (2019). Factors influencing acceptance of augmented reality in retail: Insights from thematic analysis. *International Journal of Retail & Distribution Management*, 48(1), 18–34. 10.1108/IJRDM-02-2019-0063

Pereira, L., Tomás, D., Dias, Á., d, R. L., Costa, , & Gonçalves, R. (2023). How artificial intelligence can improve digital marketing. *International Journal of Business Information Systems*, 44(4), 581–624. 10.1504/IJBIS.2023.135351

Peres, R., Schreier, M., Schweidel, D. A., & Sorescu, A. (2023). Blockchain meets marketing : Opportunities, threats, and avenues for future research. *International Journal of Research in Marketing*, 40(1), 1–11. 10.1016/j.ijresmar.2022.08.001

Perez-Vega, R., Hopkinson, P., Singhal, A., & Mariani, M. M. (2022). From CRM to social CRM : A bibliometric review and research agenda for consumer research. *Journal of Business Research*, 151, 1–16. 10.1016/j.jbusres.2022.06.028

Perez-Vega, R., Kaartemo, V., Lages, C. R., Borghei Razavi, N., & Männistö, J. (2021). Reshaping the contexts of online customer engagement behavior via artificial intelligence : A conceptual framework. *Journal of Business Research*, 129, 902–910. 10.1016/j.jbusres.2020.11.002

Perkin, N. (2023). *Agile Transformation: Structures, Processes And Mindsets For The Digital Age*. Kogan Page Publishers.

Pesämaa, O., Larsson, J., & Eriksson, P. E. (2018). Role of Performance Feedback on Process Performance in Construction Projects : Client and Contractor Perspectives. *Journal of Management Engineering*, 34(4), 04018023. 10.1061/(ASCE) ME.1943-5479.0000619

Petrescu, M., & Krishen, A. S. (2023). Hybrid intelligence: human-AI collaboration in marketing analytics. *Journal of Marketing Analytics*, 2023(3), 263–274. 10.1057/s41270-023-00245-3

Peyravi, B., Nekrošienė, J., & Lobanova, L. (2020). 'Revolutionised technologies for marketing: Theoretical review with focus on artificial intelligence', Business. *Business: Theory and Practice*, 21(2), 827–834. 10.3846/btp.2020.12313

Pham, Q. V., Nguyen, D. C., Huynh-The, T., Hwang, W. J., & Pathirana, P. N. (2020). Artificial intelligence (AI) and big data for coronavirus (COVID-19) pandemic: A survey on the state-of-the-arts. *IEEE Access : Practical Innovations, Open Solutions*, 8, 130820–130839. 10.1109/ACCESS.2020.300932834812339

Piert Espinoza, J., Cardenas Yactayo, D., & Chavez Ugaz, R. (2023, October 10). CRM Implementation in SMEs Management Processes: The Role of e-CRM and s-CRM. *Proceedings of the International Conference on Industrial Engineering and Operations Management*. IEEE. 10.46254/EV01.20230213

Pietilä, A. M., Nurmi, S. M., Halkoaho, A., Kyngäs, H. (2020). Qualitative research: Ethical considerations. *The application of content analysis in nursing science research*, 49-69.

Pine, B. J., & Gilmore, J. H. (2013). The experience economy: past, present and future. In *Handbook on the experience economy* (pp. 21–44). Edward Elgar Publishing. 10.4337/9781781004227.00007

Pinto, J. L. Q., Matias, J. C. O., Pimentel, C., Azevedo, S. G., Govindan, K., Pinto, J. L. Q., & Govindan, K. (2018). Lean Manufacturing And Kaizen. *Just In Time Factory: Implementation Through Lean Manufacturing Tools*, 5-24.

Plangger, K., Grewal, D., de Ruyter, K., & Tucker, C. (2022). The future of digital technologies in marketing : A conceptual framework and an overview. *Journal of the Academy of Marketing Science*, 50(6), 1125–1134. 10.1007/s11747-022-00906-2

Pluchart, J. J. (2017). Vers une nouvelle esthétique bancaire. *Vie & sciences de l'entreprise*, (1), 9-21. 10.3917/vse.203.0009

Ponyiam, P., & Arch-int, S. (2018). Customer Behavior Analysis Using Data Mining Techniques. *2018 International Seminar on Application for Technology of Information and Communication*, (pp. 549–554). IEEE. 10.1109/ISEMANTIC.2018.8549803

Poole, D. L., & Mackworth, A. K. (2010). *Artificial Intelligence: Foundations of Computational Agents*. Cambridge University Press. 10.1017/CBO9780511794797

Poolton, J., Ismail, H. S., Reid, I. R., & Arokiam, I. C. (2006). Agile Marketing For The Manufacturing-Based SME. *Marketing Intelligence & Planning*, 24(7), 681–693. 10.1108/02634500610711851

Poria, S., Cambria, E., Gelbukh, A., Bisio, F., & Hussain, A. (2015). Sentiment data flow analysis by means of dynamic linguistic patterns. *IEEE Computational Intelligence Magazine*, 10(4), 26–36. 10.1109/MCI.2015.2471215

Poushneh, A., & Vasquez-Parraga, A. Z. (2017). Discernible impact of augmented reality on retail customer's experience, satisfaction and willingness to buy. *Journal of Retailing and Consumer Services*, 34, 229–234. 10.1016/j.jretconser.2016.10.005

Prelec, K., & Loewenstein, G. (1998). The pain of paying: Why is cash rational in a credit card society? *Journal of Economic Psychology*, 17(6), 185–211.

Preu, L., Huang, J., & Mela, C. (2017). Will you pay more or less with a mobile wallet? Examining the moderating role of pain of paying. *Journal of Retailing*, 93(2), 182–195.

Priyanga, G. (2023). THE EFFECTS OF ARTIFICIAL INTELLIGENCE ON DIGITAL MARKETING. *ShodhKosh: Journal of Visual and Performing Arts*, 4(1SE). 10.29121/shodhkosh.v4.i1SE.2023.431

Pujol, J. (2016). *Determinants i conseqüències de la lleialtat empresarial vers les seves entitats financeres [Determinants and consequences of business loyalty to their financial entities]*. 10.5821/dissertation-2117-96128

Punj, G. N., & Et Stewart, D. W. (1983). An Interaction Framework Of Consumer Decision Making. *The Journal of Consumer Research*, 10(2), 181. Https://Doi.Org/10.1086/208958. 10.1086/208958

Punj, G., & Stewart, D. W. (1983). Cluster analysis in marketing research: Review and suggestions for application. *JMR, Journal of Marketing Research*, 20(2), 134–148. 10.1177/002224378302000204

Puntoni, S., Reczek, R. W., Giesler, M., & Botti, S. (2021). Consumers and artificial intelligence: An experiential perspective. *Journal of Marketing*, 85(1), 131–151. 10.1177/0022242920953847

Qin, H., Osatuyi, B., & Xu, L. (2021). How mobile augmented reality applications affect continuous use and purchase intentions: A cognition-affect-conation perspective. *Journal of Retailing and Consumer Services*, 63, 102680. 10.1016/j.jretconser.2021.102680

Qin, Y., Xu, Z., Wang, X., & Skare, M. (2023). Artificial Intelligence and Economic Development: An Evolutionary Investigation and Systematic Review. *Journal of the Knowledge Economy*. 10.1007/s13132-023-01183-2

Qu, M., & Tang, J. (2019). *Probabilistic logic neural networks for reasoning*. arXiv (Cornell University). /arxiv.1906.08495 10.48550

Quintana, M., Menendez, J. M., Alvarez, F., & Lopez, J. P. (2016). Improving Retail Efficiency Through Sensing Technologies: A Survey. *Pattern Recognition Letters*, 81, 3–10. 10.1016/j.patrec.2016.05.027

Raghubir, P., & Srivastava, J. (2008). Monopoly money: The effect of payment coupling and form on spending behavior. *Journal of Experimental Psychology. Applied*, 14(3), 213–225. 10.1037/1076-898X.14.3.21318808275

Rahim, R., & Chishti, M. A. (2024, January). Artificial Intelligence Applications in Accounting and Finance. In *2024 ASU International Conference in Emerging Technologies for Sustainability and Intelligent Systems,* (pp. 1782-1786). IEEE. 10.1109/ICETSIS61505.2024.10459526

Raisch, S., & Krakowski, S. (2021). Artificial intelligence and management: The automation augmentation paradox. *Academy of Management Review*, 46(1), 192–210. 10.5465/amr.2018.0072

Ramanathan, V. & Thirunavukkarasu, Meyyappan. (2019). Twitter Text Mining for Sentiment Analysis on People's Feedback about Oman Tourism. In *4th MEC International Conference on Big Data and Smart City* (pp. 1-5). IEEE. 10.1109/ICBDSC.2019.8645596

Ramdi, I. (2021). La technologie digitale et la profession d'audit: Quel impact?. *International Journal of Accounting, Finance, Auditing, Management and Economics, 2*(6-1), 126-144.

Rammer, C., & Es-Sadki, N. (2023). Using big data for generating firm-level innovation indicators—A literature review. *Technological Forecasting and Social Change*, 197, 122874. 10.1016/j.techfore.2023.122874

Ramos, C., & Pavhlichenko, I. (2022). *Creating Agile Organizations: A Systemic Approach*. Addison-Wesley Professional.

Ranaweera, H. M. B. P. (2016). Perspective of trust towards e-government initiatives in Sri Lanka. *SpringerPlus*, 5(1), 22. 10.1186/s40064-015-1650-y26759761

Rancati, G., & Maggioni, I. (2023). Neurophysiological responses to robot–human interactions in retail stores. *Journal of Services Marketing*, 37(3), 261–275. 10.1108/JSM-04-2021-0126

Rane, N., Choudhary, S., & Rane, J. (2023). Education 4.0 and 5.0: Integrating Artificial Intelligence (AI) for personalized and adaptive learning. Available at *SSRN* 4638365. 10.2139/ssrn.4638365

Rangaswamy, A., Moch, N., Felten, C., van Bruggen, G., Wieringa, J. E., & Wirtz, J. (2020). The role of marketing in digital business platforms. *Journal of Interactive Marketing*, 51(August), 72–90. 10.1016/j.intmar.2020.04.006

Rasool, A., Shah, F. A., & Tanveer, M. (2021). Relational dynamics between customer engagement, brand experience, and customer loyalty: An empirical investigation. *Journal of Internet Commerce*, 20(3), 273–292. 10.1080/15332861.2021.1889818

Rathod, H. D., Rajawat, D., Ahmed, M., Dagur, Y., & Rajpurohit, K. (2024). A Study to Know Impact of AI on CRM. *Interantional Journal Of Scientific Research In Engineering And Management*, 08(02), 1–13. 10.55041/IJSREM31253

Rauschnabel, P. A., Babin, B. J., tom Dieck, M. C., Krey, N., & Jung, T. (2022). What is augmented reality marketing? Its definition, complexity, and future. *Journal of Business Research, 142*, 1140-1150. *Scopus*. 10.1016/j.jbusres.2021.12.084

Rauschnabel, P. A., Felix, R., & Hinsch, C. (2019). Augmented reality marketing : How mobile AR-apps can improve brands through inspiration. *Journal of Retailing and Consumer Services*, 49, 43–53. 10.1016/j.jretconser.2019.03.004

Ravi, S., & Rajasekaran, S. R. C. (2023). A PERSPECTIVE OF DIGITAL MARKETING IN RURAL AREAS: A LITERATURE REVIEW. *International Journal of Professional Business Review*, 8(4), e01388. 10.26668/businessreview/2023.v8i4.1388

Rawnaque, F. S., Rahman, K. M., Anwar, S. F., Vaidyanathan, R., Chau, T., Sarker, F., & Mamun, K. A. A. (2020). Technological advancements and opportunities in Neuromarketing: A systematic review. *Brain Informatics*, 7(1), 10. 10.1186/s40708-020-00109-x32955675

Rehman, M., & Esichaikul, V. (2011). Factors influencing the adoption of e-government in Pakistan. *2011 International Conference on E-Business and E-Government (ICEE)*, (pp. 1-4). IEEE. https://ieeexplore.ieee.org/abstract/document/5887093/

Reichheld, F. F., & Schefter, P. (2000). E-loyalty: Your secret weapon on the web. *Harvard Business Review*, 78(4), 105–113.

Reinartz, W., Thomas, J. S., & Kumar, V. (2005). Balancing acquisition and retention resources to maximize customer profitability. *Journal of Marketing*, 69(1), 63–79. 10.1509/jmkg.69.1.63.55511

Reza Kiani, G. (1998). Marketing opportunities in the digital world. *Internet Research*, 8(2), 185–194. 10.1108/10662249810211656

Rick, S. I., Cryder, C. E., & Loewenstein, G. (2008). Tightwads and spendthrifts. *The Journal of Consumer Research*, 34(6), 767–782. 10.1086/523285

Rieunier, S. (2017). *Marketing Sensoriel Et Expérientiel Du Point De Vente* (5ème Édition). DUNOD.

Ritzer, G. (1999). 15 Assessing the Resistance. *Resisting McDonaldization*, 234.

Roederer, C., & Et Filser, M. (2015). Marketing Expérientiel: Vers Un Marketing De La Cocréation. 176. *Consulté À L'adresse.* Https://Books.Google.Fr/Books?Id=Yljjcwaaqbaj

Roederer, C. (2012). Contribution A La Conceptualisation De L'expérience De Consommation: Emergence Des Dimensions De L'expérience Au Travers De Récits De Vie. [French Edition]. *Recherche et Applications en Marketing*, 27(3), 81–96. 10.1177/076737011202700304

Rogers Everett, M. (1995). *Diffusion of innovations.*

Roggeveen, A. L., & Sethuraman, R. (2020). Customer-Interfacing Retail Technologies In 2020 Et Beyond: An Integrative Framework And Research Directions. *Journal of Retailing*, 96(3), 299–309. 10.1016/j.jretai.2020.08.001

Rohm, A., Sultan, F., Pagani, M., & Gao, T. (2012). Brand in the hand: A cross-market investigation of consumer acceptance of mobile marketing. *Business Horizons*, 55(5), 485–493. 10.1016/j.bushor.2012.05.004

Roman, B., & Tchibozo, A. (2017). *Transformer la banque: stratégies bancaires à l'ère digitale.* Dunod.

Rosário, A. T., & Dias, J. C. (2023). How has data-driven marketing evolved : Challenges and opportunities with emerging technologies. *International Journal of Information Management Data Insights*, 3(2), 100203. 10.1016/j.jjimei.2023.100203

Rose, S., Hair, N., & Clark, M. (2011). Online Customer Experience: A Review Of The Business-To-Consumer Online Purchase Context. *International Journal of Management Reviews*, 13(1), 24–39. 10.1111/j.1468-2370.2010.00280.x

Rowley, J., & Slack, F. (2004). Conducting a literature review. *Management Research News*, 27(6), 31–39. 10.1108/01409170410784185

Roy, S. K., Balaji, M. S., Quazi, A., & Quaddus, M. (2018). Predictors Of Customer Acceptance Of And Resistance To Smart Technologies In The Retail Sector. *Journal Of Retailing And Consumer Services, 42*, 147-160. [REMOVED HYPERLINK FIELD]

Roy, S. K., Gruner, R. L., & Guo, J. (2020). Exploring Customer Experience, Commitment, And Engagement Behaviours. *J. Strat. Market.* 1–24. Https://Doi.Org/10.1080/0965254X.2019.1642937.

Royo-Vela, M., & Varga, Á. (2022). Unveiling Neuromarketing and Its Research Methodology. *Encyclopedia*, 2(2), 729–751. 10.3390/encyclopedia2020051

Roy, S. K., Balaji, M. S., Soutar, G., & Jiang, Y. (2020). The Antecedents and Consequences of Value Co-Creation Behaviors in a Hotel Setting: A Two-Country Study. *Cornell Hospitality Quarterly*, 61(3), 353–368. 10.1177/1938965519890572

Rubin, K. S. (2012). *Essential Scrum: A Practical Guide To The Most Popular Agile Process.* Addison-Wesley.

Rust, R. T. (2020). The future of marketing. *International Journal of Research in Marketing*, 37(1), 15–26. 10.1016/j.ijresmar.2019.08.002

Ryan, K. M., & Graham, R. S. (2014). Tactics and Strategies for Creating Effective E-mail Marketing Campaigns. In: *Taking Down Goliath.* Palgrave Macmillan, New York. (https://doi.org/)10.1057/9781137444219_7

Rygielski, C., Wang, J.-C., & Yen, D. C. (2002). Data mining techniques for customer relationship management. *Technology in Society*, 24(4), 483–502. 10.1016/S0160-791X(02)00038-6

Saad, S., & Saberi, B. (2017). Sentiment analysis or opinion mining: A review. *International Journal on Advanced Science, Engineering and Information Technology*, 7(5), 1660. 10.18517/ijaseit.7.5.2137

Safi, R. (2022). What consumers think about product self-assembly: Insights from big data. *Journal of Business Research*, 153, 341–354. 10.1016/j.jbusres.2022.08.003

Sahoo, S., Kumar, S., Donthu, N., & Singh, A. (2023). Artificial intelligence capabilities, open innovation, and business performance -Empirical insights from multinational B2B companies. *Industrial Marketing Management*, 171, 28–41. 10.1016/j.indmarman.2023.12.008

Sahu, M., Gupta, R., Ambasta, R. K., & Kumar, P. (2022). Artificial intelligence and machine learning in precision medicine: A paradigm shift in big data analysis. *Progress in Molecular Biology and Translational Science*, 190(1), 57–100. 10.1016/bs.pmbts.2022.03.00236008002

Saidali, J., Rahich, H., Tabaa, Y., & Medouri, A. (2019). The combination between Big Data and Marketing Strategies to gain valuable Business Insights for better Production Success. *Procedia Manufacturing*, 32, 1017–1023. 10.1016/j.promfg.2019.02.316

Said, S. (2023). The Role of Artificial Intelligence (AI) and Data Analytics in Enhancing Guest Personalization in Hospitality. *Journal of Modern Hospitality*, 2(1), 1–13. 10.47941/jmh.1556

Salminen, J., Yoganathan, V., Corporan, J., Jansen, B. J., & Jung, S.-G. (2019). Machine-learning approach to auto-tagging online content for content marketing efficiency: A comparative analysis between methods and content type. *Journal of Business Research*, 101, 203–217. 10.1016/j.jbusres.2019.04.018

Salonen, A., Mero, J., Munnukka, J., Zimmer, M., & Karjaluoto, H. (2024). Digital content marketing on social media along the B2B customer journey: The effect of timely content delivery on customer engagement. *Industrial Marketing Management*, 118, 12–26. 10.1016/j.indmarman.2024.02.002

Sameeni, M. S., Qadeer, F., Ahmad, W., & Filieri, R. (2024). An empirical examination of brand hate influence on negative consumer behaviors through NeWOM intensity. Does consumer personality matter? *Journal of Business Research*, 173, 114469. 10.1016/j.jbusres.2023.114469

Samir, M., & Et Soumia, A. (2020). La Phygitalisation De L'expérience Client: Une Approche Qualitative. International Journal Of Marketing. *Communication And New Media*, 0(6), 56–73.

Sanchez-Hernandez, G., Chiclana, F., Agell, N., & Carlos, J. (2013). Ranking and selection of unsupervised learning marketing segmentation. *Knowledge-Based Systems*, 44, 20–33. 10.1016/j.knosys.2013.01.012

Saponaro, M., Le Gal, D., Gao, M., Guisiano, M., & Maniere, I. C. (2018, December). Challenges and opportunities of artificial intelligence in the fashion world. In *2018 international conference on intelligent and innovative computing applications (ICONIC)* (pp. 1-5). IEEE.

Sapovadia, V. (2018). Financial inclusion, digital currency, and mobile technology. In *Handbook of Blockchain, Digital Finance, and Inclusion, Volume 2* (pp. 361-385). Academic Press. 10.1016/B978-0-12-812282-2.00014-0

Sarabhai, S., Chakraborty, M., Batra, M., Kler, R., Banerjee, S., & Mishra, S. (2023, November). Using AI and Machine Learning to Predict Consumer Buying Behavior: Insights from Behavioral Economics in Case of Alcoholic Beverages. In *2023 3rd International Conference on Technological Advancements in Computational Sciences (ICTACS)* (pp. 980-986). IEEE.

Sarath Kumar Boddu, R., Santoki, A. A., Khurana, S., Vitthal Koli, P., Rai, R., & Agrawal, A. (2022). An analysis to understand the role of machine learning, robotics and artificial intelligence in digital marketing. *Materials Today: Proceedings*, 56, 2288–2292. 10.1016/j.matpr.2021.11.637

Sarkees, M., Hulland, J., & Prescott, J. (2010). Ambidextrous organizations and firm performance: The role of marketing function implementation. *Journal of Strategic Marketing*, 18(2), 165–184. 10.1080/09652540903536982

Sarker, I. H. (2022). AI-based modeling: Techniques, applications and research issues towards automation, intelligent and smart systems. *SN Computer Science*, 3(2), 158. 10.1007/s42979-022-01043-x35194580

Saßnick, O., Zniva, R., Schlager, C., Horn, M., Kozlica, R., Neureiter, T., & Nöbauer, J. (2023, April). Analyzing customer behavior in-store: A review of available technologies. In *Digital Marketing & eCommerce Conference* (pp. 243–252). Springer Nature Switzerland. 10.1007/978-3-031-31836-8_25

Saura, J. R., Ribeiro-Soriano, D., & Palacios-Marqués, D. (2021). Setting B2B digital marketing in artificial intelligence-based CRMs : A review and directions for future research. *Industrial Marketing Management*, 98, 161–178. 10.1016/j.indmarman.2021.08.006

Sauvage, M. (2019). *Stratégie Multi-Canal, Cross-Canal, Omni Canal: Laquelle Choisir?* Consulté A L'adresse. Https://Www.Inboundvalue.Com/Blog/Multicanal-Crosscanal-Omnicanal

Savastano, M., Suciu, M.-C., Gorelova, I., & Stativă, G.-A. (2023). How smart is mobility in smart cities? An analysis of citizens' value perceptions through ICT applications. *Cities (London, England)*, 132, 104071. 10.1016/j.cities.2022.104071

Sawicki, A. (2016). Digital Marketing. *World Scientific News*, 48, 82–88.

Schafer, J. B., Frankowski, D., Herlocker, J. L., & Sen, S. (2007). Collaborative Filtering recommender systems. In *Springer eBooks* (pp. 291–324). Springer. 10.1007/978-3-540-72079-9_9

Schmitt, B. (1999). Experiential Marketing. *Journal of Marketing Management*, 37-41(1-3), 53–67. 10.1362/026725799784870496

Scholz, J., & Duffy, K. (2018). We ARe at home : How augmented reality reshapes mobile marketing and consumer-brand relationships. *Journal of Retailing and Consumer Services*, 44, 11–23. 10.1016/j.jretconser.2018.05.004

Schuetzler, R. M., Grimes, G. M., & Scott Giboney, J. (2020). The impact of chatbot conversational skill on engagement and perceived humanness. *Journal of Management Information Systems*, 37(3), 875–900. 10.1080/07421222.2020.1790204

Schwaber, K. (2004). *Agile Project Management With Scrum*. Microsoft Press.

Schwartz Eric, M., Bradlow Eric, T., & Fader Peter, S. (2017). Customer acquisition via display advertising using multiarmed bandit experiments. *Marketing Science*, 36(4), 500–522. 10.1287/mksc.2016.1023

Sebastian, V. (2014a). Neuromarketing and Evaluation of Cognitive and Emotional Responses of Consumers to Marketing Stimuli. *Procedia: Social and Behavioral Sciences*, 127, 753–757. 10.1016/j.sbspro.2014.03.349

Sebastian, V. (2014b). Neuromarketing and Neuroethics. *Procedia: Social and Behavioral Sciences*, 127, 763–768. 10.1016/j.sbspro.2014.03.351

Sebei, H., Hadj Taieb, M. A., & Ben Aouicha, M. (2018). Review of social media analytics process and Big Data pipeline. *Social Network Analysis and Mining*, 8(1), 30. 10.1007/s13278-018-0507-0

Sekaran, U., & Bougie, R. (2014). *Research Methods for Business: A Skill-Building Approach* (6th ed.).

Selamat, M. A., & Windasari, N. A. (2021). Chatbot for SMEs : Integrating customer and business owner perspectives. *Technology in Society*, 66, 101685. 10.1016/j.techsoc.2021.101685

Senapathi, M., & Drury-Grogan, M. L. (2021). Systems Thinking Approach To Implementing Kanban: A Case Study. *Journal of Software (Malden, MA)*, 33(4), E2322. 10.1002/smr.2322

Shah, A. M., Eisenkraft, N., Bettman, J. R., & Chartrand, T. L. (2016). "Paper or plastic?": How we pay influences post-transaction connection. *The Journal of Consumer Research*, 42(5), 688–708. 10.1093/jcr/ucv056

Shah, D., & Murthi, B. P. S. (2021). Marketing in a data-driven digital world : Implications for the role and scope of marketing. *Journal of Business Research*, 125, 772–779. 10.1016/j.jbusres.2020.06.062

Shang, Z. (2023). Use of Delphi in health sciences research: A narrative review. *Medicine*, 102(7), 1–7. 10.1097/MD.0000000000003282936800594

Sharma, S., Islam, N., Singh, G., & Dhir, A. (2022). Why Do Retail Customers Adopt Artificial Intelligence (AI) Based Autonomous Decision-Making Systems? *IEEE Transactions on Engineering Management*. IEEE. 10.1109/TEM.2022.3157976

Sharma, A. (2023). Analyzing the Role of Artificial Intelligence in Predicting Customer Behavior and Personalizing the Shopping Experience in Ecommerce. *Interantional Journal Of Scientific Research In Engineering And Management*, 07(02). 10.55041/IJSREM17839

Sharma, P., Ueno, A., Dennis, C., & Turan, C. P. (2023). Emerging digital technologies and consumer decision-making in retail sector : Towards an integrative conceptual framework. *Computers in Human Behavior*, 148, 107913. 10.1016/j.chb.2023.107913

Sheehan, D., & Van Ittersum, K. (2018). In-store spending dynamics: How budgets invert relative-spending patterns. *The Journal of Consumer Research*, 45(1), 49–67. 10.1093/jcr/ucx125

Sheikh, H., Prins, C., & Schrijvers, E. (2023). 'Artificial Intelligence: Definition and Background', in Sheikh, H., Prins, C., and Schrijvers, E., Mission AI. Cham: Springer International Publishing. *Research Policy*, 15–41. 10.1007/978-3-031-21448-6_2

Sheikh, H., Prins, C., & Schrijvers, E. (2023). AI as a System Technology. In Mission, A. I. (Ed.), *Research for Policy*. Springer. 10.1007/978-3-031-21448-6_4

Shelley, J. (2009). *The concept of the aesthetic.*

Shih, Y. Y., & Fang, K. (2004). The Use Of A Decomposed Theory Of Planned Behavior To Studyinternet Banking In Taiwan. *Internet Research*, 14(3), 213–223. 10.1108/10662240410542643

Shrestha, A., & Mahmood, A. (2019). Review of Deep learning Algorithms and Architectures. *IEEE Access : Practical Innovations, Open Solutions*, 7, 53040–53065. 10.1109/ACCESS.2019.2912200

Shumanov, M., & Johnson, L. (2021). Making conversations with chatbots more personalized. *Computers in Human Behavior*, 117, 106627. doi:. chb.2020.10662710.1016/j

Simonofski, A., Vallé, T., Serral, E., & Wautelet, Y. (2021). Investigating context factors in citizen participation strategies : A comparative analysis of Swedish and Belgian smart cities. *International Journal of Information Management*, 56, 102011. 10.1016/j.ijinfomgt.2019.09.007

Sindhu, J., & Namratha, R. (2019). Impact of Artificial Intelligence in chosen Indian Commercial Bank – A Cost Benefit Analysis. *Asian Journal of Management*, 10(4), 377–384. 10.5958/2321-5763.2019.00057.X

Singh, H. (2022). *Artificial Intelligence in strategic marketing: Value generation and mechanisms of action NTNU.*

Singh, J., Goel, Y., Jain, S., & Yadav, S. (2023). Virtual mouse and assistant: A technological revolution of artificial intelligence. arXiv preprint arXiv:2303.06309.

Singh, P., Sharma, M., & Daim, T. (2024). Envisaging AR travel revolution for visiting heritage sites: A mixed-method approach. *Technology in Society*, 76, 102439. 10.1016/j.techsoc.2023.102439

Singh, S., Singh, G., & Dhir, S. (2022). Impact of digital marketing on the competitiveness of the restaurant industry. *Journal of Foodservice Business Research*. Advance online publication. 10.1080/15378020.2022.2077088

Singh, S., & Srivastava, R. K. (2020). Understanding the intention to use mobile banking by existing online banking customers: An empirical study. *Journal of Financial Services Marketing*, 25(3), 86–96. 10.1057/s41264-020-00074-w

Slijepčević, M., Šević, N.P. and Radojević, I. (2019) 'Limiting Aspects of Neuromarketing Research', Mednarodno inovativno poslovanje= Journal of Innovative Business and Management, 11(1), pp. 72–83.

Slimani, C. (2021, October). Traitement automatisé des données à caractère personnel: Le risque de « l'informatisation du risque ». Revue de Recherche en Droit. *Economie et Gestion*, (16), 30.

Smith, J., & Peterson, A. (2017). Demographic factors and customer churn in the telecommunications industry. *Journal of Customer Behaviour*, 16(3), 217–232. 10.1362/147539217X15024911379045

Soman, D. (2001). The tactical influence of payment on spending. *Journal of Consumer Marketing*, 18(5), 351–362.

Soman, D. (2003). The effect of payment transparency on consumption: Quasi-experiments from the field. *Marketing Letters*, 14(3), 173–183. 10.1023/A:1027444717586

Sorour, A., & Atkins, A. S. (2024). Big data challenge for monitoring quality in higher education institutions using business intelligence dashboards. *Journal of Electronic Science and Technology*, 22(1), 100233. 10.1016/j.jnlest.2024.100233

Spiess, J., T'Joens, Y., Dragnea, R., Spencer, P., & Philippart, L. (2014). Using big data to improve customer experience and business performance. *Bell Labs Technical Journal*, 18(4), 3–17. 10.1002/bltj.21642

Srivastava, A., Saxena, G., & Mishra, M. (2019). Emotional attachment and customer loyalty: An empirical investigation in telecom sector. *International Journal of Business Excellence*, 17(1), 62–80. 10.1504/IJBEX.2019.097058

Stallone, V., Wetzels, M., & Klaas, M. (2021). Applications of Blockchain Technology in marketing—A systematic review of marketing technology companies. *Blockchain: Research and Applications*, 2(3), 100023. 10.1016/j.bcra.2021.100023

Stanton, S. J., Sinnott-Armstrong, W., & Huettel, S. A. (2017). Neuromarketing: Ethical implications of its use and potential misuse. *Journal of Business Ethics*, 144(4), 799–811. 10.1007/s10551-016-3059-0

Stefanov, T., Varbanova, S., Stefanova, M., & Ivanov, I. (2023). CRM System as a Necessary Tool for Managing Commercial and Production Processes. *TEM Journal*, 785–797. https://doi.org/10.18421/TEM122-23

Steinhoff, L., & Palmatier, R. W. (2016). Understanding loyalty program effectiveness: Managing target and bystander effects. *Journal of the Academy of Marketing Science*, 44(1), 88–107. 10.1007/s11747-014-0405-6

Stitt-Gohdes, W. L., Crews, T. B. (2004). The Delphi technique: A research strategy for career and technical education. *Journal of career and technical education, 20(2)*, 55-67.

Stone, M., Aravopoulou, E., Ekinci, Y., Evans, G., Hobbs, M., Labib, A., Laughlin, P., Machtynger, J., & Machtynger, L. (2020). Artificial intelligence (AI) in strategic marketing decision-making : A research agenda. *The Bottom Line (New York, N.Y.)*, 33(2), 183–200. 10.1108/BL-03-2020-0022

Strauss, J., & Frost, R. (2014). *E-Marketing* (7th ed.). Routledge.

Suhel, S. F., Shukla, V. K., Vyas, S., & Mishra, V. P. (2020). Conversation to automation in banking through chatbot using artificial machine intelligence language. In *2020 8th international conference on reliability, infocom technologies and optimization (trends and future directions)(ICRITO)* (pp. 611-618). IEEE. 10.1109/ICRITO48877.2020.9197825

Sujová, A., & Simanová, Ľ. (2023). IMPACTS OF IMPLEMENTED CHANGES ON BUSINESS PERFORMANCE OF SLOVAK ENTERPRISES. *Central European Business Review*, 12(3), 103–122. 10.18267/j.cebr.328

Sukier, H. B., Samper, M. G., Molina, R. I. R., Karam, M. S., Palencia, D. B., Ibanez, N. P., & Ruiz, M. J. S. (2024). Analysis of Strategic Marketing in Small and Medium-sized Enterprises: Case of the Bakery Industry in Colombia. *Procedia Computer Science*, 231, 601–606. 10.1016/j.procs.2023.12.178

Sun, C., Fang, Y., Kong, M., Chen, X., & Liu, Y. (2022). Influence of augmented reality product display on consumers' product attitudes : A product uncertainty reduction perspective. *Journal of Retailing and Consumer Services, 64.Journal of Retailing and Consumer Services*, 64, 102828. 10.1016/j.jretconser.2021.102828

Sung, E. C. (2021). The effects of augmented reality mobile app advertising: Viral marketing via shared social experience. *Journal of Business Research*, 122, 75–87. 10.1016/j.jbusres.2020.08.034

Sunikka, A., Bragge, J., & Kallio, H. (2011). The effectiveness of personalized marketing in online banking: A comparison between search and experience offerings. *Journal of Financial Services Marketing*, 16(3-4), 183–194. 10.1057/fsm.2011.24

Sun, S., Luo, C., & Chen, J. (2017). A review of natural language processing techniques for opinion mining systems. *Information Fusion*, 36, 10–25. 10.1016/j.inffus.2016.10.004

Sun, T., & Vasarhelyi, M. A. (2017). Deep Learning and the Future of Auditing: How an Evolving Technology Could Transform Analysis and Improve Judgment. *The CPA Journal*, 87(6), 24–29.

Sun, Y., & Yuan, Z. (2024). A virtual gym in your pocket: The influence of augmented reality exercise app characteristics on user's continuance intention. *Virtual Reality (Waltham Cross)*, 28(1), 1–20. 10.1007/s10055-024-00959-4

Supitchayangkool, S. (2012). The Differences between Satisfied/Dissatisfied Tourists towards Service Quality and Revisiting Pattaya, Thailand. *International Journal of Business and Management*, 7(6). 10.5539/ijbm.v7n6p30

Surendro, K. (2019, March). Predictive analytics for predicting customer behavior. In *2019 International Conference of Artificial Intelligence and Information Technology (ICAIIT)* (pp. 230-233). IEEE.

Suri, A., Jones, B. C., Ng, G., Anabaraonye, N., Beyrer, P., Domi, A., Choi, G., Tang, S., Terry, A., Leichner, T., Fathali, I., Bastin, N., Chesnais, H., & Rajapakse, C. S. (2021). A deep learning system for automated, multi-modality 2D segmentation of vertebral bodies and intervertebral discs. *Bone*, 149, 115972. 10.1016/j.bone.2021.11597233892175

Suryantini, N. P. S. (2023). THE SUSTAINABLE COMPETITIVE ADVANTAGE OF SMES TOWARDS INTELLECTUAL CAPITAL: THE ROLE OF TECHNOLOGY ADOPTION AND STRATEGIC FLEXIBILITY. *Intellectual Economics*, 17(1), 30–56. 10.13165/IE-23-17-1-02

Suryawan, I. W. K., & Lee, C.-H. (2023). Citizens' willingness to pay for adaptive municipal solid waste management services in Jakarta, Indonesia. *Sustainable Cities and Society*, 97, 104765. 10.1016/j.scs.2023.104765

Syed, A. S., Sierra-Sosa, D., Kumar, A., & Elmaghraby, A. (2021). IoT in smart cities : A survey of technologies, practices and challenges. *Smart Cities*, 4(2), 429–475. 10.3390/smartcities4020024

Syed, R., Suriadi, S., Adams, M., Bandara, W., Leemans, S. J., Ouyang, C., ter Hofstede, A. H. M., van de Weerd, I., Wynn, M. T., & Reijers, H. A. (2020). Robotic process automation: Contemporary themes and challenges. *Computers in Industry*, 115, 103162. 10.1016/j.compind.2019.103162

Szczepanski, M. (2019). *Economic impacts of artificial intelligence (AI)*. EPRS: European Parliamentary Research Service, Belgium. https://policycommons.net/artifacts/1334867/economic-impacts-of-artificial-intelligence-ai/1940719/

Taiminen, H., & Karjaluoto, H. (2015). The usage of digital marketing channels in SMEs. *Journal of Small Business and Enterprise Development*, 22(4), 633–651. Advance online publication. 10.1108/JSBED-05-2013-0073

Taleb, N., Salahat, M., & Ali, L. (2020). Impacts of Big-Data Technologies in Enhancing CRM Performance. *2020 6th International Conference on Information Management (ICIM)*, (pp. 257–263). IEEE. 10.1109/ICIM49319.2020.244708

Tang, Z., Xu, X., Song, Y., & Yang, H. (2022, March). Data Analytics Applications in the Soda Industry. In *International Conference on Business and Policy Studies* (pp. 677-688). Singapore: Springer Nature Singapore. 10.1007/978-981-19-5727-7_69

Tao, X. X., & Zhang, D. P. (2021). Exploration and Practice of Talent Training Mode of Industry-Education Integration in Industrial College: Taking Big Data Industry College of Zhejiang University of Science and Technology as an Example. *Journal of Zhejiang University of Science and Technology*, 163-168.

Tavitiyaman, P., Qu, H., Tsang, W. L., & Lam, C. R. (2021). The influence of smart tourism applications on perceived destination image and behavioral intention : The moderating role of information search behavior. *Journal of Hospitality and Tourism Management*, 46, 476–487. 10.1016/j.jhtm.2021.02.003

Taylor, S., & Todd, P. (1995). Decomposition And Crossover Effects In The Theory Of Planned Behavior: A Study Of Consumer Adoption Intentions. *International Journal of Research in Marketing*, 12(2), 137–155. 10.1016/0167-8116(94)00019-K

Teixeira, S., Barbosa, B., & Pinto, H. (2019). *How Do Entrepreneurs See Digital Marketing?* Evidence From Portugal. 10.4018/978-1-5225-6942-8.ch001

Tewari, I., Bisht, S., Tiwari, A., Joshi, B., Arora, S., & Tewari, G. (2023). The Revolutionary Transformation of India's Banking Industry through Artificial Intelligence. In *2023 14th International Conference on Computing Communication and Networking Technologies (ICCCNT)* (pp. 1-5). Delhi, India. 10.1109/ICCCNT56998.2023.10307322

Thang, D. C. L., & Tan, B. L. B. (2003). Linking Consumer Perception To Preference Of Retail Stores: An Empirical Assessment Of The Multiattributes Of Store Image. *Journal of Retailing and Consumer Services*, 10(4), 193–200. 10.1016/S0969-6989(02)00006-1

Theodoridis, P. K., & Gkikas, D. C. (2019). How artificial intelligence affects digital marketing [Conference session]. Strategic Innovative Marketing and Tourism: 7th ICSIMAT [Springer International Publishing.]. *Athenian Riviera, Greece*, 2018(October), 1319–1327.

Thomas, A. R. (2017a). *'Ethics and neuromarketing', Implications for Market Research and Business Practice*. Springer. 10.1007/978-3-319-45609-6

Thomas, M., Desai, K. K., & Seenivasan, S. (2011). How credit card payments increase unhealthy food purchases: Visceral regulation of vices. *The Journal of Consumer Research*, 38(1), 126–139. 10.1086/657331

Thomaz, F., Salge, C., Karahanna, E., & Hulland, J. (2020). Learning from the dark web: Leveraging conversational agents in the era of hyper-privacy to enhance marketing. *Journal of the Academy of Marketing Science*, 48(2), 43–63. 10.1007/s11747-019-00704-3

Thrassou, A., Vrontis, D., Efthymiou, L., & Uzunboylu, N. (2022). *An overview of business advancement through technology: Markets and marketing in transition. Business Advancement through Technology* (Vol. I). Markets and Marketing in Transition. 10.1007/978-3-031-07769-2

Thümler, N. (2023). Agility In Marketing: A Bibliometric Analysis. *Business: Theory and Practice*, 24(1), 173–182. 10.3846/btp.2023.17090

Tiberius, V., & Hirth, S. (2019). Impacts of digitization on auditing: A Delphi study for Germany. *Journal of International Accounting, Auditing & Taxation*, 37, 100288. 10.1016/j.intaccaudtax.2019.100288

Tom Dieck, M. C., Cranmer, E., Prim, A. L., & Bamford, D. (2023). The effects of augmented reality shopping experiences: immersion, presence and satisfaction. *Journal of Research in Interactive Marketing*, (ahead-of-print).

Tom Dieck, M. C., & Han, D. I. D. (2022). The role of immersive technology in Customer Experience Management. *Journal of Marketing Theory and Practice*, 30(1), 108–119. 10.1080/10696679.2021.1891939

Torres, G. C. (2022). *Phygital Approaches And Intangible Cultural Heritage As A Tourism Experience Enhancer. Tradition And Innovation For A 21st Century Academic Museum Of The University Of Coimbra* [Master's Thesis, UoC].

Trabelsi, L., & Akrout, F. (2022). *Data Mining for CRM: Extracting Customer Knowledge From Data.* IGI Global. Https://Services.Igi-Global.Com/Resolvedoi/Resolve.Aspx?Doi=10.4018/978-1-7998-9553-4.Ch008

Trieu, V.-H. (2017). Getting value from Business Intelligence systems: A review and research agenda. *Decision Support Systems*, 93, 111–124. 10.1016/j.dss.2016.09.019

Trivedi, J. (2019). Examining the customer experience of using banking chatbots and its impact on brand love: The moderating role of perceived risk. *Journal of Internet Commerce*, 18(1), 91–111. 10.1080/15332861.2019.1567188

Trivedi, J., Kasilingam, D., Arora, P., & Soni, S. (2022). The effect of augmented reality in mobile applications on consumers' online impulse purchase intention: The mediating role of perceived value. *Journal of Consumer Behaviour*, 21(4), 896–908. 10.1002/cb.2047

Tsai, C. H., & Su, P. C. (2021). The application of multi-server authentication scheme in internet banking transaction environments. *Information Systems and e-Business Management*, 19(1), 77–105. 10.1007/s10257-020-00481-5

Tsai, C. H., Wu, Y. C. J., & Lin, S. D. (2020). Predicting customer churn behavior in the telecommunication industry: An integrated data mining approach. *Technological Forecasting and Social Change*, 160, 120236. 10.1016/j.techfore.2020.120236

Tsang, M. M., Ho, S. C., & Liang, T. P. (2004). Consumer Attitudes Toward Mobile Advertising: An empirical study. *International Journal of Electronic Commerce*, 8(3), 65–78. 10.1080/10864415.2004.11044301

Tsang, S. S., Kuo, C., Hu, T. K., & Wang, W. C. (2023). Exploring impacts of AR on group package tours: Destination image, perceived certainty, and experiential value. *Journal of Vacation Marketing*, 29(1), 84–102. 10.1177/13567667221078244

Tseng, H.-T. (2023). Customer-centered data power : Sensing and responding capability in big data analytics. *Journal of Business Research*, 158, 113689. 10.1016/j.jbusres.2023.113689

Tseng, H.-T., Aghaali, N., & Hajli, D. N. (2022). Customer agility and big data analytics in new product context. *Technological Forecasting and Social Change*, 180, 121690. 10.1016/j.techfore.2022.121690

Turco, M. L., & Et Giovannini, E. C. (2020). Towards A Phygital Heritage Approach For Museum Collection. *Journal of Archaeological Science, Reports*, 34, 102639. 10.1016/j.jasrep.2020.102639

Tyrväinen, O., & Karjaluoto, H. (2019). Omnichannel experience : Towards successful channel integration in retail. *Journal of Customer Behaviour*, 18(1), 17–34. 10.1362/147539219X15633616548498

Vaid, S., Puntoni, S., & Khodr, A. (2023). Artificial intelligence and empirical consumer research: A topic modeling analysis. *Journal of Business Research*, 166, 114110. 10.1016/j.jbusres.2023.114110

Vaidyanathan, N., & Henningsson, S. (2023). Designing augmented reality services for enhanced customer experiences in retail. *Journal of Service Management*, 34(1), 78–99. 10.1108/JOSM-01-2022-0004

Valdez Mendia, J. M., & Flores-Cuautle, J. J. A. (2022). Toward customer hyper-personalization experience—A data-driven approach. *Cogent Business & Management*, 9(1), 2041384. 10.1080/23311975.2022.2041384

Van Eck, N. J., & Waltman, L. (2010). Software survey: VOSviewer, a computer program for bibliometric mapping. *Scientometrics*, 84(2), 523–538. 10.1007/s11192-009-0146-320585380

Van Esch, P., Black, S., & Ferolie, J. (2018). Marketing AI recruitment: The next phase in job application and selection. *Computers in Human Behavior*, 90, 215–222. 10.1016/j.chb.2018.09.009

Van Looy, A. (2021). A quantitative and qualitative study of the link between business process management and digital innovation. *Information & Management*, 58(2), 103413. 10.1016/j.im.2020.103413

Vanheems, R., & Et Paché, G. (2018). La Distribution Face Au Consommateur Connecté: Un Monde Au Bout Des Doigts… Et Après? *Décisions Marketing, 91,* 5-21. Https://Doi.Org/10.7193/Dm.091.05.21

Varghese, P. (2022). *Neuromarketing and Artificial Intelligence for Effective Future Business.*

Vassakis, K., Petrakis, E., & Kopanakis, I. (2018). Big data analytics: applications, prospects and challenges. *Mobile big data: A roadmap from models to technologies*, 3-20. 10.1007/978-3-319-67925-9_1

Vassileva, B. (2017). *Agile Marketing Strategies: How To Transform The Customer-Brand Dynamics In Services.* Bucharest.

Veerla, V. (2021). To study the impact of Artificial Intelligence as Predictive model in banking sector: Novel approach. *International Journal of Innovative research in Technology, 7*(8), 94-105.

Velu, A. (2021). *Machine Learning Techniques for Customer Relationship Management. 9*(6).

Venkatesh, V. (2022). Adoption And Use Of AI Tools : A Research Agenda Grounded In UTAUT. *Annals of Operations Research*, 308(1-2), 641–652. Https://Doi.Org/10.1007/S10479-020-03918-9. 10.1007/s10479-020-03918-9

Venkatesh, V., Davis, F., & Morris, M. (2007). Dead Or Alive? The Development, Trajectory and Future Of Technology Adoption Research. *Journal of the Association for Information Systems*, 8(4), 267–286. Https://Doi.Org/10.17705/1jais .00120. 10.17705/1jais.00120

Venkatesh, V., Morris, M. G., Davis, G. B., & Davis, F. D. (2003). User acceptance of information technology : Toward a unified view. *Management Information Systems Quarterly*, 27(3), 425–478. 10.2307/30036540

Vergine, I., Brivio, E., Fabbri, T., Gaggioli, A., Leoni, G., & Galimberti, C. (2020). Introducing And Implementing Phy-gital And Augmented Reality At Work. *STUDI ORGANIZZATIVI, 2*, 137-163. Https://Doi.Org/10.3280/SO2019-002006

Verhoef, P. C., Broekhuizen, T., Bart, Y., Bhattacharya, A., & Dong, Q. J., Fabian, N., & Haenlein, M. (2021). Digital Transformation : A Multidisciplinary Reflection And Research Agenda. *Journal Of Business Research, 122*, 889-901. Https://Doi.Org/10.1016/J.Jbusres.2019.09.022

Verhoef, P. C., Broekhuizen, T., Bart, Y., Bhattacharya, A., & Dong, Q. J., Fabian, N., & Haenlein, M. (2021). Digital transformation: A multidisciplinary reflection and research agenda. *Journal of Business Research, 122*, 889–901.

Verhoef, P. C., Broekhuizen, T., Bart, Y., Bhattacharya, A., Dong, J. Q., Fabian, N., & Haenlein, M. (2019). Digital transformation: A multidisciplinary reflection and research agenda. *Journal of Business Research*, 122, 889–901. 10.1016/j.jbusres.2019.09.022

Verhoef, P. C., Lemon, K. N., Parasuraman, A., Roggeveen, A., Tsiros, M., & Schlesinger, L. A. (2009). Customer experience creation: Determinants, dynamics and management strategies. *Journal of Retailing*, 85(1), 31–41. 10.1016/j.jretai.2008.11.001

Verhoef, P. C., Reinartz, W. J., & Krafft, M. (2010). Customer engagement as a new perspective in customer management. *Journal of Service Research*, 13(3), 247–252. 10.1177/1094670510375461

Verma, S., & Gustafsson, A. (2020). Investigating the Emerging COVID-19 Research Trends in the Field of Business and Management: A Bibliometric Analysis Approach. *Journal of Business Research*, 118, 253–261. 10.1016/j.jbusres.2020.06.05732834211

Verma, S., Sharma, R., Deb, S., & Maitra, D. (2021). Artificial intelligence in marketing : Systematic review and future research direction. *International Journal of Information Management Data Insights*, 1(1), 100002. 10.1016/j.jjimei.2020.100002

Vicente, O. F., Fernández, F., & García, J. (2023). Automated market maker inventory management with deep reinforcement learning. *Applied Intelligence*, 53(19), 22249–22266. 10.1007/s10489-023-04647-9

Vieira, V. A., Rafael, D. N., & Agnihotri, R. (2022). Augmented reality generalizations : A meta-analytical review on consumer-related outcomes and the mediating role of hedonic and utilitarian values. *Journal of Business Research*, 151, 170–184. 10.1016/j.jbusres.2022.06.030

Viktor, Z., Alla, S., & Ol'ga, Z. (2023, April 23). Features and characteristics of business intelligence (BI)-systems as a tool for improving the efficiency of company activities. *Ukrainian Journal of Applied Economics and Technology.* http://ujae.org.ua/en/features-and-characteristics-of-business-intelligence-bi-systems-as-a-tool-for-improving-the-efficiency-of-company-activities/

Villegas, F. (2024). *Artificial Intelligence Customer Experience: What is it, Pros, Cons and Best Tools.* QuestionPro. https://www.questionpro.com/blog/tr/ai-customer-experience/)

Vlačić, B., Corbo, L., Costa e Silva, S., & Dabić, M. (2021). The evolving role of artificial intelligence in marketing : A review and research agenda. *Journal of Business Research*, 128, 187–203. 10.1016/j.jbusres.2021.01.055

Vo, K. N., Le, A. N. H., Thanh Tam, L., & Ho Xuan, H. (2022). Immersive experience and customer responses towards mobile augmented reality applications: The moderating role of technology anxiety. *Cogent Business & Management*, 9(1), 2063778. 10.1080/23311975.2022.2063778

Volkmar, G., Fischer, P. M., & Reinecke, S. (2022). Artificial Intelligence and Machine Learning : Exploring drivers, barriers, and future developments in marketing management. *Journal of Business Research*, 149, 599–614. 10.1016/j.jbusres.2022.04.007

Vongurai, R. (2021). Factors influencing experiential value toward using cosmetic AR try-on feature in Thailand. *Journal of Distribution Science*, 19(1), 75–87.

Voorhees, C., Brady, M., Calantone, R., & Ramirez, E. (2015). Discriminant Validity Testing in Marketing: An Analysis, Causes for Concern, and Proposed Remedies. *Journal of the Academy of Marketing Science*, 44(1), 1–16. 10.1007/s11747-015-0455-4

Vrontis, D., Makrides, A., Christofi, M., & Thrassou, A. (2021). Social Media Influencer Marketing: A Systematic Review, Integrative Framework And Future Research Agenda. *International Journal of Consumer Studies*, 45(4), 61744. 10.1111/ijcs.12647

Wagner, R., & Cozmiuc, D. (2022). Extended Reality in Marketing—A Multiple Case Study on Internet of Things Platforms. *Information (Switzerland), 13*(6). *Information (Basel)*, 13(6), 278. 10.3390/info13060278

Waldt, L. R., Rebello, T. M., & Brown, W. J. (2009). Attitudes of Young Consumers towards SMS Advertising. *African Journal of Business Management*, 3(9), 444–452.

Walentek, D., & Ziora, L. (2023). A systematic review on the use of augmented reality in management and business. *Procedia Computer Science*, 225, 861–871. 10.1016/j.procs.2023.10.073

Wamba-Taguimdje, S.-L., Fosso Wamba, S., Jean Robert, K. K., & Tchatchouang, C. E. (2020). *Influence of Artificial Intelligence (AI) on Firm Performance: The Business Value of AI-based Transformation Projects.*

Wang, C., Li, Y., Fu, W., & Jin, J. (2023). Whether to trust chatbots: Applying the event-related approach to understand consumers' emotional experiences in interactions with chatbots in e-commerce. *Journal of Retailing and Consumer Services*, 73, 103325. 10.1016/j.jretconser.2023.103325

Wang, F. R., & Zhao, L. (2022). A Hybrid Model for Commercial Brand Marketing Prediction Based on Multiple Features with Image Processing. *Security and Communication Networks*, 2022, 1–10. 10.1155/2022/5455745

Wang, M. M., & Pan, X. M. (2022). Drivers of Artificial Intelligence and Their Effects on Supply Chain Resilience and Performance: An Empirical Analysis on an Emerging Market. *Sustainability (Basel)*, 14(24), 16836. 10.3390/su142416836

Wang, R. J., Krishnamurthi, L., & Mathouse, E. C. (2018). When reward convenience meets mobile app: Increasing customer participation in a coalition loyalty program [V.M. Landers.]. *Journal of the Association for Consumer Research*, 3(3), 314–329. 10.1086/698331

Wang, W., Cao, D., & Ameen, N. (2023). Understanding customer satisfaction of augmented reality in retail: A human value orientation and consumption value perspective. *Information Technology & People*, 36(6), 2211–2233. 10.1108/ITP-04-2021-0293

Wang, Y., Xing, Y., Wu, Y., Yuan, N., Wang, F., Jiang, B., & Xiong, T. (2020). PMU121 APPLICATION OF REAL-WORLD DATA FROM MEDICAL BIG-DATA PLATFORM IN REAL WORLD EVIDENCE GENERATION: A PRACTICE IN POST-MARKETING RESEARCH IN CHINA. *Value in Health*, 23, S256. 10.1016/j.jval.2020.04.885

Watson, A., Alexander, B., & Salavati, L. (2018). The impact of experiential augmented reality applications on fashion purchase intention. *International Journal of Retail & Distribution Management*, 48(5), 433–451. 10.1108/IJRDM-06-2017-0117

Watson, H. J., Goodhue, D. L., & Wixom, B. H. (2002). The benefits of data warehousing: Why some organizations realize exceptional payoffs. *Information & Management*, 39(6), 491–502. 10.1016/S0378-7206(01)00120-3

Wedel, M., Bigné, E., & Zhang, J. (2020). Virtual and augmented reality : Advancing research in consumer marketing. *International Journal of Research in Marketing*, 37(3), 443–465. 10.1016/j.ijresmar.2020.04.004

Whang, J. B., Song, J. H., Choi, B., & Lee, J. H. (2021). The effect of Augmented Reality on purchase intention of beauty products: The roles of consumers' control. *Journal of Business Research*, 133, 275–284. 10.1016/j.jbusres.2021.04.057

Williams, S., & Williams, N. (2008). *The Profit Impact of Business Intelligence* (Updated and rev.[New ed.]). Elsevier/Morgan Kaufmann Publishers.

Williams, R. I.Jr, Clark, L. A., Clark, W. R., & Raffo, D. M. (2021). Re-examining systematic literature review in management research: Additional benefits and execution protocols. *European Management Journal*, 39(4), 521–533. 10.1016/j.emj.2020.09.007

Willson, M., (2016). *Algorithms (and the) Everyday, Information, Communication & Society.*

Winter, B., & Winter, B. (2015). *The Basics Of Agile. Agile Performance Improvement: The New Synergy Of Agile And Human Performance Technology*, 85-120.

Wirth, N. (2018). Hello marketing, what can artificial intelligence help you with? *International Journal of Market Research*, 60(5), 435–438. 10.1177/1470785318776841

Wirtz, J., & Zeithaml, V. (2018). Cost-effective service excellence. *Journal of the Academy of Marketing Science*, 46(1), 59–80. 10.1007/s11747-017-0560-7

Wisetsri, W. (2021). Systematic analysis and future research directions in artificial intelligence for marketing. *Turkish Journal of Computer and Mathematics Education*, 12(11), 43–55.

Wixom, B., & Watson, H. (2010). The BI-Based Organization. *International Journal of Business Intelligence Research*, 1(1), 13–28. 10.4018/jbir.2010071702

Wu, C.-W., & Monfort, A. (2022). Role of artificial intelligence in marketing strategies and performance. *Psychology and Marketing*.

Xiao, L., Li, X., & Zhang, Y. (2023). Exploring the factors influencing consumer engagement behavior regarding short-form video advertising: A big data perspective. *Journal of Retailing and Consumer Services*, 70, 103170. 10.1016/j.jretconser.2022.103170

Xue, L., Leung, X. Y., & Ma, S. (2022). What makes a good "guest": Evidence from Airbnb hosts' reviews. *Annals of Tourism Research*, 95, 103426. 10.1016/j.annals.2022.103426

Yadav, D., & Kadavath, V. K. (Eds.), *The Digital Popular in India*. Palgrave Macmillan. 10.1007/978-3-031-39435-5

Yang, X. (2021). Augmented reality in experiential marketing: The effects on consumer utilitarian and hedonic perceptions and behavioural responses. *Information technology in organisations and societies: Multidisciplinary perspectives from AI to Technostress*, 147-174.

Yang, P., Hao, X., Wang, L., Zhang, S., & Yang, L. (2024). Moving toward sustainable development: The influence of digital transformation on corporate ESG performance. *Kybernetes*, 53(2), 669–687. 10.1108/K-03-2023-0521

Yao, X. (2019). Evolving artificial neural networks. *Proceedings of the IEEE*, 87(9), 1423–1447. 10.1109/5.784219

Yaoyuneyong, G., Foster, J., Johnson, E., & Johnson, D. (2016). Augmented reality marketing: Consumer preferences and attitudes toward hypermedia print ads. *Journal of Interactive Advertising*, 16(1), 16–30. 10.1080/15252019.2015.1125316

Yim, M. Y. C., Chu, S. C., & Sauer, P. L. (2017). Is augmented reality technology an effective tool for e-commerce? An interactivity and vividness perspective. *Journal of Interactive Marketing*, 39(1), 89–103. 10.1016/j.intmar.2017.04.001

Yin, J., & Qiu, X. (2021). Ai technology and online purchase intention : Structural equation model based on perceived value. *Sustainability (Switzerland), 13*(10). *Sustainability (Basel)*, 13(10), 567110.3390/su13105671

Yoon, S., & Oh, J. (2022). A theory-based approach to the usability of augmented reality technology: A cost-benefit perspective. *Technology in Society*, 68, 101860. 10.1016/j.techsoc.2022.101860

Yusoff, Y., Alias, Z., Abdullah, M., & Mansor, Z. (2019). Agile Marketing Conceptual Framework For Private Higher Education Institutions. *International Journal of Academic Research in Business & Social Sciences*, 9(1). 10.6007/IJARBSS/v9-i1/5896

Yu, Y., Kwong, S. C. M., & Bannasilp, A. (2023). Virtual idol marketing : Benefits, risks, and an integrated framework of the emerging marketing field. *Heliyon*, 9(11), e22164. 10.1016/j.heliyon.2023.e2216438053914

Zaby, C., & Wilde, K. D. (2018). Intelligent Business Processes in CRM: Exemplified by Complaint Management. *Business & Information Systems Engineering*, 60(4), 289–304. 10.1007/s12599-017-0480-6

Zaki, S., Ismail, M. M., Rashad, H., & Ibrahim, M. (2021). Optimizing Customer Relationship Management through Business Intelligence for Sustainable Business Practices. *American Journal of Business and Operations Research*, 3(1), 70–79. 10.54216/AJBOR.030105

Zanger, V., Meißner, M., & Rauschnabel, P. A. (2022). Beyond the gimmick: How affective responses drive brand attitudes and intentions in augmented reality marketing. *Psychology and Marketing*, 39(7), 1285–1301. 10.1002/mar.21641

Zaragoza-Sáez, P., Claver-Cortés, E., Marco-Lajara, B., & Úbeda-García, M. (2020). Corporate social responsibility and strategic knowledge management as mediators between sustainable intangible capital and hotel performance. *Journal of Sustainable Tourism*, 31(4), 1–23. 10.1080/09669582.2020.1811289

Zellermayer, O. (1996). *The pain of paying*. Carnegie Mellon University.

Zemankova, A. (2019). Artificial intelligence in audit and accounting: development, current trends, opportunities and threats-literature review. *International Conference on Control, Artificial Intelligence, Robotics & Optimization (ICCAIRO)*, (pp. 148-154). IEEE. 10.1109/ICCAIRO47923.2019.00031

Zhang, D., Zhang, C., & Zheng, C. (2023). Prediction and Analysis of Customer Churn of Automobile Dealers Based on BI. *2023 IEEE 6th Information Technology, Networking, Electronic and Automation Control Conference (ITNEC)*. IEEE. 10.1109/ITNEC56291.2023.10082554

Zhao, D., & Strotmann, A. (2015). *Analysis and visualization of citation networks*. Morgan & Claypool Publishers. 10.1007/978-3-031-02291-3

Zhao, L., Tang, Z., & Zou, X. (2019). Mapping the knowledge domain of smart-city research: A bibliometric and scientometric analysis. *Sustainability*, 11(23), 1–28. 10.3390/su12010001

Zheng, R., Li, Z., & Na, S. (2022). How customer engagement in the live-streaming affects purchase intention and customer acquisition, E-tailer's perspective. *Journal of Retailing and Consumer Services*, 68, 103015. 10.1016/j.jretconser.2022.103015

Zhezha, V., Kola, B., & Melinceanu, A. M. (2023). Exploring the Landscape of Digital Marketing in Albania: Insights from Local Companies. *Academic Journal of Interdisciplinary Studies*, 12(4), 341–353. 10.36941/ajis-2023-0120

Zhou, F., Ayoub, J., Xu, Q., & Jessie Yang, X. (2020). A machine learning approach to customer needs analysis for product ecosystems. *Journal of Mechanical Design*, 142(1), 011101. 10.1115/1.4044435

Zhou, P., Zhao, S., Ma, Y., Liang, C., & Zhu, J. (2023). What influences user participation in an online health community? The stimulus-organism-response model perspective. *Aslib Journal of Information Management*, 75(2), 364–389. 10.1108/AJIM-12-2021-0383

Zhou, T. (2018). Examining users' switch from online banking to mobile banking. *International Journal of Networking and Virtual Organisations*, 18(1), 51–66. 10.1504/IJNVO.2018.090675

Zhu, Z., Jin, Y., Su, Y., Jia, K., Lin, C.-L., & Liu, X. (2022). Bibliometric-Based Evaluation of the Neuromarketing Research Trend: 2010–2021. *Frontiers in Psychology*, 13, 872468. 10.3389/fpsyg.2022.87246835983212

Ziafat, H., & Shakeri, M. (2014). Using data mining techniques in customer segmentation. *Journal of Engineering Research and Applications*, 4(9), 70–79.

Ziakis, C., & Vlachopoulou, M. (2023). Artificial Intelligence in Digital Marketing: Insights from a Comprehensive Review. *Information (Basel)*, 14(12), 664. 10.3390/info14120664

Zintso, Y., Fedorishina, I., Zaiachkovska, H., Kovalchuk, O., & Tyagunova, Z. (2023). Analysis of current trends in the use of digital marketing for the successful promotion of goods and services in Ukraine. *Financial and Credit Activity-Problems of Theory and Practice*, 3(50). 10.55643/fcaptp.3.50.2023.4080

Zouari, G., & Abdelhedi, M. (2021). Customer satisfaction in the digital era: Evidence from Islamic banking. *Journal of Innovation and Entrepreneurship*, 10(1), 1–18. 10.1186/s13731-021-00151-x

Zupic, I., & Čater, T. (2015). Bibliometric Methods in Management and Organization. *Organizational Research Methods*, 18(3), 429–472. 10.1177/1094428114562629

About the Contributors

Lhoussaine Alla is a professor in management sciences at the National School of Applied Sciences, researcher at the LAREMEF laboratory, Sidi Mohamed Ben Abdellah University, Fez, Morocco. He is a permanent professor of various marketing management modules at Sidi Mohamed Ben Abdellah University in Fez (Morocco) and in several public and private business graduate schools. He is an accredited professional expert in the fields of Training Engineering, Professional Coaching and Mentoring young entrepreneurs. After a PhD thesis on creating value for the customer and its impact on the overall performance of companies, Prof. Lhoussaine ALLA invested more in scientific research in marketing, through various scientific contributions in the form of participation in international conferences and symposia and scientific publications, in various themes inherent to Marketing (customer value creation, customer behaviour, e-marketing, customer experience, sales performance, Marketing Data Analytics, territorial marketing, territorial attractiveness, territorial economic intelligence, ...), finance (stock market performance, financial analysts, financing package,...), entrepreneurship (entrepreneur profile, startups, entrepreneurial resilience,...), tourism (tourist attractiveness, visitor behaviour, tourism, performance of tourist destinations,...), logistics (SC, SCM, SSCM, Green SCM, logistics performance,...). Prof. Lhoussaine ALLA is also (co)editor of the e-book "Integrating intelligence and sustainability into supply chains. IGI Global. DOI: 10.4018/979-8-3693-0225-5" and Publication Director of the scientific journal "Managerial and Economic Alternatives - AME", indexed on the IMIST portal, https://revues.imist.ma/index.php/AME. Prof. Lhoussaine ALLA is also (co)coordinator of many scientific events devoted to marketing research. As much scientific and educational accumulation that the publisher aims to mobilize as potential to bring together researchers and imminent experts to share the fruits of their relevant and innovative research in implementation, supervision, evaluation, Mastery and reinvention of innovative solutions developed through Data Engineering and AI in Marketing. He is now co-editor of two collective works that will be published via IGI Global: 1. Applying Qualitative Research Methods to Science and Management. 2. Utilizing Technology to Manage Territories. Prof Lhoussaine is the coordinator of a team of young researchers, very dynamic and talented, with complementary profiles, creating a friendly space for high-level scientific research.

Aziz Hmioui received his PhD in Industrial Economics and is a Professor at Sidi Mohammed Ben Abdellah University, Fez. His research focuses on tourism, logistics and territorial attractiveness. He is the author of numerous scientific articles. He has participated in numerous international scientific events (Algeria, Brazil, Canada, Egypt, Spain, France, Tunisia and Vietnam). He is a member of several scientific committees of international journals and conferences.

Badr Bentalha teaches Supply Chain and Operations Management at National School Of Business and Management – Fez, Sidi Mohamed Ben Abdellah University – Morocco. Dr. Bentalha investigates the structural dynamics and control of complex networks, applying his findings to supply chain management, Industry 4.0, risk analysis, and digital supply chains. His pioneering research has established seminal academic and practical approaches for sustainable and intelligent supply chain optimization. Using optimization, simulation, control theory, and AI, he tackles real-world supply chain and operations challenges. His work emphasizes the intersection of supply chain management, operations research, industrial engineering, and digital technology. As a professor, he teaches undergraduate, graduate, and, doctoral courses in operations management, supply chain management, logistics, management information systems, and strategic management. Through guest lectures, webinars, and scholarly presentations, he engages students and fosters an active learning environment. He aims to equip future industry leaders with the management knowledge and technological skills to build more resilient, adaptable, and sustainable supply chain operations. Dr. Bentalha's academic background includes management and economics, operations research, and supply chain management. He studied management operations and supply chain management, graduating with honors. He earned PhD degrees and completed an aggregation in economics and management. Before entering academia, he primarily worked in industry and consulting, focusing on process optimization in manufacturing, logistics, and ERP systems. His practical experience includes numerous operations research and process optimization projects for operations design, logistics, scheduling, and supply chain management. Before joining the Fez National School of Business and Management, he was a professor of economics and management preparatory classes since 2009. Dr. Bentalha's influential research is cited in supply chain management and logistics. His publication record includes over 60 papers in prestigious academic journals such as the International Journal of Logistics Systems and Management, International Journal of Business Performance Management, International Journal of Business and Technology Studies, Journal of Environmental Issues and Climate Change, and Economical Managerial Alternatives. He is also the author of three books: Netnography: Principles, Method, and Ethics, Internal Audit of Treasury and Cash Management: Report on the Audit of Treasury and Integrating Intelligence and Sustainability in Supply Chains. Professor Bentalha specializes in supply chain and operations management, operations research, and service management. He is passionate about integrating knowledge across disciplines to solve real-world problems. He has delivered numerous invited plenary talks, keynotes, and panel discussions at conferences and global webinars. He serves as Associate Editor of the Economical Managerial Alternatives journal and is on the editorial boards and advisory committees of several other publications. He regularly presents his research and has chaired organized program committees, and served on advisory boards for over 60 international conferences in supply chain management, operations, management studies, control theory, and information science. He is a member of numerous scientific committees of international journals and conferences. Since 2009, Mr. Bentalha has helped sundry companies implement an audit system, resolve issues, and improve performance.

***

Mourad Aarabe is a PhD student at the National School of Business and Management of Fez, Sidi Mohamed de Ben Abdellah University. His research focuses on tourism, marketing, digital marketing, and management.

Mohamed Badouch is a PhD student in computer science at Faculty of Sciences, Ibn Zohr University, Agadir, Morocco. He received the master degree in information systems engineering from Cadi Ayyad University in 2017. His main research is in the areas of artificial intelligence, and machine learning.

Benhayoun Issam is a part-time faculty of Accounting and Finance at School of Business Administration (SBA) – Al Akhawayn University (AUI) and an Assistant professor (full time) of Accounting and Finance at ENCG Meknes [National School of Business and Management] – Moulay Ismail University. Dr. Benhayoun holds a PhD degree in International Accounting (IFRS) from ENCG-Fez and a master's degree (ENCG diploma) in Accounting and Financial Management from ENCG-Kenitra in 2020 and 2015, respectively. His field of interest is in international accounting standardization, adoption theories, IFRS adoption, structured literature reviews, and meta-analysis.

Ahmed Benjelloun is a teacher-researcher at the National School of Business and Management of Fez, Sidi Mohamed de Ben Abdellah University.

Mehdi Boutaounte is a professor in computer science at National School of Business and Management, Dakhla, Morocco

Dwijendra Nath Dwivedi is a professional with 20+ years of subject matter expertise creating right value propositions for analytics and AI. He currently heads the EMEA+AP AI and IoT team at SAS, a worldwide frontrunner in AI technology. He is a post-Graduate in Economics from Indira Gandhi Institute of Development and Research and currently perusing PHD from crackow university of economics Poland. He has presented his research in more than 20 international conference and published several Scopus indexed paper on AI adoption in many areas. As an author he has contributed to more than 8 books and has more than 25 publications in high impact journals. He conducts AI Value seminars and workshops for the executive audience and for power users.

Ilham El Haraoui is a professor at the Faculty of Economics and Management at Ibn Tofail University. She holds a degree in Statistical Engineering and Applied Economics from the National Institute of Statistics and Applied Economics (INSEA) in Rabat, an MBA from Yonsei University in Seoul, and a PhD in Management Science with a specialization in marketing from Mohamed V-Agdal University. She teaches courses such as statistics and probability for undergraduate students, as well as multivariate data analysis and consumer behavior for master's students. Her research primarily focuses on digital marketing and the behavior of connected consumers.

Amina El Idrissi Tissafi is a Doctor of Management Economics and Professor specializing in Marketing at the Higher School of Technology, USMBA. I have participated in numerous conferences as a member of the organizing committee, scientific committee, or as an event leader. I am the author and co-author of dozens of presentations and publications.

Mustapha Elhissoufi is a Qualified Teacher of marketing and management at Institute of Hotel and Tourism Technology, Fez, Morocco. He received the master's degree in management of social enterprises and territories. He is currently pursuing the Ph.D. degree with the national school of business and management, Sidi Mohamed Ben Abdellah University, Fez, Morocco. His lecturing and research fields are intelligent marketing, artificial intelligence, consumer behavior, sales argumentation, and persuasion.

Ichrak Fahim is a PhD student in Economics and Management at The National Business School (ENCG Agadir). In Zohr University. Her research emphasis is on Neuromarketing and consumer behavior. She has a 3-years working experience in advertising agencies and she participated in understanding consumer behaviors and launching communication campaigns for multiple brands in Morocco.

Adil Garohe is a doctoral student obtained a Master's degree from the University of Moulay Ismail Meknes in Morocco. He is currently in the 3rd year of doctoral studies at Mohammed V University, Faculty of Legal, Economic and Social Sciences, Rabat

Agdal, in Morocco. His research interests include education, entrepreneurship. He is currently head of department responsible for administrative and financial affairs at the Ministry of Housing and Urban Policy in Morocco.

Farid Huseynov received his PhD in information systems in 2016 from the Middle East Technical University (METU), Turkey. He received his BS in management and MS in information systems from the METU in 2009 and 2013, respectively. His research interests encompass digital business models, behavioral issues in B2C electronic commerce, information technology (IT) acceptance and use, and machine learning. He is particularly focused on understanding the interplay between technology and human behavior, with a keen interest in exploring how machine learning can enhance and transform various aspects of digital business and consumer interactions. His researches have appeared in Interacting with Computers, Information Development, Sage OPEN, and other journals in Information Systems field.

Aya Irgui is a PhD Researcher in the Laboratory of Economics and Management of Organizations "LEMO" at the Faculty of Economics and Management, Ibn Tofail University. She is an Adjunct Professor of Digital Marketing Strategies, E-commerce & Digital Ecosystem, Digital Transformation, and Digital Project Management at both Ibn Tofail University and Hassan I University. Additionally, she is an International Digital Marketing, Branding, and Brand Strategist and Consultant. Her research focuses on the following themes: Immersive technologies in marketing and brand strategies, digital transformation, digital technologies in marketing and education, and digital marketing, branding and brand strategies.

Mohammed Qmichchou is Professor of Digital Marketing and Customer Relationship Management. He is head of the Research Master « Digital Marketing Strategies – DSM », and is a Senior Researcher and member of the research Laboratory of Economics and Management of Organizations "LEMO" in the Faculty of Economics and Management, at Ibn Tofail University. His teaching, mentoring, and research activities are centered on digital marketing, connected consumer behavior, emerging distribution channels, and understanding the Moroccan online consumer behavior.

Busra Ozdenizci Kose is an Associate Professor of Management Information Systems at Gebze Technical University. She teaches courses in a wide range of topics such as Management Information Systems, Computer Science, Business Analysis, Software Design and Development, Business Process Management, Mobile and Wireless Technologies, Near Field Communication (NFC), Internet of Things (IoT) and Blockchain. She co-authored Near Field Communication: From Theory to Practice, (2012) and Professional NFC Application Development for Android, (2013). She gives importance of academia & industry relationship, and takes roles such as project manager, researcher, and consultant for national and international companies in this manner.

Nurullah Taş earned his bachelor's degree in business administration from Istanbul University in 2012. Currently, he is actively engaged in academic pursuits, concurrently pursuing a PhD in Business Administration at Gebze Technical University and an MSc in Information Systems Engineering at Kocaeli University. His diverse research interests encompass information systems, Internet of Things (IoT), smart cities, smart transportation, and image processing, reflecting his commitment to exploring innovative and multidisciplinary areas within his field.

Rachid Zammar is a professor at the Mohammed V University in Rabat. His research focuses on entrepreneurship and management of social projects.

Zejjari Ibtissam serves as a full-time Assistant Professor in Management and Marketing at ENCG Fez [National School of Business and Management] – Sidi Mohamed Ben Abdellah University, alongside her role as a part-time faculty member in Management and Marketing at the School of Business Administration (SBA) – Al Akhawayn University (AUI). She earned her PhD degree in International Marketing from ENCG-Fez and completed her master's degree (ENCG diploma) in International Business from ENCG-Kenitra in 2021 and 2016, respectively. Her research interests focus on international marketing, consumer behaviour, education, Artificial Intelligence and bibliometric analysis.

Index

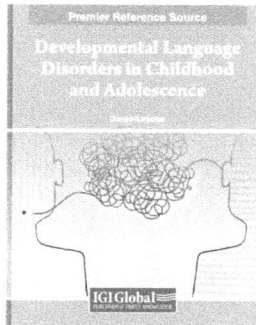

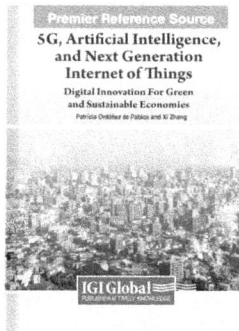

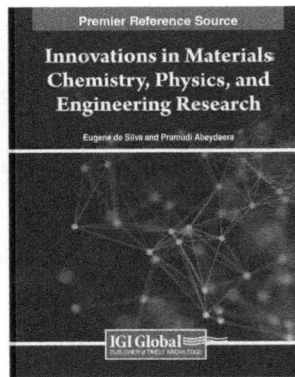

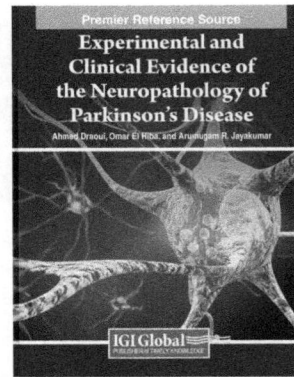

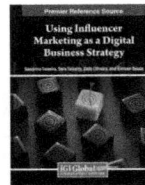

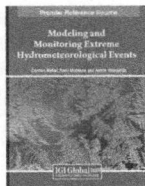

Milton Keynes UK
Ingram Content Group UK Ltd.
UKHW010228300724
446304UK00005B/106

9 798369 331729